# ENCYCLOPEDIA OF
# INVASIONS
# AND
# CONQUESTS

## FROM ANCIENT TIMES
## TO THE PRESENT

# ENCYCLOPEDIA OF
# INVASIONS
# AND
# CONQUESTS

## FROM ANCIENT TIMES
## TO THE PRESENT

PAUL K. DAVIS

**ABC-CLIO**

Santa Barbara, California
Denver, Colorado
Oxford, England

**Library of Congress Cataloging-in-Publication Data**

Davis, Paul K., 1952–
    Encyclopedia of invasions and conquests from ancient times to the present / Paul K. Davis
        p.   cm.
    Includes bibliographical references and index.
    1. History, Military—Encyclopedias.    I. Title.
D25.A2D38    1996    96-49452    355'.003—dc21

ISBN 0-87436-782-4 (alk. paper)


02 01 00 99 98 97 96    10 9 8 7 6 5 4 3 2 1 (cloth)




ABC-CLIO, Inc.
130 Cremona Drive, P.O. Box 1911
Santa Barbara, California 93116-1911

This book is printed on acid-free paper ∞.

For Jerri

# CONTENTS

# PREFACE

The greatest difficulty in undertaking a work such as this is defining the terms *invasion* and *conquest*. Both have overtly military connotations, though not all conquests are accomplished totally through military means. Still, *conquest* can best be described as the occupation and long-term domination of one country by another. Using this criterion, colonization can be defined as conquest, especially because most examples of colonization have a military aspect. Hence, the Spanish occupation of the New World, the British occupation of America, Canada, India, etc., all constitute conquests. If the colonization takes place with little military activity, the term *occupation* is used.

The definition of *invasion* is much more difficult to nail down. Any battle involves invasion of territory, even if only enemy-held ground on the other side of the battlefield. To narrow our field, we will deal only with the violation of national borders—one country invading another. This immediately removes from consideration all civil wars, since a nation fights such a war against itself. While many would argue that Union forces attacking the Confederacy constituted an invasion, this cannot fit our criteria because the Confederate States of America was never officially an indepen-

dent nation. This further removes from consideration most revolutions, unless they are against a foreign power and the revolutionaries achieve national status. The American Revolution would be covered, because the United States became a nation in the midst of revolution with formal recognition by other countries. The Texas Revolution, on the other hand, would not because Texas did not gain international recognition until after hostilities ended.

Additionally, the placement of national boundaries creates another question. For most of its history, modern Italy has been a collection of nation-states trying to establish domination over one another. Do conflicts among these neighbors constitute invasions? Would the fighting between Serbs, Croats, and Muslims in post-Communist Yugoslavia be considered a series of territorial invasions, or simply a struggle for local control? Is an attack against a neighbor, conducted with no intent of conquest (e.g., Prussia versus Austria in 1866), to be considered an invasion?

These are some of the considerations to be faced in defining the scope of this work, and in some cases, inclusion ultimately comes down to an editorial judgment call. What some might view as an invasion, we might decide was a dynastic squabble among rival factions, and modern national identities may at times be overlaid on a set of historical states that no longer exist. In general, we will explore actions by one nation against another with the intent or result of establishing the attacker's domination over the defender. By this definition, invasions almost always will be military, but ultimate conquests may be political or economic, as in the U.S. intervention in Latin American nations. Because the establishment and fall of empires normally involve the conquests of numerous enemies, these events are covered by the names of the empires, rather than listing each conquest involved in the process of empire-building. Every effort has been made to cover as much history of the world's invasions as possible—from the time Sargon the Great first expanded the borders of Akkadia to the Allied effort to reconquer Kuwait from Iraqi aggression.

I would like to thank all the contributors who aided in the production of this work: John Adams, Gary Botello, Ed Davis, Thomas E. Davis, Allen Hamilton, James L. Iseman, Edward Maier III, and Rhett Michael Schall.

I very much want to recognize the efforts of my wife, Jerri, for her patience with me during the research and writing of this work.

# PART 1
# THE ANCIENT WORLD

# Part 1
# THE ANCIENT WORLD

The numbers on the map correspond to entry numbers in the text.

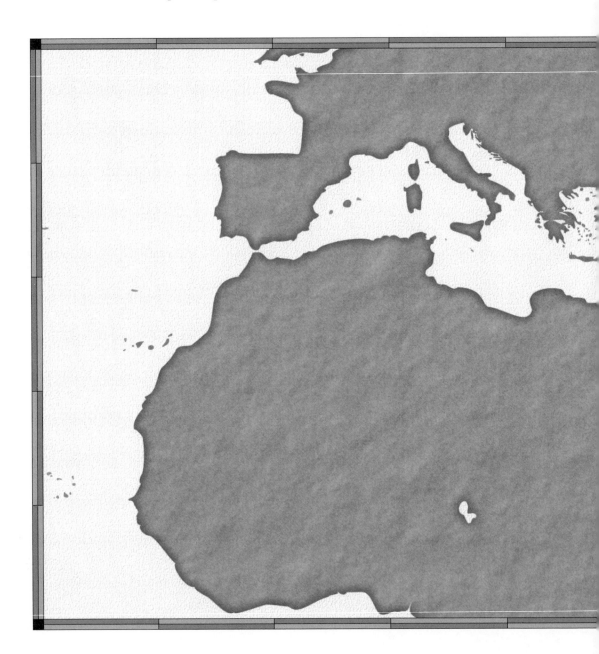

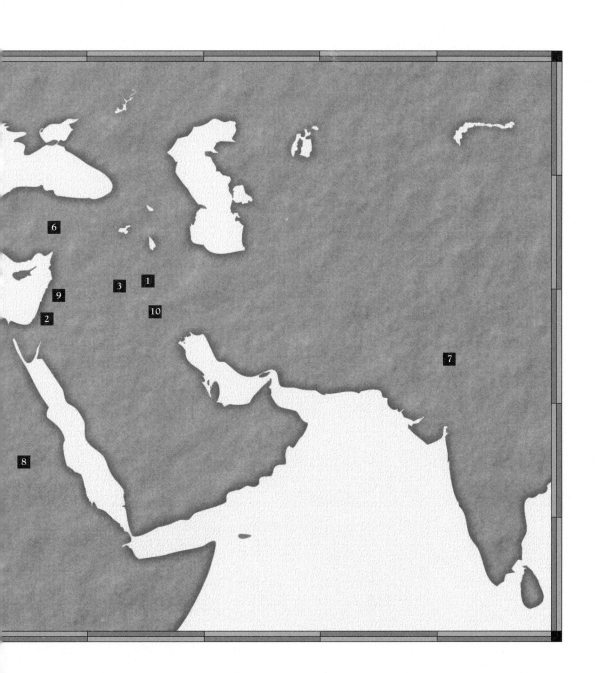

# 1 ASSYRIAN EMPIRE

The first strong Assyrian state was formed in the late Bronze Age in the wake of the decline of the Mitanni, a confederation of Hurrian tribes living along the upper reaches of the Tigris River. In the fourteenth century B.C., Ashururballit led his people in an expansion westward, during which they came to control the upper arch of the Fertile Crescent for approximately a century. The Assyrians ran up against the power of Aram (situated in modern-day Syria), which blocked their access to western trade routes. Still, the early success coupled with the continued fighting against Aram made the Assyrian army strong and experienced, able to defend itself and mount major raids far to the south and west. With this powerful military, Assyria dominated the Near East by the 900s B.C.

Initially, the Assyrians' main objective was to expand to the Mediterranean coast in order to control the major trade routes of ancient times. Assyrian armies finally overcame the resistance of nations led by Aram, and they captured the major city of Damascus in 732 B.C. Old Testament accounts tell of Assyrian attacks into Samaria and Judah and fighting against the Egyptians. Assyria established empire status under the leadership of Sargon II (722–705 B.C.), who named himself after the Sumerian leader Sargon the Great, the first well-known conqueror. Sargon II's son Sennacherib maintained the lands his father had conquered, and raided into Asia Minor after 700 B.C. Sennacherib established control over Phoenician towns on the Mediterranean coast all the way to the Egyptian frontier. The last of the great emperors was Esarhaddon (681–668 B.C.), who came to the throne by murdering his father, Sennacherib. To secure his frontiers, Esarhaddon coupled diplomacy with warfare. He entered into agreements with the

A reconstruction of the assault on the gate of Laschish by the Assyrians.

A procession of prisoners walks through the town's orchards. While many prisoners were well treated, high officials were tortured and executed for their responsibility in the rebellion against their Assyrian overlord.

Medes to the east and the Cimmerians to the north, but also invaded Egypt, a nation seemingly always in rebellion against the Assyrian demands for tribute. By the end of Esarhaddon's reign, Assyrian territory stretched from the Persian Gulf across the Fertile Crescent and halfway down the Nile in Egypt. Assurbanipal was the last of the Assyrian kings. More of a scholar than a warrior, he let his generals punish the rebellious while he established a large library at Nineveh.

The Assyrian Empire came to an abrupt end in 612 B.C. Three hundred years of warfare, both conquests and the suppression of almost constant rebellions, had put a serious strain on their manpower. The birthrate had not kept up with the casualty rate, and the Assyrians had been obliged to use conscript troops, who proved of doubtful loyalty. Agreements with neighbors lapsed, and enemies pressed from all directions. Ultimately the Medes led a coalition that laid siege to the Assyrian capital city of Nineveh, which fell after three

months, spelling the end of the empire—an end more celebrated than lamented. The biblical prophet Nahum wrote, "All who hear the news of you clap their hands over you. For upon whom has not come your unceasing evil?" Nahum summed it up perfectly; Assyria had built and maintained its empire by military force and terror, showing no mercy to any defeated foe, whether in conquest or rebellion.

They were the first people to institutionalize cruelty to control the lands they acquired. Towns destroyed in battle were left in ruins as an example to other possible foes. Ashurnasipal bragged, "I caused great slaughter. I destroyed, I demolished, I burned. I took their warriors prisoner and impaled them on stakes before their cities. . . . I flayed the nobles, as many as had rebelled, and spread their skins out on the piles [of dead bodies]. . . . Many of the captives I burned in a fire. Many I took alive; from some I cut off their hands to the wrist, from others I cut off their noses, ears and fingers; I put out the eyes of many soldiers.

I burnt their young men and women to death." This boast was not just Ashurnasipal's; every leader acted in the same fashion. It is not surprising that they had to deal with constant rebellion; they certainly inspired no loyalty from their subjects.

Despite this negative characteristic, the Assyrians contributed to society and culture. Some of the world's oldest roads were built in the time of Sargon II. This road system allowed for freer trade and the development of a postal system. The Assyrian Empire was the first to construct aqueducts. Adopting cuneiform script from the Babylonians, the Assyrians became the world's first serious historians. They established a number of libraries, where they recorded scientific knowledge acquired on their own and from Babylon. They also inaugurated the first widespread use of iron. Though iron was used by the Hittites, the Assyrians were the first to use the metal for weapons. As more iron-producing territory came under their control, it became the most common metal in tool production, far outperforming anything made from bronze. Their artists are regarded as masters of relief work, with realistic and emotional portrayals of kings at war and sport.

The Assyrians are best remembered, however, for their accomplishments in warfare. Using chariots (already invented), they were the first to add cavalry to their army, which often proved the decisive factor in their victories. Assyria was the first state, but certainly not the last, to build its society around the armed forces. They established what may be called the first true empire, because whereas most previous warriors campaigned mainly for loot and tribute, the Assyrians established political control by appointing governors in conquered lands. Had they had the statesmanship skills to match their military prowess, they could not only have lasted longer as an empire, they would have had an even greater impact on the progress of ancient society and culture.

*See also* Hittites [6]; Sargon the Great [10].

References: Bury, J. B., S. A. Cook, and F. E. Adcock, eds., *The Cambridge Ancient History: The Assyrian Empire* (Cambridge: Cambridge University Press, 1923–1939); Laessoe, Jorgen, *People of Ancient Assyria, Their Inscriptions and Correspondence* (London: Routledge & Kegan Paul, 1963); Saggs, H. W. F., *The Might That Was Assyria* (London: Sidgwick & Jackson, 1984).

# CANAAN, ISRAELITE INVASION OF

**2**

Throughout history, nations have gone to war against their enemies in the name of God, whether for punishment, revenge, or greed. Seldom has there been a war in which one or all of the participants did not try to invoke God's blessing or intercession on their behalf, no matter who their god may have been. Worse yet, a holy war is usually fought with more ferocity and less mercy.

The Israelite invasion of the area that has come to be known as the Holy Land was probably as genocidal as any in history, but it seems to have been conducted with less malice. As a racial and religious group, the Hebrews considered themselves to have been chosen by the one and only God, who had promised their forebear, Abraham, that they would have a country of their own. Thus, it became a tradition covering several centuries that the Hebrews had a mandate from God to possess this land. The people who inhabited the land were virtually unknown to the Israelites, and the only indication that the invasion was conducted with moral overtones is the biblical statement that God was punishing the local inhabitants for their idolatry.

Forty years before the invasion began, the Israelites were a captive people serving Egyptian masters in the Nile Delta region. In response to intolerable treatment, they came together under the leadership of a man named Moses, who had been raised and educated in the household of the pharaoh. Though not always popular with the rank-and-file Israelites, Moses was able to secure their release from bondage during a time of turmoil and plague, which had been attributed to God's intercession.

According to the Bible, the Israelites left Egypt some 6 million strong, but were unable to muster the resolve necessary to invade their objective immediately. They spent 40 years wandering about the Sinai desert, and by the time the actual invasion began, their numbers had considerably decreased. The Bible states that they were fielding an army of about 40,000 men as they approached Canaan, the Promised Land. The Israelites had apparently come out of Egypt unprepared for the hardships of the Sinai or the rigors of battle, but during the 40 years of wandering through the territories of various kingdoms, they had been toughened and their fighting skills sharpened by encounters with nomadic tribes.

At a date scholars place variously from the sixteenth to the thirteenth century B.C., the Israelites arrived in the area south of the Dead Sea, Canaan's southern limit. They encountered two Amorite kingdoms, Sihon and Og, and defeated both. According to God's instruction, through Moses, those occupying the land of the ancient mandate were to be killed to protect the Hebrews from contamination by idol worshippers. All the people were put to the sword, thus clearing the land, which reached from the Dead Sea to well north of the Sea of Galilee and from the Jordan River eastward almost to the Euphrates.

Though the territories of Sihon and Og were vast and a part of the Promised Land, the symbolic point at which the Israelites began the invasion was on the Jordan River just south of the ancient walled city of Jericho. Moses passed the mantle of leadership to Joshua, the general of his army, and died without ever having crossed the Jordan. Joshua gathered all his people together and instructed them to follow the priests who were carrying the Ark of the Covenant, the sacred chest containing holy relics, the most important of which were the tablets containing God's laws, the Ten Commandments. As the priests stepped into the water, the Bible says that the river ceased to flow, and all the people passed through the riverbed dry-shod.

Once across the river, Joshua ordered an altar to be built and the proper sacrifices made. He reinstituted the ancient rite of circumcision, which had been abandoned during the years of wandering. He also reconsecrated himself and his family to God and the task before them, and preparations soon began for the assault. Jericho was a strong, walled city founded on the site of an abundant spring and surrounded by palms. Seeing the Israelites' approach and terrified by the disasters that had befallen Sihon and Og, the local inhabitants fled into the walled city. They had heard that the Israelites crossed the Jordan on dry ground, and had seen with their own eyes how the Jordan had ceased to flow.

Joshua instructed his people to march around the city silently for six days; on the seventh day they would give a great shout, and the walls would fall down. This happened as Joshua predicted, and the people in the city perished—save for one family, who had harbored Israelite spies.

After the sacking of Jericho, Joshua planned to climb from the river valley to high ground and swing south, clearing the land of its inhabitants as he went.

Standing in his way was the city of Ai, another walled city partway up the mountain slope. He sent only part of his army (about 3,000 men) and was repulsed. Joshua returned with the bulk of his army, and by a ruse enticed the defenders out of the city. Cut off from the protection of the city fortifications, they were ambushed; once again, all the inhabitants were killed. Archaeologists dispute the existence of Ai, but reputedly it was very near the city of Bethel; possibly the conquests of both cities were accomplished at the same time. Whatever the explanation, the Israelites unquestionably stormed the heights, and Joshua continued his conquest.

The only exception to the policy of genocide apparently occurred at this time. The inhabitants of Gibeon took advantage of the Israelites' unfamiliarity with the country. Sending out emissaries dressed in rags and professing to be travelers from a distant land, they exacted a pledge from Joshua that he would spare their people. When Joshua learned that they lived just over the next ridge, he honored his pledge, but sentenced them to be slaves, forever "carriers of water and hewers of wood."

The land of God's mandate, now called Israel, extended roughly from the Dead Sea in the south past the Sea of Galilee in the north; it was bounded by the Mediterranean on the west and by some portion of the Euphrates on the east. After passing Gibeon, Joshua continued south along the mountains and then dropped into the lowlands, taking all the land to the south and west. Retracing his steps, he conquered most of the land in the north. In all, the Bible lists 31 kingdoms that were conquered, including Jericho. No peace treaties were made, except for that with the Gibeonites, and no one was allowed to surrender. Though the Bible states that the conquest was complete after six years and that the Israelites then rested, it is clear that some resistance still remained even when Joshua died, 25 years after the invasion began.

The chief problem lay with the Philistines, a non-Semitic people of mysterious origin occupying the area along the southern seacoast. So stubborn was their resistance, so superior their iron weapons over the bronze implements of the Israelites, and so devious their tactics that the term *Philistine* has come to mean a person of crass and base instincts. The Philistines fought against the Israelites in the time of the judges (the two centuries or so after invasion), and brought about Samson's downfall. A giant Philistine from Gath was killed by young David, setting the boy on the path to power. Not until David was king did the entire Promised Land come under complete Hebrew control. The genocidal policy was never fully implemented, and the Bible blames many of the later problems of the nation on interracial marriages, economic ties, and the worship of false gods.

For more than 3,000 years the descendants of the Israelites have possessed (in their own minds and that of many others) the Promised Land, if they have not always controlled it. This land was the geopolitical center of the then-civilized world: exposed to all cultures and religions, crossed by most of the trading caravans, and host to ships from the far places of the sea. Christianity began here and, though dominated by the Romans for centuries, this product of the land conquered and eventually possessed even that great power.

The Israelite conquest that came sweeping out of the desert one and a half millennia before the time of Christ has had more far-reaching consequences on the entire world than any other conquest in history. Though the land today is of relative insignificance in an economic sense, it continues to be a force in world affairs—a magnet for Jews, Muslims, and Christians, many with the old antipathies and genocidal tendencies intact.

—Ed Davis

References: Gaubert, Henri, *Moses and Joshua, Founders of the Nation* (New York: Hastings House, 1969); Grant, Michael, *The History of Ancient Israel* (New York: Scribner, 1984); Miller, James, *A History of Ancient Israel and Judah* (Philadelphia: Westminster Press, 1968).

# CHALDEAN (NEO-BABYLONIAN) EMPIRE, EXPANSION OF

3

Many memorable civilizations arose in the area known as Mesopotamia, the land lying between the Tigris and Euphrates rivers above the Persian Gulf. The Bible frequently mentions Mesopotamian civilizations, especially the spectacular city of Babylon. The city lay some 150 miles south of Sumer, site of the world's first civilization. The ruins of the ancient city visible today were left by the Chaldeans, or Neo-Babylonians, another Semitic group that came to prominence after the first Babylon settled by the Amorites.

The Assyrians, a warrior race based some 200 miles north of Babylon, were in total control of Mesopotamia around 750 B.C. Being a people dedicated to conquest and plunder, the Assyrians maintained a mighty army but made no loyal allies among their conquests. Hatred of the Assyrians by their conquered subjects ultimately weakened the civilization. Being forced to deal with almost continual rebellions laid them open to conquest from the outside, an invasion that came from the Chaldeans and Medes. The Chaldeans had lived in the Persian Gulf area for centuries and the Medes lived in the foothills of Persia. Together, led by the Chaldean king Nabopolasser, they destroyed the Assyrian capital at Nineveh in 612 B.C.

With the Assyrians removed from power, the Chaldeans and Medes split the territory; the Chaldeans occupied the area around Babylon, and the Medes settled in the northwest. King Nabopolasser established his capital at Babylon, ascending the throne in that city in 604 B.C. Defeat of the Assyrians did not bring peace to the Chaldeans, however. Assyria's fall encouraged the expansion of Egypt, under Pharaoh Necho, into Syria. Nabopolasser wanted to resist, but failing health caused him to send his son Nebuchadnezzar to fight the Egyptians. The Chaldeans won a major battle at Carchemish, but the Egyptians remained covetous of Syria. Allying themselves with Phoenicia and the kingdom of Judah, the Egyptians returned to the area. Again they met defeat at Chaldean hands. Nebuchadnezzar captured the capital of Judah, Jerusalem, and took a large part of the nation's population into captivity in Babylon in 597 B.C. When the Egyptians tried a third time to take Syria—and were a third time defeated—Nebuchadnezzar again took Jerusalem by siege and removed the remainder of the population.

While Nebuchadnezzar was in the Mediterranean coastal area, he made war against Phoenicia, capturing the port city of Sidon. He was unable to capture the fortress city of Tyre, though he disrupted their trade. During this expedition, Egypt caused little trouble. Nebuchadnezzar's successor, Neriglassar, took military action to defend his national borders from an invasion in the west. Neriglassar's successor, and the final Chaldean king, was Nabonidus, who spent much of his reign putting down Syrian rebellions and capturing the town of Shindini in Edom.

Though the Chaldean Empire was not as large as that of the Assyrians, they were known as the great conquerors of the Middle East because of better documentation, especially in the Bible. Nebuchadnezzar destroyed Jerusalem, burned the temple of Solomon, and hauled the people into captivity, but he was also famous for beautifying Babylon and transforming it into the cultural and economic center of its time. The city was about 81 square miles in area and surrounded by a defensive wall of brick. Eight gates into the city were dedicated to eight Chaldean gods. Babylon not only had a royal residence along the Euphrates, but sophisticated, multistory housing and paved streets. Such architectural marvels as the Hanging Gardens and huge temples (possibly even the Tower of Babel) were located in Babylon.

Babylon became the trade center of the Middle East, bringing in goods from India and Arabia. The people excelled in science, especially astronomy and astrology. The city became the center of learning in Mesopotamia, and the beginnings of literature can be traced here. The king was not considered divine, but as a mediator between the gods and the people, and he had to perform rituals worshipping Ishtar, Marduk, and Shamush.

Despite this cultural advancement, or perhaps because of it, the Chaldeans became the targets of yet other invaders. In 539 B.C., the Persian king Cyrus attacked from the east and overwhelmed the Chaldean military, which had been neglected in favor of science and the arts.

*See also* Assyrian Empire [1]; Palestine, Egyptian Invasions of [9].

References: Falls, Cyril, *The First 3000 Years* (New York: Viking Press, 1960); MacQueen, James, *Babylon* (New York: Praeger, 1965); Seignobos, Charles, *The World of Babylon* (New York: Leon Amiel, 1975).

## 4      CYRUS THE GREAT

Texts sing with endless praise of the accomplishments of Cyrus, king of Persia. One would think, therefore, that there would be few aspects of his life undivulged. However, it appears that relatively little is known of his early life and many of his achievements. The contemporary coverage focused on three battles that led to the Persian Empire and on a few decisions made at the beginning of his reign. His birth and death are shrouded with myth.

Some have speculated that Cyrus was the son of a sheepherder who migrated from the mountains north of modern-day Iraq to the plains of the Tigris River valley. We do know that his father, Cambyses, ruled over a small Persian tribe in the southern Tigris-Euphrates area. When Cambyses died, Cyrus took over and united all of the Persian tribes under his rule in 559 B.C.

The first of the three battles he is known to have fought in received limited coverage. Supposedly Cyrus moved against Astyages, King of the Medes, capturing the capital city of Ecbatana in 550. This aggressive act caused the Lydian King Croesus to turn his attention toward the rising Persian threat. The Lydians were allied with the Medians and, through Croesus's conquests, the Lydian boundaries had been extended to the Halys River, west of the newly acquired kingdom of the Persians. Croesus wasted no time in hiring Spartan mercenaries to mount an offensive against Cyrus. When he learned of this, Cyrus led his forces into Lydian territory, demanding that Croesus surrender and become his royal vassal. After a series of battles, Croesus was crushed and the Lydian capital at Sardis was captured in 546. Cyrus's generals extended his empire to the Hellespont while he attempted conquests in the east. Again, the details of his exploits have escaped modern historians. Evidently, he succeeded in extending the boundaries of the empire to the Indus River in the east and the Oxus River in the northeast.

Cyrus now sought to bring the Babylonian Empire under his control. In 539, conflict began when Belshazzar, the emperor's son and the reigning governor of Babylon, confronted Cyrus at Opis. Belshazzar was soundly defeated and the city Babylon was captured without a fight. Cyrus entered the city several days later, proclaiming himself liberator. Several factors contributed to the fall of Babylon. Nebonidus, its emperor, raised heavy taxes to pay for personal religious expeditions. He also introduced the gods of Ur, Uruk, and Eryden, which angered Babylonian priests. These actions encouraged dissidents to aid the Persians in the overthrow.

The first of Cyrus's great qualities was his ability to lead in battle. Through the strategies employed in the three battles one can see his genius. Against the Lydians he marched his troops several thousand miles through winter snows, after a standoff at Pteria, in order to surprise Croesus at Sardis. Croesus had sent most of his troops home, thinking the Persians would be delayed by the weather and terrain. Cyrus's military vision also can be appreciated in the fall of Babylon. To capture the city, he diverted the waters of the Euphrates, which flowed through the city, so his troops could enter under the wall. Cyrus organized and trained his troops better than any other ruler of his day. Organization proved to be a problem because the Persian army was composed of several different tribal and ethnic groups. Cyrus divided these groups by tribes, allowing some of their own tribesmen to lead them. The familiarity of a local leader aided the troops in their ability to trust Cyrus's decisions.

The last qualities relate to one another. They were policies that grew from an attitude of openness and toleration. The ritual of conquering nations dictated that a vassal state surrender all customs and national identity to the conquerors. The Assyrian and Babylonian empires practiced displacement of peoples and the destruction of their cultures by carrying off their gods to their respective capitals. Conversely, Cyrus allowed the conquered peoples of Babylon to return to their homeland with their gods. The Hebrew people particularly benefited from these policies, as they had been prisoners in Babylon for seventy years. When Cyrus came to power, he permitted them to return to Palestine with the sacred elements of their temple. Cyrus also funded the rebuilding of the Temple in Jerusalem, issuing a decree that gave Jewish leaders the power to secure the materials needed for construction.

These policies of tolerance led to this proclamation after the fall of Babylon: "Come forth, collect your herds, draw water for the animals, and give your families to eat. The disturbance is ended, the peace of Archaemedia prevails." The kingdom of Cyrus would be the precursor of many tolerant empires to come. Cyrus would have been forgotten as an insignificant character, and not assigned the status "the Great" afforded him today, were it not for his tolerant policies. The familiarity of his name in the Western Hemisphere grows largely out of the praise given to him in the Old Testament. The Book of Ezra elevates him to an exalted status: ". . . the Lord God of Heaven . . . appointed me [Cyrus] to build a Temple for Him at Jerusalem." The Jewish and Christian faiths recognize Cyrus as not only the king of Persia, they also call him "the Great" because of his benevolent and tolerant policies, which led to the propagation of both faiths.

*See also* Assyrian Empire [1]; Chaldean (Neo-Babylonian) Empire, Expansion of [3]

References: Huart, Clement, *Ancient Persian and Iranian Civilization* (New York: Barnes & Noble, 1972); Lamb, Harold, *Cyrus the Great* (New York: Doubleday, 1960); Sykes, Sir Percy, *Persia* (Oxford: Clarendon Press, 1922)

## 5     EGYPT, HYKSOS INVASION OF

Power slipped from the pharaohs of Egypt in the late Middle Kingdom, during the Twelfth Dynasty, in a relatively easy victory for the Hikau-Khoswet, a name originating from the Egyptian phrase meaning "rulers of foreign lands." An Asiatic group composed primarily of Semites, the Hikau-Khoswet, or Hyksos, reigned over Egypt for well over 100 years, beginning from about 1750 B.C. and ending with the establishment of the New Kingdom in 1567 B.C. The main catalysts that enabled the Hyksos to invade the Nile Delta so easily were the internal dissent among the Egyptians themselves, a counterrevolt of the nobility, and a weakening of the power of the pharaohs. Additionally, the Hyksos were said to be well trained and well armed, using tactics that included the introduction of the horse and chariot to Egypt.

During the course of their invasion, towns and cities were burned, temples damaged, and the native populations subjected to severe hardships and cruelties. Once the Hyksos gained control, they imposed heavy taxes as well as a strong military dominance. Surprisingly, the majority of Egyptians accepted this style of leadership without much resistance.

The Hyksos were not entirely preoccupied with military goals. According to William Hayes, "The Hyksos kings of the Fifteenth Dynasty brought about the construction of temples, production of statues, reliefs, scarabs, and other works of art and craftsmanship," some of which are regarded as the best examples of Egyptian literary and technical works of that time. Practical and useful inventions such as the well sweep, the vertical loom, and the composite bow, as well as the introduction of new religious and philosophical concepts, were Hyksos legacies. Until this time, Egypt was comparatively slow in its technological advancements in relation to the Middle Eastern civilizations. Egyptians were now able to learn of bronze working, the potter's wheel, and the use of arsenic copper. The Hyksos also introduced humpbacked cattle and fruit crops, and taught the Egyptians new planting and harvesting skills. Evidence suggests that the Hyksos encouraged exercise through dance and expression with new musical instruments.

On the whole, the Hyksos seem to have been a powerful and influential people, but only a few rulers can take credit for these advances. One of the six Hyksos rulers was Prince Salatis, a name that has been interpreted to mean "Sultan." During his rise to power, he banned the contemporary Egyptian rulers from the capital city of Memphis and extended his rule over most of Middle Egypt, eventually taking over Upper Egypt and Nubia as well. In the meantime, Hyksos rulers had moved the capital to Avaris, the location of which remains a mystery. Though these Semitic invaders were eventually overthrown by the Egyptians in the late 1560s, they left behind the tools and knowledge that helped build Egypt's future empire. Little information exists on the Hyksos invasion itself, but their overall accomplishments were dynamic and paved the way for future Egyptian glory.

References: Baines, J., and J. Malek, *Atlas of Ancient Egypt* (New York: Facts on File, 1980); Hayes, W., *The Scepter of Egypt* (Cambridge, MA: Harvard University Press, 1959); Van Seeters, J., *The Hyksos* (New Haven, CT: Yale University Press, 1966).

# HITTITES

The Hittites probably originated northeast of the Caucasus. They migrated into Asia Minor ca. 1900 B.C. and established a kingdom. They occupied the Anatolian plateau, ultimately extending their influence toward Syria. Their migration may have pushed other populations southward, creating the Hyksos invasion of Egypt. The Hittites probably took their name from the Plain of Hatti, which they occupied and upon which they imposed their culture and Indo-European language. Their first conquest was the town of Nesa (near modern Kayseri, Turkey) followed by the capture of Hattusha (near modern Bogazkoy).

Little is known of them until the seventeenth century B.C., when Labarna (ruled ca. 1680–1650) established the Old Hittite Kingdom and set up his capital at Hattusha. Labarna was the first major conqueror for the Hittites, spreading their control throughout Anatolia to the coast. His successors pushed their borders southward to Syria. Mursili (or Mushilish) raided deep into the Old Babylonian Empire, captured Aleppo, and set the kingdom's southern boundary in Syria. This proved to be the extent of their conquest, for they spent the next two centuries quelling internal disturbances and fighting the Mitanni of upper Mesopotamia.

Around 1500 B.C., the kingdom returned to some stability under the leadership of Telipinu, who laid down strict succession guidelines and possibly established a law code. Some 50 years later, the New Hittite Kingdom was established. The Hittites had just suffered a defeat at the hands of Egyptian pharaoh Thutmosis III and had begun paying them tribute. One of the key figures in the New Kingdom was Suppiluliuma (Shubbiluliu), who seized power about 1380 B.C., reestablished Hittite authority in Anatolia, and defeated the Mitanni. He was unable to defeat the Egyptians, however, and the two powers remained rivals for the next century. During a time of Egyptian weakness under Akhenaton, the Hittites made gains in Lebanon at Egyptian expense; they also spread their power to the Aegean, Armenia, and Upper Mesopotamia.

The key battle in the ongoing conflict with Egypt took place in 1294 B.C. at Kadesh, on the Orontes River. Pharaoh Rameses II led his army of Numidian mercenaries north to force his will on the Hittites once and for all. He captured two Hittite deserters, who informed him that their army was still many days' march away, so Rameses rode ahead of his army to set up camp near Kadesh. The two prisoners had been planted by the Hittite king Muwatallis, and the pharaoh, without most of his troops, was attacked by the Hittite army. Rameses fought bravely until his men arrived, and their appearance forced a Hittite retreat into the city of Kadesh. Without siege equipment, Rameses could not force their surrender, so he withdrew. Shortly thereafter, the two nations signed a peace agreement: The Egyptians recognized Hittite sovereignty in Syria in return for Hittite recognition of Egyptian dominance in Palestine. The alliance was sealed by a dynastic marriage, and the two nations remained at peace until the fall of the Hittite Empire, which came at the hands of the "Peoples of the Sea," about 1200 B.C.

The Hittite legacy showed itself in a mixed culture in the region of northern Syria. Some of their written and spoken language remained in the region, as did their last remaining city-states, which were ultimately overrun by the Arameans (forerunners of modern Syrians) and then by the Assyrians in the eighth century B.C. The Hittites used both cuneiform writing adopted from Mesopotamia and hieroglyphics influenced by Egypt, and their formal political writings were in Akkadian. They had a highly developed literature and historical writings. Their main strength lay in their administration; their law codes were based on those of Babylon, but depended less on retribution than on compensation. Their artwork, though recognizable as their own, was heavily influenced by Babylon, as was much of their pantheon. The Hittites are believed to be the first to smelt iron, which would account for some of their military superiority at a time when their enemies, especially Egypt, were still using bronze. Apparently, it did not prove a sufficient advantage to save their civilization from invasion.

*See also* Assyrian Empire [1]; Egypt, Hyksos Invasion of [5].

References: Ceram, C. W., *The Secret of the Hittites,* trans. Richard Winston and Clara Winston (New York: Alfred A. Knopf, 1956); Lehman, Johannes, *The Hittites: People of a Thousand Gods,* trans. J. M. Brownjohn (New York: Viking Press, 1977); MacQueen, J. G., *The Hittites and Their Contemporaries in Asia Minor* (London: Thames & Hudson, 1968).

## INDIA, ARYAN INVASION OF

**7**

The earliest known civilization in India was that of the Harappans, who established well-organized cities in the valley of the Indus River in the third millennium B.C. By about 2000 B.C., the civilization was beginning to fade, probably because of climatic changes, which brought about shifts in the rivers and widespread flooding. By sheer coincidence, as the Harappans were weaken-

ing, a group of invaders appeared from the steppes of the Caucasus. The Aryans were mostly nomadic—herding sheep, horses, and cattle—and, like most nomadic peoples, more warlike than the agricultural inhabitants of northern India. Both by migration and by force of arms, they dominated the area of the upper Indus valley and over time spread eastward down the Ganges.

The Aryans take their name from the word in their Sanskrit language meaning "noble." The Aryans themselves are identified as a language group, not a racial one. The fact that their area of origin made them lighter skinned than the people they conquered has nothing to do with the language they spoke, so equating "Aryan" with "white" is an incorrect, nineteenth-century concept made worse by some twentieth-century racists. However, the original Aryans instituted a practice that called for separation of their peoples from the conquered. Their society was based on four basic classes: priests, warriors, merchants/artisans, and laborers. This class division did not include the conquered peoples of India, and this attitude was the basis of the caste system that dominates India to this day; hence the term "outcast[e]s," or untouchables, of modern India.

The Aryans ultimately settled down to an agricultural way of life, but their early years in India resulted in the perpetuation of their herding ways. The plains of northern India provided good grazing land, and their herds of horses and cattle grew. Cattle became the most valuable of commodities, possibly foreshadowing the sacredness of cattle in the Hindu faith. The Aryans' famous horsemanship was a major reason for their military successes, as the Harappans had neither cavalry nor chariots. A military society built around the upper-class warriors was reflected in the rowdiness of the Aryans, who celebrated life with drinking, horse racing, and gambling; the latter was a national obsession.

The greatest legacy of the Aryans is the religious works passed down originally through the priesthood. The *Vedas* are a collection of religious rituals handed down through oral tradition and finally committed to writing when that skill was introduced about 700 B.C. The ceremonies practiced and the gods worshipped through the *Vedas* laid the groundwork for the introduction of the Hindu faith, the dominant religion of India for some 2,000 years.

Though they were conquerors of northern India early in the second millennium B.C. and of the northeastern plains and Ganges River valley between 1000 and 500 B.C., the Aryans became the dominant inhabitants of India as they settled into agricultural pursuits. This less mobile pastime bred, as it almost always does, a less martial society, but the Indians managed to remain fairly isolated from later conquerors. Alexander the Great spent two years fighting and negotiating in northwestern India, installing a Greek administration in some areas. After his death, however, Chandragupta Maurya overthrew the bureaucracy and established an Indian empire. Not until the Islamic invasion of India in the A.D. 800s did outside forces have much luck in penetrating the subcontinent.

*See also* Mauryan Empire [27]; India, Muslim Invasion of [53].

References: Gokhale, Balkrishna, *Ancient India: History and Culture* (Bombay and New York: Asia Publishing House, 1959); Wheeler, Radha, *Early India and Pakistan* (New York: Praeger, 1959); Wolpert, Stanley, *India* (Englewood Cliffs, NJ: Prentice Hall, 1965).

## 8   KUSH, EXPANSION OF

About 1500 B.C., Egypt conquered the area above the cataracts known as Kush. The purposes of this expedition were to establish frontier forts to protect against the aggressive Nubians and to gain access to the gold of Kush. Egypt dominated the area for about 400 years, until the collapse of the New Kingdom. In the meantime, they introduced Egyptian civilization into Kush, and the Kushites found it attractive. By the 700s B.C., Kush had grown in power and invaded Egypt in turn. Starting about 725 B.C., Kushites conquered Thebes and Memphis, establishing themselves as rulers of Egypt and beginning the Twenty-fifth Dynasty. Their occupation was relatively short-lived, thanks to the Assyrians who invaded in 664 B.C. and forced the Kushites to return home, behind the protective barriers of the Nile cataracts.

Though no longer a major factor in Egyptian history, the Kushites established a strong civilization along Egyptian lines. They copied Egyptian religion and government, and built temples and tombs heavily influenced by Egyptian architecture. Their capital at Napata, just south of the fourth cataract, was a major religious center for the worship of Amon-re. When a later Egyptian ruler raided into Kush with the aid of Greek mercenaries, the capital was moved from Napata to Meroe, which became not only the political but the mercantile center of the Kushite empire. In the few centuries prior to the Christian era, a succession of kings established their control over outlying areas and peoples, and bragged about it on inscribed memorials.

Kush reached the height of its civilization at the beginning of the Christian era, when a series of military encounters with Roman forces in Egypt brought about a treaty establishing exact borders between the two powers. By this time Meroe was the major supply center for gold as well as precious and semiprecious stones from the interior of Africa to the Mediterranean world. The profits from this trade translated into elaborate buildings and artwork. Kush made a name for itself throughout the known world, and references and artistic depictions of them spread widely through the ancient world. Indeed, it is from the Greeks that the name for the peoples of this area comes: Ethiopians, or "men with burnt faces." Kush was the first essentially negroid nation to reach great-power status. They were the first Africans to mine and smelt iron; that, plus their ability to buy horses, gave them a better armed, more mobile army than any of their neighbors.

Kush eventually fell owing to circumstances beyond its control. The area the Kushites controlled was fertile enough to support extensive agriculture and flocks at the time, but today it is almost totally desert. Historians hypothesize that overgrazing and a shift in weather patterns began to rob the land of its fertility, making it impossible to support the population. Also, the trade routes Meroe controlled along the Nile began to fall from favor after easier, seagoing trade established itself along the Red Sea coast. This lack of income, coupled with decreasing arable land, spelled the Kushites' doom, and they fell an easy prey to Axum about A.D. 350.

For 2,000 years Kush had been virtually the only point of contact between Africa's interior and the civilizations of the Middle East. Almost nothing is known of their posterity, though legends relate that the ruling families traveled west into the Sudan and were instrumental in establishing nations in central Africa.

*See also* Assyrian Empire [1]; Axum, Expansion of [35].

References: Hallett, Robin, *Africa to 1875* (Ann Arbor: University of Michigan Press, 1970); Mokhtar, G., *Ancient Civilizations of Africa* (Paris: UNESCO, 1990).

## PALESTINE, EGYPTIAN INVASIONS OF

**9**

Considering the number of times Egyptian armies entered Palestine, it is somewhat ironic that the spur for their activity was an invasion that probably came from Palestine. For about 100 years the Egyptians had been ruled by the Hyksos, who introduced new weaponry (especially the chariot) to Egypt. As is often the case, the rulers became lazy and corrupt, and in the middle 1500s B.C. Egyptian rebels overthrew them. The Egyptian army that chased them back to their homeland was the first in a long line of forces to cross the Suez into Palestine.

The Theban prince Ahmose chased the Hyksos out of Egypt and established a foothold on the eastern Mediterranean coast. Tuthmosis I led his army as far as the Euphrates River, and set up a monument to himself. His immediate successors had little to do with the area, but in the reign of Tuthmosis III (1490–1436 B.C.), 17 expeditions entered Palestine or Syria, and the Egyptians fought several times against the Mitanni, a confederation of Hurrian tribes living north of the Euphrates who raided or forced tribute from a large area in the Middle East. Tuthmosis's eighth campaign resulted in a major defeat of the king of Kadesh at the plain of Megiddo, or Armageddon. Tuthmosis personally led a flanking maneuver that crushed his opponents in what became the first recorded battle in history. He pushed Egyptian influence to the edge of Hittite authority in

Asia Minor and into northwestern Mesopotamia. This proved to be the greatest distance the Egyptian army ever traveled, because Tuthmosis III's successors merely maintained Egyptian influence in Palestine, and signed a treaty with the Mitanni in the late fifteenth century B.C.

Egypt ruled the area with a number of garrisons under the direction of provincial governors. They worked with the local princes to control the larger population centers, holding their princes' children hostage in Egypt to ensure cooperation. The governors' main duty was to provide annual tribute from the conquered territories. What, if anything, the conquerors brought to Palestine is unknown, for there are no written records from this area in that period. The Egyptians probably gave little to the people but a military presence, but they took with them knowledge, which Egypt, long isolated from the rest of the world, used along with the tribute money to build a civilization rich in architecture and culture. The Egyptians grew so accustomed to the tribute that, over time, less attention was paid to the army in Palestine, and Egyptian control began to wane.

After a series of introspective pharaohs, Egypt returned to Palestine in force during the reign of Seti I (1305–1290 B.C.); he launched a number of expeditions to reestablish Egyptian authority. The Egyptians ran into difficulties with the Hittites north of Syria and were ultimately forced to come to an accommodation with them. It would not last. Rameses II returned to Palestine with a large army in 1286 B.C. and marched to the city of Kadesh on the Orontes River. He walked into a trap, but managed to survive with the timely arrival of reinforcements. Rameses's future forays were less ambitious, and he finally signed a treaty with the Hittites in 1269 B.C. The treaty gave Egypt a nominal role in the area, but the Hittites gave little away.

Egypt's influence soon faded. Pressures from desert tribesmen to the west occupied much of their attention, and the Egyptians spent much time trying to maintain the gold supply from the southern territory of Nubia. Many historians believe the Jewish exodus, leading to the establishment of the state of Israel, took place during the reign of Rameses II. Rameses III was the last New Kingdom pharaoh to enter Palestine in order to retain it as part of the empire; he beat back several threats to his frontiers and reconquered Palestine. By the eleventh century B.C., however, Egypt had withdrawn into its shell, coming out only occasionally to unsuccessfully challenge the Assyrians or the Persians. Pharaoh Necho regained temporary sway over Palestine by defeating King Josiah in 609 B.C., but his defeat at the hands of Nebuchadnezzar of Babylon in 605 ended Egypt's role in Palestine's history.

*See also* Assyrian Empire [1]; Canaan, Israelite Invasion of [2]; Cyrus the Great [4]; Egypt, Hyksos Invasion of [5]; Hittites [6]; Kush, Expansion of [8].

References: Hawkes, Jacquetta, *Pharaohs of Egypt* (New York: American Heritage, 1965); Matthew, Eva, *The Mediterranean World in Ancient Times* (New York: Ronald Press, 1951); North, Martin, *The Old Testament World* (Philadelphia: Fortress Press, 1962).

## 10    SARGON THE GREAT

As is the case with many ancient figures, Sargon's early years are somewhat of a mystery. He was born around 2350 B.C. of undetermined parentage. Some historians

Bronze head of the Akkadian ruler
Sargon the Great.

theorize that he had either a pastoral upbringing or that he was the child of a temple
prostitute, for he did not know his father.
According to legend, the boy began life as
Moses did: cast adrift on the Euphrates by
his mother. He was rescued and raised by
others—in this case a farm family, not a
royal one. However, he managed to become
cupbearer to Ur-Zababa, the king of Kish.
He came to power either by overthrowing
the king himself or by assuming the king's
throne when Ur-Zababa was killed by the
invading king of Sumer. He took the name
Sargon, meaning "King of Universal Dominion," and made war against Sumer.

Sargon united his Semitic people into
history's first empire: the Akkadians.
Sargon set about conquering, quite successfully. He captured cities up the Euphrates
River, then crossed to the Tigris River and
worked his way up to Ashur. From there
he conquered eastward to the Persian hills,
then south to defeat Sumer, possibly gaining revenge for the death of Ur-Zababa. He
symbolically washed his weapons in the
Persian Gulf, marking the limit of his conquests in that direction. After consolidating his hold on Sumer, he marched west to
conquer Mesopotamia and possibly as far
as Syria and Lebanon, with rumors of conquests in lands as far-flung as Egypt, Asia
Minor, and India.

In order to control this vast amount of
territory, Sargon appointed representatives
of the conquered peoples to governing positions, and they answered only to him. He stationed troops in posts around the empire,
garrisoning them with forces of all nations,
though some soldiers were forced to join his
armies. Sargon was successful in battle because he initiated new tactics. He abandoned
the standard tight, phalanx-style formation
in favor of a looser one, and he adopted the
use of javelins and arrows shot from compound bows. He also maintained the first
standing army, a force of 5,400 men.

By placing so much land under one ruler,
previously uncooperative peoples became
more open to relations with neighboring
tribes, and the freer exchange of goods and
ideas resulted. New gods and religions were
adopted from conquered peoples, as were
cuneiform writing and art. The Akkadians
were the first to use writing for more than
keeping temple records. Because of this, we
have the first recorded actions of royalty;
hence, Sargon is regarded as the first clearly
identified individual in history. He set an
example for later royal chroniclers, as seen
here: "He spread his terror-inspiring glam-
our over all the countries. He crossed the
Sea in the East and he, himself, conquered
the country of the West. . . . He marched
against the country of Kazalla and turned
Kazalla into ruin-hills and heaps of rubble.
He even destroyed there every possible
perching place for a bird."

Having acquired vast amounts of land, Sargon's empire was exceedingly wealthy, controlling the known world's gold, silver, copper, and stone. With the abundant agriculture of Mesopotamia and plenty of forage to the north, Sargon seemingly had it all. He maintained control by appointing loyal governors and visiting parts of his empire on occasion to let the people know he was interested in them. He ruled for 56 years, but his reign ended with parts of the empire in revolt. The Akkadian empire lasted some 200 years, only to be overthrown by those whom they had originally defeated—a resurgent Sumerian society.

References: Edwards, I. E. S., ed., *The Cambridge Ancient History* (Cambridge: Cambridge University Press, 1980); Gabriel, Richard, *The Culture of War* (New York: Greenwood Press, 1990); Gabriel, Richard, *From Sumer to Rome* (New York: Greenwood Press, 1991).

# PART 2
# THE CLASSICAL WORLD

# PART 2
# THE CLASSICAL WORLD

The numbers on the map correspond to entry numbers in the text.

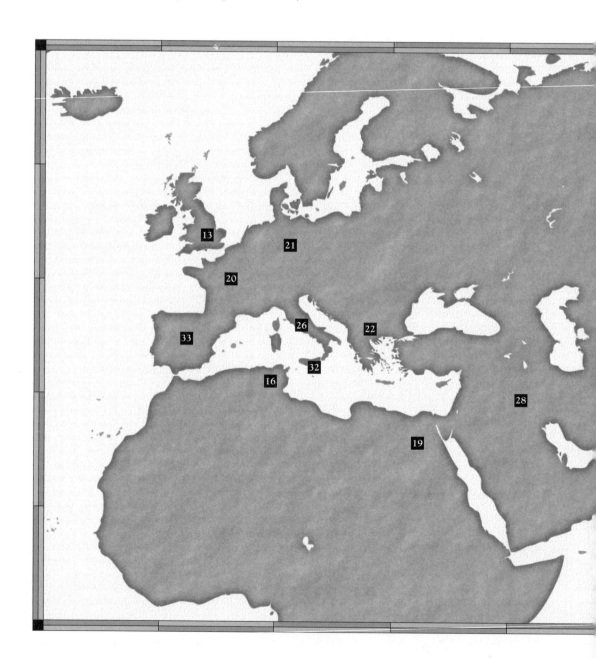

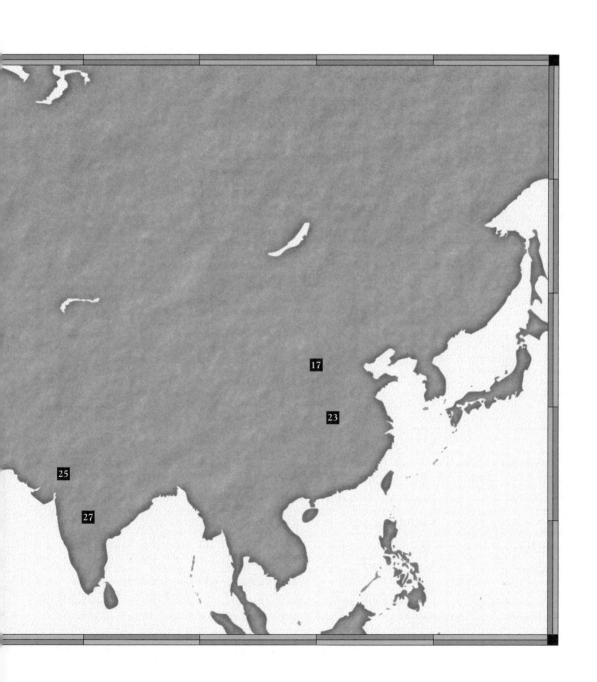

## 11     ALEXANDER THE GREAT

Alexander was born to rule and to conquer. He was the son of the great military and political leader Philip of Macedon and his first wife, Olympia. Philip was organizing the remote province of Macedon into a military powerhouse and using his well-trained and well-disciplined army to beat back the more barbaric tribes of Macedon and attack the more civilized polises of Greece to his south. He defeated the disorganized Greek city-states and obliged them to recognize him—not as their king, but as the defender of the Greek way of life against outside threats, notably from Persia. He convinced most of his defeated enemies to accept this and treated them with magnanimity, but he never converted the Athenian leader Demosthenes, who spent his life opposing Philip and Alexander. It was in the battle of Cheronaea, in which the Macedonians defeated the Athenians, that Alexander first distinguished himself in battle.

He was only 18 years old when he commanded a wing of the Macedonian army at Cheronaea in 338 B.C., but he gained the respect of all who fought with him. His father trained him well in both military and political strategies, but the two fought. Alexander's mother, Olympias, told him that his true father was not Philip but the supreme god Zeus (Ammon to the Egyptians). She also plotted against Philip and may have been responsible for his murder in 336 B.C., an act that brought Alexander to the throne. He quickly put down revolts that sprang up throughout Greece on the news of Philip's death, then marched north to defeat the tribes on Macedon's frontiers. While there, the false report of his death was circulated in Athens and Demosthenes stirred up rebellion, which Alexander suppressed as soon as he returned from the north. Like his father, he spared Demosthenes's life and left a constant irritant in Greece.

Once the rebellions were put down, Alexander marched to the Hellespont, where his father had been preparing to lead the united polises of the Corinthian League against Persia. He marched into Asia Minor in 334 B.C. with 35,000 men, liberating the coastal Ionian provinces from Persian rule. His first serious encounter with Darius III, the Persian emperor, occurred at Issus in northeastern Syria. Contemporary accounts of the Persian force claim it was 500,000 strong, but few historians believe it. Still, although it was probably larger than Alexander's force, the battle proved a fairly easy Macedonian victory. Alexander positioned himself to be in the thick of the fighting, encouraging his comrades and striking fear in his enemies. Darius abandoned the field and ran, leaving behind not only his army but his family, whom Alexander took to his camp and treated like royalty.

Rather than pursue Darius deeper into the countryside, Alexander turned south to capture the coastal cities and deny the harbors to the Persian fleet. Capturing the eastern Mediterranean coast, he entered Egypt and wintered there in 332–331 B.C. He established the city of Alexandria (the first of many) and led a small column into the desert to visit the temple of Ammon. What transpired inside the temple is unknown, but many think Alexander communed with the great god and received confirmation that he was indeed of divine parentage as his mother had told him. True or not, ever after he did nothing to stop those who would deify him. This may have been megalomania or a clever ruse to awe his enemies; no one knows for sure.

Leaving Egypt, he marched into Persia and met a new army under Darius at Gaugamela along the Euphrates River. Again, the contemporary estimates are too fantastic to believe, but Darius proved no match for Alexander. He marched on to the Persian capital at Babylon and occupied it, then captured the Persian treasury at Persepolis. With the Persian empire well under his control, he finally cornered Darius near the Caspian Sea but lost him to the swords of Darius's minions, who murdered him rather than be caught with him. From here, Alexander meandered eastward until he made his way through Afghanistan into India. Here he won victories, but they proved too costly and his army convinced him to abandon the expedition and return to Persia. He did so, taking the desert route, which proved much more difficult than he had anticipated.

Back in Persia, Alexander began to show his brilliance as a statesman. He had a vision for a world empire in which the wealth and culture of the East would meld with the rationality and drive of the Greeks. He encouraged his veterans to marry Persian women in order to facilitate the integration of the two societies. He began to act more like an Eastern potentate than a Greek general, and his men grew weary of that. He shamed them into remaining loyal, but his time was limited. Not long after his return from India, the wounds he received in battle there, along with the difficulty of the desert march and the fever he developed in Babylon, conspired to ruin his health. The stress of combat and leadership was not aided by his prodigious thirst; alcoholism too brought about his demise.

Alexander can be regarded as one of only a handful of truly brilliant leaders. Like Genghis Khan and Charlemagne, he was equally adept at both conquest and rule. He was ruthless in battle but forgiving in victory, gaining converts to his cause from among his opponents. His dream of blending the two diverse cultures of East and West was successful for some centuries, for his successors (the Ptolemaic Dynasty and

Seleucid Empire) created a Greek-like society called Hellenism, which blended the perspective and scientific bent of the Greeks with the beauty and grace of Eastern philosophies. The intellectual and artistic accomplishments of the Hellenistic societies surpassed anything that had come before and attracted the future power of the Mediterranean, Rome, to desire and fight for the mystic East. His generalship created an army that was unbeatable and soldiers who were second to none, but his successors learned only from his military lessons and not from his political acumen. They fought among themselves and by doing so laid themselves open to defeat by Rome.

*See also* Egypt, Alexander's Conquest of [19]; India, Alexander's Invasion of [25]; Persia, Alexander's Conquest of [28]; Philip of Macedon [29]; Ptolemaic Dynasty [30]; Seleucid Empire [31]; Carolingian Dynasty [39]; Genghis Khan [47].

References: Arrian, *The Campaigns of Alexander,* trans. Aubrey de Selincourt (New York: Penguin, 1958); Keegan, John, *The Mask of Command* (New York: Viking, 1987); Tarn, W. W., *Alexander the Great* (Cambridge: Cambridge University Press, 1948).

## 12      AUGUSTUS, CAESAR

Gaius Julius Caesar Octavianus, or more simply Octavian, was the grandnephew of Julius Caesar and was named in his will as heir. After Julius Caesar's assassination in March 44 B.C., his killers left Rome, Cassius going to Syria and Brutus to Macedonia. Mark Antony, consul under Julius and one of his most trusted advisers and generals, saw himself as the rightful political successor, and he was not happy to see Octavian present himself to the Senate as such. After some fighting among themselves, Octavian finally invited Antony to join forces with him and another general, Lepidus, to form the Second Triumvirate. With Senate approval they marched to do battle with Cassius and Brutus. In October 43 B.C., the forces met near Philippi, in Greece. They were evenly matched in numbers, but Antony proved the more able general. Two battles were fought; the first was a draw in which Cassius killed himself, and the second was a clear victory for the Triumvirate, resulting in Brutus's suicide soon after.

The Triumvirate soon quarreled among themselves, but at the signing of the Treaty of Brundisium in 40 B.C., the empire was divided among the three members: Lepidus controlled Africa, Octavian ruled the western provinces from Rome, and Antony ruled the provinces of the east. Antony aided Octavian in suppressing a revolt from Sardinia, Corsica, and Sicily led by the son of Pompey, a member of the original Triumvirate with Julius. In return, Octavian supported Antony's campaigns against Parthia.

Antony's popularity with his troops and his relative success in the east gave him the impetus for more power. He allied himself (personally and politically) with Cleopatra of Egypt, who urged him to seize power. Octavian convinced the Senate that Antony planned to establish rule of the empire from Alexandria in Egypt and name his sons by Cleopatra as his heirs, which motivated the Senate to support Octavian's call for war. Between 33 and 30 B.C., the two sides maneuvered for position until 2 September 31, when Octavian's forces won the naval battle of Actium, defeating Egypt's navy. Octavian proceeded to invade Egypt against a disheartened Antony and a desperate Cleopatra. After

suffering reverses at Roman hands, the two killed themselves and left Octavian supreme. He looted the Egyptian treasury, which was immense, and returned to Rome.

After years of turmoil under the Triumvirates, Rome was finally at peace, and Octavian was determined to keep it that way. Though he had not shown himself to be an outstanding soldier, Octavian used the services of able leaders, proving his eye for talent. Thus, his importance lay not in his military ability but in his political acumen, which was extensive. Octavian inherited a republic with far-flung responsibilities, and he turned it into an empire. In 27 B.C. he was named Augustus by the Senate, a title of divinity that he graciously accepted, though he preferred the title First Citizen, *princeps* of the Senate. Octavian thus avoided Julius's mistake of giving the appearance of grasping for power, and his power ultimately far exceeded that of his granduncle. Through lavish spending of his Egyptian wealth he stimulated a lagging economy, and by forgiving debts he stimulated investment; Rome's financial state was soon healthy. He dismissed 60 percent of his half-million-man army, giving them rewards and lands for pensions. He paid the remaining 200,000 men well, and distributed them around the frontiers to maintain what became known as the Roman Peace, the *Pax Romana*. He maintained a Praetorian Guard of 10,000 with which to tacitly keep control of Rome and Italy. After a 20-year enlistment, retiring veterans received land; citizenship was granted to foreigners who served in his army.

Caesar Augustus's most lasting accomplishments were the Roman Empire and the formulation of Augustan law. By synthesizing legal codes from around the known world, he created a system in which all men were treated equally before the law in a manner that did not seem alien to any of the subordinate cultures. The resulting peace created an atmosphere in which trade boomed, as did cultural advancements. Until his death in A.D. 14, Caesar Augustus oversaw the largest and most placid empire to that time. He wisely maintained the forms of republican government to which Roman citizens were accustomed, while working through those institutions to impose his will. He proved that the best government is a benevolent dictatorship; unfortunately, his successors proved more dictatorial than benevolent. Rarely has one man exercised so much positive influence on the world. Not until the reign of Constantine or Justinian would the Mediterranean world come close to being ruled by such a man of vision.

See also Caesar, Julius [14]; Constantine, Emperor [18]; Justinian [58].

References: Campbell, J. B., *The Roman Army, 31 B.C.–A.D. 337* (London: Routledge, 1994); Earl, Donald C., *The Age of Augustus* (New York: Crown, 1968); Jones, A. H. M., *Augustus* (New York: Norton, 1970).

## **13** BRITAIN, ROMAN CONQUEST OF

Between 58 and 50 B.C., prior to the time of his rise to power in Rome, Julius Caesar undertook the conquest of Gaul, an extensive territory roughly corresponding to modern-day France. He did this in order to enhance his financial and political status within Rome's governing elite. The conquest of Gaul brought Britain to Caesar's notice because of the assistance the British gave the Celts of Gaul. Rome had had a strong desire to grow from a republic to an empire, which necessitated the invasion and conquest of other territories

to amass land and riches. As Virgil wrote, "Forget not, Roman, that it is your special genius to rule the peoples; to impose the ways of peace, to spare the defeated, and to crush those proud men who will not submit." Along with the land and wealth that came to Caesar and his successors came power and glory, all of which fueled the desire to "rule the peoples."

Beginning with Julius Caesar and ending with Honorius, the conquest of Britain and its transformation to Roman rule was a process that took centuries. Caesar's invasion was almost an afterthought. During his successful conquest of the Gauls, he recognized that Britain was rich with deposits of tin and iron ore, and that, from a financial standpoint, their resources and prosperity would make Roman conquest worth the effort. Also, from a geographic perspective, England's southeastern shore was only 21 miles across the Channel from Gaul, easily visible on a clear day. During the Gallic campaign, British tribes fought among themselves, and appeals for Roman support from defeated British chieftains indicated that a conquest should not be too difficult. Finally, in light of the Celts' support of their brothers-in-arms across the Channel in Gaul, Caesar no doubt wished to teach some respect for the might of Rome.

Caesar made two forays into Britain, the first in 55 B.C. and the second a year later. Both expeditions were of minor consequence, because Rome's interest in the Britons was just beginning. On both of these attacks, Caesar crossed the Channel and entered Britain by way of Deal, after first being turned away at the cliffs of Dover. Once on land, British forces were overwhelmed and victories came easily. As was the case with all Roman conquests, demands for hostages and regular tribute followed. The significance of Caesar's invasions would not be realized immediately, but the die was cast. Britain had been brought to Rome's attention and, with the organization of Celtic Gaul into Roman provinces, the British began to feel the impact of Roman civilization.

A century went by before the emperor Claudius turned his attention to Britain, in A.D. 43. He sent four Roman legions under the command of Aulus Plautius across the Channel into Kent with the intention of bringing Britain under Roman authority. The Claudian invasion, which lasted 15 years, marked the real beginning of Roman Britain. From this moment on, the primitive culture of the British Celts was transformed by the conquering legions of a huge cosmopolitan power, and by the administrators and entrepreneurs who followed them. The invasion forces represented the best Rome had to offer: Many of the legionaries were specialists such as engineers, architects, masons, clerks, and medical staff. This mixture of soldiers was in keeping with the Roman policy of ensuring that its soldiers were highly trained, long-term professionals whose skills were as important to Rome in peace as in war. Even in garrison, the troops sometimes practiced digging defensive works or assisted civil authorities with building projects. This practice and experience in building and construction work made it possible for Roman armies to construct siege-works, build bridges, and lay roads very quickly during invasions.

In contrast to the highly skilled and organized Roman legions, the British had no standing armies. Lengthy campaigns were impractical for British troops because the majority of them were farmers, and they would leave the fields of battle for their fields of crops. During the Roman march through the British lowlands, in which there was little resistance, the British tried to fight with chariots. One of their favorite stratagems was to feign retreat to draw off small groups of Romans, and then attack them with chariotborne troops, dismounting to fight hand-to-hand.

Following the years of war after the Claudian invasion there were intermittent rebellions against Roman rule. These conflicts were peacefully resolved for the most part, but there was one significant uprising known as Boudicca's Rebellion, which took place in A.D. 60 in the British province of Iceni. This rebellion represented a critical turning point for the Romans in their quest to establish rule. Ironically, the rebellion was organized and led by Boudicca, widow of Prasutagus, king of the province of Iceni, a tribe friendly and loyal to Rome from the beginning of the Claudian invasion. Shortly before Prasutagus died, Nero ascended the Roman throne and appointed C. Suetonius Paulinus, a man of excellent military credentials, as governor of Britain. During this unstable transitional period of Roman rule in Britain, the Roman military and civil officers ransacked the Iceni kingdom of all its wealth, confiscated Queen Boudicca's property, raped her two daughters, and flogged the queen herself. Simultaneously, her neighbors, the Trinovantes of Essex, were becoming impatient with Roman rule. Many Roman soldiers had retired and settled in the colony at Colchester and, in so doing, drove the native Trinovantes from their homes and land, and treated the natives as captives and slaves. These abuses of power and the instability of Roman rule fostered the perception by the natives that perhaps now the time was ripe to rid Britain of the invaders and regain control of their homeland.

In A.D. 60, the uprising commenced. On the Roman side, considerable confusion reigned at first. The British force, led by Boudicca, was a coalition of a half-dozen tribes consisting of 230,000 men, women, and children—farmers, peasants, and soldiers. They advanced on Londinium (London), a city without colonial or municipal status at the time, but already a large and attractive prize for plundering armies. Suetonius realized he did not have a force large enough to repel the British, so he retired and left the city to its fate. Londinium fell to the rebels, and many of the same atrocities and bestialities the Iceni had suffered at Roman hands now befell the residents.

The only way to defeat the overwhelming British force was with superior Roman discipline and tactics. Suetonius could now choose the location of the decisive battle, and he drew up his 10,000 troops in a defensive position to face a force of over 200,000. He placed his men on a hill with woods behind to protect his flanks and rear, then lured the British into attacking uphill. Suetonius drove through Boudicca's force in a tight wedge, the infantry doing serious damage with the *gladius,* a short sword. The Roman cavalry next attacked the flanks of the disorganized British force. Unable to retreat, the British were butchered. Boudicca escaped, but she committed suicide shortly thereafter. Romanization recommenced in full force under peaceful conditions.

Another turning point took place during the reign of the emperor Hadrian in 117. His reign concentrated on consolidation of the empire rather than expansion— securing the borders of Roman Britain rather than conquering new lands—and he made use of the military to restore order in those parts of the empire with violent disaffection. The main effect of this emphasis on defense was three-quarters of a century of peace throughout the empire. Hadrian accomplished this goal in Britain by commissioning the construction of a wall, 70 miles long, spanning the narrow neck of land between Solway Firth and the mouth of the Tyne. The consequences were immense. Protection from the hostile tribes of Scotland brought general prosperity, which in turn caused the provincials to more readily identify with the empire, and it created a unified governing class. The universal extension of Roman citizenship to free inhabitants of the empire would be a direct result of Hadrian's reforms. An air of security allowed economic development by the southern tribes because it allowed them to concentrate on trade, farming, and manufacturing rather than be preoccupied with village defense. A long period of peace and prosperity followed, the likes of which had not been seen for almost 160 years.

For the next two and a half centuries, Roman Britain prospered. The Romans contributed greatly to the development of the British economy, and not only in agriculture. Britain had been mining long before the Claudian invasion, but the Romans introduced more efficient mining technology. They also contributed to the cultural development of Britain by introducing language, theater, art, and trade skills to its labor force. Rome's greatest contribution, though, was peace. Ironically, this reduction of military force led to the successful Visigothic invasion of Britain.

During the reign of Emperor Honorius (395–423) came the beginning of the end of Roman rule in Britain. Many of the highly skilled and trained professional Roman legionaries were replaced by local tribesmen and Saxon mercenaries, who were unable to fend off attacks by the Visigoths. Honorius rejected pleas from Britain in 410 to help defend its borders, and the barbarians ultimately prevailed. Urbanization, one of Rome's greatest contributions, halted completely, and cities and towns withered and died.

*See also* Gaul, Roman Conquest of [20].

References: Fry, Plantagenet Somerset, *Roman Britain, History and Sites* (Totowa, NJ: Barnes & Noble, 1984); Holder,

P. A., *The Roman Army in Britain* (New York: St. Martin's Press, 1982); Salway, Peter, *Roman Britain* (New York: Oxford University Press, 1981).

## 14           CAESAR, JULIUS

Gaius Julius Caesar was born 13 July 100 B.C. At age 16 he took over as head of the family upon his father's death and tended to his mother and two sisters. At age 19 he married Cornelia, the daughter of a Roman consul. After her death, Julius made a politically significant match by marrying the granddaughter of the great consul Sulla. (He divorced her after five years.) Through these contacts, and his military abilities, he rose from the relative unimportance of an impoverished noble family to contacts with the most powerful men in Rome.

Early in his military career, Julius saw service in Asia and Cilicia and was involved in battles against the Persian leader Mithradates. His accomplishments on the battlefield and his political contacts put him in position to be elected tribune in 73 B.C. As this was an elected position, it showed his growing popularity with the public. He later held other elective and appointive offices, including aedile (city administrator), pontifex maximus (head of the priests), and proconsul in Spain. He reached for the top when he allied himself with the two consuls Pompey and Crassus, forming the Triumvirate in 60 B.C. With their support in the Senate, he received the proconsulship of Gaul. There, he could enforce Roman rule and make a name for himself as a general, which was fast becoming the path to political power.

Between 58 and 51 B.C., he subdued Gaul, challenged marauding Germanic tribes, and mounted an expedition to Britain. He also tried to mediate between the increasingly hostile Crassus and Pompey.

Their failing relationship was the catalyst that ultimately led Julius to power. When Crassus was killed on campaign in 53 B.C., and Julia, Julius's daughter and Pompey's wife, died in 54 B.C., the ties binding Julius and Pompey were broken. Pompey appealed to the Senate to remove Julius from his position in Gaul, a move designed to destroy any chance Julius might have to reach the highest government position: consul. Rather than accept his recall, Julius crossed the Rubicon River and led his forces into Italy, a treasonable act that led to direct military confrontation between himself and Pompey.

Julius's reputation had preceded him, and many cities welcomed his arrival as Pompey's forces fled. Their forces finally fought at Pharsalus, where Julius was victorious. Pompey fled to Egypt, but was murdered upon his arrival. Julius followed, and fell under the spell of the Egyptian queen Cleopatra; when her brother dethroned her, Julius helped her regain the throne. Cleopatra considered a close relationship with Caesar the best security for her country, which was a declining power. After a quick campaign against the Persian Mithradates VI, Caesar returned to Rome.

Caesar did much to improve the lot of the Roman citizen. He established two colonies to drain off surplus population, and revived an old law requiring one-third of all agricultural laborers to become free men, cutting into the widespread use of slave labor long practiced by estate owners. He worked on codifying Roman law, opened the first public library in Rome, drained marshes around the city, and surveyed and mapped the empire. His longest lasting contribution was the Julian calendar, which remained the standard for date-keeping until the Middle Ages.

As a military man Caesar is best known for his Gallic War, mainly because he wrote about it firsthand in his *Commentaries.*

While in service in Gaul, he promoted the engineering aspect of Roman armies by modifying camp structure and weaponry. He improved the gathering of intelligence, the methods of training, and the art of military speechmaking. He promoted loyalty by increasing pay and benefits, and by his increased respect for the rights of soldiers. His campaign in Gaul secured the region for the Roman Empire for centuries and set up the later Roman conquest of Britain.

Rather than claim the position of king, which had been banned by the Roman Republic at its birth centuries earlier, Caesar took the title Dictator. He had himself elected to this position for single-year terms, then for a ten-year term; shortly afterward, he accepted the position for life. The difference in terminology between king and dictator was too indistinct for the Roman Senate, which Caesar had reduced to an almost powerless body. On the Ides (fifteenth) of March 44 B.C., Caesar was assassinated on his way to address the Senate. The conspirators, led by Marcus Junius Brutus and Gaius Cassius Longinus, removed the man who threatened to return the Republic to the status of a kingdom, but they had no contingency plans of their own. They were defeated shortly after by Caesar's grandnephew and appointed heir, Octavian, who instituted the position of Emperor and, as Caesar Augustus, took Rome to its greatest power. Julius Caesar did not make the Roman Empire himself, but his actions laid the groundwork for the successes of Augustus.

See also Augustus, Caesar [12]; Britain, Roman Conquest of [13].

References: Bradford, Ernle, *Julius Caesar: The Pursuit of Power* (New York: Morrow, 1984); Caesar, Julius, *Commentaries,* trans. John Warrington (New York: Heritage Press, 1955); Wiseman, Anne, and Peter Wiseman, *Julius Caesar: The Battle for Gaul* (Boston: David R. Godine, 1980).

## 15　CARTHAGE, EXPANSION OF

The city of Carthage was established by the Phoenicians late in the ninth century B.C. as a stopping place for eastern Mediterranean traders plying their business with the inhabitants of Spain and the western Mediterranean. Tyre was the parent city to Carthage, which is the Latinized version of the Phoenician Kart-Hadasht, or New City. The trading empire of Phoenicia, dealing in various metals, was well established in Spain; they also had settlement/trading posts in Sicily, Corsica, and Sardinia. Carthage represented the first major attempt to settle along the North African coast outside the Egyptian sphere of influence.

The inhabitants of Carthage lived peacefully for more than two centuries because the local Libyan population was not organized enough to resist them and whatever military action was necessary was directed from Tyre. When Phoenicia came under Babylonian control, however, Carthage lost its connection with the homeland and came into its own. While Babylon was conquering the Levant, the Greeks stirred up trouble in Sicily, where their colonies attacked Phoenician settlements around 580 B.C. Carthage provided the defensive forces for Sicily and for threatened towns in southern Sardinia. In 553 B.C. Carthage allied with the Etruscans of Italy; together, they inflicted a major defeat of a Greek fleet off Corsica. That battle made Carthage master of the western Mediterranean and gave it dominance over the Spanish trade.

Like Phoenicia, Carthage's major expansion was in the form of settlement and trade. The society was so involved in trade that its military forces were almost always mercenaries. After a defeat of its army and navy at Himera in Sicily in 480 B.C., Carthage focused its attention on expansion in North Africa, spreading its influence from Libya to the Atlantic coast of modern Morocco. The Carthaginians made little attempt to enter the interior, so their dominance was almost exclusively along the coastal strip. Though Carthage maintained settlements in western Sicily after the defeat at Himera, it took as small a part as possible in the island's politics, rising only to defend its settlements from attack by Syracuse in the east.

Carthage's relationship with Rome proved its ultimate undoing. Though the two cooperated against Greece, they had little other contact because their spheres of influence did not overlap. That came to an end in 264, when both Carthage and Rome sent forces to save a band of Roman mercenaries, employed by Carthage, fighting around Syracuse. The result was the First Punic War, which lasted 23 years and was followed by two more Roman-Carthaginian wars, the latter of which resulted in Carthage's utter destruction.

Carthage was almost unique in ancient history for having its wealth built almost completely on trade. Carthaginians became the middlemen for almost all Mediterranean trade west of Sicily, reaching as far as Cape Verde on the Atlantic coast of Africa and possibly as far as the Atlantic coast of France. Carthage displayed little in the way of culture that was particularly their own, but they served as disseminators of eastern cultures to the western reaches of the known world. The language and sciences of the East were made available to the West, and the Carthaginians established urbanization in northern Africa, where before only tribal villages existed. The transformation to "modern"

civilization in northern Africa, Spain, Corsica, and Sardinia was due to Carthaginian merchants.

See also Carthage, Roman Invasion of (Third Punic War) [16]; Italy, Carthaginian Invasion of (Second Punic War) [26]; Sicily, Roman Conquest of (First Punic War) [32].

References: Charles-Picard, Gilbert, and Collette Picard, *The Life and Death of Carthage*, trans. Dominique Collon (London: Sidgwick & Jackson, 1968); Warmington, B. H., *Carthage: A History* (London: Robert Hale, 1960).

# CARTHAGE, ROMAN INVASION OF (THIRD PUNIC WAR)

**16**

After Rome was victorious in the Second Punic War, Carthage recovered well and quickly under the leadership of Hannibal. He was as able a political leader as a military one, but as he learned in his campaign in Italy, the people of Carthage would not give him sufficient support. The Carthaginians' return to economic health made them believe that they could return to military health as well, though the terms of the treaty ending the Second Punic War denied them the ability to make war at all outside Africa, and only with Rome's permission on the continent. This control over Carthage's foreign policy laid the groundwork for the city's doom.

The Numidian king Masinissa, a one-time ally of Carthage against Rome, changed sides during the latter stages of the last war and was now trying to expand his kingdom at Carthaginian expense. He periodically demanded lands, which Carthage ceded because of Roman support of Masinissa's claims. The demands were not extravagant, but over time they chipped away at Carthage's homeland. As Carthage grew surly at this loss of territory, Rome became jealous of the revived Carthaginian economy. In Rome a merchant class arose, gaining influence in the government, and the merchants had a powerful mouthpiece in M. Porcius Cato. Cato wanted Carthage destroyed, and Masinissa's claims proved the vehicle for that destruction.

In 156 B.C. the Carthaginian government demanded that a Roman envoy come to Africa to rule on Masinissa's latest demand. Cato got the job, and observed firsthand the revival of Carthage's power. He ruled for Masinissa, provoking war. In 151 B.C. Carthage invaded Numidia, but it was a disastrous campaign and their army was virtually destroyed. As they had gone to war without Roman permission, Rome declared war on them. To Roman surprise, Carthage put up no resistance, depending on a complete surrender to guarantee lenient terms. The Romans restored lost territory to the Carthaginians, but demanded that the city itself be abandoned. The citizens would not concede their city, so Rome laid siege from 149 to 146 B.C.

The city finally fell to P. Cornelius Scipio Aemillius, son of a hero of Rome's war against Macedon and grandson of the Scipio Africanus, who defeated Hannibal. Just as Rome had demanded, no one lived in Carthage afterward because the Roman government ordered Aemillius to raze the city and sell into slavery the 10 percent of citizens who survived the siege. The destruction of the Carthaginian empire brought its territory under direct Roman control, and the city of Utica became its new capital. The province proved a valuable source of grain for Rome's expanding empire, and a century after the city's fall it was rebuilt under orders of Julius Caesar, who settled some of his veterans there. The

North African coast was so Romanized that any remains of Carthaginian influence virtually disappeared. Whatever chance Carthage had had of dominating the western Mediterranean and bringing the culture and religion of the East into Europe halted. Roman power and civilization were reconfirmed and remained dominant until the A.D. 400s, when the Vandals conquered the area.

*See also* Hannibal [24]; Italy, Carthaginian Invasion of (Second Punic War) [26]; Vandals [79].

References: Bagnall, Nigel, *The Punic Wars* (London: Hutchinson, 1990); Caven, Brian, *The Punic Wars* (London: Weidenfeld & Nicolson, 1980); Dorey, T. A., and D. R. Dudley, *Rome against Carthage* (London: Secker & Warburg, 1971).

## 17        CH'IN DYNASTY

The Chinese had been under the leadership of the Shang and Chou dynasties, but neither dynasty had been able to maintain a strong hold over a large amount of territory nor protect the citizens from nomadic raiders. The Chou dynasty established a capital at Hao, near modern Sian, in the eleventh century B.C., but was forced to move eastward in 770 B.C. by the pressure of barbarian invaders coupled with some rebellious provinces. The eastern capital at Loyang oversaw a smaller Chinese state until 476 B.C., when the Chou emperor was reduced to the status of prince. For another 250 years the provinces warred among themselves until one fought its way to the top in 221 B.C.: the Ch'in.

The Ch'in learned from the nomads the successful military use of cavalry. They also developed a militaristic society under the leadership of Shang Yang, who removed the traditional power of the aristocracy and replaced it with a ruling class based on success in battle. All the adult males were liable for military service and could rise in status by showing bravery in combat. Any member of a ruling family who engaged in private quarrels or did not fight well in battle would be punished. With an increasingly powerful military, the Ch'in also worked diplomatically to keep the other states at odds with one another so they could not combine in opposition. In 278 B.C. the Ch'in attacked and seized the capital of their neighbors, the Chou. The Chou leader fell to Ch'in aggression in 256 B.C., and the last of the five opposing states fell in 222. The next year China was declared united under one lord, who took the title Ch'in Shih Huang-ti, or Ch'in First Emperor.

Shih Huang-ti implemented a centralized bureaucracy, removing the aristocracies from the conquered states. He brought their leaders to his capital and built them luxurious homes—not from kindness, but to keep them under his watchful eye. He appointed governors to the provinces he created in his now-unified state, who had the duty of enforcing the law and mobilizing the local population for military duty. He ordered a census in such depth that it rivaled the *Domesday Book* of William the Conqueror in England. Shih Huang-ti also began the construction of a large series of internal improvements, and mandated standards for construction, language, and coinage. His administration was based on the Chinese philosophy of legalism, which punished lawbreakers but also rewarded those who aided in law keeping. Easily the most famous of the Ch'in projects was the construction of the Great Wall to protect the Chinese from northern nomadic raiders. His military power took his armies as far south as the Red River valley in modern Vietnam and onto the Korean penin-

sula. Campaigning and the construction of large palaces reflected his power but cost a lot of money, which came from increasingly high taxation. His burial in 210 B.C. also became famous; he was interred with thousands of terra-cotta soldiers and horses.

Shih Huang-ti's sons proved weak and oppressive, and soon provoked a peasant uprising. Knowing that defeat against the rebels would be rewarded with beheading, many Ch'in generals decided to change sides, and the opposition strengthened. Finally, in 206 B.C., a peasant rebel leader named Liu Pang captured the Ch'in capital at Hsienyang, and the Ch'in dynasty died. They left an empire that Liu Pang, who established the Han dynasty, would enlarge upon.

*See also* Han Dynasty [23]; Britain, Norman Invasion of [36].

References: Cotterell, Arthur, *The First Emperor of China* (London: Macmillan, 1981); Hookham, Hilda, *A Short History of China* (New York: St. Martin's Press, 1970); Twitchett, Denis, and Michael Loewe, *The Cambridge History of China*, Vol. 1: *The Ch'in and Han Empires* (New York: Cambridge University Press, 1978).

## 18 CONSTANTINE, EMPEROR

Constantine was born Flavius Valerius Constantinus about A.D. 272 in Moesia, the area of modern Serbia or Macedonia. His mother Helena bore him illegitimately, but he was adopted by Constantius I when Helena became Constantius's chief concubine. Constantius was named caesar in 305 under the newly reorganized power structure of the Roman Empire. Emperor Diocletian had divided power in the empire between two people, himself and Maximian, who were called augusti. They each appointed a subordinate, a caesar, who would rise to the position of augustus upon his superior's death or retirement. Under this system, Constantius was named caesar by Maximian, while Diocletian chose Galerius. When Diocletian retired (and forced Maximian to do likewise), Galerius and Constantius rose to become augusti. The sons of Constantius and Galerius hoped to be named caesars, but were disappointed when two others got the jobs. What Diocletian had hoped would become a peaceful progression of power became instead a struggle for inheritance.

Constantine had little formal education and turned to soldiering early. He fought with his father in a campaign in Britain, where his father died. Popular with the legions, they named Constantine augustus in his father's place. Instead, he took the title caesar rather than directly challenge the ultimate authorities in Rome. His assumption of the title, though reluctantly recognized by Rome, added fuel to the succession fire. Constantine stayed with his troops and campaigned against incursions by the Franks in Gaul.

In 306 the Praetorian Guard in Rome supported a new candidate for augustus, and the scramble for power that ensued virtually defies rational description. Not until Renaissance Italy would the world see another such convoluted struggle for leadership. At one time six men all claimed the title augustus. Constantine's army won victories at Arles and Marseilles over his rival and father-in-law Maximian in 310; the following year Galerius died, and four possible augusti remained: Maxentius and Daia, allied against Constantine and Licinius.

Learning of Maxentius's movements against him, in early 312 Constantine marched 40,000 men into Italy and won victories at Susa, Turin, Milan, Brescia, and Verona. He also recruited supporters along the way and entered his greatest fight with some 50,000 men. At Milvian Bridge across the Tiber River he received a vision; some sources say it came in a dream the night before the battle; more traditionally, it was said to come in the bright sun in front of thousands of witnesses. However it appeared, Constantine was convinced by this vision that if he placed the symbol of Christ on his soldier's shield he would be victorious. He did so, and won. As in Julius Caesar's campaign across the Rubicon into Italy, Constantine now became the master of Rome. He named Licinius augustus of the east.

After Licinius defeated Daia, it seemed inevitable that he and Constantine would oppose each other rather than return to Diocletian's original framework. They fought a series of indecisive battles until, in 323 at Adrianople, Constantine personally fought with his forces in a victory that forced Licinius into Byzantium. Constantine besieged the city and fought a final engagement at Scutari, where Licinius surrendered and was executed. Constantine was now the sole emperor.

Constantine's importance was in his role not only as the final leader of a unified Roman Empire but also as the founder of Constantinople as the new seat of empire, a second Rome. From there he directed the affairs of empire, the most important of which was his support of Christianity. In 313 he and Licinius had issued the Edict of Milan, which guaranteed religious freedom; however, Constantine became an open supporter of Christianity, and by the time of his death it was the state religion. He remained sole leader of the empire for 13 years, during which time he continued military reforms begun when he first occupied Rome. He defended the frontiers from barbarian attacks by constructing a series of forts to create a defense in depth, with mobile reserves stationed to come to the aid of any that were attacked. This strategy worked well in his time, but ultimately the increasing use of frontier recruits and the difference in pay between frontline and reserve forces created problems. To a great extent the establishment of a second capital promoted the idea of a divided empire, and after Constantine's death, the empire gradually split, with Rome ruling the west and Constantinople ruling the east. The eastern Byzantine Empire would survive until the fifteenth century, whereas the west would fall to barbarian invasions within a century.

See also Caesar, Julius [14]; Byzantine Empire [38]; Franks [46].

References: Barnes, Timothy, The New Empire of Diocletian and Constantine (Cambridge, MA: Harvard University Press, 1982); Dorries, Herman, Constantine the Great (New York: Harper & Row, 1972); MacMullen, Ramsay, Constantine (New York: Dial Press, 1969).

## 19    EGYPT, ALEXANDER'S CONQUEST OF

The Persian Empire had ruled Egypt since Cyrus the Great's son Cambyses conquered the country in 525 B.C. Cyrus's occupation was brutal, but later Persian emperors were occasionally more tolerant. Under Darius the Great, the Persians allowed unrestricted worship of the Egyptian gods. Darius studied native writing and theology, encouraged commerce, and completed a canal between the Nile and the Red Sea. The administration of his successor, Xerxes, was marked by its cruelty; he enslaved the people and robbed their temples. By the time of Darius III, Alexander the Great's Persian foe, the Egyptians had had more than enough of their rule.

The occupation of Egypt was the culmination of the first phase of Alexander's campaign against the Persian Empire, 334–331 B.C. The Persian navy far outclassed anything the Greeks could muster, so Alexander decided to control the Mediterranean coastline and occupy the port cities, thereby denying the Persian navy any base of operations. Rather than chase the defeated Darius II after the Greek victory at Issus, Alexander turned south to complete his coastal strategy. After capturing Tyre and Gaza, Alexander's forces marched into the Egyptian city of Pelusium. The city surrendered to him without a fight; indeed, the Egyptians viewed Alexander more as a liberator than a conqueror.

From Pelusium, Alexander proceeded to Memphis, on the Nile River. The inhabitants welcomed him and, so grateful were they for their deliverance from Persia, the Egyptians made Alexander pharaoh. Alexander endeared himself to the Egyptians by honoring their gods, and it was by way of religion that he not only solidified his dominance over Egypt but laid the groundwork for his own future adulation. Alexander's mother, Olympias, claimed that Alexander had been fathered not by her husband Philip but by the god Zeus, and therefore Alexander was semidivine. This claim fit neatly into the Egyptian view of pharaoh as a mixture of god and man. Prior to leaving Greece, Alexander visited the Oracle at Delphi and was told to pay close attention to the Egyptian deity Ammon-Zeus.

When Alexander decided to spend the winter of 332–331 B.C. in Egypt, he traveled to the remote desert site of the temple of Ammon-Zeus at the oasis of Siwah. The journey had all the marks of a divinely led pilgrimage. The Greek force was saved from dehydration by a freak rainstorm in the desert. A sandstorm obscured landmarks and made navigation in the desert virtually impossible, but the Greeks followed birds, which flew to the oasis. At the temple, Alexander left everyone outside and entered to commune with the priests of Ammon-Zeus. What passed between them was never revealed, but from then on Alexander did nothing to discourage the growing belief of many in the east that he was a god.

After the journey to Siwah, Alexander laid plans for the construction of a new city named—as so many of his cities were—Alexandria. The city was designed in a grid pattern to create well-organized thoroughfares. He made sure that temples to both Egyptian and Greek gods were constructed. He oversaw the start of construction prior to his return to Memphis, where he established a government to administer the country. He appointed several locals to important positions while leaving several garrisons of Greek soldiers. In the spring of 342 B.C., he left Egypt in pursuit of Darius, never to return.

After his death, Alexander's conquests were divided among three of his generals. Egypt and much of the Mediterranean coast went to Ptolemy, whose descendants ruled Egypt as pharaohs until the days of Caesar Augustus. Alexander's virtually bloodless occupation of Egypt changed both the conqueror and the subdued. Coins minted from this time depict Alexander with rams' horns (the symbol of Ammon-Zeus), and Alexander notified Greece that they could now worship him as a god. Egypt benefited greatly from the Greek occupation. Alexandria became not only one of the great cities of the ancient world, it was the site of the greatest library of antiquity, housing some 700,000 scrolls. The city became the center of learning for centuries, with public buildings, parks, and the first

museum. Alexander's legacy was one of knowledge and culture, but that of the Ptolemies was also one of exploitation of the Egyptian population and economy.

See also Cyrus the Great [4]; Alexander the Great [11]; Augustus, Caesar [12]; Philip of Macedon [29]; Ptolemaic Dynasty [30].

References: Bosworth, A. B., *Conquest and Empire* (New York: Cambridge University Press, 1988); Green, Peter, *Alexander of Macedon* (Los Angeles: University of California Press, 1991); Lane Fox, Robin, *The Search for Alexander* (Boston: Little, Brown, 1980).

## 20 GAUL, ROMAN CONQUEST OF

In Roman times Gaul made up the area now encompassed by France, Belgium, Luxembourg, and Germany west of the Rhine River. It was divided into four general areas: Provincia, Aquitania, Celtica, and Belgica. The first to come under Roman domination was Provincia, whose capital, Massalia (or Massilia), was the site of modern Marseilles. Massilia had long served as a trading center for Phoenician and Greek merchants before Rome took over; it remained a financial but not military center. The remainder of Gaul, having less contact with Mediterranean cultures, became known as Gallica Comata, or Long-Haired Gaul. The "barbarian" tribes of that area included the Suebi, Sequani, Arverni, Aedui, and Helvetii.

Population pressures forced the Gallic tribes into expansion, with the Helvetii allying with the Sequani and Aedui to escape the pressures exerted by the Suebi and other Germanic tribes pushing westward.

This combination of conquest and migration soon put pressure on Provincia, and that attracted the Roman military.

Rome had been undergoing political upheavals with a rivalry between the elected senate, which served in a strongly advisory capacity, and the growing power of individuals who hoped to exercise expanded if not supreme power. By 60 B.C. the three major figures in this rivalry were Pompey, Crassus, and Julius Caesar. Their cooperation (the Triumvirate) was unconstitutional but effective in the face of a weakening senate. Their personalities, however, guaranteed that the trio could not rule together indefinitely. The junior partner of the Triumvirate was Caesar, who lacked Pompey's military experience and Crassus's wealth. In order to gain both, he lobbied for and received the position of governor and commander of the Roman forces in Gaul. His accession to the political position in Gaul coincided with the arrival of the Helvetii, so his chance for glory beckoned.

There was no better infantry force in the world than the Roman legions, but at first they had difficulty in dealing with the aggressive cavalry of the Helvetii and their allies. Still, Caesar was successful in forcing their withdrawal in 58 B.C., while capturing the Suebi leader Ariovistus after a campaign in Alsace. The following year Caesar marched north and defeated the Belgae and Nervii, establishing Roman control over the lands of modern Belgium and northern France. He spread Roman power to the Atlantic coast in 56 B.C., thereby isolating the central Gallic tribes. An invasion by the Usipites and Tencteri forced his return to Belgium, but Caesar defeated them as well and kept his hold on the province. Campaigns in Germany and Britain accomplished little of immediate importance, but they gave Caesar more experience and publicity.

With most of Gaul under his control, Caesar spent the years 54–51 B.C. suppressing revolts. The most serious was a coalition of Gallic tribes led by Vercingetorix. Caesar cut off their supplies with scorched-earth tactics and starved them into submission, defeating them at Alesia in 53 B.C.

The immediate effects of Caesar's campaigns were to expand Rome's northwestern borders all the way to the Atlantic and beyond, laying the groundwork for a later, more successful invasion of Britain. His success and personal appeal made him immensely popular with his troops; that and the wealth he accumulated through his victories translated into personal power, for money and military support were soon to be the main factors necessary to advance in Roman politics. The death of Crassus in 53 B.C. and Caesar's military success created a rift between him and Pompey that exploded into civil war in 49 B.C. Rather than leave his army outside Rome's borders (as the law demanded) and appear before the senate alone, Caesar crossed onto the Italian peninsula at the Rubicon River and challenged Pompey and the government. Caesar proved the superior general, quickly establishing his power in Italy and Spain, chasing Pompey to Greece, and then to Egypt. Defeating Pompey, his allies, and later his sons gave Caesar ultimate power in Rome, and he became the first emperor.

In Gaul, Romanization proceeded fairly quickly in the south, mainly through the retirement and settlement of many of Caesar's veterans. In Gallica Comata, however, anti-Roman sentiment died hard. Caesar sponsored settlements only along the frontier between Provincia and the interior. The tribes so lately defeated kept nominal power in their lands, and Rome allowed them to exercise local autonomy in return for trade. These tribes also acted as a buffer against possible Germanic invasions of Roman settlements. The main part of Gaul, however, remained fairly independent. Under the reign of Claudius I some 100 years after Caesar's conquest, the provinces of Belgica, Lugdenensis, and Aquitania emerged, and they were eventually allowed to send nobles to the senate. The Roman pantheon and emperor worship were encouraged, to the detriment (and occasional persecution) of other religious practices. The later Roman Empire introduced Christianity and Latin, both of which further eroded Gallic culture. Though Gaul prospered through trade with Rome, it ultimately suffered by being first in line during the Germanic and later barbarian invasions. The territory finally was settled and divided among the new tribes, mainly the Vandals and Visigoths in the south of France and Spain, and with the Franks, Alamani, and Burgundians in the upper portion of Gaul.

See also Britain, Roman Conquest of [13]; Caesar, Julius [14].

References: Caesar, Julius, *The Gallic War*, trans. H. J. Edwards (Cambridge, MA: Harvard University Press, 1966); Drinkwater, J. F., *Roman Gaul* (London: Croom Helm, 1983); King, Anthony, *Roman Gaul and Germany* (Berkeley: University of California Press, 1990).

## 21   GERMANY, ROMAN INVASION OF

Though Julius Caesar had conquered Gaul in the middle of the first century B.C., the Roman attitude toward Germany remained undefined. Under the direction of Caesar Augustus, Rome began campaigns against German tribes in 12 B.C., ostensibly to protect Gaul from attacks by aggressive German tribes, but actually to establish a new frontier along the Elbe River. Augustus chose two generals—Tiberius and Drasus—to carry out the campaign.

The Germanic people were composed of a number of independent tribes, most of them mutually antagonistic, which kept them from making any real progress in acquiring Gallic lands or cooperating in the face of Roman attacks. Individually the Germans were courageous, but they were impaired by a lack of unity and discipline.

The Roman armies began their offensive with Tiberius pushing eastward through Switzerland to defeat the Pannonians (residing in modern-day Austria), thereby securing the southern frontier by placing Roman troops on the Danube. Drasus, meanwhile, marched north through the Brenner Pass, then down the Rhine. In a series of rapid thrusts he mastered western Germany and raided as far as the Elbe. Roman advances stopped here because Drasus's death in 9 B.C. terminated the invasion. Not until 7 B.C. did they take the offensive again, this time with Tiberius in overall command.

Tiberius consolidated the Roman hold along the Rhine by transplanting uncooperative German tribes to Gaul, where superior Roman forces could keep an eye on them. Two years later Tiberius advanced from the upper Danube into the valley of the Saale River. He also sent columns toward the Elbe River, defeating German tribes and forcing most of them to recognize Roman overlordship by 4 B.C. Rome held this position for nearly a decade.

Rome assumed that Germany was pacified. Roman merchants began to operate in the area, and forts and trading posts were constructed. The German tribes did nothing to give the impression that they resented Roman rule, and Rome took many of the German leaders and their families to Rome to teach them "civilized" behavior and language. Some of the Germans learned the Roman way of war and fought in the Roman army, sometimes with Roman troops and sometimes in command of native auxiliaries. One of the more successful students of Roman warfare was Arminius of the Cherusci. He commanded German cavalry forces in support of Roman operations; the Romans were strong on infantry and tended to use foreign troops for mounted soldiers.

Plans finalized in A.D. 5 called for Roman forces to occupy all of Germany. Again Tiberius was placed in command, but he was unable to undertake this mission because of a revolt in Illyrica (modern Yugoslavia). The operation was reinstated the following year under the command of Quintilius Varsus, who was ordered to conquer all German territory, no matter the cost. By this time, the Germans seem to have learned some lessons from the Romans, for they had formed alliances to face this threat. Led by the Cherusci tribe, the Germans launched a surprise attack on Varsus in the Teutoburger Forest. The Cherusci prince Arminius, leading the cavalry contingent of the Roman force, had lured his commander into a trap. Unable to use their standard tactics in the rugged, wooded terrain, the Romans were overwhelmed, losing three legions.

This was a major blow to Roman prestige. They feared that the Germans would follow up this victory with an invasion of the Rhine area or Gaul, but it did not happen. The Germans seemed satisfied with defending their own lands. Tiberius was soon reassigned to the area, but he decided not to push Roman luck. He solidified Rome's hold along the Rhine, but refrained from entering the Germanic wilderness. In A.D. 14, Germanicus was ordered to the region to avenge Varsus's defeat, but after campaigning among the tribes with mixed success, he withdrew to the better defended Rhineland. Tiberius, successor to Augustus as emperor, realized that if Rome did not offer a visible threat, the feuding German tribes could not maintain a solid front or pose a serious threat to Rome's frontiers.

Rome's goal became the maintenance of German recognition of their power without Rome's having to hold the ground to prove it. The frontier remained relatively peaceful until the Roman Empire began to decline in the third century. By the 220s the Goths, descended from Scandinavian immigrants, broke through the frontier and drove the Romans out of Germany, the Balkans, and central Europe.

As Roman power declined over the succeeding centuries, their former enemies became allies. Rome hired German mercenaries to man their legions, and in the process the Germans became acquainted with Roman civilization and advances. Later, Roman generals assigned to frontier garrisons became caesars thanks to the skill of their German soldiers. The people who occupied what is modern-day Germany came under a variety of influences as various peoples migrated through their territory, so Roman input into Germanic culture was but one factor among many. Germans were sufficiently impressed with Roman wealth to lust after it, and the Germans were among many who invaded and looted the Italian peninsula. They took treasures, but not much culture, and not until the Christian church came to be a dominant force in Europe did the tribes of Germany rise to the level of outside cultures.

*See also* Caesar, Julius [14]; Gaul, Roman Conquest of [20]; Ostrogoths [69].

References: Balsdon, J. P. V. D., *Rome: The Story of an Empire* (New York: McGraw-Hill, 1970); Dudley, David, *The Romans: 850 B.C.–A.D. 337* (New York: Knopf, 1970); Salmon, Edward, *A History of the Roman World from 30 B.C. to A.D. 138* (London: Methuen, 1972).

## GREECE, PERSIAN INVASION OF

Thanks to the efforts of Cyrus the Great and Darius the Great, the Persian Empire stretched from the borders of India to Egypt and from the Caspian Sea to the Hellespont by 500 B.C. However, spelling ultimate doom for the Persians was the crossing of the Hellespont into Europe. Once across that narrow strait, they faced the determined people of Hellas, ancient Greece. Though the Greeks were divided into independent city-states that were often antagonistic, in the face of an outside threat they banded together. The Greeks had attracted Darius's attention when Athens gave support to former Greek colonies in Ionia, along the western Asia Minor coast. Because they were under Persian rule, Athenian and Eretrian support of the Ionian rebellions of the 490s B.C. demanded punishment. Darius was determined to invade Greece and bring the country to heel. He sent his general, Mardonius, to subdue the northern provinces of Thrace and Macedon in 492 B.C., and massed an invasion force for an amphibious assault on Greece.

Darius gathered 50,000 men for the attack, which was commanded by Datis. With the Persians was Hippias, a former Athenian tyrant who had been deposed some years earlier and now returned with his patrons to engage in some behind-the-scenes agitation and reestablish his power. Only after the Persians attacked Eretria on the island of Euboea did the Greek mainland learn of the invasion. The Athenians prepared for battle and dispatched a messenger to the southern city-state of Sparta for assistance. The militant Spartans responded that they would arrive as soon as they had completed some necessary religious festivals. Thus, Athens marched out alone to give battle. They made their way westward to the high ground overlooking Marathon, the only available port near Athens, where the Persians had debarked their forces. Once the Athenians arrived (and were joined by a small force from Plataea), the Persians implemented their strategy. The city of Athens now stood undefended, so they embarked about half their force to sail for the city while the remainder held the Athenian army in place. The Athenian leader Callimachus ceded command of the force to Miltiades, who argued for a bold attack on the Persian force, now reduced to 20,000; that number was still half again the size of the Greek force. The Athenians advanced in a long, line-abreast formation with stronger flanks. The Persians struck the weaker center, but found their own weak flanks surrounded by the Athenians. The result, intended or accidental, was a perfect double envelopment, which broke Persian morale. They raced for the safety of the ships on the beach and escaped only by a strong holding action. The main, relatively contemporary source for the battle is the Greek historian Herodotus, who numbered the casualties as 192 Greek dead versus a loss of 6,400 Persians. The Persians sailed away, and the victorious Athenians met the Spartans arriving just after the battle's end. The Persian fleet sailed for Athens but arrived too late; the army had returned and taken defensive positions, so the Persians sailed for home.

Darius was not about to let this defeat go unavenged, but he was diverted from immediate counterattack by a revolt in Egypt. In the process of subduing the rebellion, Darius died, so the duty of punishing Greece fell to his successor, Xerxes. Xerxes planned an even larger invasion force, of probably 200,000, who marched around the Aegean, supplied by the Persian fleet sailing along the coast. At the Hellespont he ordered a bridge of boats constructed, and the Persian army marched into Europe in 480 B.C. The Greeks had spent the last ten years fighting among themselves, and now had to bury their differences to meet the foreign threat. The Persians marched through northern Greece, gaining the voluntary or grudging assistance of virtually every city-state. This time the Spartan army marched to the fore, while the Greek fleet sailed to impede the Persian navy. The Greek strategy was to separate the Persian army from its food supply onboard the ships, so the Greek fleet blocked the straits between the mainland and the island of Euboea. The Persian army continued along the coast to the pass of Thermopylae, where a Greek force commanded by the Spartan leader Leonidas awaited them. Leonidas stood on the narrow defile between mountains and sea, and for three days his 6,000 men repulsed the might of the Persian army. With the aid of a local Greek shepherd, the Persians learned of a track around the Greek roadblock and marched to surround their opposition. Learning of this move, Leonidas sent most of his force to meet it. They failed to stop the encirclement by the superior Persian force; Leonidas and his few hundred men held the pass until all were killed. The news of the Persian victory at Ther-mopylae convinced the Greek fleet to withdraw, so the Persian advance continued.

The Athenians had earlier consulted the Oracle at Delphi on the best strategy for meeting the invaders, and in true Delphic style they were told to seek refuge behind wooden walls. The debate over this response led the Athenians to determine that the oracle meant the wooden walls of ships rather than the walls surrounding the city of Athens, so the city was abandoned to the advancing Persians. The Athenians led a combined Greek naval force in the waters off Athens, but it was only about half the size of the Persian navy. Their only hope

was to use the superior maneuverability of the smaller Greek triremes in the narrow waters off the island of Salamis, near Athens. Xerxes sat atop his throne on the hillside to watch his fleet's victory, but he was disappointed. Lured on by a false promise of turncoats within the Greek fleet, the Persians found themselves unable to maneuver their unwieldy ships in the straits. Herodotus claims that the outcome was 40 Greek ships sunk for a loss of 200 Persian ships, and the remainder sailed away home. Xerxes withdrew much of his army, but left a force in the northern provinces; it was defeated in 479 B.C. The battle of Plataea broke the back of the remaining Persian force, and the Greek victory at Mycale a month later brought about the final destruction of Persian forces in Greece.

The Persian Wars rate as among the most important in history. They proved the worth of the western military mind and infantry soldier against a previously undefeated foe. The chance to continue the experiment of democracy continued unburdened by Oriental despotism, and the philosophy and culture developed by the Greeks influence Western civilization to this day. As the historian J. F. C. Fuller wrote in his *Military History of the Western World*, "With these battles we stand on the threshold of the western world to be, in which Greek intellect was to conquer and to lay the foundations of centuries to come. No two battles in history are, therefore, more portentous than Salamis and Plataea; they stand like the pillars of the temple of the ages supporting the architecture of western history."

*See also* Cyrus the Great [4].

References: Burn, A. R., *Persia and the Greeks: The Defence of the West* (London: Arnold, 1962); Fuller, J. F. C., *Military History of the Western World* (New York:

Minerva, 1954–1956); Grant, Michael, *The Rise of the Greeks* (New York: Scribner's Sons, 1987); Hignett, Charles, *Xerxes' Invasion of Greece* (Oxford: Clarendon, 1963).

## 23      HAN DYNASTY

After the successful reign of Shih Huang-ti, founder of the Ch'in dynasty, his two successors failed to live up to his standards and became the objects of rebellion. Liu Pang, one of the rebel leaders, seized power in 206 B.C. and began the Han dynasty, taking the regnal name of Kao-tsu. Kao-tsu was able to take advantage of the territorial consolidation of the Ch'in dynasty; he took over almost all of the Ch'in lands, except Yueh in the south, which he ceded to another general, Chao To, for his support in the rebellion. Kao-tsu spent the early years of his reign consolidating his power and protecting his frontiers.

Kao-tsu's main rivals on the frontier were the Hsiung-nu, known to Europe as the Huns. Dominating the steppes north of the Great Wall and often raiding south of it, their cavalry numbered as many as a quarter million. Kao-tsu's first campaign against the Huns was very nearly a disaster, for they drew him into a trap and took him prisoner. He made peace with them and sealed a treaty with the marriage of one of his harem to the Hsiung-nu leader, which secured the north for some years. Following Kao-tsu's death in 195 B.C., the Hsiung-nu honored the agreement, but after 176 B.C., new leaders began to raid into China almost as far as the Han capital at Loyang. Rather than attack the northerners directly, the Han leaders often paid other tribes to harass them.

With the accession to the throne of Wu Ti in 140 B.C., the Han challenged the might of the Hsiung-nu. Wu Ti, also known

as the Martial Emperor, took the Han dynasty to its heights of power. He launched attack after attack against the nomads, but was beaten back by their superior numbers or the hostility of the terrain. Wu Ti sought allies against his enemy, sending the envoy Chang Chien to the west to broker a pact with the Yueh Chih, or Kushan Empire, of Bactria. Chang Chien was captured by the Hsiung-nu, but escaped and made his way to Kushan. The Kushans' disastrous encounters with the Hsiung-nu convinced them not to ally themselves with China. Finally, Wu Ti led an invasion and succeeded in defeating the nomads between the Great Wall and the northern bend of the Yellow River in 127 B.C. In 121 B.C., Wu Ti sent the 20-year-old general Ho Ch'u Ping with 100,000 men to attack the Hsiung-nu capital. He was so successful that the nomads were driven north of the Gobi Desert; this victory opened the land route westward for both invasion and trade.

Wu Ti learned the value of cavalry from the Hsiung-nu, and he spent much time breeding horses and training horsemen. This proved successful in beating the Hsiung-nu at their own tactics, and gave Wu Ti the ability to defeat other, less prepared enemies. He campaigned in the south against the former Ch'in province of Yueh, capturing it, and drove southward as far as Annam and Tonkin by 109 B.C.; the chieftains of that region acknowledged Chinese suzerainty and paid tribute. In 108 B.C., Wu Ti focused his attention on the north, conquering Manchuria and northern Korea.

Not content with merely dominating China and its immediate environs, Wu Ti sent Li Kuang Li on an expedition to the west. Li Kuang Li drove into central Asia and defeated a number of tribes in the Jaxartes River region before being forced to withdraw into Sinkiang. After regrouping there, he reinvaded the region of Ferghana and forced them to acknowledge Chinese dominance. The expedition was expensive, as only 10,000 of the original 60,000 soldiers returned to China, but they brought back excellent breeding stock for Wu Ti's increasingly important cavalry.

Wu Ti spent the last years of his reign consolidating his empire, which had tripled in size under his rule. The constant warfare had cost huge fortunes, and he dedicated himself to restoring financial stability, but the overworked bureaucracy and overtaxed peasantry staged a series of rebellions. Nevertheless, China generally enjoyed relative peace with its neighbors and expanded trade, most notably along the Silk Road to India and the Middle East.

Internal troubles brought about more rebellions in the first century A.D. and led to the establishment of the Second Han dynasty in A.D. 24 under the leadership of Kuang Wu Ti. During his reign, Chinese forces under General Ma Yuan campaigned in the south and reestablished dominance in Annam and Hainan. The return of the Hsiung-nu at midcentury provoked Chinese punitive expeditions that drove the nomads farther west. Later in the first century, Chinese armies drove even deeper west, conquering Turkestan and scouting as far as the Caspian Sea. Around A.D. 90, Chinese armies inflicted the final defeat on the Hsiung-nu, expelling them from central Asia and starting them on a migration that ultimately reached Europe and produced the great leader Attila. This abandonment of the high plains opened the area to habitation by the Mongols, who began their long rise to prominence.

After the first century, the Han dynasty began to decline, mainly because of internal strife. It had been the most successful Chinese dynasty thus far, and had opened China to influences outside its culture via the Silk Road and naval expeditions into the South China Sea and beyond. Representatives of the Roman emperor Marcus Aurelius are reported to have visited Han territory. However, the internal unrest caused by the recurring problem of overtaxation weakened the dynasty, as it did so many others. Military dictators ruled at the end of the second century A.D., but after 220 the empire broke into warring states, not to be reunited with the Sui and T'ang dynasties until the late sixth century.

*See also* Ch'in Dynasty [17]; Huns [51]; T'ang Dynasty [77]; Vietnam, Chinese Conquest of [80].

References: Hookham, Hilda, *A Short History of China* (New York: St. Martin's Press, 1970); Twitchett, Denis, and Michael Loewe, *The Cambridge History of China,* Vol. 1: *The Ch'in and Han Empires* (New York: Cambridge University Press, 1978).

## 24        HANNIBAL

Often compared to Alexander the Great, Julius Caesar, or Napoleon, Hannibal dominated the military scene of his day. With the possible exception of his father, Hamilcar, Carthage never had a better political leader. Even more remarkably, this reputation was established strictly by the accounts of his enemies, because Carthaginian sources on his life do not exist.

Hannibal was born to fight Rome: At age nine his father made him swear eternal enmity to that trans-Mediterranean power. At the age of 26, Hannibal became leader of the Carthaginian Empire. He combined the policy of his brother-in-law, Hasdrubal, of building Carthaginian power by diplomacy with that of his father, who sought military conquest. Hannibal took control of Carthage's major possession, Spain, by marrying a Spanish princess and demanding hostages of the major tribes.

With this as a base, he challenged Roman authority along the Pyrenees and provoked the Second Punic War, where he established his reputation as a commander.

Hannibal seemed to have had neither personal nor strategic fear. He invaded Italy virtually without supply lines, as his crossing of the Pyrenees and Alps made resupply extremely difficult. He made the best use of his enemy's weaknesses, striking where they had the fewest forces, and he encouraged Rome's vassals to rebel and join him. He instituted a new weapon to ancient warfare—the elephant.

Hannibal knew when to take risks, and he knew his enemy. Recognizing that he might lose half of his 100,000-man army crossing the mountains to Italy, he proceeded anyway, aware that the Gauls on the other side would gladly make up his losses for the opportunity to fight their Roman overlords. Even though he lost massive numbers of men in the march, he did everything possible to take care of his troops. "In all his operations, we see supreme excellence, skill, resource, daring, an heroic spirit, the faculty of command in the very highest degree, caution, sound judgement, extraordinary craft, and last but not least, watchful and incessant care in providing for the requirements of his troops."

Hannibal's greatest legacy to military history came from his tactics at Cannae, his greatest victory and Rome's worst defeat. By withdrawing the center of his forces from Roman attack, he drew the Romans into the center of the field, where the cavalry on either end of his line could attack both Roman flanks and rear, a double envelopment that came to be known as the "Cannae maneuver." Rome entered the battle with 60,000 men and left with but 10,000. Hannibal did not follow up this victory with an assault on Rome itself, for he knew the city's defenses were too strong. He contented himself with rampaging around the country-side, living off the land, denying the Romans badly needed food supplies, and provoking rebellions against Roman rule for 15 years (218–203 B.C.). Hannibal's successes were insufficient to persuade his government in Carthage to provide him with reinforcements. All his successes went for naught when he had to return to Carthage to save the city from a Roman attack. At Zama he lost his only battle, at the hands of the Roman general Scipio.

Defeated in battle and owing the Romans tribute, Hannibal strove for seven years to rebuild his nation's fortunes. He concentrated on the traditional Carthaginian pastime—trade—to stabilize his society. He challenged the authority of the corrupt oligarchy, which had placed an intolerable tax burden on the people to pay the tribute to Rome, and forced an almost democratic system on them. His economic leadership and evenhanded treatment of the public were so successful that Carthage made enough money to pay the Roman tribute years early. But once again Hannibal was betrayed by his own government. Unable to exist in his just society, they plotted against him by telling Rome that he was planning another war. Hannibal had to flee for his life; rather than fall into Roman hands, he ultimately committed suicide.

Hannibal did it all, politically and militarily. In the end, he was too successful for his own good.

*See also* Alexander the Great [11]; Caesar, Julius [14]; Italy, Carthaginian Invasion of (Second Punic War) [26]; Napoleon Buonaparte [118].

References: Baker, G. P., *Hannibal* (New York: Barnes & Noble, 1967); Lamb, Harold, *Hannibal* (New York: Doubleday, 1958); Morris, William, *Hannibal: Soldier, Statesman, Patriot* (New York: Knickerbocker Press, 1978).

**25** | INDIA, ALEXANDER'S
INVASION OF

With the entire Middle East under his control, Alexander the Great looked for more land to bring under his domination. Determined to conquer the entire Persian Empire, he needed to occupy all the territory to the Indus River. He marched his men toward India at the urging of one of his new allies, Taxiles, who had a dispute with an Indian king, Porus. In November 326 B.C., the Greeks and their auxiliaries took two routes through modern Afghanistan: Hephaestion through the Khyber Pass to establish a bridgehead across the Indus, and Alexander paralleling him a bit to the north to defeat the tribes in the hills and secure the left flank. When the two columns reunited, Alexander's force numbered 5,600 cavalry and 10,000 infantry. Taxiles had provided a number of elephants, but Alexander used them only for transport.

Just past the Indus, the Greeks found Porus encamped on the southern side of the Hydapses (modern Jhelum) River. It was late spring and the river was rising, so Alexander had to act quickly. He spread rumors that he was going to wait until the river fell to cross, yet at the same time he built boats in plain sight of Porus's army. Unsure of Alexander's intentions, Porus reacted to Alexander's ploy of marching up and down the river, feinting at a number of places yet never attacking, in order to tire the Indians so they would soon give up following his marches and countermarches. When they quit reacting to his moves, Alexander took advantage of a well-timed storm to move his cavalry and 6,000 infantry upriver, where they crossed in the night. Spotted early the next morning, Alexander soon faced a 2,000-man cavalry force sent by Porus's son to investigate. After easily defeating them, Alexander marched down-river. The covering force he had left behind made threatening moves to cross the river opposite Porus's camp, so the Indians had to decide which threat to meet—a tactic taught in infantry schools to this day.

Porus turned to face Alexander. He stretched his men across an open plain with his anchors on the river to his left and a chain of hills to his right. He placed 300 elephants along the front of his line, supported by infantry; his 3,000–4,000 cavalry were in two equal units on the flanks. Unknown to Porus, however, Alexander had detached a cavalry force to ride behind the hills and strike the Indians from the rear after Alexander struck along the river to draw the entire Indian cavalry to that side. The assault from the rear collapsed the Indian line from the right, and the elephants ultimately lost control when the Greeks killed their handlers. The wounded Porus surrendered, but as was his wont, Alexander restored the gallant enemy to his kingdom in return for an alliance, and he settled the differences between Porus and Taxiles.

Alexander established two towns in the neighborhood of his victory and divided his force: Under Hephaestion, one-half moved down the Hydapses to its juncture with the Indus, and Alexander took the other half southeastward to the Hyphasis (Beas) River. After he defeated a force of Cathaeans there, he wanted to proceed in his search for the Indian Ocean, but for the first time, his men would not follow him. This river was perhaps the extent of the Persian Empire, and they were homesick. Alexander sulked in his tent for three days, but his men would not relent, so he finally left to rejoin Hephaestion. With his force divided, as well as hurt by unrevealed casualties he suffered at the Hydapses, certainly Alexander could not have fought his way to the ocean, though he was convinced it was not far away.

Once again reunited with the entire army, Alexander ordered ships built. The fleet was to carry many of his troops to the mouth of the Indus at Karachi and up the coast toward the Persian Gulf. While the ships were being built, he launched his last great campaign—this time against the Malli tribe, probably subjects of the old Persian Empire. He crossed to the Hydraotes (Ravi) River and attacked their main city, which fell easily. The Indians retreated to their citadel, and here the fighting was the fiercest. Alexander led the assault, but found himself inside the citadel walls with only three other soldiers. He fought with his usual tenacity even though wounded by an arrow; finally his army broke through the walls and killed all the defenders. This campaign was marked by more than the usual slaughter, perhaps an indication that the Greeks wanted to go home and not leave trouble behind.

Alexander nursed his wounds until the fleet was prepared in the autumn of 325 B.C. He intended to march along the coast and establish supply depots for the ships, but the terrain forced him to swing north. He and his troops suffered terribly from the heat and lack of supplies, but finally reached the shore and met the fleet at the Gulf of Hormuz. From there they returned to the Persian capital at Susa.

The Greek expedition to India was in some ways a reunion, because the Aryan conquerors who had established themselves in northern India a thousand years earlier may have had the same roots in the steppes of western Asia as the forebears of the Greeks; certainly there were similarities of language that suggest the possibility. As Alexander was intent on spreading Greek culture wherever he went, the establishment of cities and garrisons left some Greek imprint in the north Indian states. Though Alexander's death a few years later brought an end to Greek dominance, the Mauryan Empire that succeeded it left art and sculpture heavily influenced by Greek styles. Alexander's love of knowledge led him to debate Indian philosophy at every chance, but the long-lasting interchange of ideas is hard to pin down. Though the Greek invasion did not have abiding effects, it created a power vacuum in northern India that allowed the Mauryans to come to power, and their domination of India had positive results.

See also India, Aryan Invasion of [7]; Alexander the Great [11]; Mauryan Empire [27]; Persia, Alexander's Conquest of [28].

References: Bosworth, A. B., *Conquest and Empire* (Cambridge: Cambridge University Press, 1988); Keegan, John, *The Mask of Command* (New York: Viking, 1987); Tarn, W. W., *Alexander the Great* (Boston: Beacon Press, 1948).

## ITALY, CARTHAGINIAN INVASION OF (SECOND PUNIC WAR)

**26**

After the First Punic War, Carthage had domestic problems to overcome, mainly concerning the mercenary forces with whom it fought its wars. In the latter part of the war, these men had gone unpaid, and therefore they rebelled against Carthage. When many of the towns under Carthaginian control rebelled as well, in sympathy with the mercenaries, the appointment of Hamilcar Barca to head Carthage's defense proved a wise move. Hamilcar put down the revolt and cemented his leadership of Carthage at the same time.

Though neutral throughout the revolt, Rome soon made advances in Sardinia to support discontented Carthaginian subjects there. Rome claimed that this was part of its spoils from the first war, and Carthage could do little about it. Rome's additional demand for control of Corsica and a higher indemnity served to reignite hostility. Because Carthage was in no position to challenge Rome immediately, Hamilcar focused Carthaginian attention on expanding their power base in Spain throughout the 230s B.C. After Hamilcar's death in 229, his son-in-law, Hasdrubal, continued his work by establishing the port city of Nova Carthago (modern-day Cartagena). Rome watched with interest, as the Romans were beginning to look outward from Italy for the first time and were anxious to establish their own contacts in Spain. They entered the Iberian peninsula from Gaul as the Carthaginians were consolidating the south.

In 226 B.C. the two powers agreed to establish the Ebro River as the border between their domains, and for a few years this worked well. Hasdrubal's assassination in 221 B.C. brought Hamilcar's son Hannibal to power, and he soon had to deal with Roman expansionism. Rome persuaded the town of Saguntum, south of the Ebro, to elect a pro-Roman government. Hannibal viewed this as a violation of the spirit of the 226 B.C. treaty, and responded by laying siege to the city in 219; he captured it eight months later. As the siege continued, the militant faction came to power in Rome, and they declared war against Carthage.

Carthage had ceased to control the waters of the northwestern Mediterranean, so Hannibal had to move his forces overland to invade Italy, preempting a Roman invasion of Spain. He surprised everyone by clearing away resistance and moving his army, complete with elephants, through the Alps into northern Italy by November 218 B.C. Fighting local tribes in the mountains, coupled with the onset of winter weather, killed many of his men, but he entered Italy with 20,000 infantry, 6,000 cavalry, and a number of elephants. He quickly won two battles and went into winter quarters in the Po Valley. Hannibal's strategy was to provoke the subject tribes of Italy into revolt against Rome, which would simultaneously weaken their power and enlarge his. His apparent goal was not to destroy Rome as a major power, but to limit them to the peninsula and regain territory lost since the first war.

The Romans were unable to defeat Hannibal. He rampaged through Italy, defeating every Roman army sent against him. In 216 B.C. at Cannae, he won one of ancient history's most brilliant victories by executing a double envelopment of the Roman forces in which he inflicted 60,000 casualties for a loss of only 6,000 of his own men. The Romans appointed Fabius as occasional consul/occasional dictator during Hannibal's campaign. Fabius decided that the best way to fight Hannibal was to avoid pitched battles, instead settling into defensive positions in cities and waiting for the Carthaginians to wear out his forces. His method became known to history as Fabian strategy, and it proved successful. Hannibal did not gain as many local allies as he had hoped, nor did he have a sufficient siege train to assault the well-defended cities. He had to content himself with living off the countryside and attacking the occasional city, usually with mixed results.

Meanwhile, Rome committed its reconstituted military to Spain, attempting to deny Hannibal his base of operations. Hannibal's brother, also named Hasdrubal, fought a long and inconclusive war against Roman forces under the Scipio brothers. Both Spain and Italy saw much fighting, but no force became dominant until 209 B.C., when the son of one of the now-dead Scipio brothers came to command in Spain. Publius Scipio proved to be a match for the Carthaginian generals. He captured Nova Carthago, the capital of Carthaginian

Spain, and forced Hasdrubal and his brother Mago onto the defensive in southwest Iberia. In 207 B.C. Hasdrubal attempted to march through the Alps to reinforce his brother, but at the Metaurus River he was defeated and beheaded. Hannibal learned of his brother's fate when a Roman horseman threw Hasdrubal's head into his camp.

The fighting continued, without much success on either side, until 206 B.C., when Scipio finally consolidated Roman power in Spain. In 204 he sailed for Africa, where he raised a Numidian ally to aid him. Scipio failed to impose his will on Carthage, but he frightened them considerably. Carthage ordered Hannibal home to defend the city, but he could not comply; Rome still controlled the sea lanes. Scipio's capture of Tunes, very near Carthage, forced the Carthaginians to agree to terms. Hannibal returned to Carthage under the terms of the cease-fire to negotiate with Scipio. When they could not agree, the two powers fought the battle of Zama. Scipio, with the assistance of Numidian cavalry, became the first Roman to defeat Hannibal in open battle.

Though Hannibal had campaigned through Italy for 17 years, causing immense destruction and hundreds of thousands of deaths, the peace terms were fairly easy. Carthage lost its possessions in Spain, but maintained its merchant navy (however, the war fleet was reduced to ten ships) and trading connections. Carthage also was to pay Rome reparations amounting to 10,000 talents (more than 500,000 pounds of silver) over a 50-year period. Rome could have annexed Carthage into its new empire or denied the Carthaginians the ability to trade, which would have proven deadly. Rome did neither, and under Hannibal's political leadership Carthage was able to recover economically. The Carthaginians also recovered militarily and challenged Rome once more, a decision

that would be fatal. The main result of the Second Punic War was the establishment, somewhat by default, of the Roman Empire. Though overseas possessions had not been sought intentionally, Rome now controlled the islands of the Mediterranean as well as Spain. For the next 600 years Rome would be the dominant power in the world.

*See also* Carthage, Expansion of [15]; Carthage, Roman Invasion of (Third Punic War) [16]; Hannibal [24]; Spain, Roman Conquest of [33].

References: Charles-Picard, Gilbert, and Collette Picard, *The Life and Death of Carthage*, trans. Dominique Collon (London: Sidgwick & Jackson, 1968); Dorey, T. A., and D. R. Dudley, *Rome against Carthage* (Garden City, NY: Doubleday, 1972); Lamb, Harold, *Hannibal* (New York: Doubleday, 1958).

## 27 · MAURYAN EMPIRE

After the decline of the Harappan civilization in India, little or no organized political system existed until the arrival of Alexander the Great. Though northwestern India was considered a part of Alexander's empire, after his death the struggling inheritors of his lands could not pay attention to the distant reaches of India. What consolidation had taken place gave an opportunity to a regional Indian prince, Chandragupta, to fill the power vacuum left by Alexander's death. He came to power in 323 B.C. and cleared the northwest regions of India of Greek troops. One of Alexander's successors, Seleucus, reinvaded India in 305 B.C., but could not defeat Chandragupta's forces. Seleucus agreed to cede the Indian lands Alexander had conquered in return for 500 war elephants. This action confirmed

Chandragupta's power and extended the reach of his control.

Once solidly in control, Chandragupta organized an efficient government machinery to oversee economic and military affairs. He kept a standing army of about one-quarter the size of his wartime conscripted army, described by a Seleucid ambassador as 600,000 infantry, 30,000 cavalry, and 9,000 elephants. He also maintained a river fleet for both the Ganges and Indus, which may have protected the coastlines as well. His reserves were in the form of "guild levies," groups of craftsmen who trained together and were called up in time of emergency. One of history's first political manuals was written for Chandragupta by his closest adviser, Kautilya: the *Arthasastra,* or Manual of Politics. Like Machiavelli's *The Prince,* it spelled out the necessities for a ruler to maintain power, and included extended sections on military organization, structure, and function.

Chandragupta began the Mauryan Empire, but its greatest expansions came through his successors. His son Bindasura attacked southward and brought almost all of India under his rule, excepting only the subcontinent's southernmost tip and the island of Ceylon. Bindasura's son Asoka (or Ashoka) accomplished the last conquests, securing the eastern coast. Under Asoka, the Mauryan Empire was not only at its political extreme, it reached cultural heights previously unknown in India. Asoka became disgusted with the destruction caused by warfare and turned to Buddhism. He mandated the establishment of a Buddhist bureaucracy to maintain honesty in government affairs. Asoka spent his wealth on the construction of monasteries and temples and the erection of inscribed stone pillars extolling his accomplishments. He sent Buddhist missionaries to Ceylon, Burma, and Java, and stretched India's trading empire to those distant areas.

It is difficult to know for certain how strong the Mauryan hold in India was, or if the emperors were lords to vassal nobles who exercised local power. Whatever the case, the empire did not last long after Asoka's death in 232 B.C. The succeeding emperors lacked the will or vision of the first three, and local revolts coupled with a return of the Seleucids in 206 B.C. brought the empire down.

*See also* Alexander the Great [11]; India, Alexander's Invasion of [25]; Seleucid Empire [31].

References: Allan, John, *The Cambridge Shorter History of India* (Delhi: S. Chand, 1964); Mookerji, Radha, *Chandragupta Maurya and His Times* (Delhi: Motilal Banarsidass, 1966); Wheeler, Robert, *Early India and Pakistan to Ashoka* (New York: Praeger, 1959).

**28** PERSIA, ALEXANDER'S CONQUEST OF

Upon the death of Philip of Macedon, his 20-year-old son Alexander inherited his throne and his army. Though still young, Alexander had gained combat leadership experience from the battle of Cheronaea two years prior to his accession. His first task, however, was to restore Macedonian control over those provinces that had rebelled upon hearing of Philip's death. That accomplished, he set out to attain his father's dying goal: the conquest of Persia. Historians argue whether Alexander was originally intent on world conquest, Persian Empire conquest, or merely defeating Persian forces and gaining control of Asia Minor. Successive victories took him deeper and deeper into Persian lands, so it is difficult to gauge his original design by the outcome of his campaign.

Alexander (left) stabs a Persian soldier as he rushes to battle Darius, the Persian king, in a mosaic depicting the Macedonian victory at Issus.

Whatever his original motivation, he crossed the Hellespont in 334 B.C. The Persian emperor, Darius III, left his satraps (governors) to deal with Alexander's invasion. They met him quickly; within three days of his entrance into Asia Minor, Alexander faced a mixed force of Persian cavalry and Greek mercenary infantry at the river Granicus. Twenty thousand Persian cavalry aligned themselves along the eastern bank of the Granicus, with the infantry arrayed in phalanx formation well behind them. Alexander ignored advice to wait for dawn to make a surprise attack, and advanced immediately. He had the phenomenal ability to pick out his enemy's weak point and strike it; in this case it was the center of the Persian line, usually a strong point. Because the Persians were at the water's edge, however, they were unable to use their cavalry to build momentum for a charge. Coupled with the lack of close infantry support, this made them vulnerable to a determined assault by a mixed cavalry/infantry force. Once the center was broken, the Persians fled, and the Greeks were surrounded and slaughtered.

Alexander quickly proceeded along the coast, liberating the Greek cities of Ionia. Those that surrendered, he treated kindly; those that resisted, he pillaged or destroyed. His goal was not merely to free Greeks from Persian rule but to control the coastline so completely that the Persian navy would become superfluous. After capturing Helicarnassus, he drove inland to seize Gordium, in the heart of Asia Minor, in April 333 B.C. There he cut the Gordian knot, a feat legend said would indicate the king of Asia. He worked his way southward and then eastward to Tarsus by the autumn of 333 B.C. At this point, where the coast of Asia Minor turns southward to become the Levant, Darius arrived to fight him.

Darius reached the coast at Issus a few days after Alexander had passed, thus cutting him off from his line of communication back to Ionia and Macedon. Alexander turned about to fight at the River Pinarus, which feeds into the Gulf of Issus. Again, Alexander chose to charge the Persian center in midafternoon, and again he was successful. Darius soon dropped his weapons and fled, abandoning his army and his family. A determined counterattack by

Greek mercenaries forced Alexander to stand and fight rather than pursue, and Darius escaped. The sudden collapse of the Persian center and Darius's quick flight demoralized the Persians, and the battle was over by nightfall. Estimates of the size of the Persian force vary wildly, but it is generally agreed that it far outnumbered Alexander's, and therefore his quick victory was correspondingly amazing. The victory at Issus took Darius out of the Levant for a year and gave Alexander time to continue his conquest of the coast.

Sidon and Byblus surrendered without a fight, but Tyre resisted. The Persian garrison manned a walled fortification on an island just off the beach. The only way Alexander and his army could approach it was to build a causeway, which he began constructing in January 332 B.C. Its construction, and the defection of Phoenician ships from the Persian navy to his cause, gave Alexander the tools necessary to assault the fort. Tyre resisted for seven months before succumbing to Alexander's men; for their resistance they suffered 8,000 dead and 30,000 sold into slavery. Jerusalem fell without a fight, but Gaza resisted. Its capture and destruction in November 332 B.C. gave Alexander mastery of the eastern Mediterranean coast and open access to Egypt.

After almost a year in Egypt, Alexander marched his forces back up the coast, supplying them by sea. From Syria he struck inland for the Euphrates with 47,000 men. He marched along the edge of the Armenian hills rather than attack down the river into the waiting arms of Darius's newly raised army on the plains around Babylon. Darius grew impatient, and marched away from friendly and favorable ground to move on Alexander near the Tigris. In late September, Alexander crossed the river first and encamped near Gaugemela, just upriver from Darius's army. Darius chose the battleground, however, and placed his men in two long lines. Arrian, traveling with Alexander, numbered the Persian army at 1 million, but modern historians discount this figure and estimate between 100,000 and 250,000, a number still significantly larger than Alexander's.

Early in the battle, Darius ordered the commitment of his secret weapon— scythed chariots—but Macedonian skirmishers and light infantry disabled the horses or drivers, and they proved useless. Though Persian attacks on the Macedonian left almost broke Alexander's line, the Persian desire for loot overcame their discipline and they drove for the rear rather than turn to envelop their enemy. Alexander saw a growing gap in their line and attacked there, once again breaking the Persian lines and panicking Darius into flight. The need to protect his forces kept Alexander from pursuing, but the battle was won. After Gaugemela, Darius could do nothing but keep running. Alexander ran him to ground a year later, but could only claim the body of Darius; he had been killed by his few remaining courtiers.

In the meanwhile, Alexander marched on and occupied Babylon and the Persian capital at Susa, then captured the city of Persepolis, site of the Persian treasury. In January 330 B.C., he destroyed the royal palace at Persepolis and declared Persia to be his. Some Persian vassals resisted their new lord, and Alexander had to fight a guerrilla campaign in the northeast until 327 B.C. After that, he was poised for India.

After his return from India, Alexander ensconced himself in Babylon and proceeded to remake the known world. He dreamed of a new worldview blended from Eastern culture and Greek rationality, and Hellenism was the result. For 300 years after his death, until the Middle East came under Roman sway, Hellenism was the dominant culture of the world. The infusion of Greek settlers brought literacy and new sciences, and the massive treasury of Persepolis provided an enormous economic boost to the region that brought the expansion of trade and patronage of the arts. Though Alexander's political bequest was one of dissension, the cultural heritage brought about new philosophies, scientific discoveries, and an atmosphere of learning that was not matched again until the Renaissance.

See also Alexander the Great [11]; Egypt, Alexander's Conquest of [19]; India, Alexander's Invasion of [25]; Philip of Macedon [29].

References: Hammond, N. G. L., *Alexander the Great: King, Commander, and Statesman* (Park Ridge, NJ: Noyes Press 1980); Keegan, John, *The Mask of Command* (New York: Viking, 1987); Tarn, W. W., *Alexander the Great* (Cambridge: Cambridge University Press, 1948).

## 29     PHILIP OF MACEDON

Philip was born in 382 B.C. in Macedon. In 359 B.C., he became regent for his young nephew. The arrangement proved unworkable for the stability of the kingdom, and Philip was named the new king. At this time the Macedonian state was not unified, and the area was under incessant attack from barbarian tribes. Macedon had never been known for its military abilities and could rarely field a large force. This changed under Philip, when he quickly proved his leadership abilities. He used bribery and diplomacy to keep most of his enemies at a distance while he concentrated on the

nation's greatest threat, the Illyrians. Within 18 months of his accession to power, Philip defeated the Illyrians in one battle in 358 B.C., and celebrated the victory by marrying the first of seven wives, Olympia.

Philip proposed to unify Greece, not so much for the sake of conquest as to make sure his rear was secure for a future invasion of Asia. He gained control of Amphipolis, which provided him with the necessary wealth to continue his campaign. By capturing Pydna and Methone, he obliged the Athenian forces to withdraw southward. He next captured Chalcidice, then Thessaly. Philip made himself leader of the Thessalian League and married a Thessalian princess. This leadership position gave him access to fine herds of horses, which he used for his cavalry. After defeating a northern threat at Olynthus, he turned toward Athens. Philip laid siege to cities vital to Athens's survival and ultimately attacked Athens itself; after its capture, he surprised the inhabitants with his lenient surrender terms.

With Greece under his domination, Philip made himself leader of the Corinthian League. He hoped to use the combined power of the Greek city-states to wage war against Persia, which they voted to do in 337 B.C. Philip returned home to Macedon to prepare for the invasion, but was assassinated before the operation could start. Though the subject of some debate, historians generally believe that his first wife, Olympia, was behind the murder, as she feared for the future of her son, Alexander, because Philip was producing sons by other wives.

In his 46 years Philip accomplished a great deal. He turned a floundering kingdom into a military power and made Greece a unified state for the first time. His military organization changed the nature of classical warfare. He adopted the standard phalanx formation of the time, but lengthened the spears the formation infantry carried to between 16 and 23 feet. The extra length made it much more difficult to attack the phalanx, and extended the killing range of the Macedonian unit. Philip also made his infantry wear lighter armor so that his men could maneuver more quickly than his enemies. He used cavalry wisely in support of his infantry and employed engineers for the construction of siege engines, including the first torsion catapult. He placed members of the same community in regiments to promote unit cohesion. Troops under Philip's command were well known for their discipline, training, and loyalty.

Able as he was in military affairs, Philip preferred diplomacy and bribery to warfare. He was an intelligent leader who knew when to back away from a battle as well as when to join one. He maintained a large network of spies, and often knew his enemies' abilities better than they themselves did. He also used marriage to cement alliances and bind newly conquered states to his cause. His civil works were also notable: He founded new towns and encouraged cultural advances. Most of all, he trained his firstborn son, Alexander, to succeed him, and provided the best-trained army in the world for Alexander's own dreams of conquest. Though Philip never saw the destruction of Persia, his son accomplished that goal beyond Philip's wildest dreams.

See also Alexander the Great [11].

References: Borza, Eugene, In the Shadow of Olympus: The Emergence of Macedon (Princeton, NJ: Princeton University Press, 1990); Cawkwell, George, Philip of Macedon (Boston: Faber & Faber, 1978); Perlman, Samuel, Philip and Athens (New York: Barnes & Noble, 1973).

Late in Egypt's New Kingdom period, the ancient civilization came under the domination of foreign invaders. In the seventh century B.C. the Assyrians ruled Egypt, so weakening the local culture that the Egyptians could not withstand the onslaught of the Libyans or the Empire of Kush. When the Persians took over in the sixth century B.C., Egypt chafed under their rule, though it was more lenient than other empires that had conquered the Nile Valley. When Alexander the Great entered the country in 331 B.C., the locals viewed him as a liberator and welcomed him without resistance. Alexander's rule proved short, but Greek rule did not; Ptolemy, one of Alexander's generals, succeeded to the Egyptian throne on his leader's death in 323 B.C. Ptolemy and his heirs ruled Egypt for three centuries, until they succumbed to the power of Rome.

Having served as governor for Egypt under Alexander's administration, Ptolemy declared himself the independent ruler of Egypt in 305 B.C., taking the regnal name of Ptolemy I Soter (meaning "preserver"). He ruled as pharaoh, the divine leader recognized by Egyptian culture for two millennia. This may not have endeared him to the Egyptians, but at least it made his rule acceptable.

Ptolemy I Soter fought with his fellow successor generals, the Diodachi (Seleucus and Antigonus), who had each inherited a third of Alexander's empire. He maintained almost constant conflict with the Seleucids, in particular, over control of Syria and the eastern Mediterranean coast, and he managed to establish control over Rhodes and Palestine. Most famous for establishing the Library of Alexandria, Ptolemy I Soter resigned in favor of his son in 285 B.C.

Ptolemy II Philadelphus (meaning "brotherly") continued his father's wars with the Seleucids. He established Egypt as the major maritime power of the Mediterranean at the expense of the Seleucid king Antiochus I. He also followed in his father's academic footsteps by enlarging the Alexandrian Library and sponsoring literary and scholarly endeavors. He was also responsible for the Pharos, or great lighthouse, one of the seven wonders of the ancient world. His reign of nearly 40 years made Egypt the cultural center of its time. He was outdone only by his own son, Ptolemy III Euergertes (meaning "benefactor"), who reunited Cyrenaica (modern Libya) with Egypt and invaded Syria. Egyptian naval power grew to dominate the Aegean Sea. Ptolemy Euergertes spent even more time and money improving the library and patronizing the arts, making his 25-year reign the height of Ptolemaic power and prestige.

Successive rulers of the dynasty made alternate peace and war with the successors of the other Diodachi, as each attempted to match the empire founded by Alexander. Though they brought wealth and fame to their own spheres of influence, they could not match Alexander's military accomplishments. Frontiers moved back and forth, but the Ptolemies usually maintained control of African territory even when they occasionally ceded authority across the Suez. The Ptolemies maintained their Greek heritage by following the Egyptian practice of family intermarriage. It was a brother-sister/husband-wife combination who controlled Egypt in the middle of the first century B.C. when Julius Caesar focused Roman attention on the Egypt of Cleopatra and Ptolemy XII.

Though the Ptolemies could not be considered cruel masters, their three centuries of rule certainly did not benefit the common man in Egypt. Almost constant warfare cost significant tax money and necessitated conscription for public service, which the commoners were obliged to pro-

vide. The cultural advancements typified by the Library of Alexandria benefited only the upper classes. However, the Ptolemies maintained strict observance of Egyptian religious rites, and provided a steady flow of money to the temples for maintenance and improvement, which kept the people relatively quiet, if not happy. Rebellion was always close at hand, but the Egyptian people never had the power to defeat their Greek masters. The takeover of the country proved almost as easy for Rome as it had for Alexander, but the locals viewed them as new masters rather than liberators.

*See also* Assyrian Empire [1]; Kush, Expansion of [8]; Alexander the Great [11]; Augustus, Caesar [12]; Caesar, Julius [14]; Egypt, Alexander's Conquest of [19]; Seleucid Empire [31].

References: Beven, Edwyn, *A History of Egypt under the Ptolemaic Dynasty* (London: Methuen & Co., 1927); Foster, Edward, *Alexandria, a History and a Guide* (Gloucester: Doubleday, 1968).

## 31   SELEUCID EMPIRE

The death of Alexander the Great brought a struggle among his subordinates for succession to his throne. As many as 11 of his commanders vied for position, but it finally became a struggle between three: Antigonus controlled Macedon, Seleucus took over most of what had been the Persian Empire, and Ptolemy became ruler of Egypt. Not satisfied with their holdings, the three fought among themselves for more land; often, two of them allied against the third in an ever-changing set of partnerships. Seleucus controlled the largest of the three domains, but his successors had the most difficult time in maintaining it. Seleucus established his capital at Babylon in 312 B.C., but spent most of the rest of his life suppressing revolts by provincial governors. Syria was a continual source of trouble. His victory at the battle of Ipsus in 301 B.C. gave him control of the important trade center, but keeping it was another matter.

Upon Seleucus's death, his son Antiochus I inherited the throne and had to fight on all frontiers. He was the first to war with Egypt over Syria, losing it to Ptolemy II in the First Syrian War of 280–279 B.C. Antiochus allied himself with Antigonus after the Macedonian had to suppress several rebellions in Greece subsidized by Ptolemy. Antiochus invaded Syria in 260 B.C., and Antigonus engaged and defeated the Egyptian fleet off the island of Cos in 258. Ptolemy sued for peace in 255 B.C. Ptolemy III regained Syria in a Third Syrian War, 246–241 B.C., while Seleucus II was busy fighting a civil war against his brother. Seleucus was aided in this by the city-state of Pergamum on the Turkish Adriatic coast, which had a brief career as arbiter of Asia Minor politics.

The Seleucid Empire reached the height of its power under Antiochus III, called "the Great." He regained territory in Asia Minor from Pergamum; he fought yet another Syrian war to little effect; he suppressed a rebellion in Asia Minor (216–213 B.C.); he defeated Armenia and forced them to recognize his suzerainty; and he invaded Parthia, the power that had succeeded the Persians in the east. At the battle of the Arius in 209 B.C., he forced the Parthian king Araces III to become his vassal. Moving farther east, Antiochus III fought the Bactrians (in modern-day Afghanistan) and forced their submission, after which he marched down the Kabul River into northwestern India. In 205–204 B.C. he campaigned down the Persian Gulf to conquer Gerrha (modern Bahrain). His final successful effort was another war in Syria,

in which he took advantage of the infant king Ptolemy V. Again allying his nation with Macedon, now under Philip V, Antiochus easily defeated Egyptian forces in the key battle at Panium in 198 B.C., which gave him control over Palestine, Syria, and Asia Minor. Macedon was of little assistance because it lost battles to Pergamum and Rome.

The rising power of Rome spelled the end of Seleucid power. After defeating Philip V, the Romans continued onward toward Syria. The Romans and Seleucids fought their major battle at Magnesia in December 190 B.C. After having the upper hand early on, Antiochus's forces were broken when their elephants went berserk and trampled their own army. The Romans took the victory, but did not take territory for themselves. Instead, they gave Asia Minor and Antiochus's Greek possessions to Pergamum and Rhodes at the Peace of Apemeax in 188 B.C. This defeat and Antiochus's death in 187 B.C. brought about a general revolt throughout the Seleucid domain.

Antiochus IV managed to hold onto power for a while, even defeating Egypt twice, but he was forced by Rome to evacuate. His occupation of Palestine after that evacuation was so harsh that it provoked a Jewish revolt: the war of the Maccabees. He restored Seleucid dominance in the east, but a succession struggle broke up the empire. More revolts and the rising power of Parthia under Mithradates served to bring the Seleucid dynasty to an end late in the second century B.C.

Despite the fact that the Seleucids spent almost their entire tenure in wars, there were some positive results of their time in power, mostly in the implementation of Alexander's legacy of Hellenism throughout the Middle East. Greek settlers and retired veterans established Greek communities throughout the area, making Greek the language of science and the arts. Greek schools kept alive the sciences and philosophies of Greece and served to introduce Stoicism to the region, an outlook that had effects on the establishment of Christian doctrine. Without strict religious oversight or strong political order, the citizens of the empire were able to explore the ideas of both Eastern and European cultures and blend them into views unique to the area. Especially in religion, these views would arise as rivals to the gods of Rome and heresies to Orthodox and Roman Christianity.

See also Alexander the Great [11]; Ptolemaic Dynasty [30].

References: Bar-Kochva, Bezalel, *The Seleucid Army* (London: Cambridge University Press, 1976); Sherwin-White, Susan, *From Samarkand to Sardis* (London: Duckworth, 1993).

## SICILY, ROMAN CONQUEST OF (FIRST PUNIC WAR)

**32**

Prior to 264 B.C., the Mediterranean Basin and Asia Minor were dominated in large part by either Hellenic or Hellenistic military force and culture. However, the status quo had been inexorably changing, owing to the growing strength of agricultural Rome and commercial Carthage. According to the historian Polybius, these two powers negotiated three separate treaties prior to the outbreak of this war. The first two were basically nonaggression pacts, and the third was a mutual-defense agreement designed to neutralize or defeat a perceived common enemy, King Pyrrhus of Epirus. Rome's defeat of Pyrrhus removed the common threat, setting the stage for the Punic Wars.

Many historians believe that the First Punic War began by mistake, and some writers label the initial conflict an "accidental war." This viewpoint stems from the Roman and Carthaginian encounters in Sicily, which were centered on the Mamertine city of Messana along the Sicilio-Roman border. The Mamertines ("Men of Mars") were an unruly group of brigands who plundered and looted throughout coastal Sicily, provoking the ire of Syracuse, the dominant force on the island. The Mamertines induced Carthage to protect them from Syracuse; then, during the Carthaginian occupation, they persuaded the Romans that the citizens of Messana were Roman allies or even of Roman blood. Rome intervened on their behalf, starting the 23-year-long war. Other historians speculate that the move to save their supposed brothers in Sicily was merely an excuse for an aggressive Roman Centurial Assembly, made up of wealthy plebeians, to force the senate into a war to expand Roman power.

From Consul Appius Caudex's defeat of a combined Syracusan-Carthaginian force at Messana in 264 B.C. to the decisive naval battle at Lilybaeum, won by Consul Catalus in 242 B.C., no previous war had cost so much in lives and matériel. During the conflict at sea, the Romans lost an estimated 250,000 men and the Carthaginians 210,000; no estimate has been made regarding personnel losses suffered on land. The Romans were thought to be stronger on land and their adversary stronger at sea, but the conflict became a see-saw affair, with Rome winning many naval battles and Carthage defeating a number of Roman armies in the field. Consul Regulus, for example, soundly defeated Hamilcar's fleet off Sicily in 256 B.C.; in turn, his army was beaten and captured by Xanthippus at the Plain of Tunis.

The Romans had no navy before 260 B.C., so it is quite remarkable that they became a maritime power virtually overnight. Two key reasons for Roman success in naval warfare were their development of a boarding platform, called a "raven," and the courage, discipline, and training of the average Roman soldier or marine. The only serious naval defeats the Romans suffered came from either poor leadership or disdain for the power of nature: The majority of Roman naval losses were incurred during storms.

The Carthaginian government greatly aided the Roman cause by crucifying their own most capable admirals and generals after the loss of a single engagement, thus depriving themselves of their best leadership. They also refused to support their most successful general, Hamilcar Barca. After a series of successful raids against Roman outposts along the Italian coast, he landed his force to occupy a Roman force at Palermo. His government refused to send aid or reinforcements.

Two battles in 249 B.C. brought a major naval loss for each side, after which ensued a cease-fire of almost nine years, time the Carthaginians wasted, while the Romans rebuilt their forces. In 241 B.C., with a new 200-ship armada, the Romans sailed secretly to Sicily and caught a Carthaginian fleet unawares and overwhelmed it. The Carthaginian admiral Hanno was crucified upon his return to Carthage following this loss to Consul Catalus. This defeat swung the balance firmly in Rome's favor, forcing the Carthaginians into peace negotiations.

The immediate effects of the victory were to give Rome complete hegemony over Sicily and to provide its coffers with 2,200 talents (125,400 pounds) of silver in Carthaginian reparation payments over ten years. In the long term, Rome would henceforth view Sicily as vital to its national security. The Sicilian client-states, established after the war, would become models for Rome's governance of conquered territories during the life of the Roman Empire.

In North Africa, the Carthaginian government continued to be its own worst enemy. When the mercenaries, who made up most of the army, demanded their back pay, the government prevaricated and provoked a rebellion. Hamilcar again proved himself their most able commander. He raised a force to restore order, then convinced the government to send him to Spain to reestablish Carthaginian dominance. That move helped to provoke the Second Punic War.

Although, as stated, the First Punic War may have been accidental, it is far more likely that such a conflict was inevitable. The residents of Messana merely provided the spark to put the two powers at loggerheads. Carthaginian claims on Sicily were tenuous at best, because the powerful Syracusans lived in closer proximity to Rome than to Carthage. Polybius's writings notwithstanding, it is likely that the powerful, aggressive Romans had already decided to expand their borders beyond the Italian coast. The voices of senators who called for peace in 265 B.C. were drowned out by those clamoring for war. With consuls eager to gain fame and riches through warfare, it seems logical that they would look toward Carthage for fulfillment. At any rate, the First Punic War set the stage for Carthage's ultimate destruction and established the framework for Roman dominance in the Mediterranean.

See also Carthage, Expansion of [15]; Italy, Carthaginian Invasion of (Second Punic War) [26].

References: Charles-Picard, Gilbert, and Collette Picard, *The Life and Death of*

*Carthage*, trans. Dominique Collon (London: Sidgwick & Jackson, 1968); Errington, R., *The Dawn of Empire: Rome's Rise to World Power* (New York: Cornell University Press, 1972); Gruen, E. S., ed., *Imperialism in the Roman Republic* (New York: Holt, Rinehart & Winston, Inc., 1970).

## 33 SPAIN, ROMAN CONQUEST OF

During the First Punic War, Rome and Carthage battled each other from 264 to 261 B.C. The cause of that conflict was Rome's discontent with Carthaginian expansion into Sicily, and ultimately Rome forced Carthage back into its African domain. In 218 B.C., Rome interpreted a Carthaginian attempt to rebuild a power base in Spain as a threat to Roman interests, forcing another declaration of war on Carthage. Early in the contest, Roman success was minimal. In fact, the famed Carthaginian general Hannibal wrought havoc across the Italian countryside. Looking for new leadership, the Roman senate arranged for Publius Cornelius Scipio's son, Scipio Africanus, to be elected proconsul to Spain. Unlike most Romans, he realized that Spain was the key to the struggle against Hannibal: Spain would serve as his main base of operations and provide most of his replacements.

Scipio's first target in Spain was New Carthage (modern-day Cartagena). New Carthage was the capital, and the only Spanish port able to handle a large fleet. Furthermore, it possessed other strategic aspects: It provided a direct sea link to Carthage, the Carthaginians kept the bulk of their gold bullion and war matériel there, and it would give Scipio an essential base from which he could conduct his campaign into the south of the peninsula.

Scipio's success at Carthage was the result of his talent for deception. Cartagena was surrounded by water on three sides—a lagoon on the north, a canal on the west, and a bay and the open sea on the south. The winter prior to his assault, Scipio made careful topographical inquiries about the area. He learned from local fishermen that the lagoon was easily fordable at low tide. In the spring of 209 B.C., he launched a frontal attack on the gates of the city, which faced east, to divert their forces. He then sent a party of 500 men with ladders across the lagoon. Quickly clearing the wall, his men took the Carthaginians by surprise and opened the way for the main body of Roman troops to overwhelm the city.

This victory, coupled with Hannibal's eventual withdrawal back to Africa, left Rome in control of Spain. They had not intended to conquer all of Spain, but the law of expansion forced them to either commit themselves totally or surrender what they had captured. The more civilized eastern and western portions of Spain submitted easily to Roman rule, but it took more than 60 years to gain firm control of the country because the warlike tribes of the interior would not give in. Engaging in tribal warfare against militant Spanish bands throughout the countryside was a challenge to Rome. Coping with the type of warfare the Spanish practiced was difficult for the legionaries because the Spanish fought in small groups, taking advantage of their knowledge of the terrain to cut off and surprise Roman detachments. These tactics, employed often in the future, were given the name *guerrilla*, Spanish for "little war." Until 132 B.C., Roman armies were often defeated in the Spanish hinterland and were obliged to concede peace terms on many occasions. Nevertheless, each time the treaties were disavowed by the government in Rome or by Roman generals on the scene.

The process of Romanization was slow, not only because of the native opposition, but also because Roman ideas themselves continued to evolve until the second century A.D. Their initial contributions dealt with law and administration. Rome's administrative abilities were passed on to the Spanish through their organization of cities, towns, and governmental institutions. Even the Christian church, introduced to Spain by the Romans, was organized on the basis of Roman administrative districts, employing Roman methods and Roman law.

Thanks to agricultural and commercial successes during Roman rule, Spain amassed considerable wealth. The public works projects undertaken during Roman rule were among the most significant contributions to Spanish society. New roads and bridges—some existing in whole or in part to this day—permitted the peoples of Spain to communicate freely with one another as never before. The construction of aqueducts served as both a necessity and a convenience for expanding cities. Roman architecture in Spain had the characteristics of massiveness and strength, borrowing structural principles from the Etruscans and decorative forms from the Greeks. These qualities were most evident in theaters, amphitheaters, temples, triumphal arches, and tombs.

Spain was invaded by the Visigoths in A.D. 409, but by that time, most Roman characteristics were permanently engraved in Spanish society. Despite further invasions by barbarians from the north and the Muslims from the south, Roman influence endured. Whether or not Rome had a concrete reason for invading and occupying Spain in the beginning, the Romans were so successful in planting their culture and institutions during six centuries of occupation that much remains to this day.

See also Hannibal [24]; Italy, Carthaginian Invasion of (Second Punic War) [26]; Sicily, Roman Conquest of (First Punic War) [32]; Visigoths [81].

References: Chapman, Charles E., A History of Spain (New York: Free Press, 1966); McDonald, A. H., Republican Rome (New York: Praeger, 1966); Scullard, Howard H., A History of the Roman World: From 753 to 146 B.C. (London: Methuen & Co., 1969).

# PART 3
## THE DARK AND MIDDLE AGES

# THE DARK AND MIDDLE AGES

The numbers on the map correspond to entry numbers in the text.

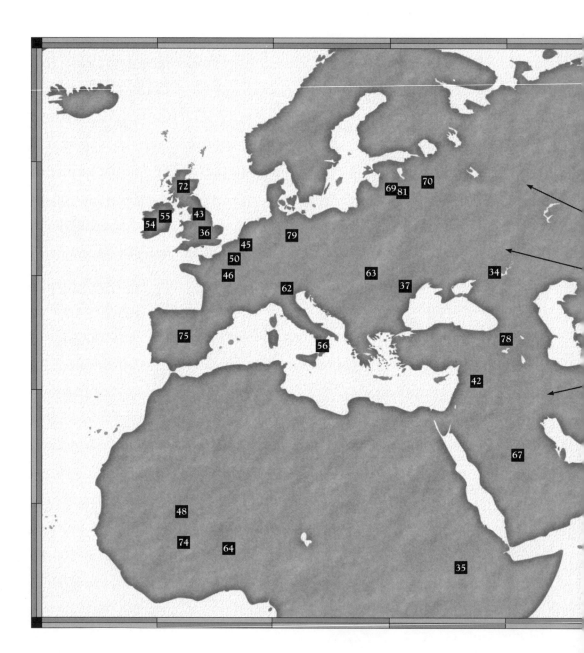

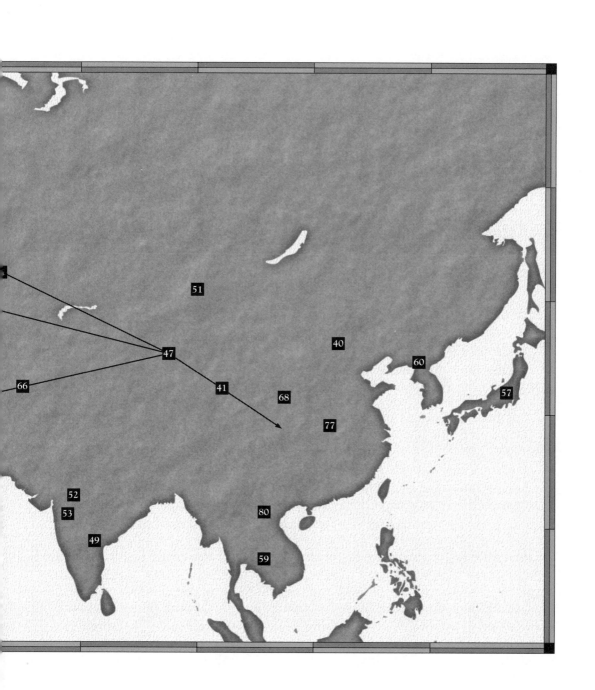

## 34          AVARS

A people ethnologically related to the Huns, the Avars are first mentioned in the fifth century A.D. as living east of the Volga River in Russia. Their first contact with Western society came in the mid-sixth century when they appeared in the Caucasus. The Avars invaded the territory west of the Dnieper River, defeating the Utigurs (the last of the Huns) and the Antes. They pillaged this territory so thoroughly that those two tribes disappeared, and the Avars then made demands on the Byzantine Empire. For a while, the Avars served the Byzantine Empire as mercenaries, but over time they grew too strong. In 561 Khagan Baian, the major Avar leader, received tribute from Emperor Justinian to stay away from Constantinople, so the Avars moved north and west. Though they met defeat at the hands of the Franks in Thuringia in 562, they allied with the Langobards in 565 to make war on the Gepids, inhabitants of the Danube valley. Together they crushed the Gepids in a huge battle in 567 and split Gepid lands between them. Rather than face a potential new enemy, the Langobards ceded their newly acquired Gepid lands to the Avars and migrated to Italy, where they became better known as Lombards.

With this cession from the Langobards in addition to their initial conquests, the Avars now controlled land stretching from western Rumania through Hungary to Bohemia and on to the Elbe River in central Germany. After attacking the Byzantine fortress at Sirmium, the Avars extorted an increased tribute from Emperor Justin II. Only on their southern frontier was there a challenge to their power: the Sclavini, the forerunner of the Slavs. This tribe had pillaged throughout the Balkans and Danube valley for years, growing wealthy in the process. Khagan Baian offered to accept the Sclavini as vassals if they would pay him tribute; they rejected his offer by killing his envoy. That was all the excuse the Avars needed. They quickly went to war against the Sclavini by moving tens of thousands of men overland and down the Danube River into their territory. The Avars made short work of the Sclavini, pillaging their land and forcing them to run for the hills of northern Greece. Justinian had hoped to play the Sclavini against the Avars, forgoing the need to commit his own forces, but the Avar victory ended that hope.

Perhaps earning the respect of the Sclavini, the Avars soon joined with the other tribe and came to be known as Avaro-Slavs. Together they invaded the Balkan peninsula, wreaking havoc everywhere. They rampaged from Constantinople to Thrace to Greece for four years, then returned across the Danube. Emperor Maurice paid the Avars tribute in return for being allowed to claim the land to the Danube as his own. In 601 Maurice's generals defeated the Avars, neutralizing the Avar threat, but a mutiny the following year gave the Avars the opening to recover their strength and counterattack. In the first decade of the 600s, the Avaro-Slavs defeated Byzantine forces in several cities along the Adriatic coast, leaving only ruins in their wake. The Sclavini returned to ravage Greece between 610 and 626. With Avar aid they laid siege to Thessalonika for 33 days, ending the siege with a treaty in 626 that gave the surrounding territory of Illyria to the Avars while allowing Thessalonika to remain free. That proved to be the high point of Avar power. In 626 they were defeated while attacking Constantinople. From that time forward they had to face rebellious tribes, including the Sclavini, who sapped their power. Migrations of Bulgars and Magyars ultimately took over Avar holdings. The final war the Avars fought was against Charlemagne in 805; after that, they ceased to exist.

The main result of the Avar conquests was the establishment of a Slavic population in eastern Europe. The remains of Avar cemeteries show a high quality of metalwork in the form of bridle bits, saber-daggers, spear points, and three-barbed arrowheads. This artistry reflected the style of eastern Asian nomads rather than any influences adapted from the peoples they conquered. Dedicated mainly to conquest and plunder, the Avars left virtually no architectural legacy.

References: Gimbutas, Marija, *The Slavs* (New York: Praeger, 1971); Hosch, Edgar, *The Balkans,* trans. Tania Alexander (New York: Crane, Russak & Co., 1972); Obolensky, Dimitri, *Byzantium and the Slavs* (London: Variorum Reprints, 1971).

*See also* Byzantine Empire [38]; Carolingian Dynasty [39]; Franks [46]; Huns [51]; Justinian [58]; Lombards [62].

## 35 AXUM, EXPANSION OF

The Axumites inhabited an area of eastern Africa lying in what is today Ethiopia. The peoples who settled here around 500 B.C. seem to have been a mixture of Semites from Yemen and settlers from the empire of Kush. The main centers of population were the city of Axum and the port of Adulis, both initially recorded in the first century A.D. For the first two centuries A.D., the Axumites controlled the Red Sea coastline and carried on extensive trade with Greek and Egyptian merchants, acting as the outlet for sub-Saharan products such as ebony, ivory, and exotic animals. By the third century, the Axumites were noted throughout the Middle East as a major empire, controlling not only the Horn of Africa but also the southern portion of the Arabian peninsula, from which they collected tribute.

The exploits of the Axumite kings were recorded on stone monuments. The first major conqueror seems to have been Aphilas, who established Axumite dominance in the Yemen area, though it is impossible to tell exactly when that took place. The leader who dominated the expansion of the empire was Ezana in the fourth century. Records show that the Axumites still controlled Yemen, and Ezana campaigned around the borders, defeating harassing tribes and ultimately conquering the faded glory of Kush. Upon securing this conquest, Ezana gave credit to the Christian God, marking the fact that Axum was converted during his reign. At its greatest extent, Axum spread from the Arabian peninsula across the Ethiopian plateau all the way to the Sahara. The last major exploit by an Axumite king took place in 525 when King Kaleb led a force of 30,000 to Nadjran on the Arabian peninsula to avenge a massacre of Christians. He succeeded in this campaign and left behind a garrison of 10,000.

Control of extensive fertile land gave Axum a solid agricultural base for its economy, to which could be added a great amount of international trade. From the third century forward, Axum was well known for its architecture and monolithic monuments. It was also the first African nation to mint coins in gold, silver, and copper. The trade network to which Axum contributed brought travelers from all over the world. Apparently the Axumites were not intolerant Christians, as evidence points to Jewish, Kushite, and even Buddhist enclaves. The empire remained important and profitable past the fall of Rome, and kept up good trade relations with the Byzantines, even though the Axumites embraced the Monophysite views of the Egyptian church, which the Orthodox church considered heretical.

With the growth of Islam, the power of Axum began to slip, though the Axumites' tolerant religious attitude is shown by the fact that early on they sheltered persecuted Muslims from Mecca. This action stood them in good stead when Muslim conquerors spread through eastern Africa. Axum remained a Christian island in a sea of Islam and maintained cordial relations with their neighbors, but gradually the political center of the country retreated inland and trade declined. Though not conquered by Islam, Axum would not regain its former influence.

See also Kush, Expansion of [8].

References: Buxton, David, *The Abyssinians* (New York: Praeger, 1970); Jones, A. H. M., and Elizabeth Monroe, *A History of Ethiopia* (Oxford: Clarendon, 1955); Mokhtar, G., *Ancient Civilizations of Africa* (Paris: UNESCO, 1990).

## BRITAIN, NORMAN INVASION OF

**36**

William, duke of Normandy, wanted to be king of England. Norman writers say that King Edward had promised the throne to him. While Harold Godwinsson, the earl of Wessex and Edward's brother-in-law, was on embassy to Normandy, he supposedly agreed to Edward's bequest and promised his support. But when Edward died on 5 January 1066, Harold was named king by England's leaders. William decided on war.

Only Norman versions of the incidents survive, so it is impossible to determine whether Edward actually promised William the throne. Harold's broken promise, however, was William's argument in gaining papal support for his cause, which allowed him to raise an army fairly quickly. The pope gave his support to William without having any sort of input from Harold concerning the truth of William's claims, which was strange considering Harold's consistent loyalty to Rome. The blessing of the church, coupled with the prospect of some serious pillage and looting in England, was sufficient reason for the aristocracy of northern France to join the expedition.

In May 1066, Tostig, Harold's exiled brother, raided England with the assistance of some Viking allies. In September he invaded the Northumbrian coast with a force provided by Harold III Hardraade, king of Norway. This obliged Harold to move many of his troops, which had been awaiting William's attack, away from the south coast. Harold was successful in defeating the Norsemen at the battle of Stamford Bridge, but immediately afterward received word that William's force had landed. He ordered his exhausted troops to march south immediately.

William had concentrated his forces at the mouth of the Dives River in Normandy in August. He probably planned to sail north and land first at the Isle of Wight, where he could establish an offshore base. He was forced to wait on favorable weather and could not sail until September, when a westerly wind allowed him to begin his expedition. The strong wind blew his ships up the English Channel, away from the Isle of Wight, and he had to regroup at Saint-Valery, still on the French coast. He had lost some ships and morale was slipping. Finally, at the end of September a southerly wind took him to England, where he landed at Pevensey and Hastings.

William organized 4,000–7,000 cavalry and infantry. After ransacking every town in the area, he found himself in a narrow strip of land bounded by the coast on one side and the forest of Andred on the other. On 25 September word came of Harold's victory over his brother near York, along with the news that Harold's army was on the march; they would arrive sooner than William had expected.

On 13 October Harold emerged from the thick forest, surprising William. It was too late in the day to continue on to Hastings, so Harold took up a defensive position along a ridge and awaited William's assault the next morning. The Normans repeatedly failed to make headway up the hill against the steadfast line the British maintained. The heavy Norman cavalry could not build up enough speed to break the English line atop the hill, nor could their archers hurt many English behind their interlocked shields. Only when the English broke ranks to pursue a repulsed Norman charge did they lose the protection of their position. In the open field, they fell prey to the Normans. The ensuing melee, and the death of Harold, spelled the end of the English army.

After the battle, William marched his force to London, defeating any resistance he met along the way. He entered the city in December and had himself crowned, like Charlemagne, on Christmas Day. William settled in to sovereignty fairly quickly. There was little resistance at first, and William set about establishing Norman control by constructing forts as centers of power across the country. In early 1068 William moved against risings in the southwest by capturing Exeter and moving into Cornwall. More castles were built in order to maintain control. Trouble in the north took William to Northumbria and York, but he gained the fealty of the northern earls and King Malcolm of Scotland. It was short-lived, for he had to return in the winter of 1069–1070 in a brutal campaign. William destroyed the agricultural production of the northern counties, burning crops and animals to deny the locals any chance of sustaining themselves. An autumn 1069 victory over Scandinavian forces under Swein Estrithson at the Humber River plus a second campaign against Scotland's King Malcolm in 1072 completed William's conquest.

Some Norman influence was present in England prior to 1066, but only after William's conquest did the whole of the British Isles begin to change. The Norman king introduced feudalism into the country, and the construction of castles throughout the country, along with the appointment of Normans to own them, created a new ruling class. At first the conquest was one of aristocracy only, as the predominantly Scandinavian rulers were replaced by continental ones, even though the Normans themselves were not that far from their Scandinavian roots. All of Britain soon felt the Norman presence when William ordered the compilation of the *Domesday Book*, a census of all the country's people, lands, and possessions for taxation purposes. Much of historians' knowledge of medieval England comes from the minute details recorded in that book.

The construction of castles and then churches changed the nature of architecture in Britain, and the new church construction signaled a change in the church hierarchy as well. Not only did the aristocracy change, but local abbots and bishops were replaced by Norman church officials; by the time of William's death in 1090, no high-ranking church official had been born in Britain. The church, being the center of learning on the continent, had a profound effect on the intellectual life of Britain. The country ceased being part of Scandinavia and began to be part of Europe.

*See also* France, Viking Invasion of [45].

References: Freeman, Edward, *The History of the Norman Conquest of England* (Chicago: University of Chicago Press, 1974); Furneaux, Rupert, *The Invasion of 1066* (Englewood Cliffs, NJ: Prentice-

Hall, 1974); Howarth, David, *1066: The Year of Conquest* (New York: Viking Penguin, 1977).

## 37    BULGARS

The Bulgars were another of the nomadic tribes of central Asia who wandered into Europe in the wake of the Roman Empire's fall. Arriving late in the fifth century, at first they were kept at bay by the power of the Byzantine Empire and that of the Avars.

The Bulgar leader Kovrat established a kingdom in 635 recognized by the Byzantines as "Great Bulgaria," but it did not last beyond Kovrat's reign. The Bulgars separated into two groups, one moving northward toward the Volga, the other establishing itself under Kovrat's son Asparuch (Isperich) on the lower Danube in 680. In 681 Byzantine emperor Constantine IV recognized Asparuch as ruler of the region stretching from the Balkan Mountains to the Dniester.

When Avar power collapsed after their defeat by the Frankish leader Charlemagne, the Bulgars moved into the power vacuum left in the eastern Balkans. The Slavs, who had been under Avar domination, fell under the power of the Bulgars; after a few generations, the nomadic Turkic Bulgars were absorbed and transformed by the peasant Slavs. The mixture of the two races created Bulgarians.

Bulgar power grew with the gradual weakening of the Byzantine defensive system in the Balkans. Though Byzantium controlled the area around Greece in the late eighth and early ninth centuries, they could make little headway against the Bulgarians. In 802 the Bulgars came under the leadership of Khan Krum, who challenged both the Byzantines and the Franks. He conquered to eastern Pannonia (modern Austria), then turned southward; he captured Sofia in 809, destroyed a Byzantine army in 811, marched to the walls of Constantinople in 813, and captured Adrianople in 814. Krum was succeeded in 814 by Omortag, who followed a more peaceful strategy with Byzantium and opened his people to Hellenistic influences. The next khan, Boris, allowed Christian missionaries into his realm.

Bulgarian tsar Simeon (r. 893–927) attacked Byzantium and won a major victory in 896, which brought an annual tribute from Constantinople. When that tribute was discontinued in 912 after the death of Emperor Leo VI, Simeon went to war again. He attacked Constantinople twice, in 913 and 924, but was unable to breach the walls. Though he called himself "Emperor of the Romans and the Bulgars," only his own people recognized the first part of that title. At his death in 927, Simeon's empire stretched from the Adriatic to the Black Sea. His son Peter signed a peace treaty that year and married the granddaughter of a Byzantine emperor; this was the closest to a juncture the two empires ever achieved.

Tsar Simeon's reign marked the height of Bulgarian power. After his time, Byzantine diplomacy brought too many allies into the picture for the Bulgarians to resist. From the 890s the Magyars, a tribe of Scandinavian descent with Turkic blood, had harassed the frontiers of both Byzantium and Bulgaria. In the middle 900s they expanded into the upper Danube plain at Bulgaria's expense. More deadly was the threat from the rising power of Russia, which Constantinople also cultivated. The emperor encouraged the Russian prince of Kiev, Sviatislav, to attack Bulgarian tsar Peter; in 969 the Russians occupied virtually all Bulgarian lands. When they were forced back to Russia by Emperor John I Tzimisces, the territory once again belonged to Byzantium and the power of the Bulgars was broken.

Bulgaria was influential in eastern Europe in a number of ways. When Christian missionaries were allowed into the territory, the representatives of the church included "the apostles of the Slavs," Cyril and Methodius. These two developed the alphabet that dominates eastern Europe—Cyrillic—and in so doing created Bulgarian literature. The long-term contact with Byzantium was not always hostile, and the culture of the Eastern Roman Empire strongly influenced Bulgar society. The introduction of Orthodox Christianity brought a Bulgarian patriarchate that lasted until the removal of the Russians. The contact with Eastern religions also brought about new interpretations of Christianity, with the incorporation of ancient Manichaean ideas that influenced the Cathar and Albigensian heresies of medieval Europe. Bulgaria was well placed to act as a transition between European and Asiatic views, creating a cultural heritage unique to the Balkans.

*See also* Avars [34]; Byzantine Empire [38]; Carolingian Dynasty [39]; Magyars [63].

References: Bury, J. B., *The Invasion of Europe by the Barbarians* (New York: Russell & Russell, 1963); Hosch, Edgar, *The Balkans* (New York: Crane, Russak & Co., 1972); Thompson, E. A., *Romans and Barbarians* (Madison: University of Wisconsin Press, 1982).

## 38     BYZANTINE EMPIRE

In the early A.D. 300s, Emperor Diocletian came to the conclusion that the Roman Empire was too unwieldy for one man to rule. He therefore appointed himself and Maximian as coemperors, or augusti, and named a subordinate to each, creating two caesars, which effectively divided the empire into quarters. After creating this format, Diocletian resigned. His planned smooth transition of power became chaos as up to six people scrambled for power. Rising to the top was Constantine, who finally subdued his rivals and established a new capital for the Roman Empire at Byzantium (renamed Constantinople) at the crossroads of east-west trade routes and Black-Mediterranean sea routes. Though it was not Constantine's intention, this shift of power to the east laid the groundwork for the Byzantine Empire. In 378 the Visigoths defeated Roman troops under Valens at Adrianople and changed the nature of the empire and its military. Valens's successor, Theodosius, made peace with the Goths and ceded them land, hoping they would act as a buffer against other marauding peoples. Upon his death in 395, the empire was divided between his sons and became permanently split into two sections.

The western half soon succumbed to barbarian invasions, but the eastern half prospered. They adapted themselves to the new fighting style of the Goths and recruited many of them into their army. They also abandoned the legion style of formation that had long served the Romans so well in favor of smaller, more mobile units. They developed a long-service professional army that rarely numbered above 100,000, but which defended the empire and at times expanded it. The basis of this new army was the *cataphract*, cavalry that could wield either lances or bows and act as either light or heavy cavalry. Heavy infantry was armed with lances and formed into phalanxes, while the light infantry used bows and javelins. By mixing these various formations in groups of 400, a Byzantine army of 25,000–30,000 had all the necessary units for attack and defense.

With these professional soldiers, Byzantine generals under the direction of Justinian expanded the borders almost to the original boundaries of the Roman Empire, reacquiring northern Africa, Italy, and southern Spain from barbarian conquerors, though they were unable to maintain that far-flung empire when the power of Islam grew. Justinian introduced an updated law code that became the model for the legal system of western Europe, but it proved too oppressive for religious groups who disagreed with Justinian's Orthodox faith. His laws were so resented that many people in the empire saw the religious toleration preached by Muhammad as a better alternative. Muhammad's warmaking, and that of his successors, was effective enough to drive back the borders of the Byzantine Empire in the seventh century and detach the distant provinces of Africa and Spain from Byzantine control.

The homeland of Asia Minor and southeastern Europe was protected by the professional army, occasionally updated and reformed along lines laid out in works like Emperor Maurice's *Strategicon* and Emperor Leo's *Tactica*. By holding the Muslim advance at bay until it settled down to consolidation, the Byzantines grew confident in their ability to defend themselves. Over time, that grew into overconfidence. When attacked by the Seljuk Turks in 1063, the Byzantines lost the battle of Manzikert, and with it much of Asia Minor. From this point forward they defended the remains of their territory against increasingly powerful and aggressive enemies on all sides. Still, they managed to survive another 400 years, until the Ottoman Turks became the first and only people to capture Constantinople. They soon controlled almost as much as the Byzantine Empire had at its height.

In 1,100 years of existence, the Byzantine Empire put the stamp of Christian and European culture on the Balkans and Middle East, while at the same time absorbing much of the East's civilization and learning. The empire's longest lasting influence was in the area of religion: The Eastern Orthodox church was born and survives to this day. Its missionaries spread Christianity from central Europe to Russia to Armenia, surviving onslaughts of Muslims and Mongols in the process. The empire likewise maintained contacts with western Europe, though usually from a position of need. Their call for assistance from Muslim attack in the twelfth and thirteenth centuries brought the Crusades to the Middle East, with a resulting shift in power and trade. The enmity between the Orthodox and Roman churches, however, kept the possible spread of Eastern learning from entering Europe until the Renaissance. The Byzantine Empire lasted long enough to cede control of the Mediterranean to Europe rather than to Islamic countries, and Western naval power ultimately translated itself into worldwide empires in the fifteenth and sixteenth centuries.

*See also* Constantine, Emperor [18]; Crusades [42]; Justinian [58]; Middle East, Muslim Conquest of the [67]; Turks [78]; Visigoths [81]; Ottoman Empire [102].

References: Browning, Robert, *The Byzantine Empire* (New York: Scribner, 1980); Byron, Robert, *The Byzantine Achievement* (New York: Russell & Russell, 1964); Franzius, Enno, *History of the Byzantine Empire* (New York: Funk & Wagnalls, 1968).

## 39 CAROLINGIAN DYNASTY

The Carolingian Empire had its roots in the migrations of the Franks into the frontiers of the Roman Empire in the third century A.D. The Salian Franks, living along the lower stretches of the Rhine, were conquered by the Romans in 358 and became their allies. When the Romans withdrew from the German frontier, the Salian Franks followed them and became the masters of territory above the Loire River in Gaul (modern France). In the late fifth century, Clovis I established what came to be called the Merovingian dynasty, and he spread Frankish power to the Pyrenees in the south and the Main River in the east. He was responsible for the defeat of barbarian tribes all around his frontiers: the Allemanni, Burgundians, Visigoths, and the Ripaurian Franks of the upper Rhine. Upon his death, however, the empire divided along traditional lines (his four sons each inherited a part), which effectively broke apart a budding empire.

The successive Merovingian kings came to depend more and more on their *mayordomo,* or mayor of the palace, who acted as a liaison between the king and his nobles and subjects. The position became one of increasing power, and was successively in the hands of the Carolingian family. The Carolingians descended from Pépin the Elder of Landin, mayordomo from Austrasia (now northeastern France), the Low Countries, and western Germany. By the time Pépin of Herstal came to the post in the late seventh century, he virtually ruled the Frankish kingdom in the Merovingians' name. He overthrew the Neustrians and Burgundians, rivals to united Merovingian rule.

The illegitimate son of Pépin of Herstal, Charles Martel ("the Hammer"), became the first high-profile leader of the Carolingian line. Charles invaded and conquered Bavaria, solidified Frankish control in Frisia and Thuringia, and turned his attentions to the south. He harassed Eudo of Aquitaine, taking advantage of his weakness after fighting the Muslims of Spain. Charles defeated Eudo and fought the Muslims at Tours in 732. This Frankish victory proved the high-water mark of Muslim expansion

in the West, forcing them to stay in Spain until the fifteenth century. He fought the Muslims again in the latter 730s, and ceded his mayordomo position to his sons Carloman and Pépin the Short.

Carloman resigned his position in 747, and Pépin moved to seize real position as well as power. He overthrew the last of the Merovingians and named himself king of the Franks in 751, thus officially establishing the Carolingian royal line. His action was sanctioned by the Roman Catholic church when Pépin was crowned by Pope Stephen II in 754. This anointing by the pope made Pépin the defender of the church, and he fulfilled that role in 754 and 756 when he led forces into Italy to fight the Lombards. He also put down a revolt in Bavaria and defeated the Saxons, forcing them to pay tribute, then turned to Aquitaine to put down a revolt there.

Pépin died in 768; following tradition, his sons Carloman and Charles inherited joint control of the throne. Carloman died in 771 and Charles became sole ruler. Through campaigning with his father, Charles had received combat experience, which he quickly put to use for the defense and expansion of Frankish lands. That experience, coupled with his natural ability, brought him the title Charles the Great, better known as Charlemagne (Carolus Magnus in Latin; Karl der Grosse in German). Charlemagne inherited the position of defender of the church from his father as well, and he soon had trouble with the church's main threat, the Lombards of northern Italy. Charlemagne married a Lombard princess in 770, but his repudiation of her, coupled with appeals for aid from Carloman's heirs, brought him into conflict with the Lombards. Pope Adrian I appealed for aid in 772, and Charlemagne marched against the Lombard leader Desiderius, his erstwhile father-in-law. The Franks were victorious in 774, and

Charlemagne named himself king of the Franks and the Lombards.

Extending the tradition of fighting the Muslims, Charlemagne invaded Spain in 777. He had mixed success, but finally drove the Muslims south of the River Ebro. He campaigned in southern Italy and Bavaria, putting down revolts, then turned eastward toward the Danube River valley. In the 790s he defeated and destroyed the Avars and conquered parts of Croatia and Slovenia. On Christmas Day 800, Pope Leo III crowned Charlemagne as emperor of the Romans. That action, and the recognition of his position by the Byzantine emperor Nicephorus I in 810, created the Holy Roman Empire. Charlemagne spent most of the remainder of his reign establishing an administration for the empire and carrying on regular campaigns against the Saxons, who alternately accepted his suzerainty (and Christianity) and rebelled against him.

Charlemagne's court, built at Aix-la-Chapelle (Aachen), became the first cultural center of western Europe since the fall of the Roman Empire. By promoting widespread literacy and schooling, building monasteries and churches, and advocating and financing art, his reign introduced the Carolingian Renaissance. He created a hierarchy of officials to rule the empire, which expanded from the Pyrenees to the North Sea, France to the Danube Valley, and south into northern Italy. Charlemagne also brought back the concept of a standing army and reintroduced the practices of the Roman Empire in his attention to logistics and transport. He built forts to protect his borders and reintroduced the art of siege warfare. All in all, he proved the best ruler of medieval times from military, cultural, and social points of view.

Tradition served him fairly well at his death, for there was only one son to inherit and thus no division of rule. Louis spent his time maintaining his father's interest in the arts and scholarship and trying with minimal success to defend his northern borders from increasing pressure by the Vikings. The Carolingian line divided again on Louis's death when his three sons divided the empire into thirds. The three spent an inordinate amount of time fighting among themselves rather than cooperating in the face of Viking attacks. The Holy Roman Empire split into German and French halves; the Saxons took over the western part in 911 and the Capetians took the French territories in 987. Those two territories became the bases of the modern states of France and Germany. The Holy Roman Empire, designed to defend the church of Rome, became more a central European political entity of waxing and waning power over the next several centuries; based more in Austria than Germany, it came under the control of the Habsburg dynasty.

*See also* Avars [34]; France, Viking Invasion of [45]; Lombards [62]; Spain, Muslim Conquest of [75]; Visigoths [81].

References: Barraclough, Geoffrey, *The Crucible of Europe* (Berkeley: University of California Press, 1976); Bullough, Donald, *The Age of Charlemagne* (New York: Putnam, 1965); Holland, Jack, *The Order of Rome* (London: Cassell, 1980).

## CHINA, KHITAN INVASION OF

40

During the declining years of the T'ang dynasty, China had little luck resisting nomadic raids from the steppes. The Khitan Mongols had learned the art of farming and iron smelting from refugees of the Han dynasty, thus developing a culture based on agriculture as well as herding. They aided a T'ang warlord in the middle of the tenth century, and for their support were awarded 16 provinces from Peking to the Great Wall, as well as a large annual monetary tribute. The Khitan made Peking their capital, and in the age of first contact with medieval Europe gave the area of northern China the name by which it was then known: Cathay.

They invaded southward when the annual tribute stopped coming, captured the T'ang capital at Kaifeng, and proclaimed themselves the Liao dynasty. Their success was short-lived; the T'ang counterattacked and drove the Khitan northward. In 960 a successful T'ang general started the Sung dynasty, and it was with this new government that the Khitan fought. Fortunately for the Sung, the Khitan were also fighting with the rising power of the Hsia kingdom farther to the west. Still, the Khitan enjoyed occasional success against the Sung. At the beginning of the eleventh century, in response to two unsuccessful Sung campaigns against them, they invaded to the gates of Kaifeng and left only with the promise of tribute totaling 100,000 taels (roughly, more than 8,000 pounds) of silver and 200,000 bolts of silk. In the 1030s the tribute was increased in response to demands and pressure by the Khitan leaders.

Thus the Sung maintained peace by bribery, not only to the Khitan but also to the Hsia, paying tribute despite the fact that they maintained a massive army of over a million men. History records the development of the first gunpowder weapons, in the form of rockets, during the Sung dynasty. They did not use them effectively enough to establish a military ascendancy, which often accompanies the development of new weaponry. The large amounts of tribute, however, had an unintended effect. The Khitan, already different from other Mongol tribes by their use of agriculture,

became increasingly Chinese in their culture and language. This not only robbed them of their fighting edge, it provoked the disdain of other Mongol tribes, notably the Juchen Mongols. The Juchen allied themselves with the Sung, and together they defeated the Khitan, destroying the Liao government. Rather than accept payment of the 16 provinces the Khitan had first won, the Juchen continued their invasion of China and forced the Sung dynasty to reestablish itself in the south. The new northern power gave up the name Juchen for Ch'in (or Kin) dynasty, and set the borders with the Sung at the Hwai and upper Han rivers.

The Khitan invasion had little effect on the Chinese socially, but the huge payment of tribute and the large standing army detailed to protect the population drained the Sung treasury and provoked peasant unrest. They became more Sinified than the Sung became Mongolized, but aggressiveness weakened the Sung while giving rise to the growing power of the Juchen, which in turn foreshadowed the rise of Mongol power under Genghis Khan.

*See also* Han Dynasty [23]; Genghis Khan [47]; T'ang Dynasty [77].

References: Hookham, Hilda, *A Short History of China* (New York: St. Martin's Press, 1970); Kwanten, Luc, *Imperial Nomads* (Philadelphia: University of Pennsylvania Press, 1979); Morgan, David, *The Mongols* (Oxford: Blackwell, 1986).

 **CHINA, MONGOL CONQUEST OF**

Genghis Khan was named leader of all the Mongol peoples in 1206, and he set about uniting the tribes and conquering large parts of Asia. One of his main interests was to conquer China, on the southern side of the Great Wall, which had long kept steppe peoples out of "civilized" lands. He first led forces across the wall on raids, stealing livestock and other goods and stockpiling them on the other side. As his army gained experience, he moved farther into China and brought land under his control. He made war against the Hsi-hsia between 1206 and 1209, finally forcing them to acknowledge his position. His war against the Ch'in dynasty was hampered at first by his lack of siegecraft, for his cavalry forces were useless against the Ch'in fortresses and walled cities. Ch'in military men who joined his cause brought with them the knowledge necessary to reduce those fortifications. In 1215 he captured and sacked Peking, forcing recognition of his dominance from the Ch'in emperor.

Mongol forces occupied northern China while Genghis and his army made war farther to the west. In his absence, the Ch'in and Hsia grew restless and allied themselves against the Mongols in 1224. Genghis named his son Ogadai as his successor should death claim him before the reconquest occurred. Genghis entered the domain of the Hsia in the winter of 1225 with 180,000 men. Across the frozen water of the Yellow River the Mongols fought a force of some 300,000 Hsia; at the end of the battle, all the khan's enemies were dead. He then divided his army—a third of it to lay siege to the Hsia capital at Ninghsia, a third under Ogadai to drive westward against the Ch'in, while he took the remainder southeastward to threaten the Ch'in southern border and block any possible reinforcements. In 1227 the Hsia emperor surrendered, but Genghis refused any peace overtures from the Ch'in. With a premonition of death, Genghis returned to Mongolia. He died along the

way, after advising his youngest son Tului on the future conquest of China.

Ogadai continued Genghis's expansionary plans, conquering Korea and then returning to deal with the Ch'in. While he and his father's most trusted general, Subotai, pressured the fortified cities of the north, his youngest brother, Tului, took a force of 30,000 southward to the Sung Empire, then swung northward to put the Ch'in armies in a pincer between himself and his brother. He decimated the Ch'in forces by wearing them down in cold mountain fighting, then chased them northward when they retreated to meet the now-attacking Ogadai. Tului died of sickness during the campaign, and Ogadai returned to Mongolia, leaving Subotai to finish off the siege of Kaifeng, the Ch'in capital. The city fell to him in 1233 after a year's siege. The Sung in the south asked for a portion of the Ch'in Empire in return for the safe passage they had granted Tului, but Subotai refused. When the Sung seized Honan, the Mongols prepared to make war on them.

War against the Sung lasted 35 years. Ogadai's nephews Mangu and Kubilai directed the campaigns. Kubilai conquered the province of Yunnan in 1253, and Mangu led the army in a series of campaigns between 1257 and 1259 that defeated Sung armies and captured fortified cities. Mangu succeeded Ogadai as the Great Khan, but his death in 1260 provoked a struggle for the position between Kubilai and his younger brother, Arik-Buka. Kubilai won after a four-year civil war and became the Great Khan, then finished off the Sungs in a campaign designed to be as bloodless as possible. It failed to be totally without killing, but Kubilai spread the news of his benevolent intentions, and many Sung generals turned against their own leaders to join him. When the seven-year-old emperor and his grandmother the dowager empress bowed to him, he declared himself emperor of China, creating the Yuan dynasty. Sung resistance in the deep south continued until he finally besieged and captured Canton. During his reign, Kubilai Khan unified China like no other emperor, yet he kept his Mongol subjects separate from the mass of Chinese he now ruled. The dynasty did not last after his death in 1294. The Mongols ruled China through the existing bureaucracy, and did little to change the country; Kubilai realized that the conquered culture was much more advanced than his own, and that he had much to learn.

Therefore, the Mongol conquest, while deadly in its establishment, had little lasting effect other than peaceful times in which to progress. During the Yuan dynasty, drama came to the fore as an art form, but the longest lasting symbol of their conquest was the construction of Kubilai's capital at Shang-tu, better known in the West as Xanadu. This garden city was Kubilai's home, though he often returned to the steppes to maintain his heritage and pursue the ancient Mongol pastime of hunting.

Kubilai carried on more attempted conquests against Japan and Southeast Asia. Sogatu, one of Kubilai's generals, advanced into the province of Annam in 1257, but he could not overcome the guerrilla war the native Annamese and Chams waged against him. Kubilai tried again to subdue the region in 1287, but it proved costly. After many deaths on both sides, in 1293 the Annamese recognized Kubilai's suzerainty; in return, Kubilai left them alone.

See also Ch'in Dynasty [17]; Genghis Khan [47]; Japan, Mongol Invasions of [57]; Kubilai Khan [61].

References: Cohen, Daniel, *Conquerors on Horseback* (Garden City, NY: Doubleday, 1970); Kwanten, Luc, *Imperial Nomads* (Philadelphia: University of Pennsylvania Press, 1979); Lamb, Harold, *March of the Barbarians* (New York: Literary Guild, 1940).

## 42        CRUSADES

During the seventh and eighth centuries, the Islamic religion swept out of the Middle East, across northern Africa, and into Spain, where it began to encroach on central Europe. During the tenth century, European Christianity went on the offensive, and by the eleventh century the tide began to turn against Islam. Christian Europe meant not only to overthrow Muslim rule, but to expel it from Europe and recover Jerusalem for Christianity.

Italian city-states exercised naval and commercial dominance, and the German empire was on the rise. Christianity was spreading into northern Europe, and the number of pilgrimages to the Holy Land and other sacred sites was on the rise. The desire to spread the gospel was mixed with a desire to open new markets and conquer new territories. Despite the opportunity for war with the Muslims, the feudal barons of central Europe engaged in private wars with one another. The need for peace compelled the pope to declare the Peace of Christ, and later the Truce of Christ, in a vain attempt to limit such conflict.

By 1095 the power and influence of the papacy, as well as the sanctity of the majority of the clergy, were on the decline, while the power and influence of the German empire were on the rise. Pope Urban II, fearing the church would lose what little influence it had, and abhorring the results of continued infighting among the Christian nobility, sought a way to unite Christendom in a common cause. In Clermont, France, he preached the First Crusade. It was a mixture of propaganda concerning the alleged cruelty of Muslims

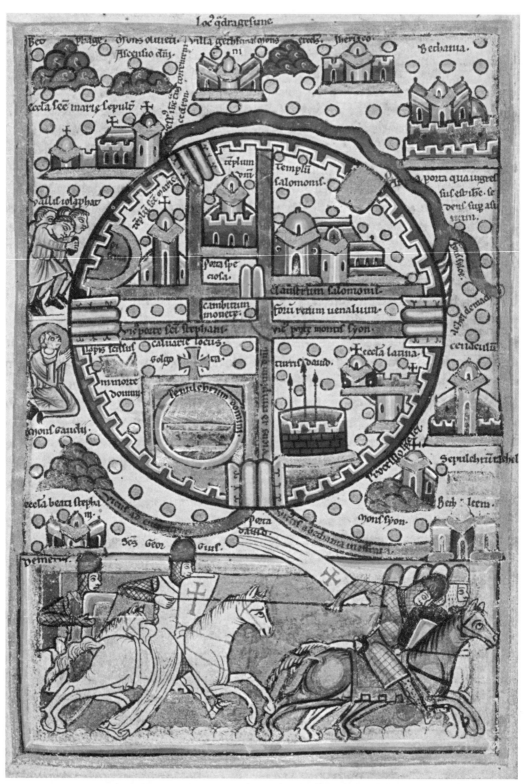

A Crusader map of Jerusalem depicts Sanctus Georgius, on a white horse and in crusader dress, defeating a group of Muslims.

to Christian pilgrims, a request for aid by the Byzantine emperor, a call for display of righteous action in the recovery of Jerusalem, and an offer of remission of sins for those who participated. The effect was overwhelming. Not only did the nobility— his prime audience—heed his call, but so did many peasants and riffraff of the cities. Others also took to preaching the crusade, most notably Peter the Hermit, whose call went mostly to peasants and street rabble.

The nobility were led by Godfrey of Bouillon (Rhinelanders), Raymond of Toulouse (Provençals), and Bohemund (Normans of southern Italy). Along with the peasants and rabble, they made up six hosts of 100,000 to 200,000 *cruciata*, or cross-signed, who traveled overland to meet in Constantinople before continuing on to Jerusalem.

The so-called Peasants' Crusade led by Peter the Hermit consisted primarily of peasants and petty criminals. It preceded the main contingents of nobility and men-at-arms, and turned into a binge of pillage, thievery, and eventual widespread murder of innocent Jews. Many of Peter's "army" died at the hands of the Turks, only a few ever reaching Constantinople.

The main forces under command of the nobility reached Constantinople in 1096. The leaders were required to swear allegiance to Alexis, emperor of the Byzantine Empire, in return for immediate gifts and a promise of future help, which was never forthcoming. Alexis's main objective was to get the Crusaders to help him regain territories lost to the Turks, who were seeking to take over his empire. Before they were allowed to leave for Jerusalem, however, the Crusaders were coerced into helping Emperor Alexis capture the city of Nicea in 1097.

The Muslim world was totally unprepared for the Christian invasion; the strength and power of the mounted knights, as well as the bravery of the common foot soldier, were more than a match for their own cavalry. The march to Palestine was marked by a decisive victory at Doryleum and the conquest of Tarsus by Baldwin and Tancred. The Crusaders and their camp followers were not prepared, however, for the long and arduous march through the Black Mountains toward Antioch. This journey meant the death of many through hunger, thirst, and heat.

Antioch fell to the Crusaders in 1098 after eight months, despite poor provisions and ill health among the besiegers. The Crusaders' confidence in the leadership of their God and the righteousness of their cause helped them to overcome numerous attempts by the inhabitants to break the siege and defeat reinforcements attempting to relieve the city. Antioch finally fell, after betrayal by one of its citizens. The Crusaders spent the next several months in Antioch recuperating, making local conquests, and repelling Turkish attempts to regain the city. Bohemund finally secured Antioch for himself as the others continued on to Jerusalem.

Tales of the seeming invincibility of the Christian army preceded it, and the march toward Bethlehem and Jerusalem was without incident. God, it seemed, was surely guiding and protecting them, and no one dared stand in their way.

They reached Jerusalem in 1099 and immediately placed it under siege. It fell to Godfrey and Raymond on 15 July. For several days, any Muslims who could be found were put to death.

After the capture of Jerusalem and the securing of the surrounding territory, most of the Crusaders returned home, feeling that they had done what was required of them by their God and their pope. Only the adventurers stayed on to establish the four states of what would be called the Latin Kingdom.

These four states, the kingdom of Jerusalem and the vassal states of Edessa, Antioch, and eventually Tripoli, were islands of Christianity in a hostile sea of Islam. The Muslim world was now much more aware of the Crusaders' presence and purpose, their strengths and weaknesses. The Muslims wasted little time in trying to regain what had been taken from them. Communications between the four Crusader cities was difficult, if not impossible, and the Christians' only hope of survival lay in reinforcements from Europe. In the meantime, however, their strength, bravery, audacity, and faith would have to keep them alive and in possession of the holy sites and the fortified cities.

With the eventual death of the last of the great leaders of the First Crusade, the bravery and piety that marked it also died. The crusading spirit they had initiated would wax and wane, but continue unbroken for the next two and a half centuries.

What are commonly referred to as "The Crusades" were actually one long, protracted conflict between Christian Europe and the Islamic Middle East over the land and holy sites of modern-day Palestine. It was the several aggressive attempts by European nobility, at the behest of successive popes, to reinforce the Latin Kingdom or regain territory lost to Islam, that give the illusion of multiple invasions. Battles would continue to be fought, cities would be won and lost, but the great Christian victories of the initial invasion would not be repeated.

The Second Crusade was preached by the pope and St. Bernard of Clairvaux after the fall of Edessa in 1144 to Zangi, governor of Mosul. This crusade was led by Louis VII and Conrad III of Germany (1147–1149). The two armies were unable to cooperate, and were separately defeated in Asia Minor. An attempt to capture Damascus failed, and the Crusaders returned home.

Muslim power was consolidated under Zangi, his son Nur-ed-Din, and later Saladin, who sought a holy war with Christianity. In 1187 Saladin's army overran the Latin Kingdom and captured Jerusalem. This caused the pope to preach a Third Crusade (1189–1192). It was led by Philip Augustus of France, Richard I of England, and Emperor Frederick Barbarossa. The emperor drowned in Asia Minor, and Philip and Richard were unable to work together because of jealousy. Philip returned home and left Richard in the Holy Land; Richard captured Acre, but was unable to recapture Jerusalem. The best he could manage was a treaty with Saladin to allow safe passage for pilgrims visiting Jerusalem.

In 1198, Pope Innocent III's influence finally brought peace to the feuding nobility of Europe, and he tried to reestablish the Crusade as a holy cause. This Crusade was led mainly by the Venetians, whose only goal was to expand their trading empire by destroying the influence of Constantinople. This they did with the sacking of Constantinople in 1204 by the Crusaders whom the Venetians had starved into compliance after they could not afford their passage to the Holy Land.

In 1215, Innocent III proclaimed the Fifth Crusade (1218–1221). Emperor Frederick of Germany obtained the title of King of Jerusalem by marriage in 1225, but was excommunicated in 1227 for delaying his start. In 1228, Frederick finally went to the Holy Land, gaining Jerusalem, Bethlehem, Nazareth, and a connecting strip of land to Acre—by treaty, not by conquest.

In 1244, Jerusalem fell to the Saracens, and a new Crusade was proclaimed by Innocent IV in 1245 and led by Louis IX of France. Though he invaded Egypt and captured Damietta, Louis was taken prisoner and Damietta was lost. Egypt revolted, and a new Muslim movement called for the recovery of Syria. Within the next few years, all remaining Christian possessions in Syria were captured and the Crusades effectively came to an end.

The major military goals of the Crusades—the driving of the Muslims from the Holy Land and the imposition of Western culture on the captured territory—were never accomplished. On the contrary, the Crusades strengthened and united the Islamic world, and weakened the Byzantine Empire until it was overcome by the Turks in the fifteenth century. They succeeded, however, in accomplishing Pope Urban II's original goals of returning the papacy to its previous position of power and influence and eventually ending feudal warfare.

The Crusades also had a profound effect on commerce and trade, both inside and outside Europe. Feudalism and serfdom disintegrated. A money economy began to predominate, which stimulated a need for banks. Spheres of influence were set up in port cities of Palestine by the trading powers of Venice, Genoa, and Pisa, providing easier acquisition of goods from both the Middle and Far East. Navigation and shipbuilding improved with the increased need for transportation of people and goods. Many of the developments attributed to the Crusades were merely the end result of changes that had begun before Pope Urban's call to retake the Holy Land. The Crusades served only to facilitate and accelerate them.

In the Middle East, the influence of Europe remained for some time to come. Italian merchants were able to establish trading privileges in the major ports of Acre and Tyre. By controlling the sea lanes of the Mediterranean, they provided Muslim merchants with access to European goods while remaining the sole distributors of Oriental goods to the West. Italian traders were able to move and work freely in dedicated districts of these cities, and gained some legal control over citizens and visi-

tors within those districts. Their basic problem was that, though they provided a conduit to the West, they could deal only with Muslim traders who handled Oriental goods, mainly spices. Therefore, the middleman remained, and the local government always got its share of the revenues. Still, there was enough money to go around, and when the trade routes shifted from Alexandria in Egypt to Damascus, Aleppo, and Antioch, the Europeans were able to expand their rights within the area. Political and military conflicts occasionally interfered with trade, but not enough to cut it off completely.

—Thomas E. Davis

*See also* Ottoman Empire [102].

References: Lamb, Harold, *The Crusades,* 2 vols. (Garden City, NY: Doubleday, 1931); Smith, Jonathan Riley, *The Crusades* (New Haven, CT: Yale University Press, 1987).

## ENGLAND, VIKING CONQUEST OF

**43**

The Vikings raided and conquered along the coasts of Europe and the British Isles from the late eighth century. They left Scandinavia for a number of reasons, overpopulation being a prime cause, but the drive for trade and/or plunder was almost equally important. The timing was perfect for them because no society other than Charlemagne's Holy Roman Empire could mount any sort of organized resistance, and after Charlemagne's death in 810, his successors had little luck in matching his military prowess. Europe was gaining in wealth, but not in the ability to defend it. Historian Gwen Dyer words this situation well: "Loot is loot in any language, and western Europe was full of it. Ireland, England,

France were the vikings' Mexico, with learning, arts, wealth, and a civilization superior to those of their northern *conquistadors,* and a similar inability to defend themselves from a numerically inferior but mobile and energetic foe."

The Danes first raided England around 789 and 793, even as Swedes pressed eastward into the Baltic and the Norwegians attacked Ireland. The Danes alternated between attacking England and France, striking both sides of the English Channel at will. In the middle 830s, they probed along the south coast as far as Cornwall, but found the raiding easier along the eastern shore, which they began to assault in 843. Not until 862, however, did large-scale landings take place, with forces numbering perhaps a thousand raiders under Yngvarr, Ubbi, and Halfdan, who attacked to avenge their father Ragnar's death at the hands of King Ella of Northumbria. They defeated an English force under Ella at York in 863, and from that date the Danes began their mastery of northeastern England.

Viking forces quickly expanded into Mercia (central England) and East Anglia, killing King (later Saint) Edmund and occupying his lands. In 870, Halfdan led men into Wessex and won many battles, but at high enough cost that he made peace and returned to the north to fight the Picts and Scots. That year marked the accession to the Wessex throne of Alfred (later to be titled "the Great"), who would mount the most successful English resistance to the Vikings. Before he could do so, however, the Danes received not only reinforcements but immigrants, and began settling in.

In January 878 the Viking chieftain Guthrum attacked Wessex and drove Alfred southwestward. Outrunning his opponents, Alfred collected a force from Hampshire, Wiltshire, and Somerset. He defeated an army of Vikings in Devon, then marched to fight Guthrum. Guthrum surrendered at Chippenham after a two-week siege, acknowledging Wessex as Alfred's and Christianity as his new religion. The conversion appears to have been successful, because the Christianization of Danes in England began to expand. It did not keep Alfred from attacking southward as far as the Thames in 880, establishing the river as the southern border of *danelaw,* that area of England ruled by the Danes. Fourteen years of relative peace followed.

Alfred was greatly assisted by an alliance with Ethelred, who was based in the southeast. United through Ethelred's marriage to Alfred's oldest daughter, the two leaders made progress against Viking pressure. Alfred was recognized as king of England in 886 (of all save *danelaw*), and Ethelred was a staunch supporter. In that same year Alfred negotiated with Guthrum a system of tributes and hostages to maintain the peace between the two peoples. It was an elusive peace at best, for while the Danes may not have made war against Alfred, they had no compunctions about assisting any countrymen who cared to try. Thus, when Hastein invaded the mouth of the Thames in 891, the successful English resistance took longer than would have been the case had the population in *danelaw* not granted aid. Alfred's improved organization and training of the levies and his construction of forts along the coasts proved invaluable in protecting the country. Further, his construction of ships, though not of the quality of the Vikings, led to some success against them and acted as a deterrent in later Viking planning.

Alfred died in 899, having been the major factor in the Vikings' failure to conquer all of England. He was succeeded by Edward, who carried the English tide northward and regained the land to the Humber River for England by the time of his death in 924. Edward's cousin Ethelwold had con-

spired with the Vikings in *danelaw* to invade the southern territories, which proved
their undoing. Edward and Ethelred were
too skillful, and the Viking losses opened
*danelaw* to English counterattack. After
Ethelred's death in 911, he was ably succeeded both politically and militarily by his
wife (and Edward's sister) Ethelflaed. The
two pressed continually northward, consolidating their gains by constructing numerous fortresses, which Viking tactics had
no way to defeat.

Edward attempted to defeat the Danes
with as little bloodshed as possible, showing himself to be a merciful victor. He did
this both to assure the Christian Danes of
retribution and to recruit their aid to fight
Norwegian Vikings from Ireland who were
beginning to settle on the west coast between Wales and Scotland. After the Norse
leader Rognvald captured York in 919, he
and Edward made peace; Edward was accepted as king of all England and Scotland—at least for a while.

The deaths of Rognvald in 921 and
Edward in 924 laid the groundwork for
further conflict between Edward's son
Athelstan and Rognvald's grandson Olaf.
The Norse Vikings of Ireland joined with
the Scots to fight Athelstan's English forces
at Brunanburh (actual site unknown) in
937. It was a decisive English victory, but
not a lasting one. Athelstan ruled well and
in nominal peace with the Danes, but after his death in 939, fighting began again.
Until 954 northern England was alternately
under English, Danish, or Norwegian rule,
but none could rule for more than a year
or two because of outside pressure or internal struggles.

England remained English through the
reigns of several kings, until the young and
weak-willed king Ethelred the Unready
(978–1016) had to stand against a second
great outpouring of Danish Vikings.
Ethelred paid for a peace treaty with the

raiding Olaf Tryggvason after the battle of
Maldon in 991. Olaf returned a few years
later, allied with the king of the Danes,
Svein Forkbeard. In 994 the two were paid
for peace; Olaf soon converted to Christianity and left England for good, but Svein
left only temporarily. His return in 1001
brought another huge ransom. The following year, Ethelred ordered the massacre of
all Danes in England. Some killing took
place, including that of Svein's sister. Svein
invaded in 1003 to avenge her death and
succeeded in pillaging as much as he liked;
only famine, in 1005, forced his withdrawal. He was back looting the next year
and took yet another massive bribe from
Ethelred. He finally came to stay in 1012;
he was received in the north by the descendants of the first Vikings, and from that
base he pillaged the entire country save
London, which he could not capture. It did
not matter, for the country surrendered to
him, and Ethelred went with his family to
Normandy.

Svein's victory was short-lived, for he
died five weeks later. His son Canute succeeded him and maintained Danish rule
over England. This also proved relatively
short, for other Viking descendants conquered England under William of Normandy in 1066. The Vikings in England
were both conquerors and conquered, as
so often happens. They adapted themselves
to a countryside that provided much more
fertile farmland than the one they had left.
The area of *danelaw* inherited influences
of law, language, personal and place names,
and social custom from the invaders. In the
long run, however, more change came from
the Norman conquest than from the
Danes.

*See also* Britain, Norman Invasion of [36];
Carolingian Dynasty [39]; Ireland, Viking Invasions of [55]; Russia, Establishment and Expansion of [70].

References: Dyer, Gwen, *A History of the Vikings* (Oxford: Oxford University Press, 1968; Layn, H. R., *The Vikings in Britain* (Oxford: Blackwell, 1995); Marsden, John, *The Fury of the Northmen* (London: Kyle Cathie, 1993).

## EUROPE, MONGOL INVASION OF

**44**

As the middle of the thirteenth century approached, the Mongols had established themselves along the Volga River, assuming the title "the Golden Horde." As they consolidated their hold on Russia, reconnaissance forces penetrated eastern Europe, returning with the news that, like the Russian principalities, the Europeans were divided and quarreling. They reported that the mightiest king, Frederick of the Holy Roman Empire, was feuding with Pope Gregory, so a Mongol advance should meet no consolidated resistance. The leader of the Golden Horde was Batu, son of Genghis Khan's illegitimate son Juchi. He preferred to settle into the steppes of Russia and enjoy his conquest, but Genghis's chief general, Subotai, under orders from Genghis's successor, Ogadai, convinced him that they must invade Europe.

Subotai commanded the invasion force, which went into motion in December 1240. Subotai chose this time because the rivers would be frozen, allowing his horsemen to cross more easily, and the poor weather would hamper the gathering of defensive forces. Their first stop was Kiev, and Subotai offered the citizens peace in return for submission. When the Mongol envoys were slaughtered, so was the population of Kiev, and the most beautiful city east of Europe was destroyed. The remainder of the Slavs inhabiting the area were driven westward until Subotai halted his men before the Carpathian Mountains. They and the nomadic Kipchaks of the south, whom the Mongols had already defeated, spread the news of the Mongols' advance and Kiev's fate. The Kipchaks fled to the court of King Bela of Hungary, offering themselves for baptism in return for his protection. Bela accepted them until Subotai wrote to him that the Kipchaks were Mongol servants who should be returned to him. Bela became convinced that his new converts were spies, so he drove them into the hills, from whence they became bandits.

On the eastern slopes of the Carpathians, Batu again counseled against entering Europe, and again Subotai overrode him. Subotai ordered his force to divide into four parts. The northernmost, under Kaidu, was to swing around the Carpathians into Poland and then ride southward to Pest on the Danube. A second column was to perform the opposite task, riding southward, then upriver. A third column was detailed to cross the mountain passes on Kaidu's left flank, while Subotai and Batu led the center column through the pass known as the Russian Gates. The four columns were to meet in one month, 17 March, in front of Pest.

Kaidu's column proved fabulously successful. He captured Szydlow, but that was on 18 March; he was well behind schedule. Cracow fell to him on 24 March. He burned the city and marched for Breslau, capturing it a week later. Before Liegnitz, he met a combined force of Moravians, Poles, Silesians, and Teutonic Knights. Kaidu's more mobile cavalry made short work of both the infantry and the heavy cavalry on 9 April. Outmaneuvering a Bohemian force marching to the battlefield, the Mongols captured and burned Moravia. Kaidu was almost a month late, but the northern flank was secure.

The southern column rode through Galicia but was slowed by the heavily wooded terrain, and they failed to reach

Pest on the appointed day. Subotai had to force his way past a stout defense in the Russian Gates, but he arrived on 15 March with his advance patrols, while Batu arrived with the bulk of the force two days later. When the second column arrived, notifying Subotai of Kaidu's progress, the Mongol general was prepared to fight with but half his army. King Bela marched his force out of Pest on 4 April. He had collected almost 100,000 men, and was not surprised when the Mongols withdrew. He followed, not realizing that Subotai was not retreating but leading him on. On 9 April the Mongols turned and attacked, and again their mobility was superior to the Europeans' heavy armor. An opening in their lines allowed the Hungarians to escape, but that too was a ruse. The road back to Pest was five days long, and the retreating men were slaughtered; some reports claim as many as 70,000 died.

The Mongols occupied Pest and sent out more patrols to scout their next operation. Through the summer of 1241, they consolidated their hold on Hungary while sending patrols toward Germany, Austria, and Italy. Europe was horrified. The defeated peoples had run west, spreading the details of the massacres, but the rivalry between Frederick and Pope Gregory was still too intense to overcome, each accusing the other of openly or tacitly supporting the Mongol invasion. Only after Gregory's death in August 1241 did the feud die. In the meantime the Mongols settled into Hungary, and peace, if not security, returned to the land. Trade flowed once again, and the Mongols proved to be less harsh masters than enemies.

Once winter approached in 1241, however, the Mongols again prepared to move. Following their strategy of a year earlier, Batu crossed frozen rivers with a portion of the army. In late December they captured and burned the city of Gran, having defeated the force of French and Lombards defending it. Passing Vienna, Batu turned southward and campaigned down the Adriatic coast, pillaging and searching for King Bela, who had escaped the slaughter outside Pest. Batu met little resistance, while Subotai waited on the eastern bank of the Danube for the German attack he was sure would come. Before it could, however, word arrived from Karakorum that Ogadai had died. All Mongol chieftains had to return for the election and installation of a new Great Khan. Again Batu argued, though now he was in favor of staying in Europe rather than returning eastward. Subotai marched home, however, and Batu was obliged to follow.

The death of Ogadai was all that saved Europe from the fate of Hungary. The Europeans had not shown any ability to defeat the tactics of the Mongol horsemen, and there is no reason to believe that any power farther west could have done so. Though the withdrawing Mongols left no doubt that this was a voluntary leave-taking, the Europeans breathed a sigh of relief; they would have time to prepare for the return of the nomads. As it turned out, the Mongols did not return; Batu settled into comfort along the Volga and did not want to leave Russia again. A rivalry among the possible heirs created a division of the Mongol Empire into four khanates, so no concerted effort to return to Europe ever materialized. Other than waste and death, the Mongols left little of their culture behind. The children they fathered went home with them, so no permanent racial infusion resulted. Their campaign had serious effects on the region, however, because the Slavs and Magyars of the region were slain by the invaders or by the resulting famine and disease after the Mongols' withdrawal. The Teutonic peoples, who had not suffered as greatly, therefore filled the power vacuum in eastern Europe. The surviving Bulgars and Magyars were pushed into the Balkan Mountains, to be dominated by Germans and Austrians for centuries.

*See also* Genghis Khan [47]; Magyars [63]; Russia, Mongol Conquest of [71].

References: Chambers, James, *The Devil's Horsemen* (New York: Atheneum, 1979); Kwanten, Luc, *Imperial Nomads* (Philadelphia: University of Pennsylvania Press, 1979); Lamb, Harold, *The March of the Barbarians* (New York: Literary Guild, 1940).

## 45    FRANCE, VIKING INVASION OF

The Vikings sailed their longships throughout the known world between the ninth and eleventh centuries, establishing both a fearsome reputation and a number of colonies. Their conquest of territory in France, however, became a pivotal event in both Scandinavian and European history, for it turned a raiding, seafaring population into a land-based military society affecting Europe and the Middle East.

As long as Charlemagne ruled the Holy Roman Empire, his military prowess kept the Norsemen at bay. After his death, however, his sons had little success in stopping Viking raids. The Vikings captured Paris in 849, holding it until Charles the Bald ransomed the city. They returned in 885 with 700 ships and 30,000 men, and besieged Paris for 13 months; again they left after receiving a ransom of 700 pounds of silver. Duke Odo and Charles the Simple protected the area around Paris—the Ile de France—and acted as something of a buffer for the inland provinces, but they did little to actively defend anything other than their own neighborhood.

Charles the Simple of Paris finally attempted to assuage the Vikings with land of their own, which could then be a buffer between the European interior and the defenseless coastline. In 911 the Treaty of St.-Clair-sur-Epte ceded land at the mouth of the Seine and the city of Rouen to Hrolf (or Rollo), leader of a group of Danish Vikings. Over the next few decades, the Norsemen stretched their borders eastward and westward along the coast, though how much was through conquest and how much through cession by Frankish leaders remains the subject of some debate. Over the next century and a half, Scandinavian and Frankish cultures mixed, with the conquered exerting a mighty influence on the conquerors.

As more emigrants moved to this territory, the Norsemen became Normans and the province Normandy, with French becoming the predominant language. As part of the 911 treaty, the Vikings accepted Christianity. In time, the Norse religions were completely replaced, and the converts became militantly Christian. In viewing the construction of buildings dating from this period, some of the oldest are monasteries and churches because the new Christians set about repairing what their pagan fathers had looted. The Normans soon embraced Christianity with a fervor, not only rebuilding but joining the monasteries in large numbers. When Norman soldiers went out into the world, they went as soldiers of God, often with papal blessing or cooperation.

The sailors soon forsook the ship for the horse; they maintained their warlike heritage, but transformed their naval prowess to cavalry power. The Normans slipped easily into the feudal system of Frankish Europe, and one of the prerequisites of nobility was leadership in battle. The Normans perfected the heavy cavalry of knighthood and developed the code of chivalry surrounding it. This development dominated the military tactics of Europe for three centuries and often ran roughshod over the lightly armed soldiers of Islam and Byzantium.

*See also* Carolingian Dynasty [39]; Crusades [42]; England, Viking Conquest of [43]; Franks [46]; Ireland, Viking Invasions of [55]; Italy and Sicily, Norman Conquest of [56]; Russia, Establishment and Expansion of [70].

References: Arbman, Holger, *The Vikings* (New York: Praeger, 1961); Brown, R. Allen, *The Normans* (New York: St. Martin's Press, 1984); Searle, Eleanor, *Predatory Kinship and the Creation of Norman Power* (Berkeley: University of California Press, 1988).

## 46      FRANKS

This group of tribes living in the Rhine River area was first recorded during the latter part of the Roman Empire. The earliest history of the Franks was written by Gregory of Tours, a contemporary of Clovis, one of the early great chieftains. Prior to Clovis's time, the history of the Franks is sketchy. The first recorded leader was Chlodio, who led the tribes into northern Gaul in the early fifth century. Chlodio was succeeded by Merovech, who fought alongside the Roman forces against Attila the Hun at Mauriac Plain in eastern Gaul in 451. The first recorded Frankish dynasty, the Merovingian, was named after Merovech. His son Childeric was on the throne by 457 and apparently remained a friend of the declining Roman Empire; he had perhaps been a captive of the Huns as a child. His Frankish forces again fought alongside Roman soldiers against Visigoths at Orleans in 463 or 464, then kept later Gothic and Saxon invaders away from Roman Gaul.

In 481, Clovis became the Frankish king, though sources indicate that he was merely the chief of other Frankish chieftains, a first among equals. He made war against the remaining Roman leadership under Syagrius, defeating him at Soissons in 486. Soon thereafter, Clovis defeated rival chieftains and claimed supreme authority among the major Frankish tribes, the Salians; Clovis can thus be named as the first real king of the Franks. He extended his authority to the Seine River with his victory at Soissons and later reached the Loire. A decade later, Clovis went to the aid of the Ripaurian Franks around modern-day Bonn and defeated the Allemanni, thus extending Frankish power into Germany.

Clovis converted to Catholicism, possibly influenced by his wife, Clotilda of Burgundy. Some sources suggest that he was a Christian when he won at Soissons, but many claim that he embraced the faith in 496. He chose Catholicism over the Arian version of Christianity, though both were practiced among the Franks. This choice had profound effects, because it started the Franks on the road to becoming protectors of the church of Rome.

First, however, there were other lands to capture and other enemies to fight. Clovis's expansion to the Loire River brought him into contact with the Visigoths, who controlled southern France and northern Spain. The Ostrogoth king, Theodoric, an Arian and related to Clovis by marriage, had long striven to maintain peace in southern Gaul, but Clovis went to war as the champion of Catholicism. He defeated the Visigothic forces under Alaric at Poitiers in 507 and sent his son to conquer as far as Burgundy. Frankish authority extended over all of France, with the exception of a southern coastal strip and the Breton peninsula. Clovis moved his capital to Paris and established a church to commemorate his victory over Alaric.

Rumor has it that despite his Christianity, Clovis plotted to murder the ruling family of the Ripaurian Franks. The truth remains conjectural, but he was elected their king after his war against Alaric. With his power solidified, Clovis was recognized as king of the Franks by the Byzantine emperor Anastasius. He was made a consul under the emperor's authority and treated as if he ruled in the emperor's name, which was hardly the case.

Clovis's four sons inherited parts of his kingdom and regularly made war against their neighbors. Under the leadership of Theudibert, the Germanic tribes were placed under tribute and the Burgunds were destroyed, which gave the Franks control over the Rhone River valley and the port city of Marseilles. Theudibert's expeditions into Italy weakened the Ostrogothic regime there to the extent that Byzantine forces came to control the peninsula.

The next great leader was Dagobert, who defeated the Avars, a Hunnish tribe threatening to expand past the Danube. He also raided into Spain and received tribute (or bribes) from Constantinople. Dagobert's reign also saw an expansion of Frankish trading power and the widespread coinage of gold and silver. He established a mint at the mouth of the Rhine and carried on extensive trade, mainly in the cloth of Frisia, in modern Belgium. He also supported the church's efforts to convert the Frisians. Dagobert, the last great king of the Merovingian dynasty, died in 639. His sons fought among themselves, and the eastern (Austrasian) and western (Neustrian) factions of the kingdom struggled for dominance.

The real power in Frankish politics was not the king but the mayor of the palace, who represented the tribal leaders before the king. Pépin II, one of the mayors, gave birth to the next Frankish ruling clan. He led Austrasian forces to victory over the Neustrians at the battle of Tertry in 687, which made him the dominant figure in Frankish politics. He assumed the role of military leader, the defender of the Frankish lands from outside attack. Pépin's conquest of Frisia brought him into close cooperation with the Irish Catholic monks who were trying to convert the Frisians, and the connection between Pépin's family and the Catholic church began to solidify. Pépin led campaigns against the Allemanni, Franconians, and Bavarians, and the missionaries followed his conquests. Pépin died in 714 as the most powerful man in Frankish politics, but still mayor of the palace.

Pépin's illegitimate son, Charles Martel, inherited the position of mayor. (His Latin name, Carolus, gave his heirs the title Carolingians.) He led campaigns against the Saxons and Bavarians to secure the northern and eastern frontiers. Like his father, he worked closely with the church to extend Christianity. Charles developed a well-disciplined military based strongly on cavalry; that army won for him his most recognizable victory. In 732 the Franks defeated a force of marauding Muslims from Spain at Poitiers in a battle widely regarded as saving Europe from Islamic influence. The battle was one of a series in which the Franks forced the Muslims to settle south of the Pyrenees. In 737 the last Merovingian king died, but Charles remained mayor of the palace with no king to whom he could represent the chieftains. He died in 741, dividing his extensive landholdings between his two sons —Carloman, to whom he granted his eastern holdings, and Pépin III, who inherited land in the west.

Carloman became increasingly interested in affairs of the soul, so much so that in 747 he ceded his lands to his brother and went to Monte Cassino to become a monk. With tacit papal approval, Pépin removed the last pretenders to the Merovingian throne and made himself king of the Franks. His successful defense of Rome against Lombard invaders endeared him to the Catholic church, which named Pépin III "King by the Grace of God." The Franks now became the official defenders of the Catholic church. Pépin spent the 750s challenging the Muslims in Spain and reasserting Frankish claims on southern France. At his death, the greatest of the Carolingian monarchs, Charlemagne, came to the throne.

To a great extent, Charlemagne's reign ends the story of the Franks. His establishment of the Holy Roman Empire changed the nature of western Europe and laid the groundwork for the nation-states that arose in the following centuries. The greatest effects the Franks had on western Europe were to serve as a stabilizing influence in the wake of the fall of the Roman Empire and to be a force for Christian missionary work in west-central Europe. Though much of this time frame is taken up with warfare, the cooperation of the Frankish tribes, under the leadership of either kings or mayors of the palace, served to facilitate trade in western Europe and the exchange of goods and ideas. Little technological innovation took place, though the development of Frankish cavalry influenced warfare throughout Europe and the Middle East.

*See also* Avars [34]; Byzantine Empire [38]; Carolingian Dynasty [39]; Huns [51]; Ostrogoths [69]; Visigoths [81].

References: Gregory of Tours, *History of the Franks,* trans. Ernest Brehaut (New York: Norton, 1969); James, Edward, *The Franks* (New York: Blackwell, 1988); Lasko, Peter, *The Kingdom of the Franks* (New York: McGraw-Hill, 1971).

## 47  GENGHIS KHAN

Certainly one of the best known and most successful conquerors was Genghis Khan, ruler of the Mongols and founder of the Mongol nation. Son of Yesugai, leader of the Borjigin tribe of Mongols, he was born probably in 1167 (though earlier dates are suspected) and named Temujin (Temuchin). Orphaned at age nine when his father was murdered, Temujin struggled to exist as an outcast in his own tribe. Stories abound as to his charismatic personality even as a youth, and he began to regain his position when an old friend of his father's gave him military support to regather his tribe and avenge himself on those who murdered his father. With the assistance of his childhood friend, Jemuka (now a prince), Temujin was immensely successful in defeating his enemies and from his earliest victories established a pattern for treating his foes: He killed the leaders and brought the commoners into his own tribe. By doing this he crushed any remaining loyalty to previous clans and required fealty to himself alone.

His early victories were directed against the tribes of the steppes and he gradually brought them under his control. He began to have some trouble, though, within his own camp when Jemuka started occasionally disagreeing and gradually challenging Temujin's authority. Jemuka led rival clan leaders in a number of attacks against Temujin, but ultimately Temujin defeated and killed his former ally. By doing so, he brought all the steppe tribes under his control. This was confirmed in 1206 when he was named emperor of the steppes and given the title Genghis Khan, meaning Universal Ruler.

With central Asia in his hands, Genghis began to look outward. With only his sons and his closest advisors for generals, he began to attack China in 1211. He established a base northwest of the Great Wall and moved quickly into Ch'in territory. By 1215 he occupied Peking. At this point he left the Ch'in conquest in the hands of General Muqali and turned toward the southwest and the Muslim nation of Khwarezm. A dispute over their treatment of a caravan under Mongol protection brought Genghis to this nation east of the Caspian Sea. When representatives from Khwarezm refused to discuss compensation, the Mongols invaded. It is in this campaign in the Oxus River area that the Mongols established their fearsome reputation. Under Genghis's direction the Mongols began destroying cities, fields, and irrigation systems.

It was also in this campaign that the Mongols began to employ new military methods. Mongol forces were made up totally of cavalry, which were unable to besiege cities. Therefore, Genghis adopted catapults and siege engines from the nations he was conquering. He also learned that there was more to empire-building than owning sufficient territory to feed Mongol horses. Cities and towns were necessary to hold territory and establish trade. With this in mind, Genghis began to stop razing cities and only engaged in wholesale slaughter on rare occasions, though often enough to maintain a reputation that he could use as a negotiating tool.

With Khwarezm conquered and under his domination by 1223, Genghis remained relatively passive, though his troops raided far and wide into Russia, southeastern China, and toward India. He died while on campaign in Russia on 18 August 1227, leaving an empire stretching from the Caspian Sea to Peking. This was expanded further by his sons and grandsons, who took the Mongol empire to its heights.

Genghis was one of those leaders who occasionally arise who is equally adept at conquest and administration. While extremely strong-willed, he was able to listen to opposing views and incorporated them into his own if he saw their merit. While believing himself divinely guided, he tolerated every religious belief his subjects practiced. Upon receiving his imperial title, he developed the Great Yasa, a code of civil, military, and economic laws that governed all Mongols, himself included. From his conquered subjects he took not only military tactics and hardware, but also adopted an alphabet, a written language, and whatever cultural accomplishments they could offer. His domination of central Asia brought about a *Pax Mongolica* that allowed the reopening of the Silk Road, bringing ideas and trade from the Middle East and beyond. Though known for the terror inspired by his soldiers, he used it for psychological ends more than for its own sake. Unlike later strongmen in the mold of Hitler and Stalin, who practiced genocide and mass murder, Genghis Khan was actually quite an enlightened and tolerant ruler.

*See also* China, Mongol Conquest of [41]; Kubilai Khan [61]; Russia, Mongol Conquest of [71].

References: Chambers, James, *The Devil's Horsemen* (New York: Atheneum, 1979); de Hartog, Leo, *Genghis Khan, Conqueror of the World* (New York: St. Martin's Press, 1989); Morgan, David, *The Mongols* (Oxford: Blackwell, 1986).

# GHANA, ALMORAVID INVASION OF

**48**

The nomads of the western Sahara, most notably the Sanhaja tribes, dominated the gold trade between Ghana and the Mediterranean in the eleventh century. This was a profitable pastime until Ghana seized control of the town of Awdaghust, at the southern end of the trade route. Because of internal dissent, the Sanhaja tribes were unable to respond to this loss of revenue and power. The king of the tribes believed something needed to be done to unite his people, and he thought that religion was the key. Islam had spread throughout western Africa since the eighth century, but it was practiced with irregular piety, and among the Sanhaja tribes of the Sahara, the people seemed to be only nominally Muslim. When their king went on his pilgrimage to Mecca, he returned with the desire to increase his people's faithfulness. He brought back a teacher, Ibn Yasin, to motivate his tribes to become better Muslims, a task Ibn Yasin was unable to accomplish.

Disgusted at the intransigence of the nomads, Ibn Yasin went into retreat along the west coast of Africa (some say near the mouth of the Senegal River, others say Mauritania or an island off the coast). Here he established a *ribat,* a fortified center for the study of religion and warfare, which attracted a following of people pious to the point of fanaticism. These "men of the ribat" came to be known as Almoravids (in Arabic, *al-muribatun*). When Ibn Yasin had about a thousand followers, mostly from the Sanhaja tribes, he declared a *jihad* (holy war). Returning to the territory of the Sanhaja, he told his recruits to either convert their people to a stronger belief, or visit God's wrath upon them. After a few defeats, the Sanhaja tribes embraced Ibn Yasin's fundamentalist stand and joined his forces, not only for religious reasons but for the promise of booty. With enlarged forces, Ibn Yasin moved north to Morocco, defeating the Berber inhabitants in 1054–1055. Here, in Ibn Yasin's homeland, the Almoravid state was established. After Ibn Yasin's death in battle in 1059, the dynasty was founded by Yusuf ibn Tashufin.

While the main Almoravid force was busy conquering Morocco, a smaller force attacked south with the intent of recapturing Awdaghust. Accomplishing this in 1054, they ultimately attacked deeper into Ghanan territory and captured the capital in 1076. For a while they instituted a strict Muslim rule in the western African state, forcing tribute and the payment of a head tax by non-Muslims. This control lasted only a few years because the Almoravids were more concerned with pillage and profit than local improvement. Even though they controlled both ends of the trans-Saharan trade route, they did not take advantage of it. When the Almoravids withdrew, Ghana remained disrupted, giving an opportunity for the expansion of Mali into the gold territory.

Meanwhile, the Almoravids in Morocco extended their campaign for Muslim fundamentalism into Spain. They attempted to revive the lethargic practices of the Spaniards and were welcomed as protection against the approaching Christian forces from Europe.

At their height, the Almoravids controlled territory from Spain through western Africa, but that rule was short-lived. They were in turn overthrown by another fundamentalist movement, the Almohads, who declared a *jihad* against them in 1122 and ultimately overthrew them in 1163. That defeat in Morocco, coupled with the inability to make a profit at the southern extreme of their holdings in the gold region of Ghana, brought the Almoravids to a rather abrupt end. The aftereffects of the Almoravid reign are mixed. Though they did not introduce Islam into Ghana, they accelerated the spread of the religion into the interior of western Africa along the Niger River to Mali and the Songhay empires. They also acted as a solidifying influence for the tribes of the Maghrib in northwest Africa; by building their capital at Marrakesh, they laid the foundation for the modern nation of Morocco. Both in Morocco and in the Sahara, the tribes were confirmed in their Islamic faith, but the fundamentalism the Almoravids preached did not last much past their demise.

*See also* Mali, Expansion of [64]; Songhay, Expansion of [74]; Spain, Muslim Conquest of [75].

References: Fage, J. D., *A History of West Africa* (London: Cambridge University Press, 1969); Hallett, Robin, *Africa to 1875* (Ann Arbor: University of Michigan Press, 1970); Trimingham, J. S., *Islam in West Africa* (London: Oxford University Press, 1962).

---

## 49      GUPTA EMPIRE

Northern India was in a state of flux for a long time after the fall of the Mauryan Empire, coming under the occasional control of the Bactrians and the Scythian Kushans. Their decline in the face of Sassanid Persia, coupled with the decline of the Andhra dynasty in southern India, left a power vacuum that was filled by Chandragupta of Pataliputra. The area of Magadha, around the lower Ganges Valley, had been the base for the Mauryan Empire, and Chandragupta claimed descent from the founder of that dynasty. He campaigned up the Ganges Valley and, having placed it under his authority, in A.D. 320 named himself Chandragupta I, King of Kings. He married the daughter of a neighboring king, and their son Samudragupta could claim noble blood from both parents.

After Chandragupta's death in 330, Samudragupta went conquering. Aiming to reestablish the boundaries of the Mauryan Empire, he attacked to the west and southwest, conquering Rajputana and the north-

ern Deccan plateau of central India. His campaign along the eastern coast drove as far as modern Madras, and the remnants of the Andhra territory paid him tribute. He attacked and was able to exact tribute from Assam, Punjab, and Nepal. After Samudragupta's death in 375, his son Chandragupta II maintained the aggressive goals of his forebears. He defeated the Punjabis and gained direct control over their territory in the northwest, then annexed the regions of Malwa, Saurashtra, and Gujarat. The empire reached its greatest extension under his rule, and saw the beginnings of a Golden Age.

Because the empire of the Guptas was not as centralized as that of the Mauryans, much local autonomy was exercised. The environment became peaceful and safe, however, and the main chronicler of the period, the Chinese traveler Fa Hsien, praises the administration for its maintenance of such a quiet land. Poetry and literature were taken to their heights, and in the sciences the value of pi and the exact length of the solar year were calculated. The world's best university at the time was established at Nalanda, near the capital city of Pataliputra, and it attracted students from all over India as well as China and Southeast Asia. By patronizing the cult of Vishnu, the Indian religious climate favored Hinduism and led to a decline in Buddhism. A number of monasteries and temples were also constructed in this time.

The empire did not long survive Chadragupta II, who died in 413. The Ephthalites, or White Huns, drove through modern Afghanistan and through the passes into northwest India. Though kept at bay temporarily by Kumaragupta and Skandagupta, the pressure proved overwhelming by 480, and the Gupta Empire collapsed. The White Huns set up a short-lived kingdom in the northwest, but the subcontinent remained fragmented until the rise of Harsha, the last of the strong native leaders. During his reign (606–647), reunification extended almost as far as the Gupta Empire, but its decentralization guaranteed its collapse into warring factions after his death. Not until the Mongol invasion of India would there again be a centralized administration.

*See also* Mauryan Empire [27]; India, Kushan Invasion of [52]; Moghul Empire [98].

References: Allan, John, *The Cambridge Shorter History of India* (Delhi: S. Chand, 1964); Basham, A. L., *The Wonder That Was India* (New York: Taplinger, 1954); Gokhale, Balkrishna, *Ancient India, History and Culture* (Bombay: Asia House, 1959).

## 50    HUNDRED YEARS' WAR

Rival claims to both land and power were the basis of conflict between Britain and France in the fourteenth century. The death of Charles VI of France in 1328 left a void in the French monarchy. The Capetian dynasty had ruled in France since 987, but there was now no direct male heir. The closest claimant was Edward III of England, grandson of Philip the Fair (1285–1314), but the French nobility had a difficult time conceiving of a foreigner as their king. They chose instead Philip VI Valois, deciding to bring the Capetian dynasty to a close. Edward resisted this choice and not only because he wanted the throne for himself but because of the fact that he was technically a vassal of the French king. Since he controlled some lands in France, he might be called upon to obey his liege lord with actions detrimental to England. The French had also supported the Bruces of Scotland in their struggle for independence from the English. Last, England coveted Flanders, nominally under French control but tied to England via the wool trade. Add to all this the traditional dislike the French and English have always harbored for each other, and war seemed inevitable.

Even though they possessed a larger and wealthier population, France did not have a strong central administration to direct military operations or collect the necessary taxes to pay for a war. England was better organized, had more consistent military leadership, and had superior weaponry in the form of the longbow.

The war was fought in three phases over the space of 116 years. First, Edward provoked trouble in Flanders by instituting an embargo on English wool, placing the merchants and trade guilds in economic jeopardy. The cities of Flanders were obliged to recognize Edward as king of France in order to reopen trade. They signed a treaty of alliance with England, but proved to be unfaithful in following it. With this foothold on the continent, Edward organized an invasion force. He drew first blood with a naval victory over the French at the battle of Sluys in January 1340, a battle which gave him control of the English Channel. He was unable to follow this up because of a lack of Flemish support, and he was forced to conclude a truce with France.

Edward broke this in 1346 when English forces invaded Normandy and won a series of victories culminating in their triumph at Crecy. He did not want to fight the French at that time, but since his ships had left Calais to evacuate wounded and booty he could not escape. While on the march for Flanders he met French forces at Crecy and had to stand and fight. Edward's army of knights and longbowmen faced a French army much superior in numbers of mounted knights and foot soldiers. He won by defense and poor French leadership. Philip attacked late in the afternoon of 26 August, before his entire army had

The Battle of Crecy during the Hundred Years'
War (from Froissart's *Chronicles of England*)

arrived on the scene. The great range and power of the longbows held French cross-bowmen at bay and drove back repeated cavalry charges. By midnight the French army was in tatters. Edward retreated to Calais, laid siege to it throughout the winter, and captured it in the spring of 1347. England controlled Calais for the next two hundred years, denying the French any opportunity to launch a counterinvasion.

Mutual exhaustion and the arrival of the bubonic plague brought the war to a halt for eight years. The second phase of the war came when England won a victory at Poitiers in September 1356. This time the key English weapon was artillery. By destroying the castle walls at Poitiers, along with the flower of French knighthood at Crecy, the French army was destroyed and King Philip became an English prisoner. Political order in France collapsed and the countryside was vandalized by roving bands of out-of-work soldiers. Scorched earth tactics employed by both armies, coupled with the pillaging of the brigands, brought destruction to all parts of the French countryside. England forced France to sign the Treat of Bretigny in May 1360, freeing Edward from his position as vassal to the king

and forcing France to recognize English control over their territories in France. Edward renounced his claim to the French throne and received 3 million gold crowns for King Philip's release.

Owing to domestic problems in England over the next few decades, they were unable to focus sufficient attention to their possessions in France and the new King Charles V. Charles was able to regain influence over much of France while English kings had to deal with peasant uprisings. After Edward III died in England in 1377, the two countries remained in relative peace. In 1396, Richard II of England married the French king's daughter, sealing a truce. Not until 1415 did the war resume, when King Henry V of England took advantage of a French power struggle and invaded, initiating the third phase of the war. He scored a major triumph at Agincourt in October. Henry's army of 8,000 defeated a French force of 25,000, again doing most of the damage with longbows against a reconstituted French armored nobility on horseback. Unhorsed knights packed into a muddy field fell victim to a swarming English infantry. Enraged by a French attack at his undefended baggage train late in the battle, Henry broke the conventions of the time and ordered his prisoners executed. Half the French nobility died at Agincourt.

Allying himself with the Burgundians, Henry held a commanding position in control of almost all northern France. He forced the French to sign the Treaty of Troyes, which created a joint monarchy. The deaths of Henry V of England and Charles VI of France in 1422 brought a single king to power, the infant Henry VI. In Paris, he was proclaimed king of both France and England, but most Frenchmen ignored the treaty and recognized Charles VII Valois.

The two countries were unified in name only. Charles VII soon set about regaining the throne, but at first had little luck. As his army inside Orleans was being besieged in 1429, France was delivered by a young girl, Joan of Arc. She gained an audience with the king and informed him that God had given her the power to lift the siege. As the war had been going so poorly and no French general could succeed, Charles had nothing to lose. Joan was just what the French military needed: a psychological boost. She had no military training, of course, but her arrival at Orleans coincided with a British retreat owing to a lack of supplies. Any French army in this position could have won, but she got the credit. Heartened by this victory and what they believed to be divine guidance, French forces built momentum and scored a series of successes over the English. Charles openly declared himself king as the English forces reeled. The Burgundians saw which way the wind was blowing and disavowed their English allies and signed an agreement with Charles in 1435. By 1453, the British agreed to peace. They were backed into a corner around Calais, which remained their sole possession in France.

The Hundred Years' War accelerated the pace of change in Europe, especially in France. The defeat of the French nobility at Crecy and Agincourt was important because the feudal system was based on the power of the knights. Without the ability to enforce the system of vassalage, feudalism began to fade. The arrival of the bubonic plague in the midst of this war brought about changes as well. By killing vast numbers of people in the cities, peasants from the countryside, no longer bound to their land by the dead or absent nobles, abandoned an agricultural life for one of business in urban areas. Decreased demand for agricultural products because of the plague, coupled with the lack of farm workers, meant that the nobles on their estates could not maintain an income. This meant

that political power shifted to where the money was, with the merchants and craftsmen of the cities. Without a strong agricultural nobility, the king became the most important political figure in the nation, and he was supported by the cities who had no traditional loyalty to one noble as the country peasants had. Feudalism fell, replaced by nationalism. Taxing power from now on lay in the hands of the king, so he used his military power to open and control trade routes, or to control foreign lands, and keep the cities wealthy.

There were changes in England as well. When the war started Edward III needed money. In order to get it, he needed the approval of Parliament, which was called upon to approve an unprecedented amount of money and supplies. This meant holding regular meetings, which resulted in a steady increase in the power of the House of Commons. Thus, as Edward tried to gain power in France, he was giving it up at home.

References: Painter, Sidney, and Brian Tierney, *Western Europe in the Middle Ages* (New York: Knopf, 1983); Palmer, John J. N., *England, France and Christendom: 1377–99* (Chapel Hill: University of North Carolina Press, 1972); Vale, Malcolm, *English Gascony, 1399–1453* (London: Oxford University Press, 1970).

## 51      HUNS

The Huns are one of a myriad of tribes who rode out of central Asia, but little can be determined of their origin. Probably they were the Huing-nu, who failed in wars against the Chinese and turned (or were forced) westward. Occasional early sources opine that they were the Nebroi mentioned by Herodotus as a semimythical people living on the fringes of territory controlled by the Scythians. Some of the earliest direct references come from clashes with the Goths around the area north of the Black Sea in the mid-fourth century A.D. The first Hun conquest was the Alans; they were then used in the vanguard of Hun attacks against the Goths or emigrated into the Roman Empire.

In 376 the Huns began to harass the Caucasus lands controlled by the Ostrogoths. After fighting around the Crimea, the Ostrogoths were pushed back across the Dnieper to the Dniester River, and began to pressure the Visigoths. The Visigoths had not fared too well against the armies of the Eastern Roman Empire, and their leader, Athanaric, had no wish to see his people defeated by a second enemy. Athanaric established his forces along the Dniester and sent a reconnaissance force east to keep an eye on the advancing Huns. This force was easily destroyed, and the Huns were on Athanaric's army before the Visigoths could finish their defenses. The Visigoths vanished into the countryside and reformed between the Pruth and Danube rivers, where Athanaric ordered a wall built. A second time the swift Hun army arrived and surprised the Visigoths, who again scattered and retreated toward the Danube. The refugees numbered between 700,000 and 1,000,000, and they settled into the forests of Transylvania.

Pressed against the frontiers of the Roman Empire, in 376 the Visigoths begged protection from the emperor Valens. The Visigoths were granted land along the Danube in return for military service. The Ostrogoths, who arrived later, also begged imperial protection, but were denied it; they crossed the Danube anyway. Emperor Theodorus I, crowned in Constantinople in 379, led Roman campaigns against the Huns, who were rampaging through the Balkans, but he could not turn them back.

The two Gothic peoples combined to fight against the Eastern Romans, which left no strong force to oppose the slowly approaching Huns. The Huns settled into Pannonia along the Adriatic coast.

By 432 the Huns were well established and a force to be reckoned with. Emperor Theodosius II paid tribute to the Hun leader, Ruas, and gave him a general's commission. Ruas's sons Bleda and Attila renewed the treaty and fought for Constantinople in campaigns against Persia. Attila grew tired of doing another's fighting and made war against the Eastern Romans. Between 441 and 443 he rampaged through the Balkans and defeated a Roman army outside Constantinople, but could not capture the city. He finally stopped upon receiving an increase in tribute. Attila killed his older brother to become sole leader of the Huns and in 447 reopened his war against the Romans. Though once again turned back from Constantinople, Attila managed to gain a threefold increase in tribute and cession of the eastern bank of the Danube. Theodosius's successor stopped paying the tribute in 450, by which time the Huns were looking westward.

Attila hoped to split the attention of the Western Roman Empire between himself and the Vandal leader Gaiseric, who was making trouble in North Africa. Further, he was invited to aid a Frankish chieftain in a succession struggle against his brother, so there seemed to be plenty of reasons to march on Gaul. He crossed the Rhine north of modern-day Mainz with 100,000–500,000 warriors, plus their families carrying supplies. With a variety of auxiliaries, the Huns advanced along a 100-mile-wide front, destroying everything in their path but Paris. The Roman general Aetius formed an army of Franks, Germans, and Alans, but could muster no more than half Attila's strength. In mid-June the two armies fought at the site of modern-day Chalons, and Attila could not prevail. He retreated eastward, and western Europe was saved from Asian domination.

Attila turned instead and attacked south into Italy. He had demanded the hand of Honoria, the Western Roman Emperor's sister, and been refused. Northern Italy was ransacked, and refugees fled to the marshlands, creating Venice. Aetius returned to face Attila, but the Huns were having problems. One of Attila's commanders had been defeated in Illyricum (northern Greece), and the Italian countryside proved to be disease-ridden and without supplies. Attila met with Pope Leo I outside Rome and, after an unrecorded discussion, turned the Huns northward and left Italy.

Attila died in 453. His sons fought for his throne while subject tribes revolted. The remnants of the Huns retreated northeast of the Danube, leaving rebelling tribes to their own devices. The last of the Huns, under Irnac, traveled as far as the Volga, but they were defeated and absorbed by the Avars. The Huns proved to be little more than plunderers, traveling from one ripe target to the next, never settling down or building cities. They accomplished nothing more than mass destruction, gaining a reputation as the "scourge of God" punishing a sinful Roman Empire.

*See also* Avars [34]; Ostrogoths [69]; Scythians [73]; Vandals [79]; Visigoths [81].

References: Brion, Marcel, *Attila: The Scourge of God* (New York: Robert McBride & Co., 1929); Bury, J. B., *The Invasion of Europe by the Barbarians* (New York: Russell & Russell, 1963); Thompson, E. A., *Romans and Barbarians* (Madison: University of Wisconsin Press, 1982).

# INDIA, KUSHAN INVASION OF

52

The arrival of the Yueh Chih, or Kushan, people in India was a result of their defeat at the hands of Shih Huang-ti of the Ch'in dynasty in China. Expelled from their traditional lands, they migrated west and defeated the Scythians of central Asia, who in turn attacked India at the time of the declining Mauryan Empire. The Scythians, or Sakas, carved out a kingdom of their own in the area around modern Afghanistan, including parts of northern India. They were supplanted, however, by the Kushans, who maintained control over the area of modern Turkistan. Late in the second century B.C., the Kushans were at the borders of Bactria, but internecine squabbling divided them into five rival clans. Kujula Kadphises subdued the other four and began to press gradually southward. Around A.D. 25, they gained control of the territory of modern Afghanistan and moved into the Kabul valley by about A.D. 50. Kujula led his people as far as the Indus River, while his son Wima occupied much of the Punjab. The third ruler, Kanishka, was the greatest of them all. The dates of his reign are a matter of some speculation, but 78–103 is generally accepted. Kanishka drove his armies eastward to capture Palitaputra (modern Patna), the capital city above the delta of the Ganges, then back to the west to occupy Rajputana. At its greatest extent, Kanishka's empire stretched from northern India to Parthian Persia to Turkistan. After his capture of India, he spent much of his time fighting border wars with China.

The Kushans played a key role in international relations in the first two centuries A.D. because their position between the Roman Empire to the west and the Chinese to the east made them valuable middlemen for the beginning of the Silk Road linking the two worlds economically and, to an extent, philosophically. Both Western and Eastern cultures blended in Kushan India, but the Kushans, like most invaders of India, were absorbed by the local society. Kanishka is known as a hero of Buddhism, spreading the faith throughout his empire and introducing it into China. It is also possible that Christianity reached India at this time; legend has it that the apostle Thomas preached there. The perspective of history sees this mingling of cultures as a great age for India and the world, but contemporary accounts (especially those written by Hindus) speak of the dark age of barbarian conquest and the upsetting of traditional values. Still, the Buddhists did well, and the Kushan patronage of the arts produced the greatest era of sculpture, much of which has Hellenistic overtones.

After Kanishka, the Kushan power began to fade. One of the Scythian satraps, Rudradaman, broke away from Kushan dominance and carved out a kingdom of his own in the northeastern portion of India, and other subordinates also broke away. The rising power of the Sassanid dynasty in Persia dealt the Kushans a defeat around 250, in which they lost their hold on their central and southwest Asian lands. Ultimately, the Kushan kings ruled over progressively smaller territories until their total absorption by Indian culture.

See also Ch'in Dynasty [17]; Mauryan Empire [27]; Scythians [73].

References: Chattopadhyay, Bhaskar, *Kushana State and Indian Society* (Calcutta: Punthi Pustak, 1975); Kumar, Baldev, *The Early Kusanas* (New Delhi: Sterling Publishers, 1973); Mukherjee, Bratindra, *The Rise and Fall of the Kushana Empire* (Calcutta: Firma KLM, 1988).

As the forces of Islam spread the faith through the Middle East in the 700s, they gained a small foothold in India by establishing a trading community in Sind, where the Indus River empties into the Arabian Sea. Not until about 1000 did Muslim conquerors return in earnest. At first, Afghan Muslims conducted raids into northern India for no other reason than plunder, but they soon added forced conversion to their raiding. Mahmud of Ghazni was the main perpetrator of this rapine, destroying as much Hindu and Buddhist culture as possible while carrying vast wealth out of the country. The cavalry tactics developed over the centuries by Turkic/Mongol peoples served the Afghan invaders well, and few of the Indian kingdoms could resist; only the military culture of Rajasthan gave the Muslims serious competition. Over time, the Muslims stayed in India rather than carrying off their plunder, and by 1200 they were in control of most of the northern part of India. Hindustan and the Punjab were incorporated into a Turco-Afghan Empire, and the invaders established a capital at Delhi, strategically located to confront the few passes giving access to Afghanistan and acting as the gateway to the agricultural lands of the Ganges and Indus river valleys. In 1206 the Delhi sultanate was formally established.

The Muslims continued to raid the countryside to extend their political control, spread Islam, and destroy the Hindu and Buddhist faiths. The population of northern India, though much larger in number than the Muslims, could not find it in their nature to organize under one leader to resist the invasion. The Muslims were successful enough in their attempt to virtually destroy Buddhism in India, the land of its birth, by killing thousands of monks and destroying temples, monasteries, and universities. Hindu temples suffered as well, because the Muslim ban on portraying the human form in artwork meant the destruction of vast amounts of sculpture. As the sultanate grew more secure, however, the later sultans carried on less persecution, and the majority of Indians who practiced Hinduism survived. They lived as second-class citizens in a Muslim society, forced to pay the head tax all non-Muslims everywhere had to pay. This bought them the right to practice their faith, and once the Muslims looked a bit more closely at the tenets of Hinduism, they found it less objectionable than first thought—it was basically monotheistic, and its lesser deities could almost be equated with the veneration of saints in some Christian societies. The rise of the *bakhti* movement, teaching a universal message of divine love, fit neatly into the Sufi teachings of Islam, so the persecution lessened considerably.

Once established, the Delhi sultanate lusted after the southern part of India, but like so many other empires they failed to make much of a dent in the forbidding Deccan plateau or the warlike Marathas who lived there. Perpetual attempts at subjugation, however, coupled with heavy taxation to pay for the military and a rising disunity in Delhi, brought the sultanate into peril. Palace cabals and discontented peasants kept the leaders from establishing a peaceful empire that could become profitable. Soldiers were often imported Mamluk slave troops, talented at their profession but also eager for power; they fought the wars but also dealt in court intrigues.

The Muslim Empire faced its most severe challenge in the early 1300s when the Mongols made their appearance on the northwest frontier. Sultan Ala-ud-din dealt the Mongols one of their rare defeats and drove them back into Afghanistan.

Ala-ud-din had already made a name for himself as an aggressive leader eager to attack the Deccan, and he had raised an agricultural tax of almost 50 percent to finance his campaigns. This gave him a ready army when the Mongol threat appeared, but it provoked the already oppressed Hindu farmers. When he died on campaign in 1316, he was little mourned.

Ala-ud-din's successors were the Tughluqs. Muhammed ibn Tughluq came to the throne in 1325 and reintroduced the forced spread of Islam, even though he fell in love with and married a Hindu. He also tried to conquer the Deccan, with only slight success, but his taxes were also heavy; further, northern India suffered a seven-year drought, from 1335 to 1342, which killed a million people. More people rebelled. Muhammed died fighting a rebellion in Sind, and he was succeeded by his cousin Firuz (1351–1388). He gave up trying to conquer, and focused on internal improvements and construction projects, building hospitals, mosques, universities, dams, and bridges. He eased the tax burdens, but enforced the strict practice of Islam and made the Hindu population know they were second-class citizens. At his death, the sultanate began to break up.

In the midst of internal dissension after Firuz's death, the timing was ripe for another invasion. The Indians seemed to fight among themselves the most bitterly when there was danger on the frontier. Tamurlane invaded with his Turkic-Mongol forces in 1398 and destroyed the city of Delhi. He left behind famine and disorder, and the Delhi sultanate never fully recovered. An attempt at resurrection was made under the leadership of Sikander (1489–1517), and a period of intellectualism flourished. Hindu and Muslim religious thought began to merge in mystic practices. Sikander's successor, Ibrahim, was the last sultan. While attempting to crush a rebellion in the northern territory of the Punjab, the local governor asked an Afghan tribe for assistance; this led to the invasion of Babur "the Tiger" and the establishment of the Moghul Empire.

The role of the Delhi sultanate in the life of the everyday inhabitant of India is difficult to assess, as little primary source material comes from this era. It was difficult for the Hindus and disastrous for the Buddhists, and the oppression did not end with the rule of the sultan. Local autocrats taxed the people for the sultan and then taxed them again for their own courts, and these local rulers gave little decent government in return. The most long-term result of the occupation was the introduction of Islam into India, giving it a hold in some areas it would never relinquish; variations on the faith are seen in groups like the Sikhs. The Muslim rule engendered no loyalty, and therefore no popular support, when it was needed most—to face another foreign invader.

See also Tamurlane [76]; Moghul Empire [98].

References: Holt, P. M., *The Cambridge History of Islam*, 2 vols. (Cambridge: Cambridge University Press, 1970); Lane-Pool, Stanley, *Medieval India under Muhammadan Rule* (Calcutta: Susil Gupta, 1951); Payne, Pierre, *The Holy Sword* (New York: Harper, 1959).

## IRELAND, ENGLISH INVASION OF

**54**

Around 1159, after hearing reports of corruption and wrongdoing in the Irish church, Pope Adrian IV gave consent to Henry II, king of England, to invade and conquer Ireland. The Irish church had been corrupt for some 25 years and, though re-form efforts were in place (including the appointment of two new archbishops), Ireland did not have the strong centralized government needed to support a state church. Henry decided against an invasion at that time, however, because of opposition from his mother.

The English invaded Ireland nine years later at the request of Dermot Macmurrough, king of Leinster in Ireland. Macmurrough was having a problem with some Irish princes who had had him removed from his lands by sanction of the high king of Ireland. Macmurrough went to Henry II for help and, with Henry's consent, obtained troops from the Anglo-Norman nobility. The invaders were foot soldiers of an English baron, Richard, earl of Pembroke. In exchange for his military aid, Richard was promised Macmurrough's daughter in marriage and succession to the throne of Leinster.

The invasion began in 1168 and lasted approximately one year. The slings and stones used by the Irish resistance were no match for the armored knights and archers of the Norman-style army. Within the year, Richard's army had seized Dublin. During this time, Richard married Macmurrough's daughter and, at Macmurrough's death, inherited the kingdom of Leinster. After Dublin's fall, Richard continued his campaign deeper into Ireland.

Richard's success made Henry nervous. Henry feared that a power-hungry Richard might use his newfound lands to rise up against England. He also worried that English nobles might divide the conquered territory into individual states independent of English rule. Henry himself had stayed out of the conflict, leaving the fighting to Richard, but now he decided to enter the country and proclaim himself lord of Ireland. He then extended English rule to the territories of Waterford and Wexford, adding them to land Richard had already conquered. In the spring of 1172, Henry returned to England, leaving in charge Hugo de Lacy, the first English viceroy in Ireland. De Lacy was given control over the territories of Waterford and Wexford as well as the province of Meath. Richard maintained control of Leinster.

The immediate effect of the invasion was that the Irish countryside was ransacked by invaders, who built castles and stole land and livestock from Irish chieftains. The Norman-English began to intermarry with the locals, and they adopted the Irish language and laws. Distraught by the assimilation, English kings passed laws prohibiting the use of the Irish language, Irish laws, Irish clothing, etc. These efforts proved futile.

Initially the invasion seemed fruitful. The English managed to move into most of Ireland, excluding western and central Ulster. However, from the very beginning their rule was challenged by Irish landholders, and over time the extent of English rule diminished. Throughout Henry's reign and that of his son John, skirmishes between the Irish and Norman-English were common. By the time Henry died, Norman control existed only in sections of the coast, land along the Shannon River, land in Leinster, and parts of Meath and Ulster. John's reign did nothing to extend that control; in fact, his attitude toward his Irish subjects further angered them and caused more rebellion.

Though Norman-style rule was diminished considerably, long-term effects of the invasion are still visible. During John's reign, the kingdoms under English rule were divided into 12 counties; those counties still exist in modern Ireland. John's main influence, though, was in the introduction of an English style of government and the adoption of English law. Even today, effects of the invasion are evident in the problems between Ireland and England. A rampart used by the invaders still stands. Robert Kee comments, "The rampart sealed off the neck of a promontory which the Normans were to use as a bridgehead. What a bridgehead into Irish history it was to prove. Eight centuries of conflict were to flow from it—a conflict that is still not over."

References: Finnegan, Richard, *Ireland: The Challenge of Conflict* (Boulder: Westview Press, 1983); Kee, Robert, *Ireland: A History* (New York: Little, Brown, & Co., 1982); Orel, Harold, ed., *Irish History and Culture* (Lawrence: University of Kansas Press, 1976).

## IRELAND, VIKING INVASIONS OF

**55**

Viking forays into Ireland began in 795 with the raid on Lambay. Twenty-five raids were recorded between 795 and 840, conducted all along the northern coast of Ireland. These raids centered mostly on churches and monasteries because the church prescribed the use of precious metals, such as gold, for its liturgical vessels. Such places were easy pickings owing to the monks' inability to defend themselves.

In 840 the character of Viking conquests changed. Thorgils, a Norse Viking, invaded and conquered the whole of Ireland. From this point on, Ireland was used primarily as a military base for expeditions to other places. Thorgils founded many garrisons that would become major cities: Dublin, Wexford, Cork, and Limerick. There was no major settling of Ireland by the Vikings, unlike the colonizing taking place in England and on the Continent. Soldiers came, served their time, and returned to Scandinavia. Also, instead of subjugating the people of Ireland, the Vikings ruled in cooperation with the seven Irish kingdoms of Connaught, Munster, Leinster, Meath, Ailech, Ulaidh, and Oriel. The Irish kings stayed kings—some working with their Viking overlords, some opposing them.

Thorgils was drowned in 845 by Mael Sechnaill, king of Meath. The Norse experienced constant conflicts for the next few years, continuing into 850 when the Danes stepped in to take over. Called the Black Strangers, the Danish Vikings raided Dublin and seized the Norse stronghold of Carlingford in 851. In 853, the Norse and Danes were united under Olaf Huiti, the son of the Norse king. In 871 Olaf returned to Norway and was killed in battle, which left Ireland to his brother Ivar, lord of Limerick. Olaf's reign had been rife with petty wars and shifting alliances, all in all an uneasy time for the Vikings. Upon assuming leadership, Ivar was dubbed "King of the Norsemen of all Ireland and Britain." This angered the Danish king Halfdan of Northumbria in England, who unsuccessfully declared war on Ivar.

These struggles, along with a reduction in reinforcements because of the settling of Iceland, weakened the Viking hold sufficiently for the Irish to rise up in 901 and reclaim their land under the leadership of Cearball of Leinster. Ireland experienced a 12-year peace—until 913, when the Vikings returned. In a four-year expedition, they retook the island and ruled it until 1000, when Brian Boru, king of Munster, defeated Sigtrygg Silkybeard.

The immediate effects of the Viking occupation were both good and bad. The slave trade became widespread throughout Ireland, but the Irish were introduced to the superior boatmaking and seamanship of the Vikings. Contacts with England were also strengthened during this time. Many of modern Ireland's major cities, such as Dublin, were founded by Thorgils. Numer-

ous Viking words found their way into the Irish language, including the words for trade, coin, and market. Excavations of parts of Dublin and other sites reveal a wealth of knowledge about the Vikings, and many examples of early Irish art are preserved in Norwegian museums. Despite some holes in our knowledge, we know the Vikings had a long-term effect on the politics, culture, and history of Ireland. Because Ireland was used mainly as a fortress-base for other expeditions, the Viking heritage here was unlike that in England, where widespread colonization occurred.

References: Arbman, Olger, *The Vikings* (New York: Frederick Praeger Publishers, 1961); Jones, Gwyn, *A History of the Vikings* (New York: Oxford University Press, 1968, rev. 1984); Richter, Michael, *Medieval Ireland* (New York: St. Martin's Press, 1988).

# ITALY AND SICILY, NORMAN CONQUEST OF

**56**

After their initial A.D. 999 foray into the Italian scene, contemporary sources dispute how soon and in what manner the Normans followed up their first appearance. The one common agreement is that they came from Normandy in relatively small groups made up of younger men who stood to inherit little if they stayed home; only by warfare could they increase their fortunes, and fortunes could be made in Italy. The Normans first acted as mercenaries for a variety of local powers, in some cases fighting on opposite sides. Their military prowess proved sufficiently valuable that they were able to obtain lands from their employers and establish a presence that grew stronger until 1042, when southern Italy was divided among them under vassalage to local lords. From this setting, the sons of Tancred de Hauteville, Robert Guiscard and Roger, spread their influence.

By 1061 the Normans were in sufficient power to extend the will of the Roman church to Sicily, dominated for 200 years by the Muslim Saracens. Internecine squabbling on the island provided a good opportunity for Robert Guiscard and his able brother/lieutenant to ally themselves with one party and insinuate themselves into an influential position. Norman knights landed south of Messina one night in May; the Normans' unfamiliarity with maritime operations made the landings a piecemeal effort, but they arrived in strong enough numbers to seize Messina and, allied with Emir Ibn at-Timnah, marched inland. They failed to seize the enemy stronghold at Enna, in the center of the island, but kept Messina as a base to stage future operations.

The conquest of Sicily took 30 years, mainly under the direction of Roger Hauteville: Palermo fell in 1072, the Saracen strongholds of Trapani and Taormina in 1077 and 1079, and Syracuse in 1085. The island was considered secure after the capture of Noto on the southeast coast in 1091. The Sicilian conquest was notable for the increasing use of sea power by Normans (both in transport and siege-craft), the aura of a Holy War taken on by the campaign as time went by, and the increasing close cooperation between Norman soldiers and the papacy. By the time Sicily was falling, however, the first great wave of Hauteville conquerors was dying: Richard in 1078, Robert Guiscard in 1085, and Roger, the "Great Count of Sicily," in 1101. From this point forward the Normans consolidated rather than conquered, ruling the Kingdom of the Two Sicilies until its incorporation into the Holy Roman Empire in 1194 under Henry VI.

The Normans left behind much, and some historians regard this conquest as the epitome of Norman accomplishment. The Normans established a feudal society patterned along the lines of western Europe. They introduced a new arm to military affairs: the heavy cavalry. The armored knight on a heavy horse proved overwhelming to the infantry and light cavalry used by their Lombard, Byzantine, and Saracen opponents. This type of warrior dominated warfare throughout the Middle Ages until its demise during the Hundred Years' War. The longest lasting legacy, however, was the spread of Norman architecture, though its description remains a point of conjecture. For a people not far removed from their Viking heritage, surprisingly the Normans seem to have pioneered castle construction. Castles appeared throughout the Mediterranean, wherever the Normans went, but in the construction of churches they adapted styles found in their travels. Churches and monasteries in Sicily and Italy reflect Greek and Muslim tile work and vaulted roof design, and no church building appears to be "typical" Norman style. Indeed, the blending of Latin, Greek, Muslim, and western European cultures shows itself in all Norman artifacts in the Mediterranean. The Norman championship of the Roman church, as well as their wars against Byzantine forces and territories, aided in the growing schism between eastern and western Christianity. Finally, their warfare against Muslim Sicily was a foretaste of the Crusades of the twelfth and thirteenth centuries.

See also Crusades [42]; France, Viking Invasion of [45]; Hundred Years' War [50].

References: Brown, R. Allen, *The Normans* (New York: St. Martin's Press, 1984); Finley, M. I., et al., *A History of Sicily* (New York: Viking Penguin, 1987).

# 57 JAPAN, MONGOL INVASIONS OF

By the time of the Mongol invasion of Japan, the Mongol leader, Kubilai Khan, was at the height of his power. The Mongol khans had conquered Russia, Poland, Hungary, and Bohemia to the west, as well as China and Korea to the east. In establishing himself in China, Kubilai had subdued his most dangerous adversaries. He could now turn his attention to Japan, the one country that had eluded Mongol domination.

The struggles on the Asian continent had very little effect on Japan. Its contact with the outside world was confined to very limited trade and visits by Buddhist priests. At the time of the Mongol expedition, Japan was under the relatively new rule of the Hojo family. The invasion would be the first test of that family's leadership.

In 1266, Kubilai Khan sent envoys to Japan requesting that tribute be paid to the Mongol Empire. The letter to the Japanese government emphasized the fact that the khan held no hostility toward Japan; he merely wanted Japan to be considered a part of his circle of friendly tributaries. The Japanese interpreted this as a Mongol attempt to subjugate them. The government was divided on their course of action; some favored conciliation and delay, while others preferred a policy of contemptuous silence. After six months, the Hojo regent Tokimune sent the Mongol envoys back without a written acknowledgment. Contemptuous silence won out. Undaunted, the khan sent further envoys to Japan, but the results were the same.

Kubilai Khan began to prepare for war in earnest. He ordered the Koreans to step up their agricultural operations in order to supply his army with food. Knowing that his men had no experience as seamen, he enlisted the aid of the Koreans to transport his army across the sea to Japan.

In November 1274, 25,000 Mongol and 15,000 Korean troops left from Korea in 900 ships manned by 8,000 Korean sailors. They began by attacking Tsushima and Iki, two islands situated in the sea between Korea and Japan. At Tsushima, a force of no more than 200 samurai held the Mongol forces at bay for a time by fighting to the death. An even smaller force repeated this feat at Iki. On 20 November, the Mongols reached the shores of northern Kyushu and were met by the troops of five Kyushu chieftains. The Mongols possessed a superior tactical system. The Japanese were trained to display their skills by engaging in single combat, while the Mongols were trained to work together as a team. If an individual samurai approached a Mongol to do battle, he would be surrounded and killed. The Mongols were excellent horsemen and could easily defeat Japanese cavalry. Despite this, the Japanese mounted a fierce resistance to the invaders. The final blow to the Mongol army came from a storm, which destroyed many of their ships and inflicted a loss of 13,200 men. They were forced to abandon the operation and return to Korea.

Kubilai Khan did not view the invasion as a defeat; he apparently believed that he had instilled fear into Japanese hearts by displaying the superior tactics of the Mongols. He immediately sent envoys to Japan to summon the emperor of Japan to Peking to surrender to him. The Japanese leaders cut off the heads of the Mongol envoys. Kubilai became more determined than ever to conquer Japan.

A second invasion was delayed for seven years because Kubilai had to subdue the last supporters of the Sung dynasty in southern China. By 1281, having taken care of his problems at home, he was ready to launch a campaign against Japan. This time, however, the Japanese were better prepared to defend themselves. They had built a long defensive wall along the coast of Hakata Bay and had trained in group-combat techniques similar to those employed by the Mongols. As a result, Kubilai's 140,000 troops were unable to penetrate the Japanese defenses and move inland. The Korean and Chinese factions of the Mongol army more than likely had no great desire to fight on, while entire families of Japanese defenders volunteered to fight at the front. The final blow to the Mongol invaders came, once again, from nature. After 53 days of fighting, a typhoon, the "divine wind" (kamikaze), destroyed the Mongol fleet and forced them to withdraw. Kubilai Khan made plans for a third invasion, but abandoned them in 1284 when he began to have problems in Southeast Asia.

Little damage was done to the Mongol Empire by the war. The Chinese contingent of the Mongol army bore the brunt of the loss—12,000 of them were made slaves by the Japanese. The Mongols lost their share of men and ships, but surprisingly little else. Mongol pride was hurt, of course; Japan held the distinction of being the only state in the Orient that did not pay tribute.

Oddly, the Japanese victory did more harm than good to the Hojo rulers. When the Mongols first arrived, the court in Kyoto appealed to heaven for help. Throughout the empire, prayers were offered, liturgies chanted, and incense burned in the temples. The priests took credit for the Japanese victory over the Mongol invaders, even claiming that they were responsible for the kamikaze, which the Japanese believed was generated by protective kame spirits against its enemies. Many of them expected, and were given, huge rewards for their help in the campaign, which created resentment among the soldiers who fought so hard for victory, as their payment for services was very small in comparison. The victory over the Mongols brought no

wealth to the victors. The invading forces had left no land as spoils of war to be divided among the Bakufu, the military leaders who were the major landowners, which lowered their prestige. Since the Bakufu had little trust in the Mongols, they did not relax their precautions against another invasion for many years to come, putting a great financial burden on the Japanese government. Eventually these factors led to the downfall of the Hojo family.

The kamikaze legend grew over the centuries, to be called upon again in the 1940s. Hoping for a man-made "divine wind" to save their empire, Japanese pilots used suicide tactics during the U.S. invasion of the Philippines in October 1944, continuing until the final surrender almost a year later.

—Gary Botello

See also Russia, Mongol Conquest of [71]; Philippines, U.S. Invasion of the [182].

References: Curtin, Jeremiah, The Mongols: A History (Westport, CT): Greenwood Press, 1972); Kwanten, Luc, Imperial Nomads (Philadelphia: University of Pennsylvania Press, 1979); Mason, R. H. P., and J. G. Caiger, History of Japan (New York: Free Press, 1972).

## 58 JUSTINIAN

After the Roman Empire split into halves following the reign of Constantine, the western half dealt continuously with barbarian invasions of Germanic and Gothic tribes. Ultimately, the area came under the nominal control of the king of the Ostrogoths, Theodoric. He and his successors established a relatively peaceful and prosperous society that practiced the doctrine of Arian Christianity. In the east, however, this doctrine was viewed as a heresy to be destroyed, and became one of the motives for conquest exercised by the emperor Justinian, who came to power in Constantinople in 527.

Justinian was born a commoner, but he had an uncle in the Byzantine army who brought him to the capital and assisted him in his military career. When his uncle Justin achieved the position of emperor, Justinian served as his closest adviser, and later as regent. Upon Justin's death, Justinian acceded to the throne. He named his wife Theodora coemperor, a wise move because of her political acumen and strong faith in her husband and herself. Together they were a powerful team who took the Byzantine Empire to its greatest heights. Though brought up in the military, Justinian's expansion of the empire was directed by two other generals, Belisarius and Narses. Justinian and Theodora had the vision, and Belisarius and Narses had the skill to accomplish the expansion.

The first order of business was to defend against Persian attacks from the east. As a junior commander, Belisarius distinguished himself in action against the Persians and thus came to Justinian's notice; he was named to the command of all the armies in the east at age 27. In his first major command, he defeated a Persian army twice his size outside the fortress of Daras. During peace talks, he learned of a flanking movement through the desert against Antioch, the richest city in the east. Belisarius quickly moved to block that assault, and the Persians withdrew.

Impressed by his young commander's skills, Justinian ordered him back to Constantinople to lead an invasion of northern Africa. Justinian wanted to return this rich grain-producing area, which had been under the control of the Vandals for the preceding century, to the empire. With but 10,000 infantry and 5,000 cavalry, Belisarius outmaneuvered the Van-

dals, capturing their capital at Carthage and defeating them in battle outside the city gates at Tricameron. Vandal power was thus destroyed, giving the province to the Byzantine Empire.

Justinian ordered Belisarius to Sicily and sent a diversionary force along the Adriatic coast to threaten northern Italy, both by their presence and by bribing the Franks to cooperate. With Gothic attention diverted northward, Belisarius easily captured Sicily and invaded the southern end of the peninsula. He quickly captured Naples, but the Gothic king Vitiges was more intent on defeating the Franks, which allowed Belisarius the opportunity to capture Rome. This caught Vitiges's attention, and he made the Franks a better monetary offer than Justinian. Vitiges then marched on Rome with 150,000, but Belisarius, with a mere 10,000, held the strongly fortified city for a year. When Vitiges withdrew toward his capital at Ravenna, Belisarius followed. He received reinforcements under the command of Narses, an older man with less military experience who nevertheless had Justinian's confidence. The two besieged Vitiges in Ravenna while Belisarius proceeded to consolidate the remainder of Italy. The Franks again intervened on the Goths' behalf, but overplundered the countryside and had to withdraw.

Belisarius was recalled to Constantinople to beat back another Persian threat. Though Belisarius did nothing to give his emperor cause for concern, he became so popular that Justinian began to fear him as a potential rival. Justinian was afraid to give him a large army, and Belisarius had to fight with undermanned forces. He performed more miracles with small forces, bluffing the Persians away from a major assault on Jerusalem and threatening their capital on the Tigris by a series of light-cavalry raids.

Belisarius returned to Italy to reconquer the lands that had fallen to newly rebuilt Gothic forces. Again, he did much conquering with few men, and was again recalled because of Justinian's paranoia. Narses was given overall command in Italy, and his victory there succeeded mainly in destroying the country so thoroughly that it was centuries before much of the land was again useful.

Belisarius gave Justinian a reunited Roman Empire, directed from Constantinople rather than Rome. Justinian tried to hold the sundry cultures together as Caesar Augustus had, by codifying laws to promise universal justice. Justinian's *Code* was a masterpiece of legal order, but it failed to reach the variety of cultures that Augustus's universal law had. By basing much of the law on Orthodox Christian bases, he offended those Christians who practiced other dogmas. Indeed, they considered the law so overbearing that they embraced the rising power of Islam in the 600s because it promised and delivered religious tolerance. The Byzantine Empire soon lost the lands Justinian brought into it, but the professional traditions of the army established in Justinian's time kept it alive for another 800 years.

See also Augustus, Caesar [12]; Constantine, Emperor [18]; Franks [46]; Ostrogoths [69]; Vandals [79].

References: Barker, John, *Justinian and the Later Roman Empire* (Madison: University of Wisconsin Press, 1966); Browning, Robert, *Justinian and Theodora* (London: Weidenfeld & Nicolson, 1971); Procopius, *The Secret History of Justinian,* trans. Richard Atwater (Ann Arbor: University of Michigan Press, 1961).

## 59    KHMER KINGDOM

The earliest records, from the first century A.D., of the population of Southeast Asia living in what is now Cambodia are of the Mon-Khmer people. The arrival of an Indian aristocrat and his marriage to the daughter of a local chief mark the beginning of the kingdom of Fu-nan, which the Chinese wrote about a century or so later. The greatest military leader of Fu-nan appears to have been Fan Shih-man, who extended his kingdom's borders east to the South China Sea, south to the Gulf of Siam, and possibly west toward Burma. Contemporary Chinese texts record the conquests and power of Fan Shih-man, who is thought to have died while on expedition to Burma. Control of the coastline along the South China Sea gave Fu-nan domination over the area's maritime trade, and his successor, Fan Chan, entered into diplomatic and economic relations with China and India. These trade contacts continued throughout the third century, gaining value as China came under the Ch'in dynasty after 280. Apparently, Indian cultural influences made regular appearances in Fu-nan over the next two centuries. The kings often had Indian names, their writing is described as resembling northern Indian script, and trade with central Asia and even the Roman Empire was noted. The greatest of the Fu-nan kings was Jayavarman, whose 30-year reign ended in 514; he was recognized by the Chinese as "General of the Pacified South, King of Fu-nan."

Jayavarman's son was probably the last king of Fu-nan, because the Chen-la are supposed to have conquered the kingdom after 539. Who the Chen-la were is a matter of some dispute, but they may have been vassals of Fu-nan who deposed their overlord. Rulers of the area at the end of the sixth century still claimed descent from the "universal monarch," presumably the king of Fu-nan, but that may have resulted from Chen-la conquerors intermarrying with the royal family. In the 590s the Chen-la leader Bhavavarman conquered the Mekong Delta, to the Mun River in the north, and to the Korat Plateau in the south. He and his brother Chitrasena seized the throne in Fu-nan, but whether as usurpers or restorers of the original royal family is unclear. Chen-la is regarded as the original kingdom of the Khmer people, the inheritors of the land and power of Fu-nan.

Bhavavarman's grandson, Ishanavarman, completed the occupation of Fu-nan to roughly the borders of present-day Cambodia. He established his capital at Ishanapura and pursued a policy of friendship toward their nearest neighbors, the Champa. Consolidation of Khmer power throughout the region continued for another century, through the reign of Jayavarman I (657–681). His death without an heir caused a time of discord and a split in the country; Chinese records speak of a "Land Chen-la" and a "Water Chen-la," corresponding to inland and coastal principalities. The one continuing factor in this time period was the widespread practice of Hinduism, for the Khmers brought the formerly popular practice of Buddhism to an end.

The period of discord brought on outside pressure, notably from the Malay Peninsula and Java. Aggressively pursuing commercial dominance of Indonesia and Southeast Asia, Java seems to have established dominance in the two Chen-las by the late eighth century. The reunification of Chen-la came about in the early ninth century when Jayavarman II ousted the Javanese. His rise to power was confirmed by a religious ceremony naming him "Universal Monarch"; his posthumous title was Parmeshvara, or "Supreme Lord," a title given to the Hindu god Shiva. He built a number of cities and established a capital at whose site Angkor was to be built.

Jayavarman's grandson Indravarman went conquering during his reign (877–889), returning the Korat Plateau to the northwest to Khmer control. He sponsored irrigation projects and built a huge reservoir. Canal and reservoir construction for irrigation, as well as the building of temples and monasteries, remained royal projects for generations. The next several monarchs devoted themselves to public and religious works; not until the reign of Suryavarman (1010–1050) did more expansion take place. During his reign, Khmer power extended into the Menam Valley and to the west of the Great Lake, hitherto a wasteland. Also by his time, a resurgence in Buddhism took place. His sons struggled against internal revolts and attacks from the Cham tribe; the two sons joined the Chinese, however, in an unsuccessful campaign against Dai-Viet.

A new dynasty was established in 1080 by a Brahman who took the throne name of Jayavarman VI. His grandnephew, Suryavarman II, took the Khmer kingdom to its heights. He launched invasions of Dai-Viet in 1128, 1138, and 1150, conquering as far as the Red River delta. He conquered Champa, holding it for four years, and briefly occupied the land of the Mon kingdom. Contemporary Chinese sources state that the Khmer kingdom stretched from Burma to the east coast of the Malay Peninsula. Suryavarman II also constructed Southeast Asia's most notable structures at Angkor Wat, which became his mausoleum, overseen by the Hindu god Vishnu. Rebellions broke out after his death sometime after 1150, but events of the following century and a half are sparsely recorded. Not until the end of the thirteenth century do Chinese accounts describe a fading civilization, though the Khmer again gained control over the Cham territories in the early 1200s. Later that century, a Mongol force entered the area, and records indicate that the Khmers paid tribute to the Chinese emperor Kubilai Khan. After a series of conflicts with the rising power of Siam, the Cambodian capital of Angkor fell to them in 1431. Though the Khmer recovered much of their strength and territory by the middle of the sixteenth century, the Siamese returned to defeat them. Only the arrival of the Portuguese, who gave military assistance to the Khmer king, enabled them to retain some power. From this point forward, too many internal struggles and outside forces—the influences of Portugal, Holland, and Islam—conspired to allow the Khmer to be powerful again. Finally, France took control of all of Southeast Asia in the mid-1800s, establishing a protectorate over Cambodia in 1863.

See also Ch'in Dynasty [17]; Kubilai Khan [61].

References: Audric, John, *Angkor and the Khmer Empire* (London: R. Hale, 1972); Briggs, Lawrence, *The Ancient Khmer Empire* (Philadelphia: The Philosophical Society, 1951); Coedes, G., *The Making of South East Asia,* trans. H. M. Wright (Berkeley: University of California Press, 1966).

## KOREA, MONGOL INVASION OF

60

The Mongol armies invaded China and took control of its northern provinces by 1234. As they attacked the remains of the Sung dynasty in the southern part of China, other Mongol forces invaded Korea. The Mongols had been raiding into Korea since 1231, periodically devastating the country. When the capital city of Kaesong was attacked, the ruling family (under King Kojong) and the government (under the leadership of the Ch'oe family) withdrew to an island off the coast, to which the land-bound Mongols could not follow. They established a new capital and, with taxes collected from the southern part of the peninsula, constructed palaces and pavilions. The government ignored the conditions on the mainland, where Mongols were killing and enslaving tens of thousands of people.

The government depended on prayers to Buddha to keep them safe on the island, but in 1258 Prime Minister Ch'oe Ui was assassinated, and the royal family decided to make peace with the Mongols. The crown prince traveled to the Mongol capital to apologize for the government's resistance; he returned as vassal to the Mongol government. In 1274, Ch'ungnyol Wang, married to a princess of the Mongol Yuan dynasty, ascended the throne and the two nations were united. The Koreans paid tribute to the Mongols and in return were treated as members of the family, though Yuan officials were posted throughout the country to keep tabs on events. Peace was bought at the price of independence.

The Yuan dynasty enlisted the aid of the Koreans in their attempted forays against the Japanese, and the Korean peasants virtually had to starve themselves to feed the armies preparing for the expedition. When they revolted, a combined Chinese and Korean army suppressed them. Even though the invasions of Japan failed, the relations between Korea and the Mongols grew stronger, which meant that the Mongols' influence increased and the Koreans adopted Mongol forms of government and culture. The peasants continued to suffer, their torment increased by a coincidental wave of raids by Japanese pirates along the entire coastline. The marauders, or Wako, so pillaged the coastal farms and shipping that the peasants withdrew to the interior, and the coasts became wastelands. Throughout the era of Yuan dominance, the peasants suffered continually and slavery expanded. A feudal system of sorts was established that kept most people tied to an estate, owned by a Mongol or a Korean supporter of the Yuan dynasty.

The Mongol rule in Korea came to an end when the Mongol rule in China ended. In the 1350s, power struggles within the Mongol ruling family, coupled with rebellions, strained their ability to rule. Bandit uprisings harried the Mongol administration, and the Red Turbans were the most dangerous. Korea was called upon to provide troops to fight the Red Turbans, but they were defeated. The Red Turbans followed up their victory with attacks on Manchuria and Korea in 1359 and 1361. A Red Turban leader declared himself head of a new dynasty, the Ming dynasty, and made war against the Yuan dynasty from the Ming capital at Nanking. Seeing an opportunity, the Korean king, Kongmin Wang, killed the Mongol leaders in his country and sent the army to reoccupy the northern portion of the peninsula. When the Mings established their authority, Korea rushed to recognize it and swear allegiance.

See also China, Mongol Conquest of [41]; Japan, Mongol Invasions of [57]; Ming Dynasty [68].

References: Charol, Michael, *The Mongol Empire; Its Rise and Legacy* (London: George Allen & Unwyn, 1961); Hatada, Takahashi, *A History of Korea*, trans. Warren Smith and Benjamin Hazard (Santa Barbara, CA: ABC-Clio, 1969); Henthorn, William, *Korea: The Mongol Invasions* (Leiden: E. J. Brill, 1963).

In the early thirteenth century, the steppe tribes were united under the dynamic leadership of Genghis Khan, who directed his people to conquests establishing the largest empire in history. That empire, however, was destined to a rather short life. Though Genghis spelled out directions for succession, which his children followed with little trouble, his grandchildren divided the empire beyond the hope of reunification. After the death of Ogadai, one of Genghis's sons, Ogadai's son Mangu ruled as the Great Khan, or Khakhan. Upon Mangu's death there was a struggle among his brothers. The youngest (designated "Keeper of the Hearth" to rule over the Mongol homeland) was Arik Buka, who had the support of his brother Baiku of the Golden Horde and his nephew Kaidu, who lived on the steppes to the north. However, the next in line for the throne was Kubilai. Arik Buka's supporters rejected Kubilai's leadership because he had become too Chinese and not sufficiently Mongol in his actions.

Kubilai had been Mongol enough to lead the armies of the steppes into southern China against the Sung Empire. Using the techniques developed by Genghis and the siege engines adapted from Chinese and Muslim forces, Kubilai proved as capable and successful as any Mongol general. He had seen the advantages of Chinese culture—its wealth and scientific accomplishments—and he embraced them as adjuncts to the traditions and military prowess of the Mongols. His interest in Chinese culture seemed a betrayal to the more conservative Mongols in the homelands.

In 1260, Kubilai made a quick truce with the Sungs, then turned his forces northwest toward his younger brother's base at Karakorum. Kubilai captured the city and held it against Arik Buka's counterattacks until, in 1264, the younger brother submitted to the older's leadership. Kubilai forgave him and gave him lands of his own, but punished his brother's advisers for urging the revolt. Kubilai returned to China, never to see the Mongol capital of Karakorum again. His nephew Kaidu refused to submit and spent the next 30 years harassing China's borders.

Kubilai returned to his garden city of Shang-tu, better known to Westerners as Xanadu. He also returned to his campaign against the Sung, who had violated the truce in his absence. Kubilai blended traditional Mongol tactics with a new one: He depended on Chinese familiarity with past Mongol cruelties to cities that resisted, then offered peaceful terms to any that would submit willingly. That promise, coupled with benevolent treatment of refugees, won the hearts of most of the Sung people, so that by 1276 the seven-year-old Sung emperor and his dowager empress grandmother surrendered to him. Kubilai had to continue campaigning against Sung supporters in the southeast, capturing Canton and waging a naval war against the final holdouts, but with the submission of the emperor the war was won.

Kubilai's significance lies not in new military developments, but in his political leadership. Many areas of Chinese life improved during the new Yuan dynasty. Public works were of prime importance, and new roads and canals were constantly constructed while he was emperor. Kubilai proved to be a benevolent master to the poverty-ridden peasantry, providing the first public-assistance program in China and introducing the practice of stockpiling surplus supplies in good years for redistribution during lean times. He maintained the Chinese bureaucracy, yet kept the Mongols as a separate class in society. He sponsored intellectual pursuits by ordering the printing of many books and the construction of observatories for updating astronomical observations. The expansion of printing brought Chinese drama to heights never before experienced, and spread its influence widely over the population.

He was not, however, without his failings. Kubilai maintained a large military, the cost of which was a severe burden on the taxpayers. He also sponsored two disastrous invasions of Japan, which cost money and thousands of Chinese lives. In order to maintain the splendor of his palaces, he collected vast sums of silver for his treasury, but introduced printed money to the Chinese economy, overprinting it to the point of high inflation. Though he protected China from the raids of his nephew Kaidu and unified the country into a form it would basically hold to present times, the costs to the peasant taxpayer proved too much of a burden. Though called Kubilai the Wise, he laid the groundwork for the fall of his dynasty. He also oversaw, somewhat by default, the breakup of the Mongol Empire. Birkai of Russia never acknowledged his supremacy and made his portion of the empire independent; Hulagu established an independent state of the Il-Khans in Persia. Kaidu also maintained his own independence in the northern steppes. Thus, Kubilai was left with China, a nation that reached new heights under his leadership but which quickly overthrew his successors and reestablished Chinese dominance in the Ming dynasty.

See also Genghis Khan [47]; Japan, Mongol Invasions of [57]; Middle East, Mongol Invasion of the [66]; Ming Dynasty [68]; Russia, Mongol Conquest of [71].

References: Cohen, Daniel, *Conquerors on Horseback* (Garden City, NY: Doubleday, 1970); Lamb, Harold, *The March of the Barbarians* (New York: Literary Guild, 1940); Rossabi, Morris, *Khubilai Khan: His Life and Times* (Berkeley: University of California Press, 1987).

## 62           LOMBARDS

The Lombards were a tribe of northern Germany who came to recorded history during the latter stages of the Roman Empire. The Romans gave them their name—*langobard,* or "long beard." Though known to fight occasionally against either their neighbors or the Romans, the Lombards tended to be peaceful, pastoral people. Through the fourth and fifth centuries, they began to migrate southward into the Danube River region known as Pannonia (modern Austria). The Lombards fought for Byzantine emperor Justinian in his campaigns against the Ostrogoths in Italy and received favored status during his rule. His successors, however, favored the Gepids, a neighboring hostile tribe. Fearing a war against the Gepids supported by the Byzantines, the Lombards under King Alboin allied themselves with a tribe newly arrived from central Asia, the Avars. Together they were victorious and split Gepid lands between them.

In the middle of the sixth century, the Lombards established a new tribal organization based on an aristocratic hierarchy. Dukes and counts commanded clans organized into military units (*farae*), all serving under a king. With this new organization, the Lombards, now in fear of the Avars, decided in the late 560s to migrate farther, to Italy. The long-running war between the Ostrogoths and the Byzantine Empire had left a power vacuum in northern Italy, and the Lombards were able to move in and take over fairly easily. Under Alboin's leadership, by 572 they had conquered the entire northern peninsula to the Po River, and occasional districts in southern and eastern Italy.

Alboin was murdered shortly after the Lombards' arrival in Italy, and for the next few decades the tribe struggled internally while they exploited the Italian people and countryside. The Lombards established themselves as the dominant force in northern Italy, but they adapted readily to the existing agricultural framework in the area, believing that whatever the Romans had organized was the best format for agricultural production. The tribal dukes exercised the most power, with little or no central control. Only when threatened from outside, by the Franks, did the Lombards again form a united front. In 590 the Lombards elected the duke of Turin, Agiluf, to the kingship, and he reconsolidated Lombard power and established a capital at Pavia. King Rothari, who ruled in the mid-600s, issued a legal code for his people along the lines of that produced by Justinian in Constantinople. The leading Lombard king was Liutprand (712–744), who further focused on the internal needs of his kingdom. Later in his reign he reinstituted the campaign against Byzantine power in Italy.

The Lombard incursion into Italy frightened the pope. At first the Lombards practiced Arian Christianity, which denied the equality of God and Jesus. Their military success, coupled with their heretical views, posed a threat to orthodox Catholicism. Even though they converted to orthodox views in the late seventh century, their power was a source of concern to the pope. When the Lombards under King Aistulf captured Ravenna in 751 and threatened Rome in 754, Pope Stephen II appealed to the Franks for deliverance. Pépin the Short, first of the Carolingian dynasty, marched to Italy and defeated the Lombards in 754 and 756. Pépin recaptured Ravenna and gave land to the church, creating the Papal States; in return, the pope anointed Pépin as king of the Franks and defender of Rome.

Aistulf remained as king of the Lombards, but his successor, Desiderus, was defeated by another Frank, Pépin's grandson Charlemagne, in 773. Charlemagne made himself king of the Lombards and incorporated northern Italy into the Holy Roman Empire, thus bringing to an end the Lombards' existence. Though their rule in Italy was often harsh, the Lombards contributed to the country's heritage. Much of the legal system of the area descends from Lombard practice. King Rothri, who reigned in the mid-600s, issued a law code patterned along the lines of that compiled by Justinian in Constantinople. One of the most important aspects of Rothri's code was the attempt to end the practice of vendetta. The personal feud was to be replaced by monetary payment for damages, known as *guidrigild*, which appears in later Scandinavian cultures as *weregild*. The Lombards' greatest effect, however, was indirect, in that they removed once and for all Byzantine power in Italy, which ended any chance of Eastern Orthodoxy challenging papal authority in western Europe. In the eleventh century, Lombardy played a major role in dominating the trade routes from the Mediterranean into the continent, and the resulting wealth gave them commercial and financial leadership that later translated into political power: They formed the Lombard League, which resisted the invasion of Frederick Barbarossa of Germany in 1176.

*See also* Avars [34]; Franks [46]; Justinian [58]; Ostrogoths [69].

References: Bona, Istvan, *The Dawn of the Dark Ages: The Gepids and the Lombards* (Budapest: Corvina Press, 1976); Hallenbeck, Jan, *Pavia and Rome: The Lombard Monarchy and the Papacy in the Eighth Century* (Philadelphia: American Philosophical Society, 1982); Paul the Deacon, *History of the Langobards*, trans. W. D. Foulke (Philadelphia: University of Pennsylvania Press, 1974).

## 63    MAGYARS

There are two rival claims as to the source of the Magyars. Legend has it that they were descended from Nimrod, a descendant of Noah's son Japheth, who left Babel after the construction of the Tower of Babel. Nimrod had two sons, Hunor and Magyar, who began the two great tribes of the Huns and the Magyars. Following the direction of a magical elk, they moved to the Caucasus, where the two tribes lived in peace. As time passed and the tribes grew, the Magyars remained in the Caucasus and the Huns began a nomadic life that ultimately took them past the Volga into Europe. Under the leadership of Attila, the Huns terrorized Europe. After Attila's defeat and death, his sons returned to the Caucasus and pleaded with the Magyars to return with them to Europe where they could find new lands and opportunity.

Aside from the legend of a Middle Eastern origin, in reality the Magyars seem to have had Finn-Ugaric origins with traces of Turco-Tartar elements. They had long practiced a nomadic lifestyle in central Asia and finally migrated westward past the Ural, Volga, Don, and Dnieper rivers, and at last the Danube. In this movement, they had to successively fight and defeat other nomadic tribes, such as the Bulgars, Khazars, and Petchenegs. The pressure of the Petchenegs and Bulgars finally drove them into Europe. As they entered eastern Europe, they encountered the power of the Byzantine Empire, which hired them as mercenaries and introduced them to Christianity; likewise, German kings hired them to aid in fighting the Slavs.

By the ninth century A.D., the Magyars moved into central Europe under the leadership of Arpad. They entered the Hungarian plain with some 150,000 men, defeated the Slavs and Alans, settled, and used the area as a base for further raiding into German and Italian lands. The Magyars became the permanent occupants of this region, and came to be known as Hungarians. Under Arpad, Magyar soldiers ranged successfully into Italy as far as Milan and Pavia in 899, finally leaving upon receiving sufficient bribes. The Magyars fought in much the same style as the Huns and were precursors to the Mongol invasion of Europe. Employing mostly light cavalry and archers, they avoided close contact with their enemies, harassing them into exhaustion and then exploiting any openings. The heavy cavalry developed in Europe at this time did not succeed against the Magyars at first, but the Europeans eventually adopted some of the Eastern tactics and began to have more success.

By 907, Magyar interest in Germany forced their rivals into defensive cooperation. Luitpold of Bavaria allied with Ditmar, the archbishop of Salzburg, but their efforts proved futile when the Magyars defeated them at Presburg. In the 920s the Magyars raided as far as the Champagne region of France, again into northern Italy, and as far as the Pyrenees. The Magyars created as much terror as the Vikings from the north, but the Germanic nobles soon began to prevail. Henry the Fowler defeated the Magyars in 933 at Merseburg, inflicting 36,000 casualties. He and his successors began fortifying the frontier, which lessened the frequency of the Magyar raids,

and Bavarians began to raid Magyar lands. In 954, up to 100,000 Magyars attacked deep into Germany and France, taking advantage of the revolt of Lorraine against Otto the Great, Henry's son. They made a huge pillaging sweep through France and into northern Italy and back to the Danube Valley, but Otto defeated them the following year at Lechfeld; after that, the Magyars were on the decline.

At home in Hungary, they settled down to a more stable and civilized lifestyle under the leadership of Duke Geyza in the 970s. Christianity replaced their Asiatic animistic and totemic beliefs, and they began showing a toleration and acceptance of other cultures. King Stephen (997–1038) defended his homeland from takeover by the Holy Roman Empire and acquired authority from the pope over a national church. Stephen oversaw the construction of monasteries and cathedrals, and for his efforts and example was later canonized. The Magyar language became, and remains, the official language of Hungary; but for the battle at Lechfeld, it might have become the language of much of western Europe. For all their terrorism of the West, the Hungarians nevertheless defended western Europe from the Ottoman Turks as they fought to bring down the Byzantine Empire and expand the Muslim faith into Europe.

*See also* Bulgars [37]; Byzantine Empire [38]; Carolingian Dynasty [39]; Europe, Mongol Invasion of [44]; Huns [51]; Ottoman Empire [102].

References: Bartha, Antal, *Hungarian Society in the 9th and 10th Centuries*, trans. K. Baazs (Budapest: Akademiai Kiado, 1975); Macartney, C. A., *The Magyars in the Ninth Century* (Cambridge: Cambridge University Press, 1968); Vambery, Arminius, *Hungary in Ancient, Medieval, and Modern Times* (Hallandale, FL: New World Books, 1972).

## 64     MALI, EXPANSION OF

By the beginning of the thirteenth century, the large gold-producing nation of Ghana had lost its power. Islamic attack by the nomadic Almoravids from the Sahara had devastated Ghana's main trading centers, and tribes previously under Ghana's dominance began to exert their independence. The Soso tribe was influential for a few decades, but ultimately they fell to the growing power of Mali.

Sundiata, leader of the Malinke clan of Mali, came to power in 1230. The Malinke were originally pagan, but saw the economic potential of Islam. Embracing the faith would not only give them equality with Arabic traders, it would also lessen the chance of being attacked by aggressive Muslims such as the Almoravids. Thus, Malian traders spread Islam in their travels. Also, Sundiata and his successor *mansas,* or emperors, attempted to impose military dominance in order to maintain peace on their own terms, a peace that would be beneficial to trade. The empire of Mali claimed descent from Muslim roots, as did most of the West African nations that embraced the religion. Most claimed descent from white forebears, but Mali claimed negroid descent: Bilali Bunama (Bilal ibn Rabah in Arabic) was Muhammad's first muezzin, and his grandson supposedly settled in the territory that became Mali, establishing power from the Niger to the Sankarani River.

Sundiata was the earliest recorded leader, using military ability to bring area tribes under his direction and establish a capital city at Niani on the Niger River. Niani was well placed for defense and trade, amidst good farmland and iron deposits. As the Mali came to control territory previously dominated by Ghana, they grew in influence and replaced Ghana as the main producer and distributor of gold.

A succession of leaders of irregular quality managed to maintain dominance in the area, but the strongest and best known, Mansa Musa, emerged in 1312. His 25-year tenure was widely reported and praised by contemporary Muslim writers. He became famous for making the pilgrimage to Mecca in 1324 and spending incredible amounts of gold along the way. He also extended the power of the empire by bringing the town of Timbuktu under Mali's control, turning it into the major trade and intellectual center it would remain for generations. Mansa Musa was followed by Mansa Sulayman, who maintained strong contracts with powers as far away as Morocco.

Under the strong leadership of Sundiata and Musa, Mali extended its influence from the Niger River in the east to the Atlantic Ocean in the west. Its power was based on cooperation of vassal kings and chieftains rather than on military control, apparently sufficient to maintain a peaceful and profitable empire. However, after Mansa Musa's reign, a series of weaker kings and internal power struggles brought a lack of direction at the top, and former vassals began to break away from the empire. In the 1400s, Berbers from the north conquered the upper reaches of Mali's empire, and the trade centers of Timbuktu and Walata fell under nomadic control. Malian emperors lost their power to internal dissent and the rising power of Songhay to the west.

*See also* Ghana, Almoravid Invasion of [48]; Songhay, Expansion of [74].

References: Hiskett, M., and Nehemia Levtzion, *Ancient Ghana and Mali* (London: Methuen, 1973); Oliver, Roland,

*A Short History of Africa* (New York: New York University Press, 1962); Trimingham, John, *A History of Islam in West Africa* (London: Oxford University Press, 1970).

## MEXICO, AZTEC CONQUEST OF

**65**

Much of Central America was dominated by the Toltec peoples until their dissolution about A.D. 1200. The power vacuum that followed coincided with the arrival of nomadic tribes from the north. One tribe came to be known as Aztecs, or People from Aztlan. They drifted into the valley of central Mexico and became subject to whichever power was able to achieve temporary hegemony. The Aztecs ultimately settled on the western side of Lake Texcoco, where they adapted themselves to the already established practice of building "floating gardens" of built-up silt. They established the city of Tenochtitlán in the mid-fourteenth century; a second city, Tlatelolco, was built by a second Aztec faction. The two cities put themselves under the protection of rival powers: Tenochtitlán under Culhuacan, Tlatelolco under the Tepanecs.

Through the latter part of the fourteenth century, the Tepanecs dominated the valley, and they expanded their power across the mountains to the west to encompass an area of perhaps 50,000 square kilometers. This consolidation was performed by the Tepanec king Tezozomoc, but after his death in 1423 the various city-states began to rebel. Three powers—one of them the Aztecs of Tenochtitlán—joined in a Triple Alliance to replace the Tepanecs. Despite the occasional disagreement, the three worked fairly well together and dominated central Mexico for 90 years. From 1431 to 1465 they consolidated their hold over the former Tepanec domain, then

began a period of expansion. The Aztecs became the dominant partner in the triumvirate, but the three tribes collectively spread the empire from the Atlantic to the Pacific and as far south as the modern-day border between Mexico and Guatemala. Only two tribes remained recalcitrant, and the Aztecs established garrisons along disputed borders. Though they occasionally warred with the Tlaxaltecs and the Tarascans, they never subjugated them.

The Aztecs led the expansion for a number of reasons. Primarily they wanted to expand their trading routes and incorporate a larger tax base among the conquered peoples. They also fought for religious reasons. The Aztecs worshipped, among others, the god of the sun, Huitzilopochtli. The Aztec religion taught that history moved in cycles, the end of which came with the destruction of the sun. To keep the god healthy and shining, he required sacrifices to eat, and the Aztecs went conquering for sacrificial offerings. The pyramids dominating the city of Tenochtitlán were large altars where prisoners of war were executed daily. On days of special celebration, several thousand would be sacrificed. This need for offerings drove the Aztecs to conquest, but did not encourage loyal subjects.

Once in control of their empire, the city of Tenochtitlán was expanded and beautified. The city reached a population of perhaps 200,000, possibly one-fifth of the Aztec population; the total number of subject peoples is estimated to have taken the empire's population as high as 6 million. The capital city was laid out in logical order with straight streets and many canals, along which trade moved by boat. When Montezuma II came to power in 1502, the Aztec empire was well established, and he was responsible for much of the city's lavish architecture and decoration. Their sister-city, Tlatelolco, which they took under their control in 1475, became a commercial center with the largest market in Central America. The Spaniards under Hernán Cortés estimated that 60,000 people attended the market days.

The constant need for sacrificial victims created a resentment among all the subject peoples, and when the Spaniards arrived they were easily able to gain allies to assist in their attacks on the Aztec Empire. Though the Aztecs were in many ways more advanced than the Europeans, they lacked the necessary weaponry and resistance to foreign diseases to defeat their invaders. They had created outstanding works of art and developed an extensive hieroglyphic writing system, but their scientific knowledge was limited. Even without the arrival of the Spaniards, it is questionable how much longer the tribes of Central America would have accepted the military dominance and religious practices of the Aztecs.

See also Cortés, Hernán [91]; Western Hemisphere, Spanish Occupation of [110].

References: Berdan, Frances, *The Aztecs of Central Mexico* (New York: Holt, Rinehart & Winston, 1982); Carrasco, David, *Moctezuma's Mexico* (Niwot: University Press of Colorado, 1992); Henderson, Keith, *The Fall of the Aztec Empire* (Denver: Denver Museum of Natural History, 1993).

## MIDDLE EAST, MONGOL INVASION OF THE

**66**

In 1219 the Mongols under Genghis Khan had spread their influence as far as the Caspian Sea. The shah of Khwarezm offended the Great Khan by declining to extradite one of his governors for the death of two Mongol merchants. His refusal provoked an invasion and the destruction of Khwarezm, and led to the Mongol onslaught of the Middle East. Four Mongol armies engaged in the punishment: Genghis led one army that burned Bokhara, Samarkand, and Balkh; his son Juchi defeated the shah's forces at Jand, reportedly killing 160,000 men in the victory; another son, Jagatai, captured and sacked Otrar; yet another son, Tule, led 70,000 men through Khorasan and pillaged everywhere he went. All the armies proceeded undefeated, capturing and despoiling Merv, Nishapur, Rayy, and Herat.

Genghis returned to Mongolia, but the steppe horsemen stayed. After Genghis's death his successor, Ogadai, sent 300,000 men to put down a rebellion launched by Jalal ud-Din. Ogadai was victorious at Diarbekr in northern Persia, and in the wake of their victory, the Mongols proceeded to pillage Armenia, Georgia, and Upper Mesopotamia. In 1234, Genghis's grandson Hulagu led a force into Iran to defeat the Assassins at Alamut, then turned his men toward Baghdad. Though Hulagu was a Buddhist, his primary wife was a Christian, and he carried on his grandfather's policy of religious toleration. Therefore, his attack on Baghdad was intent on conquest, not religious persecution.

Hulagu drew on the assistance of troops from the Golden Horde to capture Baghdad. Caliph Al-Mustasim Billah refused to offer allegiance to Hulagu; he also failed to heed his generals' warnings to strengthen the city's weakened walls and military. The caliph depended on his position to draw sufficient defensive manpower, but that prestige had long ago faded. He was forced to choose between the Mongols and the Mamluks, slave-soldiers who had come to power in Egypt and whom he had long scorned. Too late he looked to his city's defenses; in 1258 the Mongols breached the walls and spent eight days sacking the city. Baghdad lost most of its several hundred thousand inhabitants, plus its libraries, universities, mosques, and treasures. Never again would it serve as the intellectual capital of Islam.

The destruction of Baghdad had a religious significance Hulagu never intended. On the one hand, his Christian wife urged him to ally himself with the Crusaders based in Syria. On the other hand, his relative Birkai, chief of the Golden Horde, had converted to Islam and refused to aid him any longer; indeed, he offered aid to the Mamluks of Egypt in an Islamic coalition. With Crusader assistance, Hulagu took Aleppo and Damascus and was aiming for Jerusalem when news came to him that changed the fate of the Middle East. The Great Khan Mangku had died, and it was Hulagu's duty to return to Mongolia. Though advised to the contrary by his wife, generals, and the Crusaders, Hulagu left for home. He left behind a contingent under Kit-Boga.

In Egypt, the new sultan, Kotuz, and his brilliant general, Baibars, had been preparing for battle. They took advantage of Hulagu's withdrawal and marched toward Syria. Kit-Boga advanced to meet them and the two forces converged on the Plains of Esdraelon at Ain Jalut (Goliath's Well). The outnumbered Mongols fell to Baibars's Mamluks, who used Mongol tactics to defeat the invaders. Hulagu decided to turn around and avenge Kit-Boga's death, but the Golden Horde now presented a threat to his rear. He marched into Russia instead, surprising his kinsmen at the River Terek in the winter of 1262. The two forces fought each other almost to exhaustion, but neither was able to gain the upper hand. Hulagu retreated to Persia and hoped to rekindle his alliance with the Crusaders, but his death in 1264 ended that plan. His son Abaka marched for Egypt in 1281, but was met in Syria and defeated by Kalawun, Baibars's successor, at the battle of Homs. The Mongols

retreated across the Euphrates and established the dynasty of the Il-khans.

Hulagu's descendants ruled in Persia and Mesopotamia until 1337. The greatest of his successors was Ghazan Khan, who broke with the Great Khan Kubilai of China. He established the capital of his independent state at Tabriz, where he received envoys from as far away as Spain and England. He ruled wisely and well, stabilizing the currency, protecting the peasants, and building the city into a showpiece that rivaled Baghdad. He built mosques (the Il-khans converted to Islam in 1294), schools, an observatory, a library, and a hospital, then set aside the tax revenues from certain pieces of land to finance these institutions. Travelers passing through Tabriz (including Marco Polo) noted its magnificence, and some estimated its population to be 1 million. Ghazan's brother Uljaitu followed as leader of the Il-khans and patron of the arts and sciences. Literature, art, and architecture reached new heights during his reign. His successor, Abu Sa'id, proved to be the last ruler of a short-lived dynasty. After his death in 1335, factional fighting weakened the regime, making it easy prey for Tamurlane's forces in 1381.

The Mongol invasion of the Middle East was relatively short, the actual fighting taking place over approximately four decades. It proved decisive in confirming the Muslims as the dominant influence in the region, because the Mongols and Crusaders never cooperated as fully as they might have. Kit-Boga's defeat at Goliath's Well, though a relatively small battle in itself, proved to be the Middle Eastern version of the Muslim defeat at Poitiers. Just as Christian Europe had held back the forces of Islam, so Muslim Egypt turned away the forces that could have ended their hold on the Middle East, possibly driving them back to the deserts of Arabia and the Sahara. The Mongols exercised the well-known tactics of destruction and terror, killing hundreds of thousands of people and destroying much of Islam's literature and scientific writings, though the Il-khans strove to renew that intellectual atmosphere during their short dynasty.

*See also* Genghis Khan [47]; Russia, Mongol Conquest of [71]; Tamurlane [76].

References: Allsen, Thomas, *Mongol Imperialism* (Berkeley: University of California Press, 1987); Chambers, James, *The Devil's Horsemen* (New York: Atheneum, 1979); Lamb, Harold, *The March of the Barbarians* (New York: Literary Guild, 1940).

## 67    MIDDLE EAST, MUSLIM CONQUEST OF THE

Muhammad led his followers to control of the cities of Mecca and Medina, which in turn dominated the area known as the Hejaz, along the Red Sea's eastern coast. His charisma held the faithful together, but at his death, many of the Arab tribes who had followed him proved to be less than faithful. Without a clear successor, the tribes fell back into their independent raiding ways. When Abu-Bakr rose to the position of caliph, the successor to Muhammad's political power, he embarked on a war to force the tribes back under one banner. Abu-Bakr knew that the ways of the Bedouin—raiding and plunder—must be rechanneled because Islam forbade fighting among believers. Therefore, they must find nonbelievers to attack.

Abu-Bakr challenged the authority of the Byzantine Empire in Palestine. He sent his best general, Khalid, on raiding parties that ultimately joined together to defeat a larger Byzantine force at Ajnadain between Jerusalem and Gaza on 30 July 634.

Abu-Bakr's successor, Umar (Omar, 634–644), captured Jerusalem. He then sent forces in all directions to challenge both Constantinople's power and that of the Sassanid dynasty of Persia. Again Khalid was successful, taking Damascus by treachery in 635 and occupying Emesa (modern Homs) by the end of that year. He ceded the city back to a 50,000-man Byzantine army the following spring, then outmaneuvered and annihilated them in August 636. The Byzantine forces, though twice the size of Khalid's, had to deal with a hostile population made angry by years of taxation and religious persecution. Though not Muslim themselves, the people welcomed the invaders as liberators from the repression of Constantinople. Coupled with the fact that the Byzantine Empire had been fighting itself to exhaustion against the Sassanid Persians, that made them fall an easy prey.

The Sassanids were just as disliked among their subject peoples, and the Muslim invasion brought about that dynasty's swift downfall. They lost their first battle to Muslim invaders in the autumn of 635, and within two years the Muslim forces controlled the Persian capital at Ctesiphon, then Mesopotamia and Irak. The eastern Muslim forces under Said ibn Wakkas drove farther, taking the ancient Persian capital of Ecbatana in 641, controlling the Persian Gulf by 645, and occupying Khorasan by 652.

At the same time, a third Muslim force, under Amr ibn al-As, captured Egypt. Amr defeated the Byzantine defenders at Heliopolis in 640 and received Alexandria's surrender on terms in 642. To give themselves a buffer zone, the Muslims spread through Cyrenaica along the Mediterranean coast. Several decades later, the Muslims pushed farther along the coast, capturing Carthage in 695 and bringing to an end the last of Roman influence in

North Africa. Alliances with the local Berber tribes gave them the impetus to reach the Atlantic and turn north into Europe.

These events occurred during the Umayyid dynasty, which lasted until 750. The ultimate goal of the Muslims was not the plunder of nonbelievers (though they certainly did not ignore it), but the capture of Constantinople itself—a dream this dynasty, and others, would not live to see. Umar's successor, Uthman (Oth-man, 644–656), tried it first in 655. His early naval success came to naught when he was assassinated a year later. After some factional struggles among the Muslim leadership, which included an armistice while the question of succession was argued, the Umayyids returned under Muawiya in 668. He crossed into Thrace and attacked from the landward side, but did not lay siege. An attempt to force the straits and control the Bosporus failed in 677; afterward, Constantinople suffered only intermittent raiding, though the reach of the Byzantine Empire was much diminished. Caliph Walid tried again in 715, by which time Muslim armies had reached India and the borders of China. He died in the attempt, and the next caliph, Suleiman, did not succeed either. After a year-long siege, the Muslims were defeated by Byzantine naval forces at sea and by Bulgar allies operating in the Balkans. That, and the threat of Franks arriving from farther west, convinced Suleiman to withdraw. A storm wrecked the remains of his fleet, and Muslim sea power was destroyed; their troop losses are estimated at 170,000. The Byzantine emperor Leo III saved eastern Europe from Muslim domination and, after another victory in 739, regained control of western Asia Minor. This stand, coupled with the defeat of the Muslims at Tours in France in 732, kept Europe Christian.

For a few centuries the Muslims consolidated their hold rather than extend it, other than the occasional independent action such as the entry into India. In all their Middle East conquests, they benefited from a weakening of their rivals' military power as well as the aid rendered by disgruntled subjects. The Muslims had a reputation as conquerors forcing their faith on the defeated, but this happened only occasionally. For the most part, Muslim rulers followed Muhammad's dictates to respect the rights of other faiths. The levying of a tax on nonbelievers, however, encouraged many of the poor to convert and began the long history of Islamic faith in that part of the world. Also, the Arabic language became widely used, replacing the Koine Greek or Aramaic spoken for centuries. The Muslims fought among themselves for centuries over Muhammad's true successor, and to this day various factions, most notably the Shi'ites and Sunnis, claim authority from one or another of the original converts or family members. Occasional conquerors would pass through the Middle East in centuries to come, but none was able to dissuade the inhabitants from their adopted religion. Islam's homeland may not always have been militarily secure, but no one was able to shake the security of their faith.

*See also* Byzantine Empire [38]; India, Muslim Invasion of [53]; Middle East, Mongol Invasion of the [66]; Spain, Muslim Conquest of [75]; Tamurlane [76].

References: Armstrong, Karen, *Holy War* (New York: Macmillan, 1988); Koprulu, Mehmed Fuad, *Islam in Turkey after the Turkish Invasion* (Salt Lake City: University of Utah Press, 1993); Serjeant, R. B., *Studies in Arabian History and Civilisation* (London: Variorum Reprints, 1981).

## MING DYNASTY

Under the Yuan dynasty the Mongols ruled China and established extensive contacts with the West. Trade along the Silk Road was brisk, and Christian monks traveled to spread their faith. They found a rich culture that the Mongols had appropriated for themselves, but one that they never completely assimilated. After the death of the great Kubilai Khan in 1297, no other leader could match his ability, and the dynasty weakened. In the middle 1300s, a group called the Red Turbans attacked the Mongols. That assault, coupled with decades of mistreatment of the Chinese peasants, led to a peasant rebellion that ultimately overthrew the Mongols. The leader of this rebellion and the first emperor of the newly established Ming dynasty was Chu Yuanchang, a former Buddhist novice.

Chu established the capital of the new dynasty at Nanjing in 1368. Despite his early Buddhist training, Chu was a ruthless emperor who strove to reestablish Chinese traditions in the wake of Mongol rule. He also set about reestablishing China's suzerainty over its neighbors. Within ten years the Chinese court was receiving tribute from Okinawa, Borneo, the Malay Peninsula, Java, and the Indian coast, and they had set up trade contacts with those countries plus Japan and the Middle East.

The next Ming emperor of note was Yong Le. He not only maintained China's military position, but extended the empire's strength to include a powerful navy. Between 1405 and 1433, Admiral Zheng He, a eunuch of Muslim descent, led seven expeditions that reached as far as Persia, Arabia, and eastern Africa. The fleet grew to 62 ships and as many as 28,000 men, and they were a feared organization throughout the China Sea and the Indian Ocean. Their captains demonstrated organizational and navigational skills not matched until the arrival of the Portuguese in the 1500s.

The Chinese military was used mainly to protect the borders and enforce the will of the emperors upon their subjects. Chu persecuted the remaining Mongols in China and forced them to marry Chinese people rather than their own, for he would not allow purely foreign groups to exist and create trouble from within. After total control was established, arts and culture once again began to flourish, financed by the income from the far-flung Chinese traders. The famous Ming porcelains were developed in this era, and the construction of palaces in Nanjing, and later Beijing, reflected the Ming desire to reassert Chinese culture. Science and technology had few advances, but literature and philosophy experienced a renaissance.

The later Ming rulers proved less and less capable. The growing power of the Jurchen and Manchu tribes in the northeast threatened those frontiers, while peasant uprisings in the northwest kept the army busy in that sector. A Japanese invasion of Korea in the 1590s brought Chinese armies into Manchuria, where they were weakened in a victorious war that forced a Japanese withdrawal. The Manchus now had the impetus to conquer Korea and, with their rear protected, make war against the Ming. The cost of war could not be paid because the peasant taxpayers were in revolt, so Ming power slipped. The final Ming emperor hanged himself in 1644, and the invaders established the Ching (Manchu) dynasty.

*See also* Ching (Manchu) Dynasty [90]; Kubilai Khan [61].

References: Hucker, Charles, *The Ming Dynasty: Its Origins and Evolving Institutions* (Ann Arbor: University of Michigan Press, 1978); Spence, Jonathan, ed.,

*From Ming to Ching* (New Haven, CT: Yale University Press, 1979); Tong, James, *Disorder under Heaven* (Stanford, CA: Stanford University Press, 1991).

## 69            OSTROGOTHS

The Goths were a Germanic tribe who possibly came from Sweden in the early centuries A.D. By the third century, they had come into contact with the Roman Empire and often clashed with Roman armies on the northern and northeastern frontiers. They arrived in the region of the lower Danube River, and from there plundered the Balkans and Greece. At the height of their powers they controlled the lands from the Black Sea to the Baltic Sea. In about A.D. 370, the Goths split into two nations: The eastern Ostrogoths were based in the Black Sea area into modern Ukraine and Byelorussia, while the western Visigoths inhabited the Danube Valley.

The Ostrogoths were among the first in Europe to feel the wrath of the Huns. By force or circumstance, they fought alongside the Huns, especially Attila, during the Hunnish invasion of Gaul in 451. They were obliged to fight their Visigothic kinsmen, who were allied with Rome, but after the Hun defeat at Chalons, the Ostrogoths exerted their independence. They agreed with the Roman Empire to settle into Pannonia, an area roughly equivalent to parts of modern Austria, Hungary, and Slovenia. While settled here, the greatest of the Ostrogothic kings came to power: Theodoric. He allied his people with the Eastern Roman Empire, especially the emperor Zeno, and with Constantinople's support, the Ostrogoths invaded Italy in 488. The Ostrogoths defeated Odoacer, the first Germanic ruler of Italy, in a number of battles. They finally captured Odoacer's capital at Ravenna, after which Theodoric murdered him and took his place as ruler of Italy.

Though he was not officially given the title of Western Roman Emperor, Theodoric surely exercised the power of an emperor. Under his rule of 33 years, the Gothic kingdom in Italy recovered much of its lost productivity and culture. Raised in captivity in Constantinople, Theodoric appreciated the finer points of Roman culture and brought Roman ways to his people. He practiced Arian Christianity, considered heresy by both the Roman church and the Eastern church, but he was tolerant of all beliefs in his realm. Roman law was the basis of the Italian state, but traditional Gothic laws also applied to Goths in Italy. Theodoric's rule was peaceful and progressive, but his death in 526 marked the beginning of the decline of the Ostrogoths. The growing military power, ambition, and religious intolerance of Emperor Justinian in Constantinople spelled doom for Gothic peace. Eastern Empire armies under the command of Belisarius destroyed the power of the Ostrogoths, and they finally broke apart and were absorbed by other tribes who established power in northern Italy, mainly the Franks and Burgundians. They absorbed more Roman culture than imparted characteristics of their own, so little of Gothic society remained after their demise.

*See also* Huns [51]; Justinian [58]; Visigoths [81].

References: Cunliffe, Barry, *Rome and Her Empire* (London: Constable, 1994 [1978]); Heather, Peter, *Goths and Romans* (Oxford: Clarendon, 1991); Thompson, E. A., *Romans and Barbarians* (Madison: University of Wisconsin Press, 1982).

## RUSSIA, ESTABLISHMENT AND EXPANSION OF

Russia's first political foundations lay deep in myth. Vikings, or Varangians, had alternately traded and plundered through the area east of the Baltic coast since the middle 700s, occasionally staying long enough to establish settlements and exact tribute from local tribes. By the middle 800s they were forced out of the area of the upper Volga and Neva rivers by the Slavic tribes they had once subdued. According to the traditions of the *Russian Chronicle*, the tribes fought among themselves until they jointly agreed to bring in an outside ruler. They asked the Swedish tribe of Rus, or Rhos, to rule over the tribes and protect them from their enemies. The family of Rurik accepted and, with his two brothers, Rurik moved the Rus tribe to the Neva River area. He established himself in Novgorod in 862, placing his brothers in charge of Beloozero and Izborsk. When they died, Rurik took control over the entire area, and his descendants ruled for generations. From them comes the title Russia.

Being Vikings, the Rus continued their practice of trading and plundering, at the same time defending their new subjects from the Bulgars and the Khazars, who lived above the Caspian Sea between the Volga and Dnieper rivers. At times the Russians grew strong or bold enough to approach Constantinople, sometimes in peace and other times as invaders. They made little progress in their military expeditions against the Byzantine Empire, but they succeeded in carrying on a profitable trade in their more peaceful endeavors. They also managed to successfully defend their territory from invaders, both the aggressive Khazars and the raiding Petchenegs, and they man-

aged to completely drive the Bulgars from their frontiers into eastern Europe. It remains debatable just how well the Russians were organized at this time; some say they had established a state, others that they were merely a strong group of warrior chiefs under the leadership of an overlord. The latter seems more likely.

The matter of defense probably took the Rus from their original base at Novgorod to Kiev. The *Chronicle* relates that two of Rurik's subordinates, Askold and Dir, captured Kiev from Slavic tribes to expand both their defensive perimeter and trade routes. It seems likely that, in the wake of the collapse of the Khazars in the eleventh century and the arrival of the Pechenegs from farther east, the Slavic tribes came together under Rus leadership to provide a more solid defensive stance. For three centuries Kiev played the key role of defensive outpost and vital trading center on the route to Constantinople. Through the 900s the Rus had a trade agreement with Byzantium, but they also sent a number of military expeditions against Constantinople as well, maintaining the seemingly traditional Viking link between trade and plunder. In the meanwhile, the Rus dominated the Slavic tribes, forcing them either into slavery or to the status of tributary, the main tribute being paid in kind or in Arabic coinage. Sometime in the tenth century the Russians embraced the Eastern Orthodox faith; it was named the state religion by Vladimir I (978–1015), who was later sanctified.

Throughout the tenth century, Kiev was the dominant city-state, if not the capital of a political entity. From there the "Grand Duke" held sway over the other dukes, or governors, who usually were his younger relatives. Thus, what passed for a Russian state was actually a large feudal arrangement based on the oldest male controlling

Kiev and the others granting him the highest status.

Early in the eleventh century, feuding between successors brought about the end of Kiev's preeminent position. The Rus split into two more or less equal "states" along either side of the Dnieper, then were rejoined in 1035 under Yaroslav I. Yaroslav made war against the Finns, Poles, and Pechenegs, and mounted the last (disastrous) expedition against Constantinople. On his deathbed, he willed the land of the Rus to his five sons and a grandson, directing them to aid one another and follow the lead of the eldest son in Kiev. Rather than continue the rule from Kiev as Yaroslav had hoped, the brothers took a series of actions to break away from Kiev's domination. Over the next several decades the territories given to the sons became separate entities, often at odds with one another. By 1097 they were held together by a loose confederation bound together only by promises to defend their lands from outside threats.

Yaroslav was the last of the strong Russian leaders until the rise of Ivan the Great in the mid-1400s. He was an effective ruler who codified Slavic law, built numerous churches, and sponsored the translation of religious literature from Greek to Slavic. He also established ties with western Europe by giving his daughter in marriage to King Henry I of France. Though the Rus had expanded from a Scandinavian tribe to an important population stretching from the Baltic to the Black seas, Yaroslav's legacy was the destruction of the feudal system holding the Russians in a somewhat unified culture into one of squabbling brothers and cousins who failed to defend their homeland from Pecheneg and Cuman nomadic raiders from the steppes and from the ultimate conquerors from the east, the Mongols.

See also Byzantine Empire [38]; Russia, Mongol Conquest of [71].

References: Carmichael, Joel, A History of Russia (New York: Hippocrene Books, 1990); Chirovsky, Nicholas, A History of the Russian Empire (New York: Philosophical Library, 1973); Florinsky, Michael, Russia: A History and an Interpretation (New York: Macmillan, 1947).

## RUSSIA, MONGOL CONQUEST OF

71

During the time of Genghis Khan, his general Subedai rode westward on a reconnaissance in force to scout the steppes of southern Russia. Subedai and Jebe Noyan, another general, roamed over the vast plains west of the Volga, searching for possible invasion routes and testing the mettle of the inhabitants. Their main opponent was the Cumans, Turkic-Mongols who had moved to the area from central Asia some centuries before. The Cumans had established themselves as bandits and pillagers throughout the area north of the Black Sea, making themselves enemies of the Russian principalities. Only after the Cumans had been sorely defeated and forced to retreat into Russian lands did the Russian princes reluctantly join with them to resist the Mongols, or Tartars (Tatars), as the Russians called them. In 1223 the combined Russo-Cuman force was defeated at the Kalka River along the northern shore of the Black Sea, but the Mongols did not follow up on their victory; instead, they joined with Genghis's son Jochi, and returned to report to their leader. The invasion seemed like a bad dream to the Russians, who prayed that the Mongols would prove to be no more than passing raiders.

After attacking and destroying the Bulgars at the junction of the Volga and Kama rivers in 1236, the Mongols returned to the trans-Volga steppes. This time they came not as raiders but as invaders, because the entire tribe of Genghis's heir Batu migrated into the area. It is questionable whether any Russian defensive measures could have halted the Mongol onslaught, but it certainly could not be stopped by the divided, squabbling nobles who inhabited the Russian principalities.

Batu's invasion was made easier by the inability of the princes to cooperate. The Mongols crossed the Volga in late 1237 and entered the state of Riazan. They made their way easily across the territory, capturing land and burning cities. By 1239 they had defeated the major noble in the area, Yuri of Vladimir, and seemed to be taking aim at the city of Novgorod. Instead, they turned back onto their invasion path and moved southeast to the territory of the Cumans, whom they again defeated and now drove into Hungary. With a secure flank on the Black Sea, the Mongols drove on to Kiev, capturing the city in December 1240. The Russian princes would not cooperate, even with much of their land under foreign control, so Batu drove his forces into Poland and Hungary. He returned to Russia in 1241, possibly on news of the death of Ogadai, the Great Khan who succeeded Genghis.

Batu settled into Russia, creating what came to be known as the Khanate of the Golden Horde. He established the city of Sarai as his capital, and for the next 200 years the Mongols dominated Russia. The princes of Russia became his vassals, and none could rule without Mongol permission. The settling of the Mongols into one place, however, diminished their traditional warlike manner, and they soon began to act more like the Russian nobles, arguing over succession and wealth. The Russian princes, bound by their oaths to provide taxes for the Mongol overlords, soon got the job of collecting it themselves; they jockeyed for favor in the Mongol court by promising higher tax revenues in return for political appointments. Of course, this meant more suffering for the peasants paying the taxes to keep their prince in the good graces of the Mongols. The Russians paid nominal service to the Mongols, occasionally revolting but always finding a Mongol army in response. Between 1236 and 1462, the Mongols made 48 military expeditions into Russian lands, either to put down rebellions or to aid one Russian faction vying with another. In all that time, only once did the Russians score a major victory.

In the mid-thirteenth century, the Golden Horde assisted some of its Mongol brethren in an assault on the Islamic Middle East. Genghis's grandson Hulagu led his forces against the Muslims in Mesopotamia, capturing and sacking Baghdad in 1258. He killed most of the city's inhabitants and destroyed its mosques and libraries, bringing to an end Baghdad's reign as the intellectual capital of Islam. His treatment of the caliph, however, offended the Golden Horde's Muslim ruler, Birkai. He withdrew his support and, after Hulagu had allied himself with the Crusader armies, Birkai offered an alliance to the Mamluks defending Syria and Egypt. That threat to Hulagu's rear while facing Muslim forces under the brilliant general Baibars gave Hulagu too many enemies. After the defeat of one of his contingents by the Mamluks, Hulagu retreated across the Euphrates and ended his quest for Egypt and his ties to his cousin in Sarai.

Ultimately bringing the Golden Horde to its demise was the fate suffered by so many conquerors: They lost their fighting edge by easy living and personal greed. They took advantage of their position to profit from the Asian trade with Europe, dealing in silks, carpets, and wine from Persia and China; furs from Russia; jewels from India; and their own horses and leather goods. After the Golden Horde broke from the control of Mongolia in the latter part of the fourteenth century, they spent much of their time on court intrigues. Other, more vigorous nomads wrought havoc on the sedentary Mongols when Tamurlane's invasion in 1395 destroyed the capital city of Sarai. The Golden Horde split into two factions in the middle 1400s, creating the Kazan Mongols along the upper Volga and the Crimean Mongols around the Black Sea. That split so dissipated the military power of the Mongols that Russians under the leadership of Muscovy finally defeated the Mongols and reestablished Russian independence.

*See also* Genghis Khan [47]; Middle East, Mongol Invasion of the [66]; Tamurlane [76].

References: Chambers, James, *The Devil's Horsemen* (New York: Atheneum, 1979); Florinsky, Michael, *Russia: A History and an Interpretation,* 2 vols. (Toronto: Collier-Macmillan Canada, 1947); Saunders, J. J., *The History of the Mongol Conquests* (New York: Barnes & Noble, 1971).

## 72 SCOTLAND, ENGLISH CONQUEST OF

Relations between the northern and southern neighbors of the island of Britain have always been tense. In 1138 and 1149, the king of Scotland tried to gain land at English expense, but in failing to do so lost to the English the province of Northumbria. The Scots tried to regain the land under William the Lionhearted in 1165 by aiding a rebellion against Henry II. That failed as well, and William was forced to sign the Treaty of Falaise, wherein Scotland swore loyalty to England. The Scots were released from that treaty in the reign of Richard I,

who received in return 15,000 marks of silver, roughly equivalent to one-fifth of the annual English royal revenues.

Relative peace was kept for a century, but in the 1280s the Scots began chafing at English dominance. Alexander III of Scotland died in 1286, leaving his daughter as heir to the throne. When she died childless, the line came to an end and various claimants scrambled for the throne. Edward I of England stepped in to support the claim of John de Baliol, who was crowned in 1292. The country became divided: One group of nobles recognized English suzerainty, while another group, supported by the common people, resented English interference. After meeting constant demands to provide soldiers for wars against France, Baliol succumbed to the popular will in 1295 and allied Scotland with France, hoping to gain total Scottish independence. Again the Scots backed the losing side, and England's military occupied Scotland after the battle of Dunbar in 1296, annexing it to their own domain.

Soon Scottish forces under William Wallace rose up against the English, winning at Stirling Bridge in 1297 but losing the following year at Falkirk; Wallace was ultimately betrayed to the enemy. Robert Bruce came to the throne in 1307 and massed forces to break away from England's power. Edward I died en route to fight him, and Robert was able to consolidate his power throughout Scotland by 1314. In that year Edward II marched north to defeat at Bannockburn, and Scotland was freed from English overlordship. In 1328 Edward II of England signed the Treaty of Northampton, which recognized Scottish independence and Robert's throne.

Within five years there were challenges to the Scottish throne. John Baliol challenged David Bruce; John defeated David at Halidon Hill with the aid of England's Edward III. Many Scots rejected John for dealing so freely with the English, and two decades of unrest followed, with the French covertly aiding David's supporters. David invaded England in 1346, but lost and was taken captive; he was ransomed in 1357 and ascended the Scottish throne, ruling until 1371.

The Bruce line ran out rather quickly, ending with Robert's grandson, and was followed by the Stuart line. The Scots fought among themselves and against the English for decades. In 1502 the two peoples tried to ease the tensions between them through marriage, and James IV married Henry VII's daughter Margaret the following year. This laid the groundwork for the union of the two nations under one monarch, but not as the English intended. When Elizabeth I died childless in 1603, James VI of Scotland was the closest blood relative, and he ascended the throne of England, taking the name James I. Relations between the two nations grew somewhat closer, but both operated separate governments. James's son Charles I, however, returned the two peoples to hostility by taking stands more to the liking of the English than the Scots. Scottish soldiers were ordered into combat in Europe during the Thirty Years' War at Charles's behest. He also alienated Parliament, which overthrew him in a civil war, bringing Oliver Cromwell to power in London. Cromwell exercised a tight rein on both English and Scottish subjects, and he temporarily united Scotland and England under one government. After his death, however, the new monarch, Charles II (another Stuart), could not keep the two countries together.

In 1707 the Scots finally agreed to join with England. They had accepted the kingship of William III of England, who reigned as William II of Scotland, 19 years earlier. For some years Scotland had suffered from severe weather and poor harvests, causing thousands of deaths, which was perhaps the last straw that broke the will to independence. The two nations signed the Act of Union, which allowed the Scots to maintain local laws and church policies, plus have members in both houses in Parliament, and the Scots also received equal trading rights. Under one crown since 1603, the two countries now came under one government.

Two fairly serious attempts were later made to exert Scottish dominance. With the aid of France, two Stuarts tried to restore their line. In 1715 the Jacobites failed to provide any successes for James Edward Stuart, and the death of Louis XIV in France ended any chance of worthwhile outside aid. In 1745 Prince Charles ("Bonny Prince Charlie") again tried to raise the Stuart standard and drew a fairly large number of Scottish supporters, but their defeat at Culloden in 1746 ended any further endeavors toward restoring Catholic Scottish rule.

Though it seemed a joining of equals in 1707, the English had almost always enjoyed the dominant position. They had been able to hold Scottish royalty hostage from time to time. For example, the first James Stuart was held by the British and sent to France; when he was later released, he had to pay 40,000 pounds sterling as the "cost of his education." The English also had long drawn on Scottish manpower for foreign wars, which weakened the ability of the northerners to rebel and laid for the London government the foundation of control. Scottish soldiers made a lot of history for the British Empire; a long-standing comment was, "There will always be an England (as long as you've got the Scots to do your fighting for you)." Even today the union has its critics, and a Scottish secessionist movement occasionally tries to return the northern country to its old status.

*See also* Thirty Years' War [108].

References: Lee, Maurice, *Road to Revolution: Scotland under Charles I* (Urbana: University of Illinois Press, 1985); Levack, Brian, *The Formation of the British State* (Oxford: Clarendon, 1987); McKenzie, W. M., *Outline of Scottish History* (London: Adam & Charles Black, 1907).

## 73        SCYTHIANS

Most of the information available on the Scythians comes from the pen of Herodotus (of whom one must often be leery) and from modern archaeology and anthropology. They were an Indo-European tribe who made their way from central Asia into southern Russia in the eighth and seventh centuries B.C., though some elements of their culture can be traced to Siberian tribes of the third millennium B.C. Centered in the steppes north of the Black Sea, they built an empire with an equally strong military and economic base. They inherited the territory from the Cimmerians and ultimately ceded it in the third century B.C. to the Sarmatians. All three cultures possibly were related; certainly they had many similarities. The Scythians fought the Cimmerians for 30 years before conquering them and taking their land.

The Scythians were fierce warriors whose organization in some ways presaged that of Genghis Khan. The king was the army's leader, and they were always prepared for battle. Most of their success came from their mastery of the horse, and their enemies usually could not match the Scythian mobility. The king provided ⌐ly food and clothing; all other pay in the form of booty, which the soldier could share in return for ⌐an enemy. They wore bronze Greek pattern and carried ⌐ bows with trefoil arrows.

At their greatest penetration into the Middle East, the Scythians reached Egypt, but mainly they were penned into the steppes by the Persians. They fought the Persian king Darius I in 513 B.C., and held off his invasion of southern Russia. However, they could not hold off the Sarmatians in the third century. The two peoples had been clashing for decades along the Asia frontier; the Scythian military finally was defeated, but their economic legacy remained.

Though a minority, the Scythians ruled a vast territory. Their location made them middlemen for trade from Asia into eastern Europe and the Middle East. Apparently they were able businessmen, because the graves of their aristocrats held artwork and weaponry of gold and other precious metals. The graves also held the dead man's wife, household servants, and horses. Two types of artwork were discovered in their tombs: animal subjects, which they made themselves, and Greek objects gained through trade. Steppe art traditionally deals with animal subjects, and the portrayal of two animals fighting was a popular theme. The artwork was rarely large, for their nomadic ways never left them, and their art was usually carved onto easily transportable items such as jewelry, weapons, and cups. The artwork in gold is regarded as excellent, and they also worked in wood, leather, bone, iron, and silver. The Scythians left a legacy of horsemanship, great warriors, well-stocked tombs, and fine artwork.

*See also* Genghis Khan [47].

References: Minns, Ellis, *Scythians and Greeks* (Cambridge: Cambridge University Press, 1913); Rostovtzeff, M., *Iranians and Greeks in Southern Russia* (New York: Russell & Russell, 1969); Tompkins, Stuart, *Russia through the Ages* (New York: Prentice-Hall, 1940).

## 74

SONGHAY, EXPANSION OF

The Songhay tribe apparently got started about A.D. 670 along the eastern banks of the Niger River, where they established the two main population centers of Gao and Koukia. The leading family was of Berber extraction, and their line ruled the Songhay into the 1300s. In 1005, the current king, Kossi, converted to Islam; about the same time, Gao became the capital city and the Songhay became a vassal to Mali. When Mali's Emperor Mansa Musa made his famous pilgrimage to Mecca in the 1320s, his return trip brought him through Gao, where he took two royal sons back to his capital as hostages. One of the boys escaped and returned to Songhay in 1335, taking the name Sonni, or savior. He established a new dynasty and began the resistance to Mali that ultimately brought independence for his people.

The rise of the Sonni dynasty coincided with the decline of Mali. When Mali's power slipped away in the late 1300s, the Songhay threw off their vassalage, but did not come into their own until the latter half of the 1400s. King Sonni Ali was the greatest ruler of his dynasty and brought Songhay to imperial power. He captured Timbuktu from the nomads in 1468 and invaded Mali's old empire with a strong military force based on a river fleet operating on the Niger. The major trading center of Jenne fell to Songhay forces in 1473, but little inland progress was made against the remains of Mali's people. Not until 1492, when Sonni Ali died, did Songhay troops make inroads into Mali's countryside. Under the leadership of Askia Muhammad al-Turi, founder of a new dynasty, an improved infantry became strong enough to break away from the river fleet and strike inland. Askia Muhammad drove along the northern frontier of the old empire, defeating the last of Mali's leaders and gaining vassals for himself. He dominated the old Ghanian empire and took control of the gold trade that had made the area rich and famous. Though kings of Mali remained in control of factions deep in the rugged countryside, they ultimately surrendered to reality and recognized Songhay's control, paying them tribute. After Askia Muhammad was overthrown by his son in 1528, a series of dynastic struggles ensued. Ultimately his grandsons Ishaq and Dawud ruled successfully from the 1530s to the 1580s.

The Askia dynasty embraced Islam much more strongly than the Sonnis. Askia Muhammad imported Muslim scholars to Gao, Timbuktu, and Jenne, and he continued to maintain Timbuktu as the intellectual center of western Africa. He used the vast wealth of the empire to support Muslim clerics and build mosques, but the majority of the peoples he dominated remained loyal to their local gods. Under Askia Dawud, the Songhay Empire reached its intellectual and economic zenith. Trade across the Sahara became of greater importance than ever before, and Dawud supported the arts and sciences with royal patronage.

The Songhay ultimately fell to invaders from the north. After fighting upstart tribes in the southern part of the empire as well as sending forces to engage Berbers in Morocco, the empire was defeated by Moroccans with firearms. The empire broke up quickly in the wake of this defeat in 1591. In a matter of just a few years, the Songhay were reduced to their original holdings around Gao.

See also Mali, Expansion of [64].

References: Levtsion, Nehemia, *Ancient Ghana and Mali* (London: Methuen, 1973); Trimingham, John, *The History of Islam in West Africa* (London: Oxford University Press, 1970).

## SPAIN, MUSLIM CONQUEST OF

**75**

One of the most distinctive invasions of history was that of the Moors upon the Iberian Peninsula. Its unusual aspect lay in the fact that it was a relatively peaceful invasion that permitted three distinct cultures—Christians, Muslims, and Jews—to coexist and flourish. The Arab occupation of Spain was not a preconceived plan of conquest; they were able to convince the natives of the many local tribes to surrender to attractive offers, which led to Arab control of three-fourths of Iberia for some 700 years.

It began during the seventh century when the Visigoth Empire in Spain suffered through a period of instability and rebellions, instigated by the sons of Visigothic king Witiza. During Witiza's reign (701–709), Arab forces of the caliphate had conquered northern Morocco and laid siege to Ceuta, the last Byzantine possession in the area. Julian, the imperial governor of Ceuta, sent his daughter Florinda to the court of Toledo to be educated. Unfortunately, she caught the eye of Witiza's successor, Don Rodrigo, who dishonored her. In retaliation, Julian ceded his control of the Ceuta to the Arabs and incited the Arab viceroy in North Africa, Musa ibn Nasair, to attack Spain and ally with Witiza's rebellious sons.

The Arab invasion began with a series of excursions by Tarik ibn Zair, the governor of Tangier. Under orders from the viceroy, he attacked across the Straits of Gibraltar in 710 with a force of 7,000 men, mostly Berbers. Reinforced by an additional 5,000 men, Tarik moved to Laguna de la Janda to await the arrival of Spanish forces under Don Rodrigo. On 19 July, Don Rodrigo was defeated and killed. Witiza's sons and supporters, who had withdrawn during the battle, now joined with Tarik and encouraged him to advance northward

to seize Toledo and Cordoba. In June 712, Musa crossed from Morocco with an army of 18,000 Arabs and captured Sevilla and Merida. Dispatching his son Abdul Aziz to the southwest, Musa joined forces with Tarik at Talavera, then took up residence in Toledo. In 714 he captured Zaragoza and, with Tarik, made an expedition into Leon and Galicia before returning to Damascus. After occupying Portugal, Abdul Aziz completed the conquest of Granada and Murcia.

On the whole, the invaders met with little opposition. The sons of Witiza and the other great Visigothic families, whether or not they converted to Islam, paid tribute in return for extensive domains. Freed from persecution, the Jews were eager allies, and the serfs gained a measure of freedom. Most of the population converted to Islam, and the converts, known as *Muwallads*, became active in the general Moorish population. The unconverted, called *Mozarabes*, suffered little discrimination and formed prosperous communities in the Muslim cities. Too few to colonize the country, the Arabs formed the administrative and military cadres in the Zaragoza region. The Berbers settled mainly in the central and mountainous regions, which resembled their native Atlas Mountains and favored their anarchic tendencies.

Viewed as a whole, the conquest was not a great calamity. In the beginning there was a period of anarchy, but the Arab government soon repressed racial and tribal discord. In many respects the Arab conquest was beneficial. It brought about an important social revolution and put an end to many of the ills that had engulfed the country under the Visigoths. The power of the privileged classes, the clergy, and the nobility was reduced and, by distributing confiscated lands to the population, a peasant proprietorship was established.

The conquest ameliorated the condition of the peasants; the Moors provided many of the Christian slaves and serfs with an easy path to freedom. They brought Iberia a comparatively advanced culture and new technologies, and introduced economically important crops and new agricultural techniques. Moorish culture influenced architectural styles and native music and dances, and ancient learning, preserved by the Arabs, was reintroduced to this part of Europe.

*See also* Visigoths [81].

References: Byng, Edward J., *The World of the Arabs* (Plainview, NY: Books for Libraries, 1974); Chejne, Anwar, *Muslim Spain: Its History and Culture* (Minneapolis: University of Minnesota Press, 1974); Glick, Thomas, *Islamic and Christian Spain in the early Middle Ages* (Princeton, NJ: Princeton University Press, 1979).

## 76 TAMURLANE

Timur, which translates as "iron," was born 8 April 1336 near the central Asian city of Samarkand, into the Turkic-speaking Muslim tribe of Barulas Mongols. Later, he became known as Timur-i-leng, or Timur the Lame (for an injury to his right leg sustained in a sheep-stealing raid); Tamurlane is the westernized pronunciation. Timur was illiterate, but he had an active interest in history. In later life he kept slaves to read to him and keep accounts of his campaigns.

By the age of 25, Timur had a following of several hundred men, a force with which he began his rise to power. He placed himself and his men under the direction of the ruler of Moghulistan, Tughlug-Timur. For his loyalty, Timur was soon promoted to regional governor of Samarkand. Upon Tughlug-Timur's death, Timur-i-leng took over as ruler of Transoxiana, the area east of the Aral Sea. He made Samarkand his capital, and over the years it benefited from the booty of his conquests.

Timur built a powerful military force of cavalry, infantry, and engineers. His standard tactic was to absorb the enemy's attack with his well-trained infantry, then exploit the confusion with his cavalry. Like Napoleon in the nineteenth century, he depended on vanguards and flanking units for scouting and for screening his movements. He also had no hesitation in marching his men great distances. He believed that campaigning over a wide area and attacking in random directions kept rivals from having time to establish themselves. He did not really care to absorb the peoples he defeated; he just plundered them. He calculated that a return campaign every few years would give an area time to recover economically without having the opportunity to build up militarily.

In 1381 Timur moved south and west toward Herat in Afghanistan, then advanced into territory covered by modern-day Iraq and Turkey. Having taken his fill of plunder there, he turned northward in 1384 to campaign against the Mongol Golden Horde occupying Russia. For four years he fought against Tokhtamysh, leader of the Golden Horde, defeating him and protecting his northern frontier. This so weakened the Golden Horde's power that Russia was able to arise into an independent state. In 1392 he began the "Five Years Campaign," during which he conquered Iran, then Baghdad, and moved northwest into the valley of the Don River north of the Black Sea. Rather than attack the rising nation of Russia, he reattacked the remains of the Golden Horde, capturing and pillaging Sarai and Astrakhan.

Timur turned toward India in 1398. Like most of his campaigns, this was for loot rather than conquest. He followed a force led by his grandson, who captured Multan across the Indus River. After Timur joined his forces to his grandson's, they attacked Delhi and razed the city. In 1399 he was out of India and on the campaign trail for his last operation. Covering much of the same ground as he had pillaged at the end of the Five Years Campaign, he drove southward through Georgia into eastern Turkey. He defeated the Ottoman sultan Bayezid I, after which he invaded Syria and closed out the year 1400 with the capture of Aleppo. The following season he took Damascus, then once again captured and looted Baghdad, murdering the inhabitants and destroying the city. After taking Smyrna in 1403, he turned for home. He stayed in Samarkand a short while before deciding to invade China, then under the Ming dynasty. Timur died on the road to China on 18 February 1405. His son and grandson succeeded him, creating the Timurid dynasty, but they lacked his talent and drive, and the clan came to an end within a hundred years.

Timur the Lame goes down in history as a masterful military leader who, unlike his forerunner Genghis Khan, lacked the necessary ability to rule. He is remembered as a cruel conqueror and for little else; hundreds of thousands of people died at his direction. His excesses in mistreating defeated soldiers (beheading, burying alive, etc.) made him a man to be feared, but never one to be respected. He left behind little but his reputation; only the expansion and beautification of Samarkand was a positive, lasting contribution to society. His grandson, Ulugh Beg, studied astronomy and oversaw the Timurid period of culture, but it was short-lived.

Timur's conquests had several side effects. His defeat of the Othman Turks in Anatolia hurt them, but did not keep them from rising to power. His campaigns past the Black Sea destroyed Venetian and Genoese trading centers, which spurred them toward maritime rather than overland trade routes, and they would dominate the Mediterranean as seamen. He also bypassed Moscow, leaving the inhabitants unharmed while defeating the Mongol Golden Horde that dominated the region, and the state of Russia was born.

See also Genghis Khan [47]; Napoleon Buonaparte [118]; Ottoman Empire [102]; Russia, Establishment and Expansion of [70]; Russia, Mongol Conquest of [71].

References: Lamb, Harold, *Tamurlane, the Earth Shaker* (New York: R. M. McBride, 1928); Manz, Beatrice, *The Rise and Rule of Tamurlane* (Cambridge: Cambridge University Press, 1989).

## 77 T'ANG DYNASTY

With the dissolution of the Sui dynasty in the early A.D. 600s, the T'ang, one of the rival factions struggling for power, finally rose to the top. The first in the T'ang line was Kaotsou. His son Lichiman was his chief general and did most of the conquering for the T'ang. Lichiman captured the capital city of Loyang and destroyed the Sui palace to prove that their dynasty had indeed come to an end; he then pensioned the Sui survivors. Lichiman went on to establish control over all of northern China and defeat a confederation of Turkic tribes on the eastern frontier. So successful was he that Kaotsou abdicated in 620 so Lichiman could rule. On taking the throne from his father, Lichiman took the royal name Taitsong.

Taitsong continued to fight, pacifying the entire Chinese realm by 624. He captured the king of the Tartars, forcing the barbarians to sue for peace. As usual, peace was fleeting, and Taitsong fought the nomads for years. In the first year of his reign, the Tartars attacked with 100,000 men and invaded almost to the capital city. Taitsong turned them away almost single-handedly. He met with the Tartars accompanied only by a small escort, shaming them, and convinced them to abide by the terms of the previous peace and return home.

Taitsong built a standing army of 900,000, placing one-third of them along the frontier and two-thirds behind them, creating not only a defense in depth, but a mobile reserve that could react to any crisis. This was China's first standing professional army, and Taitsong became a warrior-king, the first to do so voluntarily. He spent so much time on training and discipline that when his army went on their first campaign, again against the Tartars, the Chinese were so impressive that the nomads gave up without a fight. At this point he named himself Khan of the Tartars and took the power to regulate their affairs. This action brought Chinese control into the Gobi Desert and spread its influence even farther.

Taitsong was as good an administrator as he was a military leader. He lowered taxes, instituted a fair civil service, and set the example for his government to follow. As a Confucian, he believed that it was necessary for a leader to promote the harmony of his people by personal excellence. He was assisted in administration by his wife, a woman as dedicated and wise as he. They both lived a simple life, without imperial fanfare. She died in 636, leaving as her legacy a college and the Imperial Library.

Taitsong cultivated Chinese relations with Tibet in 634. After initiating talks, the Sanpou, the Tibetan head of state, requested a Chinese bride to seal their relationship. Taitsong refused, and the Sanpou prepared for war. Taitsong's superior army defeated the Tibetans at the western border. Tibet became China's vassal, and Taitsong rewarded the Sanpou with a Chinese wife—his own daughter. The Tibetans began to adopt Chinese culture and abandon barbarism. That same year, Chinese forces won another victory over Turkic tribes at Kashgar, which extended Chinese authority as far as eastern Turkistan, the greatest limit of national authority until the Mongols' dynasty.

Taitsong's only reverse came in Korea. A usurper in the Korean palace refused to recognize the T'ang line and mistreated Taitsong's ambassadors. The Chinese responded to this insult by invading Korea in 646. The Korean usurper decided he had better pay tribute rather than face the invading army, but Taitsong refused his gifts, deciding to teach the Korean a lesson. The Chinese massed 100,000 men and 500 boats for a combined land-sea operation. Telling the Korean people that he had no quarrel with them, Taitsong proclaimed a war against the king only. However, the Korean people resisted, and after an easy start the Chinese force lost a quarter of its force in a siege at Anshu on the northwest coast, which they were unable to capture. Because winter was coming and Taitsong's forces were short of supplies, he retreated. Taitsong never went back, dying in 649.

When he saw his end approaching, Taitsong wanted to leave a legacy for his successors. He wrote the *Golden Mirror*, a text on statecraft, for his son. Taitsong is regarded as probably the finest of all Chinese emperors of any dynasty, and among the best rulers anywhere and anytime. As is usually the case, his descendants did not measure up, starting with his son, Kaotsong.

Kaotsong married one of his father's concubines, an extremely ambitious woman who came to be known as Empress Wu. She was the power behind the throne, and when Kaotsong died she seized power openly, one of the only women ever to do so in Chinese history. She ruled with an iron hand and with mixed success in foreign policy. Her armies lost twice to Tibet in 670 and signed a truce to keep the Tibetans out of Chinese territory, then broke the truce and as a result, the army was virtually wiped out. From then on, she could do little more than defend the western frontier from the occasional Tibetan invasion.

Empress Wu had more luck in Korea. Chinese forces fought there for ten years, ultimately forcing the Koreans to appeal to Japan for aid. Her forces defeated the combined forces in four battles and destroyed the Japanese fleet. Though the Chinese established predominance, they had no long-term advantage. Empress Wu also received appeals from India to assist in repelling invading Muslims, but she wisely refrained from sending her armies so far afield. In 692 she directed her forces to regain preeminence in Tibet, which they did, though they had to continue fighting to maintain their position. Empress Wu's greatest, and last, failure was in dealing with the threat of Khitan Mongols in the north. She allied herself with a Turkic chief, Metcho, in 697 and armed his forces to aid her against the Mongols. Instead, Metcho took the weapons and invaded China himself.

After Empress Wu's death in 705 at age 80, a succession of poor leaders followed. Border wars continued against the Tibetans in the west and the Khitan Mongols in the north. In the middle and latter part of the eighth century, the Chinese depended more and more on Turkic mercenaries, who proved able soldiers for the Chinese; at the same time, Turkistan received Chinese aid to keep the Muslims at bay. The constant warfare took its toll on Chinese society. Early in the 700s the Chinese census numbered 52 million; by 764 the population had dropped to 17 million. The T'ang dynasty stayed in power until 906, when the final emperor conceded power to one of his generals. At the height of the dynasty, the T'angs spread from Korea to Turkistan to the Persian frontier to the borders of Vietnam. They spread Chinese culture, maintained trade relations with the West, and acted as a bulwark against Muslim expansion. The dynasty contained 20 emperors (including one empress), but none as good as Taitsong, who took them to their greatest limits.

*See also* Vietnam, Chinese Conquest of [80].

References: Boulger, Demetrius, *The History of China*, 2 vols. (Freeport, NY: Books for Libraries, 1898); Capon, Edmund, *Tang China* (London: Macdonald Orbis, 1989); Wei, Cheng, *Mirror to the Son of Heaven*, ed. and trans. Howard Wechsler (New Haven, CT: Yale University Press, 1974).

## 78      TURKS

The peoples known as Turks originated not in the Turkey of today, but in Turkistan in central Asia. In the middle of the sixth century A.D. they formed themselves into a large tribal confederation, then shortly thereafter split into eastern and western factions. The eastern Turkic tribes interacted strongly with the Chinese, most notably the T'ang dynasty, and alternately aided or were defeated by Chinese societies. The western Turkic tribes, however, were better known as conquerors for their occupation of territory stretching from the Oxus River to the Mediterranean Sea.

Their first major entry into Western history came through contact with Arabs spreading Islam past Persia and toward central Asia. The pastoral Turks became exposed to the civilizations of Persia and the Byzantine Empire, and began a gradual conversion to Western religions, mainly but not exclusively Islam. Soon Turkic soldiers served in Muslim armies, either as volunteers or as slave-soldiers, forerunners of the Mamluks or the janissaries of the Ottoman Empire. They soon became *ghazis,* or border warriors, hired by Muslim governments to protect the northeastern frontier. At this point the western Turks also split, the eastern faction becoming the Ghaznavids and the western becoming the Seljuks.

## THE GHAZNAVIDS

Most of the Turks embraced the more orthodox Sunni branch of Islam, and they spread the faith as well as practiced it. Based in the city of Ghazna (some 150 kilometers southwest of modern Kabul, Afghanistan), in the tenth and eleventh centuries the Ghaznavids spread their power and religion eastward into India. Their original holdings were a land grant from the Samanid dynasty of Muslims given to them as a reward for military services. Under the leadership of Sebuktegin (977–997) and his son Mahmud (998–1030), the Ghaznavids conquered the area today covered by eastern Iran, Afghanistan, the Punjab, and past the Indus River into parts of India. Their most notable achievement was the introduction of Islam into India, but their use of forced conversions often made them more feared than welcomed. They were defeated not by Indian resistance, but by the Seljuks.

## THE SELJUKS

Named for their first major leader, Seljuk or Selchuk, the western Turkic tribes also served Muslim governments. Their position on the Asian frontier attracted growing numbers of Islamicized Turkic tribes, and soon the land grants ceded by the Muslims proved inadequate for the needs of so many pastoral people. Their multiplying numbers gave them an increased military strength as well as a growing need for grazing lands. As the Muslim Buyid dynasty grew weak and the Ghaznavids looked toward India, the Seljuks found conquest of the lands west of Persia relatively simple. They defeated the Ghaznavids in 1040, and occupied Baghdad in 1055. They did not take the city to pillage it, but to return it to Sunni control from the less orthodox Shi'ites. The wedding of the Seljuk chief to the sister of the caliph (religious leader), and the Seljuk's resulting promotion to the position of sultan (temporal leader), established them as the premier military and political force in the Middle East.

Filled with religious zeal, the Seljuks conquered Armenia, the Levant, and moved into Asia Minor; Malik Shah, the most successful Seljuk military leader, scored a major victory over Byzantine forces at Manzikert in 1071. Despite their desire to reestablish the Sunni sect of Islam, they did not undertake the forced conversions practiced by the Ghaznavids in India. Though they made subjects of Christians and Jews, they did not persecute them; the Seljuks followed Muhammad's teachings of religious tolerance. Once established in Asia Minor, they chose as their capital city Konia, a site occupied since the Hittites at the dawn of recorded history, which became a center for culture and learning. The Turks did not create so much as they copied, but their adoption of Persian and Arab knowledge and art was extensive. Seljuk rulers exchanged educators and religious leaders with Constantinople, and seemed for a time to pursue the concept of finding a common belief for both Christian and Muslim to embrace.

Such a noble dream of religious cooperation was not to be. The orthodoxy of the
Sunni Seljuks frightened Europeans, who
rejected peaceful interaction for militant
Christianity and mounted the Crusades. The
enlightened rulers Ala-ed-din and Jelal-ed-
din, promoters of positive religious contact,
had no effective counterparts in Europe.
Though the Crusades brought about no
lasting European presence in the Middle
East and the Seljuks remained in power,
they were doomed to destruction in the
same manner that brought them to power:
hordes from central Asia, the Mongols of
the thirteenth century. The Seljuks left behind a positive legacy, for the most part.
They spread Persian learning and culture,
and established universities and religious
schools from the Mediterranean to the
Caspian. Their occupation of Asia Minor
ultimately weakened the Byzantine Empire
to the point that it fell to the successors of
the Seljuk, the Ottoman Empire.

*See also* Byzantine Empire [38]; Crusades
[42]; T'ang Dynasty [77]; Ottoman Empire [102].

References: Koprulu, Mehmet, *The Seljuks
of Anatolia,* trans. Gary Leiser (Salt Lake
City: University of Utah Press, 1992);
Muller, Herbert, *The Loom of History*
(New York: Harper & Brothers, 1958);
Rice, Tamara, *The Seljuks in Asia Minor*
(New York: Praeger, 1961).

### 79        VANDALS

The Vandals were one of the tribes who
migrated from the area below the Baltic Sea
during the late Roman Empire. They were
of the same racial stock as the Goths, but
traveled across Germany more directly than
did the Goths, who migrated at the same
time but took a more southerly route be-

fore moving westward across Europe. Little
is known of their early history, but they
crossed into Germany about the time Rome
was loosening its grip on the area in the
A.D. mid-300s. The Vandals were actually
the leaders of a group of tribes, and were
themselves divided into two groups, the
Asdings and the Silings. They led and conquered with the Sueves, another Germanic
tribe, and the Alans, who were a non-
Germanic people driven into Europe by the
advance of the Huns.

The Vandal coalition moved across Germany as the Western Goths (Visigoths)
were occupying northern Italy and Dacia,
and the two fought each other. The
Visigoths had the better of the encounter,
and the Vandals seemed to disappear for a
time. In 406 they emerged again to lead
their forces across the Rhine River. Their
passage into western Europe was bloody;
the Vandals pillaged through Gaul (areas
covered by modern-day Belgium, Holland,
and northern France), then turned south
and cut a wide swath of destruction to the
Pyrenees. This territory officially belonged
to the Roman Empire, and the emperor
tried to convince his Visigothic allies/mer-
cenaries to save Gaul. By the time they
turned to face the Vandal threat in 409,
the tribes had moved into northern Spain.

Like the Goths, the Vandals were Arian
Christians. The two peoples were of the
same heritage and spoke a similar language.
The Goths had established themselves in
Italy as occasional allies to what remained
of the Roman Empire. They therefore went
to Spain to regain control of the area for
Rome and to carve out whatever good lands
they could acquire for themselves, even if
it meant making war against people much
like themselves. The four Vandalic tribes
had spread quickly over much of central
and western Iberia, and the Goths operated out of the eastern part of the peninsula. After a failed attempt to cross over to

North Africa, the Goths made war against the Vandalic tribes. After a few defeats, the Vandals appealed to Rome for protection; the emperor played one tribe against another by granting or denying favors. Imperial aid went mainly to the Asdings and the Suevians, so the Goths continued to fight the Silings and the Alans. The Silings were virtually exterminated, and the Alans, after losing their king, retreated westward to join the Asdings. The ruler of the remainder came to be called "King of the Vandals and the Alans."

Once the Visigoths went about establishing their own claims, the remaining Vandals were left to themselves. An argument soon arose between the Vandals and the Sueves and, after a battle, they parted company. The Sueves stayed in northwest Iberia, and the Vandals and Alans moved to the south. On the way, they fought and defeated a Roman force, and established themselves in the province of Baetica. The Vandal king Gunderic raided into other areas of Spain and possibly across the Mediterranean into Mauritania. His brother and successor, Gaiseric, saw the potential of the farmland of North Africa, which had long been Rome's primary food source. He was leader of the Vandals when chance called them to Africa.

The general commanding Roman forces in Africa was Boniface, loyal to Rome and a strong Christian. However, he took a second wife who was an Arian, and this placed him in opposition to the Roman Catholic church. He refused to return to Rome to answer to the government, and Boniface defeated the first army that came after him. The second one defeated him, however, and Boniface fled to the Vandals. He invited them to come to Africa; if they would fight alongside him, he would reward them with land. Boniface provided shipping, and 80,000 people crossed the Mediterranean, 15,000 of whom were fighting men.

The Vandals proved to be unmerciful in their treatment of the Mauritanian population. They killed and looted towns and churches, caring nothing for Catholic shrines or priests. Gaiseric proved an able military leader and a cunning diplomat. His treatment of Roman citizens encouraged other groups who disliked Rome to join in the fray. Moors and Egyptian Donatists attacked eastward along the Mediterranean shore, and other groups branded as heretics saw a chance to get vengeance on their Roman oppressors. Attempts to negotiate with Gaiseric proved futile. He not only fought the Roman armies sent against him, but turned on Boniface as well and drove him back into Roman arms. In 430 the Vandals invaded Numidia and besieged the city of Hippo, home to St. Augustine, which held out for a year. When Boniface joined with an army sent from Constantinople in 431, Gaiseric defeated them as well, then turned back and captured Hippo.

In Rome, internal power struggles kept the government from any effective resistance to Gaiseric. Finally the Visigoth general Aetius was able to speak for Rome and convince the Vandals to stop fighting. In 435 they were ceded the Mauritanian provinces and part of Numidia in return for acknowledging the overlordship of the Roman government. Gaiseric consolidated his hold on northwestern Africa, but continued to consider his options. Basing himself in Carthage, Gaiseric built a fleet and began raiding at sea. His forces raided Italy and occupied Sicily and Sardinia. The Vandals did not long survive Gaiseric, however. Roman forces ultimately returned and reconquered the area, bringing the Vandal tribe to an end.

Though Vandal power lasted about a century, they left behind little cultural heritage. Their time in Spain was sufficiently brief that they had no impact there, and even in North Africa they built and contributed little. The effect of the Vandal migrations and conquests was not small, however. By their very presence in North Africa, controlling the grain-producing lands that had fed Italy for centuries, the declining power of Rome declined even faster. Without the logistical support of Africa, Roman forces could not aggressively respond to threats in Europe, mostly in Gaul. The advances of the Huns and the Ostrogoths, then of the Franks, came about more easily because Rome could not support enough troops in the field. Roman power fell faster and German influence rose more quickly in Europe because the Vandals, at Rome's back door, split the attention of the fading empire.

See also Huns [51]; Ostrogoths [69]; Visigoths [81].

References: Bury, J. B., *The Invasion of Europe by the Barbarians* (New York: Russell & Russell, 1963); Isadore of Seville, *The History of the Goths, Vandals and Suevi*, trans. Guido Donini and Gordon Ford (Leiden: E. J. Brill, 1970); Thompson, E. A., *Romans and Barbarians: The Decline of the Western Empire* (Madison: University of Wisconsin Press, 1982).

## VIETNAM, CHINESE CONQUEST OF

**80**

In 221 B.C. the Chou dynasty in China was overthrown, replaced by the short-lived Ch'in dynasty. Though this was the first centralized empire in China, it lasted but one generation. However, it was a busy lifetime: All of China was under one rule and the emperor Shih-huang-ti planned an expedition to conquer territory in the far south, called Yueh (pronounced Viet in the south). He began planning the attack in 221 B.C., but was not able to launch it until 218. The invasion was both political and economic; Shih-huang-ti hoped to spread Chinese influence and to profit from that spread by accessing the ivory, rhino horn, tortoiseshell, pearls, spices, aromatic woods, and exotic feathers for which Chinese silk had long been traded. The Chinese already had merchants in place in Yueh and were well aware of its potential.

The first invasion was fairly easy. The indigenous tribes retreated before the Chinese advance, marshaling their forces until they could outnumber the invaders. Chinese leader Chao T'o (Trieu Da) called for reinforcements, and the lower levels of Chinese society were plumbed for men. The early success was limited to the plains around modern Canton; the Red River delta was left untouched for a while.

Shih-huang-ti's death in 209 B.C. brought civil war, ending in the establishment of the Han dynasty in 202. While civil war raged in China, the governor in the south saw an opportunity to declare independence, but he was unsuccessful. He was replaced by the returning Chao T'o, who executed all officials still loyal to the Ch'in and, in 207 B.C., assumed the title King of Nan-yueh (Nam Viet). The Han dynasty recognized him as king in return for his acknowledgment of Chinese suzerainty. In a later trade dispute, Chao T'o declared his independence, and defeated the Chinese force sent against him. He forced the population living farther south, called the Lo (Lac) people, to recognize his position. The Lo lived in a feudal society along the Red River delta and the coastal plains to the south. Even after Chao T'o made peace with China and again recognized their overlordship, this territory continued to recognize his leadership. The area came to be designated a military district called Chiao-chih (Giao-chi).

The Lo princes remained vassals to Chao (Trieu) and his successors. When Nan-yueh broke from China in 112 B.C., it was invaded by the Han emperor Wu-ti. He was quickly victorious and incorporated Nan-yueh into the Han Empire as a protectorate. He divided it into nine military districts; six of them took up the modern provinces of Kwangtung and Kwangsi in China, and the remainder lay in what is now Vietnam. Despite the incorporation, Wu-ti did not establish a Chinese administration in Nan-yueh, but treated the military districts as colonies with a minority Chinese population. The local lords were confirmed in their positions under Chinese suzerainty, and maritime trade with China opened up.

Not until A.D. 1 did the Chinese begin to impose their culture on the people of Chiao-chih. Through the efforts of Governor Hsi Kuang (Tich Quang), who ruled from A.D. 1 to 25, the Chinese language became more widely used. The influx of Chinese immigrants also aided in the sinicizing process; many of them were scholars and officials fleeing from the rule of the usurper Wang Mang (A.D. 9–25). Schools were widely established in this time, and Chinese inventions such as the metal plow were introduced to Chiao-chih society. Hsi Kuang also mandated Chinese clothing styles and marriage ceremonies, and he trained a militia along Chinese lines and with Chinese weaponry. This provoked a rebellion in A.D. 34 by the Lo lords, who feared a loss of power, but by 43 it was suppressed through the efforts of one of China's most able generals, Ma Yuan (Ma Vien). This failed rebellion resulted in the further sinification of the administration in Chiao-chih as the Lo nobles lost their position. From then on, Chiao-chih was treated not as a protectorate, but as a province of the empire.

China dominated the area for the next several centuries, making its culture increasingly Chinese. Under the governorship of Shih Shieh (Si Nhiep), traditional Confucian studies were introduced and Vietnamese students began to go to China to take the civil service exams, which further solidified Chinese culture and administration. Also during this time, the first Buddhist missionaries appeared in Chiao-chih, as did proponents of Taoism and Confucianism.

China ruled the area for almost a thousand years. Those years were mainly peaceful, though plagued by resistance from some of the hill tribes who resented foreign occupation and by the Champa people farther south who occasionally attempted to spread their influence into Chiao-chih. Periodic revolts of either local chieftains or recalcitrant governors proved unable to dislodge Chinese authority, even when Chinese dynasties changed. The successors to the Han, the T'ang dynasty, reorganized the administration of the area in the 600s, renaming the Chiao military districts An-nan (An-nam), meaning "pacified south." The name survives to the present day as a state in modern Vietnam.

By the 800s rebellions became more common and the Chinese had to work to keep control. The growing aggressiveness of neighboring peoples like the Champa (in the neighborhood of Hue) and the Laos kept Chinese troops busy, and even seaborne Javanese raiders attacked occasionally. The fall of the T'ang dynasty in 907, however, was the event that eventually brought Chinese control to an end. Local governors and chieftains successively struggled for control in the area while the disruption of politics in China kept any punitive expeditions from being sent. In 968, Dinh Bo Linh proclaimed himself emperor of the territory, which he renamed Dai Co Viet, and in 970 he received recognition from the new Sung dynasty, as long as he would swear to remain a Chinese vassal.

The country that ultimately became Vietnam remained independent from

China, though they often had to fight to repel successive Chinese dynasties. Meanwhile the Chinese administrative structure was maintained, giving them a centralized government stronger than any in Southeast Asia. Strengthened by the nationalism that grew in repeated wars of defense against China, the government served as motivation for Vietnamese expansion southward. By the 1800s they had conquered the Champa and Khmer peoples along the east coast of Indochina to establish basically the same borders that the country maintains today. Of all the Southeast Asian cultures, only the Vietnamese were strongly affected by the Chinese; the others were more influenced by India. Not long after their consolidation, however, the Vietnamese became the target of French colonization.

See also Ch'in Dynasty [17]; Han Dynasty [23]; T'ang Dynasty [77]; Indochina, French Occupation of [135].

References: Cannon, Terry, *Vietnam: A Thousand Years of Struggle* (San Francisco: People's Press, 1969); Coedes, G., *The Making of Southeast Asia,* trans. H. M. Wright (Berkeley: University of California Press, 1969); Taylor, Keith, *The Birth of Vietnam* (Berkeley: University of California Press, 1983).

## 81            VISIGOTHS

The Goths were a Teutonic tribe probably originating in Scandinavia who arrived in northeastern Europe in the third century A.D. Coupled with their countrymen, the Ostrogoths, the Visigoths ravaged the lands of eastern Europe as far as Asia Minor and Greece. The first serious conflict between Goths and Romans occurred when a number of Gothic mercenaries aided the

usurpation attempt of Procopius in Constantinople in 366. Following Procopius's failed attempt and subsequent execution, the Roman emperor Valens launched an attack on the Goths across the Danube. After an inconclusive war, the two sides agreed on the Danube River as the boundary between their claims. About 370 the two Gothic groups separated, the Visigoths occupying the land from the Dneister River to the Baltic Sea, the Ostrogoths living east of them to the Black Sea.

In 376 the Goths found themselves threatened by the migration of the Huns from central Asia. The Ostrogoths fled westward to pressure the Visigoths, who appealed to Valens for protection and aid. Valens agreed to allow them across the Danube in return for surrendering their weapons and male children under military age. Under the leadership of Fritigern and Alavius, the Visigoths agreed and gave up their boys, but resisted relinquishing their weapons. The Romans abused the Visigoths and provoked their retaliation after killing Alavius during a parley. Fritigern attacked and defeated Roman forces at Marianopolis (in modern Bulgaria), then called on the Ostrogoths for assistance. Emperor Valens, fighting against the Persians, secured a truce there and moved to protect his northeastern frontier. The two fought an indecisive battle at the mouth of the Danube in 377; then the Goths escaped and raised a general barbarian revolt along the frontier. The Romans finally began to regain control in the province of Thrace by 378, but met defeat while launching an attack on the Gothic forces near Adrianople. Spurning a request for peace talks, Valens attacked the Goths before reinforcements arrived. The Gothic force of perhaps 200,000 warriors (roughly half Visigothic infantry and half mixed barbarian cavalry) badly defeated Valens, who died in the battle along with two-thirds of his 60,000 troops. The Visigothic king Fritigern was in overall command.

Valens's successor, Theodosius I, learned from his countryman's defeat and, after rebuilding an army and restoring order in Thrace, defeated the Goths and then invited them into his army. The Visigoths served Theodosius, but upon his death in 395 they chose their own leader: Alaric. He had earlier raided Roman lands from across the Danube, but was captured and incorporated into the Roman army. Upon his election as king, Alaric led the Visigoths through Thrace and Greece. His only serious enemy was Stilicho, a Vandal general in Roman service who had served Theodosius. The Visigoths remained relatively unbothered, however, because the Eastern Roman emperor Arcadius ordered Stilicho to remain in Italy. Alaric spent the mid-390s ravaging Greece, then turned toward Italy.

Visigothic forces marched through Pannonia (along the eastern Adriatic coast) and crossed the Alps in October 401. He overran some of the northern provinces, but Stilicho's delaying actions kept him in the north. During the winter Stilicho ordered forces from Gaul to Italy and did some personal recruiting among German tribes. The resulting army attacked Alaric's forces, who were besieging Milan. Alaric withdrew and marched south, looking for Stilicho's incompetent emperor, Honorius. After two difficult battles in March and April 402, Alaric asked for negotiations and agreed to leave Italy. Instead he marched for Gaul, left unprotected. Stilicho learned of this maneuver and blocked him, defeating the Visigoths at Verona. Alaric again withdrew and Honorius moved the imperial capital to Ravenna, behind whose marshy outskirts he felt safe from attack. Alaric decided to cooperate with Stilicho and was named master-general of Illyricum. When in 408 Honorius ordered Stilicho murdered, the general's followers appealed

to Alaric to invade Italy; he did so gladly. After two attacks on Rome were called off (owing to successful Roman bribery), Alaric marched his forces to Rome. On 24 August 410, Rome fell to foreign invaders for the first time in a thousand years. Alaric marched south to invade Sicily, but died on the way.

Under the leadership of Athaulf, the Visigoths invaded Gaul in 412, supposedly to recover it for Honorius. Athaulf accomplished the conquest by 414 and was rewarded with marriage to Honorius's half sister. He followed Honorius's direction to reconquer Spain, but died in the process in 415. His successor, Wallia, defeated a number of barbarian tribes in Spain and was rewarded with a kingdom of his own in southern Gaul.

The Visigoths settled into lands ranging from the Rhone River into Spain. Their greatest king was Euric, who established a law code based on a mixture of Roman and Germanic legal traditions. The one thing he could not do, however, was establish a hereditary line, for the nobility forbade it. The monarchy was elective, and therefore subject to too much political infighting. This lack of unity laid the Visigothic kingdom open to outside pressure, and in 507, Clovis, the founder of the Merovingian dynasty of the Franks, defeated Alaric II and acquired much of the land north of the Pyrenees. Though the Visigoths managed to maintain their hold on Spain in the face of pressure from the Vandals, they ultimately fell to Muslim invasion. The last Visigothic king, Roderic, was defeated and killed in 711, and the remaining Visigothic tribe was confined to the province of Asturias.

The Visigoths played an important role in the fall of the Roman Empire in the West. Like many of the barbarians who flooded the empire, they converted to the Arian view of Christianity and thus often had troubles with the Roman Catholic church, which viewed them as heretics. As soldiers they proved themselves so talented that the Roman army in the East, based in Constantinople, reconfigured itself to adapt to Gothic cavalry. They had little effect on the future course of European history, however, because they spread themselves too thinly—from the Balkans to Spain—and were finally defeated and absorbed by more powerful enemies.

*See also* Franks [46]; Huns [51]; Ostrogoths [69].

References: Cunliffe, Barry, *Rome and Her Empire* (London: Constable, 1994 [1978]); Heather, Peter, *Goths and Romans* (Oxford: Clarendon Press, 1991); Thompson, E. A., *The Goths in Spain* (Oxford: Clarendon Press, 1969).

# PART 4
## THE RENAISSANCE AND THE AGE OF EXPLORATION

# PART 4
# THE RENAISSANCE AND THE AGE OF EXPLORATION

The numbers on the map correspond to entry numbers in the text.

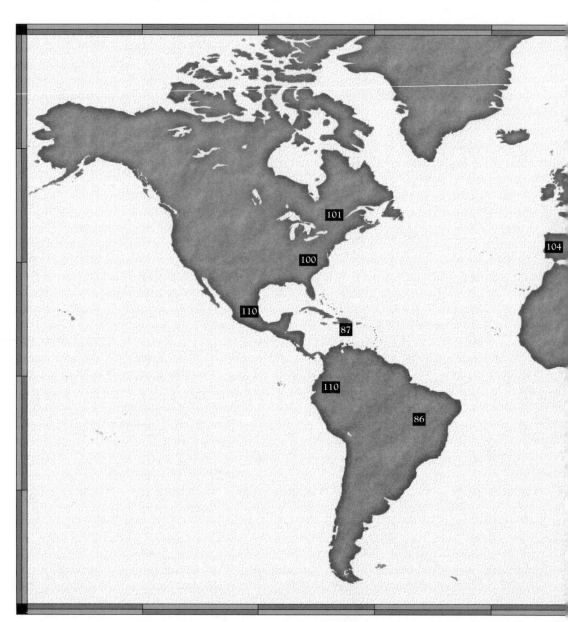

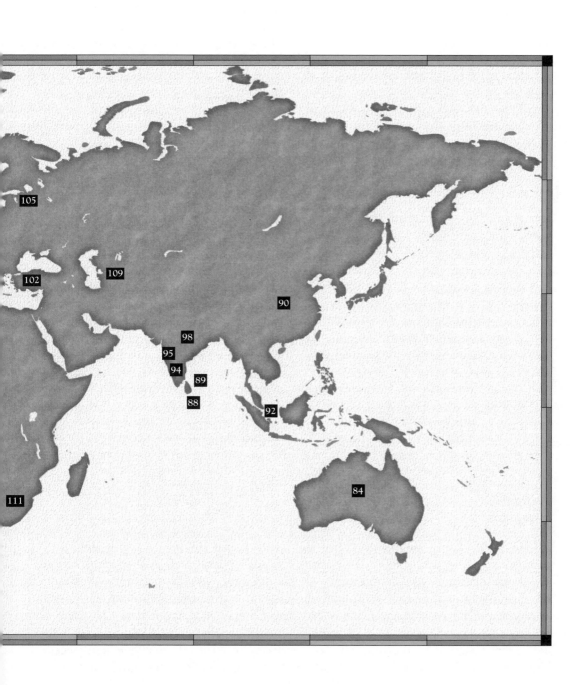

## AFRICA, DUTCH OCCUPATION IN

**82**

The Dutch first considered the idea of establishing trade with Africa even as they were fighting for their lives against their overlord, Philip II of Spain. Their first contact with the maritime routes to Africa came from Jan Huyghen van Linschoten, who for seven years was the servant of the archbishop of Goa, the Portuguese settlement on the western coast of India. Van Linschoten wrote detailed geographical descriptions of his travels for the archbishop and published them as the *Itinerario*. The information contained in this book proved valuable to the first Dutch sailors to Africa.

In 1595 the Dutch launched their first trading expedition, which went to the Guinea coast near the mouth of the Niger River. They exchanged salt, wine, cloth, copper, flax, timber, and wood products from all over Europe for the gold and ivory for which the area was famous. Within three years, five fleets totaling 22 ships were trading in African harbors. However, their first trading post was not established until 1617, when they concluded a treaty with a local chieftain on the island of Goree, among the Portuguese-held Cape Verde Islands. Twenty years later they attacked Portuguese settlements, and by the early 1640s were masters of the Gold Coast.

The major Dutch colonial venture in Africa was not along the Gold Coast but at the continent's southern extreme. After a shipwreck, survivors of the *Haarlem* discovered the potential of the land that would become South Africa. Their descriptions of the area to the Dutch East India Company convinced the Dutch to establish a base there, for they were in need of a shipping resupply point for carrying on trade with India and the Spice Islands. The company built a fort near the southernmost tip of Africa, around which Cape Town grew up.

The project to found Cape Town and the accompanying fort was directed by Jan van Riebeeck, who arrived on site 6 April 1652. Van Riebeeck quickly realized that the fort and town's survival required colonists to exploit the rich agricultural region nearby. Therefore, in 1657 the company began granting land to retiring employees; within a year the colonists were enslaving the local population, but the colony took root. The Castle of Good Hope was constructed between 1666 and 1679, and a second fort was built at Newlands. The nearby mountain was an ideal location for vineyards, receiving the name Wynberg, or Wine Mountain. Through the remainder of the century and into the 1700s, the colony grew slowly, increasing with the immigration of political exiles from the Netherlands and interbreeding with the local population.

The financial fortunes of Cape Town rose and fell with the Dutch competition with Great Britain. Britain had failed to capture the colony during the Seven Years' War, but the defeat of Holland's ally, France, left the colony exposed. When Napoleon conquered the Netherlands, Britain took over the colony to keep it from falling into Napoleon's hands. When Napoleon was defeated in 1815, Britain acquired South Africa (the Cape Colony). Though Britain had political control, the Dutch settlers, or Boers, were slow to cooperate with the new owners, and ultimately warfare between the two broke out.

The strongest heritage of modern-day Cape Town is from the Dutch. The whitewashed walls, spacious and lofty interiors, and massive furniture are all relics of the Dutch era. The Dutch Reformed church dominated the religious life of the Boer settlers, persuading them that they were a chosen people in a heathen land with divine sanction to do whatever was necessary to master it. The Dutch dialect of

Afrikaans remains one of the official languages of the country.

See also East Indies, Dutch Occupation of the [92]; Saxony, Prussian Invasion of (Seven Years' War) [106]; South Africa, British Occupation of [144].

References: Collins, Robert, Europeans in Africa (New York: Knopf, 1971); Hepple, Alexander, South Africa: A Political and Economic History (London: Pall Mall Press, 1966); Israel, Jonathan, Dutch Primacy in World Trade, 1585–1740 (Oxford: Clarendon Press, 1989).

## AFRICA, PORTUGUESE OCCUPATION OF

**83**

The Portuguese did not intend to settle Africa, only to sail around it. The Muslim Middle East controlled the spice trade, and prices were high for European consumers, so in the early 1400s the Portuguese established a new overseas trade route to compete with the Muslims. They also hoped to spread Christianity through the assistance of the legendary Prester John, a Christian king reportedly located somewhere in Africa. An alliance with John would aid both in fighting the Muslims (if necessary) and giving Portugal sites for trading bases to the Spice Islands and the interior of Africa, where the Muslims also controlled the trans-Saharan gold trade.

The first expeditions down the northwest African coast began in the early 1440s. The Portuguese set up bases at Sao Tome, the Cape Verde Islands, the mouth of the Senegal River, and Guinea. Each expedition traveled a bit farther south and brought back new information for the next voyage. By the 1480s settlements were set up in Angola. Vasco de Gama's trip in 1497–1498 took the Portuguese around the Cape of Good Hope, and soon afterward Mozambique, on the Indian Ocean coast, was settled. From there Portuguese merchants had access to the spice trade in the Indian Ocean.

The early Portuguese settlements along the western coasts attempted to access the gold and ivory of the region, but the interests of the merchants soon transferred almost exclusively to slaves. The trading posts turned from their original intentions of promoting local agriculture and trade goods to dealing with the already flourishing slave trade from the interior. Native prisoners of war had long been owned as slaves or sold to Arab merchants, but the Portuguese soon cornered the market. Through their bases (each of which was part trading post and part fort) they dealt with local slavers, who provided an almost unlimited supply. It was such a lucrative business that it attracted almost every element of Portuguese colonial society, from the bureaucrats to the clergy. Slaves were taken by the Portuguese administration in exchange for taxes, then sold abroad or used for local agricultural or mining ventures operated by the Portuguese.

The Mozambique colony was originally used as access to the Rhodesian gold fields and as the major stopping point for ships sailing from Europe to India. When the gold revenue did not meet expectations, the Portuguese moved farther inland up the Zambezi River, not to colonize but to get closer to the gold supply. In 1569 Portugal's King Sebastian sent an expedition up the Zambezi to secure control of the gold mines, dislodge the Swahili traders, and gain access for Catholic missionaries. The thousand-man force was almost completely destroyed by disease, and they had no luck in establishing permanent control. The missionaries had little success in converting the area's natives, and by the end of the eighteenth century most missions were abandoned. By 1836, Mozambique shifted its focus to slave trading as well.

The Portuguese rarely controlled extensive landholdings, but their presence along the coastlines had numerous long-term effects. Many of the early settlers were convicts or other undesirables banished from Portugal who intermarried with the locals and became Africanized. They were probably more influential in spreading Catholicism through their marriages than the church was through its missionaries. Large-scale Jesuit and Dominican missionary ventures had little success in converting the local populations, most of whom remained true to their native religions or found more comfort in Islam. The missionaries involving themselves in the slave trade also did little to promote willing conversions. Still, what little European culture filtered into Africa through the Portuguese came through the efforts of the church. As the traditional venue for education, the missionaries ran the few European-style schools in the Portuguese colonies. Little attempt was made to educate the mass of Africans, focusing rather on educating those few needed to assist the Portuguese in exploiting their property.

The Portuguese had the longest lasting colonial experience in Africa, but some of the least effect on the local populations. Because their primary goal was exploitation, little dissemination of culture or education succeeded, or was intended. When the last Portuguese colony, Mozambique, gained its independence in 1975, its population was mainly illiterate, diseased, and poverty-stricken. The colony of Angola was no better; though blessed with rich mineral resources, its people lacked the education and dedication necessary to use those resources for the general good. The long-term Portuguese presence proved far more destructive than positive.

*See also* Ceylon, Portuguese Occupation of [89].

References: Duffy, James, *Portuguese Africa* (Cambridge, MA: Harvard University Press, 1968); Ferreira, Eduardo, *Portuguese Colonialism in Africa* (Paris: UNESCO Press, 1974); Newitt, Marilyn, *Portugal in Africa* (London: Longman, 1981).

## AUSTRALIA, BRITISH OCCUPATION OF

**84**

The continent of Australia became predominantly British in heritage because the Dutch did not follow up their discovery. The Dutch East India Company did not care to pursue the exploration of the land they called New Holland, despite Governor Anthony van Damien's assurances of the availability of gold and silver. The company preferred to focus on the established spice trade in the Indies, viewing the north and west coasts of Australia (all they had knowledge of) as a barren land.

The English first viewed Australia from the more inviting east coast. In 1688 a shipload of buccaneers landed onshore, and among the crew was William Dampier. He used his descriptive talents to advertise the country when he returned to England, and was able to gain enough backing to charter the *Roebuck* in 1699 for a more intense exploration. It was largely a failure, but he brought back enough information to keep some interest alive in England. That interest was pursued by a tiny band of adventure-minded citizens; the interest of the British government was still three-quarters of a century away.

The Royal Society commissioned another expedition, which sailed on the *Earl of Pembroke* in 1769. The ship carried a

Aborigines with spears attack Europeans in a touring boat in this 1830 drawing by Joseph Lycett

group of astronomers interested in viewing Venus as it crossed the face of the sun, an event best viewed deep in the Southern Hemisphere. Captain James Cook was chosen to command the ship, and he was given leave to explore Australia while the astronomers explored the sky. Cook sailed along the coast in the summer of 1770, mapping it and charting possible landing or colonization sites.

The exploration was well timed, because an upsurge of crime in England, coupled with the impending loss of colonies in North America, meant that the government had to find another dumping ground for its criminals. The newly passed Enclosure Laws, which denied public land to poor farmers and shepherds, forced a number of country folk to the cities, where crime became an even more pressing problem.

"Transportation" as punishment for crime was well established in English law; some 50,000 people had been sent to North America in the 60 years prior to the revolution. Australia began to look quite appealing as an alternative for the removal of undesirable elements.

At the instigation of Sir Joseph Banks, James Matra, and Sir George Young, the Transportation Act of 1784 officially created the Australian colonies. Matra had sailed with Cook, and he proposed that the government investigate Australia as a site for a penal colony and also as a possible headquarters for trade with the Spice Islands, China, and Japan. Three years later, six vessels sailed from Portsmouth, reaching Botany Bay on 26 January 1789; Captain (then Governor) Arthur Phillip led the expedition. He soon rejected Botany Bay, the primary location indicated by Cook, as a colonization site. Instead, the group established Port Jackson at the site that ultimately became Sydney. Over the next 40 years, other settlements would be founded at Norfolk Island, Melbourne, and Hobart.

The first convict-settlers were apparently little motivated, and the colony gained few free settlers in its early years. By 1820 the census named only 2,201 colonists as "free immigrants," the remainder were convicts who had either served their time or were still incarcerated. When land was granted as a retirement bonus to military officers and convict labor was made available free of charge, the country became more attractive. It took some time for the colony to become more than a penal colony, but in the nineteenth century, whaling, sealing, flax and cloth production, and sheepherding became important industries. The food supply increased, as did livestock after breeding for the Australian climate was perfected.

The natives of Australia benefited little from their contact with the outside world. The aborigines lived a Stone Age hunter-gatherer lifestyle, and had little interest in the white settlers. Governor Phillip's original orders called for him to establish close and friendly relations with the aborigines, and to punish anyone who harmed them. Unfortunately, the natives had no concept of private property and therefore could not grasp the practice of claiming land or trespass. Thus, less enlightened settlers persecuted them through greed or ignorance, and some historians believe that the 1789 smallpox epidemic among the aborigines was started intentionally. Contact with white society had a major impact on them, and little of it for the better.

By 1850 Australia was a burgeoning colony. There was an expanding economy based on trade and manufacture, and 1851 brought a gold rush. Australia was eventually divided into six colonies, which federated in the 1880s. After many complaints to London concerning its local needs, Australia was granted commonwealth status in 1901. It remains a member of the British Commonwealth of Nations, and its English ties took Australian soldiers to South Africa in the Boer War, Europe and the Middle East in World War I, and North Africa in World War II.

References: Eddy, J. J., *Britain and the Australian Colonies* (Oxford: Clarendon Press, 1969); Frost, Alan, *Convicts and Empire* (Oxford: Oxford University Press, 1980); Shaw, A. G. L., *Convicts and the Colonies* (London: Faber & Faber, 1966).

## AUSTRIA, TURKISH INVASION OF

85

After the Ottoman Turks destroyed the remains of the Byzantine Empire by capturing Constantinople in 1453, they had a strong hold on southeastern Europe and wanted to expand their power and their religion farther into Europe. The Turks were turned away after an unsuccessful siege of Belgrade in 1456, but Serbia fell to them in 1459, a year after they captured Athens with no resistance. Bosnia accepted Turkish dominance and Islam in 1463, and Albania fell to them in 1479. Hungary, however, kept the Turks at bay into the sixteenth century. In 1514 Hungary declared a crusade against the Turks and called for troops. Massive numbers of peasants responded; once armed, however, they attacked the nobility instead. The suppression of the revolt forced an even more oppressive dominance over the peasantry and left the country open to possible invasion.

The Ottoman leader who staged the invasion was Suleiman, called the Wise by his people, the Magnificent by the West. In 1521 he invaded Hungary and captured Szabacs and Belgrade, then turned against the Knights of St. John in Rhodes, whose position threatened Muslim control of the eastern Mediterranean; he secured the island on 1 January 1523. In 1525 Suleiman received a request from Francis I of France,

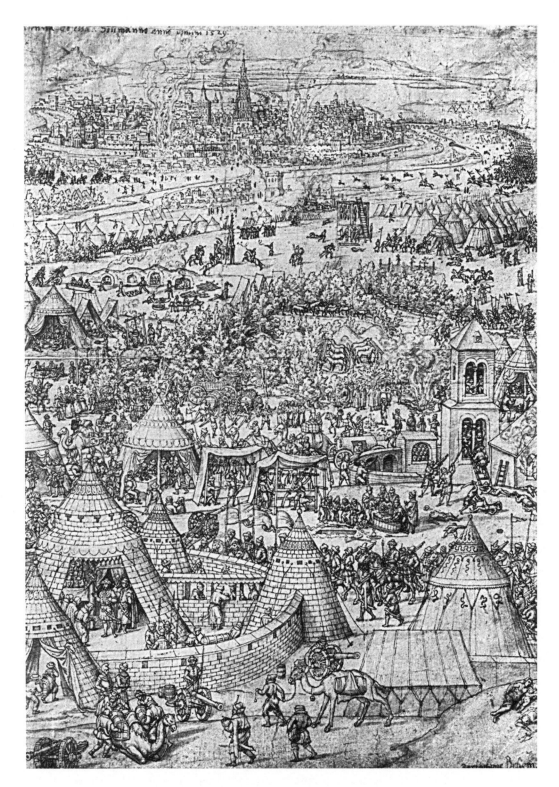

The Turkish camp surrounding Vienna, 1529

inviting him to invade Hungary in order to weaken the power of Habsburg emperor Charles V. Turkish forces marched in April 1526, and the pope called for the Christian faithful to resist the Muslim invaders. Martin Luther persuaded his followers not to respond to this call, and even Charles declined to fight. Suleiman's force of some 75,000 scored a difficult victory at Mohacs, and Christianity suffered a moral defeat as well. Suleiman made Hungary a tributary under the control of Transylvanian John Zapolya.

Zapolya consolidated his power in Hungary, but drew the attention of Ferdinand of Habsburg, who defeated him at Tokay. Zapolya appealed for aid, and Suleiman marched in 1529, bringing 80,000 soldiers; Zapolya provided 6,000. Buda fell after a five-day siege and, aided by a flotilla on the Danube, the Turks approached Vienna in late September. They surrounded the city, and for three weeks bombarded and attempted to mine the walls, but failed to breach them. Suleiman withdrew in mid-October to go into winter quarters, but he was pursued by the Austrians, who harassed him constantly and severely damaged his flotilla at Bratislava.

Suleiman returned in force in 1532, but after inconclusive fighting he retreated. Pressed by Persia to his rear, Suleiman decided to make peace with Ferdinand of Habsburg in 1533. He had to pay tribute to the Turks, but he gained control of about a third of Hungary. Ferdinand was granted, in Suleiman's words, an eternal peace if he would but observe it; he did not. At the urging of Charles V, Ferdinand joined other European forces invading Turkish Hungary in 1537. They were defeated and virtually destroyed during their retreat. Suleiman led his army back into Hungary and annexed it to his empire. Ferdinand attacked at Pest in 1542 but was repulsed, and Suleiman

entered Austria, armed with a veteran army and an alliance with France. He pillaged throughout the country until 1544, when France abrogated the treaty. Suleiman again made peace with Ferdinand under the terms of their first agreement.

Ferdinand could not leave well enough alone. He invaded Transylvania in 1551 and was repulsed, but he managed to defeat a Turkish counteroffensive. After desultory fighting, the two leaders renewed their treaty in 1562 at the Peace of Prague. The Austrian Habsburgs were at peace, but Suleiman was still engaged in a war with the Holy Roman Empire. When the emperor Maximilian ordered another attack on Hungary, the 72-year-old Suleiman returned to Austria at the head of a 100,000-man army. The Turks won a month-long siege of Szigeth, but Suleiman died just before the city fell, so the Turks returned home.

After Suleiman's death, the Ottoman Empire came under the rule of Selim, known as the Sot. After Selim's navy was defeated at the battle of Lepanto in 1571, Ottoman power began to decline. Fighting with Austrian and Holy Roman Empire forces in the 1590s weakened the Ottoman hold on Hungary and Turkish possessions in the Balkans. The Thirty Years' War diverted European attention away from the Balkans until the 1660s, when the Turks returned to advance on Vienna under the leadership of Fazil Ahmed Koprulu Pasha. They were checked at Neuhause in September 1663 and postponed their attack until the following spring, by which time the Austrians were stronger and better prepared. The battle of St. Gotthard Abbey was fought as peace talks were being held, and the Turks were forced to retreat to Belgrade. The Peace of Vasvar, signed in August 1664, called for a 20-year peace and ceded Transylvania to Turkey.

After the 20-year truce, the Turks were back in 1683. Hungary was in the process of rebelling against Austria, so the Austrians were pressed by a number of enemies: the Hungarians, Transylvanians, and Turks. Muhammad IV arrived at Vienna in June with 150,000 men to besiege a city defended by a mere 15,000. The Turks had little siege artillery, but they managed to breach the walls in a few places. They could not break through in strength, however, and Vienna was spared by the timely arrival of Pole Jan Sobiesky, who arrived at the same time a German force marched to help. A mixed Austrian-German-Polish force of 70,000 engaged the Turks outside Vienna on 12 September. After an all-day battle the Turks fled, and the city was saved. Sobiesky later pursued the Turks and captured Grau and much of Hungary, which came under Habsburg control over the next five years.

Suleiman II made the last serious threat toward Habsburg territories in 1690, but his defeat at Szalankemen in 1691 and at Zenta in 1697 ended that dream. In January 1699 the two powers signed the Treaty of Karlowitz, which ceded Hungary to Austria and left the Turks in control of Serbia.

The defeat of the Turkish invasions served to consolidate Habsburg control in central and southeast Europe, but also stopped Islam from expanding past the Balkans. The Catholics and Protestants had more than their share of struggles, but Christianity in one form or another would remain the religion of most of Europe. Hungary, under Habsburg rule, was later incorporated into the Austro-Hungarian Empire, but the ethnic struggles of the myriad populations of that region simmered under Habsburg control, and to a great extent continue to this day.

See also Byzantine Empire [38]; Ottoman Empire [102]; Thirty Years' War [108].

References: Held, Joseph, *Hunyadi: Legend and Reality* (New York: Columbia University Press, 1985); Kinross, Patrick, *The Ottoman Centuries* (New York: Morrow, 1977); Spielman, John, *The City and the Crown: Vienna and the Imperial Court, 1600–1740* (West Lafayette, IN: Purdue University Press, 1993).

## 86   BRAZIL, PORTUGUESE COLONIZATION OF

When the Portuguese explorer Cabral discovered Brazil in 1500, it was fortuitous that this landmass was dedicated to Portuguese ownership. In 1494, at the direction of the pope, the Spanish and Portuguese signed the Treaty of Tordesillas, in which the world was divided in half for the two signatories to exploit. Spain colonized most of the Western Hemisphere without competition, and the Portuguese dominated trade and exploration along the coasts of Africa and Asia. The only part of the Western Hemisphere ceded to Portugal by the treaty was an area several degrees of longitude from South America's east coast into the interior.

Unlike the riches of Central America and Peru, Brazil had little to offer in the way of resources or labor. However, the Portuguese produced agricultural surplus when they introduced sugarcane from the Caribbean and slaves from Africa. With these assets Brazil grew rich and, as more colonists explored the interior, valuable metals were discovered. Portugal focused its colonization efforts on Brazil because the populations of Africa and Asia resisted Portuguese attempts at settlement, though they gladly engaged in trade. As Portugal's military and economic power ebbed in the African and Asian markets, its interest in the continuing success of Brazil grew.

Portuguese colonists dominated the economic and political life of Brazil, but socially they were open-minded. While it was virtually impossible for a nonwhite to attain high political office, whites, natives, and blacks mingled freely in society and culture. The Brazilian Portuguese were as brutal in their treatment of slaves as any owners anywhere, but they treated free blacks with openness. Mixed-race marriages were common, and children of these unions were accepted without social prejudice. Of all the imperial experiences, only the British in New Zealand approached the racial openness of Brazil. Perhaps this was why Brazil did not chafe at Portuguese control; either they enjoyed the public equality or, by being denied education, had little knowledge of nationalism. Even though large sums left the country for tribute and taxes, the Brazilian upper classes remained loyal.

Brazil gained independence almost by accident. The royal family fled Lisbon for Rio de Janeiro in 1808 when threatened by Napoleon's forces. Not only did they find a country richer and more populous than the one they had left, it had many of the comforts of home and a society that spoke their language, worshiped in the Catholic church, and held many of their values. Because of the presence of royalty, Rio de Janeiro became the capital of the Portuguese Empire. In 1815, Brazil was declared a full sister kingdom, which opened the country to foreign trade previously restricted to Portugal. Brazil grew even more wealthy as it established further contacts with the outside world. This wealth, coupled with the spectacle of lavish royal spending, the stronger authority of Portuguese courts and officials, and the more direct exploitation of resources (little of which benefited the native population), caused a more rebellious attitude. Rio grew more powerful at the expense of outlying provinces, which began rebelling in 1817.

When Britain's Duke of Wellington dislodged French forces in 1811, the royal family was free to return to Lisbon. King Juan VI liked Rio, however, and he stayed until 1820. By then Portugal was chafing at being a virtual colony of Brazil. The Portuguese at home resented the extended presence of the British, the diminution of the international trade they once enjoyed, and the lack of Brazilian income, which stayed with the royal family. Demands for a liberal constitutional government brought King Juan back to Portugal in 1821, leaving his son Dom Pedro as regent. The Portuguese government demanded a return to the old ways, with Portugal the center of the empire and Brazil the colony, but the Brazilians had little desire to part with their newly acquired rights and privileges. When Dom Pedro agreed to become king of Brazil and adopt a liberal constitution, the nation declared its independence.

Brazil became officially independent in 1825 when Lisbon recognized its status through the diplomatic efforts of Great Britain. In return, Brazil assumed a large debt that Portugal owed Britain and bought King Juan's estates. Brazil also received British recognition and trade treaties, but at the cost of abolishing the slave trade. Dom Pedro, now Emperor Pedro, tried to maintain family control of both Portugal and Brazil by having his daughter (from Brazil) marry his brother (in Portugal), but he was unable to do so. Brazil remained a constitutional monarchy until the establishment of a republic in 1889.

See also Western Hemisphere, Spanish Occupation of [110]; Napoleon Buonaparte [118]; New Zealand, British Occupation of [139].

References: Diffie, Bailey, *A History of Colonial Brazil* (Malabar, FL: R. E. Krieger, 1987); Macaulay, Neill, *Dom Pedro* (Durham, NC: Duke University Press, 1986); Prado, Caio, *The Colonial Background of Modern Brazil* (Berkeley: University of California Press, 1967).

## CARIBBEAN, EUROPEAN OCCUPATION OF

**87**

When Christopher Columbus arrived in the Caribbean in October 1492, he was the first European to sight the numerous islands of that sea, and he laid claim to many of them for Spain. The Spanish dominated the area for at least a century, but the islands changed hands periodically through conquest or treaty. Wars in Europe often brought about changes in ownership of Caribbean islands, and the use of these islands as diplomatic bargaining chips did not stop until the nineteenth century.

### THE BAHAMAS

The Bahamas were probably the first islands Columbus saw in the Western Hemisphere, but the site of his first landing is the subject of debate. The island Columbus called San Salvador is probably Samana Cay. The first established colony was not Spanish, however, but British. A century and a half after Columbus, the British settled the islands of Eleuthera and New Providence. Though often attacked by the Spanish, they remained under British control. The Bahamas served as a base of operations for buccaneers who struck at the Spanish and any other handy island or ship. At the turn of the eighteenth century, the islands came under the direction of the American colony of Carolina, but the British Crown reassumed direct control in 1717. During the American Revolution, some of the islands were held briefly by foreign powers: The Americans occupied Nassau, and the Spanish were in control at war's end. British rule was restored by the Treaty of Paris, which ended the revolution. The islands suffered economically for decades when slavery was abolished, and again when a cholera epidemic ravaged the population. Proximity to the United States, however, proved profitable when the islands were used by Confederate blockade runners during the Civil War and by alcohol smugglers during the 1920s era of Prohibition. The British granted local autonomy in 1964 and independence in 1973.

### BERMUDA

Like the Bahamas, Bermuda was first discovered by a Spaniard but settled by the British. Juan de Bermudez was shipwrecked on the islands in 1503, but no settlement ensued for a century. In 1612, while on his way to Virginia, the British sailor George Somers found himself shipwrecked there as well. The islands bore his name for a time, and were under the direction of the colony of Virginia until 1684, when the Crown took them over. With the introduction of African slaves and the importation of Portuguese laborers from the Azores, the population grew. The Bermuda Islands served as havens for Confederate blockade runners and, at the turn of the twentieth century, as a holding location for prisoners from the Boer War. British warships were based there throughout the nineteenth and twentieth centuries, and the United States received 99-year leases for naval bases under the lend-lease arrangement between United States and Great Britain.

### CUBA

Christopher Columbus made landfall at Cuba on his first voyage and found the island inhabited by the Ciboney, a tribe related to the Arawak. He left some men behind, but the first colony was not established until 1511, when Diego Velázquez founded the settlements of Baracoa, Santiago, and Havana. Cuba was used mainly as a supply base for expeditions to Florida and Mexico. Only after the indigenous population died through disease and abuse did the island become dedicated to agriculture, with labor provided by African slaves. It was often the target of both pirate raids and more organized attacks by the British or Dutch navies, but Cuba remained firmly in Spanish hands until the Seven Years' War, when the British captured Havana. Complete control of the island returned to Spain after the Treaty of Paris of 1763, and they instituted a liberalized administration encouraging settlement and commerce. By 1817 the population of the island had grown to half a million. Trade laws continued to be liberalized, but the local administration grew more harsh. By the 1830s the first independence movement formed to rebel against the tyrannical rule of the captain-general, Miguel de Tacon. This revolt and others that followed were suppressed, usually with great loss of life. In the early 1850s, Spanish-American general Narciso López plotted with U.S. officials in Europe to seize Cuba for the United States, but the discovery of the plot and the execution of López ended the scheme.

The United States occasionally offered to buy Cuba, but could never interest Spain in selling the island. Still, whenever the local population rebelled, the United States took an interest and sheltered refugees. In 1873, in the midst of the Ten Year War, the United States nearly involved itself when some U.S. citizens were executed for gun-running, but a Spanish apology and payment of damages calmed the situation. Not until the revolution of the 1890s, led by José Martí, did the United States finally intervene. Spain left a legacy of bitterness in Cuba, but also a culture that is heavily Spanish in its religion, language, and arts.

## FRENCH WEST INDIES

The French joined the Spanish, English, Dutch, and Danes in the Caribbean colonization game in the seventeenth century, settling colonies on a number of islands. None had the production capacity of Haiti, nor the official notice, but some stayed in French hands much longer. Only Guadaloupe and Martinique (with five small islands nearby) survived as French colonies. Other islands the French had colonized, such as Grenada, St. Kitts, Dominica, St. Martin, and St. Eustatius, were extremely valuable as sugar producers in the eighteenth century and became pawns in European politics. Most were ceded to Great Britain when France lost a number of conflicts on the Continent. Still, they served as profitable markets for American colonists, and played a role in the growing conflict that led to the American Revolution. France made the French West Indies an overseas department in the Fourth Republic in 1946.

## HISPANIOLA

First discovered and settled by the Spanish, the island of Hispaniola was originally populated by an Arawak tribe, the main people (along with the Caribs) of the region. Exploitation under Spanish rule and the introduction of European disease soon made the Arawaks extinct. Thus, the main population of the island came to be slaves imported from Africa. Spain maintained control over the entire island until 1697, when the Peace of Ryswick (ending the War of the League of Augsburg) transferred the western third of the island to the French, who established the colony of Saint-Domingue (now Haiti). The Spanish neighbor on the remainder of the island was Santo Domingo, now the Dominican Republic.

The French invested in their section and it flourished, but Spain's other, more profitable islands kept their portion from growing. In fact, the Spanish cared so little for their share of the island that they ceded it to France in 1795.

The following decade proved tumultuous. Local general Toussaint L'Ouverture first freed the slaves of Haiti, then aided the new French republic in dislodging invading British troops, and established local rule under his leadership. Napoleon sent forces to recapture the island; they took L'Ouverture prisoner but at such a high cost in manpower that Napoleon abandoned the colony. General Jean Jacques Dessalines declared the independence of Saint-Domingue in 1804, and renamed the new nation Haiti.

After Dessalines's assassination in 1806, the island changed leadership regularly, and the eastern section declared itself independent of Haiti. The Spanish reoccupied Santo Domingo and in 1814, after Napoleon's defeat, instituted a harsh government. The abuse provoked a rebellion in 1821 and a declaration of independence, but Santo Domingo was soon invaded and occupied by Haiti. In 1843 Haitian rule was finally overthrown and the independent nation of the Dominican Republic was created. The Dominicans argued among themselves over whether to offer themselves to Spain or the United States; Spain reestablished control in 1861, but left four years later. The incessant political infighting and lack of economic promise kept the Spanish from regretting their decision.

The United States came to the economic rescue of a heavily indebted Dominican Republic in 1906, but rioting forced the establishment of a military government in 1916. Fighting in Haiti also led to U.S. Marines landing there in 1915. After the liberation of Haiti from the French and the Dominican Republic from the Spanish, the United States became the island's major influence. The two sections of the island, particularly the black and mixed-race populations, maintain strong cultural influences from their original colonizers, and the use of the French and Spanish languages is widespread.

## JAMAICA

The original inhabitants of this island were Arawak, and their word for "isle of springs" gives the island its name. Sighted by Columbus on his second voyage to the hemisphere, Jamaica received its Spanish colonists in 1509. As in Hispaniola, the Arawak population was soon completely wiped out and replaced by African slaves. The island was attacked and captured by British forces under Sir William Penn in 1655; his original assignment from Oliver Cromwell was to capture Santo Domingo, but that effort failed. The middle 1600s was an active time in the Caribbean, with Spanish, English, and Dutch forces attacking one another's possessions, and many islands gaining and losing temporary masters. Jamaica, however, remained British by the Treaty of Madrid in 1670, in which the British promised to halt piracy and the Spanish ceded control of the island.

The British made Jamaica an economically strong island, overseeing the production of cacao, sugar, and timber. Their success brought about an even greater demand for slaves, and Jamaica became one of the world's largest slave-trading markets. For 150 years slavery was an integral part of Jamaican life, but in the 1830s the British government outlawed the practice throughout their empire. Some 310,000 slaves were freed in 1838, and they immediately took over unclaimed land; the production of the past decades dwindled almost to a halt. Increased taxation and discriminatory laws provoked an uprising by the black population in 1865, but it was quickly and brutally suppressed. The local autonomy enjoyed by the island was removed, and Jamaica became a crown colony.

Jamaica is one of the most "British" of Caribbean islands because, even when it was not thriving economically, it was an important military base for the Royal Navy. It has a parliamentary government patterned after Great Britain's, and recognizes as head of state the British monarch, who has a governor-general resident on the island. Power is exercised through a cabinet headed by a prime minister, and the legal code is based on English common law.

## PUERTO RICO

The island of Puerto Rico was captured by Ponce de León in 1509, and he was named its first Spanish governor. The island was populated by the Borinqueño but, as happened so often, they were wiped out by abuse and disease. The Borinqueño were used as forced labor by the Spanish, but after their extermination the African slave trade brought replacement labor for the plantations and sugar mills. Pirates frequently raided the island, and the Spanish built a number of forts for defense. The forts were stout enough to defeat an attack by the famous British pirates Sir Francis Drake and Sir John Hawkins in 1595; Hawkins died of wounds received in the fight. The Dutch attacked the capital city of San Juan and burned it in 1625, and the British sacked Arecibo in 1702.

None of this was sufficient to remove the island from Spanish hands, and the island received positive treatment from the homeland: Foreign trade was allowed in 1804, and the Puerto Ricans were granted a seat in the Spanish Parliament in 1808. Nevertheless, the population occasionally rebelled during the nineteenth century. The most serious uprising was the El Grito

de Lares in 1868 but, like all the others, it was suppressed. Spain granted the island local autonomy in 1897, but lost possession to the United States in the Spanish-American War the following year.

## THE VIRGIN ISLANDS

Like so many other Caribbean islands, this group, lying east of Puerto Rico, was first located by Columbus, who named them after St. Ursula and other virgin martyrs. They were first settled in 1648 by the Dutch settlers, but one of the islands, St. Thomas, was settled by Denmark, which used it as a base for the Danish West Indies Company. The company controlled the three islands of St. Thomas, St. Croix, and St. John, which were bought by the Danish king in 1755. As on most of the other islands, slavery was practiced, and sugar was the main export.

St. Thomas was occupied by the British during the Napoleonic Wars but restored to Denmark after 1815. Sugar continued as the main crop, but the abolition of slavery in 1848 brought about a decline in production. In 1867 the United States entered into negotiations to buy the Danish West Indies, and an agreement was reached in 1917. The United States continues to govern the islands, but since 1968 the people have been allowed to elect their own governor.

The remaining Virgin Islands belong to Great Britain, who acquired them from the Dutch in 1666. Once a popular pirate haven through the 1600s, today most of its visitors are tourists, from whom the islands draw much of their income. They also have a British-style government, though the governor is appointed from London.

See also Palatinate, French Invasion of the (War of the League of Augsburg) [103]; Saxony, Prussian Invasion of (Seven Years' War) [106]; Western Hemisphere,

Spanish Occupation of [110]; Napoleon Buonaparte [118]; Cuba, U.S. Invasion of [131]; South Africa, British Occupation of [144]; Latin America, U.S. Interventions in [169].

References: Claypole, William, *Caribbean Story,* 2 vols. (San Juan, PR: Longman Caribbean, 1989); Hamshere, Cyril, *The British in the Caribbean* (Cambridge, MA: Harvard University Press, 1972); Severin, Timothy, *The Golden Antilles* (New York: Knopf, 1970).

## CEYLON, DUTCH OCCUPATION OF

88

Portugal's fading mercantile power in the 1600s, coupled with difficulties in cooperating with the local population, provided an opening for the rising power of the Netherlands in the affairs of Ceylon. Unlike the Portuguese, who wanted to spread Catholicism as well as trade, the Dutch were interested in trade only. They allied themselves with the mountain kingdom of Kandy to fight the Portuguese, and in 1656 established themselves as the dominant foreign power on the island. Through the Dutch East India Company, a civil administration was established, directed by a military governor. The Dutch introduced a civil service that, like the Portuguese system, worked with the local government in trade (especially cinnamon) and civil works such as fort and canal construction.

The Dutch soon had troubles with their erstwhile ally, Kandy. The Kandyans were a fiercely independent monarchy, and they raided Dutch forts, for which they suffered Dutch retribution. The Kandyan king Rajasinha II was the major irritant to the Dutch. He hated all whites, and mistreated any with whom he came in contact, whether prisoners or ambassadors. He

constantly broke his agreements with the Dutch, and punished any native who cooperated with them. Unable to remove him from his mountain home, the Dutch ultimately left the island's interior to Rajasinha and confined themselves to the coastal areas.

Ceylon was a profitable possession for the Dutch, but eventually the home government grew less interested. When the Netherlands had to deal with the rising power of France in the 1790s, they sold their Ceylonese interests to the British.

During their time on the island, the Dutch established a new law code based on Dutch and Roman law, much of which remains in effect today. They maintained a fair administration, and provided public services to the local population. Other than the law codes, they had little long-term effect on the island. With no distinctive architectural legacy and few remnants of Dutch in the local language, they left behind less of themselves than had the Portuguese.

*See also* Ceylon, Portuguese Occupation of [89].

References: Beny, Roloff, *Island Ceylon* (London: Thames & Hudson, 1970); Codrington, Humphrey, *A Short History of Ceylon* (Freeport, NY: Books for Libraries, 1926); Tresidder, Argus, *Ceylon: An Introduction to the Resplendent Land* (Princeton, NJ: Van Nostrand, 1960).

## CEYLON, PORTUGUESE OCCUPATION OF

89

For centuries the Muslims had trade connections with Ceylon, which created some friction when the Portuguese arrived in 1505. The Iberians had been fighting to remove the Muslims from their homeland for a couple of centuries, so there was no love lost between the two cultures. Portugal, the sole European trading power in Asia, did not want economic competition from anyone. When Dom Laurenço de Almeida landed at Colombo, he had to establish a Portuguese power base to protect their national interests, so he began construction of a fort at the harbor town. The king of the lowland Sinhalese population, at the capital city of Kotte, welcomed the Portuguese. He was impressed by their guns and armor, and asked their protection in return for an annual tribute to be paid in cinnamon. King Parakrama Bahu VIII hoped to use the Europeans to secure his position against threats from the Tamil peoples in the northern part of the island, the highland king of Kandy, and the Moors.

The Portuguese built forts along the western coast of the island and soon dominated the export market from Ceylon. The island's traders were ruled by a governor-general on the island of Goa, who directed their economic activities throughout Asia. Working with the existing power structure, the Portuguese eventually expanded their trade dominance to political control as well. By allying themselves with the successive kings of Kotte and protecting them against the other powers on the island, they could dictate to the Sinhalese leaders. At one point the island was divided among three rival Sinhalese brothers. When a secret embassy to Portugal in 1540 asked the government to bless an infant heir to the throne of Kotte, the Portuguese did so, then sent troops and Franciscans to aid in the young king's rule. This event did much to consolidate Portugal's hold on the economy and the population.

The only serious threat to Portuguese power was King Rajasinha I of the local kingdom of Sitawaka. Learning from the Europeans, Rajasinha built an army fur-

nished with modern weapons and defeated Portuguese troops, after which he laid siege to Colombo. He built a navy and harassed Portuguese shipping. He also made war against the other kings on the island and defeated them. At the height of his reign, which lasted from 1554 to 1593, Rajasinha controlled all of Ceylon except Colombo and the kingdom of Jaffna on a small island off Ceylon's north coast. In the end, he was brought by a rival leader, not the Portuguese. Rajasinha renounced the dominant faith of Buddhism and became Hindu, and he persecuted Buddhist priests on Ceylon. However, he was regarded as a national champion for defending the island from foreign invaders.

During their struggle with Rajasinha, the Portuguese earned the enmity of the Ceylonese by capturing a sacred relic, one of Buddha's teeth. The Tooth Relic was the island's most sacred possession, and losing it to a foreign power was devastating, especially when the Portuguese archbishop at Goa ordered it burned as a heathen talisman. This action, along with the resistance of the islanders under Rajasinha, badly hurt Portuguese chances of recovering their former political or trade position. When the Dutch began to expand their international trade routes, they were able to break into the Ceylon market because of Portuguese weakness.

Surprisingly, 150 years of Portuguese presence in Ceylon produced few lasting results. The main effect was the introduction of Catholicism, a faith followed to this day by a significant minority of Ceylonese. Catholic priests sent to the island by the Portuguese usually acted on behalf of their converts against government persecution, and thus made a favorable impact. Their presence during the Portuguese dominance is regarded as the major reason Islam never took strong hold in southern India or Ceylon. The Portuguese also introduced a number of new food crops, which the Ceylonese turned to the island's benefit.

See also Ceylon, Dutch Occupation of [88].

References: Beny, Roloff, *Island Ceylon* (London: Thames & Hudson, 1970); Codrington, Humphrey, *A Short History of Ceylon* (Freeport, NY: Books for Libraries, 1926); Tresidder, Argus, *Ceylon: An Introduction to the Resplendent Land* (Princeton, NJ: Van Nostrand, 1960).

## CHING (MANCHU) DYNASTY

**90**

In the early 1600s the Nuchen tribe was a burgeoning power in Manchuria, to the northeast of the Chinese Ming dynasty. They came to prominence under the leadership of Nurhachi, who united them in 1616 and began to wage war against Ming China. He constructed a strong fortress in his capital, Liaoyang, then began training his soldiers along Ming lines. He divided them into four commands, or "banners," which later formed the basis of the Manchu political administration. In 1618, Nurhachi led his forces to war, seizing a Ming stronghold at Fushun and defeating the punitive force sent to recapture it. To counter this invasion, the Mings called on their traditional allies in Korea for reinforcements.

Nurhachi drove southwest into China, capturing Mukden in 1621. He could advance little farther, however, because the Ming army introduced artillery provided by European Jesuits, and these weapons were the deciding factor. Nurhachi gave up the assault on China for the moment, and turned west to attack Mongolia. When Nurhachi died in 1626, his son Abahai took over. In 1627 Abahai launched an invasion

of Korea to cover their rear for his proposed reinvasion of China. He forced the Koreans to recognize his sovereignty, then returned in 1636 to conquer the peninsula. Repeated raids into China in the early 1630s had proved fruitless, so Abahai began to develop an artillery arm for his forces.

In 1636 Abahai proclaimed the Ching dynasty in Mukden, and the Nuchen-led invaders came to be called the Manchus. Abahai took the regnal name of Ch'ung Teh. The Manchus expanded their power into the Amur River basin in four expeditions lasting through 1644. Ch'ung Teh died in 1643, leaving the throne to his five-year-old son Shun Chih; the young emperor's uncle Dorgon acted as regent. With the addition of Mongol troops who deserted their own army to join his and because of the widespread rebellions against Ming authority, Dorgon was able to take advantage of the faltering dynasty. A Ming general asked for cooperation in suppressing a peasant rebellion, and the Manchus aided him. The rebel leader Li Tzu-cheng seized Peking, but lost to the combined Ming-Manchu forces just south of the Great Wall; the Manchurians occupied Peking, then attacked south. The Ming emperor established a capital at Nanking and challenged the advancing Manchus, but lost to Dorgon in a seven-day battle near Yangchow. After slaughtering the defeated army and the inhabitants of the area, Dorgon captured Nanking. From this point, the Ming dynasty died. Though claimants to the throne resisted the Manchus for decades, their rivalry allowed the Manchus to defeat them in detail.

Through 1647 the Manchus swept southward, capturing Fukien province and Canton. Dorgon ran into some resistance from the last Ming emperor, Kuei Wang, but defeated him and consolidated control of southern China by 1651. Manchu forces gained control of the southwestern

A portrait of Emperor Ch'ing Ch'ien-lung painted by William Alexander

provinces by 1659, but had trouble from the sea. The pirates of Cheng Ch'eng-kung, or Koxinga, championed the Mings and raided along the coast of China, fighting both the Manchus and the Dutch, who had trading posts in the area. The Manchus withdrew their population from the coast and established a barrier ten miles inland; only Koxinga's death allowed them to regain control. The Manchus later cooperated with the Dutch to defeat the pirates, and the Manchus annexed Taiwan from them in 1683.

Meanwhile, the Russians pressed from the northwest. After a number of campaigns in the 1680s, the Ching emperor signed the Treaty of Nerchinsk, which removed the Russians from the Amur River valley. The Manchus also had to deal with aggressive nomadic tribes in Mongolia. Some tribes resisted the cession of suzerainty granted the Manchus at the Congress of Dolonor in 1689, but Manchu military power ultimately prevailed. With 80,000 men supported by artillery, the Manchus crushed the main resistance, led by Galdan of the Dzungars, in 1696.

The Manchu expansion to the northwest came under the 60-year reign of Emperor K'ang-hsi (1662–1722). To secure his hold on Mongolia, K'ang-hsi ordered forces to the Tibetan border. A dispute over the Dalai Lama took Manchu troops into Tibet in 1705 to support their candidate against the opposition of most Tibetans. The Dzungars intervened with 6,000 men in 1716, capturing the capital of Lhasa and imprisoning the Dalai Lama. The Manchu force sent to his rescue was ambushed and destroyed. K'ang-hsi responded with two armies in 1720, one of which reestablished control in Tibet; the other invaded and subdued Dzungar lands. For the first time the Mongols fought with muskets, but they were no match for the experience of the Manchus. K'ang-hsi installed a more ac-

ceptable Dalai Lama, but he also installed a Manchu garrison in Lhasa. Troubles with Tibetans and Dzungars continued through the mid-eighteenth century.

Though successful on the frontiers, an unforeseen source spelled the Manchus' doom. The Ching Dynasty had cooperated with the Dutch and with Portuguese Jesuits, but the increasing presence of Europeans began to diminish their power. The Manchus had incorporated the Ming bureaucracy upon their takeover and embraced the Confucian philosophy upon which the bureaucracy was based. This brought about an ultraconservative view that stagnated progress in China at the same time that growing numbers of Europeans, especially the British in the nineteenth century, brought technology the Chinese could not rival. Demands for trade enforced by military might gave the British a foothold in China that encouraged other Europeans to demand and receive trade and territorial concessions. The conservatism of the imperial court brought about its fall in the early twentieth century.

The Manchus were a foreign invader who established dominance in China, as did the Mongols under the Yuan dynasty. They kept a cultural separation between Manchurians and Chinese, though they adopted most of the Chinese traditions, economy, and technology. The Manchus forced their mode of dress on the Chinese, but for the most part they absorbed more of Chinese ways than they altered the lives of the common people.

*See also* China, Mongol Conquest of [41]; Ming Dynasty [68]; China, British Invasion of (Opium War) [130].

References: Hookham, Hilda, *A Short History of China* (New York: St. Martin's Press, 1970); Hsu, Immanuel, *The Rise of Modern China* (New York: Oxford

University Press, 1975); Twitchett, Denis, and John Fairbank, eds., *The Cambridge History of China,* Vols. 9 and 10 (New York: Cambridge University Press, 1993).

## 91      CORTÉS, HERNÁN

Hernán Cortés was born in Medellín, Spain. Like many other Spaniards who set sail to the New World in the 1500s, he was a minor noble. Minor Spanish nobles of his era often became conquistadors, for they were wealthy enough to travel to unsettled lands but not rich enough to be assured of the future security of their family fortunes in Spain. The prospect of attaining riches and fame as the first settlers of a newly discovered land recently claimed by the Spanish Crown appealed to many Spaniards of Cortés's generation.

Cortés first distinguished himself in Cuba, where he took part in the Spanish conquest of that island in 1511. At the time of the invasion, he was an officer under the command of Diego Velázquez, who led the military expedition to Cuba and became its governor.

In 1518 Velázquez authorized Cortés to undertake a very important mission. The Spaniards who had studied Columbus's 1492 voyages to America believed there was a kingdom close to Hispaniola that possessed vast quantities of gold. Columbus, who conquered much of the Caribbean and touched on the mainland of America, claimed that the natives of Hispaniola had revealed to him that such a kingdom existed. Cortés was to sail west toward the mainland of the Americas to search for this rich kingdom.

As Cortés prepared to sail west with a military expedition, Velázquez, a highly impulsive and temperamental man, abruptly relieved him of his duties. Velázquez's relatives and cronies had pressured him to grant them the privilege of undertaking the voyage, and they persuaded him to issue orders demanding that Cortés relinquish his command. When Cortés heard of Velázquez's change of heart, he hastily ordered his men (who still believed him to be its authorized commander) to board ship and speedily set sail from Cuba. Cortés's ships landed at Trinidad for provisions, and two messengers from Governor Velázquez brought him orders to return to Cuba under arrest. Having invested virtually all of his personal financial resources in the venture, Cortés resentfully defied the orders and headed for Mexico. His heavy personal investment in the mission, as well as his relationship with the governor of Cuba (he had married Velázquez's niece), perhaps accounts for Cortés's unflinching resolution to complete his voyage and establish himself as ruler wherever he landed. Essentially a fugitive, he had much to gain and little to lose as he headed for the Mexican coast.

When he landed in Mexico on Good Friday in 1519 (in the area where present-day Veracruz is located), he learned that the area was ruled by a vast empire extending throughout Mexico. His own force consisted of only about 600 men. Many were armed with steel swords or bows and arrows, and only 13 carried guns. Cortés also had 14 cannon and 16 cavalry horses. His soldiers were naturally intimidated at the prospect of invading a vast empire with such a paltry force, so Cortés burned their ships to forestall any desertion.

Cortés bluntly stated his ambition to quickly enrich himself in Mexico, proclaiming, "I have come to win gold, not to plow the fields like a peasant." By 1520 he had his gold, for in the summer of that year he became ruler of an empire with some 5 million subjects.

Ultimately, the king of Spain richly rewarded him with lands in Spain and ordered him to return. He was granted the title of marquis, and lived quietly in Spain until his death in 1547.

—John Adams

*See also* Mexico, Aztec Conquest of [65]; Western Hemisphere, Spanish Occupation of [110].

References: Innes, Hammond, *The Conquistadors* (New York: Knopf, 1969); Marks, Richard, *Cortes: The Great Adventurer and the Fate of Aztec Mexico* (New York: Knopf, 1993); White, John, *Cortez and the Fall of the Aztec Empire* (New York: St. Martin's Press, 1971).

## 92 EAST INDIES, DUTCH OCCUPATION OF THE

Pieter Coen, founder of the port of Batavia in Java, which is now Jakarta.

In the latter part of the 1500s, the Dutch acted as middlemen between the Portuguese bringing spices from Asia and the customers of Europe; Portugal handled the importation, Holland handled the distribution. The arrangement was mutually profitable until King Philip II of Spain, in an attempt to crush the power of Protestantism in Holland, closed the port of Lisbon to Dutch shipping and cut off their ability to distribute the spices. Holland had no choice but to bypass Portugal and establish its own contacts in Asia. By 1596, Dutch ships cruised the East Indies, or Spice Islands, looking for markets.

Competition between Holland and Portugal meant increased prices for the Spice Islanders' products. Equally important, the Dutch were uninterested in converting anyone to Catholicism or any other religion. This pleased the Spice Islanders, most of whom were Muslim. The Dutch signed agreements with local sultans and soon began to force the Portuguese out of business. Portugal's resources were stretched thin by maintaining government and trade relations from East Asia to Brazil, so they were unable to mount any serious opposition. They were soon out of the picture when the Dutch, with local assistance from the sultan of Jahore on Sumatra, laid siege in late 1640 to the major Portuguese trading center at Malacca, on the Malay Peninsula. It fell after six months, and the Portuguese ceased being a threat in the area. The Dutch had mild competition from England, but the English were busy with North America and did not press the Dutch in East Asia.

Soon Holland established a monopoly on spices heading for Europe, and they saw the potential for making even more money controlling the trade within Asia. Holland built settlements and forts to protect their interests and carry on trade, but had to stamp out local competition as well if they were to dominate the Asian market. In

Portrait of Jan van Linschoten and the title page from his *Itinerario*, published in 1596

1618 the Dutch governor-general, Pieter Coen, established the town of Batavia on the island of Java as the Dutch area headquarters. From here the Dutch controlled the Sunda Straits, the most popular trading route through the islands. Throughout the 1600s the Dutch spread their contacts through the area, and because of their monopoly were able once again to lower their buying costs. The local producers had to pay Dutch prices or not sell anything, so the Dutch grew very rich. Dutch ships patrolled the waters of the East Indies to keep out foreign ships.

The only trouble the Dutch had for decades came from local powers who did not like the low prices the Dutch paid. Occasionally the Dutch forced sultans to cooperate at gunpoint rather than sell their wares to other Asian ships that might venture to trade with Europeans. The Dutch wanted to monopolize the tin exports from Perak, on the west coast of the Malay Peninsula. In 1652 they tried to build a trading post that would control the purchasing

in the area; the Perak forces destroyed it. The Dutch built a fort in 1670 to guard access to the country and fought the locals to keep the fort; the sultan of Perak looked for other ways to ship and sell his tin, and the Dutch were never able to establish a monopoly on the product.

Throughout the Dutch tenure as the dominant European power in the area, the local tribes struggled among themselves over matters of local interest. By and large the Dutch had little concern in these relations as long as they could maintain a relatively peaceful atmosphere and keep the trade flowing. Usually the Dutch did not interfere in the politics of the area unless it directly affected their income. Occasionally a tribe would challenge Dutch power, as did the Bugis of Celebes in the 1780s. The Bugis were mercenaries whose activities affected the rise and fall of sultanates in the East Indies, and they gradually came to influence the politics of many of the states of the area, much as the Mamluks of Egypt turned from warriors to rulers. The

Bugis challenged the Dutch by laying siege to Malacca in 1784, attempting to exert control over the area from Jahore on Sumatra. The six-month siege failed when the Dutch brought in reinforcements and defeated the Bugi naval contingent. After the Bugis were removed from the area, the Dutch signed an agreement with the sultan of Jahore (now freed from Bugi control) that gave Holland dominance on Sumatra.

The cost of European wars in the 1790s caused the most damage to the Dutch in the East Indies, but through the 1700s they had seen the power of the British East India Company rise in Asia. Britain's major enterprise in Asia was Indian and Chinese tea, a market they dominated. By the late 1700s the British were also looking toward Borneo, an East Indian island the Dutch had ignored as lacking trade potential, considering it merely a haven for pirates. Thus, when Napoleon conquered continental Europe, the British were establishing themselves in the area, and suddenly the Dutch in the Indies had no support from home. They lost Malacca to the British in 1795 through an agreement with the Dutch government-in-exile that Britain would occupy Dutch possessions around the world (to deny them to Napoleon for the duration of hostilities). Though Malacca was returned to Holland in 1815, Britain regained the town in 1824.

The Dutch lost their preeminent trading position in the area, but the political control they had established from Batavia through various treaties with area sultans made them masters of the East Indian islands. Britain came to dominate Southeast Asian trade, but Holland maintained the East Indies as colonies until after World War II.

See also Singapore, British Occupation of [143]; Dutch East Indies, Japanese Invasion of [153].

References: Hyma, Albert, *A History of the Dutch in the Far East* (Ann Arbor, MI: George Wair Publishing Co., 1953); Ryan, N. J., *A History of Malaysia and Singapore* (London: Oxford University Press, 1976); Vlekke, Bernard, *The Story of the Dutch East Indies* (Cambridge, MA: Harvard University Press, 1945).

## ENGLAND, SPANISH INVASION OF (SPANISH ARMADA)

**93**

The gold and silver of the New World brought untold wealth to Spain, riches that the Spanish kings translated into military power. Kings Charles I and Philip II built armies not just for national purposes, but for religious reasons as well. Strong Catholic rulers, they believed their nation was meant to exploit these newfound riches because God smiled on them, and he smiled on them because they were good Catholics. Therefore, they believed it was Spain's duty to do God's work, which meant not only converting the inhabitants of the Americas, but defending in Europe the one true church from attacks by Protestants, whom the pope viewed as heretics. Philip sent his armies across Europe to smite the heretics, and if Spain should come to control some territory along the way, so much the better. The Protestant nation causing Philip the most grief, however, was not so easy to smite: England.

Since the early 1500s the Catholic church in Britain had been in a state of flux. British king Henry VIII rejected the pope's authority and made himself head of the church in England. After his death, his daughter Mary (raised a strong Catholic by her mother) recognized the pope's authority and, to prove herself and her country, married Philip of Spain. The Catholic champion could thus focus on continental heretics and not worry about England—not for five years, at least, for that was how long Mary ruled. Her death brought Elizabeth I to the throne, and Elizabeth was her father's daughter. She not only rejected the pope's power and made herself head of the church, she removed Catholicism altogether and created the Church of England, or Anglican church. Philip lost the security he had enjoyed regarding England and, to make matters worse, in power was a monarch who supported Protestant movements in Europe. Thus, not only was the Catholic champion challenged, so was the church itself.

England in the 1500s was not a major power, but Elizabeth dreamed it might become one. Power required a strong navy, which cost money, and most of the real wealth was under Spanish control. Unable to get the money at its source, Elizabeth secretly commissioned privateers to raid Spanish treasure convoys in the Atlantic. It was more than Philip could stand. Not only was this woman challenging his church, she was stealing his money to do so. Thinking that he could control England as he had done with Mary, Philip proposed marriage to Elizabeth. She declined the offer. Philip considered England to be his because of his earlier marriage into the royal family, so he felt he had no choice but to take direct action against Elizabeth. He would invade England and enforce his will on the country.

In the mid-1580s Philip began bringing ships together in an invasion fleet. Men and supplies were to be taken by 130 ships up the French coast to Flanders, where a 10,000-man force was currently fighting Dutch Protestants. This force would be ferried to England, and Elizabeth would be overthrown. The British army (such as it was) certainly had no reputation, and no naval force could resist the largest fleet in the world, so Philip saw no reason why the

most powerful nation in the world should not be able to defeat a second-rate country such as England. He assembled a force of mixed nationality: Portuguese, Italian, and even Levantine ships and crews were in the Spanish Armada. The ships were placed under the command of the duke of Medina-Sidonia. The duke had never been to sea, but he was of royal blood, and could command the mixed force with that authority.

The lengthy time required to prepare the armada allowed plenty of time for word to filter to England. The English gathered 102 ships, a mixture of royal and privately owned vessels. Command was given to Lord Howard of Effingham who, like Medina-Sidonia, was not a sailor but had sufficient royal authority. Luckily for England, Howard was surrounded by experienced captains such as Francis Drake, Martin Frobisher, and John Hawkins, all of whom had made a name for themselves as privateers and were able to work together.

The armada left Lisbon harbor on 29 May 1588, but bad weather soon drove them into Corunna, on Spain's northwest coast. Three weeks later they sailed for Flanders and rounded the French coast. By 19 July they had entered the English Channel. Most of the English ships were in port at Plymouth, and they rushed to leave the harbor. It was a slow process against adverse winds, but by 21 July they formed up behind the armada and followed, looking for an opportunity. The westerly winds made it impossible for the Spanish to turn and fight, so they continued up the Channel until they reached Calais, where Medina-Sidonia could resupply and send a message to the Duke of Parma's forces in Flanders that he was on his way.

The Spanish ships anchored in a tight crescent formation. In the 1500s the standard method of fighting at sea was not long-range cannon fire until one ship surrendered or sank. Instead, ships would sail alongside each other, and marines would do battle; whichever force of soldiers prevailed won the battle, and the defeated ship was taken as a prize, virtually undamaged. Therefore, a tight formation was the best method of defense because the interior ships could not be reached by an attacker. This standard defense, however, doomed the Spaniards. Lord Howard took eight of his ships, filled them with gunpowder, armed all the cannon, and set them afire. The prevailing wind carried them directly into the midst of the armada, burning and exploding.

The previously disciplined Spanish fleet broke apart. Each commander was concerned with his own ship as he tried to get away from the other burning ships, for which they had no defense but maneuver. The massed Spanish force disintegrated and, running for the open sea, ran into the waiting English fleet. The Spanish tried to continue their journey to link up with their army, but Dutch rebels denied them landing and the English continued to harass them. With the way home blocked and the coastline hostile, the Spanish had no choice but to sail home the long way, around Scotland and Ireland. The English chased them until their supplies of food and powder ran low, then abandoned the armada to nature. Heavy weather plagued the Spanish and caused shipwrecks from the Orkneys to the Shetlands to Ireland to Cornwall. The armada lost 64 ships and 10,000 of its 30,000 men.

Like the Battle of Britain 350 years later, the Spanish invasion attempt is important for its failure. The year 1588 marked the high point of Spanish power. With so many ships destroyed, their stranglehold on the Atlantic began to slip. Though Spain continued to be a power for some time to come, never again were the Spanish as fearsome. At the same time, the battle that cost the English so little brought their fleet into some prominence, and they could now ply the Atlantic with more freedom. England had long lusted after Spain's New World riches and could now freely plant colonies of its own. The British could not go to Central and South America for gold and silver because Spain's power there was still impregnable, but colonies along the North American coast began to sprout in the decades following the armada's defeat. The decrease in Spanish power mirrored an increase in English strength; the British Empire would soon be in sight. Further, Elizabeth was able to continue her support of Protestant movements in Europe, and the Dutch soon gained their independence from Spain's rule.

To a great extent, the world as it is today dates from 28 July 1588. North America is predominantly British in its heritage rather than Spanish. Had the armada succeeded, Elizabeth's forces could not have withstood Spain's invading army. The British Empire, if it ever came to exist, would have been seriously delayed, and the Spanish would have colonized North America as well as the southern part of the hemisphere. A well-timed northwesterly breeze—the "Protestant Wind," as it came to be known—blew those fire ships into the armada and saved England. Had the wind blown from another direction, our world would have taken a different direction as well.

*See also* North America, British Occupation of [100]; Western Hemisphere, Spanish Occupation of [110]; Britain, Nazi Invasion of (Battle of Britain) [149].

References: Lewis, Michael, *The Spanish Armada* (New York: Thomas Y. Crowell, 1968); Martin, Colin, *The Spanish Armada* (New York: Norton, 1988); Mattingly, Garrett, *The Armada* (Boston: Houghton Mifflin, 1959).

**94** INDIA, BRITISH
OCCUPATION OF

European sailors reached India in the 1500s, when the Moghul Empire was at its height. The country's riches attracted Portuguese merchants, followed in later years by the Dutch, French, and British. The Portuguese lost the necessary sea power to maintain distant trading posts and the Dutch concentrated more on the spice trade in the islands of Indonesia, which left France and Britain as the main rivals for Indian trade. France's East India Company gained the first foothold, but lost their position on the subcontinent through military defeat in India and diplomatic exchanges of land as the result of wars in Europe. The British became the main European power in India almost by default.

Britain established its first trading post in 1639 when the British purchased a harbor from a south Indian ruler; that acquisition, on India's southeastern coast, became the port of Madras. The British built fortifications and began buying up the high-quality Indian cotton textiles. An attempt to enter the north Indian trade ran into the fading power of the Moghuls and the growing power of the Bengalis, both of whom barely tolerated British merchants. With the construction of a fortified base on the Hooghly River, part of the Ganges Delta, the trading center of Calcutta was born in 1690. To attempt entry into western Indian markets, the British gained the defunct Portuguese port of Surat, where the Tapti River empties into the Arabian Sea. All three ports were operated by the British East India Company, which held sole trading rights.

The British solidified their position in the north in a rather odd fashion. The Moghul emperors contracted out tax collection, and the British gained the concession in the areas around Madras and Calcutta. When the Moghul Empire collapsed and factional fighting all over India ensued, the British kept collecting taxes and began to form military units to protect their trading posts and routes. The mixture of European and local troops became the basis of the Indian army, which at first was a business venture rather than a governmental one. Because the British could maintain a measure of stability in an increasingly disrupted Indian society, their trading posts began to attract Indian merchants looking for a secure place to do business. Their soldiers proved their ability to defeat bandits and keep the peace, and various kings began to contract with the company. Military expertise in return for trading rights became standard East India Company procedure, and it aided the British merchants in gaining a major hold on the markets of all parts of India.

With control over Bengal, Madras, and Calcutta, the British settled down to maintaining order in the areas immediately around those cities, which grew rapidly with Indian merchants and artisans looking for a peaceful place to do business. The East India Company gradually began to act like a government, for the warring states offered no justice in their courts or taxation. British control extended in the 1750s via the Seven Years' War, wherein an Anglo-French war in Europe had colonial side-effects. The French plotted with local powers to gain a military advantage, but the British defeat of the French and their ally of Hyderabad in the south spelled the beginning of the end of French involvement in the region. The Anglo-French conflict was timely because the Moghul Empire, already on its last legs, was battered even further by invading Afghan armies. The downfall of the Moghuls encouraged other states to exert their authority. Bengal attacked Calcutta in 1756 and forced the British to evacuate. An avenging force from Madras under the leadership of Robert Clive (who had defeated the Franco-Hyderabad alliance) recaptured the city and defeated the Bengali army at Plassey, giving the company control over Bengal. A victory over a Bengali-led coalition in 1764 removed any serious competition in northern India.

The arrival of Warren Hastings as governor-general in the mid-1770s marked the establishment of Britain and the East India Company as the masters of India. By posing as an Oriental-style absolute monarch, he commanded Indian respect. He enforced just and fair practices in law enforcement, taxation, and the courts that had not been experienced in India since the days of Ashoka. These tactics won him local support, and Hastings intervened in factional squabbles along the frontier, both to extend company power and to divide and conquer the remaining recalcitrant states, notably Maratha in the northwest. Passage of the India Act of 1784 in London cut into his authority, and he resigned.

Hastings was followed by Lord Cornwallis. He furthered the company policy of fair taxation and extended company control to Mysore in the south. His successor, Richard Wellesley, sent British forces up the Ganges from Calcutta to force the cooperation of the state of Oudh, and the British gained control over the main trade route in India. Wellesley also entered into Ceylon, establishing a British presence there to take advantage of the harbor at Trincomalee and to "protect" the Dutch colony from Napoleon's forces. After Napoleon's defeat in Europe, all French influence in India was removed.

The British became overlords of India somewhat by accident. Originally interested only in trade, their fair business practices attracted many Indians to British settlements. Rejection of the weak and rapacious local rulers left a power vacuum, which the East India Company filled, originally to maintain safe trade routes but ultimately to maintain order for the entire population. The growing bureaucracy solidified British authority and, by attracting Indians to the burgeoning civil service, created a partnership. While the British tradespeople benefited the most, many Indians profited as well. The mass of Indians remained poor, but the opportunity to live in peace and expect justice made the British the favored choice over the local kings, even if that meant outside domination. Along with Hindi and Urdu, English became an accepted language and the path to success in the British civil service and trading circles. For 100 years the Indians lived peacefully under British suzerainty, but in 1857 revolted against the company. It was disbanded, and the British government took over its operation. India remained the "jewel in the crown" of the British Empire until its independence in 1948.

The relationship between the British and the Indians is somewhat strange. Many British were fascinated by Indian culture and studied it in depth. For the most part, the Indians were allowed to continue their cultural practices, but slavery and *suttee* (the ritual immolation of wives with their dead husbands) were banished. The Indians also took on some British practices. Not only did English become widely spoken, British pastimes like soccer and cricket became Indian passions as well. Still, the British generally did not mingle with the locals, and they tried to re-create some of England in India rather than "go native." The British prejudice against nonwhites showed itself in interpersonal relations, which kept the two races generally distinct, but that did not usually affect the business of running the country. As Kipling described the attitude, the British believed they were "taking up the white man's burden" to assist India. The Indians did not appreciate this viewpoint, but they valued the stability Britain brought, and responded by assisting the British Empire in its wars, sending troops around the world to fight alongside Australians, New Zealanders, South Africans, and others. The British exit in 1948 revived some of the old tribal differences, but a tradition of democracy is well established.

*See also* Mauryan Empire [27]; East Indies, Dutch Occupation of the [92]; India, French Occupation of [95]; Moghul Empire [98]; Saxony, Prussian Invasion of (Seven Years' War) [106]; Southern United States, British Invasion of [123]; Ceylon, British Occupation of [126].

References: Chamerlain, Muriel, *Britain and India* (Hamden, CT: Archon Books, 1974); Griffiths, P. J., *The British Impact on India* (Hamden, CT: Archon Books, 1965); Mason, Philip, *A Matter of Honour* (London: Jonathan Cape, 1974).

## INDIA, FRENCH OCCUPATION OF

**95**

As with most of France's international endeavors in the colonial period, the French looked more for trade than empire. In 1664 the Marquis de Colbert formed a government-sponsored company to exploit the Indian trade for French merchants rather than buy from the British and Dutch. Colbert's company inherited few assets from previous private attempts to break into the Eastern trade; only Port Dauphin on the island of Madagascar was a French-controlled port of call. Still, previous merchants had established some contacts upon which the new company was able to expand.

The French effort had many of the aspects of a government, most particularly the right to enter into trade agreements and the right to negotiate peace or declare war with non-Europeans. The company had government-appointed directors in Paris, but investment was open to the public, who proved less than enthusiastic: Only about half the shares made available were publicly purchased. The venture ran into hard times because of its inability to compete with the established British and Dutch traders and because of national rivalries being fought out in Europe. By the time of relative peace in 1713, the company was too deep in debt to survive. An attempt to revive it under John Law in 1719 fell apart in four years. The government again stepped in and ran it under the name Compagnie de Indes. The company was granted a monopoly over all international French colonial trade; again, the directors were appointed by the crown and acted as civil servants, which meant that the company did not have to pay them a salary and all trade was profit.

By 1723 the company was able to take advantage of earlier acquisitions, though Madagascar was abandoned in favor of Île de France (Mauritius) and Bourbon islands in the Indian Ocean. Pondicherry was the French trade headquarters in India. The company built "factories" (trading posts) along the Indian coastline, and began to compete more successfully with the British and Dutch. The government provided all necessary naval support, and the company hired soldiers to protect their interests. All went well until 1763, when France and its allies in Europe lost the Seven Years' War. The French governor-general in India, Dupleix, was unable to defeat the forces of the British East India Company and lost some factories as a result. France was able to continue operating in India, and indeed, the profits were considerable, but the losses in ships and the costs of war were too great for trade to overcome. Rather than invest more government money to keep the operation afloat, Paris decided to remove the company's monopoly status and turn the factories into colonies.

Independent merchants were able to profit in India, but not so well that all of France's trade should pass through them. A new company was begun in 1785 with a monopoly on trade, but without the previous powers of government. It survived, but only because it bought through British agents; the French had lost any contacts of their own. The British victory in the Seven Years' War virtually guaranteed that their enterprise, the British East India Company, would dominate the India trade and have the lion's share of the subcontinent's riches. With the political upheaval of the French Revolution, the Compagnie de Indes became low priority for the Paris government. French trading posts existed, unfortified, through 1815, but in the wake of Napoleon's defeat the British acquired all the French holdings. In the long run, France had little impact on India; the subcontinent's European influence came almost totally from Great Britain.

*See also* Saxony, Prussian Invasion of (Seven Years' War) [106]; Napoleon Buonaparte [118].

References: Mason, Philip, *A Matter of Honour* (London: Jonathan Cape, 1974); Miles, William, *Imperial Burdens* (Boulder, CO: L. Rienner Publishers, 1995); Sen, Siba Pada, *The French in India* (Calcutta: University of Calcutta Press, 1947).

## ITALY, AUSTRIAN INVASION OF (WAR OF THE SPANISH SUCCESSION)

96

In 1700, Charles II of Spain died childless, naming as heir his somewhat distant relative Philip of Anjou. Normally the situation would not have created much of a problem, but Philip was the grandson of King Louis XIV of France, an absolute monarch who had made his nation the most powerful in Europe and had dominated European affairs for decades. If his grandson Philip, of the house of Bourbon, did not cede any future claim to the French throne, then the potential for united Franco-Spanish power was too great for the remainder of Europe to contemplate. One of France's traditional rivals, Austria, was ruled by Leopold I, who also held the position of Holy Roman Emperor. He was a Habsburg (as Charles II had been) and believed that his second son, Charles, should inherit the Spanish throne. He therefore planned to fight for his son's rights, and there was no shortage of European countries willing to assist him to restrain French power.

Louis provoked the war, as he had often done in the past, by invading the Netherlands and seizing fortifications along the frontier, moves he claimed were defensive. Leopold claimed the Spanish Netherlands as his own, so the French attack was all the excuse he needed to go to war. Not only did Leopold want his son on the Spanish throne, he hoped to expand Austrian territory in the process. His first move was to commit troops to Italy, much of which was under Spanish control, under his most able commander, Eugene of Savoy. Eugene entered northern Italy in 1701 and faced a superior Franco-Spanish force, which he finally drove back into Mantua.

The other concerned European countries soon entered into an alliance initiated by Great Britain, whose King William III had recently finished a war against Louis. Under William, Parliament raised a large army to counter not only French ambition, but also in response to Louis's recognition of the young James III of the Scottish house of Stuart as king of England and Louis's initiation of economic warfare against England. William died of an accident in 1701 and was succeeded by his daughter Anne, who continued to support the conflict. The Grand Alliance attracted the membership of England, Austria, Holland, Prussia, and most German principalities. Only Austria had a direct interest in the succession; the others joined to limit French expansion.

The British army was led by John Churchill, the earl (later duke) of Marlborough, one of the finest British generals of all time. He commanded an allied force that invaded the Spanish Netherlands in June 1702; some 12,000 of the 50,000 troops were British, the remainder Dutch and German. His Dutch allies troubled him the most, because their political leaders often overrode his decision to fight when they would not allow him to commit Dutch forces. As he invaded, forces of the empire threatened the French possession of Strasbourg. Marlborough finally convinced the Dutch to allow him to assault fortresses along the Rhine, which he captured by the autumn. He hoped to link up with the Austrians, but the entrance of Bavaria on the French side threatened such a connection. Maximilian, the elector of Bavaria, joined Louis on the promise of the throne of the Holy Roman Empire if Austria were defeated. He was joined in May 1703 by a French force under General Claude de Villars, who urged an attack on Vienna, but Maximilian preferred to seize the Tyrol and attempt a link with French forces in Italy, a venture that failed. Through the latter part of the summer of 1703, Villars enjoyed success against Austrian forces and the German state of Baden, defeating them separately in the Danube Valley. When his second suggestion for an attack on Vienna was refused, Villars resigned. French forces under Tallard also enjoyed success along the middle Rhine.

Meanwhile Marlborough was being frustrated in the Netherlands, either by his hesitant Dutch allies or his French counterpart, Villeroi. The success of the Franco-Bavarian forces drew his attention in 1704, and Marlborough marched to join his army with the forces of Eugene in Austria, who had recently been recalled from Italy. After a series of maneuvers to defeat or baffle the French, Eugene and Marlborough joined forces in August in Bavaria. Together their 56,000 men faced a 60,000-man force of French and Bavarians under French general Tallard and Maximilian. The resulting battle of Blenheim was a smashing allied victory; the defeated Bavarian forces withdrew, and Maximilian's dream of becoming emperor died when his province was annexed by Austria. The battle also destroyed the myth of French invincibility that Louis's armies had held for years.

Despite this turn of events, neither side showed any inclination toward negotiations. The year 1705 brought nothing but stalemate on all fronts. That was broken on the Netherlands front in 1706 when Marlborough scored another victory over French forces at Ramillies, near Namur. This enabled him to consolidate the Spanish Netherlands by October. In 1706 the main theater of war shifted back to Italy, where French general Vendome regained territory lost earlier to Austria. This French success took Eugene back to Italy to lead Austrian forces. In the battle of Turin in September, Eugene defeated Vendome's replacement, the duke of Orleans, and drove the French completely out of Italy. Austrian dominance would be established there for more than a century.

Little happened in 1707, but in 1708 the French once again aimed toward the Netherlands. Vendome had been given command of French forces, and he went on the offensive against Marlborough. The British commander had planned to join

Eugene, but before the juncture could take place, Marlborough engaged the French at Oudenarde, winning another victory on 11 July. Vendome turned him back at Ghent shortly afterward, but Marlborough captured the city in a winter campaign, and in January 1709 the French withdrew to defenses along their borders. Louis offered to begin negotiations, but he refused to accept the allied peace terms, which he considered overly harsh, and the war continued. Through the summer of 1709, Marlborough and Eugene tried to break through the French defensive line or force them out into the open field. When they began the siege of Mons, Louis ordered Villars to fight; he marched to Malplaquet to threaten the allied rear. Marlborough turned to meet him there and the resulting battle on 11 September proved inconclusive. The allies lost too many men to follow up, but the French failed to relieve Mons, which fell at the end of October.

In 1711, Marlborough was recalled by a new English government, never to command again. Negotiations began soon thereafter and continued throughout 1712. As talks proceeded, Eugene wanted to continue fighting to gain leverage at the conference, but the Dutch were overly cautious. The French, under Villars, seized the initiative and recaptured some fortresses along the frontier, which gave the French bargaining power. The Treaty of Utrecht was signed 11 April 1713. Louis recognized the Protestant succession in England and ceded some French property in the Americas to England. Philip of Anjou was recognized as King Philip V of Spain, and Louis guaranteed that Spain and France would remain separate. Louis also agreed to cede the Spanish Netherlands as well as Spanish territory in Italy to the Austrian Habsburgs, but the Holy Roman Emperor (now Charles VI) refused to agree. He

wanted both Austria and the Spanish throne he had claimed at the beginning of the war, so he continued fighting. His lack of success, however, forced him to sign the Treaty of Rastatt (as the emperor of Austria) and the Treaty of Baden (as Holy Roman Emperor), making peace with France. He took control of the Netherlands and the ceded Italian provinces, but he refused to recognize Bourbon rule in Spain.

The war accomplished the goal of the Grand Alliance by constraining French expansionism and maintaining a balance of power, though that shifted somewhat. Spain, long a declining power, lost the most: its Netherlands and Italian holdings to Austria, and Gibraltar, Minorca, and its slave trade with the Western Hemisphere to England. France also ceded Newfoundland and the Hudson Bay to England, thus beginning the French expulsion from North America. Though Louis succeeded in keeping his country from being surrounded by Habsburgs again, France had passed its prime. The English were becoming ascendant in the world through their dominance of maritime trade, and future French conflicts with England too often proved futile. The cost of the war severely damaged the French economy, and the cession of overseas possessions did nothing to alleviate that loss. France was perhaps the most grateful for the quarter-century of peace that followed, for they could finally recover from Louis's constant warmaking. Louis XIV died in 1715, and no other monarch was able to exercise his absolute, divine rule. Though Louis became the most significant figure of his age, France's power did not long outlast him.

See also North America, French Occupation of [101]; Palatinate, French Invasion of the (War of the League of Augsburg) [103].

References: Hassel, Arthur, *Louis XIV and the Zenith of French Monarchy* (Freeport, NY: Books for Libraries, 1972); Kamen, Henry, *The War of Succession in Spain, 1700–15* (Bloomington: University of Indiana Press, 1969); Lossky, Andrew, *Louis XIV and the French Monarchy* (New Brunswick, NJ: Rutgers University Press, 1994).

## ITALY, FRENCH INVASIONS OF

**97**

It may be impossible to find a more confusing set of political circumstances than that of Renaissance Italy. The peninsula was full of rival city-states with occasional links to European royal houses and an ever-shifting set of alliances among those royal houses and themselves. During the fifteenth and sixteenth centuries, no ruler held particularly strong ties to any other, and the armies of Italy were mercenary *condotierri* who fought for anyone who paid their price, often shifting sides during battle for a higher offer. The various warring *condotierri* bands knew one another well enough that the battles were often little more than pantomimes of combat, the mercenary leaders deciding among themselves who should win. Needless bloodshed was avoided, but it created a soldiery that became both more professional and less talented, which did not serve them well when outside armies invaded.

The French under Charles VIII entered Italy a number of times with an ever-changing set of allies and enemies. Charles had a relatively strong claim to the throne of Naples, but his entrance into Italian politics came by way of an invitation from Ludovico Sforza, the duke of Milan. In 1494, Sforza found the Italian city-states of Naples, Florence, and the Papal States arrayed against him, so he called on Charles for assistance, promising him military aid and access to his throne in Naples. It is a matter of some debate how eager Charles was to claim that throne, but it seems clear that he was eager for adventure, if nothing else. His father, Louis XI, had expanded French territory by conquest and inheritance, making France a strong military power, but he had always remained wary of getting involved in Italian politics. Charles had no such qualms, and he responded to Sforza's invitation.

His army of 25,000 (including some 8,000 Swiss mercenaries) joined with Sforza to conclude a quick and successful campaign. Within a year Charles had defeated the Florentines and forced them to cede the city of Pisa to him; he occupied the Papal States, and he easily occupied the kingdom of Naples. He considered launching a crusade against the Turks in Constantinople or the Muslims of Jerusalem, but the League of Venice—consisting of Venice, his former ally Milan, the Holy Roman Empire under Maximilian, Spain, England, and Pope Alexander VI—joined together to threaten his line of communications back to France. He marched north in 1495 and engaged a *condottieri* force under Giovanni Francesco Gonzaga. On 6 July they fought in the pass at Fornovo, and the French artillery proved too effective and aggressive for the Italians, who retreated after losing almost ten times as many men as the French. Charles decided to return to France rather than Naples.

Naples retained a French army, but its king, Ferrante, had familial ties to the house of Aragon in Spain. Spain sent forces to his aid in 1495, and took advantage of Charles's departure. After an initial loss, the Spanish general Fernández de Córdoba fought a war of attrition against the French and wore them out over a three-year period. When he left in 1498, the French had been removed, but a civil war the following year brought them back to Naples.

Charles's son Louis XII returned to claim his throne in 1499. His main ally was Pope Alexander VI, who turned to him to counter the increasing power of Venice. Though Louis entered into an agreement with Ferdinand of Aragon to divide the kingdom of Naples between them, he invaded and provoked a war with Spain. Louis easily conquered Milan, and his larger force took over Naples as Spanish ships occupied the harbor at Taranto and blockaded the major French base at Barletta. At the battle of Cerignola on 26 April 1503, Spanish forces under Córdoba defeated a combined Franco-Swiss force by breaking a cavalry charge with harquebusiers, making it the first battle in history decided by gunpowder small arms. Córdoba quickly occupied Naples and spent the remainder of the year harassing French forces. On 29 December 1503, Córdoba launched a surprise attack at the Garigliano River and crushed the French; they were allowed to leave Italy by sea under terms concluded on 1 January. In 1505, Louis ceded his claims in Naples to Ferdinand.

France was not through with Italy yet, however. Louis XII was back in 1508, allied this time with Maximilian, the Papal States, and Spain in the League of Cambrai, formed to resist Venetian power. France scored a major victory at Agnadello in May 1509 and Venice lost much of its territory to Spanish forces, but disunity within the league allowed Venice to recover most of its lands. Yet another combination of forces was created in 1510 when the Papal States sponsored the Holy League to unite against the French and Maximilian's German troops. Spain joined in the league with Pope Julius II and Venice, but there was little fighting of consequence until 1511, when a new French commander arrived: Gaston de Foix, 21-year-old duke of Nemours. He took the initiative and drove away a besieging force from Bologna, then turned northward against Venetian troops at Brescia, besieging and capturing that city in February 1512. At a fierce battle at Ravenna, Gaston routed a Papal-Spanish force but was killed in the pursuit, robbing the French of a potentially brilliant general.

Just when things seemed to be going well for France, Maximilian changed sides and withdrew his troops from the French army. Joining with Swiss forces, Maximilian drove the French from Italy. Prince Louis de La Tremoille led the French force back into Milan in 1513, but was soon driven back after losing a battle at Novara in June. The French ignored Italy for a while when English forces under Henry VIII invaded France. Switzerland took a French bribe to stay out of the invasion, and Henry VIII and Maximilian quarreled over strategy. All the members of the Holy League made peace with France in 1513 or 1514.

Not content to leave well enough alone, Francis I of France now allied himself with Venice and Henry of England against Spain, Milan, Florence, Switzerland, the pope, and the Holy Roman Empire. Francis's capture of Milan was sufficient to break the alliance against him, and he ended the war in possession of most of northern Italy. Five years later he was at war with Charles I of Spain, soon to become Holy Roman Emperor as well. His invasion through the Pyrenees in 1521 sparked renewed fighting in Italy. France was forced out of Italy by a defeat at Milan, but marched back in 1523. Defeats in the spring of 1524 were followed by an abortive invasion of France in the late summer. French troops came right back in October 1524. Francis's army besieged Pavia, but was defeated by a relieving force in February 1525. Francis was captured by the Spanish and taken to Madrid, where he was forced to buy his freedom with a treaty abandoning all claims in Italy.

Francis renounced the treaty as soon as he returned to Paris, and he was soon on the campaign trail again. His war in Italy lasted until 1529, during which time French forces fared poorly. In the Treaty of Cambrai in 1529, he once again surrendered any right to Italian claims. He spent the next seven years reorganizing his army, and invaded Italy in 1536. After a cease-fire, signed in 1538, Francis did the unthinkable for a Christian European: He allied himself with Suleiman the Magnificent, sultan of the Ottoman Empire, who was then threatening the Holy Roman Empire. A Franco-Turkish naval force sacked Nice in 1543, and Francis won the battle of Ceresole, south of Turin, in April 1544. It was a short-lived victory, because French forces were soon home to defend France from invasions by the Holy Roman Empire and England. Emperor Charles soon abandoned the invasion to spend more time on the Turkish threat, but Henry VIII kept French forces tied down until 1546. France tried one more invasion in 1552 under a new king, Henry II, but it failed to restore French power in Italy. Warfare against the Holy Roman Empire until 1559 kept them so busy that the French never returned to the Mediterranean.

It might be said that the Franco-Italian wars brought an end to the Renaissance, because the almost constant warfare for 50 years kept the dukes and princes who had so strongly supported the arts and sciences from spending their money on these peaceful and cultural pursuits. The rampaging armies dealt so much destruction to the countryside and the cities, while the rulers taxed the citizens unmercifully, that the peninsula was ruined economically. Every major city saw fighting and destruction to some extent; Rome was sacked for the first time since the Byzantine days. It reconfirmed the political discord of the peninsula, which would not see unity until the

end of the nineteenth century. Italy would become a battleground again in the future, but it no longer showed itself to be a leader in any field.

The theorist Machiavelli wrote his discourse *The Art of War* in the wake of these invasions, arguing that the centralized power of the French government proved superior to the fragmented power of the Italian city-states. The wars also established a long lasting hostility between the royal houses of Valois of France and Habsburg in Spain, especially after the Habsburgs succeeded to the throne of the Holy Roman Empire. The Austrian branch of the Habsburgs maintained a hostility with France until World War I, enmity that showed itself in repeated power struggles. From a military point of view, the war was the first postmedieval conflict showing the major use of wheeled artillery and individual firearms in the form of harquebusiers and muskets. Firepower began to replace the shock attack of heavy cavalry, and fieldworks began to make their appearance as protection for those cannon and musketeers.

*See also* Austria, Turkish Invasion of [85].

References: Rice, Euguene, *The Foundations of Early Modern Europe, 1460–1559* (New York: Norton, 1970); Taylor, F. L., *The Art of War in Italy, 1494–1529* (Cambridge: Cambridge University Press, 1921); Waley, D., *The Italian City-Republics* (New York: Longman, 1988).

## 98     MOGHUL EMPIRE

After Tamurlane's invasion of northern India in 1398, the area was fragmented among squabbling tribes. A clan of Afghans, the Lodis, captured the capital at Delhi in 1451, but could not extend their rule outside the immediate area of the Punjab in the upper Indus River valley. They persecuted the local Hindus, and provoked rebellions and attacks from all directions. Seeking outside assistance against the Lodis, a Punjabi governor appealed to Babur, the ruler of Afghanistan. A descendant of both Tamurlane and Genghis Khan, Babur "the Tiger" marched his steppe army into northern India. His better trained troops outfought a larger Lodi army at Panipat in 1526. He defeated the warlike Rajputs in 1527, and seized power with his victory over the Delhi sultanate in 1529. At this point he proclaimed the Moghul (or Mughal) Empire (from the Persian word for Mongol).

Babur's reign was short; he died in 1530. His son Humayun was expelled from India in 1540 by one of Babur's Afghan generals, and he went into exile in Iran. He returned to power at the head of an avenging army in 1555, but like his father, Humayun lived only a year after taking the throne. His 13-year-old son Akbar succeeded him, and the Moghul army defeated an immediate Hindu challenge to Akbar's throne, again at Panipat. At age 20, Akbar assumed full responsibility as emperor. He spent 20 years extending Moghul power through the northern half of the Indian subcontinent, establishing in the process one of the greatest dynasties in India. By allying himself with defeated tribes, he built an army as he conquered. After his conquest of Rajasthan he took Gujarat, on the west coast, in 1573; by 1576 he controlled Bengal, on the east coast, and by 1581 he had captured most of Afghanistan.

Though he was born outside the country, Akbar considered himself Indian. He realized that to have a successful empire, he needed to promote loyalty. He was tenacious in battle, but when he defeated a rival tribe he did not punish them, but made them allies. The militaristic Rajput

tribe, for example, became the primary source of his military advisers and generals. More important for Indian peace and culture was Akbar's religious tolerance. He was raised Muslim, but he studied and practiced a variety of modes of worship. His four wives were Christian, Muslim, or Hindu. He governed wisely and well, promoting all religions and tribes equally within his administration. He removed taxes that had long been targeted at Hindus, and by bringing peace to a large area of India, he promoted trade. The revenues he collected were dedicated to promoting the arts and building monuments to his empire and his culture. His court became internationally known for its wealth, beauty, and intelligence. Akbar himself wrote and painted, but most of his free time and energy were spent in religious study. He attempted to introduce a new religion that would incorporate aspects of all faiths and unite his country, but the belief did not survive him.

In 1606, Akbar died at the hands of his eldest son, Jahanigir ("World Seizer"). Jahanigir and his Persian wife Nur Jahan expanded the Persian influence in the Indian court and spent even more on construction. His dedication to luxury meant that the Moghul Empire did not expand in his reign, which ended in 1627. Again, the eldest son came to power by plotting against his father. This time it was Shah Jahan, who killed his nearest relatives and removed his mother so there would be no challenges to his throne. He ruled for 30 years and lived as profligate a life as did his father, benefiting neither the people nor the empire. He returned to the practice of heavy taxation, and left behind only two major contributions to India: the Taj Mahal and a new capital city at Delhi modeled on Akbar's Red Fort at Agra.

As usual, Shah Jahan's sons plotted against him. He favored Dara, whose interests followed those of Akbar, but the

Three Muslim emperors, who ruled India successively during the peak of Moghul power, are shown side by side on canopied thrones. In the center is the greatest of the emperors, Akbar, with his son, Jahanigir (right), and his grandson, Shah Jahan (left)

more ambitious Aurangzeb killed Dara and imprisoned Shah Jahan. Another purge of relatives left Aurangzeb in total control by 1658. Unlike the previous rulers, he turned his back on religious tolerance and re-started the mandatory practice of Islam. His persecution of Hindus caused revolts, as did his increased taxes to pay for the suppression. Aurangzeb took up the expansionist attitude of Akbar and tried to conquer the southern Indian area of the Deccan, but he had only limited success and usually was obliged to surrender whatever gains he had bought at a high cost in money and lives. His army reached the Cauvery River in the south, but could not maintain dominance because of local resistance and the need to suppress rebellions in other parts of the empire. Aurangzeb brought forth such hatred that he had to fight virtually every tribe or state in India. The Marathas, Rajputs, and Sikhs—groups that would influence India for centuries—rose to prominence as defenders of India against the Moghul despotism.

Aurangzeb's legacy was one of destruction. The heavy taxation, the devastation from the fighting, and the disruption of trade impoverished the country. At his death in 1707, the empire was splintering. The Moghuls remained emperors by title until 1858, but after Aurangzeb they were little more than figureheads. His persecution of faiths other than Islam divided the country into so many factions that after their common enemy was defeated, they were unable to agree on anything.

The Moghul Empire took India both to its heights and to its depths. At the beginning, Akbar introduced Persian as the official language, which helped create the languages of Hindi and Urdu, the two native languages of India today. Honest and efficient administration made India incredibly wealthy, and the construction he sponsored made it incredibly beautiful. Never before or since has India been as unified in its politics and religious toleration. During his reign, India was the equal or superior of almost any culture on earth. Successive self-indulgent rulers ruined Akbar's accomplishments. Though they added to India's cultural heritage, they did not pursue the sciences, and there were virtually no Indian achievements in technology and agriculture. By the time the Europeans arrived in the 1700s, the country was destitute and divided, and the foreign incursions proved that the rest of the world had passed India by.

*See also* Genghis Khan [47]; Tamurlane [76]; India, British Occupation of [94]; India, French Occupation of [95].

References: Harrison, John, *Akhbar and the Mughal Empire* (St. Paul, MN: Greenhaven Press, 1980); Prawdin, Michael, *Builders of the Mogul Empire* (London: Allen & Unwin, 1963); Sharma, G. N., *Mewar and the Mughal Emperors* (Agra, India: Shiva Lal Agarwala, 1962).

## 99 NETHERLANDS, FRENCH INVASIONS OF THE

The Netherlands of the seventeenth century was a disjointed group of provinces. The northern area was known as the United Provinces and was controlled by the Dutch, whereas the southern provinces (modern Belgium) were under the control of the Spanish Habsburg monarchy, which had ruled all of the Netherlands prior to the successful Dutch rebellion in the sixteenth century. The southern provinces first attracted French interest when King Louis XIV decided to establish a more secure northern border at the expense of the Spanish, who had long been French rivals.

Louis believed that the Scheldt River should serve as a natural northern boundary for France, and in 1667 he set about to make it so.

Louis had an extremely tenuous legal claim to that territory through his marriage to Spanish princess Maria Theresa, who was the daughter of Philip IV by his first marriage. Though Charles II came to the throne, he was the son of Philip's second marriage. Louis claimed that Maria Theresa's inheritance should outrank that of the progeny of Philip's second marriage and, therefore, the Netherlands were Maria Theresa's by right. It was an incredibly weak claim, but almost no one was in a position to challenge it. Louis had created one of the largest European armies ever, numbering some 120,000 men, and he entered the Spanish Netherlands on 24 May 1667. He enjoyed early success against the unprepared Spanish. By October, Louis's general Turenne captured a vast number of towns and forts and controlled the entire area. Having accomplished such easy victories in the north, Louis turned eastward in 1668 to occupy the Habsburg province of Franche-Comté, on the Swiss frontier.

No one was prepared for Louis to launch a winter offensive, but he ordered Condé, the governor of Burgundy, to do just that. Condé's force of 15,000 invaded the province on 3 February 1668 and conquered it in two weeks. Louis rode to Franche-Comté to accept the surrenders of the local leaders, so within three weeks the province was in French hands before any other country could react.

Louis had spent the last months of 1667 negotiating with possible rivals, and he had threatened or bribed many into submission, or at least cooperation. Most German princes accepted his bribes and stayed clear of his military power. In January he concluded a secret treaty with Leopold, Holy Roman Emperor, in which Louis would cede to him the Spanish throne upon the imminent death of Charles II; he would also give up French claims in the West Indies, Milan, and Tuscany. In return, Louis would receive the Spanish Netherlands, Franche-Comté, Naples, Sicily, and Spanish possessions in Africa and the Philippines. Though the treaty would reward him handsomely and confirm his possession of France's northern frontier, it depended on Charles II's death, and that could not be predicted. Therefore, Louis continued plans for invading deeper into the Netherlands.

Afraid of his aggression, three nations allied themselves to oppose Louis. Holland convinced Sweden and England to join forces, and the alliance proposed a negotiation period through May 1668, beyond which the three nations would make war against France on land and sea. Louis's advisers were divided on the wisdom of continuing the fighting. Spain had been unable to provide troops for the defense of the Netherlands because of problems at home, but the Spanish had made peace with Portugal and might now turn their attention to Louis. The possibility of being surrounded convinced Louis that the secret treaty with Leopold was worth waiting for, so he entered into negotiations with his opponents and signed the Treaty of Aix-la-Chapelle on 29 May 1668. Under this treaty Louis kept only two small pieces of land along the northern French province of Artois.

The invasion Louis launched in the summer of 1667, sometimes called the War of Devolution, was nothing more than a precursor of fighting to come. It proved his ability to handle international diplomacy, and it was the first serious military campaign in which he himself participated; this gave him increased confidence in the ability of his nation and his subordinates, and it provided France with a small province that acted as a buffer for possible Austrian or Swiss invasion into northern France. The peace signed in May 1668 proved to be nothing more than a cease-fire, and Louis invaded the Netherlands again in 1672.

Louis realized that to gain control of the Spanish Netherlands as soon as he hoped, he would have to break the Dutch, who feared France as an immediate neighbor. Between the two wars, Louis broke the Triple Alliance of Holland, England, and Sweden. Sweden had long had profitable trade relations with France, and was easily convinced to change sides. Remarkably, England proved almost as easy. Though the two nations had long been at odds, England's King Charles II was a Catholic ruling a predominantly Protestant country, and he had continual troubles with Parliament. Louis offered moral support not only as a fellow Catholic but as a fellow monarch, one who exercised more power in his country than did Charles in England. The thought of gaining personal power at the expense of Parliament (as well as strengthening English naval dominance at Dutch expense) appealed to Charles, and he fell in with Louis's plans in 1670. The Holy Roman Empire maintained the neutrality it had pledged in the secret 1668 treaty, and most German princes were quiet or cooperative with French bribes. Holland was isolated, and Louis could depend on the British navy to counter the Dutch fleet.

Britain struck first, declaring war on Holland in March 1672. Louis was quick to follow up with an army much strengthened since the end of the last war. Aided by the talented general Turenne, who had trained his army, and the brilliant fortification engineer Vauban, Louis had what seemed to be an unbeatable force. French armies rolled into Holland, and towns fell to it with remarkable ease. The country seemed helpless before the onslaught, and was saved only by Louis himself, who ignored Turenne's advice for a quick drive

on Amsterdam in favor of laying siege to a number of forts that he could easily have bypassed. The hesitation in attacking Amsterdam saved the Dutch. They sacrificed years of work for their own defense: They broke the dikes and flooded the approaches to the capital city.

No one expected such a radical maneuver, and it brought French operations to a halt. A change of government in Holland brought William of Orange to power, and he proposed to cede Maastrict and the Rhine towns and pay a large indemnity. Louis refused that and a later, more generous offer. Louis's pride cost him dearly, because he gave up the chance to gain virtually all he wanted for little cost. Instead, he demanded that the Dutch demilitarize their southern border and pay a higher indemnity, which they refused. War was declared, but the flooding ended campaigning in the Netherlands for a while. The following summer, a new coalition formed to oppose Louis, made up of the Dutch, the Holy Roman Empire, and the Spanish. They successfully captured cities in German states Louis had previously bribed. Louis's money proved too little an inducement to resist the new coalition; most German states began to join it because they were Protestant and feared Louis's increasingly Catholic viewpoint. Britain also pulled out of the conflict when Parliament forced Charles II to make peace with Holland.

Louis was now isolated but undaunted. He ordered Turenne to invade the Franche-Comté, which he had so easily conquered in 1668. The campaign took six months and provoked a response from the coalition. In August 1674 they drove Turenne back along the Rhine frontier and threatened to invade, held back only by the arrival of winter. Turenne surprised them with another winter offensive just after Christmas and secured the French frontier by a successful campaign in Alsace. After that, the war settled into one of defense. Turenne died in July 1675, and Louis lost his most able general. Condé replaced Turenne, but failing health forced his retirement by the end of the year.

Louis spent his time between the battlefield and Versailles, and in the spring of 1676 was back with his troops. He was in a position to score a significant victory over William's forces near Valenciennes, but hesitated when he received conflicting opinions from his advisers. He returned to his favorite pastime of siegecraft, and the Dutch army remained intact. The French navy was successful in the Mediterranean in 1676, but the lack of progress on land, coupled with a rising discontent among segments of the French population, gave Louis pause. The destruction in the frontier provinces was costly, and he had had to increase taxes and revert to the sale of offices to pay for this war. There was little active campaigning in 1677 other than some successful sieges, but William of Orange married Mary, daughter of England's James II, which could presage a closer Anglo-Dutch bond, and this worried Louis. In 1678 he agreed to peace terms at Nijmegen in Holland, then concluded separate treaties with Spain and the Holy Roman Empire. Though required to surrender many Dutch towns, he acquired many more in the Spanish Netherlands and had a belt of fortresses covering his northern frontier reaching from Dunkirk to the Meuse River. The two conflicts against the Netherlands had taken France to the height of its prestige, power not to be seen again until the time of Napoleon. The financial cost had provoked some domestic discontent, but Louis's success solidified his strength as absolute monarch. It also whetted his appetite for more glory and more secure borders, both of which he pursued in later campaigns: the War of the League of Augsburg and the War of the Spanish Succession.

*See also* Italy, Austrian Invasion of (War of the Spanish Succession) [96]; Palatinate, French Invasion of the (War of the League of Augsburg) [103]; Napoleon Buonaparte [118].

References: Hassall, Arthur, *Louis XIV and the Zenith of French Monarchy* (Freeport, NY: Books for Libraries, 1972 [1895]); Israel, Jonathan, *The Dutch Republic: Its Rise, Greatness and Fall, 1477–1806* (Oxford: Oxford University Press, 1995); Sonino, Paul, *Louis XIV and the Origins of the Dutch War* (New York: Cambridge University Press, 1988).

## NORTH AMERICA, BRITISH OCCUPATION OF

**100**

By the time English settlers began arriving on the east coast of North America in the late 1500s, the Native American tribes had already had experience with Europeans in the form of passing Spanish ships. The English settlements along the coast of present-day Virginia were situated in the midst of an Indian confederation led by the local chief, Powhatan. He had domination over a number of tribes and led a population of perhaps 14,000 people, from whom he could draw over 3,000 warriors. He had successfully built a political organization in the neighborhood, and saw the English as little threat—they could either be killed or used for supplies to fight his enemies. Indeed, the earliest attempts at colonization faced extermination both through disease and Indian warfare.

The settlement in 1607 at Jamestown changed the situation. Powhatan continued to believe that these new white people could be used or killed as necessary, and the early experiences of the Jamestown settlers seemed to bear that out. However, under the leadership of John Smith, the English began to practice both military defense and diplomacy. Powhatan traded corn for copper, the metal best known and most valued by the area tribes. Because he commanded a number of tribes, he was able to negotiate with the English through one tribe while attacking them with another. English reinforcements began to change the balance of power, and they actively courted Powhatan's enemies. Powhatan continued to trade with the English even as he persecuted them, but the large supply of English copper deflated its value, and he began to demand weapons (especially muskets) in return for food. By 1610 fighting between the two sides over land and food was common, and the alliances with Powhatan's enemies began to pay off. He refused to pay the exorbitant ransom demand made by his Anglo-Indian foes when they kidnapped his daughter Pocahontas. Instead, after a brief skirmish in 1614, Powhatan accepted Pocahontas's marriage to an English colonist who was investigating the export potential of tobacco. That ended the war.

The English imported more people as the Indians suffered through some bad harvests. Now they were forced to buy English corn, and the English were beginning to make serious profits with tobacco. More settlers were lured to the New World with promises of free land; that land, however, had to be taken from the Powhatan Confederation. Increased immigration brought English culture, but Powhatan's successor was able to obtain muskets in return for allowing the teaching of Christianity. In 1619 a government was formed, the House of Burgesses, which banned the supplying of muskets to the Indians. Closer ties also brought more death from European diseases. The withdrawal of firearms provoked Opechancough, Powhatan's successor, to launch a surprise attack against English farms up and down the James River in 1622. The Indians massacred 342 men, women, and children, and the remaining English withdrew into fortifications and were soon besieged. The English broke out on occasional sorties to loot the ripe cornfields of the Indians, which forced a food shortage that took warriors out of battle to plant new crops. Slaughter continued on both sides, and the English began underhanded diplomacy: They lured large numbers of Indians into negotiations, then poisoned them. Shortly thereafter, the first reported scalping took place—by the English. The more heavily armed English soon gained the upper hand, killing more Indians in battle and regularly stealing their food. By the early 1630s the Indians negotiated a truce, which was often violated by both sides. Opechancough's massacre in 1622 seemed to be all the excuse the English needed to make their settlement heavily militarized and their colonization one of complete domination. The establishment of militia units and their increasingly modern weaponry, coupled with a determination to conquer the land for their own agriculture, made warfare with the Indians a virtually constant pastime.

Relations between colonizing Englishmen and Indians to the north took a somewhat different turn. Early expeditions to fish and trade along the New England coast brought Indians back to England as prisoners. They were taught English and used as interpreters and scouts for later colonists. Only intermittent contact between the two peoples occurred in the first two decades of the seventeenth century, but it was enough to bring about a devastating epidemic in 1616–1618 that wiped out about 90 percent of the local Wampanoag tribe. Their loss of population made them targets for aggressive northern tribes armed by the French or Dutch, so when the English arrived, the Wampanoags hoped to gain an alliance that would aid in protecting their territory.

The first serious attempt to establish a permanent colony came in 1620 with the arrival of the Pilgrims, fundamentalist Calvinists who left England and Holland to get away from worldliness and temptation. They came armed and surly, with a professional soldier, Myles Standish, as military adviser. After early aggressive actions against the locals, the Pilgrims made peace with the local Wampanoag chief, Massasoit, through the intermediary Squanto, a captured Indian interpreter. The Pilgrims hoped to use Massasoit as their agent to collect tribute from the area tribes; Massasoit hoped to gain weaponry from them to defend his lands from enemies. Increasing numbers of colonists, not all of them Pilgrims, caused social friction that resulted in a second settlement at Boston. The new arrivals ran afoul of the Massachusett tribe, and relations between Indians and whites became strained. Massasoit used this strain to convince Standish to attack the Massachusetts, thereby eliminating a Wampanoag rival.

The Pilgrims got into the fur trade as the fastest way to pay off their debts. They began growing corn, then traded the corn for furs. From the Dutch they learned the value of wampum, strings of beads made from seashells. These were a mark of status among area Indians, and because European tools made the production of wampum much easier, wampum soon replaced corn as the medium of exchange. Its increased availability brought about intertribal rivalry in the rush to trade with the Europeans, which also led to increased rivalry between the English and Dutch in the area. A smallpox epidemic killed many members of the Pequod tribe of Connecticut, where the Dutch had established a trading post. The aggressiveness of the Pequods brought about a response by Connecticut settlers in 1637 in what came to be called the Pequod War. An attack on their main settlement, in alliance with some of the area tribes chafing under Pequod dominance, ended in a slaughter of the tribe in May. The tribe's destruction came through fire and genocide, as the English killed men, women, and children in a fashion unknown to the Indians at that time. It set the example for most of the later conflicts in the New England area as the Puritans and later colonists set about to clear the land of whatever stood in the way of European progress.

The English imposed treaties on the defeated Indians throughout their New World colonies, but these usually marked temporary truces rather than lasting peaceful relations. Though the settlers gained from the Indians the knowledge necessary to survive in North America, whether in agriculture or fur trading, the Europeans gave little in return. The arming of the Indians inflamed preexisting hostilities among tribes and gave later settlers an excuse to make war on armed natives. In the long run, the resources of America benefited only the Europeans; the native people gained little but disease, weaponry with which to kill one another, and exploitation of their land and produce. Not until the white settlers dominated the country did they seriously attempt to educate the Indians or convert them to Christianity, about the only positive influences the English could provide.

References: Stannard, David, *American Holocaust* (New York: Oxford University Press, 1992); Steele, Ian K., *Warpaths: Invasions of North America* (New York: Oxford University Press, 1994); Wright, Ronald, *Stolen Continents* (Boston: Houghton Mifflin, 1992).

## NORTH AMERICA, FRENCH OCCUPATION OF

**101**

Within five years of Columbus's voyage to the Americas, French ships were harvesting cod in the coastal waters off Newfoundland. They competed with other countries doing the same, but in 1524 the explorer Verrazano claimed for the French king the North American coast from Newfoundland to Spanish Florida. In 1534, King Francis I sent Jacques Cartier with two vessels to explore the coast of this new world. Cartier found Indians who attempted to engage in trade with him, which indicated that they had had previous customers for their furs, but other than that, he reported little of value. Cartier took two Iroquois with him to learn French and act as future interpreters, and in 1535 he brought them back and sailed up the river now called the St. Lawrence. They wintered at the site of modern-day Quebec and suffered the fate of almost every expedition to New France: scurvy. The French also entered into a practice that would come to dominate their experience in the New World: intervening in the affairs of warring tribes. This immediately brought them into conflict with the Iroquois, a relationship that came to haunt them.

For the remainder of the sixteenth century, the French attempts at colonization suffered from Iroquois hostility, scurvy, and the Spanish. Early in the seventeenth century, King Henry IV tried to establish a colony to maintain the French claim in the Western Hemisphere, and to do so he authorized Pierre du Gua, sieur de Monts, to form a trading company with monopolistic rights. Europeans were becoming enchanted with beaver fur, and the French wanted to control the trade. The monopoly faced fierce competition from independent traders, but de Monts set up his headquarters at Port Royal on the Newfoundland coast in 1604. De Monts and his associate, Samuel de Champlain, made connections with tribes of the Algonquin peoples, traditional enemies of the Iroquois, and both sides benefited. The French gained suppliers for their furs, while the Indians received French weaponry to use in their own intertribal conflicts. The Port Royal settlement was short-lived. De Monts lost his monopoly in 1607 and British settlers from farther south destroyed the village in 1612, marking the beginning of the other major rivalry engaging the French in North America.

Champlain attempted another trading center farther up the St. Lawrence, returning to Cartier's landing site, Quebec. He found fewer Indians, and they were both peaceful and enemies of the Iroquois, so they again entered into a mutually beneficial partnership. Still suffering from scurvy, the French held onto Quebec and promised to aid the local Algonquin tribes in their wars. Champlain's firearms helped make the Huron tribe masters of the area; they also made the French an enemy of the Mohawk tribe, who would plague the French for years to come. Though desirous of trading with the Europeans, the Mohawk had to look elsewhere; they established ties with the Dutch in the area that became upper New York.

Champlain wanted the Hurons to take him farther inland so he could explore new trade possibilities, but they were reluctant. The Hurons dominated the upper St. Lawrence economically as well as militarily; why should they introduce the French to other tribes when they could act as middlemen? Champlain found that he could operate only as freely as his Huron allies would allow. Still, the partnership was profitable, and Champlain was able to advertise his settlement in France. In 1626 he received the assistance of the Catholic church when eight Jesuit priests arrived, sent by the multifaceted Cardinal Richelieu, King Louis XIII's prime minister. In 1628, Anglo-French fighting in Europe caused the new interest in Quebec to suffer. Over time, British and French possessions in North America and around the world would often change hands at European peace conferences. The French lost possession of their holdings for a few years, but returned in 1632. When the war ended, the church sent even more priests as well as nuns to minister to the Hurons and establish settlements, which included Montreal.

During the French absence from their settlements, the Mohawk returned, eager to assert claim to the St. Lawrence area. An agreement between the Mohawk and some Algonquins over trading privileges brought the Mohawk and French back into conflict. Beginning in 1635 they entered into three decades of intermittent fighting. The Hurons were losing their power as allies, possibly as a result of their contact with the priests, who exposed them to European disease as well as Christianity; epidemics in the late 1630s cut the Huron population by one-third to one-half. Many Hurons embraced Christianity, which divided families along cultural lines that ultimately became political lines. The once powerful tribe began to break apart, and by 1650 had virtually ceased to exist, the remnants drifting off to join other tribes. After years of fighting the Mohawk with minimal success, the French stood by as the Mohawk persecuted their old Huron enemies.

Intertribal warfare nearly destroyed the fur trade, and by the mid-1600s the French were losing money. French soldiers made a futile attempt to take the war to the Mohawk in 1770, but the Mohawk also began to fade because of constant warfare with neighbors and occasional epidemics.

When King Louis XIV came to the throne in 1661, he put the North American venture under royal control. Louis worked closely with his economic adviser Jean-Baptist Colbert in strengthening French colonies around the globe. The king sent over 1,000 soldiers and a military governor, and he directed the training of militia units in Canada. Forts were built along major Mohawk trading routes, and the soldiers challenged the Mohawk and the Iroquois directly. By 1665 the Iroquois had negotiated a peace. Sixteen years of peace gave the colony the breathing room it needed to solidify and grow.

Peace allowed for exploration, and the French began to travel the Great Lakes and beyond. René-Robert Cavelier de La Salle oversaw the construction of trading posts from Niagara to the Mississippi River; he navigated that river to its delta in 1682, and claimed all the land drained by it for the king of France, giving the French supposed control over everything from the Rocky Mountains to the upper Ohio River valley.

In general, the French experience in North America differed greatly from the Spanish and British. The Spanish came to conquer and the British came to work the land, but the French seemed to be more financially motivated. Whether it was fish or furs, the primary inducement for French settlement was trade. The alliances facilitated that trade, and the combat in which they engaged often came about because of arguments over which tribe was going to be the primary middleman. The French did not come to North America in the overwhelming numbers that the British and Spanish did and, especially in the cases of the priests and the independent French trappers, seemed to be less intentionally threatening to the Indians' lifestyles. As did the British and Spanish, they introduced diseases for which the Indians had no natural immunity, but the twin goals of profit and conversion argued against the violent methods of the Spanish or the high-handed methods of the British. The French learned that many times things had to be done the Indians' way, and they came to accept that; the Iroquoian diplomatic rituals came to be the norm for French negotiations with Indian tribes, and the French often sponsored intertribal councils. The French also learned that the Indians had learned how to negotiate among themselves economically long before the Europeans arrived, and their ability to drive a hard bargain forced the French to provide value for value. The Indians often grew wealthy in the eyes of their own kind, and many became powerful warriors thanks to French goods. The Indians knew the value of fur, and what they could get for it.

The French had the most cooperative European experience with the Indians, but their struggles with the British (in North America, Europe, and India) spelled the end of the French presence. After defeat at the hands of British soldiers and colonists in the French and Indian War (1755–1760), in addition to defeat in Europe during the Seven Years' War (1756–1763), the Treaty of Paris of 1763 took away all French lands east of the Mississippi River and awarded them to the British; a separate agreement ceded the French claims west of the Mississippi to the Spanish. Except for fishing rights off Newfoundland, the French colonial experience was over.

See also North America, British Occupation of [100]; Saxony, Prussian Invasion of (Seven Years' War) [106]; Western Hemisphere, Spanish Occupation of [110].

References: Eccles, W. J., *France in America* (East Lansing: Michigan State University Press, 1990); Steele, Ian, *Warpaths:*

*Invasions of North America* (New York: Oxford University Press, 1994); Wrong, George, *The Rise and Fall of New France* (New York: Octagon Books, 1970 [1928]).

## 102　OTTOMAN EMPIRE

In the wake of the Mongol invasions in 1243 that broke up the Seljuk Turk Empire, Anatolia was filled with small, rival principalities. The group that finally rose to the top was led by Osman, or Othman, who resided in the north-central part of the peninsula at Sogut. According to legend, Sogut's mountaintop location was established by Hannibal, who advised the local rulers at the end of his life. Hence, the great enemy of Rome may have founded the town that brought about the end of the Roman Empire at last: Osman's followers, the Ottomans, delivered the killing blow that finished off the Eastern Roman Empire.

Osman spent his life making war against the Byzantine Empire. His major victory, accomplished as he lay dying in 1326, was the capture of the city of Bursa after a nine-year siege. This city in the northeast part of Anatolia put his son Orkhan in a position to strike across the Dardanelles into Europe. He also spread Ottoman rule eastward to Ankara. Unlike his father, Othan sometimes cooperated with the Byzantines, crossing the straits to aid them in beating back European enemies. The third time he did this, he did not go back but began to expand into the Balkans. His son Murad established Ottoman dominion in the Balkans with the defeat of powerful Serbia at the battle of Kosovo in 1389, though Murad died in the battle. Bayezid followed Murad's lead and laid siege to Constantinople in 1395. This provoked a response from Christian Europe, with the king of Hungary leading a coalition of English,

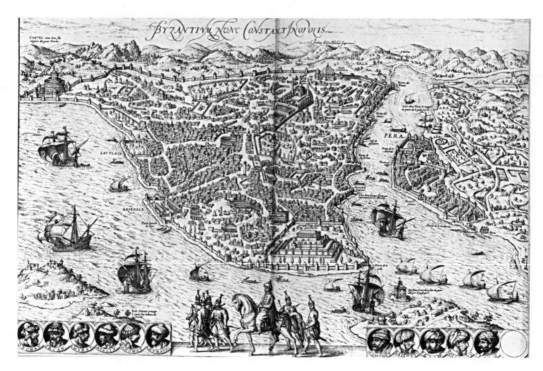

A late–sixteenth-century map of Constantinople, the imperial capital of the Ottoman Empire.

French, German, and Balkan forces. They lost to Bayezid at Nicopolis, and the Ottoman Turks became the dominant force in the Balkans, transferring their capital from Bursa to Edina in Thrace.

The unbroken string of successes came to an end when Bayezid turned against traditional policy by attacking eastward, into the strength of the great conqueror. He lost his freedom and his lands when Tamurlane defeated his forces at Ankara in 1402. After a struggle for power among his four sons, Mehmet (Mehmed) came to power in 1421. He reestablished Ottoman power, and his successor, Murad II, reigned for 30 years. Murad extended Ottoman rule farther into Europe, though he had a lot of difficulty with the Hungarians.

Mehmet II came to the throne in 1451, and he took the Ottomans to the height of their power. The remnants of the Byzantine Empire, huddled around Constantinople, finally died at Turkish hands.

Mehmet took the city in 1453, but he was not the barbarian the inhabitants had feared. After a mere three days of pillage, Mehmet began rebuilding. He made the city his new capital, and his tolerant policies promoted a quick peace. After centuries of strict Orthodox Christianity, the open-minded Mehmet made the city as cosmopolitan as had any previous ruler. He did not stop with this victory, however. Ottoman forces captured Greece and drove to the banks of the Adriatic; they landed at the tip of Italy, and only Mehmet's death prevented a major invasion. His successor, Bayezid II, did more building than conquering, and his passive nature led to his overthrow by his son Selim, called "the Inexorable." Selim's gunpowder-armed soldiers created the Ottoman Empire, anchoring the east at the head of the Persian Gulf in 1514 and defeating the Mamluks to occupy Egypt in 1516. Ottoman power stretched to include Mecca, Medina, and Jerusalem.

The string of able sultans reached its height—and its end—with Suleiman, known to Europe as "the Magnificent" and to his people as "the Lawgiver." Ruling from 1520 to 1566, he presided over the capture of Rhodes and the North African coast, defeated the Portuguese in the Red Sea and the Hungarians on land, and laid siege to Vienna. Suleiman's devotion to a secondary wife became not only his undoing, but that of the Ottoman Empire. After killing one son and exiling another from a previous marriage, his son Selim II, "the Sot," succeeded him. Ten brilliant leaders were followed by centuries of misrule.

The secret of Ottoman success was in the nature of their soldiers. Like the Seljuks before them, the Ottoman Turks recruited boys and young men from subdued Christian populations. They were called janissaries, raised in isolation and brought up on a mixture of Islamic teaching and strict discipline, learning loyalty to Allah and the sultan. They never left the barracks except to go to war; like the Spartans of ancient Greece, their military unit was their family. Other captive youths were trained in administration skills as well, and they ran the Ottoman bureaucracy. The rulers believed that such trainees would have no loyalty to any faction other than those in power and therefore would operate the government and the military in a focused and unbiased manner. Through ten sultans they performed their tasks well and took the empire to its domination of the eastern Mediterranean world. However, Ottoman strength ultimately became its weakness; weak rulers from Selim II onward became the tools of the talented few who could exercise political and military power. The bureaucracy, rather than the sultans, came to run the empire. The more power the bureaucrats exercised, the more they craved, and they soon turned away from the practices that made the empire

strong. Instead of recruiting from the population, they made their sons and nephews janissaries and administrators. The intense discipline and loyalty faded, and show began to replace substance. Weak sultans and military defeat saw the early promise of the Ottoman Empire decline from the late 1500s onward.

The naval defeat at Lepanto in 1571 marked the turning point of Ottoman fortunes. Expansion ended; instead, they defended their gains. By 1699 they began to cede territories in the Balkans, and in another century they were "the sick man of Europe." The Ottoman military decline coincided with an economic one. The wealth of the Western Hemisphere and the spread of ocean trade by the Europeans bypassed the traditional overland routes that had made the Middle East wealthy since the time of the Crusades. Political concessions to Europeans living and trading in Ottoman territory—the Capitulations—laid the groundwork for foreign infiltration of the economic and political system. Added to this was the increasing tax burden required to maintain the increasingly inefficient military; the decline of empire was inevitable. In the nineteenth century the Turks lost control of their frontiers in Europe and Africa, and by World War I had to pin their hopes on an alliance with Germany to keep up the facade of power.

*See also* Byzantine Empire [38]; Tamurlane [76]; Turks [78]; Austria, Turkish Invasion of [85].

References: Kinross, Baron Patrick Balfour, *The Ottoman Centuries* (New York: Morrow, 1977); Shaw, Stanford, *The History of the Ottoman Empire and Turkey* (Cambridge: Cambridge University Press, 1976); Wheatcroft, Andrew, *The Ottomans* (London: Viking, 1993).

## PALATINATE, FRENCH INVASION OF THE (WAR OF THE LEAGUE OF AUGSBURG)

**103**

French forces captured Strasburg and Luxembourg from the Habsburgs, and King Louis XIV was rewarded with an unchallenged 20-year occupation of them in the Truce of Ratisbone, signed in the summer of 1684. This aided Louis's constant quest for more secure frontiers, but it frightened many Europeans. Hence, the League of Augsburg was formed on 9 July 1686, made up of the Holy Roman Empire, Spain, Sweden, Holland, and various German principalities including Saxony. Pope Innocent XI secretly joined, and Savoy and Bavaria joined openly the following year. Louis responded by demanding that the Truce of Ratisbone be made a permanent peace and that he be permanently rewarded with his conquests. Louis hoped for the assistance of English king James II, a fellow Catholic and occasional rival of William of Orange, leader of the United Provinces of Holland.

Louis wanted Luxembourg as a further buffer for any possible threat from central Europe, and he also hoped that the pope would recognize him as the champion and defender of the church. The older Louis became, the more he seemed to embrace an aggressive Catholicism, which made many German princes distrustful. In June 1688, their suspicions were reinforced when the archbishop of Cologne died and Louis rushed to install one of his puppets as elector of Cologne; French troops occupied the city, and Furstenburg was named —not elected—elector. Louis immediately followed up this action with a move toward the Palatinate, deeper in German territory. The sole survivor of the ruling family was the wife of the duke of Orléans, and Louis demanded that she be named ruler of the province even though she did not want the position. Louis hoped that by occupying Cologne and the Palatinate, Europe would concede to his demand over the Ratisbone truce.

Louis's invasion of German territory gave a respite from French pressure to William of Orange, who sailed for England and was awarded the throne in the Glorious Revolution of 1688. James II had strong suspicions that he was about to be removed, but he had rejected Louis's offer of aid as condescending. William's enthronement brought a return to Protestant rule in England and guaranteed Anglo-Dutch cooperation against France. Had Louis invaded the Netherlands rather than the Palatinate, William's accession to the English throne would have been delayed if not undone; William could never have abandoned his country's defense.

The alliance of two strong Protestant nations strengthened the resolve of the Protestant German princes to resist French aggression. Further, Louis's revocation of the Edict of Nantes, which had long guaranteed Protestant rights in France, did nothing to allay German fears. Louis seemed unprepared for the strong German response, and also for that of the Holy Roman Empire, which was currently fighting Turkish aggression. Rather than hold a position too far away from France, Louis decided to abandon the Palatinate—but not before destroying it. French forces burned the countryside and leveled the towns in a manner not seen in Europe since the Thirty Years' War. This wanton destruction also intensified German hostility.

Rather than force Europe to concede to his wishes, Louis had enraged virtually every country. His main problem now was deciding which opponent to face first. He chose the Anglo-Dutch alliance, and launched an invasion of Ireland in an attempt to install James II as king there. A Catholic ally in Ireland would strengthen

Louis's strategic position vis-à-vis England, but it was not to be. French troops landed and encouraged anti-English sentiment, but the French defeat at the battle of Boyne on 1 July 1689 ended any serious chance of success. Two years of sporadic fighting in Ireland confirmed English rule and forced the exile of some 12,000 Irish soldiers who had entered French service. However, France managed to win a costly victory at sea, the battle of Beachy Head on 10 July 1689. It kept their fleet operational in the English Channel, but hurt them sufficiently that ultimate victory against the combined English and Dutch navies would be nearly impossible. Louis maintained the dream of invading England itself and reestablishing Catholic rule, but a naval defeat by English forces off La Hogue in May 1692 reestablished Anglo-Dutch naval dominance.

Meanwhile, Louis had continental enemies to face. In 1690 he made demands on the duke of Savoy; when they were not met, he invaded. He captured Savoy, Nice, and much of the Piedmont; the rest of that province fell to him in October 1693. On the Rhine front, the fighting remained mainly defensive. Louis had no talented general here, so the French showed little initiative, but the continuing struggle against Turkey kept the empire from launching any offensives. The most important action took place in the Netherlands, where Louis engaged in his favorite pastime of laying siege. Aided by Vauban, the master engineer of the time, Louis captured Mons in April 1691. In May 1692 he besieged Namur, one of the strongest fortified cities in Europe, and captured it in June. At that point, Louis could have launched a decisive invasion of Holland, but he was not a talented field commander, and preferred sieges to set-piece battles. Holland was saved by Louis's unreadiness to pursue his advantage.

Louis returned to the field for the last time in June 1693 as French forces began the siege of Liege, but they failed to take the city. For the remainder of that year, as well as 1694 and 1695, only sporadic and inconclusive fighting along the Rhine and the Spanish border took place. Louis could make little headway in breaking the league militarily, but he finally did so diplomatically. In 1696 he bribed the duke of Savoy to break with his allies; after returning most of the land he had captured in the southeast to Savoy, Louis had an additional 30,000 troops he could transfer to the Netherlands front. However, he offered to hold peace talks, and the allies agreed rather than face what could be a long conflict in the Netherlands.

Representatives met at Ryswick in May 1697, and in September Louis signed a treaty with Holland, England, and Spain. He withdrew from Luxembourg, allowed the Dutch to fortify their frontier, gave them a favorable trade treaty, and recognized William of Orange as King William III of England, promising not to aid any plots against his rule. In October he signed a second treaty with the empire and the Germans, wherein he withdrew his claims to Cologne and the Palatinate, abandoned all land east of the Rhine (though he fortified the west bank), and abandoned Lorraine. He kept Landau, Strasburg, and Alsace, much to the indignation of the Germans. He further angered them by demanding that Catholicism remain predominant in whatever territory he ceded.

Louis hoped that he could reestablish friendly relations with the Germans in the face of the rising power of the Holy Roman Empire, but they had had enough of his actions. The destruction of the Palatinate and his aggressive Catholic policies turned them against France permanently; Franco-German hostility reappeared constantly over the following three centuries. Louis failed in his original aim of permanently occupying Luxembourg, but that was his only loss after nine years of war. He broke the league formed to oppose him, kept France well protected and strong, and was in an excellent position to influence events soon to come concerning the rule of the house of Habsburg. Though French pride and power were maintained, Louis's position as the supreme power in Europe declined. It also marked the beginning of the end of the power of divine right and absolute monarchy; the democratic, constitutional monarchies of England and Holland were the wave of the future.

See also Austria, Turkish Invasion of [85]; Italy, Austrian Invasion of (War of the Spanish Succession) [96]; Thirty Years' War [108].

References: Hassall, Arthur, *Louis XIV and the Zenith of the French Monarchy* (Freeport, NY: Books for Libraries, 1972 [1895]); Lossky, Andrew, *Louis XIV and the French Monarchy* (New Brunswick, NJ: Rutgers University Press, 1994); Treasure, G. R. R., *Seventeenth Century France* (London: Rivingtons, 1966).

## PORTUGAL, SPANISH OCCUPATION OF

**104**

In 1578, King Sebastian of Portugal was killed while fighting Muslim forces in Morocco. Sebastian died without an heir, bringing to an end the house of Aviz. The Portuguese throne was open, and the nearest claimant was Philip II of Spain, whose mother was a Portuguese princess. Spain was in need of the territories that Portugal controlled because, despite the wealth of the Americas, Spanish finances were drained in attempts to suppress revolts in the Low Countries.

Philip's major rival for the throne was Don Antonio de Crato of Beja. He fought Philip for two years, but was finally defeated at the battle of Alcántara on 25 August 1580 by Philip's general, the duke of Alva. Crato fled for France to plan for his return. Philip assured the Portuguese government, the Cortes, that he would not take advantage of the country. He promised to recognize the rights of Portuguese citizens; all civil, military, and judicial offices would remain in Portuguese hands; all the dignities of the church and orders of knighthood would be respected. He also promised that goods from Portuguese territories would be carried only on their own shipping and that the revenues from the trade with Africa, Persia, and India would remain in the country, kept separate from Spain's revenues. Further, he promised to grant the sum of 3,000 crowns from his own treasury to redeem prisoners, repair cities, and relieve the miseries of sickness among the people.

Three times Philip had to fight to keep his new possession. Crato attempted to return and seize the throne with both French and British assistance. He tried to capture the Azores with a French fleet in 1582, but was defeated by the Spanish admiral Álvaro de Bazán. He tried the same thing the following year with the same result, confirming the power of the Spanish fleet in the Atlantic. In 1589, the year following the disaster of the Spanish Armada, Philip again turned away Crato's attempt to return to Portugal. Crato landed his forces on the coast with the aid of Sir Francis Drake and Sir John Norris of England; the people not only failed to rise to his call, they turned against the invaders because of English plundering.

Philip kept his promises. The Portuguese held important positions, taxes were not raised, and the laws remained the same. As long as Philip II remained in power, things ran smoothly. The same cannot be said of his sons, however. Philip III and Philip IV saw Portugal as a source of revenue to be tapped and a source of political positions for their associates. Philip II's evenhanded rule collapsed, causing resentment in the country. The Portuguese possessions overseas became the targets of English attacks, and the Spanish did little or nothing to protect them.

The Spanish were experiencing their own problems, with revolts in the Netherlands and in the Spanish province of Catalonia. In 1640, Philip IV asked the Portuguese duke of Bragança to bring troops to Spain. The duke raised troops, but used them to seize the throne with the blessing of the Cortes, the church, and the people. Bragança tried to establish relations with the Dutch to maintain pressure on Spain from two sides and regain Portuguese possession of territories lost over the past several years, but the Dutch-Portuguese economic rivalry was too great to overcome. They established a ten-year truce, which allowed the Dutch to trade with Brazil, but the peace did not last. Portuguese forces regained some trading posts in Angola and forced the Dutch trade centers in Brazil to shut down. The two countries finally agreed to a trade treaty in 1654. Portugal entered into a mutual-defense alliance with England in 1661 that guaranteed protection in case of renewed Spanish pressure.

Spain was much too busy with revolts to seriously try another occupation. Attempts at invasion in 1644 and 1665 were turned back; a peace treaty between the two countries was signed in 1668. The "Sixty-Year Occupation" had little effect in Portugal; the only serious result was the loss of overseas trading posts owing to the lack of Spanish defensive measures. Considering the small size of the Portuguese navy in comparison to the growing fleets of England and the Netherlands, the loss of those trading posts may have been inevitable.

References: Marques, A. H. de Olivera, *History of Portugal* (New York: Columbia University Press, 1976); Payne, Stanley, *A History of Spain and Portugal* (Madison: University of Wisconsin Press, 1973); Stephens, Morse, *The Story of Portugal* (New York: AMS Press, 1971).

## RUSSIA, SWEDISH INVASION OF (GREAT NORTHERN WAR)

**105**

In 1655, Sweden's king Charles X took his country to the greatest extent of its power and territorial conquest. His defeat of Denmark and concessions from Poland made Sweden the dominant force in the Baltic region. The First Northern War came to an end with Charles's death in 1660. The Second, or Great Northern War was much longer and bloodier. Sweden was under the able leadership of Charles XII, only 18 years old. Upon Charles's accession, Poland's king Augustus II saw an opportunity to break away from the domination his nation had suffered since 1660. He led the formation of the Northern Union, made up of Poland, Denmark, and Russia. Russia gave him the greatest support because Tsar Peter, known as the Great, longed to replace Sweden as the major Baltic power.

Instead of letting the Northern Union make the first move, Charles attacked Denmark, his closest and weakest enemy. The Swedes invaded Zealand and threatened Copenhagen; Denmark soon sued for peace. In the Treaty of Travedal, signed 28 August 1700, Denmark ended hostilities and promised no further action for the duration of the conflict, but the Danish fleet remained intact and Charles considered it a threat to his lines of communication.

Charles next landed 8,000 troops at Livonia to relieve the city of Riga. However, he learned after debarking that Narva was under siege, the attacking Russians outnumbering the defenders by at least four to one. Taking advantage of a blinding snowstorm on 20 November, Charles surprised the Russians and defeated them, killing or capturing 10,000 men while forcing another 30,000 to retreat and abandon all their artillery and supplies. Charles now made a fateful decision. Instead of advancing on Moscow and taking Russia out of the war, he turned his army around and marched on Poland, which he believed to be the greater threat. The Swedes invaded Poland in 1702 and proceeded to capture both Krakow and Warsaw.

Augustus II was forced to surrender in 1706. The Treaty of Altranstadt on 24 September stated that Poland had to withdraw from the war and Augustus must abdicate the Polish throne in favor of the Swedish puppet Stanislas Leszczynski. The Swedes also gained permission to winter in Saxony and await recruits and equipment for the upcoming campaign against Russia. Meanwhile, Tsar Peter made the most of the time Charles gave him after the defeat at Narva. He had gained control of the Neva River, and had begun work on his new capital city of St. Petersburg at the river's mouth. He also began building a navy on the Baltic Sea while making significant changes in his army, which was now much improved over the force that performed so poorly at Narva.

Charles led 50,000 men across the Vistula River on 1 January 1708 with the goal of advancing directly on Moscow. He defeated the Russians at Holowczyn on 4 July, but the scorched-earth policy employed by the retreating Russians forced Charles to march south in hopes of acquiring supplies from his new ally, hetman of the Cossacks Ivan Mazepa. This southward move separated Charles from his badly needed supply train and reinforcements,

led by General Carl Emil Lewenhaupt. Peter maneuvered his army between Charles and Lewenhaupt, and at the 9 October battle of Lesnaia, he used his four-to-one superiority in troops to defeat Lewenhaupt. The Swedish general was forced to abandon his artillery and burn his supply wagons; of the 11,000 men he was taking to join Charles, only 6,000 arrived.

These men, along with the Cossacks Mazepa brought, raised Charles's army to around 40,000. A particularly cold Ukrainian winter and constant skirmishing with the Russians diminished the force to about 20,000 by the spring of 1709. Instead of regrouping, in May Charles chose to continue his advance on Moscow. Between his army and Moscow lay the Russian stronghold at Poltava on the Vorskla River. The Swedes laid siege to the city but found themselves surrounded by a force of 50,000 when Peter arrived in mid-June. Short of artillery and gunpowder and cut off from his supply line, Charles had to break out of the encirclement. He launched his attack on 9 July and achieved early success, but the superior number of Russian troops and cannon (100 to 34) wore the Swedes down. After 18 hours of fighting, Charles was driven from the field and fled southeast to the Dnieper with Mazepa and about 1,500 cavalry; he sought refuge with the Turks. Lewenhaupt was obliged to surrender with 16,900 prisoners at Perevolchna.

Poltava and the subsequent surrender at Perevolchna signaled the demise of Sweden and the rise of Russia. The victory brought a pause in the war as well as a geographic shift in the fighting to northern Germany and the Baltic region. Russia's victory reunited the Northern Union and brought in the additional support of Hanover, Prussia, and Saxony; further, Augustus II was restored as Polish king in 1710. During the five years that Charles spent with the Turks, Peter continued to strengthen Russia's position in the eastern Baltic. Charles returned to Sweden in 1714, but he was unable to stop the momentum of the allied armies in northern Germany. Sweden abandoned its last possession in Germany—Stralsund—in 1715. Charles spent the next two years rebuilding his army, which had been at war for almost 20 years. In 1717 he invaded Norway, then a Danish province, and was killed at Fredriksten on 11 December 1718.

With Charles's death, the Great Northern War began winding down. In 1719 and 1720, Sweden signed the Treaties of Stockholm with Poland, Saxony, Denmark, Prussia, and Hanover. Hanover was given Bremen and Verden in return for a large indemnity; Prussia acquired parts of west Pomerania and the city of Stettin; Denmark retained only Schleswig. Peace with Russia did not occur until 1721, when the remaining two belligerents signed the Treaty of Nystadt on 30 August. Russia acquired Livonia, Estonia, Ingermanland, part of Karelia, and a number of islands in the Baltic. Most of Finland went to the Swedes, as did a large indemnity in payment for the Baltic islands. At this point Russia controlled the Baltic coast from Vyborg to Riga.

The implications of the Great Northern War were enormous. Russia replaced Sweden as the major Baltic power and began a century of expansion southward and westward, finally acquiring its "window to Europe," which allowed economic ties to the West. Peter, who worked desperately to westernize his nation, found the new respect from European powers quite helpful in attracting intellectuals and engineers to Russia. While this contact brought a great degree of advancement for the Russian upper class, the mass of Russian citizens benefited little. All they felt was the tax burden of paying for Peter's ambitions and conscription into the armies fighting for his glory. The Swedish cession of the Baltic provinces laid the foundation for Russian proprietary interest in them to this day.

—James L. Iseman

References: Hatton, R. M., *Charles XII of Sweden* (London: Weidenfeld & Nicolson, 1968); Massie, Robert, *Peter the Great, His Life and World* (New York: Knopf, 1980); Robert, Michael, *Sweden's Age of Greatness, 1632–1718* (New York: St. Martin's Press, 1973).

## SAXONY, PRUSSIAN INVASION OF (SEVEN YEARS' WAR)

106

In the wake of the War of the Austrian Succession, the major European powers remained suspicious of one another; indeed, the Treaty of Aix-la-Chapelle was more of a truce than a real peace settlement. Empress Maria Theresa of Austria chafed at the loss of the rich province of Silesia to Prussia's Frederick II, and she directed her chief minister, Count Wenzel von Kaunitz, to feel out possible allies for an attempt to regain her lost lands. Her recent ally, England, had been making overtures to Frederick in hopes of protecting the lands of Hanover, from whence came the English royal family. Austria's centuries-old rival, France, was now afraid of Prussia's growing power and desirous of extending its sway into the Netherlands, which Austria controlled and England wanted. Austria also found a sympathetic ear in Russia because Czarina Elizaveta feared Prussian designs on Poland. Even Sweden had a grudge against Prussia for lands lost years earlier. Last, the German elector of Saxony felt more comradeship with Catholic Austria than with Protestant Prussia. Kaunitz's design, ultimately successful, was to draw these powers into line against their common foe.

Frederick realized that his hold on Silesia was tenuous, and that Maria Theresa wanted it back. He welcomed England's proposal of friendship, even though England had little army with which to assist him should he be pressed on all sides. However, England had an agreement with Russia, which Frederick hoped (in vain, it proved) would keep Russia away from him. Learning of Kaunitz's discussion through his spies, Frederick decided that a preemptive strike was necessary. His English allies were already fighting France over their North American colonies, so an attack by France was certainly plausible. When he asked Maria Theresa for guarantees against aggression, her evasive answers provided all the justification Frederick needed to begin fighting.

Frederick possessed the finest army and possibly the best military mind in Europe. His 150,000-man army was no match for the combined forces arrayed against him, but it was the equal or better of any of them individually. He attacked Saxony at the end of August 1756, and occupied the territory easily. He acquired and published documents proving Maria Theresa's plot against Prussia. She sent an army from Bohemia to challenge him, and Frederick won the first battle of the war at Lobositz on 1 October. He returned to capture the one remaining Saxon stronghold, at Pirna, then incorporated the 14,000 prisoners into his army, declared Saxony conquered, and drew on its finances to pay for the war. He spent the winter in Dresden.

The European monarchies rallied to Austria, condemning Prussian aggression. Only the English remained at Frederick's side, and then only halfheartedly; William Pitt (Frederick's greatest supporter in England) was removed and later recalled as chief minister. While awaiting England's financial (and token military) support, Frederick's 145,000-man army

faced a combined force in excess of a third of a million men. His only hope to survive was to make sure they did not combine. Frederick spent the next six years marching and countermarching to face one foe after another, in the process earning the appellation "the Great." It was a title he did not acquire easily.

Frederick invaded Bohemia in the spring of 1757 and won a narrow victory over the Austrian forces outside Prague, which he was unable to successfully besiege; he had to abandon the effort after a defeat at Kolín at the hands of the great Austrian general Leopold von Daun. Feeling depressed at the military loss as well as the death of his mother, Frederick sent out tentative peace feelers, but they were rejected. The allies saw no reason to negotiate now: A French force defeated a Hanoverian force under English king George II's son at Hastenbeck, Swedish troops arrived in Pomerania, 100,000 Russians overran a 30,000-man force in East Prussia, and a force of Croats attacked Berlin. Frederick contemplated suicide, but at last he turned to face French forces (aided by German principalities) at Rossbach, near Leipzig.

Having left garrisons or forces under other commanders at various spots around his frontiers, Frederick had a mere 21,000 men under his direct command at Rossbach. Nevertheless, he staged one of the great victories of his career. He surprised the German forces with a rapid cavalry assault, then pounded the approaching French with artillery. The Prussians inflicted 7,700 dead to a loss of only 550. Silesia, however, fell to Austrian forces in November. Frederick raced to recover the province, and met retreating Prussian troops and the Austrian army near Leuthen on the road to Breslau. Though outnumbered almost two to one, Frederick attacked in echelon, a maneuver unheard of in military circles of the time. The maneuver confused the Austrians as to the true focus of his attack, and they were overwhelmed: They lost 20,000 prisoners, 116 artillery pieces, and more than 3,000 men died. The twin victories of Rossbach and Leuthen etched Frederick's name into the list of masterful generals.

The end of 1757 brought renewed promises of support from England and fresh confidence to the Prussian king. He would need it, for in 1758 he was constantly on the move facing one threat or another, often losing battles. Frederick's rebuilt army had to abandon the siege of Olmütz to face a Russian army marching toward Berlin, fighting the larger Russian force to a bloody stalemate. Daun again defeated him in Silesia in October, but the winter gave Frederick time to regroup; once again, he rejected suicide.

The Prussians had a hard time of it in 1759. Leaving a holding force near Dresden to keep Daun at bay, Frederick marched to meet a Russian threat to Berlin. After a hard-fought battle at Kunersdorf, the Prussians were at last overwhelmed and routed, but Frederick reformed the survivors and marched back toward Berlin. He found no Russians, because supply problems forced their retreat, and he turned once again to face Daun. Frederick arrived at Dresden too late to save it from Austrian occupation for the winter of 1759–1760.

He tried to recapture Dresden in the summer of 1760, but had to abandon that siege as well to march to Breslau. He entered the city in triumph after defeating an Austrian force at Leignitz, but at a later battle at Torgau on the Elbe River in November, the best Frederick could manage was a draw and a winter in Breslau. In 1761 much diplomatic maneuvering but little military action took place. The high financial cost of the war wore on every monarch, and peace feelers were extended in every direction. In England, George II died and his successor did not share his passion to defend Hanover; Pitt resigned rather than abandon Frederick, but the English government grew tired of subsidizing Frederick in the wake of their gains in North America at French expense.

Frederick was saved not so much by his endurance and talent as by events beyond his control. The czarina died in 1762, and Peter III replaced her; an ardent admirer of Frederick, he not only signed a peace treaty but allied himself with Prussia. The French could no longer afford to send subsidies to Austria, and the Turks were attacking Austrian territory. Austrian chancellor Kaunitz refused to deal with an English government now hostile to Frederick, and the loss of Russian assistance was too much for Austria to handle. Frederick finally got the best of Daun at Burkersdorf in July, then defeated the Austrians at Schweidnitz in Saxony; in October, a separate Prussian force defeated the Austrians in Saxony, and the war was as good as over.

Reluctantly, the monarchs began to talk peace. The French, no longer in possession of a navy, their North American lands, or very much money, made peace with Britain in return for Caribbean islands. Spain, which had been of slight help to France, gained some concessions, and these settlements left Austria standing alone, facing 100,000 Turks in Hungary. Maria Theresa proposed peace and Frederick agreed, signing a treaty in February 1763. A war begun strictly for political reasons had few direct political results other than a return to the status quo antebellum. Austria lost Silesia for good, and ran up a huge debt. Maria Theresa gave up the title Holy Roman Empress for empress of Austria-Hungary; the German principalities that had for centuries given grudging fealty to the Holy Roman Empire began to drift toward Prussian power. Russia lost 120,000 men, but gained a seat in European councils and laid the groundwork for a partition of Poland. Prussia gained the most in political respect, but lost the most in territorial devastation because most of the war was fought across its lands. Frederick claimed some 180,000 soldiers dead through combat or captivity; the total loss to the country was 500,000 people, out of an original population of 4.5 million. Britain came out of the war richer in territory but much poorer in cash; this could have marked the birth of the British Empire, but England's attempts to recoup financial losses via its North American colonies would provoke rebellion in 12 years.

The war brought about a new economic point of view that mass armies needed massive amounts of supplies, so the military-industrial complex was about to be born. The experience of destruction brought about a pessimism that resulted in a renewal of religious faith in the face of earthly futility. Further, the Protestant faith was finally safeguarded in central Europe, as an Austrian victory could have meant a forced return to Catholicism, much as had been seen prior to the Thirty Years' War.

See also Silesia, Prussian Invasion of (War of the Austrian Succession) [107]; Thirty Years' War [108].

References: Duffy, Chris, The Military Life of Frederick the Great (New York: Atheneum, 1986); Ritter, Gerhard, Frederick the Great, a Historical Profile (Berkeley: University of California Press, 1970).

## SILESIA, PRUSSIAN INVASION OF (WAR OF THE AUSTRIAN SUCCESSION)

**107**

Unlike the War of the Spanish Succession, this conflict did not involve the inheritance of the throne by a foreigner, but by a woman. Emperor Charles VI of Austria had succeeded his sonless brother Joseph in 1711, but Charles also was unable to sire a male child. For 20 years he planned to give his throne to his daughter Maria Theresa, and received the promise of the major European powers to acknowledge the pragmatic sanction, a document through which the traditional law of crowning only males on the Habsburg throne was temporarily put aside. It also overrode whatever claim Joseph's daughter may have had to the throne (she had married into the ruling family of Bavaria). When Charles died in 1740, the promises of most European countries proved useless.

The first to react to this female monarch was Frederick of Prussia. He had inherited from his father the best trained army in Europe and, at age 28, was anxious to prove his leadership ability. Frederick offered his services as defender of Austria in return for cession of the province of Silesia; he revived a 200-year-old claim to the land. When Maria Theresa proved unwilling to pay the price for his protection, as he knew she would, Frederick ordered his army into Silesia in December 1740. Maria Theresa immediately appealed to the guarantors of the pragmatic sanction, but she found few supporters. Bavaria wanted to push the claim of Joseph's daughter Maria Amalia, France wanted the Austrian Netherlands (modern Belgium) and therefore allied with Bavaria, and Saxony and Savoy saw an opportunity to gain land at Austrian expense. Only the English, whose King George II was also elector of Hanover and had no desire to see that province under Prussian or French dominance, and the Dutch, fearful of French aggression, promised aid to Austria, though their motives were more self-centered than altruistic.

Frederick's first military experience did not prove as glorious as he had hoped. His army met the Austrians at Mollwitz in April 1741, and Frederick fled the field when threatened by Austrian cavalry. Only the steadiness and military acumen of his chief general, Field Marshal Kurt von Schwerin, saved the day; Frederick was 20 miles away when he heard of the Prussian victory. During the summer and fall of 1741, the war widened with a Franco-Bavarian invasion of Bohemia, followed by the capture of Prague and the crowning of Bavarian prince Charles Albert as the new emperor of Austria. His rule was short-lived, because he was quickly forced to return to Bavaria to respond to the Austrian capture of Munich in his absence. A weak French force stayed in the Prague area. The following spring Frederick threatened Vienna, then withdrew into Silesia. The pursuing Austrians found Frederick waiting for them at Chotusitz, where he defeated them and recovered from the disgrace of the previous year. A few weeks later Maria Theresa conceded to Frederick's demand for Silesia, and he withdrew his nation from the war.

For two years Frederick stayed idle while Austrian forces drove back the French. They were so successful that Frederick grew worried about rising Austrian power, and in 1744 he was back in the war. He quickly invaded Bohemia and captured Prague, but withdrew to Silesia just as quickly when superior Austrian numbers marched toward him, and spent the winter in Silesia unhindered. Charles Albert died in December; his son and heir decided not to follow in his father's footsteps and rejected any claim to the Austrian throne, for which he was rewarded by the return of all Bavarian possessions captured by Austria.

In January 1745, Maria Theresa created the Quadruple Alliance, entering into a mutual-defense agreement with Saxony, Holland, and England in opposition to Prussia and France. In May the French quickly dealt the English a defeat at Fontenoy, while Frederick defeated an Austro-Saxon force in June at Hohenfriedeberg and at Kesselsdorf in December. Once again Maria Theresa made peace with Frederick, reaffirming his ownership of Silesia in return for his guarantee of the pragmatic sanction. The addition of 16,000 square miles of territory and 1 million subjects earned him the appellation "the Great." The war continued until 1748, with the Netherlands becoming the main theater of war. France's Louis XV had some success there, but it was offset by naval and colonial losses to the British. The war came to an end with the signing of the Treaty of Aix-la-Chapelle.

Maria Theresa lost Silesia, but gained a large measure of respect; after this war, no one questioned either her right to rule or her ability. The loss of Austria's most productive province, however, spurred Maria Theresa to implement a series of reforms in her empire. Prussia's centralized government had proven more efficient in both command and civil administration, and Maria Theresa learned that her government also needed to move away from feudal aristocracy toward a more enlightened form of government. She reformed the tax codes to her benefit (at the expense of the aristocracy) and broadened legal rights for peasants, making it easier for them to support their families and better able to pay taxes. She was unable to successfully incorporate the Hungarian and Slavic citizens of the empire's bureaucracy, however, and they remained somewhat discontented.

Prussia proved to be the big winner in the war, not only gaining land but establishing itself as a power to be reckoned with and Frederick as a general of no mean talent. The military he perfected became the standard of comparison throughout Europe until Napoleon embarrassed it in the early 1800s. England and France continued their long-standing hostility, but neither came out of the war much richer, because the treaty that ended the fighting called for a return of colonial possessions. American militia fighting in Canada for England resented this because they had scored their first major military success by capturing Louisburg; its return to France created ill feelings, which became one of the many causes of revolution. The peace of Aix-la-Chapelle proved no more than an eight-year armistice, because in 1756 Maria Theresa tried to take Silesia back in what became known as the Seven Years' War.

*See also* Italy, Austrian Invasion of (War of the Spanish Succession) [96]; Saxony, Prussian Invasion of (Seven Years' War) [106]; Prussia, Napoleon's Invasion of [121].

References: Addington, Larry, *Patterns of War through the Eighteenth Century* (Bloomington: Indiana University Press, 1990); Crankshaw, Edward, *Maria Theresa* (New York: Viking, 1969); Duffy, Chris, *The Military Life of Frederick the Great* (New York: Atheneum, 1986).

| 108 | THIRTY YEARS' WAR |

In 1555 the Peace of Augsburg became the law of the Holy Roman Empire, which included modern-day Germany, Holland, Belgium, Austria, Switzerland, and the Czech Republic. The ruling Habsburg dynasty was divided into two branches, one in Austria and the other in Spain, each with its own responsibilities and territories. The Augsburg declaration was an attempt to defuse the rampant religious and political feuding in central Europe, especially in the Germanic principalities. It stated that each prince had the power to decide for his provinces what its official religion would be. Thus, Catholic and Lutheran provinces

were officially recognized; the growing Calvinist denomination, however, was not. The Peace worked for several decades, but by the early 1600s religious alliances became more and more political. A clash between Protestant and Catholic states was inevitable.

In the northern states of the empire, Frederick V, the Calvinist ruler of the Palatine, a province along the Rhine River, organized the Protestant Union. In the south, Archduke Maximilian of Bavaria countered this move with the formation of the Catholic League. Their first encounter took place in Bohemia in 1618. When Ferdinand of Styria (south of Bohemia) became the Bohemian king in 1617, he was determined to impose his strict Catholicism on the province. The Bohemians tolerated a variety of religious views in their country and had little desire to have Ferdinand impose his will on them, so they threw the imperial governors literally out the windows of the castle in Prague. They raised an army and offered the throne to Frederick V, who accepted the crown, bringing the Protestant Union and the Catholic League in conflict.

The war was brief. The Catholics, under the brilliant general Baron von Tilly, defeated Frederick's forces in 1620. Ferdinand proceeded to impose Catholicism on Bohemia, and widespread killing and destruction ensued, ruining the nation's economy. The ruling aristocracy was replaced by Ferdinand's supporters who received large estates. Protestant religious practices disappeared in Bohemia over the next ten years of persecution while the Catholic Habsburgs reasserted their authority.

The protestant Lutherans and Calvinists were so suspicious of each other that the Lutherans actually assisted the Habsburgs in Bohemia. Though the power of Catholic Spain frightened the northern German Protestant states, they could not agree among themselves to present a united opposition. The king of Denmark offered his assistance to the Protestants, but he was motivated more by a desire for north German lands than religious unity; the Spanish under Czech adventurer Baron Albrecht von Wallenstein defeated Danish forces in 1625. Wallenstein led a well-trained force that numbered as many as 125,000, but he had personal ambitions above serving the Habsburgs. He planned to use this army to defeat the Habsburgs' enemies, then carve out a kingdom in central Europe for himself. The Habsburgs came to suspect this, and by the late 1620s the Catholic forces were beginning to quarrel almost as much as were the Protestants. Still, with Wallenstein's army supreme and the momentum on their side, the Catholic League urged Ferdinand to restore all lost Catholic lands in northern Germany. This decision mean the resumption of war. The loss of their lands as well as their faith finally motivated the Lutherans to action.

At this point, a Protestant champion stepped forward: Gustavus Adolphus, king of Sweden. Gustavus had wisely exploited his country's natural resources of copper and timber to build a strong economy, and he organized the world's first modern professional army based on universal conscription. His army was equipped with the first artillery light enough to maneuver on battlefields, improved muskets, regular pay, uniforms, and discipline. From 1611 through 1629, Gustavus's army had won victories over Poland, Denmark, and Russia, making Sweden the dominant force in the Baltic. It was this dominance that he wanted to protect from Wallenstein's encroachment. Gustavus committed his forces too late to prevent the destruction of the city of Magdeburg, the cruelest incident in a cruel war, but his forces soundly defeated imperial troops at Breitenfeld in Saxony in the fall of 1631.

That setback obliged the Habsburgs to recall Wallenstein, whom the Catholic League had come to mistrust. His presence was not enough to save the Catholic forces at Luetzen, which proved to be not only Gustavus's greatest victory but his last, for he died during the battle. Without his leadership, the Protestant cause floundered, but with Wallenstein assassinated on Ferdinand's orders, the Catholics had difficulty rallying to take advantage. Imperial armies stopped the Swedes in 1634, but Gustavus had saved Protestant Germany.

With both sides fighting themselves to exhaustion, a new player entered the game: France. France's chief minister Cardinal Richelieu had allied his country with Denmark earlier but, owing to domestic problems, had been unable to directly assist in the war. He now saw an opportunity to strike a blow against the Habsburgs who, by their control of central Europe and Spain, had his country surrounded. Though mostly Catholic, the French made allies of the Protestants, especially the Dutch, who had long suffered under Spanish rule and had been trying for a few decades to confirm their independence. When the Swedish army was defeated in 1634, Richelieu decided France had to intervene directly. The French declared war on Spain and allied themselves with Holland and the German states. The armies on both sides continued to slog through Europe for another 17 years, the war turning into a conflict between the French Bourbon and Spanish Habsburg monarchies. At last Spain, more tired than the others, called it quits. Rebellion in Portugal and Catalonia had weakened the Spanish effort and the allied victory at Roicroi in 1643 crushed the Spanish army. With Swedish forces besieging Prague and approaching Vienna, the two sides sat down in 1644 and began negotiations. The political leaders that began the war died off through the late 1630s and early 1640s, and the new generation could no longer sustain the cost of war with their countries devastated and unproductive.

The Congress of Westphalia, which continued until 1648, was Europe's first major, general peace conference. No such international gathering had been held since the Council of Constance had met in the early 1400s to attempt church reform. The Protestant movements discussed at Constance reached their fruition at Westphalia, for the rival factions were now recognized as legitimate faiths. The status quo established by the Peace of Augsburg, which allowed each nation to choose its own religion, was restored in 1648. This time Calvinism was accepted as one of the European denominations. The Holy Roman Empire was officially disbanded, more than 300 German states gaining recognition of their independence, as did Switzerland and the Netherlands. The relative positions of Catholic Germans in the south and Protestant Germans in the north was little altered from before the war. The Catholic church had lost its preeminent position in Europe to the Protestants.

By the time this was fought, the role of the military had evolved. The widespread introduction of firearms changed the nature of warfare and politics. It established equality on the battlefield, as any peasant with a gun could take the life of a nobleman; it mattered little about their respective training, position, or ability to lead. As equipping large numbers of men with firearms and procuring the newly perfected artillery were both very expensive propositions, only national governments could afford the cost. Hence, nations began to arm and war became an extension of political will and not a moral crusade to fight for the church, as combat had been for centuries. From this time forward, one sees the rise of standing armies and professional soldiers.

The struggle between rival monarchies of Spain, France, and Sweden wrought its destruction on the people being invaded by so many nations, the Germans. Politically, it caused a major upset in the balance of power. Spain saw its strength seriously reduced and the Peace of Westphalia was a serious military setback for a nation that had lost its naval dominance in the wake of the defeat of the Spanish Armada by the British in 1588. The Dutch Republic was created in the Netherlands, and the Swiss Confederation was formed out of the now-defunct Holy Roman Empire.

The Thirty Years' War was the most destructive Europe had seen up to that time, and they would not see its like again until World War I. The victories usually degenerated into wholesale pillage and plunder by both sides and entire towns disappeared in the process. Cities lost population, agriculture was virtually halted, livestock was wiped out, and the resultant lack of food brought about starvation and disease that killed more people than did the war itself; 4 (some say as many as 8) million people died out of a central European population of 21 million.

*See also* England, Spanish Invasion of (Spanish Armada) [93].

References: Parker, Geoffrey, ed., *The Thirty Years War* (London: Routledge and Kegan Paul, 1984); Robb, Theodore, ed., *The Thirty Years War* (Lexington, MA: Heath, 1972); Wedgwood, C. V., *The Thirty Years War* (Gloucester, MA: P. Smith, 1969).

109 UZBEKS

A Turco-Mongol tribe, the Uzbeks first appeared as followers of Shayban, who had been allotted land east of the Ural Mountains on the death of his grandfather, Genghis Khan, in 1227. The height of Uzbek conquest came in a short time period. In the fifteenth century, Abu'l-Khair built an empire that stretched from the Ural River to the Syr Darya. He failed to hold the land, but his grandson Muhammad Shaybani conquered land from the collapsing Timurid dynasty between the Syr Darya and the Amu Darya, or Oxus River. Muhammad Shaybani filled the vacuum left by the Timurids, the descendants of Tamurlane, by conquering as far as Herat and Tashkent; by 1503 he was the most powerful figure in central Asia. The Uzbek khans could not make much headway against the Persians and the Khirgiz, but they stabilized control over much of western Turkistan, including Bokhara and Samarkand.

A civil war among the Safavids of Persia in 1526 encouraged the Uzbeks to investigate the potential of acquiring land at Safavid expense. The Uzbeks captured Tus and Astarabad, and moved at will through Khurasan. By 1528 they were laying siege to Herat, in modern Afghanistan. The siege was lifted by a relieving force under Shah Tahmasp, who defeated the Uzbek leader 'Ubayd Allah Khan in a touch-and-go battle. 'Ubayd, though wounded in this battle, returned five times between 1524 and 1538 to invade Khurasan. These invasions, coupled with habitual raiding, gained the Uzbeks plunder, but little territory.

Internal Safavid troubles attracted the Uzbeks again in 1588. Once more they laid siege to Herat, which they captured in February 1589. The city in hand, the Uzbeks drove deeper into Safavid territory, conquering half of Khurasan. They exercised nominal control over the area until finally meeting the forces of the greatest of Safavid leaders, Shah 'Abbas, in 1598. The death of the Uzbek leader 'Abd Allah II was the major cause of 'Abbas's success. He marched from Isfahan on 9 April 1598, and the Uzbeks withdrew before him. He marched on Herat in early August, hoping to bring the Uzbeks, now under Din Muhammad Khan, to battle. 'Abbas showed himself to the defenders at Herat, then withdrew, leaving agents behind to spread the rumor that he had returned to deal with political problems at home. The ruse drew the Uzbek force out of the city to follow him; he turned and attacked on 9 August. Though his horses were exhausted from a forced march and the Uzbeks outnumbered him 12,000 to 10,000, 'Abbas charged. The charge broke Uzbek ranks and, when Din Muhammad was wounded, the army retreated. 'Abbas's forces chased them until the horses could no longer run, and they killed some 4,000 Uzbek soldiers. This victory, at Rabat-i-Pariyan, regained Herat for the Safavids and secured Khurasan's northwest frontier. A series of treaties ended hostilities between the two peoples.

The Uzbeks began as illiterate nomads, but they improved their society by learning from the cities they captured. They became Sunni Muslims and adopted many Persian elements into their culture. For a time they grew rich by controlling the caravan routes through central Asia, but the rising maritime powers of Europe ultimately took away that overland trade. With less income, the Uzbeks began to quarrel among themselves and lose tribal cohesion. By the nineteenth century, they fell under the control of either the Afghan or Russian government. The last Uzbek emirate to fall was Bokhara in 1868, which accepted protectorate status from Russia. Bokhara came under the control of the Soviet Union in 1920.

The last of the Uzbeks live in either Afghanistan or the former Soviet Union. Though they long ago gave up their nomadic ways, some traces of that lifestyle still exist. Even now, some Uzbeks abandon their houses in the summer for the felt tents of their ancestors.

*See also* Genghis Khan [47]; Tamurlane [76].

References: Haidar, Muhammad, *A History of the Moghuls of Central Asia* (New York: Praeger, 1970); Kwanten, Luc, *Imperial Nomads* (Philadelphia: University of Pennsylvania Press, 1979); Savory, Roger, *Iran under the Safavids* (New York: Cambridge University Press, 1980).

## 110 WESTERN HEMISPHERE, SPANISH OCCUPATION OF

Christopher Columbus's discovery of a "new world" in 1492 led to one of the largest invasions ever undertaken. In this case, it was not merely a neighboring country or region that fell, but an entire hemisphere. Reports of gold led many adventurers across the Atlantic, but they were merely the forerunners of a huge influx of settlers who occupied vast territories at the expense of the native inhabitants.

In 1520 a Spanish conquistador named Hernán Cortés conquered the Aztecs of Mexico. When the Spaniards arrived, the Aztec population was about 5 million, so Emperor Montezuma II had thousands of warriors at his disposal. Cortés had only 553 soldiers, 13 of whom were armed with relatively crude Renaissance muskets. Most of the rest were armed with steel swords, though Cortés also possessed 10 cannon and 16 horses.

In 1532 another Spaniard by the name of Francisco Pizarro brought down the Inca Empire. The Incas were situated in the area where Peru, Colombia, Ecuador, and Chile are located today, and had come to dominate the region only a few years prior to the Spanish arrival. They established an extensive bureaucracy to control their subjects, and drafted defeated warriors into the Inca military. Only a few weeks prior to Pizarro's appearance, the Incan emperor Atahualpa came to the throne after a civil war between rival claimants. The Incas are estimated to have had an army of between 40,000 and 80,000 men, but they were defeated by Pizarro's 200-man force, 62 of whom were cavalry.

The cost of defeat to both the Aztecs and the Incas was exceedingly high. The Mexicans and Peruvians of the pre-Columbian era were subject to no one and, indeed, enjoyed mastery over subject peoples, extracting tribute from their neighbors. Their cultural heritages were long and rich, and the Spaniards who conquered them were often envious of the sophistication of the local buildings, the refinement of their culture, and the abundance of goods in vast markets. The Spaniards deliberately and systematically destroyed temples, seized property, and committed acts of violence, theft, and vandalism from the first days they arrived on American soil.

Obviously, the Aztec and Inca civilizations did not submit willingly to Spanish domination, and both cultures fiercely resisted the invaders. How, then, did so few Spaniards triumph over such a huge population? European racists in the centuries following the conquest, such as the French philosopher Voltaire, would claim that the Aztecs and Incas were docile by nature and otherwise inferior to the Spaniards. In recent decades, such simplistic and naive explanations have yielded to more compelling ones.

One of the most important factors in the triumph of Cortés and Pizarro was probably disease. The New World, separated from Europe by a vast ocean and from Asia by the frozen Bering Strait, was sealed off from European and Asian diseases for thousands of years. American Indians, who had migrated from Asia in prehistoric times, had never been exposed to such diseases as measles, smallpox, and influenza, and thus had no antibodies to combat them. Unwittingly, the Spaniards created the conditions that led to their victory by simply breathing in the presence of the natives. By some estimates, 90 percent of the population of the Americas died from diseases that Europeans often experienced as resistant carriers. Particularly rampant among military commanders in the Aztec and Incan ranks were smallpox and measles, both potentially fatal and often debilitating when experienced by adults. Little did Aztec and Incan officers know, as they interrogated Spanish prisoners, that in gathering information they were hastening their own doom.

The Spaniards also had a tactical advantage. Europeans of the 1500s immediately charged upon enemies with swords drawn once they approached the field of battle. Warfare among the Spaniards' opponents was governed by different rules. Aztec and Inca warriors often engaged in preliminary rituals, in which fighting was preceded by confronting the opponent face-to-face unarmed. When Pizarro captured the Inca emperor and massacred his elite guard, which had served him well enough in battles against other American tribes, they were essentially unarmed, anticipating that the actual battle would take place later in the day.

Mexicans and Peruvians suffered yet another disadvantage, one that was truly bizarre. As mysterious diseases raged and mighty armies fell before the strange invaders, Aztecs and Incas looked to their most ancient prophecies. In both cultures, the earliest seers had recorded that white gods across the oceans would emerge one day to signal the end of the world. The legends of Quetzalcoatl in Mexico and Viracocha in Peru thus gave the Spaniards a profound

psychological advantage because their opponents were burdened by the necessity of first determining that they were mortal human beings before resolving to combat them.

With dumb luck so uncannily slanted in their favor, it is not surprising that the Spaniards were triumphant. The societies that existed in modern-day Central and South America were almost completely destroyed, as Europeans brought with them habits and cultures that were imposed on the natives. Today, it is virtually impossible to hear the sounds of Aztec or Incan language or music (though some Andean tribes still speak the Incan Quechua), understand the nuances of their religion, or see the beauty of their artwork because European chauvinism could not appreciate the contributions the peoples of the Americas had made to the world and could have made to their own cultures. The main purpose of the invasion, to acquire American gold and silver, was so successful that Spain became the dominant political and military power in the world for more than a century, seriously affecting the political situation in Europe.

—John Adams

*See also* Cortés, Hernán [91].

References: Díaz del Castillo, Bernal, *The Discovery and Conquest of Mexico* (London: Routledge, 1928); Liss, Peggy K., *Mexico under Spain, 1521–1556* (Chicago: University of Chicago Press, 1975); Means, Philip A., *Fall of the Inca Empire and the Spanish Rule in Peru, 1530–1780* (New York: Gordian Press, 1971).

 ZULUS, EXPANSION OF

The Zulu nation began in southeastern Africa as a vassal of the neighboring

Mtetwa tribe. The Mtetwa first rose to prominence under the direction of Dingiswayo, who became chief in 1795 at the age of 25. Dingiswayo organized his people along regimental lines, establishing a military framework for his tribe. After intensive training, he went on campaign, beginning a series of wars that the area tribesmen came to call the Mfecane. He defeated virtually every neighboring tribe and made them tributaries. The one tribe he failed to bring totally under his sway was the Ndwande, whose chief Zwide would be Dingiswayo's undoing. Dingiswayo refused to allow his warriors to slaughter captives, preferring tribal unification and growth through intermarriage. By this practice he created a confederation of tribes with the Mtetwa as the leaders. He also established trading contracts with the Portuguese at Delagoa Bay.

Dingiswayo took under his tutelage a young exile from the Zulu tribe who had escaped to the Mtetwa with his mother. Shaka, the illegitimate son of the Zulu chief, had had to leave his homeland to escape persecution from his brothers. He distinguished himself in combat, gaining Dingiswayo's attention, and ultimately rose to the rank of general. Shaka became one of the tribe's leading figures through performance and studying at his chief's side, but he thought that a better strategy in dealing with defeated enemies was destruction and forced integration rather than peaceful absorption. Still, Shaka was devoted to his leader and followed orders.

Word came in 1810 that Shaka's father had died, replaced by one of Shaka's half brothers. By this time Shaka was hoping for an independent leadership role, and he wanted the chieftainship of his old tribe. He arranged to have his half brother assassinated, and persuaded Dingiswayo to appoint him chief instead. Shaka took over the Zulu tribe in 1816 at age 32, though he

remained a vassal to Dingiswayo and continued to fight in his campaigns, including three against the Ndwande. All were successful, but Zwide, though openly swearing loyalty, still would not submit. Zwide ultimately captured Dingiswayo in battle and executed him in 1818. By general acclamation, the tribal confederation recognized Shaka as Dingiswayo's successor.

Zwide wanted the position for himself, and two wars ensued between Shaka and the Ndwande tribe. The first began with an invasion of Zululand in April 1818. At the battle of Qokli Hill, a force of some 4,300 Zulus defeated an army more than twice its size, but the remaining Ndwande forces escaped with a large number of Zulu cattle. The second took place 14 months later. Shaka ordered his people to hide all available food, then withdrew his army before a poorly supplied invading force of some 18,000. After leading them deep into Zululand and wearing them down, Shaka attacked the Ndwandes before they could withdraw to their homeland for more supplies. The Zulus scored a solid victory and followed it up with a fast-moving raid on Zwide's royal kraal. Zwide escaped, but caused no more trouble. With the Ndwandes out of the way, Shaka conquered other neighboring tribes while incorporating the tribes he inherited from Dingiswayo into the Zulu nation.

Shaka now became leader of all the tribes in the Natal area of southeast Africa. He built on Dingiswayo's idea of organizing society along military lines, and created one of the most powerful military forces in history. At their height, the Zulu forces numbered 600,000 men and Shaka's empire covered 11,500 square miles. Shaka established a training program second to none; for example, warriors were barred from wearing sandals in order to toughen their bare feet. His men developed the ability to move rapidly over long distances,

Shaka, the founder of the Zulu nation, in a drawing by James Saunders King

being able to run 50 miles in a day and go straight into combat. Shaka controlled society by requiring military service of all males and forbidding their marriage until retirement age (in their mid-thirties). At that point they would be awarded some cattle from the king's herd and could build a homestead. This system made maximum use of the supplies available and produced young warriors who could fight without worrying about family attachments (Shaka awarded a share of the spoils of war to the parents of the slain).

Shaka established a road system to facilitate intertribal communication, a system of unbiased courts to fairly enforce the laws, an equal opportunity for advancement in the military for anyone of any tribe who joined him, and an effective intelligence network to keep him informed of potential trouble. This failed him in the end, because his spies did not work within his own capital. Shaka was assassinated by yet another half brother, Dingane, in 1838.

The Zulus remained the major native power in southern Africa, and their expansion forced the migration of other peoples out of the area that would come to be known as Natal. This depopulation was fatefully timed because Dutch farmers soon arrived in the area, looking for lands to settle. No other tribe could challenge the Zulus, but ultimately they could not stand up to the superior weaponry of the colonizing Europeans.

Like Genghis Khan, Shaka forced his defeated enemies to swear loyalty to him and become members of his tribe, thus creating a nation rather than a confederation as Dingiswayo had done. Similar to the Spartans of ancient Greece, he created a society in which the military was the raison d'être. He used highly disciplined troops skilled in weapons designed for hand-to-hand combat and motivated by national and regimental pride to defeat every native opponent. While perhaps not quite as enlightened a ruler as Genghis Khan, Shaka's reputation for ferocity was at least the equal of the Mongol leader's, and the Zulu warrior provoked as much fear as any steppe horseman.

*See also* Genghis Khan [47]; South Africa, British Occupation of [144]; Zululand, British Invasion of [146].

References: Ritter, E. A., *Shaka Zulu* (London: Longman, 1955); Selby, John, *Shaka's Heirs* (London: George Allen & Unwin, 1971).

# PART 5
# THE AGE OF REVOLUTIONS AND NAPOLEON

# PART 5
# THE AGE OF REVOLUTIONS AND NAPOLEON

The numbers on the map correspond to entry numbers in the text.

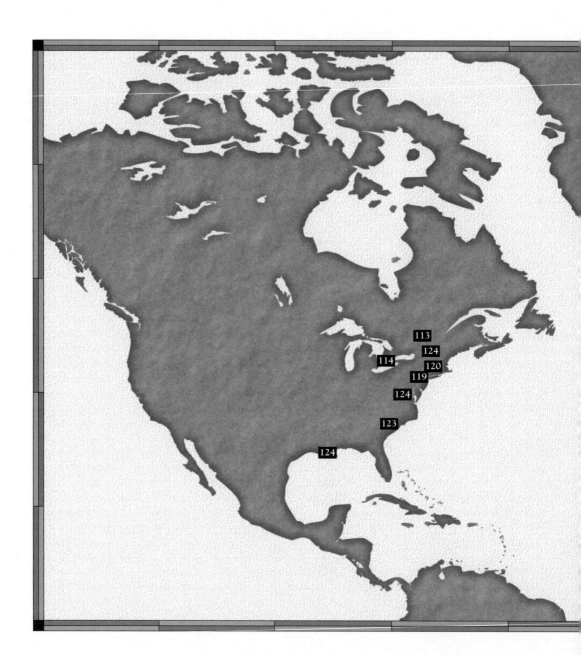

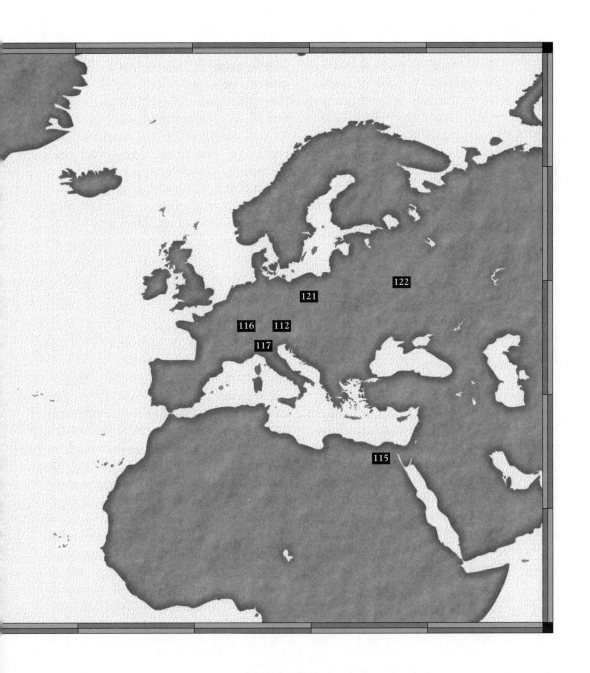

## AUSTRIA, NAPOLEON'S CONQUEST OF

**112**

After his return from the Middle East, Napoleon Buonaparte staged a coup d'état and named himself First Consul of the French government, virtually a dictatorial position. He proposed peace terms to European countries allied against him, but no one accepted his offer. He set about to quickly reconquer Italy, then made plans to amass an invasion force for the conquest of "that nation of shopkeepers"—England. As he gathered forces near the Channel coast, he was diverted by the rise in late summer 1805 of an Austrian force that, coupled with an approaching Russian army, planned to attack both Italy and the French positions west of the Rhine. Napoleon put his English expedition on hold and, more quickly than any of his enemies expected, marched his army toward Austria.

Austrian general Baron Karl Mack von Leiberich led 50,000 men to the city of Ulm, near Lake Constance, where he awaited the arrival of 120,000 Russians. He knew nothing of Napoleon's movements until the second week of October, when French cavalry forces appeared out of the Black Forest before his western front. He focused on them, having no idea that the remainder of Napoleon's force was making a massive encirclement of his position. A halfhearted attempt to break out of the encirclement was futile, and Mack was obliged to surrender almost his entire force to Napoleon after one of the most brilliant maneuvers in all military history. After this almost bloodless victory, Napoleon sent several corps to seal off Austrian troops in northern Italy. From there, Napoleon's subordinate André Masséna drove the Austrians through the Tyrol, forming a second French thrust into Austria. The proposed Russo-Austrian junction with Mack's forces never took place; instead, Russian general Mikhail Kutuzov found himself faced with a French army, which drove him backward as Napoleon marched toward Vienna.

Napoleon had moved too swiftly for his enemies to respond, but he had placed himself in a dangerous situation. The Russian army remained formidable; Austrian archduke Ferdinand commanded another Austrian force at Prague, and two more Austrian archdukes were leading 80,000 men out of Italy toward Austria by way of Hungary. If these armies could join, Napoleon would be outnumbered a long way from his bases in France. Indeed, they saw the opportunity and marched to cut off the French in Vienna from their supply lines to Paris. Napoleon anticipated their move, and lay in wait for them near Austerlitz. He placed his army on low ground and in an extended position, making it an attractive target to the better placed Russo-Austrian force commanded by Kutusov. The bulk of French forces, however, were out of sight. The allied force attacked early on 2 December 1805 and had early success against the French right flank. As they pressed it, however, they extended their own lines so thinly that a French counterattack broke through. With the well-timed arrival of his hidden forces, Napoleon's army divided and encircled the Russo-Austrian force, and by the end of the day, it had virtually ceased to exist. Brilliant as the victory at Ulm had been, that had been a triumph of strategic maneuver. Austerlitz was a masterpiece of tactical planning and entrapment, and it went down in history as one of the greatest battles of all time. Two days later, Austrian emperor Francis agreed to an unconditional surrender as the remains of Russian forces hastily retreated home. The Treaty of Pressburg, signed 26 December 1805, took Austria out of the Third Coalition, and ceded Austrian territory in Italy and Germany to Napoleon. The brilliance of Napoleon's victories was tarnished by the news of the defeat of his navy at the hands of British admiral Horatio Nelson at Trafalgar, off the Spanish coast. It doomed his plans for invading England, and allowed the British to obtain mastery of the sea, with which they began a blockade of continental Europe.

Napoleon's victory over Austria placed him in a position to continue his ambition of conquering all of Europe. In the following two years, his armies devastated the forces of both Prussia and Russia. When Napoleon suffered setbacks at the hands of the British in Spain, Austria decided to try its luck again in 1809. Invasion forces marching into Italy and Bavaria had early successes and raised a revolt against the French-supported government of Bavaria. Napoleon's arrival in April immediately reversed French fortunes. In a series of battles from 19 to 23 April, French forces pushed back the Austrians through Abensburg, Landshut, Eggmühl, and Ratisbon. In a week, Napoleon had undone whatever successes the Austrians had achieved, and in May he was once again in Vienna. Napoleon's forces suffered their first setback along the Danube at the battle of Aspern-Essling, but a reinforced French army of 200,000 prepared to win back the initiative. At the battle of Wagram on 5 and 6 July, Napoleon assembled the largest mass of artillery ever placed in one location and blasted a hole in the Austrian center. His infantry broke through and drove the Austrians from the field. Again, Emperor Francis asked for peace terms. At the Treaty of Schönbrunn, Austria surrendered 32,000 square miles of land and 3.5 million inhabitants to Napoleon and his allies.

The defeat forced Austria to join Napoleon's Continental System, his economic warfare against England. French forces occupied Austria for a relatively peaceful three years, until Napoleon's invasion of Russia and the debacle resulting from that operation once again encouraged Austrian resistance. Their last uprising, aided by a rejuvenated Prussia and a Russian army full of momentum from their victory in 1812–1813, finally brought Napoleon down at the 1813 Battle of the Nations. Austria maintained its empire, and the subject ethnic groups of southeastern Europe did not profit from the philosophy of the French Revolution as had many other occupied populations. Not for another century—in the aftermath of World War I—would they gain *liberté* from Austrian rule; to this day, the questions of *égalité* and *fraternité* remain unanswered.

*See also* Egypt, Napoleon's Invasion of [115]; Napoleon Buonaparte [118]; Prussia, Napoleon's Invasion of [121]; Russia, Napoleon's Invasion of [122].

References: Arnold, James, *Napoleon Conquers Austria: The 1809 Campaign for Vienna* (Westport, CT: Praeger, 1995); Chandler, David, *The Campaigns of Napoleon* (New York: Macmillan, 1966); Connelly, Owen, *Blundering to Glory* (Wilmington, DE: Scholarly Resources, 1987).

## 113   CANADA, AMERICAN INVASION OF

When the 13 American colonies sent delegates to the Continental Congress in Philadelphia, Pennsylvania, in September 1774, they made decisions that inevitably led to rebellion against Great Britain. Judging that armed conflict would come soon, the Congress hoped to gain allies in the British colony of Quebec. Because the entire area, from the mouth of the St. Lawrence River to the Great Lakes and beyond, had been a French colony until the Treaty of Paris of 1763, the Americans

The death of General Montgomery during the attack of Quebec in December 1775.

were sure that the predominantly French population would be glad to take up arms against a traditional enemy. Their delegations to French leaders, however, received no widespread promises of aid. Still, Congress assumed that while the Canadians might not openly support rebellion, they would not hinder American efforts to expel the British.

When Ethan Allen captured Fort Ticonderoga and Crown Point at the southern end of Lake Champlain from the British in early May 1775, a natural invasion route was opened. Two plans were developed to launch the conquest of Quebec. One would drive northward up Lake Champlain into Canadian territory and thence to Montreal. From there a force could float downstream to the main prize: the city of Quebec. A second attack would move through Maine, up the Kennebec and down the Chaudiere rivers to the St. Lawrence, just opposite the city of Quebec. Both plans were implemented in the fall of 1775, and both were doomed because of timing.

The Continental Congress judged correctly that British forces in Canada were too few to defend both Montreal and the city of Quebec. Hence, with a two-pronged attack, at least one must surely succeed. General Philip Schuyler received directions from Congress to attack Montreal. He spent the summer of 1776 gathering men and arms, both of which were in short supply. A man of irregular temperament, Schuyler did not get his expedition of 1,700 men moving until September, then abandoned it to his second-in-command, Richard Montgomery, when the Americans reached St. John's, some 30 miles east of Montreal. Montgomery had too few men to either storm the British position or leave a detachment behind and bypass it. He therefore was obliged to lay siege. The British held out 55 days, a delay the Americans could not afford.

Sir Guy Carleton, the governor of Canada and commander of British forces, had spent the summer trying to raise troops amid a disinterested population. He had three infantry regiments and three artillery companies in the entire country; with one regiment and one company assigned to protect Detroit and Niagara, there was precious little left with which to defend Montreal and Quebec. The fort at St. John's held 600 men, all lost when the American siege was successful on 2 November. Meanwhile, Montgomery had been receiving some reinforcements and was partially successful in finding a few Canadians willing to assist. Carleton was obliged to abandon Montreal on 16 November when the inhabitants told him they would not help him fight the Americans. He lost even more of his men, and he himself only narrowly escaped, during the withdrawal down the St. Lawrence toward Quebec.

In the meantime, the second American advance was under way through Maine. Led by Benedict Arnold, these 1,100 men were also too late in getting started; they did not move up the Kennebec River until 25 September. They soon ran into harsh weather, and began to run low on supplies. Arnold pushed his men through the freezing wilderness in October and November, losing many to disease and desertion. Gaining some aid from local Frenchmen, Arnold managed to reach the St. Lawrence opposite Quebec on 10 November, his force reduced to 500 men. A quick assault on the city would have found it undefended because the troops assigned to it were out on patrol. However, Arnold was unable to cross the river for three days, and the defending troops returned in time to hold off an attack on the walled city.

Montgomery and Arnold joined forces on 2 December some 20 miles upriver, their combined army numbering almost 1,000 men. As at St. John's, there were too few men to take the city by storm, so another siege began. It was doomed; the British had more supplies than their besiegers, and the winter weather bothered them much less. The few attacks the Americans made were repulsed (and Montgomery was killed), and Carleton was smart enough not to sally out of his defenses. The Americans suffered through the cold until spring 1776, when reinforcements arrived from Britain. Arnold withdrew to Montreal, but his force was decimated by smallpox, and the Canadian population there would not support him. By June the Americans had abandoned the invasion.

An earlier beginning to the campaign would almost certainly have made the difference, because Carleton's defensive measures were taking effect just as the Americans arrived. If the revolutionaries had gained control of Quebec and Montreal, the French inhabitants would probably have joined with them. Whether they could have withstood a determined British army and navy in the spring and summer of 1776 is open to question, but an inspired population could have mounted just as effective a guerrilla campaign as the Americans later did in the Carolinas. Instead, Britain maintained control of the country.

A successful invasion in 1775–1776 would have made the war of 1812 unnecessary. The second American invasion of Canada in 1812 again failed to bring Canada into the American union. Hostility between the two countries was ultimately laid to rest with the settlement of border differences in the 1840s, and since then the United States and Canada have become two of the most friendly nations in the world. Indeed, the two countries share the world's longest undefended border. Canada remained a British colony until the

1850s, when it gained dominion status, but it nearly became the fourteenth original American state. What the Americans would do about current Quebecois nationalism, or if it would even exist, must remain a matter of speculation.

*See also* Southern United States, British Invasion of [123].

References: Alden, John R., *The American Revolution* (New York: Harper & Row, 1954); Lawson, Philip, *The Imperial Challenge: Quebec and Britain in the Age of the American Revolution* (Montreal: McGill-Queens University Press, 1990); Wrong, George McKinnon, *Canada and the American Revolution* (New York: Macmillan, 1935).

## CANADA, U.S. INVASION OF

**114**

Britain's resistance to Napoleon in Europe had side effects that brought about war with the United States. The Royal Navy's blockade interfered with the Americans' right of free trade, but then so did Napoleon's Berlin and Milan decrees, which forbade neutral trade with Britain. The Royal Navy's need for sailors, however, brought the greatest American outcry. Without government authority to conscript from the public, the Royal Navy was unable to raise more crewmen in Britain. Searching far and wide for sailors to enter into the harsh service at sea, the British began to stop American merchant ships on the high seas. They took away anyone who spoke English—speaking English was proof enough for the British warships that a crewman on an American ship was a British deserter. While this was true in a few cases, most of the men pressed into British service were American citizens, and the United States loudly protested the British government's piracy.

The United States was unable to gain any satisfaction in reference to the trade or the impressment troubles, and in the late spring of 1812, President James Madison asked Congress for a declaration of war; they complied. The American people, though angry at British high-handedness, also had less legitimate reasons for wanting war. Americans living in the western states desired Canada, not only to secure the northern border from possible British interference, but also to expand American farmland northward. Westerners believed that the British authorities in Canada were supplying Indian tribes south of the Great Lakes with weapons. Because of the long-standing antipathy between white and native Americans, white frontiersmen would not accept anyone, especially outsiders, helping their traditional enemies. With Britain busy in Europe in 1812, the time seemed ripe to seize Canada for the United States, a dream many had cherished since the American Revolution.

Even though the forces protecting Canada were small, the United States was unprepared for war against anyone. The standing army had less than 3,000 men. There was no command structure to speak of, no logistical framework for supplying armies, and no staff structure to plan or coordinate operations. The constitution allowed the federal government to call out the militia for domestic use only; many men, called up by their state governments, refused to cross the border into Canada. In order to raise forces for the regular army, volunteer units were needed; these were raised by individuals, some of whom had little military experience, so the quality of both recruits and commanders was irregular.

American secretary of war William Eustis exercised what little control the military had. He realized that the forces Britain

The battle of Queenston Heights, 13 October 1812.

could raise to defend Canada were limited. There were no more than 4,000 British and Canadian regulars, with a varying number of militia and Indian allies of uneven quality. The Canadians could expect little assistance from Britain, but their major advantage lay in the quality of their opponent: Eustis gave them little to worry about. He planned an overly ambitious campaign to seize Canada, and had there been more rapid communications and movement of men and supplies, the plan would have been a good one, but for 1812 it was impossible. Eustis's plan called for a four-pronged offensive to strike simultaneously at Detroit, Niagara, Sackett's Harbor, and Montreal. By spreading the British/Canadian defenses thin, any or all of the thrusts should have broken through. Since the inhabited portion of Canada stretched only some 50 to 100 miles north of the American border, from the Great Lakes to the

mouth of the St. Lawrence, there was not all that much of Canada to conquer. It all seemed so easy.

The attacks, when they took place at all, were totally uncoordinated. William Hull gathered a force of more than 2,000 men in northern Ohio and marched for Detroit in May and June 1812. He crossed the Detroit River into Canada and seized the town of Sandwich, which he began to fortify. Hull issued a proclamation calling for Canadians to flock to his banner and throw off British rule; the document also threatened instant death for anyone caught fighting alongside an Indian. Many locals responded to his entreaty, and the British defense forces in the neighborhood found their numbers reduced to less than 500. However, this was the best Hull could do. Though a veteran of the revolution, he lacked the dash necessary to seize the moment. While Hull hesitated and worried about his supply lines, the British, under Isaac Brock, governor of upper Canada, reinforced. As more Indians joined in with the British and Brock began harassing Hull's supply lines, the American commander lost his nerve. He retreated across the river to Detroit, then gave in to Brock on 16 August. His entire force of almost 2,500 men was surrendered without a fight because Hull was mistakenly convinced that huge numbers of Indians (of whom he had an almost pathological fear) were about to attack. Hull was later tried on charges of cowardice and ordered executed, but President Madison pardoned him. The United States' first invasion attempt gained no more than one mile of Canadian territory, and ended in the loss not only of Detroit but all of the Michigan territory.

The second attack, at Niagara, was delayed so long that Brock was able to secure Detroit and return to direct the defense of Queenston and Fort George along the Niagara River. A force of 6,000 militia was poised to invade, but because of a mix-up in command and a poor supply situation, they did not go into action until October. They gained an early advantage over the defending forces and captured Fort George. Brock was killed in the battle, and the Americans were on the verge of driving the British from the field and capturing Queenston. Only the refusal of New York militia, held in reserve on the other side of the Niagara River, to cross into Canada and provide the coup de grace prevented an American victory. The British regrouped and forced the Americans back across the river. The second attempt was close to success, but failed for lack of will.

Meanwhile, the force that was to advance up Lake Champlain and assault Montreal should have been gathering all summer under the main American general, Henry Dearborn. Instead of organizing his force at Albany, he left for Boston, where he did little but inspect coastal defenses and try to convince Massachusetts legislators to increase their aid. When his British opposite learned of the British government's willingness to discuss American demands, he proposed an armistice, to which Dearborn agreed. However, President Madison rebuffed any peace talks, and Dearborn finally went into action. American troops advanced northward in November to Plattsburgh and met a small Canadian force near the border at the La Colle River. The resultant battle was so confused that Americans fired at one another as often as at the enemy. It seemed the better part of valor to retreat to Plattsburgh for the winter. The forces at Sackett's Harbor, on the eastern end of Lake Ontario, contented themselves with building a small fleet to try to gain control of the lake, and saw no action. The year 1812 ended not with a bang but a whimper.

The year 1813 saw but little improvement in American progress. In April an American force sailed across Lake Erie and captured the Canadian capital at York (modern-day Toronto). Rather than capitalize on this victory, however, they burned the city and withdrew. A second attack against York at the end of July brought the same result. Why they refused to use this city as a base of operations to fight the war in Canada, as opposed to fighting it along the frontiers, remains a mystery. American forces captured the strategic Fort George at Niagara, but they were defeated in attempts to drive inland from there. When the militia's term of enlistment ran out in November and they went home, Fort George could not be held. The neighboring town of Newark was burned, but the fort was not, and the British reoccupied it. At the eastern end of Lake Ontario at Sackett's Harbor, Americans under the command of James Wilkinson (regarded as quite possibly the worst general the country has ever produced) vacillated over how to attack Montreal. Piecemeal troop commitments and arguments among the generals produced only defeat late in the year at Chrysler's Farm just across the Canadian border. Americans went no farther north in this area in 1813 than they had the previous year.

The only real accomplishment occurred in September. American ships under Oliver Hazard Perry defeated a roughly equal number of British ships at Put-in-Bay on the western end of Lake Erie. That victory gave the Americans control of the lake and made it possible to ferry across troops who could cut off the British forces garrisoned at Detroit. Before that could happen, the British withdrew from the city; the Americans reoccupied it in October. Kentucky militia led by William Henry Harrison chased the retreating British and Indians, catching up to them along the Thames River. American cavalry made short work of the few hundred British soldiers and, in hand-to-hand combat, American infantry broke the Indian forces by killing their leader, Tecumseh. Again, rather than take advantage of the momentum, Harrison withdrew his men to Detroit for the winter. Whatever successes the Americans accomplished in 1813 they did not exploit.

What had originally appeared to be an easy target defended by few British troops had, at the end of two campaigning seasons, proven too difficult for the disorganized American forces to conquer. The year 1814 would be their last chance. Unfortunately, Wilkinson still held command in the northeast. He led some 4,000 men across the Canadian border and engaged a force of 200 Canadian militia at La Colle Mill. When Wilkinson could not reduce the stone mill by bombardment, he returned home. He was brought up on charges for his incompe-

tence and removed from command. His successor, Jacob Brown, tried to regain the initiative along the Niagara River. His forces, led by young Colonel Winfield Scott, won a resounding victory over quality British troops at Chippewa in June, but they failed to make further headway. The British kept their hold on the Niagara forts, and there were no more invasion attempts. Napoleon had been defeated in Europe, and British veterans were on their way, so American forces were soon on the defensive.

The desires of some Americans to remove the British from their northern border and to incorporate Canada into the United States came to naught. Had the American government pursued a strategy of negotiation with disaffected Canadians in 1812, it is possible that a revolution there would have accomplished those goals. By launching invasions, the United States forced Canadians into the arms of the British government so they could defend their lands from aggression. Further, by sacking and burning Toronto, Newark (outside Fort George), and other towns, the Americans caused such resentment among the Canadians that the two nations remained suspicious of each other for years. Not until the 1840s did Canada and America settle some border disputes and become friends, a relationship that remains to this day. No serious attempt at union between the two countries ever arose again, though there were occasional splinter group activities toward that goal.

See also Canada, American Invasion of [113]; United States, British Invasion of [124].

References: Berton, Pierre, *The Invasion of Canada* (Boston: Little, Brown, 1980); Coles, Harry L., *The War of*

*1812* (Chicago: University of Chicago Press, 1965); Mahon, John K., *The War of 1812* (Gainesville: University Presses of Florida, 1972).

## 115 EGYPT, NAPOLEON'S INVASION OF

By 1798 Napoleon Buonaparte was a national hero in France for his capture of Toulon and his brilliant campaign in Italy. That fame potentially made him a dangerous political rival to the ruling Directory, so he was assigned to a campaign outside the country. The first proposal was an invasion of England, but France lacked the naval power necessary to accomplish that. Thus, the Directory supported Napoleon's plan to invade Egypt, for it would take fewer ships and men. Napoleon hoped by this attack to secure a French colony in Egypt, which would open a path to India, from which the French had been dislodged 30 years earlier. The French government authorized the creation of the Army of the Orient in April 1798, and the force sailed from Toulon in May. The French fleet slipped past the British fleet under the command of Horatio Nelson and made first for Malta. Napoleon secured the island on 12 June from the decrepit Knights of St. John and left a garrison as he sailed for Egypt with 32,000 troops and a large number of scientists.

After a delay for repairs needed because of a storm, the British sailed quickly for Egypt and arrived two days before the French. Thinking he had missed Napoleon, Nelson sailed for Sicily, allowing the French to arrive and debark in Egypt unmolested. The French quickly captured Alexandria on 2 July and marched for Cairo. Along the way they were harassed by bedouins, and then met a force of the ruling Mamluks, the Muslim soldier-leaders of Egypt. Un-

accustomed to European-style warfare, the Mamluk cavalry rashly charged the French defensive squares and were slaughtered; the French counterattack destroyed the Mamluk camp. With most of the serious opposition defeated at what came to be called the Battle of the Pyramids, Cairo fell easily on 22 July.

Everything seemed to be going as Napoleon had planned until he learned that Nelson had destroyed the French fleet off Alexandria in Aboukir Bay. This left the coastline in British control and Napoleon's forces without a means of escape. He did not worry, but proceeded to establish a government made up of local religious figures along with a few French commissioners. Napoleon painted his arrival in Egypt not as an invasion but as a liberation from the Mamluks, who resisted the political and religious will of the Ottoman Empire, which the French supported. He mandated that his troops honor Muslim sensibilities, and negotiated a *fetwa* (directive) from the religious leaders of the Mosque of El Azhar that the French were official allies of Islam. He did everything in his power to allay Egyptian fears that the French were there to persecute them, but he soon admitted that French authority would in the end rest not on good deeds but on military strength.

After escaping the battlefield near the Pyramids, the Mamluk general Ibrahim fled to Syria and began raising a force with which to reconquer Egypt. Napoleon struck first, sending a force up the Nile to secure the southern flank while he marched toward Syria with 8,000 men in January 1799. He won the battles of El Arish and Jaffa fairly quickly, which gave him a false sense of security concerning the port city of Acre. He attacked without siege artillery and was thrown back, but he laid siege to the city in mid-March. Though he defeated a Turkish force that marched to relieve Acre, Napoleon was obliged to lift the siege and march away when plague struck the city and began to spread to his own forces. He was constantly harassed on his march back to Cairo, and returned with more than a quarter of his force dead of wounds or disease. The British aided a Turkish invasion force that landed at Aboukir Bay, but the French successfully defeated them in late July. At that point, a British captain sent Napoleon newspapers that updated him on events in Europe, events that showed political upset in Paris and the loss of Italy. A second alliance of nations was forming to threaten France, including Russia and the Ottoman Empire, and Napoleon's military talents would be necessary on the Continent. Needing to look out for his own career as well as gain reinforcements for the expedition in Egypt, Napoleon arranged for a secret escape and returned safely to France.

Napoleon went to Egypt intending to establish a colony and use it as a base for operations against British India. He also played the role of Alexander the Great in this expedition by taking with him a number of leading scientists and intellectuals to investigate the history of Egypt and the potential of constructing a canal linking the Mediterranean with the Red Sea. The discovery of the Rosetta Stone during this expedition, wherein a single message was written in hieroglyphics, Greek, and Latin, made possible the first translation of hieroglyphics and created the field of Egyptology. The administration Napoleon left on the island of Malta was a much more efficient government than had existed under the Knights of St. John who had ruled the island for more than 100 years; he brought an end to both slavery and the nobility, and gave a number of local students the chance to travel to France to study. In the long run, the invasion of Egypt was little more than an expensive sideshow,

but a French success there could have changed the course of the Napoleonic era by obliging the British to reapportion their naval forces away from a blockade of Europe and forcing the European powers to focus more attention on the Ottoman Empire. A French victory over the Ottomans, giving Napoleon control of Constantinople and the access to the Black Sea, could have changed the direction of his aim for empire and altered the balance of power in the Mediterranean for a long time to come.

See also Alexander the Great [11]; Napoleon Buonaparte [118].

References: Chandler, David, The Campaigns of Napoleon (New York: Macmillan, 1966); Connelly, Owen, Blundering to Glory (Wilmington, DE: Scholarly Resources, 1987); Markham, Felix, Napoleon (New York: New American Library, 1963).

## 116   FRANCE, EUROPEAN INVASION OF

The success of the French Revolution in July 1789 had an extremely sobering effect on the monarchies of Europe. If the king of France could lose his power so soon after the Americans had removed British king George III's power from the American colonies, what might that mean for the remainder of Europe if the idea of successful revolution should spread? Rather than wait for such a subversive philosophy to reach other countries, Prussian king William II joined Emperor Leopold II of Austria in August 1791 to isolate France and attempt to restore the monarchy. Russia and Sweden promised to contribute troops with Spanish subsidies. England did not join, but continental Europe was threatening the French Revolution. At the urging of French émigrés, Austria and Prussia formed a joint military command in February 1792 and sent troops toward the French frontier; the north Italian kingdom of Savoy joined in soon afterward. The French legislative assembly, having called for the formation of a larger army the previous August, declared war against the Austro-Prussian alliance on 20 April. Patriotic volunteers flocked to the colors, but they lacked discipline. The veterans of the army maintained a formal organization, but the removal of pro-monarchy officers somewhat hurt its effectiveness. The invading Austrians had little trouble disposing of the first French forces they met near Lille, and they began a siege of the city.

In July the invading army came under the command of Karl Wilhelm, the duke of Brunswick. He led 80,000 soldiers and, marching from Coblenz, quickly captured the French fortresses of Longwy and Verdun. Because the commander of the French army was the Marquis de Lafayette, his defeat was sufficient for a Paris mob to demand that the French king Louis XVI be stripped of the last vestiges of power. Lafayette was replaced by the more politically acceptable Charles Dumouriez, who joined his new command with that of French general François Kellermann to stand in the path of the advancing coalition force. At Valmy, 36,000 French soldiers of irregular quality faced 34,000 veterans under Brunswick. What should have been an easy victory for the invaders proved to be a defeat, thanks to the superior quality of the French artillery. Brunswick withdrew his forces to Germany.

In the meantime, other French forces were enjoying more success; in northern Italy they captured Nice, and other forces captured Mainz and marched toward Frankfurt in western Germany. This helped bring about the formation of the National Convention in September 1792, which formally ended the monarchy in France. Dumouriez scored one more success that year, invading Belgium and defeating an Austrian force near Jemappes, leading to the French capture of Brussels and the besieging of Antwerp. Though the coalition had been thrown on the defensive, Brunswick's recapture of Frankfurt in December ended the year on a positive note for them.

The beheading of Louis XVI in January 1793 provoked the English monarchy into joining the coalition against France. In return, France declared war on England, Holland, and Spain. Revolutionary fervor ran high in the wake of the execution and the growing threat to the nation, and the new government declared national conscription. Dumouriez was ordered to invade Holland, but before he could organize the assault, the coalition invaded again. Brunswick attacked Mainz with 60,000 Prussians, while 40,000 Austrians crossed the Meuse River to recover Belgium. More troops formed up along the Rhine River and in Luxembourg. Dumouriez was defeated at Neerwinden in March; when he was accused of treason, he fled to the invading forces. His replacement was killed in action, and more coalition victories resulted in the beheading of defeated revolutionary generals. The success of the invading forces, coupled with the Reign of Terror in Paris during the summer of 1793, nearly brought about the defeat of the revolution. British forces invaded the French coast at Dunkirk and occupied the harbor of Toulon in the south, which, along with Marseilles, had declared itself in favor of a return to the monarchy.

The governing body in Paris, the Committee of Public Safety, ordered the Levée en Masse, the drafting of every adult male.

Fourteen armies numbering almost a million men were soon created, and aided in the recapture of Marseilles. The massive numbers of French recruits proved successful. Even though they had no training and were poorly armed, they overwhelmed enemy forces by the sheer weight of numbers and the nature of their attacks. The soldiers flooded the battlefields, causing coalition generals to withdraw or be surrounded, a battlefield tactic unlike any the generals had ever faced. The English retreated after the battle of Hondschoote in early September; the Dutch ran from the field at Menin a week later. The victory over the Dutch did not lead to a retreat by the Austrians, however, and the French commander found himself a head shorter.

At this point the military adviser to the Committee of Public Safety, Lazare Carnot, was appointed head of the army. He became known as the "Organizer of Victory" for his ability to create order out of the chaos of the Levée en Masse. By mixing large numbers of the new draftees into existing units manned by a cadre of veterans, the army began to take shape. The veterans set a good example for training and operations, while the recruits provided the ardor and bravery. The new armies turned the tide of battle in the second half of 1793 by recapturing Toulon, invading Alsace, defeating both a Prussian and an Austrian force in successive battles in December, and recapturing Mainz.

In 1794 the new armies continued to grow and overwhelm the forces of Prussia, Austria, and England. French armies completed the occupation of Belgium, drove the English away at Antwerp, and occupied territory up to the west bank of the Rhine. Further victories in Italy and the Pyrenees extended French power past its frontiers. By April 1795, the invaders could stand it no longer. Prussia was the first to make peace at the Treaty of Basel, and the other German principalities of Saxony, Hanover, and Hesse-Cassel followed suit. Some political upheaval followed the overthrow of the Committee of Public Safety and the installation of the five-man Directory in August, but the armies held their own or expanded their successes. By 1796, Carnot's military was able to abandon the defensive and go on the offensive to spread the revolutionary gospel. The archduke Charles of Austria, however, outfought two French armies attempting to invade Bavaria and drove them both back. His transfer to Italy gave the French the opportunity to restart their invasion in the spring of 1797. French successes near the Rhine, coupled with the victories of Napoleon Buonaparte in Italy forced the Austrians to sue for peace.

By October 1797, France had defeated all its continental rivals, and only England remained at war with the French. The success of the French came partly from the lack of coordination on the part of the coalition forces, and partly from the new style of warfare they introduced. The mass patriotic army proved that in many cases courage could overcome an enemy's discipline, and the burgeoning Industrial Revolution made it possible to arm and equip the massive army France raised. From then on, national armies raised by conscription came to be the norm, and smaller, professional armies became obsolete. The intoxication of the revolution inspired men not only to join the army to defend their new government, but also to take the message of their philosophy to other peoples. That proved to be a two-edged sword, however; as the countries Napoleon occupied learned of the joys of *liberté*, *égalité*, and *fraternité*, they yearned for liberty from French domination. The nationalism inspiring the French success later energized the resistance movements that helped to defeat the armies of Napoleon. From this time forward, wars would be fought not by armies, but by nations.

See also Italy, Napoleon's Invasion of [117]; Napoleon Buonaparte [118].

References: Best, Geoffrey, *War and Society in Revolutionary Europe, 1770–1870* (New York: St. Martin's Press, 1982); Chandler, David, *The Campaigns of Napoleon* (New York: Macmillan, 1966); Sydenham, M. J., *The First French Republic, 1792–1804* (Berkeley: University of California Press, 1973).

## ITALY, NAPOLEON'S INVASION OF

**117**

By 1796 the European continent had been in constant turmoil for seven years, brought on by the revolution of the French populace against the aristocracy and church. With the 1793 execution of King Louis XVI and his queen Marie Antoinette, and the spread of the ideas of *liberté, égalité,* and *fraternité,* the royal courts of Europe mobilized thousands of troops to subdue the French armies and restore the monarchy. They were unsuccessful, and by 1796 only England and Austria remained at war with France. On 27 March 1796, command of the French Army of Italy was given to the little-known Napoleon Bonaparte, setting in motion a series of events that forever changed the face of France and Europe. Napoleon earned the notice of the French rulers by his defense of the governing Directory at Toulon in 1792. The Army of Italy was his first major command.

Napoleon joined the army at its headquarters in Nice. Following a review of the ragged and demoralized troops, he spoke with his divisional officers and outlined his strategy to divide and conquer the opposition—Austria and the Italian state of Piedmont, which was defended by Sardinian forces. By gaining the central position between the two, he planned to quickly eliminate one and then marshal his resources against the second. Though older and more experienced than their new commander, the divisional officers yielded to his domineering attitude and inspirational manner.

Napoleon planned to start his offensive on 15 April, but the Austrians moved first. Their forces, commanded by General Baron Johann Beaulieu, marched on 10 April for the town of Allesandria, northwest of Genoa. A second Austrian force of 20,000 under General de Argenteau marched to Montenotte west of the city, while a Piedmontese force of roughly the same size encamped across a valley at Ceva. Napoleon reacted quickly, dividing his force of 37,000: One force held the Piedmontese to the French left, while Napoleon led the majority of the troops against Argenteau on the right of the valley. At daybreak on 12 April, Argenteau found himself confronted and flanked by Napoleon; the Austrians soon withdrew from an untenable position.

Having driven Argenteau back, Napoleon turned to throw the weight of his forces at the Piedmontese. He drove them from Ceva back to the town of Mondovì, then forced them to run some 50 miles to their nearest base at Turin, abandoning most of their supplies and artillery, both badly needed by the French. The Piedmontese king offered peace terms, which Napoleon immediately accepted without first notifying Paris. This separate peace removed Piedmont from the conflict and gained for France the provinces of Savoy and Nice.

Napoleon had now secured his rear, so he could concentrate on the Austrians. Beaulieu had withdrawn from Allesandria northward to defensive positions behind the Po River. Anticipating French river crossings, he secured the fords and bridges along his front. Napoleon left two divisions across from Beaulieu to keep his attention, while the remainder of his force marched far to the east and crossed the Po at Piacenza on 7 May. This move threatened to sever Beaulieu's communications with Austria, and he was forced to abandon his position and move rapidly to Lodi, north of Piacenza. A quick battle at Lodi forced Beaulieu to withdraw again, this time to the Adige River far to the east past Lake Gardo.

Rather than follow Beaulieu immediately, Napoleon marched northwest to Milan and entered the city on 15 May. he was acclaimed by the public, and arranged treaties with the surrounding duchies. He also received orders from the Directory to surrender half his army to General F. C. Kellermann, commander of the French Army of Germany, and take the remainder south to intimidate the pope. Napoleon threatened to resign his command rather than see his small force made smaller still; his growing popularity with the French public gave weight to his demands, and he kept his army.

Beaulieu meanwhile moved his army south of Lake Gardo to the city of Mantua, where he soon found himself besieged by the French. Suddenly Napoleon had too many things to do: Maintain a siege, keep an eye on the papal forces to the south in Lombardy, secure his own lines of communication, and keep his army supplied. Without reinforcements or effective action from Kellermann in Germany, Napoleon had to go to an active defense. The Austrians reacted by sending another force under General Count Dagobert Wurmser to deal with the French. Wurmser marched toward Mantua, while secondary forces marched against the French advance post at Verona (to the east of Lake Gardo) and down the west coast of Lake Gardo to cut off any line of French retreat toward Milan.

Napoleon maintained a good intelligence network, and when he learned of the three-pronged attack, moved to defeat each one separately. He abandoned the siege of Mantua and quickly moved to blunt the thrust along the west coast of the lake. The unsuspecting Austrians found themselves facing a superior French force on 3 August and beat a hasty retreat to the Tyrol. The French wheeled to face Wurmser, defeating him at Lonato the next day, forcing his return to Austria. For a loss of 40,000 casualties, his artillery, and his supplies, Wurmser had managed to get only food to Mantua, which was once again besieged. Leaving a covering force at the city, Napoleon marched northward with the remainder of his army and engaged the newly reinforced Austrians marching south from the Tyrol. Rapid marching once again allowed him to meet the Austrian forces before they could join against him, and Napoleon defeated them at Rovoreno, Primolano, and Bassano in early September. His victorious forces were now placed between the Austrians and their homeland, and less than 40 miles from the Gulf of Venice on Italy's east coast. Wurmser retreated southward toward Mantua.

The Austrian government raised yet another army, and attempted again to drive along Lake Gardo to Verona. Napoleon met the Austrians, led by General Baron Josef Alvintzi at Caldiero, east of Verona. Failing to dislodge them from strong positions, Napoleon withdrew toward Verona, then swung his forces around and behind Alvintzi, attacking his flank and rear at Arcole on 15 November. A three-day battle ensued that forced the Austrians to withdraw yet again. Unwilling to concede defeat, another Austrian force marched to reinforce Alvintzi. Unsure of Napoleon's position or intentions, Alvintzi stretched his forces thin and launched multiple attacks toward Verona, Lognano, and Rivoli. Napoleon massed his strength at Rivoli and drove Alvintzi back yet again after a hotly contested struggle that effectively smashed the Austrian army. These setbacks, when reported to Wurmser in Mantua, compelled his surrender of that city in February 1797.

So impressed was the Directory with Napoleon's victories that they decided to reinforce the Army of Italy, planning on a triumphant campaign against Vienna itself. With new French troops, plus a number of recruits from the newly conquered Italian provinces, Napoleon crossed the Alps on the way to Vienna in the spring of 1797. Austrian forces under Archduke Karl Ludwig did their best to stem the tide, but the French successively stormed or turned each Austrian position. When the French were 100 miles from Vienna, Karl decided it was time to negotiate. Napoleon's lines of communication were stretched perilously thin, but Karl did not know that; the French commander blustered, and the Austrian commander gave in. The Treaty of Leoben ended the hostilities between France and Austria.

Napoleon rocketed from semiobscurity to national prominence after the Italian campaign. The lightning maneuvers he used to open the campaign stunned the Austrians, leaving them witless. His maneuvers were not new, but they had not been used in the late eighteenth century. By the rapidity of his marches, his flanking movements to threaten his enemy's rear, and his army's ability to live off the land, Napoleon was able to accomplish much more than expected against superior forces. His personal direction of each offensive and his placement of units for easy mutual support enabled him to bring to bear considerable forces at the most opportune

moments. With a superior intelligence service and his own uncanny ability to outguess his opponents, he consistently caught his opponents unaware of his presence, defeating them one at a time.

After a campaign in Egypt, Napoleon was back in Italy in 1800. He staged one of his greatest victories at Marengo, and placed the northern part of the peninsula under French control.

Napoleon brought Italy the first semblance of unity it had had since the Roman Empire. The French attempted to educate the Italians in revolutionary doctrine, but the mostly illiterate population was more accustomed to repression than political freedom, and they were slow to respond. The Italians bridled at the lack of respect shown the pope by the foreigners, but they soon began to work within the bureaucracy installed by the French; thousands acquired hands-on experience in political administration. The French also built schools (even for girls), improved the road system, abolished serfdom, and introduced the Napoleonic Code. Even the British blockade had positive effects, for it forced the start of industrialization and the cultivation of a new variety of crops. When Napoleon was defeated in 1815, much of Italy returned to disunity or Austrian control, but that first taste of national unity would be fulfilled in the 1840s.

—Rhett Michael Schall

See also Napoleon Buonaparte [118].

References: Britt, Albert Sidney, The Wars of Napoleon (Wayne, NJ: Avery Publishing Group, 1985); Chandler, David, The Campaigns of Napoleon (New York: Macmillan, 1966); Gibbs, M. B., Napoleon's Military Career (Chicago: Werner Co., 1895).

On the small Mediterranean island of Corsica in August 1769, the second surviving son of Carlo and Leticia Buonaparte was born. He was given the name of a rare saint, Napoleone, a name that in only a few decades would become world-renowned.

Proving his aristocratic Italian bloodline, Carlo was able to enroll his eldest sons in French schools at royal expense. At the school in Brienne, Napoleon immersed himself in his studies, especially mathematics, history, and geography. At military school, he completed his education as an officer in the French army. He graduated earlier than usual, with the rank of first lieutenant, and was posted to an artillery regiment.

The French Revolution's early stages had little effect on Napoleon. However, once the National Assembly had established itself, he was quick to embrace the concepts and ideas the revolution professed. He sailed to Corsica to spread the revolution to his homeland, but was unsuccessful in his attempts to bring about its independence. Arousing the anger of Corsica's citizens, the Bonaparte family was forced to flee to France.

Napoleon's career wavered between active and inactive duty during the infancy of Republican France. Not until he was called upon to take command of the artillery at the siege of Toulon was he able to show his talents. The siege's successful outcome elevated Napoleon's status; events would increase or decrease his popularity, once even to the point of a brief prison stay. Nevertheless, political events changed drastically, and brought Napoleon again to the forefront of popularity.

To eliminate any opportunity for a dictatorship, the National Assembly was disbanded in favor of the Directory. Alarmed by the outcry of the Paris mobs, the Directory called upon Napoleon for protection. His "whiff of grapeshot" kept the Directory in firm control and elevated him to second-in-command of the Army of the Interior. In 1796, Napoleon fell in love with and married Rose de Beauharnais, known better as Joséphine. With his marriage only days old, Napoleon was dispatched to take command of the Army of Italy against Austria, one of the two remaining antagonists of Republican France.

In an explosive, masterful campaign across northern Italy to the frontiers of Austria, Napoleon forced a peace treaty in 1797. Returning to Paris to the acclaim of the populace, he began to feel that the future of France and his destiny were intertwined, but the time was not yet right to seize power. Instead, he gladly took the Directory's orders to undertake a campaign in the Middle East. Through another stunning example of generalship, he was successful in subduing Egypt, but the campaign was brought to a halt at the walls of Acre and by the British devastation of the French fleet at Aboukir. In newspapers and letters that filtered through the British blockade of Alexandria, Napoleon learned of the disasters befalling the Republican government. Deciding the time was ripe, he gathered a small group of faithful followers, slipped past the British blockade, and returned to France. Once more in Paris and acclaimed by the population, Napoleon intrigued to become the first consul of the new government.

The consulship was to be a three-person government, but Napoleon soon showed his domineering and persuasive personality, and assumed sole power. He immediately went to work addressing the needs of France. To sooth the populace he permitted the return of émigrés, the aristocrats who had sought refuge outside France. He reestablished the Catholic

Buonaparte, the Consul. An unfinished but
most celebrated portrait of Napoleon
in his prime by David, 1798

ences were patronized so that with their finest work he could transform France, and Paris in particular, into the capital of the European continent.

Compelled by internal and external events, Napoleon spent the majority of 1805–1807 in the position of commander in chief of the newly formed Grande Armée. The genius he brought to military thinking became most evident during this time period. Napoleon reworked the French army into a corps system, which maneuvered in an entirely new fashion. Marching with four corps in a loose diamond fashion, the *bataillon carré*, each force could forage for itself and defend itself when attacked, holding an enemy in place until the other units came to its support. Two corps would flank the enemy, while the remaining one would act as a reserve. Thus, any enemy force finding itself with a superiority in numbers soon found itself flanked by the rapidly moving French response. Mobility and speed marked his actions, and his enemies usually found themselves defeated by their own ponderous tactics.

In astounding campaigns he would humble the Austrians, the Prussians, and the Russians. After each one, the sphere of his influence and control spread throughout Europe. With his passion for family ties, he created various realms from the territories he acquired to give to his brothers, sisters, and military/political associates to administer (under his direction). However, he was unable to come to grips with his one major rival, Great Britain. The loss of his fleet, and that of his ally Spain, at the battle of Trafalgar forced Napoleon to devise a means to humble that "nation of shopkeepers." Napoleon established the Continental System: All commerce between the Continent and Britain was to cease and all ports were to close to British shipping, thereby damaging the British eco-

church as the state religion, but provided protection for other faiths. He centralized the bureaucracy to better control and oversee district government agencies, and he established the Banque de France to regenerate the sagging and disrupted national financial situation.

Napoleon's greatest endeavor was restructuring and establishing a set of civil laws equitable to all citizens. His short prison term during the revolution had given him the opportunity to read the one book available in his cell, *Justinian Law*. Reworking these ideas into the basis of France's new law, he created what became known as the Civil Code, later the Napoleonic Code. Taking four years to fully codify, the Civil Code would be the greatest achievement of Napoleon's government.

To eliminate the nation's poverty and civil disrepair, Napoleon instigated various public works. Roads were constructed throughout the provinces, while avenues were cleared and widened within major cities to accommodate the movement of commerce and troops. The arts and sci-

nomically, since he could not deal with them militarily.

At home, events and emotions over the future of France compelled Napoleon to divorce Joséphine. In her place he married Marie Louise of Austria for political reasons, and to produce an heir, which Joséphine was unable to provide. For the next two years (1810–1811) Napoleon spent his time on the policies of empire and playing with his son. He soon grew displeased with the constant smuggling of goods through European ports and especially into Russia. Seeking to regain his dominance and influence over the youthful and inexperienced Tsar Alexander, Napoleon called forth over half a million men to invade Russia.

Napoleon left the army during its retreat from Moscow, and returned to Paris to build a new army and forestall a reported coup attempt. During the years 1813–1814, he endeavored to maintain his empire by conducting campaigns against combined enemy forces. Eventually forced back behind the frontiers of France, he conducted a brilliant but futile struggle to keep his throne. The attempt to turn over the reins of empire to his son failed; for the good of France, Napoleon abdicated. Sentenced to exile on the island of Elba in the Mediterranean, he tried to accept the inevitable conclusion of his life. However, the reestablishment of the Bourbons reasserted his belief that his destiny was tied to that of the French people. Escaping from British surveillance, Napoleon returned to French soil and easily regained the throne. His attempts to pacify the European governments so he could maintain his crown failed when the Congress of Vienna outlawed him as a danger to the peace of Europe.

Never one to take the defensive, Napoleon raised an army of 100,000 to take the field against the British and Prussians in the Belgian lowlands. In one of the most famous battles in modern history, Napoleon was beaten at Waterloo and forced once more to abdicate. His punishment for again disrupting Europe was exile to the remote island of St. Helena in the south Atlantic. With little more to do than stroll the limits of his house and grounds, Napoleon spent most of his time dictating his memoirs.

Even though Napoleon attempted to control the vast continent of Europe through his own hands and those of his puppet rulers, today his greatest achievement is considered the *Code Napoleon*. It has changed little since its institution, and has had an effect on the laws of Italy as well as many other European nations. Napoleon is better remembered as a great military commander, but his compassion for the French people brought about their resurgence in civil works and in the arts and sciences, and a greater belief in the concepts of liberty and equality for all individuals.

—Rhett Michael Schall

See also Egypt, Napoleon's Invasion of [115]; France, European Invasion of [116]; Italy, Napoleon's Invasion of [117]; Prussia, Napoleon's Invasion of [122]; Russia, Napoleon's Invasion of [122].

References: Abbot, John S. C., *Life of Napoleon*, 4 vols. (New York: Harper & Brothers, 1855–1856); Chandler, David, *The Campaigns of Napoleon* (New York: Macmillan, 1966); Markham, Felix, *Napoleon* (New York: New American Library, 1963).

## NEW YORK, BRITISH INVASION OF (1776)

In March 1776 revolutionary forces under George Washington were successful in forcing a British withdrawal from their

Colonists pull down the statue of George III after the signing of the
Declaration of Independence in 1776.

main base in Boston, Massachusetts. This effectively curtailed British operations to put down the rebellion until they could reestablish control over a port through which to commit troops and supplies. The next best harbor was at New York City. Washington also understood the British need for a harbor, and guessed correctly that New York would be the target. However, he was handicapped by the forces at his disposal. Even though the revolution was a year old, he was still unable to form a regular army, having a force made up almost entirely of volunteer militia. They were of irregular quality, but fairly well motivated because of the success they had thus far enjoyed. After all, they had inflicted three times as many casualties as they had suffered on the war's opening day at Lexington and Concord in April 1775. They gave a good account of themselves at Breed's (Bunker) Hill the following June; though they were forced from the field, they inflicted almost 50 percent casualties on the British. The bombardment of Boston, which forced the British almost totally out of the country, capped a year of positive results on the battlefield that ultimately convinced the revolutionary leadership to declare American independence.

Washington knew that ultimate victory would come only with a regular army that could beat the British in the open field, but the supplies and government support he needed to accomplish this were irregular, since the Continental Congress had not been able to establish the authority to collect taxes. Therefore, training and organization were slow. Still, he took what men he had and moved to New York to prepare for the invasion he knew would come.

Washington's next problem was the placement of his troops. He was under orders from the Continental Congress to build defenses to protect the city—almost an impossibility. There were just too many directions from which an invading force could be landed: Staten Island, Long Island, Manhattan, either bank of the Hudson River. Washington tried, but the job was too big for his 20,000 men, of whom more than half were short-term militia. Luckily for him, General William Howe, his British adversary, would be cooperative. The advance guard of the British army under Howe landed on undefended Staten Island on 4 July 1776, but did nothing to slow down Washington's preparations. With the assistance of his older brother, Admiral Richard Howe, General Howe tried to negotiate with the rebels. This occupied about six weeks of his time to no avail, because the revolutionaries stood by their Declaration. Finally, with reinforcements up to a total of 34,000, Howe went into action against Washington's 8,000 men on Long Island on 22 August.

With superior numbers, the British overwhelmed or outmaneuvered the rebels, and Washington was forced to abandon his forward entrenchments and withdraw into prepared defenses on Brooklyn Heights, backed up against the East River. These were untenable should the British navy position itself behind him, so Washington withdrew his army under cover of darkness and heavy weather, extricating his entire force without British knowledge until the operation was completed.

Not terribly aggressive even at the best of times, Howe missed a golden opportunity to crush the rebel army and possibly capture Washington himself. Howe had commanded the forces assaulting the rebel

position on Breed's Hill outside Boston the previous summer, and the appalling casualties his force suffered remained in his memory. He often had opportunities to crush the Americans, yet always hesitated at key moments and took the more cautious and careful option, which gave Washington time to react or escape. Though he ultimately occupied New York City, his lack of audacity robbed him of the complete victory he might have accomplished.

Howe did not follow Washington's men across the river until 11 September, by which time the rebels were already preparing to withdraw farther north. Washington was chased to Harlem Heights, where his forces stood temporarily and stalled the British pursuit, giving Howe another opportunity to be cautious. Howe began to consolidate his hold on New York City, and did not move toward the rebels again until 9 October. He missed another chance to corner Washington, who retreated to White Plains with his forces reduced to about 14,000. Washington dug in, and the British finally attacked him on 28 October. Again the British were victorious, and again the rebels were allowed to slip away.

In November the British had New York City well in hand, and Washington was on the run toward Philadelphia. Howe allowed the chase to halt outside New Brunswick, New Jersey, and began the traditional practice of settling into winter quarters. By 1 December, his forces controlled everything from the Delaware River to Newport, Rhode Island, and he put the war on hold until the spring, as was the common procedure of the time. Howe accomplished part of what he set out to do: He regained a port through which Britain could supply the war. By failing to seize many opportunities to crush the rebellion by destroying its armed force, he allowed Washington to fight another day, and would ultimately live to regret it.

The British held New York City throughout the remainder of the war, but the lack of dash on the part of their commander became a habit practiced by Howe's successors as well. The invasion was a short-term success that for a time disheartened the patriot cause, but in the long run the British were not able to follow up on it.

References: Alden, John R., *The American Revolution* (New York: Harper & Row, 1954); Dupuy, R. E., *An Outline History of the American Revolution* (New York: Harper & Row, 1975); Gruber, Ira, *The Howe Brothers and the American Revolution* (New York: Atheneum, 1972).

## NEW YORK, BRITISH INVASION OF (1777)

**120**

When General William Howe captured New York City in the latter half of 1776, the British believed that they were in a strong position to bring the American Revolution to an end. They controlled a wide circle of land surrounding the city, stretching from New Jersey to Rhode Island, and had dealt George Washington a set of serious defeats in the process. Despite the fact that Washington had regained some initiative with victories at Trenton after Christmas and Princeton in the new year, the British authorities did not view the rebels as serious opposition. The only problem the British faced was a lack of direction on how to finish off the rebels. Without a planning staff in London, or one person who exercised total command and control, the generals on the spot were left to develop strategy. This lack of coordination would ultimately spell the doom of the British war effort.

In New York City, Howe proposed attacking Philadelphia. It was the site of the Continental Congress, the capital city, as it were, of the revolutionary movement. Capture the capital and the movement would die, he believed. He sent this plan to London, and received approval from Lord Germain, secretary for America in the British government. However, Germain's approval of an alternate strategy that in some ways contradicted Howe's would ultimately bring about disaster. General John Burgoyne proposed an offensive out of Canada into New York. Burgoyne viewed New York as the linchpin of America, as did Washington himself. By gaining control of the state of New York, the revolution would be physically split, with the heart and soul of the revolutionary spirit in Massachusetts cut off from the supplies of the less ardent southern states.

The idea was a good one, but lacked the key element of coordination, or at least communication. Burgoyne was to lead a major offensive down Lake Champlain to the Hudson River and on to the capital at Albany, which would give him control of upstate New York. Simultaneously, a second and smaller thrust would be led by Barry St. Leger from Lake Ontario eastward down the Mohawk River, thus gaining control of the center of the state. To complete the operation, Howe should march north up the Hudson from New York City and join the other two in Albany, thereby controlling the southern part of the state and dividing the country in two. Burgoyne knew that Howe was dedicated to an attack on Philadelphia, in another direction from his assigned role in this strategy, but the two generals and Germain in London all agreed that Philadelphia would fall quickly enough for Howe to dispatch troops to Albany. Certainly the two strategies should crush the revolution.

Depending on William Howe for speed was a mistake, though in this case the fault was not totally his own. Instead of marching directly for Philadelphia (his forces already controlled most of the route), Howe decided to embark his troops on ships and sail up Chesapeake Bay, where he would debark and attack Philadelphia from the southwest. Not only was this a very roundabout way to reach his objective, it depended on cooperation from the Royal Navy, which was not readily forthcoming. There was no overall commander to order the navy's cooperation, and the navy and army rarely got along very well. It took much of the summer for 260 transport ships to be collected to carry Howe's force, and they did not set sail until late July. The troops did not debark until 25 August, and Howe did not contact Washington's defensive force until 10 September. By the time he defeated the rebels at Brandywine Creek and Germantown to take possession of the city, it was October and time to settle into winter quarters. He could not possibly dispatch troops to assist Burgoyne at that late date, and the troops left behind to garrison New York City were given no orders to cooperate with Burgoyne's offensive from the north. One-third of the operation would never materialize, but Howe could not quickly communicate that to Burgoyne.

In the meantime, Burgoyne had made good progress. He traveled along Lake Champlain and captured the American fort Ticonderoga on 6 July. Burgoyne maintained a stable supply line by water most of the way back to Canada, but from Ticonderoga onward he had to move overland and build a road as he went. This slowed his progress and allowed the American commander in the area, Horatio Gates, time to set up a defensive position along the Hudson near the town of Saratoga, halfway from Ticonderoga to Albany. During this slow advance southward, Burgoyne began to run into trouble. A well-known young loyalist lady, Jane McRae, affianced

to an American officer fighting with Burgoyne and awaiting the arrival of the British forces, was murdered and scalped by an Indian guide hired by Burgoyne. Burgoyne wanted to punish the murderer, but he could not afford to alienate his guides so deep into enemy territory and let the offender go. Though the victim was a loyalist (and upper New York had many of them), the long-standing enmity between colonist and Indian was aroused. Even those supportive of Britain could not tolerate Burgoyne's decision, and many New Yorkers rose up to either join Gates at Saratoga or harass the British supply line back to Canada. When Burgoyne ordered his mercenary Hessian troops to acquire supplemental supplies from the countryside, they were none too gentle in their treatment of the locals, and this further provoked the New Yorkers. Burgoyne found himself in a suddenly hostile countryside with a growing force of rebels ahead and behind, but he had to push on for Albany.

The eastward prong of the attack, from Oswego down the Mohawk Valley, was having even less success. They were slowed by a rebel force of some 850 men behind the strong defenses of Fort Stanwix, at modern-day Rome, New York. Difficult fighting and the arrival of a relief force commanded by rebel general Benedict Arnold disheartened the 1,000 Indians of St. Leger's force. They forced his 800 British, Canadian, and Tory troops to retreat or face the Indians as well as the rebels. St. Leger ordered a withdrawal to Oswego in late August, and Burgoyne was left without the second force he was to meet at Albany. Like Howe in Philadelphia, St. Leger was unable to get word to Burgoyne.

Thus Burgoyne was alone when he ran into Gates's defenses at Freeman's Farm outside Saratoga in mid-September. Checked by the rebel forces, Burgoyne spent almost a month building defenses and probing the American lines. When he tried again to push through the Americans at nearby Bemis Heights, he was repulsed. The rebels counterattacked under the leadership of Benedict Arnold, recently arrived from the Mohawk Valley. They forced the British back to their defensive lines and surrounded them. Cut off from his supplies, Burgoyne soon realized that neither St. Leger nor Howe would arrive to extricate him. He surrendered his force of 8,000 men on 17 October.

The American victories near Saratoga became the turning point of the revolution. First, they took a large force of British out of the war. Second, they kept the British from controlling New York and splitting the colonies. Third, and most importantly, they impressed the Europeans, whose support the Americans were so desperately courting. The French in particular began to take a serious look at recognizing American independence. They had refrained from doing so in the past for fear of British retribution, but Burgoyne's defeat convinced the French government that the revolution had a serious chance to succeed. Loss of its colonies had to weaken the British, and the French could only profit thereby. They recognized the United States, and signed a mutual-defense treaty with the new nation in February 1778. This brought a steady supply of war matériel, which the colonists had to have in order to continue the war and ultimately win it. The French provided arms and ammunition, supplies, money, ships, and troops. Their decision also prompted other European nations, notably Spain and the Netherlands, to recognize American independence as well. Britain now had to guard its interests nearer to home, and could no longer focus its full attention on America. Though the war would continue until 1783, for all intents and purposes the Americans' independence was assured after Saratoga. The very

existence of the United States, and what it has meant to the history of the world, was guaranteed in October 1777.

References: Chidsey, Donald B., *The War in the North: An Informal History of the American Revolution in and near Canada* (New York: Crown Publishers, 1967); Furneaux, Rupert, *The Battle of Saratoga* (New York: Stein & Day, 1971); Mintz, Max, *The Generals of Saratoga: John Burgoyne and Horatio Gates* (New Haven, CT: Yale University Press, 1990).

## PRUSSIA, NAPOLEON'S INVASION OF

121

By 1804, Napoleon was on the road to mastery of Europe. He had proclaimed himself emperor of France in the wake of the French Republic, and with his personal genius and his well-trained, experienced army he had humbled Austria and taken control of Italy and Spain. The powers of Europe, encouraged by Napoleon's devious diplomacy, could not cooperate against him. Prussia was the only power that remained neutral through Napoleon's rise. Prussia was the possessor of a rich military heritage via Frederick the Great, but its victories were 50 years in the past, and its army had lost its quality leadership and training. Prussian king William III lusted after the state of Hanover, home of the English royal family but currently under Napoleon's control. William remained neutral until he could determine whether England or France would be the best ally to satisfy his territorial ambitions. His vacillation provoked Napoleon's contempt.

In May 1804, William got off the fence by joining the Third Coalition, allying Prussia with Austria, Russia, and England. Though Austria went on the offensive into Bavaria in September, William remained a passive partner. He would not commit his troops, even when French troops crossed the Prussian principality of Ansbach. William signed the Convention of Potsdam, wherein the Russian tsar called for the commitment of Prussian troops to the coalition's defense, but still he would not honor the treaty. Napoleon's victory at Austerlitz was therefore gained at the expense of Austrian and Russian troops only.

William sent an envoy to Vienna after Austerlitz to try to convince Napoleon that Prussia had not been a member of the coalition. Napoleon was not fooled, and proposed a treaty in which Prussia would cede some of its territory to France and sever all ties with the former coalition members, allying itself only with France. In return, Hanover would become Prussia's possession, only because Napoleon knew it would act as a point of contention between Prussia and England. As William vacillated over signing this Treaty of Vienna, Napoleon added more conditions: All North Sea ports had to be closed, and all English ships and goods seized. William signed.

Unsatisfied with his humiliation of Prussia thus far, Napoleon established the Confederation of the Rhine, an organization of smaller German states, which threatened traditional Prussian influence in northern Germany. Prussia was further hurt by English actions; England declared war on Prussia over Hanover and seized hundreds of German ships in English ports. When William learned that private peace feelers were extending from London and Moscow toward Paris, his wife Louise convinced him to stand firm and avenge his country's honor.

Prussia's army was in no condition to face Napoleon's Grande Armée. Though it retained its reputation and numbered a quarter million strong, the Prussian army had not been tested in battle for decades. Its weaponry, tactics, and organization were long out of date, and its youngest high com-

manders were in their sixties. They completely failed to grasp any of Napoleon's past strategies, and predicted he would assume a defensive position when they approached him. Their mobilization program was slow and had poor security, so Napoleon learned of their moves and embarked with his traditional speed to beat the Prussians to the punch. On 7 October 1807, Prussia declared war on France, but Napoleon's armies were already on Prussia's frontiers.

The first battle took place the following day, and Napoleon was victorious at Rudolstadt, killing Prussia's prince Louis in the process. A week later, at Jena, Napoleon scored yet another of his impressive victories. Napoleon slaughtered a Prussian corps while his subordinate, Marshal Davout, in a diversionary attack, actually found the bulk of the Prussian army at Auerstadt. Though outnumbered, Davout's aggressive handling of his forces forced a Prussian retreat. By 24 October, Prussia was crushed, and Napoleon was in Berlin. He levied heavy reparations on Prussia but, rather than collect them quickly, Napoleon decided to stay in Prussia and use it as a base for possible operations against Russia.

After the French victory at Friedland in 1807, Tsar Alexander signed the Treaty of Tilsit with Napoleon, promising to make common cause against England. In return, Napoleon forced Prussia to cede its possessions in Poland to Russia. With his eastern flank secured, Napoleon now collected the remainder of Prussian reparations. French humiliation of Prussia caused a groundswell of popular feeling against Napoleon. The Prussians ached for vengeance, and the army learned that it could not rest on the laurels won by Frederick the Great.

Napoleon's occupation of Prussia planted the seeds of his destruction. Though the people came to hate him, Napoleon brought to Prussia the lessons of the French Revolution. The nationalism that saved France from European enemies became the same force that motivated Prussia. Prussia joined with the remainder of Europe to take advantage of Napoleon's weakness in 1813 and was involved with his ultimate defeat at Leipzig in 1814 and Waterloo in 1815. The Prussian General Staff was re-formed to modernize the military and focus on learning the lessons of this and every other war. It became a military organization the world would model in the late nineteenth century. This reconstituted military became the symbol of national power and pride, leading to German unification in 1871 and the German Empire shortly thereafter.

See also Austria, Napoleon's Conquest of [112]; Russia, Napoleon's Invasion of [122].

References: Chandler, David, *The Campaigns of Napoleon* (New York: Macmillan, 1966); Horne, Alistair, *Napoleon, Master of Europe, 1805–1807* (New York: Morrow, 1979); Markham, Felix, *Napoleon and the Awakening of Europe* (London: English Universities Press, 1954).

## 122    RUSSIA, NAPOLEON'S INVASION OF

By 1807, Napoleon controlled all of Europe, directly or indirectly. Only Britain remained completely free from French control, but Russia had bought some time and security by signing the Treaty of Tilsit. Tsar Alexander agreed to boycott British goods and import mostly French products, but poor Russians could not afford them. Aside from economic sacrifices, Russia looked askance at Napoleon's political desires. He firmly controlled the duchy of Warsaw, which seemed to Russia a good

launch point for an invasion of their country. Further, Napoleon was looking longingly at the Dardanelles, long a strategic goal of Russian foreign policy. He had done little to assure Russia of long-term friendly intentions, and short-term financial woes pressed on the Russian economy. By 1812, Alexander's advisers convinced him to ignore Napoleon's Continental System barring British goods from all of Europe. The Russian government ignored Napoleon's plea to impound a large number of British ships sailing for St. Petersburg, and for Napoleon that was the last straw. He was determined to punish Russia for violating his economic warfare policies, lest other European countries follow suit.

Napoleon's invasion force numbered over half a million men, but included a large percentage of non-French troops whose loyalty and cooperation might prove doubtful. Alexander also had foreign aid; he had been negotiating with Sweden, Poland, Prussia, Turkey, and Britain, and many of the generals Napoleon faced were not Russian. Even though he outnumbered his Russian foe, Napoleon's advisers counseled against the invasion. Their advice went unheeded. Napoleon planned on a relatively easy campaign, because he took few horses and ordered the troops to carry only four days' rations. Regularly placed supply depots, plus the army's traditional ability to live off the land, would provide for his needs. The long march, however, forced the army to shrink in size: Depots needed garrisons, and forage parties also needed men.

French forces crossed the Nieman River in June 1812. Well aware of Napoleon's prowess, Alexander withdrew his forces before the advance and ordered a scorched-earth policy. Thus, the French could rarely come to grips with a sizable Russian force, and they found it virtually impossible to live off the land. The French expected the peasants to welcome them as liberators, but instead they cooperated with the tsar's orders. Tsar Alexander wanted to lead his forces himself when the two armies would finally meet, but his wife and advisers convinced him to stay in the capital and give command to the baron Barclay de Tolly. The baron followed the plan to avoid confrontation, but was soon criticized and relieved for retreating too quickly. His replacement was the aged general Prince Golinischev-Kutosov, veteran of earlier encounters with Napoleon.

No battle of import was fought until Kutosov found a good place to stand some 70 miles from Moscow, near the village of Borodino. The battle cost a total of 70,000 lives and could be called little more than a draw, but Kutusov abandoned the field and withdrew toward Moscow. He soon vacated that city as well, as did virtually the entire population. Napoleon sent a messenger to the city to demand its surrender, but no one of any authority remained there. He occupied the empty capital, and claimed an empty victory. The city was soon on fire, the blazes set by retreating soldiers and civilians, and those valuables that could be saved from the flames loaded down the looting French soldiers. After no more than a few days, there was nothing in the city unburned or unplundered.

With cold weather approaching and Moscow unsuitable for spending the winter, Napoleon had little choice but to declare victory and go home. He left on 19 October 1812 and found the road out of Russia as difficult as the one coming in. His army became an easy target—slowed by rain and snow, bogged down by the burden of their loot, and harassed by raiding Russian units. The lack of food and shelter, coupled with the constant sniping, caused many more deaths than did battle. Total casualty counts vary, but of the 600,000-plus men that entered Russia in June, Napoleon led no more than 100,000 out; some sources claim that as few as 10,000 survived. Probably 125,000 of the total were battle deaths.

Napoleon's fortunes dwindled rapidly. Proven to be fallible, the countries he had conquered quickly rose against him. Napoleon reached Paris and raised a new army before news of his disaster reached his country, but his new forces lacked the training and experience of the Grand Armée that had taken him to glory. A coalition of European countries formed and defeated him in 1814 at Leipzig in the so-called Battle of the Nations, and he went to exile in Elba. A short-lived attempt to regain power in 1815 left him defeated again at Waterloo in Belgium; thereafter, he was exiled to St. Helena in the middle of the South Atlantic, too far away to be rescued or exert influence.

The invasion of Russia and Napoleon's defeat serve as landmark events in that nation's history. The world enjoys two enduring tributes to these events—Tchaikovsky's *1812 Overture* and Tolstoy's *War and Peace*. The Russian tsar's power remained strong, but the peasants who sacrificed for the cause gained no reward for it. Autocratic rule remained in Russia for another hundred years, but to this day the people of that nation depend on Mother Russia and Mother Nature to save them from any invasion.

*See also* Austria, Napoleon's Conquest of [112].

References: Cate, Curtis, *The War of Two Emperors* (New York: Random House, 1984); Palmer, Alan, *Napoleon in Russia* (New York: Simon & Schuster, 1967); Tarle, Eugene, *Napoleon's Invasion of Russia in 1812* (New York: Farrar, Straus & Giroux, 1971).

## SOUTHERN UNITED STATES, BRITISH INVASION OF

**123**

After the British failure to split the rebellious American colonies in half by the campaign in New York in 1777, British leaders had to rethink their goals. Possession of New York City and Philadelphia had not brought about the expected collapse of revolutionary resistance nor the expected uprising of loyalist pro-British support among the citizenry. When General Sir William Howe was relieved of his command in the summer of 1778, General Sir Henry Clinton replaced him as head of the British forces in America. In London, American Secretary Lord Germain decided that the wisest course was to move the sphere of action to the American south, where revolutionary feeling was not nearly as intense and loyalist sentiment was supposed to predominate. Building a power base in the south would deprive the rebels of much of their supply source, and the British could pin the revolutionary forces between advancing British troops from the south and the existing British positions around New York City.

Germain ordered Clinton to initiate this southern strategy, and British troops began their campaign in the state of Georgia in December 1778. Savannah fell easily by the end of the month, and by the end of January the entire state was in British hands. They brought back the former royal governor, who reestablished a British regime for the following three years. With the Georgia operation such an easy victory, the British hurried on toward South Carolina.

The Continental Congress, directing the American military operations, sent Benjamin Lincoln to restore the rebel fortunes, but he was defeated above Savannah and retreated to South Carolina. A second attempt to recapture Savannah, this time with French troops and naval support, failed in late October 1779. Lincoln spent the winter of 1779–1780 reinforcing at Charleston, South Carolina, where he faced a large British force in April. Surrounded by superior numbers and cut off from the sea by the British fleet, Lincoln surrendered the city and its garrison of 5,000 men in mid-May. The loss of such a large number of men, along with 300 cannon, severely hurt revolutionary morale.

The British had received reinforcements in the Carolinas who came under the command of Lord Cornwallis, with some 8,000 troops at his disposal. The expected enlistment of loyalist forces finally came as hundreds of locals rushed to join the winning side. Many Americans considered the southern states lost because the British occupied forts all across South Carolina. The Continental Congress sent Horatio Gates, victor of the battle at Saratoga, to mount a defense in the south. Without the large number of men he had had in upstate New York, Gates's deficiencies as a general, and the fact that he had many more militiamen than trained regulars, were his undoing. Cornwallis defeated him at Camden in mid-August and followed the retreating rebels into North Carolina.

The only bright spot in the American effort came from small guerrilla groups operating independently in Georgia and South Carolina. They successfully harassed British supply lines and outposts, but their small successes could not make up for Gates's glaring failure; ultimate British success seemed assured. Only the British could hurt the British, which is exactly what they did. Cornwallis outran his supply lines, and the North Carolina loyalists did not appear in the large numbers he had hoped. Cornwallis withdrew his hungry troops back to Camden for the winter of 1780–1781.

Gates's failure caused American commander in chief George Washington to plead for a replacement, and Nathaniel Greene got the job. Greene was the best possible choice because he understood the realities of the American military strength. He launched an almost completely guerrilla campaign throughout South Carolina, in which he simultaneously lost most of his battles and hurt the British badly—dancing them around the state, making them tired, hungry, and frustrated, unable to pin him down and destroy him. Greene used his small forces to their best advantage, moving more quickly than the British and denying them control of any territory. They had to chase him, and thus could not occupy any area long enough to establish their authority. In the end, the British controlled the cities and the rebels held sway over the countryside.

Cornwallis chased the American forces into North Carolina in the spring of 1781. Despite a marginal victory at Guilford Court House, Cornwallis again found himself a long way from his supplies, and Greene's force was still intact. Cornwallis marched to the coast to get supplies from the Royal Navy at Wilmington, then marched to Virginia. Greene stayed behind and continued to make life miserable for the British and the loyalist allies in the Carolinas. After marching around central Virginia, and receiving some assistance from a force newly dispatched under Benedict Arnold, Cornwallis marched to the coast to establish a base at Yorktown. He and Clinton still hoped to squeeze the main portion of the revolutionary army between them.

Cornwallis then made a fatal mistake. In July he began digging defensive positions to protect his base, but he allowed the

rebels to operate and concentrate immediately west of him. Cornwallis's position at Yorktown was on the end of a peninsula formed by the York and James rivers, and the rebel forces commanded by the Frenchman Marquis de Lafayette had him in a corner. Should French ships arrive offshore in Chesapeake Bay, he would be as effectively cut off as Lincoln had been at Charleston. Still, he dug in and awaited word from Clinton on cooperative operations. Without a British force on the loose in Virginia, the revolutionary forces were able to move about freely. Lafayette called for Washington to come from Rhode Island to strengthen the American position against Cornwallis. Leaving a screening force to hold Clinton in place, in late August 1781 Washington marched some 2,000 American and 5,000 French troops unmolested past New York City and through New Jersey and Pennsylvania to Virginia. Simultaneously, the French fleet left Newport to deny Cornwallis succor from the Royal Navy. By mid-September, Cornwallis's 8,000 men were outnumbered two to one by the Franco-American force. Coupled with the 5 September victory by the French navy over a smaller British fleet in Chesapeake Bay, the British position was untenable. French and American troops moved their siege lines gradually closer to the British through September and October. Cornwallis made a vain attempt to escape across the York River, then asked for terms on 17 October. His forces laid down their arms two days later.

If the American victory at Saratoga was the turning point of the American Revolution, Yorktown was the coup de grace. Six years of futility was more than the British population was willing to accept, and once word of Cornwallis's surrender reached London, the ruling government's days were numbered. Prime Minister Lord

North resigned in March 1782, and the new cabinet called for negotiations with the Americans. Talks began in Paris in the summer and dragged on for more than a year. The desires of France and Spain, both of which had contributed significantly to the American victory, were rarely compatible with each other or with those of the United States. Finally the Treaty of Paris was signed in November 1783, in which Great Britain recognized American independence and established the United States' borders as between the Atlantic and the Mississippi River, and from the Great Lakes down to but not including Florida, which reverted to Spanish ownership. Within the United States there were a large number of loyalists in despair at the outcome of the war, and they could not accept the results. More than 100,000 people left the country, most going to Canada.

The American Revolution, completed after this failed British campaign, changed much of the world. It signaled the first break in the colonial system that Europe had been building, and would continue to build, for more than another century. Whatever colonies were established in the future, the seeds of discontent were already sown by the Declaration of Independence and the democratic tradition begun by the infant United States in the 1770s and 1780s. Never before had a republican form of government successfully operated in a large nation, but now it became the goal of colonial dreamers worldwide.

*See also* New York, British Invasion of (1777) [120].

References: Alden, John R., *The American Revolution* (New York: Harper & Row, 1954); Dupuy, R. Ernest, *An Outline History of the American Revolution* (New York: Harper & Row, 1975); Pearson, Michael, *Those Damned Rebels: The American Revolution as Seen through British Eyes* (New York: Putnam, 1972).

## 124   UNITED STATES, BRITISH INVASION OF

While the British were occupied with other European countries attempting to defeat Napoleon, the United States declared war on Great Britain. In an attempt to maintain a blockade against Napoleon's European empire, the British had impressed American sailors into the Royal Navy and had kept the Americans from carrying on free trade with Europe. Since the summer of 1812, the United States had attempted to conquer Canada with little or no success, but had not had to worry about fighting many British troops. When Napoleon was defeated at the Battle of Leipzig in 1813 and sent into exile in 1814, the British had plenty of veteran troops to send to the United States to bring a quick end to the war.

In the early summer of 1814, British troops sailed for North America as the British made invasion plans. The United States would be attacked from three directions. First, the British would move from Canada southward down Lake Champlain, a route used by invading armies since the French and Indian Wars of the 1750s. Second, they would attack the American capital at Washington, D.C., to put pressure on the government to surrender. Third, British forces would attack the Gulf Coast in an attempt to carry the war to the western states, where support for war was greatest, and they could also gain control of the Mississippi River. Seeing the Americans' inept manner of fighting displayed thus far, the British (and many Americans) were sure that the veterans of war against Napoleon would walk over any opposition in North America.

The route from Montreal down Lake Champlain was much the same path General John Burgoyne had followed in 1777. The British now had 15,000 men to draw on, while the Americans could muster no more than 4,000, mostly militia. The Americans were in a good defensive position, however, with three blockhouses along a narrow front at Plattsburgh, New York. Further, Captain Thomas MacDonough had a force of gunboats ready to fight the British ships sailing along with the advancing British army. The two forces met on 11 September. Though the British army and navy were supposed to launch a simultaneous assault, the navy went into combat virtually alone. Because of headwinds, the British ships could not maneuver past the anchored American vessels, so the two sides faced each other and pounded away. After two hours the American gunners had the better of the fight, and the remnants of the British fleet, minus their dead commander, retreated to Canada. Seeing his main source of supply sail away, British general Sir George Prevost withdrew his men and followed. His troops outnumbered the Americans at Plattsburgh almost four to one, but Prevost did not care to advance against the blockhouses, and went home. His veterans had little opportunity to prove their superiority, and the first part of the British grand strategy died aborning.

The second plan, to attack the American capital at Washington, proved much easier. British forces under General Robert Ross numbered over 4,000 and had just arrived from France. Since the American army, such as it was, had been stationed along the Canadian frontier since 1812, the east coast was relatively undefended. The Royal Navy harassed various harbors up and down the coast, but focused their main attention on Chesapeake Bay as the door to Washington. Ross landed his men southeast of the city at Benedict, Maryland, on

22 August without opposition. The American high command had dithered all summer, and had produced virtually no plans to defend the capital. Militia units were not called up until British troops had landed, and they had little chance to succeed. Mustering 6,000 men, they attempted to defend their capital by standing at Bladensburg, due east of the city, but they were untrained, disorganized, and poorly commanded. They stood for longer than could be expected when Ross's men advanced against them on 24 August, but retreat soon turned into rout. The British occupied a deserted Washington and set many of the public buildings on fire, paying the Americans back for the burning of the Canadian capital at York the previous year. Finding no one with whom to negotiate, and with a tornado striking the next day, the British returned to their ships on the evening of 25 August. The ships sailed for Baltimore, hoping to find more booty and punish the pirates who had been harassing British shipping throughout the war.

Baltimore proved a tougher nut to crack. The citizens were led by Samuel Smith, senator and Revolutionary War veteran. He was a determined man, and he had some able lieutenants. The city's defenses had been improved through the war, and the gunners at the main bastion, Fort McHenry, were well trained and motivated. On 13 September, Smith placed riflemen along the path the British would have to take to march on the city, and they did a good job of holding back Ross's advance. When Ross was killed, the British went into bivouac; meanwhile, the British fleet attacked Fort McHenry. Some 1,800 shells landed in and around the fort during 25 hours of bombardment, but the defenders would not surrender. Two more sorties against American troops were repulsed, and the British decided the target was too expensive; they reboarded their ships and sailed to Jamaica. The second British offensive also came to naught.

The British had great hopes for their southern thrust. Reinforcing at Jamaica, the British sailed through the Gulf of Mexico. American forces in the south were commanded by Tennesseean Andrew Jackson. Since the summer of 1813, his forces had been fighting the Creek Indians in the Mississippi Territory. Jackson's victories cleared the area of the Indians' presence and gave his men battle experience. The government assigned the defense of the Gulf Coast to Jackson. This area stretched only between Spanish Florida and Spanish Texas; there really was not much to cover. Indeed, only two sites offered themselves as potential targets: Mobile, Alabama, and New Orleans, Louisiana. When Jackson learned that a small British force had occupied Pensacola (in Spanish Florida), he was sure that Mobile was in imminent danger. Jackson arrived at Mobile on 27 August and began organizing the defenses. With reinforcements from Tennessee, he raided into Spanish Florida and destroyed the forts guarding Pensacola, denying the town to the British. This secured his flank and further intimidated Indians aiding the British.

In late November, Jackson left for New Orleans with 2,000 men. He left 1,000 behind in the Mobile defenses and sent another 1,000 to Baton Rouge to act as reserves, ready to support either location should the British attack. In New Orleans he found local militia units forming and preparing to defend their homes. Jackson set about blocking as many routes to the city as possible, hoping to funnel the British into a trap. The British ships could get no closer than 60 miles because of shallow water, so they needed to control the eastern approaches to assault the city from that direction. On 12 December the British captured the five American gunboats covering the city via Lake Borgne. They

brought up men and matériel through Lake Borgne without Jackson's knowledge, but moving through inundated countryside was slow going.

Jackson's one great need was artillery, as he had left most of his cannon back in Mobile. Local pirate leader Jean Lafitte had turned down a British offer to join the attackers, and now he offered his professional gunners and ordnance to Jackson, who accepted them in return for granting Lafitte a pardon for all his crimes.

By 23 December, Jackson was well armed, and just in time; word came of British troops massing just below the city. Jackson led a raid against the British camp that night, setting the British timetable back a couple of weeks. Not until 8 January were they ready to advance on New Orleans. By then Jackson had 5,000 men behind a defensive wall along a dry canal 1,000 yards wide, stretching from the Mississippi River on his right to an impenetrable swamp on his left.

When the British veterans marched out of the morning fog, they were an impressive sight, but they were being led to slaughter. The massed musket and artillery fire tore huge holes in their ranks and, unable to maneuver in the narrow battleground, they found themselves in a killing field. Of the 6,000 men led by General Sir Edward Pakenham, 2,000 died or were wounded before 8:30 in the morning; American losses totaled 45. Jackson decided against taking his men over to the offensive, and the British decided against another attack. After a truce to bury their dead, on 18 January the British withdrew to their ships and sailed away.

The battle at New Orleans proved to be the one clear-cut and overwhelming victory the Americans scored in the entire War of 1812. To an extent it was also pointless, because American and British diplomats had ended the war with the signing of the

Treaty of Ghent on 24 December 1814. Had the British won at New Orleans, however, they could well have kept it and controlled access to the Gulf of Mexico, no matter what may have been agreed in Ghent.

Though the battle turned out to be a disaster for the British, it became a morale boost for the United States. It turned an otherwise dismal military experience into one that could be viewed, however misguidedly, as another American triumph over Britain. Along with the British failures to punish the Americans at Plattsburgh or Baltimore, the victory at New Orleans brought the people together in a new sense of nationalism. Though the issues that forced a declaration of war in 1812 were not addressed by the peace treaty, the end of the war against Napoleon brought an end to British violations of American rights on the high seas; Americans convinced themselves that their force of arms had secured the rights for which they originally went to war. Freedom of trade after the war, along with an increased measure of respect from Europe, brought a new financial security, and the United States grew in confidence. The rapprochement between the United States and Britain, showing itself in the settlement of trade and border disputes, allowed the Americans three decades of isolationism to grow economically and physically until the nation established borders on the Pacific Ocean.

*See also* Canada, U.S. Invasion of [114]; Napoleon Buonaparte [118]; New York, British Invasion of (1777) [120].

References: Coles, Harry, *The War of 1812* (Chicago: University of Chicago Press, 1965); Lord, Walter, *The Dawn's Early Light* (New York: Norton, 1972); Mahon, John, *The War of 1812* (Gainesville: University Presses of Florida, 1972).

# PART 6
# THE AGE OF EMPIRES

# THE AGE OF EMPIRES

The numbers on the map correspond to entry numbers in the text.

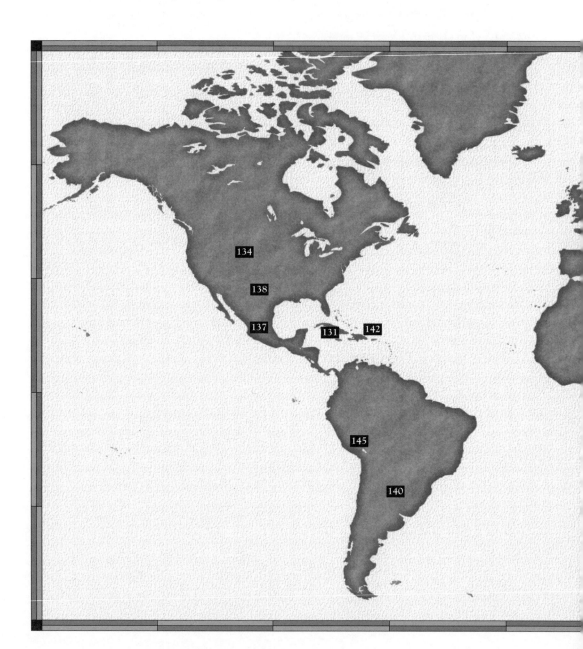

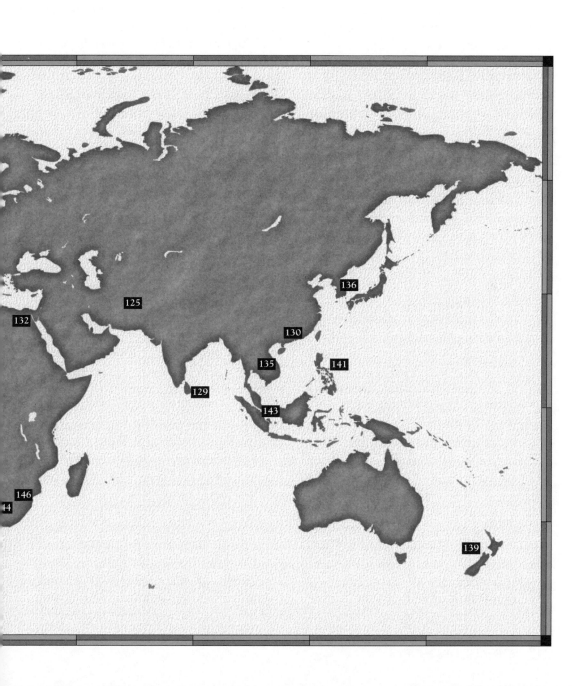

## 125 AFGHANISTAN, BRITISH INVASIONS OF

The British army and the forces of the British East India Company were regularly successful in India, but they found the inhabitants of Afghanistan more difficult to defeat. Even when the British and Indian forces won clear victories in the field, the political victories were nebulous. The British interfered in Afghan affairs twice in the nineteenth century, and lived to regret both experiences.

### THE FIRST AFGHAN WAR

The mountainous country of Afghanistan had little that the British wanted or needed, but they continually worried that another country would gain influence there and be in a position to attack India. The amir of Afghanistan in the 1830s was Dost Muhammed, who was quite surprised when the British took his courtesy seriously. In a diplomatic letter to Lord Auckland, governor-general of India, he ended by saying, "Consider me and my country as yours." This formal phrase meant nothing more than "I am very truly yours" at the end of a Western letter. Still, it seemed an invitation too good to resist. When a British spy in Afghanistan stumbled into a Russian-led Persian army invading the country, he undisguised himself and offered his services (successfully) to the Afghan army. Rather than bring about closer ties, it led to a British expedition into Afghanistan. If Dost Muhammed could not successfully repel outside incursions, then Britain needed to assist him whether he liked it or not. In fact, it seemed a good idea to bring along a replacement amir more amenable to British intentions: Shah Shuja, who happened to be very unpopular with the Afghan population.

In retrospect, it seems ludicrous that the British would believe the Afghans would welcome another power deposing their leader with a despised lackey for the doubtful purpose of saving them from the Russians or the Persians (neither of whom had proven their ability to invade successfully), and to further impose on them this new leader whose troops practiced the Sikh religion, hated in Afghanistan. The Army of the Indus formed up in late 1838 and entered Afghanistan early the next year. The British officers traveled in style through the forbidding country, harassed constantly by small Afghan bands, but met with no resistance they could not overcome. The capture of the fort at Ghazni in July was the major obstacle, and the British marched into the capital city of Kabul in August. Shah Shuja was installed as amir before a sullen populace.

The British attacked pockets of resistance in the area for the next few months. The exiled Dost Muhammed threw himself on the mercy of the khan of Bokhara; for his trouble, he ended up in jail. He was imprisoned with other foreigners as well, including a few British and Russian citizens, so the British decided they needed to deal with the khan and capture Dost Muhammed before the Russians did. Both Russian and British envoys were dismissed, imprisoned, or executed, but the khan received no retribution; when he allowed Dost Muhammed to escape, the political justification for invasion was gone. Besides, trouble in Afghanistan diverted British attention.

The British envoy in Kabul, Sir William Macnaghten, decided to stop tribute payments to hostile tribes who had traditionally controlled the passes into India. Those tribes immediately began to close off British lines of communication, which coincided with an uprising in Kabul in 1841. The British and Indian forces quickly found themselves besieged in Kabul, Ghazni, and Kandahar. The Afghans were better armed than the British, and better marksmen as well; their sniping into the fort at Kabul was deadly. An attempt at negotiation ended in Macnaghten's murder. In early January 1843, the British decided, unwisely, to abandon Kabul for the long march back to India. Some 14,500 men, women, and children (4,500 of them British and Indian) left the city and headed toward the British fort at Jelalabad 60 miles east of Kabul. A week later a lone horseman staggered into Jelalabad—the sole British survivor. A few Indian soldiers and captured wives and children were recovered later.

Jelalabad was surrounded before the defenders could obey orders to withdraw to India. They built and rebuilt walls around the city, and held the Afghans at bay. In April an attack from the fort drove the Afghans away, and the defenders captured the hastily abandoned enemy camp. A British-Indian force stormed the Khyber Pass, a feat never before accomplished by any army in history, and relieved Jelalabad on 16 April. By September they were in Kabul. They freed British prisoners and burned down the Great Bazaar, then marched home. Honor was satisfied, but the original intent of the British government was not accomplished. The First Afghan War was a bitter pill for the British.

## THE SECOND AFGHAN WAR

The second time the British tried to establish residence in Kabul was in 1879, long enough after the first debacle for the British to have forgotten its lessons. They demanded that the Afghans allow a British diplomatic mission into their capital, as they had just welcomed one from Russia. The amir was Shere Ali, one of the seven sons of Dost Muhammed, who retook power when the British left in 1842. Shere Ali had as little desire to allow the British into his country as his father, because he feared that any political concession to Britain was the

first step toward annexation. Knowing their demand would fall on deaf ears, the British had an invasion force ready to go: 45,000 men divided into three columns. The major fighting took place in the valley of the Kurram River, which crosses the border 65 miles southeast of Kabul. The smallest column, 6,500 men under F. S. Roberts, fought brilliantly against superior forces in narrow defiles. Wise maneuvering and brave fighting took the British to Kabul. Shere Ali fled for Russia and died on the way, leaving his son Yakub Khan in power. Yakub Khan negotiated the Treaty of Gandemuk in May 1879, in which the British gained everything they wanted: an envoy in Kabul, territorial cessions, freedom of trade for British/Indian merchants, a telegraph line from Kabul to India, and total control over Afghanistan's foreign policy.

It was, as often happens, too good to be true. A British force remained in Kabul, but it was merely a personal guard of some 100 men for the envoy, Major Pierre Louis Napoleon Cavagnari; most of the British forces went home to India. The unpopularity of the treaty and of Yakub Khan for signing it fed local animosity. A mutiny in the Afghan army resulting from a demand for back pay led to an attack on the British residency, where the soldiers were sure money could be found. After an all-day battle, the Afghans wiped out the British force in Kabul, losing only 600 men. Roberts, a national hero for his exploits earlier in the war, was ordered to avenge the slaughter, marking the beginning of the second half of the war, sometimes regarded as the Third Afghan War. As Roberts's force moved northwestward up the Karrum Valley, Yakub Khan went there to plead his innocence in Cavagnari's death and hopefully slow down the British advance. Roberts had little time for him, and continued marching his force of 6,600 men toward Kabul. Twelve miles short of the city, the British met their first serious resistance. A sharp engagement on 6 October 1879 at the bridge at Charasia resulted in a British victory and control of Kabul. Roberts followed his orders to find and publicly execute Cavagnari's killers; with this completed and the British installed in Kabul, it seemed a quick end to rebellion.

Roberts bivouacked his men in a well-fortified camp, but did not occupy the major Afghan fortress overlooking Kabul. In the countryside, religious leaders stirred up the tribesmen against the British, and once again lines of communication were harassed or cut. By the end of 1879, several Afghan forces began moving on Kabul, and Roberts's force was besieged on 14 December. He was well supplied and his troops well disciplined, so they held the much larger Afghan army at bay. The siege was short. Failing to overcome British defenses during a major assault on the night of 22–23 December, the Afghan troops left the city. Still, Roberts was not safe. A British-Indian force under Sir Donald Stewart marched northward from the fort at Kandahar, some 300 miles southwest, to relieve Roberts. His army of 14,000 secured the British hold on the city when they arrived in May 1880, but word soon arrived that Kandahar was under siege and a British force at Maiwand in southern Afghanistan had been badly beaten. Stewart, the ranking officer in Kabul, sent Roberts to relieve Kandahar. This march was followed closely by the British public and further secured Roberts's reputation. He left Kabul on 9 August with 10,000 men. As he approached Kandahar on 25 August, he received word from the garrison that the besieging forces had left to attack his column. Kandahar was relieved on 31 August, and Roberts's men dealt a severe defeat to the Afghan army the next day. Now seemed like a good time to go home.

The British left Afghanistan, the terms of the treaty now forgotten. They had no representative in Kabul, nor did they direct Afghanistan's foreign affairs. The Second Afghan War, like the first, was of no value to the British Empire. Britain continued to fear Russian incursions into the country as late as World War I, but without reason. The Afghans proved too tough a nut for the British to crack; victory on the battlefield did not translate into political victory, and the Afghans remained fiercely independent. In the 1970s they educated the Russians with the same lessons they taught the British in 1842 and 1880.

References: Adams, James Truslow, *Building the British Empire* (New York: Scribner's Sons, 1938); Bilgrami, Ashgar, *Afghanistan and British India, 1793–1907* (New Delhi: Sterling Press, 1972); Farwell, Byron, *Queen Victoria's Little Wars* (New York: Harper & Row, 1972).

# AFRICA, FRENCH OCCUPATIONS IN
**126**

After losing its claims in India in the late 1700s, France turned toward Africa and the Far East for colonies. French success in Africa was mixed; along the Mediterranean coast, France gained territory almost by accident, while deeper in the interior, the expansion was gradual and driven mainly by the men on the spot.

## EQUATORIAL AFRICA
France had held trading posts on the far western African coast at Senegal since the late 1700s, and from there the French looked inland. Through the first half of the nineteenth century, European outposts on the west coast had been involved mainly in suppressing the slave trade, but the growing commercial relations with local tribes created European rivalry by the 1860s. In

order to gain the dominant share of nuts, palm oil, and other local products, France and Britain began making treaties with as many local chieftains as possible. Between 1854 and 1864, the French carried out a war against the Tukulors, and that fighting took them toward the Niger River. They spent the next 25 years solidifying their hold on the upper Niger area, then fought three wars against the Mandingo of the Ivory Coast, finally claiming that area by 1898. Meanwhile, forces from the French possessions along the Congo River joined with troops invading from Algeria to capture Chad. France was now predominant in the Sahara, and aimed toward a possible transcontinental link reaching from the Atlantic to the Indian Ocean, where France had a colony at Somaliland. French troops reached Fashoda on the upper Nile in 1898, but faced a much larger British force recently arrived from Egypt. After a tense period, the French government ordered a withdrawal, and the British kept alive their own dream of a transcontinental Cape-to-Cairo land link.

## MADAGASCAR

During the initial rush in the 1600s for Far East markets, France established a temporary settlement at Fort Dauphin on Madagascar, off Africa's eastern coast. It failed to maintain itself, and for a time France settled for posts on the smaller islands of Île de France (Mauritius) and Bourbon. By the 1800s, France had secured treaty rights for protection of French nationals on Madagascar, but the dominant Hova government leaned more toward British than French interests. In 1883, French warships bombarded the towns of Majunga and Tamatave and landed troops, forcing the acceptance of a French protectorate. The locals resisted the French presence, sometimes under the direction of British officers. The resistance provoked another bombardment

of Tamatave in 1894, followed by an invasion the following year. French general Jacques Duchesne landed 15,000 men on the island and began a methodical invasion against violent resistance. By 1896 the island was declared a French colony. A military government deposed the queen and continued to fight the revolts, finally suppressing the locals by 1905.

French colonization was undertaken more for European prestige than for profit or raw materials. Almost none of the colonies made money, and most cost unreasonable amounts to acquire. After the suppression of piracy on the Mediterranean coast, France had no real interests there, and the acquisition of the Saharan colonies gained land but little else. By World War II, French possessions across the upper part of the continent included Mauritania, Senegal, Dahomey, the Ivory Coast, Guinea, French Guinea, French Sudan, Upper Volta, and Niger. Chad, Gabon, and the Middle Congo made up France's equatorial colonies, and the mandates acquired after the Versailles Treaty gave it Togoland and Cameroon. For much of the nineteenth century, France exercised the traditional mercantilist view of colonies, that they should exist for the benefit of the mother country. Exclusive import and export rights were maintained not only for French profit but to keep out other European countries. The population of the colonies remained subject to French rule, with little chance of gaining French citizenship and legal rights. Only Algeria came to be regarded as a department in the French governmental system. Local French administrators attempted to apply French political philosophies, but found the native populations so hostile to their presence that the governors resorted to whatever measures were necessary to maintain order. Only after World War II did France begin to let its colonies go. In 1960 almost all French colonies in Africa became sovereign states, though most maintained some ties with France. Only French Somaliland remained an overseas territory.

## NORTH AFRICA

France first acquired land in Algeria in the north and moved east and west from there. Gaining Algeria was expensive, and further expansion was not politically popular at home, but Tunisia almost begged to be taken over. The ruler of Tunisia, the bey of Tunis, borrowed heavily from France and other European powers to finance an independence movement to break away from the Ottoman Empire. Once accomplished, Tunisia needed more money for modernization. Ultimately, it was too heavily in debt to meet the payments, and in 1869 a multinational European commission entered the country to administer its finances. France was the largest creditor, but had no desire to annex the country. When Italy showed an active interest in taking over, however, French forces crossed the border in 1881 and obliged the bey to sign an agreement making his country a French protectorate. During the expedition, there was a local uprising against the French and the bey, and French forces occupied the entire country. Though the bey remained in nominal control after the revolt, for all intents and purposes Tunisia was a French possession.

With such strong control over a stretch of the Mediterranean coast, it is not surprising that the French became interested in Morocco to the west. Italy also showed an interest, but an agreement in 1900 ceded French interests in Morocco in return for Italian interests in Tripoli (Libya). Both were off-limits according to international agreements protecting the property of the Ottoman Empire, but in the rush for African colonies at the turn of the twentieth century, those pacts carried little weight. Owing to their ever-friendlier relationship from 1904, Britain granted France permission to act; when Moroccan bandits raided across the Algerian border, the French responded. France demanded control of the Moroccan police forces to maintain order in the deteriorating political environment; the Moroccan government was under pressure not only from Europe but from popular uprisings in the hinterland. When Germany objected to French actions and began to show interest in the country as well, international hostilities loomed. Only the Algeciras Conference of 1906–1907 kept the peace; France and Spain were given equal rights in Morocco, with an Open Door economic policy for the rest of Europe. The ongoing popular unrest brought French naval bombardment of Casablanca in 1907, followed by occupation of the city; Fez was occupied in 1911 for similar reasons. The Treaty of Fez in 1912 made Morocco a French protectorate, and, as resident general, General Louis Lyautey began forging a closer relationship between the two nations.

*See also* Algeria, French Occupation of [128]; Indochina, French Occupation of [135].

References: Collins, Robert, *Europeans in Africa* (New York: Knopf, 1971); Fieldhouse, D. K., *The Colonial Empires* (New York: Dell, 1966); Pakenham, Thomas, *The Scramble for Africa* (New York: Random House, 1991).

**127**

## AFRICA, GERMAN OCCUPATION OF

Germany first began considering colonization in Africa in the Frankfurt National Assembly of 1848. Acquiring territory in Africa seemed a good way to handle surplus population displaced by changes in German agriculture, as well as provide a focus for national pride in an active foreign policy. Not until the 1880s, however, did any serious colonization begin. By then, Chancellor Otto von Bismarck had led the new German nation into world affairs, and German economic interests viewed Africa as a good source of raw materials. Besides, foreign control of the coastlines by other powers could prove costly to German trade.

Bismarck had long been leery of the idea of colonies, believing them too expensive to administer and defend, but he finally saw them as a tool of international diplomacy. In 1885 he hosted an international conference in Berlin, where ground rules were laid for African land claims by European powers. At the time, few other European diplomats considered Germany a player in the colonization game. The first colony Germany claimed was Cameroon in 1884. German trading posts had been in the area for some years, and it appeared the British might claim the land first, but Dr. Gustav Nachtigal signed treaties with the two main kings in Cameroon and declared it a German protectorate. Cameroon was not an economically successful venture, and its acquisition often came under attack by anticolonial factions in Germany. German plantations were successful, but not lucrative enough to pay for the colony's administration. In the 1890s and early 1900s, the colony was newsworthy in Germany for the scandals perpetrated by its governor, Jesco von Puttkamer. He was accused and convicted of financial misadventures and gross mistreatment of natives, both common and royal. He was fined only slightly, however, and recalled from his post.

About the same time the Germans took over Cameroon, they signed agreements with the chiefs in Little Popo, or Togoland. The most successful of the German colonial ventures, Togoland became a model

colony, consistently showing a trade surplus and paying for its administration. Local profit meant a looser rein from Berlin, so Togoland also became the scene of scandal and abuse of the native population. Though profitable, Togoland did not hold enough raw materials or profits to be more than a minor success.

The largest of the German colonies was Southwest Africa, stretching from the Portuguese colony of Angola southward 900 miles to the Orange River, beyond which lay the British Cape Colony. The Portuguese originally discovered this territory, but their missionaries had little success there, and it was transferred to the control of the Rhenish Missionary Society of Germany. Bismarck stated that the "missionary and trader must precede the soldier," and within ten years German clerics had established missions in a number of tribal capitals. The political and military presence was not far behind; German forces intervened in tribal warfare between the Herero and Nama tribes. The Herero signed a protection treaty with the German imperial commissioner in 1885; when the Nama waged guerrilla warfare instead, the Germans led punitive expeditions against them until their surrender in 1894.

There was little source of income in Southwest Africa. The Nama and Herero were cattle herders who did not care to trade their herds to the Germans until 1897, when a plague of rinderpest virtually wiped out their cattle, and they had to sell their lands and possessions to buy vaccinations or new cattle. The German colonists gained the best land available, and the already poor natives were in even more dire straits. Many came to the missions for aid and conversion, and German governor Theodor von Leutwein was sure that his administration was maintaining peace and a prosperity of sorts. The German settlers robbed the natives and made them as subservient as possible, which provoked a Herero rebellion in January 1904. Some 200,000 Africans lived in the colony, compared to a German population of about 4,700. The Herero killed every German male who could bear arms, but spared women, children, and non-Germans. They slaughtered inhabitants of isolated farms, but were unable to assault the better fortified towns.

By February, Leutwein seemed back in control, but Berlin replaced him with General Lothar von Trotha, who had orders to put down the rebellion by any means necessary. The small number of German soldiers in the country could not keep the rebellion down, but with reinforcements from Germany, Trotha attacked the Herero and drove them into the desert, placing guards at every waterhole. The Herero defeated, Trotha next had to deal with a Nama revolt in October 1904. Guerrilla warfare raged for a year, and both sides suffered badly. Trotha was eventually ordered home in disgrace, but the Nama capitulated in October 1905.

The colony of German East Africa was claimed in the 1880s as well, though German and British traders had long dealt with the sultan of Zanzibar for goods from the interior. In 1885, Carl Peters, the head of the Company for German Colonization, snuck into the region and made a number of suspect treaties with local chiefs, all of which Bismarck supported. In 1888 the sultan of Zanzibar granted Peters's company the administration of the southern coast of East Africa in return for a percentage of the profits. The high-handed German administration insulted Muslim sensibilities and tightened tax collection. German troops and warships enforced their will and challenged the authority of the sultan in his own territory, provoking a revolt among the locals that lasted through the spring of 1889. The British had long supported the

sultan, but in this instance they sided with Germany to "suppress the slave trade" by blockading the coast and allowing the Germans to send in troops. Germany established itself as the dominant European power, but could only hold onto the colony until World War I.

Germany entered Africa in search of prestige and raw materials, but gained only the former. Though Togoland proved somewhat profitable, none of the other colonies financially justified German efforts. Sending major military support was too costly, so when World War I occurred, the Germans did nothing to save their colonies or take advantage of the raw materials they might have provided. The League of Nations mandated all the German colonies in Africa, mostly to Great Britain. The Germans left behind little but a memory of European abuses.

*See also* East Africa, British Invasion of [154].

References: Pakenham, Thomas, *The Scramble for Africa* (New York: Random House, 1991); Smith, Woodruff, *The German Colonial Empire* (Chapel Hill: University of North Carolina Press, 1978); Townsend, Mary Evelyn, *Origins of Modern German Colonialism* (New York: Howard Fertig, 1974).

## ALGERIA, FRENCH OCCUPATION OF

**128**

Long a part of the Ottoman Empire, the regency of Algiers was one of the bases of the notorious Barbary pirates, who harassed or extorted bribes from international shipping passing through the western Mediterranean. The country's Ottoman occupiers never numbered more than 15,000, so the French had little trouble removing the

Turkish janissaries during their 1830 invasion. An insult by the local Ottoman ruler to the French consul after a dispute over debt payment provoked the attack. The French discovered that Ottoman rule was limited merely to coastal and urban areas, while the outlying countryside held only the occasional Turkish garrison cooperating with a few Arab tribes. The Berber population in the rugged terrain was beyond the direct authority of the Turks. The Turks recognized their inability to establish control in the mountains, so did not try.

At first, the French copied Ottoman practices, but they became too ambitious. Presenting themselves as liberators from Ottoman rule, the French moved into the countryside and found only resistance. The only local groups who would cooperate with them were the urban Jews, long a despised segment of the local population. By allying themselves with the Jews, the Christian French did nothing to endear themselves to the Muslim majority of the country. From the first, the Algerians resented the French occupation and resisted it.

The Algerians organized themselves behind the leadership of Abd al-Kadir, who wanted not only to free his country from outside dominance but also to establish a united Muslim state. Abd al-Kadir took the title of amir and led a *jihad*, or holy war, against the French. Under his direction, the frontier population organized a Muslim administration that maintained a tax system, a standing army of 10,000, strategically placed forts, and Muslim schools and courts. Initially, the French were willing to recognize Abd al-Kadir as ruler of the interior, but conflict was inevitable. By 1846 more than 100,000 French troops were in the country, and the Arabs could not defeat such superior numbers. In 1847, Abd al-Kadir surrendered and went into exile.

For the first 20 years of their occupation, the French had administered Algeria (so named in 1839) via the Ministry of War, which appointed governors-general to rule. They were later assisted by the establishment of an Arab Bureau, which proved to be more condescending to the locals than helpful to the military. The French solidified their hold on the country by encouraging immigration, and by the time Abd al-Kadir was defeated, the new citizens numbered some 109,000 from all parts of the western Mediterranean. The majority were laborers and craftspeople, but some wealthy French bought large estates. Most of the immigrants had been forced from France after the revolution in 1848, or fled political upheaval in Alsace and Lorraine after the Franco-Prussian War, or moved to new vineyards when a blight destroyed much of the French wine industry in 1880. The new population tended to settle along the coast, but were protected from the hostile country folk by large numbers of French soldiers.

Uprisings by native tribes were put down through the remainder of the nineteenth century, and French control over the entire country was established in 1900. The most significant resistance to the French government occurred in 1870; the French military put down a revolt in the mountain area of the Kabyles and confiscated most of the land. That same year the European population rebelled against the rule of Napoleon III, who quieted them by granting local autonomy and reducing the power of the military. Algeria had been declared legally a part of France in 1848, but a French-style government was not installed until 1871.

The country was soon divided into three major areas: the coastal zone, mainly populated by Europeans; the countryside, mainly populated by Muslim Berbers; and the Sahara, which had numerous nomadic tribes and was the province of the army. The Europeans dominated the government and the courts. The native Berber population interacted with the French by working for them, occasionally going to French schools, and often moving to France to work. By 1831, the centenary of the invasion, the French occupation appeared to be a rousing success. French writers trumpeted the civilizing influence of the French presence and the economic progress the country had enjoyed.

Underneath the facade was a growing discontent among the Muslim population. Education in French schools had taught them about the ideals of the French Revolution—liberty, equality, fraternity. The Berbers enjoyed none of these rights. The first hint of resistance came in 1912 when native organizations called for equality under the law in return for conscription into the French military. After World War I, during which Algerian soldiers fought and died in the trenches of France, the calls for equality grew louder. In 1920 two native movements began, one calling for equality and assimilation into European Algerian society and the other calling for independence and a severing of ties with France.

Through the 1930s and 1940s, more organizations sprang up to demand either equal rights or liberation. During World War II the Algerians again demanded equal rights in return for military service, but the Vichy government suppressed the protest groups, and the Free French under Charles de Gaulle granted only minor concessions. By midcentury, the native population had plenty to complain about. More than one-third of the 8 million Muslims in the country were landless, another 1 million were underemployed, 90 percent of the Berber population was illiterate, and a quarter of them spoke only Berber. The French military in Algeria was made up of foreign soldiers, with few Algerians. The European population owned 90 percent of the indus-

try and 40 percent of the best land. After the Europeans rigged the elections of 1948, 1951, and 1953 to maintain their power in the government, violence seemed the only alternative for native resistance groups. Egyptian president Nasser offered military officers to help organize a revolt.

Violent protest broke out under the leadership of the Front de Liberation Nationale, or FLN. The FLN started a campaign of terrorism in November 1954 aimed not at removing their enemies but at removing the moderates who encouraged assimilation of the two societies. They hoped this would provoke a massive response by the French military that would create hostility on the part of the population. Instead, the government in France installed a new, more liberal governor-general; he appointed large numbers of Muslims to positions in the government and civil service, and forbade reprisals by the local gendarmes. The FLN responded by initiating a program of genocide toward the European population, a strategy that provoked the violent government response originally intended. Both the FLN and the government forces engaged in slaughter, with thousands of innocents caught in the middle. In January 1957 the government gave the military carte blanche to deal with the FLN in any manner they desired, legal or not. The murder and torture that resulted provoked a critical response in France, which called for negotiation with the FLN to lead toward Algerian independence.

The French army generals, both in Algeria and France, were loath to lose to the terrorists. When it seemed that the government was going to give in to public opinion, the generals threatened a coup, which brought Charles de Gaulle out of retirement and into the government. The Fifth Republic was established and de Gaulle was elected president in late 1958. Thus, the generals got what they asked for, but not what they bargained for. President de Gaulle had long ago realized the futility of continuing colonial rule anywhere, and he was determined to remove France from Algeria. Publicly he continued to support the generals and their policies, but privately he worked to secure his own power base so he could accomplish his goals.

The referendum that created the Fifth Republic also allowed colonies to decide for themselves whether to stay with France or go their own way. De Gaulle began removing the same generals who had brought him to power. He opened negotiations with the FLN in mid-1960, and the Algerians voted for independence in January 1961. The military in Algeria was furious, and rogue generals created the Organization de l'Armée Secrete (OAS) to fight their government's decision. So intent were they on maintaining French power in Algeria that they tried twice to assassinate de Gaulle. They also initiated the same type of terror campaign the FLN had started, and again the innocents suffered. The government approved any and all measures to destroy the OAS, and once again torture and imprisonment were rife. The vote for independence meant that the European population was in danger from Algerian Muslims, who attacked Jewish businesses and synagogues. In 1962 the Europeans left in large numbers, first destroying many of the things they had created: hospitals, schools, libraries, a university. Some 1.3 million inhabitants left for France, leaving anyone who had cooperated with them at the mercy of the new regime. Thousands of locals who could not afford to leave were murdered by the government created by the FLN.

The departure of the French after 130 years in Algeria left the country in dire straits. The first president of the new government later commented that the only accomplishments during the first 20 years of local rule were negative: Agriculture was

destroyed, there was no industry, the government was full of corruption, and the leaders fought among themselves. The terrorism brought to the country by the FLN was exported when Algeria became a training base for terrorists of all kinds. The crime and disorder in which the country was born presaged similar conditions in other African countries that gained independence from the 1960s onward.

*See also* France, German Invasion of [160]; France, Nazi Invasion of [161].

References: Gordon, David, *The Passing of French Algeria* (London: Oxford University Press, 1966); Henissary, Paul, *Wolves in the City: The Death of French Algeria* (New York: Simon & Schuster, 1970); O'Ballance, Edgar, *The Algerian Insurrection* (Hamden, CT: Archon Books, 1967).

## 129 CEYLON, BRITISH OCCUPATION OF

The Dutch were the dominant European power in Ceylon from the 1650s. They exploited the island's trade goods, but in general treated the natives fairly. Britain wanted the island nation, not so much as a trading center but for its harbors, most particularly Trincomalee on the east coast. When Napoleon took control of Europe, Britain went after the continental countries' colonies to put economic pressure on the French dictator's holdings. At this time, the British moved seriously against Ceylon. In 1796 they worked their way around the island's perimeter, capturing its ports, until the major Dutch base at Colombo fell without a fight.

The island was initially controlled by the British East India Company, which replaced the Dutch East India Company as ruling body. Unlike the Dutch and Portuguese, the British refused to cooperate with the local power structure, and their high-handed manner provoked local revolts. In 1798 the Crown took over the country, installing Frederick North as the governor-general. By dealing with unscrupulous pretenders in Ceylon's royal families, North managed to perpetuate the natives' hostility to the British. The most serious resistance came, as previous foreign powers had learned, from the mountain kingdom of Kandy. Sri Wickrama Rajasinha fought the British until 1815, when he was finally captured and deported to India, ending a 2,300-year-old line of rulers. Having established control, the British tried to make up for their shaky start. They brought in legal and political reforms through a paternal administration, hoping to bring about progress for the native population. They improved the road system, abolished forced labor, and, with the Colebrook Reforms of 1833, broke down the feudal system that had dominated the island since time immemorial. They promoted agriculture (mainly the beginning of coffee plantations), opened schools, and brought in the civil service system from India, to which locals could apply after they learned to speak English.

The ruling power, however, remained in British hands. They set up and appointed a legislative council to act in an advisory capacity to the governor-general. The British believed the island was too racially divided to fairly govern itself. In time, as the local population pressed for more say in the government, seats were added on the council (some of them elective), but the council stayed in an advisory role. Open revolt in 1915, though it was put down, brought attention to the people's need for more voice in the government. The British made the council popularly elected by constitutional change in 1924, but the franchise was so limited by education and property restrictions that only 4 percent of the people could vote. A British government commission in 1927, the Donoughmore Commission, called for a new constitution, which went into effect in 1931. This document granted universal suffrage in Ceylon, the first Asian country to have it.

Some popular resentment, mainly from the Tamils in the northern part of the island, still remained. The country pressed for dominion status in 1942, and it was finally granted in 1947. Ceylon was declared independent in 1948. True to the original British fear, there was enough ethnic division in the country to create trouble. When the dominant Sinhalese made their language the official language of the nation in the 1950s, the Tamils (who were strong in the civil service to that time) protested. Through the next several decades, the Tamils led a violent resistance to the ruling Sinhalese.

See also Ceylon, Dutch Occupation of [88]; Ceylon, Portuguese Occupation of [89]; Napoleon Buonaparte [118].

References: Beny, Roloff, *Island Ceylon* (London: Thames & Hudson, 1970); Codrington, Humphrey, *A Short History of Ceylon* (Freeport, NY: Books for Libraries, 1926); Tresidder, Argus, *Ceylon: An Introduction to the Resplendent Land* (Princeton, NJ: Van Nostrand, 1960).

# CHINA, BRITISH INVASION OF (OPIUM WAR)

**130**

The British had been trading in Chinese ports in a mutually profitable enterprise from the 1790s, but a wise observer could have foreseen trouble from the start. The two peoples were too much alike, both convinced of the superiority of their culture over all others and unwilling to concede anything to the other. When the first British ambassador refused to kowtow to the emperor in Peking in 1792, the clash of cultures began. The British military action beginning in 1839 came to be known as the Opium War, but that was merely a handy excuse, much like the destruction of tea in Boston leading to the American Revolution.

The illegal importation of opium from India to China was practiced openly and proved lucrative for both parties, but the wide introduction of the drug offended many in Chinese society, who saw it as a foreign attempt to weaken their culture. Chinese officials were easily bribed until January 1839, when an unbribable imperial high commissioner from Peking began a crackdown. He withdrew all Chinese labor from foreign warehouses and laid siege until 20,000 cases of opium were surrendered. It was all handled peacefully, so the British had no excuse for military intervention. Six weeks later, a brawl in Kowloon ended with a Chinese death at the hands of a British or American national, and the Chinese government demanded the culprit's surrender for punishment. The foreign refusal led to another withdrawal of Chinese labor and the exile of British personnel to the rugged island of Hong Kong. Chinese smugglers under the protection of two British frigates supplied the British in Hong Kong. The Chinese government sent 29 war junks to stop the smuggling. Shots were exchanged, and the Chinese suffered losses.

This was excuse enough for action. The British government ordered a siege of Canton until the Chinese signed a treaty guaranteeing British trading rights. The forts around Canton fell fairly easily, and on 20

January 1841 representatives of the two nations signed the Convention of Chuenpi. This agreement ceded Hong Kong to the British, awarded them $6 million in damages, and granted open trading rights in Canton. Both the Chinese and British governments repudiated the agreement. Chinese forces began gathering near Canton, but the British struck first and attacked the city in late May 1841. A naval victory, coupled with the occupation of the heights overlooking the city, convinced the Chinese army to withdraw. The British force of 3,500 prepared to occupy a city of some 1 million inhabitants. The British government representative, Sir Charles Elliot, stepped in and negotiated another $6 million ransom, which saved the city.

Queen Victoria's government did not care for this arrangement either. Elliot was replaced by Sir Henry Pottinger, and more troops and ships were sent. Major General Sir Hugh Gough's forces marched north, capturing four cities before settling in for the winter. Chinese counterattacks in the spring of 1842 were repulsed, with heavy Chinese losses. The British captured the ports of Hangchow and Shanghai with few losses in the first occupation and none in the second. They soon captured Chinkiang, and were at the gates of Nanking by August. The emperor had had enough. The Treaty of Nanking laid China open to foreign exploitation by guaranteeing trading rights that favored outside interests. It also gave the British $21 million; entitled them to exclusive use of the "treaty ports" of Canton, Amoy, Foochow, Ningpo, and Shanghai; set low tariffs; and gave the British legal jurisdiction over their own nationals. There was no mention of opium.

The British actions in China altered the economic patterns of the world. The practice of granting treaty ports soon extended to other countries, and by the end of the nineteenth century, Britain, France,

Russia, Germany, and Japan had staked out the entire Chinese coast in separate economic spheres of influence. In 1899 this began to change when the United States lobbied for an Open Door policy allowing all foreigners equal access to all of China. This arrangement permitted a rapid response in 1900 when a multinational force entered China to save foreign nationals from the Boxer uprising, which strengthened the positions of the outside powers and cost China even more indemnities.

The Chinese fear of foreign corruption of their culture also came true. The close trading contacts brought Western ideas and technology into their country. This flow of goods and information lasted until the Japanese invasion of China in 1937 and the Communist takeover of the government in 1949. After that, China's isolation lapsed only through one port—Hong Kong. For the British, Hong Kong was easily the most significant result of the Opium Wars. Its location off the Chinese coastal city of Canton and the island's outstanding harbor turned Hong Kong into an economic treasure for Britain. Though granted ownership of the island in the Convention of Chuenpi, the agreement's repudiation meant Britain and China ultimately had to come to another arrangement. The current arrangement ends in 1997 with the termination of the British lease on the island. However, the economic base the British established in the 1840s became, and remains, China's main economic outlet to the world.

See also China, Japanese Invasion of [151].

References: Farwell, Byron, Queen Victoria's Little Wars (New York: Harper & Row, 1985); Owen, David E., British Opium Policy in China and India (Hamden, CT: Archon Books, 1968); Steeds, David, China, Japan and Nineteenth Century Brit-ain (Dublin: Irish University Press, 1977).

## 131 CUBA, U.S. INVASION OF

Cuba was one of Spain's last remaining colonies in the Western Hemisphere, but they had no desire to remain one. Throughout the nineteenth century, Cuba staged a series of revolts, all of which were put down by the Spanish. The United States had always taken an interest in Cuba, even considering purchase or invasion of the island at one time or another. The United States was nearly drawn into one of the revolutions in 1873 when a Spanish warship captured a ship running guns to the rebels and executed the crew for piracy; the crew included eight Americans. The Spanish quickly paid damage claims to keep the United States out of the conflict, but the Americans kept a close eye on Cuban affairs.

Another revolution in 1895 directly involved the United States. Thousands of refugees fled to American soil, and told of brutal treatment at the hands of the Spanish military. William Randolph Hearst and Henry Pulitzer, pioneers in "yellow journalism," exploited the stories of the Cuban refugees for their own profits, and demanded that the United States intervene. The United States was again beginning to view itself as a nation of destiny, fated to "take up the white man's burden," so the public was sympathetic to the idea of protecting its weak neighbor against a European oppressor.

The stories coming out of Cuba were indeed horrible, but slanted in favor of the rebels. The newspapers ignored the guerrillas' tactics of assassination and destruction. The Cubans thought that by employing a scorched-earth strategy, they could make the island economically useless to the Spanish, and therefore convince them to leave. The Spanish policy to fight the guerrillas became the focus of American press attention. To deny the rebels public support, Spain instituted a policy of *reconcentrado,* rounding up the civilian population and concentrating them in a number of camps around the island. After this was accomplished, anyone outside the camp was immediately assumed to be a rebel and shot on sight. Unfortunately, because the camps lacked basic sanitary facilities, regular water and food supplies, and decent medical care, 200,000–250,000 people died in them. The American public was informed about the situation by the newspapers, and they wanted it stopped. By late 1897, American public opinion was growing stronger in favor of intervention, but the *reconcentrado* policy had nearly brought the revolution to an end.

Two events in February 1898 finally brought American action. The first was the publication of a private letter written by the Spanish ambassador to the United States. He had written to a friend in Havana that American president William McKinley was weak and would do nothing to interfere in Cuba. The letter was stolen and given to Hearst, who published it as "the worst insult to the United States in its history." On 15 February, the USS *Maine,* an American battleship in the Havana harbor to evacuate Americans should the need arise, mysteriously exploded. Two investigation commissions, one American and one Spanish, came to two opposite opinions; the Americans announced that the sinking resulted from an external explosion, while the Spanish investigation claimed it to have been internal. No one ever determined the true culprit, but the

Soldiers board a transport at Tampa Bay for the invasion of Cuba.

sinking was too well timed not to have had rebel connections.

McKinley had to accede to the public outcry for war. Congress authorized military action, and a blockade of Cuba was begun, provoking a Spanish declaration of war. First blood went to the United States when its Pacific fleet destroyed the Spanish ships based in Manila Bay in the Philippines. U.S. action in Cuba had to wait until volunteer units could be raised because the American army was at its normally small peacetime size. After a tragicomedy of errors getting men, horses, and matériel to Cuba, the fighting was very brief. Once the American forces defeated Spanish troops on the hills outside their main base of Santiago in late June and early July, and the U.S. fleet blockaded the Santiago harbor, the Spanish forces surrendered.

The Treaty of Paris of 1898 that ended the war removed Spain from the Western Hemisphere, bringing to an end a presence the Spanish had maintained since 1492. Because the U.S. Congress pledged not to annex Cuba, but merely to free it from Spanish rule, the treaty stated that the United States would occupy the island only until it was determined that the Cubans could rule themselves. This decision came in 1902. After helping the Cubans write a constitution, the United States agreed to leave under certain conditions. Cuba promised never to contract a debt it could not pay or to sign any treaty that might endanger its independence. Cuba also had to agree to an American-sponsored sanitation program aimed at combating yellow fever. The United States further demanded the purchase or lease of a naval base on the island, reserving the right to intervene in Cuba to protect it. Intervention was intended only during times of external threat, but American forces intervened in 1906 after the second Cuban presidential election. The outgoing president refused to concede de-

feat, and announced that he was rejecting the constitution. American forces removed him from power and oversaw peaceful elections. Over the next three decades, the United States periodically intervened for similar reasons. In 1934, President Franklin Roosevelt allowed the Cubans to give up the promises concerning debts and treaties, though the naval base at Guantánamo Bay remained in American hands.

Even when the American armed forces were not on the scene, the Cubans saw plenty of American influence in their country. American investment dominated the Cuban economy, draining much of the wealth from the island. Cuba endured a string of corrupt leaders as well, almost all of whom enriched themselves at public expense. The average inhabitant lived in poverty with minimal chance for advancement. So, in both war and peace, the United States benefited from its involvement in Cuba. The American victory in this "splendid little war" brought the country into world power status and solidified the American attitude toward treating Latin America as a little brother it could protect or direct as necessary.

See also Philippines, U.S. Invasion of the [182].

References: Friedel, Frank, *The Splendid Little War* (New York: Dell, 1962); Millis, Walter, *Martial Spirit* (New York: Literary Guild, 1931); Trask, David F. *The War with Spain in 1898* (New York: Macmillan, 1981).

# EGYPT, BRITISH OCCUPATION OF

**132**

In the latter part of the nineteenth century, Egypt was a tributary of the Ottoman Empire. Turkey, the base of the empire, was a fading power, the "sick man of Europe." Still, most European countries preferred even a weak Turkey in control of the Bosporus rather than have a strong country, especially Russia, dominate it. Therefore, whenever Turkey got into trouble (such as the occasional Balkan war, or war with Russia), the rest of Europe and Great Britain in particular stepped in to maintain Turkish independence. Britain was also obliged to act in Ottoman territory if British interests were threatened, since Turkey did not have the power to do so. Because of this, Britain came to dominate Egypt.

The event that brought the British to Egypt concerned the Suez Canal. Built by a French company and completed in 1869, the canal became the most popular sailing route to the Far East, and British shipping made up 80 percent of its traffic. The khedive of Egypt, Ismail Pasha, controlled 44 percent of the canal company's shares. Ismail wanted to improve and modernize Egypt, and he spent lavishly. He also spent handsomely on himself, all with money borrowed from foreign investors, mainly British and French. Between 1862 and 1875, Egypt's debt rose from £3 million to £100 million. When the Egyptian government could not pay, Ismail bought some time by selling his shares in the canal company to the British government for a mere £4 million. The sale staved off his creditors for no more than a few months, and the Egyptian government was declared bankrupt in May 1876.

To recover their lost investments, a debt commission appointed by the French government took over Egypt's finances, administering revenues and collecting taxes fairly. Rather than allow the mostly French commission to have too much authority, Britain decided to play a more active role. However, Ismail removed the foreigners from their governmental duties and replaced them with his son Tewfik, who had

little success in restoring Egypt's fortunes. In 1879 the Ottoman sultan removed Ismail as khedive and replaced him—not with someone responsible, but with Tewfik. This situation soon proved too much for the Egyptian military. Disliking Tewfik and disgruntled with foreigners in the government, a colonel named Arabi led a revolt that ousted Tewfik in September 1881.

The British government was not in the practice of using their military to bail out troubled businessmen in foreign countries, but this case was different. As part owner of the canal, the British could not allow any domestic disturbance that could potentially translate into restrictions on trade. At the urging of the French president, Britain agreed in early 1882 to join a Franco-British intervention to maintain both order and income. The arrival of foreign troops provoked an even more violent popular uprising. Rather than reinforce, the French parliament voted to withdraw their forces. Britain remained, and took action against Arabi. In July 1882 the Royal Navy bombarded defensive positions around the harbor at Alexandria, then followed this with an invasion in September. Arabi was quickly defeated, and the British placed Lord Cromer in the position of commissioner to restore financial stability.

The British took control on what they assumed would be a temporary basis, but it lasted until after World War II. They had hoped to place a popular liberal ruler in power, but none could be found except Arabi, who was anti-British. At first Cromer had no official position, but he had the British army to maintain himself; he stayed 23 years. Despite a lack of cooperation in the Egyptian government and occasional foreign-policy problems (most notably a Muslim uprising in the Sudan), Egypt benefited from Britain's administration. The government's finances were better handled; the Egyptian army grew larger and better trained; irrigation, school, and railroad projects were begun; and taxes were levied and collected more fairly.

Britain remained a dominant factor in Egyptian affairs until after World War II, and continued to maintain their interest in the Suez Canal. The Egyptians nationalized the canal in 1956, and an abortive attempt to overthrow the Egyptian government and retake control proved to be Britain's last gasp in the region.

*See also* Ottoman Empire [102].

References: Marlowe, John, *Cromer in Egypt* (London: Elek, 1970); Porter, Bernard, *The Lion's Share* (London: Longman, 1975); Robinson, R. E., and J. A. Gallagher, *Africa and the Victorians* (New York: Macmillan, 1961).

## FRANCE, PRUSSIAN INVASION OF (FRANCO-PRUSSIAN WAR)

**133**

Germany's dominant state in the middle 1800s was Prussia, which had risen to prominence mainly through its military. Ever since their defeat at the hands of Napoleon in 1806–1807, the Prussian military had dedicated itself to becoming the best in the world, both to return to the glory days of Frederick the Great and to ensure that such embarrassment at the hands of the French was never repeated. They developed the world's first General Staff, promoting excellence in all phases of military activity. The system proved itself in 1866 when Prussia easily defeated Austria in a border dispute; that war seemed almost a tune-up for a return match with France. Under the leadership of Chancellor Otto von Bismarck, Prussia gathered the lesser German states around it in a North German Confederation and aimed toward the

unification of all Germanic principalities into one state. A war with France would serve as a focus for German nationalism.

After the revolution of 1848, Napoleon III of France had reigned as head of state. The Second Empire was a shadow of the First Empire established by Napoleon Buonaparte, but France hoped to maintain a major role in world affairs, even if it could not reach the heights of grandeur of the beginning of the nineteenth century. During the war between Prussia and Austria, Napoleon had given Prussia tacit support in return for generalized promises of reward. France hoped to gain border lands along the western Rhine after that war, but Bismarck refused to cede any such territory to non-Germans. He then stood in the way of a proposed French purchase of Luxembourg from Holland. When Napoleon hoped to gain some expansion at Belgium's expense through heavy French investment in that country's rail system, Bismarck reminded England of possible French control of the Channel coast, and English opposition halted French aims. In the face of these French attempts, Bismarck convinced the southern German state of Bavaria to join in a defense pact.

The question of a new heir to the Spanish throne brought Franco-Prussian difficulties to a head. After Queen Isabella was deposed in 1868, the government reorganized itself as a constitutional monarchy, but the Spanish were in need of a monarch. They secretly appealed to Prince Leopold of the house of Hohenzollern, a distant cousin of Prussian king Wilhelm. Negotiations to offer the crown to Leopold were conducted between the Spanish government and the Prussian court. Wilhelm had little interest in the matter, and occasionally spoke against the scheme, but Bismarck pushed Leopold's cause. When the French learned of the negotiations, they feared being surrounded by Hohenzollerns;

they had fought such possibilities since the Holy Roman Empire of Charles V and the War of the League of Augsburg. The French ambassador to Prussia met with Wilhelm in Holland and secured the withdrawal of Prussian support for Leopold, but then he pressed his luck by demanding that no future claimant would ever come from the Hohenzollern dynasty. When Bismarck received word of this demand in a telegram, he doctored the communication to make it appear that the French were rude to Wilhelm and that the kaiser had dismissed the ambassador. This provoked French public opinion to the point of war; Napoleon, frustrated by Prussia at every turn, complied.

The French army was not as prepared for war as French public opinion. Despite minor improvements to the French military over the last two years, they were no match for the Prussians. Under the military leadership of Count Helmuth von Moltke, the German General Staff was prepared for almost every contingency, and they could field an army twice the size of the French. Moltke planned on drawing the French army into a trap, but aggressive action on the part of a Prussian general warned the French of the impending danger. They slowed their advance to the frontier, but this did little but delay the inevitable. Napoleon divided most of his army into two sections, to be based around the cities of Sedan and Metz. Prussian forces outperformed the French in all phases of warfare, and both French armies found themselves surrounded. On 1 September 1870, French forces in Sedan under Marshal Maurice de MacMahon surrendered some 100,000 men, including Napoleon III himself. A month later the fortress at Metz, under the command of Marshal François Bazaine, also surrendered. Meanwhile, Prussian forces drove across northern France toward Paris.

Hearing of Napoleon's capture, the government in Paris was overthrown; a revolutionary government under Léon Gambetta tried to rally the public to the French colors. The forces they raised could not compete with the crack Prussian troops, and Paris was soon surrounded. The siege of the Paris Commune lasted until January 1871. As Prussian forces besieged the city, Wilhelm was named kaiser, emperor of a united Germany. Bismarck had finally succeeded in unifying the German states, which had not been under one rule since the time of the early Holy Roman Empire under Charlemagne's grandsons.

The French defeat brought an end to the Second Empire, but more importantly for Europe, it brought the French a burning desire for vengeance. The rapid military defeat, the surrender of the head of state, and the forced payment of reparations totaling some $3 billion were embarrassing, and the French military and population began looking for the next war to return the humiliation. France created a General Staff along the lines of Prussia's and laid plans for a decisive attack sometime in the future. Plan XVII was 40 years in the making, and would prove ineffective when the time came for its implementation in August 1914. The French people and government also felt the humiliation, and Franco-German relations, never cordial, remained strained. The two nations struggled with each other diplomatically in the world of empire-building at the end of the nineteenth century, and their rivalry over Morocco almost brought about World War I in 1905. The alliance systems built up by each side laid the groundwork for the Great War of 1914–1918.

See also Carolingian Dynasty [39]; Italy, Austrian Invasion of (War of the Spanish Succession) [96]; Palatinate, French Invasion of the (War of the League of

Augsburg) [103]; Saxony, Prussian Invasion of (Seven Years' War) [106]; Napoleon Buonaparte [118]; Prussia, Napoleon's Invasion of [121]; France, German Invasion of [160].

References: Carr, William, *The Origin of the Wars of German Unification* (London: Longman, 1991); Howard, Michael, *The Franco-Prussian War* (New York: Collier, 1961); von Moltke, Graf Helmuth, *The Franco-German War of 1870–71* (New York: Harper Brothers, 1901).

## INDIANS OF NORTH AMERICA, U.S. CONQUEST OF

**134**

From the time Europeans first set foot on the American continent, they attempted to force their will on the native Americans, or American Indians. The major source of these conflicts was land—the Indians had it and the Europeans wanted it. As waves of settlements swept westward, one tribe after another was wiped out. After the United States broke away from the rule of England, the conquest of the Indians accelerated at the hands of the aggressive young nation.

By the 1840s the United States had come up against the Plains Indians, those peoples who lived on the Great Plains of North America, an area that ran from Canada south to the Gulf of Mexico, and from the Mississippi River west to the Rocky Mountains. The Plains Indians tribes included the many nations of the Sioux, Cheyenne, Arapaho, Pawnee, Shoshoni, Crow, Kiowa, Comanche, and, to a lesser degree, Apache. All these peoples (with the exception of the Apache) shared a common culture—the horse culture, based on the buffalo and the horse.

The buffalo furnished the Plains Indians with all the necessities of life: food, clothing, housing, fuel. With great herds of tens of millions of animals at their disposal, the Indians had a seemingly inexhaustible supply. Horses had been introduced onto the plains by the Spanish around 1550 and instantly adopted by the Indians, who had been following the buffalo herds on foot for thousands of years. The horse gave the Plains Indians a mobility that other North American Indians lacked, and made them into fearsome warriors. They could cover a hundred miles in a day, strike at the weakest, most exposed points in the frontier settlement lines, and be long gone with their spoils before they could be apprehended. Plains Indian societies were intensely militaristic, with advancement in a tribe based on deeds in war and in the hunt. The nearby white settlers, living on isolated farms and ranches, and usually with only themselves for protection, offered opportunities the Indians could not resist. No military force could catch these swift raiders, and no militia could handle them. Armed with lance, shield, rapid-fire bow, and, later, firearms, the Plains Indians easily comprised the finest light cavalry in the nineteenth-century world.

In comparison, the U.S. Army of the post–Civil War period was poorly trained, badly equipped, and subject to a desertion rate sometimes approaching 50 percent in some regiments. From a peak strength of over 2 million men at the end of the Civil War, the army was reduced by Congress to less than 25,000 by 1870, and only ten regiments were cavalry. Called upon to build, garrison, and maintain the frontier forts, patrol the settlement lines, protect mail and stage lines, enforce the law, and intercept and punish Indian raiders, the 5,000 or so troopers of the U.S. cavalry found themselves badly overtasked.

Surrender of Geronimo (left center, seated) to General George Crook Cright
(seated in helmet) in 1866.

With a single dramatic incident in 1871, all this began to change. General of the Army William Tecumseh Sherman, the highest ranking officer in the U.S. Army and the man who had helped bring the American South to its knees, came to Texas on an inspection tour. Traveling with only a 16-man escort, Sherman was nearly ambushed by a party of over 200 Plains warriors; he escaped only because the Indians decided to wait for a richer prey to come along. After this close brush with death, General Sherman decided to bring the might of the U.S. government to bear on the Plains Indians.

During the American Civil War, Sherman had developed the idea of "Total War," the concept of waging war not just on an enemy's armies but on its people too, thus breaking their will to resist. Following this notion, Sherman had burned Atlanta and marched across Georgia, burning and destroying everything in a 50-mile-wide path from Atlanta to the sea. This ruthless aggression achieved its purpose, destroying the supply base of the Confederate armies and making the war unpopular with the southern people. Sherman reasoned that this same strategy would work against the Plains Indians.

The first step was to attack the Indians' supply base: the buffalo. Sherman encouraged the New England tanning industry to start using buffalo hides in their manufacturing process; they worked just as well as cowhides and were far cheaper, needing only to be "harvested." The tanning industry hired small armies of buffalo hunters who descended on the plains, shooting hundreds of animals a day merely for their skins, leaving behind a prairie full of rotting carcasses. When the killing began in 1872, there were perhaps 20 million buffalo in the United States; by 1884 there were less than 1,200. General Philip Sheridan reflected the army's position on this slaughter when he told the Texas legislature, "Let them kill, skin, and sell until the buffalo is exterminated, as it is the only way to bring lasting peace and allow civilization to advance."

This government-sanctioned extermination removed the sustenance of the Plains tribes. Sherman next struck at the tribes themselves. He had studied the Indians' lifestyle, and realized that their vaunted mobility was not complete. Indian ponies ate prairie grass, and during the dead of winter when there was no grass, they were too weak to carry riders. Thus, in the cold months, the Plains Indians were almost completely immobile, and passed the winter in box canyons and other remote hidden places. In the spring, almost as soon as the grass was up, the ponies would regain their strength and the Indians would be off again on their epic journeys and raids. Wintertime gave Sherman a window of opportunity to strike at the tribes. Army horses ate grain, which could be carried in wagons, along with infantry reinforcements. In truth, the cavalry was not much slower in the winter than they were in the summer. But at least they could operate, which was more than the Indians could do.

Thus, in 1874–1875, Sherman launched a campaign that became known as the Red River War. Thousands of cavalry and infantry crisscrossed the plains of Texas, Oklahoma, and Kansas, looking for hostile Indians in a great search-and-destroy mis-

sion. As the Indian encampments were uncovered, the army attacked. Inevitably, the army would drive off the Indian defenders and overrun their camps. At Sherman's order, all captured material was destroyed. Clothing, weapons, food, the irreplaceable hide tepees—all were burned. Indian horses that fell into the army's hands were shot, as many as 1,500 killed at a time; at some places, their bones could still be seen in the twentieth century. Dismounted and devoid of the necessities of life, the dispirited remnants of the southern tribes walked to their reservations and surrendered.

Sherman's tactics, which had worked so well against the southern Plains tribes, faltered against the northern tribes mostly due to problems in leadership, the most notorious example being Lieutenant Colonel George Armstrong Custer. In 1874, Custer led an expedition into the Black Hills of Dakota, land sacred to the Sioux. Numerous civilian gold miners accompanied Custer, and they discovered gold in the Black Hills, setting off a rush that violated the Indians' treaty guarantees. The army did nothing to stop these incursions, and when the Sioux attacked the interlopers, the army was ordered to move against the Indians. In June 1876, Custer led his famous Seventh Cavalry regiment in an ill-advised attack on some 5,000 Sioux and Cheyenne warriors under Chiefs Sitting Bull and Crazy Horse along the banks of the Little Big Horn River in the Montana Territory. Custer's entire command of 270 men was wiped out. Sheridan and Colonel Ranald Mackenzie were dispatched to avenge Custer, and within three years the Sioux and Cheyenne had been broken like the southern tribes.

In the mountains of the Southwest, the Apaches fought on under leaders like Cochise and Geronimo until 1886, when their resistance was overwhelmed. The once proud tribes of the plains were now confined to reservations. In the late 1880s a new religion, the Ghost Dance, swept the plains. It promised the return of the buffalo and all the dead warriors, and the destruction of all whites if the living would perform a ceremonial dance at every new moon. The desperate Indians embraced the new religion so strongly that the government became alarmed. In December 1890, during an effort to prevent the dance at the Wounded Knee Agency in South Dakota, hostilities erupted between Sioux tribesmen and elements of the Seventh Cavalry. Some 200 Indian men, women, and children and 25 cavalrymen died in the bloodbath. With Wounded Knee, the period of the Indian wars was officially over. In 25 years, the U.S. Army had fought over a thousand actions, with 932 men killed and 1,061 wounded, and the Plains Indians had suffered an estimated 5,519 killed and wounded. In addition, the culture of the Plains Indians was destroyed. The war between the United States and the Plains Indians had been a guerrilla-type, fast-moving, light-marching war, pitting a brave and savage foe against a modern world power. Though their struggle had been epic and, in some cases, the stuff of which legends are made, the outcome was inescapable. The days of the lance, bow, and shield were gone forever. The reservation system, developed prior to the Civil War, became the forced habitation of all Native American tribes. Poor funding, corruption, and a lack of national interest virtually guaranteed that the reservation lifestyle would make the Indians overlooked, second-class citizens in a country they once dominated.

—Allen Lee Hamilton

References: Hamilton, Allen, *Sentinel of the Southern Plains* (Fort Worth: Texas Christian University Press, 1990); Leckie, William, *The Military Conquest of the Southern Plains* (Norman: University of Oklahoma Press, 1963); Utley, Robert, *Frontier Regulars* (New York: Macmillan, 1973).

## 135   INDOCHINA, FRENCH OCCUPATION OF

France first became interested in Southeast Asia in the late 1700s when French missionaries began witnessing to the inhabitants. At first the missionaries were protected by the king of Annam, the southeastern portion of the Indochinese peninsula, but after 1820 new monarchs began to persecute the missionaries. This persecution became most extreme under the reign of Tu-Duc (1847–1883), who was determined to stamp out Christianity in his kingdom. Appeals to France brought a quick response. Through naval demonstrations off the coast, the French tried to force Tu-Duc to guarantee the missionaries' rights and safety, but without success. Another naval demonstration in 1858 did little better. Rather than allow Frenchmen to be harassed, French emperor Napoleon III sent troops to Annam. They invaded and captured the territory around Saigon and the Mekong River delta.

The success of French troops convinced Tu-Duc in 1862 to grant the guarantees the missionaries demanded, and he also ceded to France the three provinces of Cochinchina and the island of Pulo Condore. France's new territory needed a French administration, so bureaucrats were soon installed. Jealous of their land, the civil servants and the newly arrived French merchants pressured the French government to expand its control to create buffer zones around Cochinchina. Thus, France expanded its influence deeper into the peninsula: Cochinchina was declared a colony in 1874, and Annam was declared a French protectorate. Civil disturbances and the activities of Chinese pirates brought more French troops, and in 1884 they occupied the northern province of Tonking.

In 1887 France created the Union Indochinoise, combining the protectorates of Tonking, Annam, and inner Cambodia with the colony of Cochinchina, all under the direction of a governor-general. Two years earlier, France had begun to experience problems in the neighborhood when Britain invaded and occupied Burma; the British believed the French had been secretly supporting Burmese nationalists making trouble along the Indo-Burmese border and harassing British merchants in Burma. The French hoped to extend their economic influence deeper into Southeast Asia, particularly Siam, but this put them into confrontation with Britain. In 1892, France proposed a border between their spheres of influence by claiming everything east of the Mekong River, which would include Laos, then under Siamese control. When Britain hesitated, France invaded; in 1893 they sent an invasion force and a flotilla up the Menam River to Bangkok. At gunpoint they demanded Laos for themselves and a return of Angkor and Battambang to Cambodia. Britain decided not to intervene on Siam's behalf, and France got what it wanted. Siam remained independent, however, because both the British and French realized that a buffer between their territories would be a good idea. These agreements were confirmed by a series of treaties: the Franco-British entente of 1904, a Franco-Siamese treaty in 1907, and an Anglo-Siamese treaty in 1909.

French administration in the area brought French schools and culture, and therein lay the seeds of their own destruction. They taught the French revolutionary principles of *liberté, égalité, fraternité*, which encouraged the growing intelligentsia to consider their own liberty; they also favored the Asians who embraced Catholicism over those who remained Buddhist, and this discrimination fostered resentment. By 1919 young intellectuals were considering the benefits of independence. Ho Chi Minh traveled to Versailles after World War I to urge American president Woodrow Wilson to extend his 14 Points' tenet of national self-determination to all colonies, not just those of the defeated Central Powers. When he failed to accomplish this, he returned home via Moscow and learned the strategies of subversion. In the 1920s he formed the Viet Minh and began the struggle against French imperialism.

When Vichy France turned over Indochina to Japan in September 1940, the Viet Minh fought the Japanese. After the Japanese surrendered to the Allies in 1945, Ho Chi Minh hoped for a breakup of empires that would give his country independence; again, he was disappointed.

The United States did nothing to stand in the way of French desires to reoccupy Indochina, and the Viet Minh resumed fighting the French. The United States initially thought that France should give up its empire, but when the Cold War began and the suspicions of communism increased, President Harry Truman supported France as an obstacle to the spread of communism. American military aid to the French increased through the early 1950s, but the growing numbers of the Viet Minh and the increased support they received from China and the Soviet Union tipped the balance. In 1954, as French and Indochinese representatives met in Geneva to achieve a solution, word arrived that the major French bastion of Dien Bien Phu had fallen to the Viet Minh. The French public was tired of the fighting, and France conceded defeat.

The Geneva Conference declared a timetable for French withdrawal and the independence of the Indochinese countries of Cambodia, Laos, and Vietnam (the former Tonking and Annam). The French were to withdraw in 1956, and elections would be held to determine the new leaders. Though the United States was not a signatory to the Geneva agreement, the Americans did not wish to see Ho Chi Minh elected. Therefore, President Dwight Eisenhower recognized the regime of Bao Dai, a French functionary who oversaw the French withdrawal from the southern provinces. With American support, the country of South Vietnam was created, and the struggle between North and South Vietnam began.

*See also* France, Nazi Invasion of [161].

References: Hammer, Ellen, *The Struggle for Indochina* (Stanford, CA: Stanford University Press, 1955); Randle, Robert, *Geneva 1954* (Princeton, NJ: Princeton University Press, 1969); Thompson, Virginia, *French Indo-China* (New York: Macmillan, 1937).

## KOREA, JAPANESE INVASION OF (SINO-JAPANESE WAR)

**136**

In the early 1600s, Japan fought and lost a war in Korea during which the widespread use of firearms had a lasting effect on Japan's rulers. The samurai warriors who dominated Japanese society could not bear the thought of a peasant having the power to kill one of his betters with a gun. They therefore withdrew from the world rather than allow this technology to upset their culture. Japan remained isolated until 1854, when American commodore Matthew Perry sailed a fleet of ships into Tokyo Bay and demanded that Japan receive diplomatic representatives. The government bowed before the threat of Perry's artillery; they also saw that the only way to

protect themselves was through the adoption of new technology. The samurai lost their political power in the 1868 Meiji Restoration, and Emperor Meiji embarked Japan on an industrial path to modernity.

Japanese society advanced 300 years in four decades. By the 1890s, Japan had a modern navy and well-equipped army, yet maintained the martial spirit that had long dominated Japanese culture. They learned from the world how to build modern weaponry, and they learned that to be powerful in the late nineteenth century a country needed colonies. Traditional martial values coupled with modern weapons and international attitudes meant that Japan would soon be looking for opportunities outside its borders.

China had exercised suzerainty over Korea for two centuries, but in the early 1880s, Japan attempted to enter the Korean markets. Within the Korean royal family there was an ongoing struggle over the role of foreigners: One side (led by Taewon-gun, the king's father) was xenophobic, while the other (led by Queen Min) wanted progressive reforms and considered recent Japanese reforms to be models. In 1882 the two factions clashed, and China sent in troops to restore order. Japan also sent troops, but they were outnumbered and forced to withdraw. Taewon-gun was captured and removed to China, and the Chinese government began to control the Korean government through the Min government. A pro-Japanese faction staged a revolution in 1884, seizing power for a short while. Another Chinese military demonstration compelled the withdrawal of Japanese forces, and the Chinese were once again firmly in control. The best the Japanese could gain was the Treaty of Tientsin in 1885, whereby both countries would pull their forces out of Korea and both would send troops into the country in case of internal violence.

Japanese status in Korea was low, and economic progress was almost nil.

The "internal violence" appeared in the form of a peasant rebellion in 1894. When the Koreans appealed to China for military assistance to suppress the rebellion, Japan feared the possibility of a Chinese army so close to its shores. Therefore, under the provisions of the Treaty of Tientsin, Japan used the rebellion as an opportunity to establish a dominant position in Korea. Tokyo committed the Japanese First Army to Korea and captured the capital at Seoul in July; war was officially declared on 1 August. Outside observers gave tiny Japan little hope against huge China, but the Chinese military was poorly organized and led, and in Korea they were outnumbered. The larger Chinese fleet failed to move aggressively against the Japanese at the battle of the Ualu River in September and had to concede th naval initiative, which the Japanese never surrendered. Free to move troops across the Tsushima Straits and the Yellow Sea, the Japanese attacked at will. By 15 September they controlled the Korean peninsula and looked to invade China itself.

The First Army continued north and crossed the Yalu River into Manchuria while the Japanese Second and Third Armies landed on the Liaotung Peninsula. By the end of 1894, Japanese forces had captured the Weihaiwei and Port Arthur, giving themselves a port of entry into China. Though the Chinese manned well-constructed fortifications, they did not mount a serious defense; Japan lost many more men to winter weather and disease than to combat. A second naval battle off Weihaiwei resulted in the destruction of most of the Chinese fleet, while the Japanese army moved deeper into China. By the spring of 1895, Peking was threatened and probably would have fallen had the Chinese not sued for peace. The Treaty of Shimonoseki brought the war to an end.

Japan acquired the Liaotung Peninsula and Formosa, and forced the Chinese to pay a large indemnity, supplanting the Chinese as the dominant power in Korea. The Japanese earned these concessions, but European nations considered them to be too threatening. Russia and France put diplomatic pressure on Japan to return the Liaotung Peninsula, which they did. It soon became a base for the Russian Pacific Fleet, which began a diplomatic feud resulting in the Russo-Japanese War in 1904. By fighting so poorly, the Chinese showed themselves incapable of fielding a disciplined or well-supplied army; central coordination was nonexistent, and corruption among commanders was rampant. European powers were soon making increased demands on China for economic and political concessions.

Once Japanese forces gained control of Korea and the fighting shifted to China, the Japanese launched an ambitious reform program. Among other things, slavery was banned, civil rights were to be granted to certain lower-class professions, feudal rights of the upper classes were removed, family punishment for the deeds of one of its members was banned, political free speech was opened up, tax reform was initiated, and attempts were made to clean up government corruption. These reforms aimed much higher than any the Min faction had ever planned, so much so that later reforms in 1895 banned royal family interference in the government. Most importantly, Japan now exercised the political and economic power that China had possessed for 200 years. Japan began to look past Korea's borders toward Manchuria.

Even though the Japanese and Chinese both fought a "civilized" war with few atrocities, the Japanese destruction of Port Arthur after the discovery of tortured Japanese prisoners was a foretaste of what conquered peoples would experience at Japanese hands in World War II. During this war, however, they treated most of their prisoners and the conquered people with consideration; it was their later administration (after the Russo-Japanese War) and exploitation of the Koreans that dominate the cultural memory. The Western countries paying attention to this war saw little to change their idea that offense was the dominant aspect of military thinking, a view that would haunt them in World War I. Japan, on the other hand, got a taste for imperialism that did not wane until the end of World War II.

Manchuria was under increasing Russian influence, and the Russians had their eyes on Korea. They quickly moved to exercise influence over Queen Min, who had recently taken their side against Japanese influence. The struggle between the two foreign factions in the Korean government effectively halted any implementation of reforms. In October 1895, Queen Min was killed and the pro-Russian ministers were removed from office. The Russians responded by kidnapping the king and killing pro-Japanese officials in February 1896. A pro-Russian government took power while the king ruled from the Russian legation. Japan could only negotiate minor trading concessions to stay in the country.

Meanwhile, in 1900 Russia enlarged its army in Manchuria in response to the antiforeign Boxer Rebellion in China. When Russia refused to remove its troops, a worried Great Britain entered into an alliance with Japan in 1902, setting the stage for a Russo-Japanese showdown. As the war was being fought (1904–1905), the Japanese regained their influence in the Korean government and soon took control. In a series of agreements, Japan took over Korean foreign policy, acquired military bases, and installed a resident-general whose permission was required before the Korean government could act in foreign or domestic affairs. This put Japan in de facto control of Korea, but in August 1910

the country was officially annexed to Japan. Instead of implementing the reforms they had outlined 15 years earlier, the Japanese took over the entire economy of the country, using the physical and human resources of the country for their own ends until 1945. Despite resistance from unemployed Korean soldiers, Korean intellectuals, and ex–government ministers, the Japanese held control until their defeat in World War II.

*See also* Manchuria, Japanese Invasion of (1904) (Russo-Japanese War) [171].

References: Conroy, Hilary, *The Japanese Seizure of Korea, 1869–1910* (Philadelphia: University of Pennsylvania Press, 1960); Dowart, Jeffrey, *The Pigtail War* (Amherst: University of Massachusetts Press, 1975); Lone, Stewart, *Japan's First Modern War* (New York: St. Martin's Press, 1994).

## 137 MEXICO, FRENCH OCCUPATION OF

Mexico suffered through a civil conflict, the Three Years War, between 1857 and 1860. The ultimate victors—the liberal faction, under the leadership of Benito Juárez—attempted to institute reforms the conservatives had resisted. Rather than accept defeat, the conservatives appealed to Europe for assistance. Great Britain, France, and Spain all responded positively; they had suffered uncompensated economic losses during the war, and foreign bondholders were unable to redeem their investments from a bankrupt Mexican government. With sufficient reasons to intervene, in October 1861 the three European countries agreed to send troops to Mexico in an attempt to recoup their investments by force.

The coalition force captured the port of Vera Cruz in January 1862. After receiving assurances from the Mexican government that they were doing all they could to make good the European losses, Britain and Spain decided to withdraw. France, however, remained behind. French emperor Napoleon III had plans for Mexico. Assured by conservative factions in the country that the Mexican population would welcome the French presence, Napoleon planned to establish dominance over what he hoped would become a Mexican empire, giving him economic and political standing in the Western Hemisphere. He persuaded an unemployed aristocrat, Archduke Ferdinand Maximilian of Habsburg, brother of Austrian emperor Franz Josef, to rule in Mexico.

Expecting to be welcomed as liberators, French troops marched inland from Vera Cruz westward to Puebla. They found a population far from welcoming. Fierce resistance by poorly equipped Mexican troops in the city forced a French withdrawal on 5 May 1862, but they returned in March 1863 with 30,000 reinforcements and took the city after a two-month siege. Having lost a significant portion of his army at Puebla, President Juárez decided to take his government out of Mexico City, and fled northward into the interior. French forces occupied Mexico City on 10 June and were welcomed by the clergy and conservatives, if not the general population. By the end of the year, the French occupied the major cities of Monterrey, Saltillo, San Luis Potosí, and Querétaro.

Possession of the cities meant little because the population, mostly loyal to Juárez, controlled the rugged, empty, roadless countryside. Nevertheless, the French thought they were off to a good start. In October 1863, Mexican conservatives offered Maximilian the crown. He responded that he would take it only after consulting with the Mexican people, so a referendum was held. Staged by the French and conservatives, it was not surprising that the results were overwhelmingly in favor of Maximilian, and he accepted the throne in April 1864. Maximilian disappointed the conservative Mexicans, who thought they could easily regain the positions they had held before the Three Years War. Instead, he favored the foreign investment that had come into the country with his accession. Still, he did what he could to keep the conservatives happy while simultaneously courting the liberals. He convinced some of them that he wanted to be fair with all Mexicans—an enlightened monarch—and he gained some converts in the cities. The countryside, however, remained hostile to the foreign invaders.

Trouble hit Maximilian in 1866. Viewing the French occupation as a violation of the Monroe Doctrine, the United States threatened possible military action to liberate Mexico. At the same time, domestic problems in France and an increasingly aggressive Prussia brought Napoleon III to the realization that he needed all his forces at home. As French troops boarded ships for the return home in 1866, the generals begged Maximilian to abdicate and go with them. Instead, he listened to those Mexicans who insisted that he could maintain his hold on power. In early 1867 they convinced Maximilian to go to Querétaro to take command of forces preparing to fight an approaching force loyal to Juárez. Rather than leading his troops to victory, Maximilian was captured on 14 May and soon executed by firing squad.

With all European troops out of his country, Benito Juárez resumed the presidency and attempted to institute the reforms he had tried to begin before the invasion. He started with putting government finances back on a sound footing by cutting expenses, in this case by firing two-thirds of his army. This resulted in a series of revolts he was obliged to suppress. With the remaining budget, he spent heavily on education. Within a few years Mexico had 8,000 schools with 350,000 students. Juárez also ordered the construction of a railroad line from the port of Vera Cruz through Puebla to Mexico City. In the cities, the first attempts at labor reform and the beginnings of trade unionism began. Juárez's attempts to bring capitalism to agriculture were also successful, but at a high price. He wanted to make farming profitable at the expense of the Indian tribes, who controlled much of the arable land. With government assistance, the landowners brutally put down Indian revolts. The Indians suffered from violence, government confiscation of their lands, and fraud by unscrupulous land speculators.

References: Keen, Benjamin, and Mark Wasserman, *A Short History of Latin America* (Boston: Houghton Mifflin, 1984); Meyer, W. C., and W. L. Sherman, *The Course of Mexican History* (New York: Oxford University Press, 1979); Roeder, Ralph, *Juárez and His Mexico*, 2 vols. (New York: Viking, 1947).

## MEXICO, U.S. INVASION OF

138

When Texas successfully secured its independence from Mexico in 1836, the Texans immediately applied for statehood. The U.S. Congress rejected them, so Texas established a republic and operated as an independent nation for nine years. Early in 1845 Congress relented and offered statehood. The only problem lay in the designation of Texas's border with its former owner. Though the Mexican government had never recognized Texas's indepen-

dence, Mexico had not seriously tried to bring the recalcitrant state back into its union. Upon learning of the state's annexation into the United States, the Mexican government was willing to let Texas go, but only on the condition that the borders follow the land grants Mexico had originally given to American settlers in the 1820s. Those borders stretched from the Nueces River in the south to the Red River in the north, territory that today encompasses central and east Texas. The Texans, however, claimed the Rio Grande as their border with Mexico, and claimed it to its source, which meant Mexico would have to cede about three times as much land, including its main northern settlement at Santa Fe. If the United States accepted the Texas claim to the Rio Grande, Mexico promised war.

American president James Polk sent John Slidell to Mexico to negotiate the purchase of the disputed territory and anything else Mexico might be willing to sell (such as California). The Mexicans not only refused his $15 million offer, they refused to recognize his very presence in their capital. This diplomatic insult, slight though it may have been, was fuel to the expansionist fires burning in American society, fires that Polk stoked in his election campaign. Coupling this incident with Mexico's refusal to pay any damage claims for raids their army had conducted in Texas during the republic period, Polk felt justified in threatening Mexico.

Polk sent troops under General Zachary Taylor from New Orleans to Texas, ordering them to cross the Nueces and establish a presence along the north shore of the Rio Grande. Taylor began building Fort Polk and Fort Brown near the mouth of the river in March 1846. In mid-April a cavalry patrol was ambushed and captured by Mexican forces. The Mexicans felt justified because they considered their country

Landing of the U.S. Army, under General Scott, on the beach near Vera Cruz on 9 March 1847

invaded as soon as American forces crossed the Nueces. For Polk, however, it was the final justification for war. He sent a message to Congress in early May, saying, "American blood has been shed on American soil" (a view not shared by Mexico). Congress agreed, and declared war.

After two fairly easy victories in early May at Palo Alto and Resaca de la Palma, Taylor drove Mexican forces back across the Rio Grande. His forces crossed the river in June and worked their way upstream along the southern bank. In the meantime, the Mexican government had promoted Antonio López de Santa Anna to the command of their forces. As dictator in 1836, Santa Anna had been defeated at San Jacinto, and it was he who signed the document that the Texans claimed gave them their independence. In 1844, Santa Anna had been removed from power a second time and exiled to Cuba. Some military historians regard him as one of the worst generals ever, but he had the ability to rise

to leadership positions in Mexico over and over again.

Taylor arrived outside Monterrey with about 6,000 troops in the middle of September. He anticipated little difficulty in capturing the city despite the fact that the Mexicans had fortified the high ground around the city and dug extensive defenses across the more level approaches. The battle for Monterrey took three days, but the defending Mexican general asked for terms after American forces attacking from two directions had captured the high ground and were making their way through the city. Taylor occupied the city, allowing the Mexican army to withdraw.

Meanwile, volunteer units were forming in the United States. The largest belonged to Stephen Kearny, a regular army colonel leading 1,500 frontiersmen, who marched westward from Kansas in the summer of 1846. He and his men were assigned to secure the New Mexico Territory, and by mid-August they raised the American flag over Santa Fe, declaring it and the territory to be U.S. possessions. Not a shot was fired on the campaign. In September, Kearny and 300 men marched for California. They arrived in December to find that forces from Oregon under John C. Frémont, along with naval forces under command of John Sloat and then Robert Stockton, had liberated the California Territory but were facing a popular uprising around Los Angeles. Stockton's sailors and marines joined with Kearny's small force to secure Los Angeles by early January. Mexican resistance in the territory was ended; the only struggle yet to come was between Kearny and Frémont over who was actually in command in the territory.

As Kearny marched through the Southwest toward California, several hundred men from his original force left Santa Fe and headed south. Alexander Doniphan and his men enjoyed singular success in their expedition. They captured El Paso after a brief fight in late December; after a month of rest and recreation in the city, Doniphan's force marched for the city of Chihuahua. Another brief battle (suffering 2 killed and 7 wounded while inflicting 800 casualties on the Mexican force) gave them control of that town, followed by another month of R and R. They next marched for Monterrey to join with Taylor's forces, arriving there too late for Taylor's last major battle, at Buena Vista. They marched to the coast, sailed for New Orleans, were mustered out of service, and went home. They had claimed north-central Mexico for the United States by right of conquest, having accomplished the entire mission without regular army troops, orders, or leadership.

Northern Mexico was coming under American control, but Taylor was having his problems at Monterrey. Even though he was winning his battles, and had extended his hold southward to the town of

Saltillo, the government was reining him in. President Polk, a Democrat, feared Taylor's rising popularity, and he wanted to derail any future run Taylor might make toward high office as a Whig. Taylor was ordered to go on the defensive, but he chafed at these orders. Taylor widened his hold on the area around Saltillo, and ran into Mexican forces under Santa Anna. The Mexican force of 20,000 had marched across the desert to reach Buena Vista, south of Saltillo, in late February. After difficult fighting on 23 February 1847, Taylor's forces held their ground, and Santa Anna retreated. It would be the last major battle in the north.

Newly arrived American general Winfield Scott siphoned off some of Taylor's forces and sailed for Vera Cruz. Scott captured the port city fairly easily, and began to march west for Mexico City. Santa Anna had returned to the capital after his defeat at Buena Vista, and began to direct the defense of the city. Scott's advance through difficult terrain was harassed periodically by Mexican guerrillas, but he approached the city by late August. The two sides negotiated a cease-fire to discuss peace terms, but Santa Anna was only buying time to improve his defenses. By early September the armistice was over and Scott's forces drew nearer the city.

Unwilling to have Scott negotiate a peace treaty and make him even more popular than his military victories were doing, President Polk sent Nicholas Trist to Mexico to talk with the Mexican government. Congress had returned to Whig dominance after the last election, and they did not support the war. Polk hoped to secure the original goals of this war: the disputed area of Texas and possibly American possession of California. Certainly Mexico had suffered enough to concede to these demands.

Trist entered Mexico City under a flag of truce and found the government in chaos and unwilling to negotiate. He withdrew and sent word to Polk of his lack of success. The message took six weeks to reach Washington owing to travel time, and the reply took equally as long. Trist's original communication had been sent in late July, and the reply did not arrive in Mexico City until November: Forget the negotiations and come home. By then Scott had captured Mexico City, Santa Anna had been deposed, and the new Mexican government was negotiating with him. Still operating under his original orders, Trist was in a quandary. Should he continue to negotiate, or follow the latest directive to go home? He stayed.

In the meantime, Polk learned of the success at Mexico City and saw an opportunity not only to gain Texas and California, but all of Mexico. He sent a new directive to Trist to forget the original instructions and demand complete capitulation. That message arrived after Trist had negotiated the treaty and left for Washington. Under the terms of the treaty of Guadalupe-Hidalgo, Mexico ceded the disputed area of Texas and gave up all lands west toward the Pacific. In return, the United States would pay the originally offered $15 million, plus $3.25 million in damage claims held against Mexico by American citizens. The United States had just fought a year and a half to force Mexico to sell land.

When Trist arrived in Washington, unaware of the president's last message, he proudly visited the White House to display the fruits of his labors. Polk was furious, almost murderous. The United States might have taken all of Mexico without paying anything, if only Trist had better understood his president's expansionist attitudes. Had he exercised personal initiative and seized the moment, he could have seized the entire country. Polk did not want the treaty, but knew that congressional opposition would not allow him to continue the war; he re-luctantly signed it and sent it to the Senate for ratification. No one in the Senate liked it either, thinking that it took too much, or too little, from Mexico; they ratified it as a compromise. The Mexican government did not like parting with any land at any price, but they were in no position to make demands; they ratified it as well.

The Treaty of Guadalupe-Hidalgo is one of the great might-have-beens of history. The future of the United States and all of Latin America would have been radically altered if the United States' southern border had become the Yucatán peninsula. For example, what would have been the policy concerning slavery in this new territory? Could the southern states have gained power in Congress with new slave states sending representatives and senators to Washington? What would that have meant in 1861? Would the Civil War have been averted if the South had had more say in Congress? Would Mexican states have seceded from the Union and fought for the Confederacy? Further in the future, what problems would the United States have avoided in terms of illegal immigration, or in trade questions like the North American Free Trade Agreement?

Questions aside, there were concrete results from the war. The United States achieved its "manifest destiny" by reaching from sea to shining sea. Within a year of possessing California, gold was discovered and the rush was on. Having two distinct coastlines gave the United States the opportunity to expand overseas trade to the Orient as well as to Europe. The United States benefited greatly from the land gained, despite the fact that the slavery question over this new land almost directly led to civil war. Combat experience gained in Mexico showed itself in just a few years when junior officers under Taylor and Scott became senior officers in Union and Confederate uniforms.

In terms of foreign relations, Latin America began to view the United States with increasing suspicion. The nation that had seemed a defender of the region with the Monroe Doctrine in the 1820s came to be viewed as a bully taking what it wanted from a weaker neighbor on trumped-up charges. The United States never lost that reputation, and did little in succeeding years to ameliorate it.

References: Connor, Seymour, *North America Divided* (New York: Oxford University Press, 1971); Eisenhower, John, *So Far from God* (New York: Random House, 1989); Singletary, Otis, *The Mexican War* (Chicago: University of Chicago Press, 1960).

## 139 | NEW ZEALAND, BRITISH OCCUPATION OF

In the wake of the American Revolution, the British needed a new land into which to send their criminals and chose Australia. The islands east of Australia, known as New Zealand, were used as a British whaling station and remained relatively untouched by civilized hands. After the whalers advertised the beauty and fertility of the islands back in England, land speculators and settlers began to arrive. So many people emigrated that by 1840 the British government annexed the islands in order to save the local population, the Maori.

The Maori had a different view of land ownership than the English; they believed that the land belonged to everyone and therefore could not be sold. British missionaries helped to muddle things; on the one hand, they defended the natives from aggressive land speculators and, on the other hand, they themselves were aggressive in their attempts to convert the Maori to Christianity. The Treaty of Waitonga made the Maori British subjects, but allowed them to retain control of the land. This worked for a few years until the formation of the New Zealand Company, which brought in some 30,000 settlers. The original intent of the New Zealand Company was to re-create British culture in a foreign land, and the new arrivals felt that the recognition of Maori rights robbed their own attempts of proper appreciation. The settlers therefore had little consideration for the natives. The decision in 1852 to allow local self-government to the settlers foreshadowed conflict, because the Crown was the sole agent allowed to acquire land from the Maori.

In 1860 an individual Maori sold a piece of land to the British government, but the Maori's tribe nullified the sale, saying he had no right to sell property collectively owned. The British took control of the land anyway, and war began. For five years, British troops fought against the Maori. They forced a peace treaty on Maori king Wiremu Kingi, though a violent resistance movement among irreconcilables continued through 1881. The defense of settlers' rights proved too expensive for the British Colonial Office, however, and they withdrew their troops in 1870. The Colonial Office hoped that by shifting the expense to the settlers, they would stop fighting to save money. For the most part, this worked.

The settlers had obtained the right to confiscate land, but surprisingly did not abuse that right. Most New Zealanders established cattle or sheep ranches that provided a good income but did not cover huge areas of land. When the first refrigerated ships arrived in 1881, the New Zealand economy really began to prosper. The export of wool was supplemented by dairy products, and almost all of it went to Britain. The profitable export market, coupled with a gold rush in the early 1870s, gave New Zealand a high standard of living.

These events came at a time in British society when humanitarian impulses were strong, resulting in experiments in social legislation that marked the island nation as truly progressive.

The Maori were able to take advantage of this as well. They maintained control over large tracts of land through the mid-1800s, but in time, European contact brought the same result faced by other native populations: death by disease. By the beginning of the twentieth century, the Maori population had decreased from over 200,000 to just over 40,000, which may account for their absorption into mainstream white society in New Zealand. They did not have sufficient numbers to pose a threat, nor did the whites need large amounts of cheap labor because they kept their landholdings fairly small. The humanitarianism of the time, coupled with the Maoris' ultimate embrace of European culture, created one of the world's few truly interracial societies.

Though the New Zealanders planned in the late 1800s to expand into the southern Pacific region, such dreams never came about. New Zealanders are often considered more British than the British in their rural outlook, but they have far outperformed their role models in the institution of government programs that successfully deal with labor, health, and culture.

See also Australia, British Occupation of [84].

References: Cain, P. J., *British Imperialism: Innovation and Expansion, 1688–1914* (London: Longman, 1993); McLeod, A. L., *The Pattern of New Zealand Culture* (Ithaca, NY: Cornell University Press, 1968); Thomson, Arthur, *The Story of New Zealand* (New York: Praeger, 1970).

## 140 PARAGUAYAN WAR

After the removal of Spanish rule in South America in the 1820s, Paraguay resisted Argentine domination by declaring its independence from the previous viceroyalty of Río de la Plata. Under two successive dictators, Francia and López, Paraguay established a progressive and prosperous nation. The Paraguayans established economic and cultural ties with Europe; phased out slavery, yet had little feudalism or peonage; and had one of the highest literacy rates on the continent. Francisco Solano López came to power in 1862 upon the death of his father.

In 1864, López felt threatened by Brazil's interference in a civil war in neighboring Uruguay, through which landlocked Paraguay had access to the port city of Montevideo at the mouth of the Uruguay River. If a hostile government were to come to power there, Paraguay would have to depend on the goodwill of Argentina to allow sea access through Buenos Aires. López's protests concerning Brazilian interference in Uruguay fell on deaf ears, so he decided to apply direct pressure by attacking the Brazilian province of Mato Grosso. This being a rugged and uninhabited territory, the attack had no effect. López then asked permission of Bartolomé Mitre, Argentina's leader, for access through his country to assist Uruguay, a request he refused. Considering this an unfriendly act, Paraguay declared war on Argentina in March 1865 and launched an invasion.

The attack brought about the formation of the Triple Alliance of Brazil, Argentina, and Uruguay on 1 May 1865. A secret clause in the treaty called for the alliance to confiscate about half the Paraguayan territory and divide it between Brazil and Argentina. The coalition of three nations—two of them the largest in South America—seemed overwhelming in its power. Though the well-trained, 70,000-man Paraguayan army outnumbered the combined coalition forces, López was unable to press his invasion of Argentina, and was soon on the defensive. Alliance troops invaded across the Parana River in April 1866 and maintained their momentum. They won a hard-fought victory over a Paraguayan force at Fort Humaita in August 1868, then occupied the capital city of Asunción in January 1869. López was unable to strengthen his army, but the alliance forces, mainly Brazilian, continued to grow. López's last stand came on 1 May 1870. He was killed in battle after being cornered against the Brazilian border, and his death meant the end of Paraguayan resistance.

A prosperous and independent Paraguay was no more. The country's population was devastated by the war, three-fourths of the 500,000 citizens dying from combat, disease, starvation, or the brutal Brazilian occupation; the adult male population was reduced to only 30,000. As agreed during the formation of the Triple Alliance, Brazil and Argentina annexed about half the country and forced the Paraguayans to pay heavy reparations. Brazil established a puppet government of former Paraguayan generals, and proceeded to dismantle the decades of progress the country had enjoyed. Most of the land was sold to foreign investors at extremely low prices, and the economy came under the control of Brazilian investors.

Paraguay was not the only country affected by the war. Argentina had to raise taxes to pay for its involvement, which provoked a number of provincial uprisings during the conflict. The Argentine government was so busy suppressing these rebellions that by 1867 the Argentinians had virtually withdrawn from the war. Nevertheless, Brazil honored the agreement to give Argentina half the annexed land and half the reparation money.

References: Keen, Benjamin, and Mark Wasserman, *A Short History of Latin America* (Boston: Houghton Mifflin, 1984); Warren, Harris, *Paraguay and the Triple Alliance* (Austin, TX: Institute of Latin American Studies, 1978); Williams, John, *The Rise and Fall of the Paraguayan Republic* (Austin, TX: Institute of Latin American Studies, 1979).

## PHILIPPINES, U.S. OCCUPATION OF THE

**141**

Even though the American declaration of war against Spain in 1898 was brought about by events in Cuba, the United States prepared to make war against Spanish possessions around the world. The first military action the Americans initiated was the U.S. Navy's destruction of the Spanish fleet at Manila Bay on 1 May. While this was an overwhelming victory, it had its drawbacks. Foremost among them was that ships cannot occupy ground, and therefore the Spanish army in the Philippines remained untouched. Because the U.S. Army was rapidly expanding to fight the war, and the main focus would be on Cuba, troops could not be expected to arrive in the Philippines anytime soon. The actions taken by Admiral George Dewey to secure control of the islands laid the groundwork for a long struggle for American control.

Prior to the outbreak of war, the Filipinos, under the leadership of Emilio Aguinaldo, had engaged in struggles against the Spanish occupation. They failed, and the Spanish deported Aguinaldo to Hong Kong. By sheer luck, the U.S. Pacific Fleet was anchored in Hong Kong when war broke out against Spain. Assistant Secretary of the Navy Theodore Roosevelt cabled Dewey to proceed against the Spanish at Manila, and Dewey took Aguinaldo along with him. What transpired between

Hong Kong and Manila is the subject of some debate. Dewey claimed that he asked Aguinaldo to go ashore and rouse his freedom fighters to control the countryside and keep the Spanish army penned in the cities. Aguinaldo claimed that Dewey promised freedom for the Philippines if Aguinaldo would cooperate, which Dewey denied. Whether freedom was guaranteed or implied, the Filipinos believed it was theirs.

When the U.S. Army finally arrived to take possession of the Philippines, the peace negotiations between the United States and Spain were under way in Paris. Officially still at war, the Spanish commander did not want to surrender freely, yet he realized that his forces could not survive extended combat with the Americans. The two forces agreed to stage a mock battle for Spanish home consumption, then hold surrender ceremonies, and honor would be satisfied. This agreement, however, was just between American and Spanish officers. When the firing started, the Filipinos thought it was a real battle and joined in, killing several surprised Spanish soldiers before the Americans could stop the shooting. This exclusion from the official capture of Manila, their own capital, offended the Filipinos and set the stage for strained relations between native and "liberator."

When the Treaty of Paris of 1898 awarded possession of the Philippines to the United States in return for $20 million, the Filipinos assumed that this was a temporary measure, just as the American occupation of Cuba was to last only until the Cubans could govern themselves. After all, the U.S. Senate had stated prior to hostilities that they would not annex Cuba. True, but the declaration did not state that they would not annex anything else. The United States also acquired Guam and Puerto Rico from the Spanish along with the Philippines, and it planned on keeping them all.

Aguinaldo and his followers felt betrayed, and warfare erupted. The Filipinos had occupied the string of blockhouses outside Manila since the beginning of the occupation, and they now occupied trenches overlooking the city. With their superior training and firepower, the Americans were able to throw them out in a few days of hard fighting in early February 1899. The Americans pursued Aguinaldo's forces into the interior, where the Filipinos attempted to fight a conventional war, but they were hopelessly outclassed and outgunned. By May the war seemed to be over, and the American commander, Elwell Otis, settled in for the rainy season with bright prospects.

Otis informed Washington that the rebellion was over and that with the return of the dry season he could begin to impose American will. After all, the Americans viewed themselves as the harbingers of civilization and wanted only to improve the lot of their "little brown brothers." Once civic improvements were begun, the Americans would be welcomed. There was only one problem: The fighting was not over. The Filipinos had failed to win a conventional war, so they turned to the guerrilla tactics for which their nature and the countryside were much better suited. Simultaneously, most of the American troops, who were volunteers, were coming to the end of their enlistment and were slated to go home. Hence, Otis would be losing much of his force at a time when more intense warfare was about to begin.

When new volunteer forces began to arrive in the fall of 1899, the early action seemed to confirm Otis's views. More of Aguinaldo's forces were defeated, and many of his main lieutenants were captured. With only "scattered resistance" left, Otis began the reform projects: road and bridge construction, increased access to health care and education, railroads, and telephone and telegraph lines. These projects were successful, and illiteracy began to drop, as did infant mortality and deaths from cholera, smallpox, and the plague. Otis was quite surprised when the fighting continued in the countryside.

The country folk, long used to dealing with rugged terrain and banditry, became successful guerrillas immediately. Aguinaldo hoped that protracted warfare would disillusion the American public and bring support from Asian weapons suppliers. Hand in hand with guerrilla war against the army was terrorism against those who cooperated with the Americans.

Shadow governments operated in villages and controlled the people when the American forces were not on the scene. Collaborators were punished with either destruction of their property or torture and death. Captured American soldiers suffered similarly grisly fates, provoking equally harsh responses from the army. The army, accustomed to dealing with Indian tribes in the United States, with atrocities committed and received, had little trouble continuing the process in this climate.

Otis was replaced in May 1900 by Arthur MacArthur. He continued Otis's reforms and expanded them, but began a more intensive campaign against the guerrillas. He trained friendly Filipinos to guide and fight with American forces, gather intelligence, and protect the villagers. He invoked General Order No. 100, first issued during the Civil War, which stated that war was to be fought between armies; partisans and guerrillas operated outside the law and would not be treated like soldiers, but punished like criminals. MacArthur was able to get more U.S. troops committed to the country, and by early 1901 he commanded 70,000 men. They began sweeping the countryside and harassing the guerrillas, keeping them away from villages that might provide them with supplies. He started a Filipino political

party to have input into local administration as an alternative to Aguinaldo's political aspirations. When Aguinaldo was captured in March 1901, the underground leader soon issued a statement calling for an end to hostilities and cooperation with the Americans. For the most part, the guerrillas gave up the fight, but two large bands (more bandit than patriot) continued the struggle.

The final actions against the *insurrectos* were brutal. Further atrocities provoked the Americans into corresponding behavior. Field commander Jacob Smith ordered his troops, "I wish you to kill and burn; the more you kill and burn the better it will please me. I want all persons killed who are capable of bearing arms in actual hostilities against the United States." Any male over ten was to be targeted. While this mandate was not rigorously enforced, burning and destruction were, and they ended the activities of one of the guerrilla groups. The other group, operating in the southern part of the main island of Luzon, saw a different tactic used against them. The Americans rounded up 300,000 citizens in concentration camps, denying any public support to the guerrillas. Though many died of disease in these camps, just as many Cubans had, it served its purpose. By April 1902 the fighting was ended.

After such a difficult experience establishing control, it is somewhat surprising that the Americans ever gained the friendship of Filipinos. The continued efforts at reform, even in the midst of the brutality, bore fruit. The occupation forces tried to show themselves as helpers who had to deal with bandits in unpleasant ways in order to bring about improvement. The quick assimilation of Aguinaldo and other political figures into the civil administration helped to prove the Americans' desire to cooperate with the locals. Despite the fact that 20,000 Filipino soldiers died and an estimated 200,000 civilians perished from disease or mistreatment, the Americans and Filipinos managed to grow fond of each other. When World War II broke out and the Japanese invaded the islands, American and Filipino troops fought side by side, and then suffered side by side in prison camps. A relationship born in hostility became, through improved administration and cooperation, a close friendship.

*See also* Cuba, U.S. Invasion of [131]; Philippines, Japanese Invasion of the [181].

References: Gates, John M., *Schoolbooks and Krags: The United States Army in the Philippines* (New York: Greenwood Press, 1973); Karnow, Stanley, *In Our Image: America's Empire in the Philippines* (New York: Random House, 1989); Miller, Stuart, *"Benevolent Assimilation": The American Conquest of the Philippines* (New Haven, CT: Yale University Press, 1982).

## 142   PUERTO RICO, U.S. INVASION OF

Puerto Rico was one of only two remaining Spanish possessions in the Western Hemisphere when it became the target of American efforts to rid the Caribbean of Spanish influence in the Spanish-American War. Though the main fighting of the war took place in Cuba, which was secured by 17 July 1898, Puerto Rico seemed a tempting target. The Spanish government here was more liberal than in Cuba, allowing the Puerto Ricans a modicum of self-rule, but the Americans were perceived as liberators who would give the island its independence rather than hold it as a colony.

General Nelson Miles commanded the 3,300 troops who landed on the island 21 July 1898. Fearing a direct attack on the capital of San Juan would prove too costly, they first captured the port of Ponce. The landings went smoothly, against minimal opposition, and reinforcements were soon on hand. The soldiers began to believe the occupation would be bloodless; the only trouble they had was with street vendors and large numbers of welcoming politicians. After a weak of easy duty, Miles ordered his force to move across the island along a number of routes, all heading for San Juan. Only the lack of initiative on the part of the Spanish army kept this from being a bloodbath, because the rugged terrain could easily have disguised any number of ambushes. The most difficult engagement turned out to be no more than a skirmish, resulting in six American wounded and six Spanish deaths.

The Americans methodically made their way across the island, capturing town after town against little or no resistance. There was no battle for San Juan, because word came on 13 August that an armistice had been signed. The capture of Puerto Rico seemed ridiculously easy, but Miles's multipronged offensive was designed to outflank any large Spanish force, and the Spaniards rarely stood to fight. Dismissed as a "picnic" by some writers, correspondent Richard Harding Davis gave the credit for success to Miles. "The reason the Spanish bull gored our men in Cuba and failed to touch them in Porto Rico [*sic*] was entirely due to the fact that Miles was an expert matador; so it was hardly fair to the commanding General and the gentlemen under him to send the Porto Rican campaign down into history as a picnic."

The inhabitants of the island were not happy to learn that the United States would not grant them independence. Unlike the situation in Cuba, the United States had made no promise about freeing Puerto

Troops raising the American flag at the Governor's Palace, San Juan

Rico. Instead, Congress voted to make the island an "unincorporated territory," which meant that the Puerto Ricans became citizens of no nation. Wealthy Americans bought up the best lands for agricultural production, and the locals had to work for them. However, there were benefits for the Puerto Ricans. Prior to the U.S. invasion, only two or three improved roads existed on the island, there were no banks, and only about one-fifth of the land was being farmed. U.S. investment and interest improved sanitation, utilities, and roads, though mainly within or between cities, leaving the peasants in the countryside lagging behind. The education system improved until some 80 percent of the island was literate, much higher than most Caribbean countries. Despite this, most of the profits that accrued from the outside investment resulted in those profits leaving the country. By 1930 the United States controlled 50 percent of the sugar production, 80 percent of the tobacco, 60 percent of the banks, 60 percent of the public utilities, and all of the shipping.

In 1917 Congress finally agreed to grant Puerto Ricans U.S. citizenship, and in 1947 they received the right to elect their own governor. To this day, the inhabitants remain divided about the island's future, roughly equal numbers wanting independence, statehood, or to keep things as they are.

*See also* Cuba, U.S. Invasion of [131].

References: Carrión, Arturo Morales, *Puerto Rico, a Political and Cultural History* (New York: Norton, 1983); Friedel, Frank, *The Splendid Little War* (Boston: Little, Brown, 1958); Millis, Walter, *The Martial Spirit* (Boston: Houghton Mifflin, 1931).

## 143

## SINGAPORE, BRITISH OCCUPATION OF

While the Dutch maintained a trade monopoly in the East Indies in the 1700s, the British stayed out of Southeast Asia and concentrated on the tea trade with India and China. By the end of the century, however, Dutch reverses in European wars led to a weakening of their economic strength in the area around Malaysia. The growing power of the British East India Company drew the attention of the British government to the area, and they soon saw the need for a naval base on the eastern side of the Bay of Bengal. Francis Light, a trader well connected with Malay leaders, negotiated a British lease on Penang on the west coast of the Malay Peninsula. The base established there proved valuable to Britain's military needs, but the trade port failed to make as much money as Britain had hoped.

During Holland's occupation by Napoleon, Britain occupied Dutch possessions around the world in an attempt to deny them to the French dictator. Because of this, the British took control of Malacca, farther down the Malay coast. Originally a Portuguese stronghold, the Dutch had seized the town in the 1640s. Britain moved into the port in 1795 and was reluctant to return it to the Dutch after Napoleon's defeat in 1815. Stamford Raffles, an active agent for the East India Company, convinced his superiors of the necessity of dominating Malacca and the peninsula in general if the British were to challenge Dutch trading interests in Southeast Asia. Thus, Raffles was directed to find a suitable site to challenge the Dutch monopoly.

In 1819, Raffles chose Singapore, a small island off the tip of the Malay Peninsula. It had an excellent harbor and was sparsely populated; though the island was in the Dutch sphere of influence, they had no one on it. To gain title to the island, Raffles had to deal with a pretender to the sultanate of Johore, on the island of Sumatra across the Malaccan Straits. By recognizing the pretender, in opposition to the de facto sultan recognized by the Dutch, Raffles placed Britain in a precarious position should the Dutch challenge his occupation of the island. Challenge they did, but the negotiations dragged on from 1820 through 1823, during which time the importance and profits of Singapore grew to the point that the British were not about to abandon their claim. By making Singapore a free port, trade from all over Asia flocked there, away from the Dutch trade center at Batavia. The island's population skyrocketed from 150 when Raffles entered into the lease to 10,000 by the end of 1820. The trade center at Penang, never profitable, slipped even further into mediocrity.

The Dutch finally conceded British occupation of Singapore in the Treaty of London in 1824. Not only did they drop their opposition, they received delineated spheres of influence to maintain at least a partial monopoly. Britain could control Singapore and the Malay Peninsula, and Holland would dominate the islands south of the Malaccan Straits. Thus, Britain exchanged its one settlement on Sumatra for the Dutch settlement of Malacca. Trade in Borneo, however, remained contested. The ports of Penang, Malacca, and Singapore collectively became known as the Straits Settlements, and the British government viewed them as protection for trade to China. It would be decades before Britain moved deeply into Malay trade and politics.

By conceding the East Indies to the Dutch, the British abandoned Raffles's idea of creating a British colonial empire in Southeast Asia. The states of the Malay Peninsula were freed from the domination of the sultan of Johore on Sumatra and pro-

ceeded on their own course; Siam dominated the interior for decades. In 1824 the
British concluded a new agreement over
Singapore. The original had given Britain
permission to build a settlement; the new
pact gave Britain the island forever in return for a cash payment and a pension to
the local chieftains.

The British may not have established an
empire, but Singapore grew to dominate
the Southeast Asian trade. By the middle
1800s the city was handling almost as much
trade as all of the East Indies. Banks, trading companies, and insurance companies—
the extra necessities for commerce—
centered themselves in Singapore. The
livelihood of most of the population was
bound up with shipping, trade, and port
labor, and its financial success attracted
migration from all over, especially China.
From 10,000 people in 1820, the city grew
to more than 16,000 by 1830, more than
doubled by 1840, and reached almost
60,000 by 1850. By 1860, of the 80,000
inhabitants on the island, 50,000 were
Chinese, 13,000 were Indians, and the rest
were Malays.

The Chinese dominated trade and the
population with their financial success and
introduced secret societies to protect their
interests. These occasionally caused disturbances when they fought among themselves, and large riots occurred every few
years. The fact that British administration
for the settlement came from India probably explains the slack control. In 1867,
Singapore came under the direction of the
Colonial Office in London, but they practiced little direct control. The importance
of Singapore as a trading center fluctuated,
especially with the establishment of Hong
Kong as the major port of egress from
China, but with the opening of the Suez
Canal and the increase in trade from Australia and New Zealand, the Straits Settlements became profitable enterprises.

Britain controlled the island and its success up to the outbreak of World War II,
after which the situation changed.

See also East Indies, Dutch Occupation of
the [92]; Singapore and Malaya, Japanese Conquest of [189].

References: Hahn, Emily, *Raffles of Singapore, a Biography* (Garden City, NY:
Doubleday & Co., 1946); Ryan, N. J., *A
History of Malaysia and Singapore* (London: Oxford University Press, 1976).

## 144 SOUTH AFRICA, BRITISH OCCUPATION OF

The southern portion of the African continent was the last to attract serious attention from Europeans. It is not surprising
that the Dutch were the first to settle
people there, because they had most of the
shipping going around the Cape of Good
Hope en route to the East Indies. They
established a way station there in 1652,
from which a colony began to grow. The
victualing station needed farmers to provide food and soldiers to provide protection, so a number of Dutch moved in to
begin a new life of farming, ranching, or
hunting. The inhabitants called themselves
Boers, the Dutch word for farmer. Eventually, the Boers expanded their population
and moved northward, pressing back the
native population with mixed results: The
Hottentots became laborers, the Bushmen
became targets of genocide, and the numerous Bantu tribes, such as the Zulus and
Matabele, became rivals for control of the
land.

When French forces occupied the Netherlands in 1795, the British responded by
occupying the Dutch colony at the Cape.
Increased British trade with India could
not be threatened by French forces in

southern Africa, though the British saw no economic value in the colony itself. Still, they took it as their own in 1806, and this was confirmed in the peace process in Europe after Napoleon's defeat.

Keeping the colony would not prove nearly as easy as gaining it. When the British began to export settlers to the colony, the Boers resented the intrusion. They had grown accustomed to settling huge ranches, and did not want a foreign population robbing them of what they considered their lands. The British could not abide the relationship the Boers had with the Hottentots, which was one of virtual slavery. When the new British administration began to act in favor of native rights, the Boers decided it was time to move. They pushed northeastward, paralleling the coast, into the area known as Natal, recently left empty because of native wars. When the British would not or could not commit sufficient forces to defend the frontiers expanded by the Boers, the Dutch saw it as "kaffir-loving," a policy of favoring "colored" over white. They decided to move again, this time far enough to get away from British politicians. Thus began the Great Trek.

Beginning in 1835, 14,000 people ultimately migrated into the veld land farther north, lands occupied by native groups who did not want to leave. The Zulu and Ndebele tribes resisted, and their societies, which emphasized military training, were willing to fight the Boers at every turn. Superior firepower became the deciding factor, and small Boer republics sprang up wherever they settled to raise their crops and herd their livestock. The Boers became even more conservative in their views: They believed that they were a people chosen by God, the land was theirs to take, and the natives were an inferior race permissible to use or abuse as they saw fit. When the British annexed Natal in 1842,

some Boers stayed, while others moved even farther north across the Vaal River, establishing the Transvaal Republic.

The two white communities began to tolerate each other. Then, in 1867, major changes came to the area: Diamonds were discovered just south of the Vaal River. There was a mining rush, mainly British, and the Boers were able to keep few claims. The new wealth created problems. The discoveries were in territory claimed by both Boer trekkers and British; the British bought out the Dutch claims just south of the Vaal. The main labor force in the mines consisted of natives who, though they worked for much less than white miners, still made plenty of money—money they spent on firearms to take back to their tribes. The traditional hostility between native and Boer grew sharper, and British policies were sufficiently irregular to keep the whites hostile to each other as well. The Boers believed the British were too conciliatory to the natives, yet, at the same time, the British occasionally treated the Natal tribes much like the Americans treated their native tribes during the westward expansion, putting them on reservations, then persecuting them when the whites wanted the land. As native labor became more in demand, and therefore more expensive, both the needs of white businessmen and the fears of black power grew.

In 1852 the British recognized the independence of the Transvaal, but the Dutch did not manage their republic too well. Owing to expensive campaigns against local tribes and a defaulted foreign loan, the republic was in dire financial straits. In 1877 the British offered to annex the Transvaal, delivering the Boers from their financial problems and providing protection on the frontiers. The local government reluctantly agreed to temporarily accept the annexation while their representatives traveled to London to get it reversed. The reversal did not happen, but the Boers were in no financial or military state to halt the course of events. Britain wanted the Cape Colony to federate all the lands available, much as in Canada, and the Transvaal was necessary for that goal. If the British could establish a united native policy throughout the federation, certainly peace and prosperity would follow. Also necessary was domination over all native lands. The British invaded Zululand in 1878–1879 on trumped-up excuses and established control there; the Pedi were defeated and scattered a few months later, and most other tribes saw the futility of resistance. Momentarily at least, the British had made good on their promise to protect the Boers from hostile natives.

With no native threat, the Boers believed the British presence had become unnecessary, and that the Transvaal should have its independence restored. When the British refused ("As long as the sun shines over South Africa, the British flag will fly over Pretoria"), the Boers began cleaning their rifles. After the British provoked an incident over a Boer who would not pay his taxes, the Boers began organizing. Under the leadership of Paul Kruger (nicknamed "Oom," Dutch for uncle), who had gone to London to protest the annexation, the Boers declared their independence in November 1880. They raised a force of 7,000 men, three times the number the British had in Transvaal, sent men to besiege British garrisons in Transvaal towns, and began to fight a guerrilla war. In November, December, and January they fought three battles, and in each defeated a superior British detachment. The embarrassed British government hastily approved negotiations to give the Boers independence. The general on the spot, Sir George Colley, disagreed with the government's offer and decided to press on. He died, along with the majority of his force of 400 men,

at the battle of Majuba Hill in late January 1881. Kruger accepted the offer to negotiate, and in late March the Transvaal was again independent, though the British did retain the right to direct the Boers' foreign policy.

Gold was soon discovered in the Transvaal. In order to exploit the mines, foreign (Uitlander) engineers had to be imported, and they tended to be British. By the late 1890s a large British population had migrated to the Boer republic to work the mines. Despite the wealth they now enjoyed, the Boers remained wary. British expansionists, led by gold and diamond magnate Cecil Rhodes, had acquired land to the north of the Transvaal, effectively seizing the mineral rights, but more importantly denying the Boers room to expand. With British territory above and below them, the Boers felt sure they would soon be obliged to defend their lands. When Rhodes sponsored a raid into the Transvaal, hoping futilely for a British uprising to grab the country and its riches for the empire, the fears of the Dutch farmers were confirmed. They responded by further denying political rights to Uitlanders in their country, keeping them in the position of second-class citizens. The native population, of course, remained beyond the hope of even that lowly status.

This was not a social position the British were prepared to accept. They appealed to the British government to protect them and, desiring not only wealth but the geographic position of Boer lands, the government responded. By controlling Egypt and having a dominant position in countries to the south, a transcontinental Cape-to-Cairo railroad was possible. This would mean wealth and political power for the British Empire if they could build it, but to do so they needed to gain control of the right-of-way through the Boer republics of the Transvaal and the Orange Free State on its southern border. Additionally, there were soldiers in the British army, still chafing from the defeat the Boers dealt them in 1880–1881, who would truly savor revenge. The British public received a steady diet of anti-Boer propaganda to prepare them for the war that seemed inevitable.

Paul Kruger, now president of the Transvaal, saw the British designs and responded by launching preemptive attacks against British towns in Natal and along the southern and western borders of the Orange Free State. If the Boers could control Natal (which they believed the British stole from them after the Great Trek), the British would have a difficult time bringing in reinforcements. After all, the Cape Colony, even though long under British rule, had a Boer majority among its population.

Britain was confident that the Boers could again be easily overcome. Instead, British garrisons were quickly besieged, and Boer forces drove 100 miles into the Cape Colony. When the British finally began to arrive in large numbers in November, the Boers stopped to consolidate. When the British attacked in December, the Boers thrashed them three times in one week, and by Christmas, the British had suffered 7,000 casualties. The growing British forces, however, ultimately forced the Boers to resort to guerrilla tactics. As the British made their way into Boer territory, the enemy melted into the hills and harassed them with ambushes. The British responded with the one proven method of dealing with a guerrilla movement. As Mao Tse-tung would later write, the population is the sea in which the guerrilla fish swims. Take away the population, and the guerrilla has no one to provide food, information, or refuge. The British rounded up the Boer population of women and children and placed them in concentration camps from which they could provide no assistance. Then they began a slow, expensive process to literally corral the Boers, crisscrossing the countryside with barbed-wire fencing and regularly placed strong points. By building more and more fences, they gradually lessened the area inside which the Boers could operate, and any attempt to break through brought quick responses from the strongpoints. With a smaller and smaller area in which to operate and gather supplies, the Boers were finally starved into submission.

The fighting went on until May 1902, when the exhausted Boers reached the bitter end and signed a peace treaty. They were promised self-government sometime in the future plus immediate financial relief for the losses they suffered—and losses there were. Owing to poor initial management of the concentration camps, huge numbers of civilians died from typhoid, dysentery, and measles: some 28,000 white women and children out of a total of just over 111,000; 14,000 out of almost 44,000 native internees; and 7,000 Boer men killed in combat. The British lost 20,000 men and spent £200 million, but they had control over the land. The Boers and the British ultimately managed a relatively peaceful coexistence. When World War I came in 1914, the South African contingent helping the British was led by Jan Smuts, who had been one of the primary commanders of Boer forces.

The Peace of Vereeniging, which ended the South African War of 1899–1902, had long-lasting aftereffects. The treaty stated that the native population would receive political rights after the nation received its independence, without spelling out exactly when "after" would be. When provincial autonomy was granted in 1906 to the Transvaal and in 1907 to the Orange Free State, the Boer population controlled the government in those provinces, as well as in Natal and the Cape Colony. They also dominated the gold and silver mining, and therein lay a problem. Britain needed the wealth the mines could produce, but the British people had a difficult time with the Boers' policies in regard to their labor, both natives and imported Asians. The Boers kept them in a state of semislavery and allowed them no political rights. The British government tried to protect the rights of the abused, but could not legally do so because they had granted self-government to the provinces. When the provinces united in 1910 to create the Union of South Africa, the descendants of the ultraconservative, God-fearing, self-perceived Chosen People instituted the policy of apartheid that made the country infamous in the latter half of the twentieth century. The country grew to become the wealthiest in Africa, a wealth built on gold and diamonds, but the native population was not included in the spoils.

*See also* Zulus, Expansion of [111]; Egypt, Napoleon Buonaparte [118]; British Occupation of [132]; Indians of North America, U.S. Conquest of [134]; Zululand, British Invasion of [146].

References: Nuttingham, Anthony, *Scramble for Africa: The Great Trek to the Boer War* (London: Constable, 1970); Pakenham, Thomas, *The Scramble for Africa: White Man's Conquest of the Dark Continent* (New York: Random House, 1991); Porter, Bernard, *The Lion's Share* (London: Longman, 1975).

## 145 WAR OF THE PACIFIC

In 1874–1879 the South American nation of Chile experienced a depression caused by falling copper and wheat prices, a dropping off of exports, and rising unemployment. The only bright spot in the economy was the expanding nitrate business, but its mining eventually caused war between Chile and its neighbors, Peru and Bolivia. Nitrates were mined in the Atacama Desert along the Chile-Bolivia border. Most of the work was done by Anglo-Chilean companies, which operated in the Bolivian province of Antofagasta and the Peruvian province of Tarapacá. An 1866 treaty between Bolivia and Chile set their border at the 24th parallel, with both countries able to mine nitrates between the 23d and 25th parallels; tax revenues collected by either country along the frontier would be split with the other country. This taxation arrangement was altered in 1874 when Chile agreed to give up its share of Bolivian tax revenue in return for a promise that taxes on Chilean profits in Bolivia would not be raised for 25 years.

Though Chile had no border with Peru, aggressive Chilean miners pushed into the Peruvian desert to mine nitrates. By 1875 some 10,000 people were employed in mining and subsidiary operations in the Peruvian Tarapacá desert region. Peru had thus far said little about the Anglo-Chilean operations in its province, but in 1875 a faltering economy forced the Peruvian government to nationalize the nitrate companies. The Peruvian government paid for the companies with government bonds paying 8 percent, payable in two years. When the bonds came due, they were unable to honor their financial commitments and the bonds' value plummeted. The Anglo-Chilean companies were able to absorb the loss of the Peruvian assets, but when the Bolivians decided in 1878 to raise taxes on the Chileans along the frontier in violation of the 1876 agreement, the loss of profits was too much to take. Chile refused to pay the higher taxes even when Bolivia threatened to nationalize the operations as the Peruvians had done. According to the 1876 agreement, an arbitrator should have been called in to handle the dispute, but Bolivia refused.

The Bolivian government felt secure in its ability to back up its threats because of an 1874 secret mutual-defense treaty with Peru, but the Bolivians failed to consult the Peruvians in advance. In February 1879, Bolivia nationalized the mining companies, and Chilean troops went into action. On 14 February, they occupied the port of Antofagasta against no opposition; soon they were in control of the entire province. Not wanting to get involved in the fighting, Peru offered to mediate a peace settlement. Chile then learned of the secret treaty and, accusing the Peruvians of duplicity, declared war on them on 5 April 1879.

The combined Bolivian and Peruvian effort appeared daunting, especially as they had a combined population twice that of Chile, and Peru had a fairly good navy. However, Chile had a stronger and more stable central government, a more motivated population, a well-trained army, and a navy armed with two modern ironclads. Also, the main theater of operations was handier to Chile; the Bolivians had to cross the Andes, and the Peruvians had to cross the desert. All three countries were in economic trouble, but Chile was in the best financial shape and had the assistance of the British because the mining operations were mainly theirs. Both Bolivia and Peru had defaulted on British loans and had angered the British by nationalizing the companies, so they had no qualms about supporting Chile.

The key battle of the war took place at sea on 8 October 1879, when the Chilean ironclads captured a Peruvian commerce raider, the *Huascar*, that had been hurting their trade and logistical operations. With control of the sea, Chile could supply their troops more efficiently, and the army was soon marching through Bolivian territory into Peru. Bolivia withdrew from the conflict in mid-1880 when Chilean troops oc-cupied large parts of Peru. After a difficult battle, the Chileans captured the capital city of Lima in January 1881, effectively winning the war. Peruvians continued to fight a guerrilla war for two years, but on 20 October 1883 they gave up and signed the Treaty of Ancón. The treaty gave Chile the province of Tarapacá forever and two other provinces for ten years, after which a referendum was to be held to determine their nationality. The referendum never took place, but in 1929 the two countries agreed to return the province of Tacna to Peru while Chile kept the province of Arica.

The Bolivians signed an armistice with Chile in April 1884, in which they ceded the province of Antofagasta to Chile, but cession was not official until 1904, when a treaty was finally signed. That treaty obliged the Chileans to pay an indemnity and build a railroad from the Bolivian capital of La Paz to the coast of Arica, which was completed in 1913.

With their army already mobilized, the Chilean government decided to use it to deal with the Araucanian Indians, a tribe that had been fighting for their land since colonial times. Hopelessly outnumbered and outsupplied, after two years the Indians were forced to sign a treaty in 1883 that placed them on reservations, though they were allowed to maintain tribal government and laws. Chile consolidated the rugged territory that had been the Araucanian homeland. With Peru bankrupt and Bolivia isolated, Chile became the strongest nation on South America's west coast. Control of the area's copper and nitrate meant an improving income, but close ties to Britain kept them from enjoying it totally. Chile decided to honor the Peruvian bonds issued when the Tarapacá mines were nationalized, and British speculators had been buying them up ever since Peru could not fulfill them. Thus, the British were able to control 70 percent of the nitrate production by 1890, as well as profit from their own construction of banks, railroads, and subsidiary businesses. Longstanding ties between Britain and the Chilean upper class made the British acquisition smoother, and some Chileans were able to profit from investments in British concerns.

References: Keen, Benjamin, and Mark Waserman, A Short History of Latin America (Boston: Houghton Mifflin, 1984); Loveman, Brian, The Legacy of Hispanic Capitalism (New York: Oxford University Press, 1979); Sater, William, Chile and the War of the Pacific (Lincoln: University of Nebraska Press, 1986).

## ZULULAND, BRITISH INVASION OF

**146**

Queen Victoria's reign (1837–1901) marked the high point of British expansion and colonialism, with not a single year in which her soldiers were not engaged in combat somewhere in the empire. Of the many tribes the British fought in Africa, none were as feared and respected as the Zulus, the last great native empire on the continent.

The British army was equipped with the latest arms and technology. The officer corps came from Britain's elite, while the enlisted men were the lowest of society, suffering harsh discipline during their long term of service. The rank and file were among the best soldiers of their era, but the quality of the officers varied widely because promotion was a matter of wealth rather than ability, a factor of some consequence in the war against the Zulus. The British were better armed than their enemies and relied on superior firepower to compensate for their inferior numbers. The typical British strategy was to form one large or several small squares, each side two to four ranks deep, to provide virtually continuous fire. The greatest handicap was the British logistical system. Transporting the army's supplies required huge numbers of wagons and animals, often overloaded with officers' personal effects to make the campaign trail more comfortable.

The Zulu army was created by the great chieftain Shaka, who introduced a number of reforms that increased the army's ability. Shaka outlawed the use of hand axes and throwing spears, introducing as the main weapon the *iklwa*, a short-shafted stabbing spear with a long, leaf-shaped blade. With the *iklwa* and a five-foot-high shield, the Zulus became masters of hand-to-hand fighting. Another favorite weapon was the knobkerrie, or *iwisa*, a club made from ironwood. The Zulu warrior was trained to ignore hunger, cold, and fatigue, and to go barefoot in order to be able to move more rapidly in battle. The standard battle formation was patterned after the charging buffalo: The central body was the head, followed by reserves immediately behind (the loins), and two flanking units were the horns. The tactic was to hold the enemy with the head while the horns attempted a double envelopment.

The Zulu military system was an integral part of Zulu society and culture, and training started early in life. Boys age 13 to 18 were organized into military kraals where they served three years as cadets, practicing military skills while herding cattle and working in the fields. When their training was over, they went to a regiment assigned to them by the king, where they would await his permission to get married. This would occur around age 35, at which point the warrior would leave the regiment and build a homestead.

The principal reason for war among the Zulus was cattle. Cattle played an

The battle of Ulundi inside the square

important part in Zulu life by providing milk, raw materials, and meat for ceremonies. All cattle captured in battle became the property of the king, who distributed them to men who had reached marrying age and had proved themselves in battle. The importance of putting an age restriction on marriage can now be understood. Had there been none, not enough cattle would have been available for all those who wanted to marry, and Zulu society would have broken down. This cultural practice would become a key factor in the outbreak of hostilities with Britain.

The British goal in 1871 was to form a confederation of the various white colonies in South Africa and create an economy directed to the benefit of England. To accomplish this, the British government sent Sir Henry Bartle Frere, a distinguished colonial officer, to become governor of the Cape Colony. By accepting the position, Frere hoped to advance his personal fortunes and status, but such was not to be. Frere's first attempts to bring about the desired confederation met opposition from the local Dutch/Boer population, who threatened armed resistance. Further, in July 1878 a British commission appointed to decide a boundary dispute between the Zulus and the Transvaal found in favor of the native population. If Frere enforced this decision, it would increase white resistance and make the Boers even more angry. On top of these factors, many of the conquered African tribes pointed out that the British had failed to conquer the Zulus. Frere felt that in order to control those tribes, the Zulus must be defeated. All in all, a successful war against the Zulus seemed to be the answer to his problems.

On 11 December 1878, Frere issued an intentionally unreasonable communiqué to King Cetshwayo and the Zulu nation. He demanded the complete dismissal of the entire Zulu army, the discontinuation of the

Zulu military system, and permission for Zulu males to marry when they desired. Frere demanded an answer in 21 days, knowing it could not be fulfilled. King Cetshwayo was in a difficult position; it was impossible for him to disband the army, as it was not assembled and had not been for 20 years. Unlike European armies, the Zulus did not spend their time in barracks waiting for action. To fulfill Frere's demands would bring about the end of the Zulu social system, as there were not enough cattle to go around and no more could be acquired without going to war. As Cetshwayo put it, he felt like a man "trying to ward off a falling tree." On 11 January the ultimatum expired unanswered. The British army was immediately on the march.

The British commander, Lord Chelmsford, invaded Zululand along a front of about 200 miles, aiming for the Zulu capital at Ulundi. Three columns invaded at different points, while two more stayed on the border in reserve. The first contact came at Isandlwana. A force of 20,000 Zulus marched to engage Chelmsford's column of 4,700. Chelmsford ordered that their position not be fortified, contrary to the advice of several of his officers. He then split his force, leading half to search out the Zulus and leaving the other half to defend the overly large baggage train. On 22 January, the 1,300 British troops left behind were overrun and slaughtered. The greatest British liability—their arrogance—was exposed. At Isandlwana they learned a hard lesson, one they would not forget.

By the time Chelmsford returned to find his camp in ruins, the Zulus had already moved on. They attacked a small force of 130 men at a mission station on the Buffalo River called Rorke's Drift. Here the discipline of the British soldier showed at its best, as they repeatedly beat back attacks over a period of two days. Use of

the infantry square and firing in ranks, tactics that had not been used at Isandlwana, proved too much for the Zulus to overcome.

That same firepower and discipline proved decisive on 4 July at Ulundi, the Zulu capital, when the main Zulu army was defeated. Cetshwayo escaped, but his military power was gone. The British victory at Ulundi was credited to Lord Chelmsford, but he was in the process of being superseded by Sir Garnet Wolseley, who presided over the destruction of Zulu independence. Cetshwayo was captured a month after the battle at Ulundi and sent to England, where he met with Queen Victoria. After two years, he was returned to Zululand as king, but without any real power. In 1897, Zululand was annexed into Natal Province; there was a final attempt at freedom in 1906, but the rebellion was quickly suppressed. In the 1970s some of the historical Zululand was incorporated into the province of KwaZulu, and then remerged to form the province of KwaZulu/Natal for the multiracial elections of 1994.

The Zulus, who had once dominated southern Africa, became just another native tribe under British rule. To this day they maintain a tribal heritage, and they played a significant role in the Republic of South Africa's first postapartheid elections, but their trademark cowskin shields and short stabbing spears are tourist items now rather than the weapons of war that shocked the British nation in 1879.

See also Zulus, Expansion of [111].

References: Farwell, Byron, Queen Victoria's Little Wars (New York: Harper & Row, 1972); Morris, Donald, The Washing of the Spears (New York: Simon & Schuster, 1965).

# PART 7
# THE TWENTIETH CENTURY

The numbers on the map correspond to entry numbers in the text.

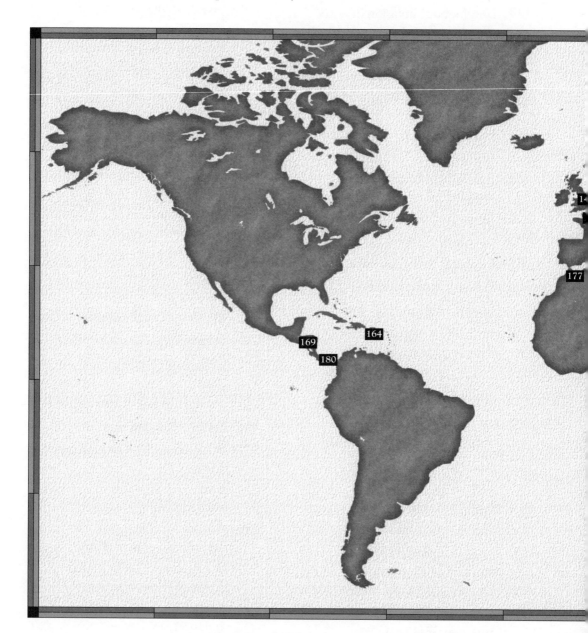

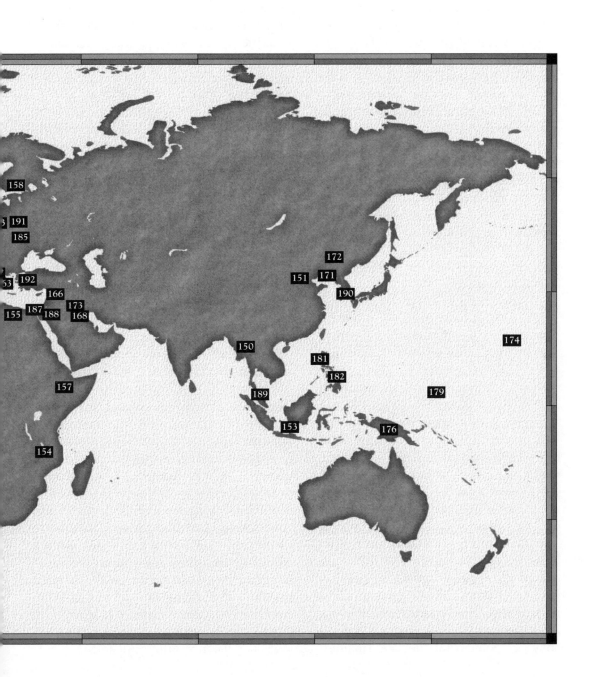

# ALBANIA, ITALIAN CONQUEST OF

**147**

In the wake of World War I, Albania came under the leadership of President Ahmed Zogu, who declared himself King Zog. Though he attempted to bring about some modernization and reforms, Zog tied the country to fascist Italy. In 1926 the two countries signed the Pact of Tiranë, in which Italy promised to maintain the status quo in Albania. The following year the two entered into a 20-year defense alliance, which had the effect of binding the weaker Albania to the stronger Italy. The Italians took advantage of this by making themselves indispensable to Albania, giving them no-interest loans and gifts in return for Albanian acceptance of Italian technical aid, military aid and advisers, economic investment, and exploitation of Albanian natural resources. Albania was viewed by most of the world as almost an Italian possession.

As fascism began to spread in the late 1930s, Albania began to fear for its independence, such as it was. When Germany occupied Czechoslovakia in the spring of 1939, Mussolini felt that his ally was overshadowing him and that Italy needed to reassert its aggressive nature. Albania seemed a natural acquisition. When rumors flew in the world press about tensions between the two countries, Mussolini denied it, though plans were already under way for military action. Three Italian warships anchored off the Albanian coast on 6 April, and troops landed the next day.

Fighting was brief. Within a week Italy had installed a puppet government, which offered the crown to Italy's King Victor Emmanuel III. Albania became a part of Italy; foreign ambassadors were sent home, Albanian ambassadors recalled, and the army incorporated into the Italian military.

Because Italy's dominant role in Albanian affairs had long been recognized, most countries had no complaint about Italy's actions, though perceptions varied. Mussolini saw the invasion as yet another step on his road to reestablishing the Roman Empire. Further, he wanted to establish a presence in the Balkans as a counter to Hitler in Czechoslovakia, and he hoped the countries of the region would prefer him to the Nazis. He also hoped to gain British and French recognition of this anti-Nazi move, and possibly establish closer ties. Britain and France refused to see it that way, seemingly rebuffing Mussolini, while Hitler heaped praise on his ally and appeared to be Italy's only friend. Yugoslavia had no qualms about an Italian invasion next door because they hoped to work with the Italians to gain some border concessions. Greece had similar views; once assured that Italy had no designs on the island of Corfu, Greece also hoped to expand at Albania's expense. Within Albania itself, few people missed the exiled King Zog.

Relations between Britain, France, and Italy remained cordial until the Italian invasion of France in May 1940. With relations broken, Britain began to plan possible support of resistance movements in Albania. This proved difficult; even though the population did not care for the elites placed in power by the Italians, they had no leadership to organize resistance. Zog had so little support in the country that Britain refused to recognize him as head of a government-in-exile. Not until Italy attacked Britain's ally, Greece, from Albanian bases did any serious planning take place to begin a guerrilla movement in the country. Albanians themselves were of mixed emotions; some appreciated the opportunity to regain territory in southern Yugoslavia populated by ethnic Albanians.

Ultimately the most effective resistance movement was that of the Communists. A Communist party had existed in Albania since the 1920s, but even they were split into factions. Only after Josip Tito sent agents from Yugoslavia did the Communist resistance become effective. When Mussolini was deposed and Italy resigned from the war in September 1943, German forces occupied the country. A Soviet military mission arrived in September 1944, and Communist power grew. As the war progressed, they gained control of the southern part of the country and began to make war against not only fleeing Nazis but also other, more nationalistic resistance groups. By the end of 1944 most of the country was in their hands. Ignored by the major powers in wartime conferences, Albania ultimately came under the control of the Communists because no other group had any real organization or ability to challenge them. A Communist government was established in April 1945, and recognized by the major powers. Of those nations falling under Communist dominance in the postwar world, Albania fared more poorly than most. It is regarded as the least advanced, least economically viable country in the Balkans, if not all of Europe. Even with the fall of the Soviet Union, Albania seems to be the forgotten satellite.

See also Czechoslovakia, Nazi Occupation of [152].

References: Barker, Elizabeth, British Policy in Southeast Europe in the Second World War (New York: Barnes & Noble, 1976); Haines, C. G., and R. J. S. Hoffman, The Origins and Background of World War II (New York: Oxford University Press, 1947); Logorici, Anton, The Albanians (Boulder, CO: Westview Press, 1977);

Lowe, C. J., and F. Marzari, Italian Foreign Policy, 1870–1940 (London: Routledge & Kegan Paul, 1975).

## 148 AUSTRIA, NAZI OCCUPATION OF

In his book Mein Kampf, Adolf Hitler stated that it was necessary for all German-speaking peoples to be under one government, and this outlook dominated his pre–World War II foreign policy. He was able to slowly extend German power in the middle 1930s despite the fact that the Versailles Treaty, which ended World War I, was designed specifically to keep Germany weak for as long as possible. First, an area known as the Saar, bordering France, returned to Germany. It had been under French occupation since World War I, but in a 1935 plebiscite the population voted ten to one to return to German control. In March 1936, the Nazis occupied the Rhineland, the area between the French border and the Rhine River. Under the terms of the Versailles Treaty, this area, along with a 50-mile-wide strip of land east of the Rhine, would remain demilitarized. When France and Britain refused to challenge Germany's action, Hitler felt confident he could implement his policy of expansion with no foreign interference.

Austria was Hitler's first target for expansion outside Germany itself. He wanted the land of his birth under German control, and supported the establishment of an Austrian Nazi party to lay the groundwork. In July 1934, Austrian Nazis assassinated the Austrian chancellor, Englebert Dolfuss, in an abortive attempt to stage a coup. Italy's dictator, Benito Mussolini, threatened to intervene to protect Austria, and this, coupled with Germany's lack of a strong military, forced Hitler to refrain from

A Nazi rally during the occupation of Austria.

grabbing power. Instead he moved to bring Germany and Italy closer together, a strategy that worked when he was the only world leader to support Italy's invasion of Ethiopia. After the signing of an alliance, Mussolini would not interfere in Hitler's moves against Austria.

Like Dolfuss, new chancellor Kurt von Schuschnigg was a virtual dictator in Austria. Knowing Hitler's aims and fearing the growing Nazi movement in his country, Schuschnigg tried placating Hitler, making sure nothing happened that Hitler could turn into an excuse for an invasion. He seemed to be worrying over nothing. In May 1935 Hitler publicly stated that he had no desire to violate Austrian sovereignty, and in July 1936 he signed an agreement with Austria, reaffirming that stance. The agreement, however, had some secret clauses in which the Austrian Nazi party would provide some members to the Austrian cabinet.

By early 1938, Hitler was ready to bring Austria under his control. He met with Schuschnigg in February and, after accusing Austria of subverting German progress for generations, demanded that Schuschnigg resign and appoint members of the Austrian Nazi party to most of the key positions in the government. After being subjected to a two-hour tirade and a threat of invasion, the Austrian chancellor agreed. He returned to Vienna, but rather than immediately implement Hitler's directives, he called a national plebiscite. This infuriated Hitler, who began to make good on his threat to invade Austria if Schuschnigg did not follow orders. Hitler called in his military commanders and ordered them to mass the army on the Austrian border.

By 11 March the troops were on the march, and at dawn on 12 March they were in position. Seeing that the invasion would take place and not being prepared to oppose it, Schuschnigg resigned, and German troops crossed the border to an enthusiastic reception. Hitler entered the country not long after. He spent the night in Linz and visited his mother's grave, then traveled to Vienna, where he spoke to a huge crowd. Hitler announced that Austria was henceforth incorporated into the German Reich, and many Austrians, especially the young, welcomed the idea.

The "invasion" of Austria proved valuable to Hitler and his army. They discovered that their military was not as well organized or supplied as they had assumed, and they set about to address that deficiency. Hitler was reinforced in his assumptions that Britain and France would do nothing to oppose his expansionary dreams, just as they had done nothing substantial when he reacquired the Saar and Rhineland. This lack of action certainly fueled his ambition to bring about the occupation of Czechoslovakia, which occurred six months after the Austrian escapade.

Austria became a German state, giving up its independence, and the new Nazi government set about persecuting anyone who had opposed the Austrian Nazi party prior to the *Anschluss,* or "joining." Such persons became subject to the whims of the Nazi government and liable for service in the German military, and Austrian Jews received the same fate as the Jews of Germany and the remainder of Europe. Though little if any fighting took place in Austria during World War II, the country was occupied by Allied soldiers and an Allied administration after the war.

*See also* Czechoslovakia, Nazi Occupation of [152]; Ethiopia, Italian Invasion of [157]; Hitler, Adolf [165]; Rhineland, Nazi Occupation of the [184].

References: Churchill, Winston, *The Gathering Storm* (Boston: Houghton Mifflin, 1948); Payne, Robert, *The Life and Death of Adolph Hitler* (New York: Praeger, 1973); Shirer, William, *The Rise and Fall of the Third Reich* (New York: Simon & Schuster, 1960).

## BRITAIN, NAZI INVASION OF (BATTLE OF BRITAIN)

**149**

By June 1940 Hitler had conquered or placed under his control most of Europe. With France in his hands, Hitler was in a position to attack his last remaining opponent—Great Britain. Luckily, Britain had been able to recover most of its army via the Dunkirk evacuation, but the problem facing Hitler was not with the British army, but with that centuries-old British defensive barrier, the English Channel. He believed he could defeat the army if only the Channel could be crossed, but the Royal Navy was ready to bar that route. Hence, Hitler had to neutralize the British fleet. He lacked the naval power to face the British head-to-head, but his battle-tested air force, the Luftwaffe, should be able to clear the Channel of British warships long enough to complete his planned invasion, Operation Sea Lion. This plan, however, brought up yet another obstacle—the Royal Air Force. The Germans needed air superiority to defeat the Royal Navy in order to cross the Channel, so air operations must precede all else. The Luftwaffe began to prepare for what would become known as the Battle of Britain.

Britain had an air force approximately half the size of Germany's, but the British had a technological advantage. Within the past few months, British scientists had perfected radar, with which they could detect German air attacks in advance. This early warning system would make constant standing patrols over the coast unneces-

sary, and allow the Royal Air Force sufficient time to assemble defending aircraft over German targets. Learning of radar and its abilities, Luftwaffe chief Hermann Goering attempted first to knock the radar antennas out of action. Though his Stuka dive-bombers had the pinpoint accuracy to accomplish this, their slow speed made them easy targets for British fighters, and the attacks on the towers were rarely successful. Another strategy had to be developed.

Working on the assumption that the Royal Air Force could not resist if their airfields were out of operation, the airfields became the Luftwaffe's next targets. Intensive bombing of the airfields of southeastern England proceeded through the rest of the summer. This strategy was more successful than the radar attacks, and the British ability to maintain their aircraft suffered when hangar facilities were destroyed. However, the airfields had dirt runways, which made them easy to repair, and the planes continued to use the fields even if aircraft maintenance was hampered. With the Royal Air Force continuing to operate, German authorities decided to target aircraft factories also. If British aircraft could not be replaced, then superior German numbers would soon wear them down. This tactic proved very effective, and soon the British were in desperate straits.

The major change in German strategy that ultimately saved Britain came in response to an air raid on Berlin in August. Enraged that the British would attack civilian targets, Hitler ordered that England be repaid in kind. Attacks on the airfields and factories were called off to focus on British cities. This decision took pressure off the factories and the Royal Air Force, which could now replace their losses and improve aircraft maintenance and repair.

The blockade around England closes as German *recce* (spotting) and
fighter aircraft fly above the English Channel coast

Hitler's decision to give up his successful war of attrition with the Royal Air Force in favor of the negligible results of bombing population centers guaranteed that he would not achieve air superiority. Without it, the Germans could not control the Channel, and therefore could not invade. By mid-September it was too late in the year to attempt a Channel crossing; Operation Sea Lion was postponed, never to be revived. Much like the attempted invasion by the Spanish Armada more than three centuries earlier, the failed invasion attempt in 1940 had long-term effects. As long as the British Isles remained free, they could be used as the staging point for the Allied war effort for the remainder of the war. Had Hitler taken Britain, it would have been difficult if not impossible for the United States to intervene in Europe, and the Third Reich probably would have had much more than a 12-year life.

See also England, Spanish Invasion of (Spanish Armada) [93]; France, Nazi Invasion of [161].

References: Hough, Richard, and Denis Richards, *The Battle of Britain* (New York: Norton, 1989); Macksey, Kenneth, *Invasion* (New York: Macmillan, 1980); Wood, Derek, and Derek Dempster, *The Narrow Margin* (New York: Coronet, 1969).

## BURMA, JAPANESE INVASION OF

**150**

In the months prior to the outbreak of hostilities in the Pacific, Burma seemed an unlikely arena for fighting. The land was too rugged and jungle-covered to fight through, or so the British thought. Having only recently become independent from India in 1937, Burma was just beginning to field an army of its own, and it was unprepared for serious combat. As war became imminent, the Burmese army was placed under the control of the British General Staff, but still paid and supported by Burma. When the Japanese finally began the war in early December 1941, total control of the Burmese forces came under the auspices of the Indian army, which had the assignment of defending the country if necessary. The prospects of success against a Japanese attack were minimal: A new and relatively untrained Burmese force, an Indian army weakened by transfers of units to assist Britain in North Africa, and two understrength British brigades seemed to provide little in the way of a defense force. Still, no one believed the Japanese would come.

Japan began the war in command of Indochina and very quickly seized control of Siam (Thailand) by capturing Bangkok on 8 December. Burma seemed safe, because Japanese forces moved southward down the Malay Peninsula toward Singapore. Britain viewed Burma as a giant buffer zone to protect India, but they were unable or unwilling to commit large forces to protect the country, even when they realized the Japanese were coming. To make matters worse, the forces protecting Burma were once again transferred to another command, that of ABDA (American-British-Dutch-Australian), based in Java, and given the task of protecting all of Southeast Asia and Indonesia. The constant shifting of command responsibility made planning virtually impossible.

The Japanese invaded Burma from two sites. On 15 January 1942 a division crossed the border heading north from Victoria Point, the southernmost tip of Burma. Five days later, another division attacked out of Siam west toward Moulmein, a move that would cut off the southern peninsula of Burma. The British-Burmese-Indian forces were stretched too thinly, trying to hold a cordon defense across the entire frontier. At the start of the invasion, one Burmese and one Indian brigade, 8,000–10,000 men, were assigned to protect 500–800 miles of frontier. The troops found themselves quickly outflanked by more mobile Japanese forces, which forced Allied unit after unit to retreat or face annihilation.

The Japanese air forces bombed the capital city of Rangoon, bringing its harbor operations to a gradual halt. The British air defense consisted of 16 obsolescent fighter aircraft, soon supplemented by the American Volunteer Group (AVG), the "Flying Tigers," on loan from the Chinese. The AVG harassed the air raids, but could not stop them. Luckily for the defenders on the ground, the Japanese close air support was not very successful.

Heavily engaged Allied forces fought the Japanese to a standstill, but at such a cost that they could not hold out indefinitely. By mid-February the commander in the field asked permission to withdraw to more defensible positions behind the Sittang River. When finally permitted to withdraw, the troops had to do it under fire and air attack during hot and dry weather, short on food and water. It was a textbook withdrawal, but the Japanese again staged a flanking attack. Light tanks and newly arrived Gurkha troops were rushed in to assist in the ferocious battle for the one major bridge across the Sittang River. Having barely held the Japanese at bay, the British command ordered the bridge destroyed, even though two-thirds of the Indian 17th Division were on the opposite side. Luckily, the Japanese committed more troops to the flanking movement, and most of the men were able to escape across the river.

The Allied forces were exhausted, and pulled back from the Japanese attacks. On 8 March, Rangoon fell, though the defenders managed to extricate themselves shortly before the city was surrounded. The Japanese had the initiative, and the Allies were obliged to pull back toward the Indian frontier.

Chiang Kai-shek offered to supply Chinese troops to assist the Allies, but without logistical support of their own, they had to be supplied with whatever meager aid the British could provide. The American general Joseph Stilwell commanded the Chinese forces, and put himself under the direction of the British commander, General Harold Alexander. The two cooperated closely, but the convoluted chain of command sometimes created delays.

The Japanese attacked northward up three rivers—the Irrawaddy, the Sittang, and the Salween—and the Allied forces, including the Chinese, had to withdraw. By mid-April the retreating Allies were forced to destroy millions of gallons of crude oil stored in tanks at Yenangyaung. With little air power, the British were unable to bring in much reinforcement of supplies, and even the introduction of more Chinese troops in April could not stem the Japanese tide. On 29 April the Japanese captured Lashio. Lashio was the starting point of the Burma Road, the one roadway to carry supplies overland to China, and its capture spelled an end to direct overland aid to China until January 1945.

The Japanese were unable to destroy the Allied forces, but they pushed them out of Burma. The British-Indian-Burmese forces reached the Indian frontier at the perfect time: the monsoonal season. The weather held the Japanese at bay, while the exhausted British and Indian forces reorganized and prepared defensive positions to protect India.

The expected Japanese invasion of India after the monsoon did not materialize. The Japanese seemed content to hold the country and exploit its oil and rubber rather than challenge the mountainous terrain along the Burma-India border. In India, Stilwell and his British counterpart, General Archibald Wavell, trained their men and made plans for reconquest. As they did so, the British tried a new strategy. Orde Wingate, an eccentric British leader, organized and led a guerrilla group into the jungles to harass the Japanese. These "Chindits" survived by air supply, a logistical innovation pioneered by Wingate. The men suffered as they learned how to deal with the jungle and the Japanese, but they succeeded in disrupting Japanese operations. In the meantime, the Americans attempted to keep the flow of supplies into China uninterrupted by flying "over the Hump"—the Himalayas. Until a new overland route could be established starting at the northern Burma town of Ledo, air supply was the only option.

Not until 1944 did the British and Americans feel prepared to go back into Burma, and they planned to enter from the north with a mixed Sino-American force, from the northeast with a Chinese force sent by Chiang Kai-shek, and from the west with the British 14th Army. The invasion was thrown off-schedule by a Japanese attack toward the border. The Japanese intended to strike toward the railroad terminal at Ledo, cutting off the attempts to reestablish land communication with China. After early success, they bogged down around the towns of Imphal and Kohima, where the 14th Army under General William Slim held out through a siege and pushed the Japanese back in the summer of 1944. From then on, the Allied effort went consistently forward. Stilwell and Frank Merrill led the American and Chinese troops southeast from Ledo to Myitkyina, capture of which gave the Allies a forward air base to bypass the Himalayas into China. By the end of 1944, British forces had captured the port of Akyab on Burma's west coast and had crossed the Irawaddy River toward Mandalay, the large rail junction in the center of the country. Too hard-pressed in other theaters to reinforce Burma, the Japanese lost ground consistently. Mandalay fell in April 1945, and Rangoon in May, effectively marking the recapture of the country.

The battle for Burma was one of the most physically trying of the entire war. Fought almost completely in jungle terrain, with which Western soldiers were unfamiliar, the challenges of terrain, weather, and disease sapped the strength of all soldiers. The necessity of recapturing Burma has since been questioned. The main American reason for the operation was the need to reopen the supply line to China. The United States was convinced that China could tie up masses of Japanese troops, though the British thought that Chiang Kai-shek was more concerned with stockpiling weapons to fight the Communist Chinese than to fight the Japanese. The campaign proved the effectiveness of long-range strike forces such as Wingate's Chindits, and the ability of air forces to provide such operations with supplies and medical evacuation. Certainly the need to deny the Japanese the natural resources of the country was important, but the Allies overestimated Japan's intentions. They did not seriously threaten India's frontiers until 1944, and by then Japan's inability to reinforce meant that no major invasion of India could have taken place even had the

British and Commonwealth soldiers not stood fast at Imphal and Kohima.

References: Bidwell, Shelford, *The Chindit War* (New York: Macmillan, 1980); Romanus, Charles, *Time Runs Out in CBI* (Washington, DC: Office of the Chief of Military History, 1958); Slim, William, *Defeat into Victory* (New York: D. McKay, 1961).

## CHINA, JAPANESE INVASION OF

**151**

The onset of the international depression of 1929 led to the seizure of power by militaristic leaders in Japan. Many of these leaders came from a rural background, and the agricultural section of the economy had been hit particularly hard. The farmers' inclination was to blame politicians and the wealthy for the poor economy; thus, the common people supported the new regime, which stressed honor and devotion to the emperor above all else. The militarists saw themselves as the natural saviors of the downtrodden. Historically, victims of economic woes have often sought solution in military action.

In 1931 the Japanese military flexed its muscles and precipitated a conflict that resulted in their occupation and domination of the Chinese province of Manchuria. With that relatively easy victory, they began to think in terms of the total domination not only of China, but also of Southeast Asia, Australia, and India, creating the Greater East Asia Co-prosperity Sphere.

The military launched the Manchurian campaign without the government's knowledge; presented with a fait accompli, the cabinet accepted the army's explanation of events and assumed control of the resource-rich province. Events in 1937 followed much the same path, though it is unclear how much actual planning went into the clash of Japanese and Chinese soldiers at the Marco Polo Bridge along the Sino-Manchurian border near Peking in July 1937. Because of the Boxer Protocol of 1901 (forced upon the Manchu government after the abortive Boxer Rebellion), the Japanese military had the right to engage in maneuvers in the area, and the Japanese had been expanding their economic influence into the area for some time. Though the Japanese had the right to protect their interests, the location and timing of the Marco Polo Bridge incident point to deliberate provocation.

The Japanese worked on the assumption that they would be able to take over the five northern provinces of China without large-scale military action. This proved not to be the case, surprisingly so because the Chinese government under Chiang Kai-shek was fragmented and venal, having a power base that included warlords, gangsters, and drug kingpins. Chiang himself rose to power and kept it through the machinations of the Green Gang boss and the strength of the immensely powerful Soong family, which virtually controlled the banking and taxation systems in China. Through his wife, American-educated Soong May-ling, Chiang had access to the highest levels of American government and society, and it was largely through this connection that he was able to get the assistance he needed to fight the Japanese.

China's government was also engaged in a long-running struggle with the Chinese Communists under Mao Tse-tung, and the Chinese were unsure of how to fight a war on two fronts when neither had much popular support. The result was that the Nationalists under Chiang fought a war of delay and retreat into the vast interior of the country, relying on what support they could gain from outside the country. For a time Chiang was aided by Prussian military advisers, but they left upon the signing of the Tripartite Pact, which allied Germany and Japan in 1940. Soviet pilots were the mainstay of his air force until Claire Chennault and the American Volunteer Group (the "Flying Tigers") arrived in late 1941 to fight his air battles.

Japan blockaded Chinese ports and poured masses of men and matériel into the fight. Japanese casualties were heavy and they lost the occasional battle, but the losses of manpower on the Chinese side were staggering, and the ferocity and wanton killing of unarmed civilians by Japanese soldiers (highlighted by the infamous Rape of Nanking in 1937) left little doubt that the Japanese would prevail. By the end of 1938, the Japanese realized their goal of capturing north and central China; they had also captured the port of Canton in the south.

Of the unconquered territory remaining, a quarter of it was under Communist control in the northwest. The Communists had as much reason to fear the Japanese as the Nationalists, but even though they stopped fighting each other for a time, there was no united effort or cooperative planning against the common enemy.

By July 1939 the Japanese consolidated and extended the territory they had gained in 1938, including additional ground around the ports of Canton and Nanking. Chiang had been driven back into the interior in a series of major retreats, and he finally established a new capital at Chungking. By the time the Japanese navy attacked Pearl Harbor in late 1941, the Japanese perimeter in China had been extended to control the principal Chinese railroad in the south.

When the United States came into the war, economic and military aid for China increased dramatically. Chennault continued his efforts to strengthen and expand the air war against the Japanese, and General Joseph Stilwell was sent to command ground operations. Stilwell was often at odds with Chiang and Chennault, and he was openly contemptuous of the incompetence, corruption, and internal dissension that made Chinese actions and American support ineffective. After Stilwell was replaced by General A. C. Wedemeyer late in the war, the U.S. government expressed strong interest in giving aid to the Communists as a viable alternative to Chiang's regime. Because of political considerations, it was not done, however, and by the end of the war Wedemeyer had succeeded in reshaping the Nationalist armies to the point where they could go on the offensive against the Japanese.

The initial adventuring of the Japanese militarists on the Chinese mainland may not have had the wholehearted support of the entire Japanese government, but the operations in China provided the military machine with the opportunity to test its skills, train its men, and develop its military hardware for the later execution of its expansionist policies, culminating in the confrontation with the United States and its allies in the Pacific theater of operations. Ineffective as the Chinese armies often were, they forced Japan to maintain a large percentage of its force that could otherwise have been used for operations against the advancing Americans.

As stated earlier, the Nationalists and Communists never cooperated in their war against the Japanese, so the war was not long over in 1945 before the two rival factions were fighting each other again. The United States continued to support Chiang Kai-shek, but that support lessened as time went by, and the Nationalist leadership proved no less corrupt after the war than before or during it. In September 1949,

Mao's Communist forces finally forced the Nationalists to abandon the country and set up a government-in-exile on the island of Formosa. The United States continued to recognize their claim as the legitimate government of all the Chinese, even though many countries extended recognition to the Communists as the de facto government on the mainland. This difference in recognition has provided some interesting times in the United Nations, because China has a permanent seat on the Security Council. Mao Tse-tung established himself as not only the leader of China, but virtually its god, and his personal policies or whims affected tens of millions of individuals through economic policies, purges of political rivals, and the occasional foreign military venture. Japan's invasion may have postponed Mao's seizure of power in China, but the years of struggle endured by the common Chinese citizen certainly aided his consolidation of power, if for no other reason than as an end to years of fighting and destruction.

—Ed Davis

See also Manchuria, Japanese Invasion of (1931) [172]; South Korea, North Korean Invasion of (Korean War) [190].

References: Hi, Hsi-sheng, *Nationalist China at War* (Ann Arbor: University of Michigan Press, 1982); Liu, F. F., *A Military History of Modern China* (Princeton, NJ: Princeton University Press, 1956); Tuchman, Barbara, *Stilwell and the American Experience in China* (New York: Macmillan, 1970).

## 152 CZECHOSLOVAKIA, NAZI OCCUPATION OF

After the successful Nazi occupation of Austria in March 1938, Hitler focused his attention on Czechoslovakia in accordance with his policy, spelled out in *Mein Kampf,* of bringing all German-speaking people under one government. The far western area of Czechoslovakia, the Sudetenland, had a large German minority, and Hitler claimed they were being treated unequally by the Czech government. Within a few weeks of the Austrian *Anschluss,* Hitler had his generals working on invasion plans; meanwhile, his agents in the Sudetenland were engaged in a propaganda campaign to blow out of proportion any slights the Czechs may have inflicted on Germans.

The Czech government followed two strategies: Negotiate with Germans in the province, and make sure the defense treaty with France would be honored. The German spokesman, Czech Nazi leader Konrad Henlein, proposed a plan that would give German communities in the Sudetenland local autonomy, a scheme to which the Czech government had little opposition. Despite Czech willingness to cooperate,

rumors persisted of a German military buildup along the border. Nevertheless, Czech president Edvard Beneš twice received assurances from the French government that their defense commitments to Czechoslovakia would be honored.

With a British mediator on hand in Prague, Czech officials entered into negotiations with Henlein on 3 August 1938. After several days, talks stalled. France continued to assure the Czechs, but the French also quietly asked Britain what support they would supply if France mobilized against Germany. The British replied that they would defend French security, but could not give an assurance in advance concerning any other country without first consulting with the dominions of the empire. Talks continued in Prague through September, but finally broke down on 12 September.

The Nazis in the Sudetenland began rioting, provoking the intervention of Czech troops and the declaration of martial law. German intervention seemed inevitable,

Parade of German troops at Wenzels Square in Prague to celebrate *Tag der Wehrmacht* (Army's Day).

and Britain's prime minister, Neville Chamberlain, asked to meet with Hitler. At Hitler's private estate at Berchtesgaden on 15 September, Chamberlain offered agreement to "far-reaching German proposals" in order to avoid war, including support for a referendum in the Sudetenland and its cession to Germany. Though Hitler demanded "the return" of the 3 million Czechs of German descent, in reality this area had never been under German control, but that of Austria. Hitler agreed to postpone any action until Chamberlain spoke with the French. Over the next several days, Chamberlain convinced the French to agree to cession of the territory, and the Czech government saw their foreign support slipping away.

Unknown to Western sources until after the war was the resistance to Hitler's actions within Germany. The German military was convinced that the French and British would never allow an invasion of the Sudetenland but would mobilize and invade Germany, which did not have the necessary defensive works constructed along the French frontier. Within the high command, several generals plotted to overthrow Hitler if he gave the order to invade. Since they had to plot in secret, they made no attempt to inform Britain or France of their intentions. Such information surely would have stiffened the British and French resolve and avoided another world war.

In Chamberlain's second meeting with Hitler on 22 September, the prime minister informed Hitler that France had agreed to support the cession of the Sudetenland. Pleased that he had averted war, Chamberlain was shocked when Hitler added another demand: immediate German military occupation of the area. When Chamberlain could not guarantee French or Czech acceptance, he was met with yet another demand: total Czech withdrawal from the Sudetenland beginning on 26 September, to be completed by 28 September. By coincidence, immediately after this demand was made, word came that the Czechs had ordered the mobilization of their armed forces. Chamberlain knew he certainly could not convince the Czechs to withdraw in so short a time period, if at all. Hitler granted a concession: He would wait until 1 October. Chamberlain jumped at it, not knowing that 1 October had been the German target date all along. Unfortunately, neither the British cabinet nor the French government would agree to Germany's latest demands. France ordered a partial mobilization.

Czechoslovakia had much to fight for. Though it was a new country, formed by the Versailles conference out of the old Austro-Hungarian empire, the Czechs had a strong nationalist feeling. Further, loss of the Sudetenland would not be merely the cession of a piece of land, but of the defensive fortifications that protected the country, located in the nation's most rugged terrain. Giving up that land would mean giving up their one natural defense. They had an army of some 800,000 men, equal to what Hitler could mobilize, but they believed Hitler's bluff that his military was much larger. Without the defenses of the Sudetenland, without the assurances of aid from France, the Czech government was not sure they could defeat Germany. An existing defense agreement with the Soviet Union was useless, because the Soviets were denied access through Poland or Rumania to give assistance.

A last attempt to avert war came when Mussolini invited Chamberlain and French president Édouard Daladier to meet with him and Hitler at Munich on 29 September. Czech representatives were not invited. In this conference, Britain and France gave in to Hitler's demand that his army begin entering the Sudetenland on 1 October, finishing the occupation by 10 October.

The Czech government was informed that if they did not agree to this arrangement, they could face Germany alone. The agreement signed by Hitler, Chamberlain, Mussolini, and Daladier gave the Germans control of the Sudetenland, but guaranteed the remainder of Czechoslovakia. Hitler stated, "I have no more territorial demands in Europe. I want no more Czechs." With this agreement in hand, Prime Minister Chamberlain told the British public, "We have peace in our time."

The Czech government gave in and ceded the territory. Within a matter of months, their country ceased to exist. A German-backed Slovak independence movement removed that segment of the country from Czech control; because the borders that had been guaranteed by the Munich agreement no longer existed, Britain did not lift a finger to stop the German occupation and annexation of the remainder of the country in March 1939. Neither did the Czech government ask their population to resist. As with the occupation of Austria, the Germans had added another conquest to their list without a shot being fired. All Czech provinces became German protectorates, including Slovakia. Acquisition of Czechoslovakia put Germany into a commanding strategic position in relation to Poland, putting Nazi forces on both the western and southern borders. Later that same year, Germany would quickly invade and subjugate Poland as well.

Some historians argue that the Munich agreement bought time for England and France to prepare their respective armed forces for the war they knew would be coming. If that argument is accepted, they did not spend their time wisely. The best summation of the actions of Britain and France was given by Jan Masaryk, Czech minister to Britain. He told Chamberlain and Foreign Minister Halifax, "If you have sacrificed my nation to preserve the peace of the world, I will be the first to applaud you. But if not, gentlemen, God help your souls."

*See also* Austria, Nazi Occupation of [148]; Poland, Nazi Conquest of [183].

References: Churchill, Winston, *The Gathering Storm* (New York: Houghton Mifflin, 1948; Shirer, William, *The Nightmare Years* (New York: Little, Brown, 1984); Shirer, William, *The Rise and Fall of the Third Reich* (New York: Simon & Schuster, 1960).

## 153 DUTCH EAST INDIES, JAPANESE INVASION OF

As Japanese forces fought against Chinese Communist and Nationalist forces, they needed more and more oil to fuel their war machine. At the same time, the United States, their major supplier, began to negotiate with the Japanese to halt their war with China and even withdraw from the territories they had already occupied. The Japanese goal of dominating Asia economically as well as militarily would not allow them to withdraw, so negotiations dragged. When Japan joined Germany and Italy as one of the Axis powers in September 1940, Japan received free access to the French colony of Indochina, ceded to the Japanese by the French Vichy government.

Japanese troops in Indochina and the strong coastal position the Japanese held in China frightened the United States. Japan seemed to be slowly working its way around the Philippine Islands, controlled by the United States since 1898. American president Franklin Roosevelt decided to begin an embargo of oil and scrap iron to Japan, hoping to pressure the Japanese into more serious negotiations over China. Denied their primary supplier, the Japanese had to make a decision: Give in to

American demands, which would weaken their plans to dominate Asia and entail a great loss of face, or continue their expansion and find a new source of oil. The only source near at hand was in the Dutch East Indies. The United States knew that as well, and U.S. Secretary of State Cordell Hull warned Japan that if it invaded those islands, the United States would go to war, even though the Americans had no direct interest there.

Japan and the United States continued to negotiate through 1941, but the talks served only to drive the two sides further apart. By late summer, the Japanese government decided to continue conferring with the Americans but simultaneously prepare for war in case the talks failed. By late November, Tokyo bowed to the inevitable—war against the United States—because Japan had to have oil. As naval forces secretly left Japan to launch the strike against Pearl Harbor, other Japanese forces embarked for attacks against American possessions in the Pacific, the British base at Singapore, and the British colony of North Borneo. On 7 December 1941 (8 December on the other side of the international date line, Japanese troops were seemingly everywhere at once.

Within a month Japanese forces controlled most of the Philippines, and the southern island of Mindanao became their base of operations for the invasion of the Dutch East Indies. Allied forces in the area knew the invasion was imminent and tried to mount an effective defense, forming the ABDA (American-British-Dutch-Australian) Command under the direction of British general Archibald Wavell. Naval and air forces were under subordinate American command, and land forces were commanded by the Dutch. Even though the Dutch had the most intimate knowledge of the sea lanes in the area, they were rarely consulted on naval matters.

The Japanese planned three separate invasion forces. The Western Force assembled at Cam Ranh Bay in Indochina to attack southern Sumatra and Java. The Central Force left the base of Davao, on Mindanao, for attacks along the eastern coast of Borneo, to be followed by aiding the attack on Java. The Eastern Force also left Davao, heading for the islands of Celebes, Ambon, and Timor. The ABDA forces could do little to stop these onslaughts, for none of the countries represented could commit large forces to the area. Holland was under German occupation, Britain was fighting in North Africa, and the United States was still trying to get its military organized and operating in the wake of Pearl Harbor.

Japan began the operation on 7 January 1942 when elements of the Eastern and Central Forces left the Philippines. The Eastern Force landed on 10 January on Celebes's northeastern coast at Manado, and in three days was in control. On 24 January they captured the new airfield near Kendari on the southeast coast. From here, Japanese aircraft could harass shipping throughout the area and attack targets in Java. The island of Ambon was secured on 5 February; Timor was attacked by amphibious and airborne forces on 17 February and secured a few days later.

The Central Force was just as successful. The main Dutch oil and coal sources were on Borneo, and its towns fell with frightening rapidity: Tarakan on 13 January, Balikpapan on 24 January, Bandjermasin on 10 February. Borneo's oil production and refining were now in Japanese hands, and the Dutch had only one remaining oil field, Palembang on the island of Sumatra. The Japanese prepared to assault this spot with the Western Force, which began by securing the island of Banka on Sumatra's east coast on 14 February. Amphibious forces sailed up the Musi River toward

Palembang, and resistance by ABDA naval forces proved futile, both because of a lack of Allied coordination and because of Japanese air superiority. Palembang fell on 16 February, one day after the British surrender of Singapore. Though reinforcing the Allies was impossible, planning for the area's defense proceeded, for political if no other reasons.

The Japanese juggernaut moved on. On 18 February they struck Bali. The Allies attempted to stop the landings, but failed. A mixed Dutch-American naval force sustained much more damage than they inflicted, and they withdrew to try again later. On 27 February the naval forces tried to forestall the invasion of Java, and the resulting Battle of Java Sea became an Allied disaster. The two sides had roughly equal numbers, but the Japanese were more experienced and had practiced working as a unit. The American, Dutch, and British ships had never worked together in combat, and they had difficulty communicating. After an early exchange of shots that caused light damage on both sides, the Japanese began to register deadly hits with torpedoes and shell fire. Three Dutch ships and a British ship were sunk, and the damaged American and British ships had to withdraw. The invasion of Java was delayed but one day. By 9 March the Japanese were in a position to demand, and receive, unconditional surrender from the remaining Dutch forces. The entire operation to control the Dutch East Indies took three months, half the expected time.

The Japanese occupation of the islands got off to a good beginning. So disliked were the Dutch that the Japanese were welcomed as liberators, particularly by the Javanese. The Japanese encouraged anti-Western feeling by allowing the display of the Indonesian flag and the playing of the national anthem, both of which the Dutch had outlawed. Within six months, all Dutch and Eurasian inhabitants still on the islands were rounded up and committed to camps. This caused a major loss of civil servants, but the Japanese replaced them with Indonesians, a policy that both ensured a loyal following in the islands and gave the locals experience in running the bureaucracy. Japan promised that they would soon allow the Indonesians a self-governing state, and they promoted Indonesian nationalism through the creation of a home guard of 120,000 men and the support of Sukarno, the leading prewar advocate of independence from Holland. Japan tried to use Sukarno to encourage local support for Japanese war aims, created an Islamic forum to obtain religious support, and opened the educational system to all, regardless of ethnicity.

All these programs bought the Japanese the goodwill of the people, but they also gave the Indonesians a taste for education and political advancement that could only be satisfied through independence from all outside domination, whether Dutch or Japanese. Further, by creating a national guard, the population became armed, as well as ambitious. The political leaders who trained in Japanese schools graduated not as supporters of Japan, but as Marxists, which did not spell good news for a Japanese occupation. As the war turned against the Japanese, they gave more and more promises to the Indonesians concerning independence, which they finally awarded in March 1945. Rather than bind the locals to Japan with friendly feelings of gratitude, it made them more anxious than ever to rid themselves of the Japanese.

On 6 August 1945, the day the first atomic bomb was dropped, the Japanese were prepared to cede all political power to the Indonesian Nationalists; on 17 August, Sukarno declared independence, and the following day the nation of Indonesia was organized. With the war over, the

Dutch assumed they would reoccupy the islands and pick up where they left off in 1942, but the British were assigned occupation duties. The Allied political leader in Southeast Asia was Britain's Lord Mountbatten, and the military leader of occupation forces was American general Douglas MacArthur. They decided to recognize Sukarno's government, and did nothing to reestablish Dutch authority. Thus, Indonesia benefited from Japan's conquest more than any other country, because it brought them independence, if somewhat by default.

See also China, Japanese Invasion of [151]; Egypt, Italian Invasion of [155]; France, Nazi Invasion of [161]; Philippines, U.S. Invasion of the [182].

References: Collier, Basil, *Japan at War: An Illustrated History of the War in the Far East* (London: Sidgwick & Jackson, 1975); Hyma, Albert, *The Dutch in the Far East* (Ann Arbor, MI: George Wahr Publishing, 1953); Ryan, N. J., *A History of Malaysia and Singapore* (London: Oxford University Press, 1976).

## 154 — EAST AFRICA, BRITISH INVASION OF

When World War I broke out in August 1914, German colonies around the world became targets. Germany had entered the empire-building race late in the 1800s and was not as successful in claiming productive territories as its European rivals. The main location for action during the war was the colony of East Africa, which was surrounded by other colonies controlled by or allied to the British. Though the German colony was enclosed, it would give Germany the opportunity to strike in several directions while maintaining interior lines

of communication. As soon as war was declared, the German officer in charge, Paul von Lettow-Vorbeck, began doing just that.

Lettow-Vorbeck could draw on a force of about 1,800 active-duty soldiers and 5,000 reservists, backed by several thousand *askaris* (native troops). He had been an observer with the Boers during their war with Britain and had learned their impressive guerrilla commando tactics. The Germans used this hit-and-run fighting style to keep the British Ugandan Railway in a constant state of disrepair.

The British responded by creating Force B of 8,000 soldiers from the Indian army and Force C of 4,000 Indian army soldiers stationed in British East Africa. Force B was to land on the Indian Ocean coast, then drive inland to link up with Force C. It never happened. On 4 November 1914, the invasion was first held at bay by a lone German machine gun, then by hastily dispatched German reinforcements. Street fighting in the town of Tanga the next day was fierce enough to cause 2,000 British-Indian casualties and force their withdrawal. The British spent the next year training local units to handle the fighting; Lettow-Vorbeck spent the time continuing his raids against the Ugandan Railway.

Another conflict was going on simultaneously that had more prestige than military value. The Germans armed several boats to control Lake Tanganyika, and the British and Belgians responded. In a series of clashes reminiscent of the movie *The African Queen*, the Allied force ultimately prevailed with the assistance of aircraft sent from Britain. By midsummer 1916 the lake was in Allied hands. The other naval aspect of this theater was the appearance of a German cruiser, the *Koenigsberg*, which had been harassing Allied shipping in the Indian Ocean. British warships chased the cruiser into the delta of the Rufiji River, but the deeper draft British ships could not follow. Nevertheless, they pounded the cruiser with their big guns until the *Koenigsberg* settled into the mud. Lettow-Vorbeck salvaged some 4.1-inch guns and some sailors to handle them, and used them in his campaign.

In January 1916, 30,000 newly trained African troops were ready to take the offensive. They came under the command of South African Jan Smuts, one of the Boers who had given the British fits almost 20 years earlier. Smuts planned a two-pronged offensive around the north and south sides of Mount Kilimanjaro to catch the Germans in a pincer. Poor communications and extremely difficult terrain argued against a well-coordinated effort; the Germans were able to hobble the attacks and then fall back southward. A large battle in March pitted Lettow-Vorbeck's small force against an entire division under Smuts. The Germans and *askaris* took the most casualties, but were again able to slip away. The British forces had to give up the chase because of a lack of food and water as well as a growing casualty list from disease. Still, one of the main objectives was achieved: The Germans were never again in a position to cut the Ugandan Railway.

The British attempts to flank the Germans and cut them off came to grief owing to the terrain and the weather, which exhausted the supply animals as well as the men. In September, however, the British occupied the port city and capital, Dar es Salaam. Lettow-Vorbeck's force was down to 1,100 Germans and 7,300 *askaris* after the fall of the city, and he received news that the Portuguese were committing 7,000 men from the Congo to aid the British. Nevertheless, the British were still unable to catch the Germans. By the end of 1916, the white British and South African forces were relieved by West Indian and Nigerian units better acquainted with the tropical climate; 15,000 British soldiers

were discharged and sent home as medically unfit.

The Allied forces finally came to grips with the Germans in October 1917. Their 4,000 men outnumbered Lettow-Vorbeck's force two to one, most of his men being *askaris*. The two armies fought hard, often hand to hand, in a four-day battle. Once again, Lettow-Vorbeck was able to withdraw and continue his movement south. In late November he ordered all his sick and wounded to surrender to the British, while he took his remaining men into Portuguese East Africa. The British forces gave chase, and through most of 1918 the two forces circled each other, but with little contact. Lettow-Vorbeck crossed back into German territory in early November and fought his last battle on 12 November, one day after the armistice was signed in Europe.

Lettow-Vorbeck and his remaining 200 German troops were taken back to Germany, where they were treated as heroes in Berlin. He remained in the army for two years and aided in suppressing rebellions in the chaotic postwar German society. He served in the government throughout the 1920s, but gave it up rather than work with the Nazis. He kept in contact with his old enemy Smuts, who sent him food parcels and suggested to German conspirators in 1944 that Lettow-Vorbeck be named head of a new government should the Nazis be overthrown.

In East Africa, the Germans left behind a country that had flourished before the war. They had built railroads, schools, and hospitals and established a profitable trade in sisal. The League of Nations decided that all German colonies in Africa should be assigned as mandated territories, which European powers would administer under the general direction of the league. The British were assigned German East Africa, which they renamed Tanganyika. They inherited a rail system badly damaged by the Germans during the war and a number of plantations left derelict for four years; the native population suffered from hunger and influenza. The most economically rich areas of the country, Rwanda and Burundi, were detached as nations of their own. The British administration was slow to act, but finally in the 1920s the country began a slow climb back to normality.

See also South Africa, British Occupation of [144]; France, German Invasion of [160].

References: Harlow, Vincent, ed., *History of East Africa,* 2 vols. (Oxford: Clarendon Press, 1965); Hoyt, Edwin, *Guerilla* (New York: Macmillan, 1981); Lineberry, William, *East Africa* (New York: Wilson, 1968).

## 155   EGYPT, ITALIAN INVASION OF

Since the Italian peninsula unified into one country in the 1870s, they had harbored the desire to dominate the Mediterranean. When Benito Mussolini came to power in the early 1920s, he set about preparing the Italian military to accomplish this dream. It seemed logical to extend Italian power from its existing location in Sicily through to Tunisia, thus controlling the central Mediterranean. France, however, had a protectorate in Tunisia. That fact had driven the Italians into an alliance with Germany prior to World War I (which they withdrew from early in the war) and was the main motivating factor in Mussolini's support of Hitler's invasion of France in May 1940. Italian troops also invaded southern Italy, but the Germans were so successful in overrunning the country that Italy gained little control and could thus demand little in the way of

spoils. The German-controlled Vichy government in the south of France maintained a tenuous hold on French colonies, in Africa and elsewhere.

Unable to take advantage of his Axis alliance to gain a stronger position in Africa, Mussolini turned toward Egypt, long protected by Great Britain. Using the Italian colony of Libya for a base, plus the southern position of Ethiopia that Italy had conquered in 1937, Mussolini had troops sufficient (he thought) to defeat the British. Early success against the badly outnumbered British in Somaliland confirmed this notion. Control of Egypt would not only give Italy dominance in the Mediterranean, it would give the Axis powers possession of the Suez Canal, a vital seaway for British supplies. Unfortunately for Italy, Mussolini was looking at Eastern Europe as well as Africa, and this split focus cost him in both regions.

Mussolini had some 200,000 troops in Libya, as opposed to only 63,000 British Commonwealth forces in Egypt, Palestine, and East Africa. Field Marshal Graziani's invasion in September 1940 seemed destined for success. British General Archibald Wavell was a long way from the strategic or logistic decision center in London, so he had to make do with what he had on hand. It was enough. The Italian attack drove 60 miles into Egypt, reaching Sidi Barani. It was at this point Mussolini hurt himself. He launched an invasion of Greece at the same time as the Egyptian campaign opened. On the one hand, that forced a division in British interests which had long-range results, but it hurt the Italians more. Early November saw a series of Italian disasters. The British Royal Navy dealt a punishing blow to Italian naval forces at Taranto, the invasion of Greece bogged down in the face of the rugged Greek resistance and terrain, and Wavell launched a counterattack in Egypt.

Although Wavell's attack was merely meant to recapture Sidi Barani, it was so successful he decided to exploit his advantage. The Italians lost 38,000 prisoners in this one engagement, and soon lost more. By February 1941, Wavell had captured the Libyan port of Tobruk and surrounded and captured the majority of the Italian army at Beda Fromm. Two months' of campaigning netted the British 130,000 prisoners plus the destruction of 500 Italian tanks and the destruction or capture of almost all their trucks and heavy guns. British losses were 2,000 men. Wavell proposed to march west and capture all of Libya, but such was not to be. With attacks on so many fronts, Prime Minister Winston Churchill could not spare any men or matériel. Instead, he ordered Wavell to set up a defensive position and send some of his forces to assist the Greeks. When Mussolini had suffered his reverses there, Hitler had driven through Yugoslavia to aid him and the Greeks were sorely pressed. That British diversion of men to a lost cause cost the Allies dearly in the African desert.

Not only did Hitler bail Mussolini out in Greece, he diverted two divisions under Erwin Rommel to assist in Libya. Rommel had proven himself to be an audacious leader of armored forces in the invasion of France, and he reinforced that reputation in Africa. Like Wavell, Rommel was ordered to hold a strong defensive position; also like Wavell, he took the opportunity to exploit a small victory. In March 1941 he quickly overran Wavell's holding force and, forced to leave a besieging force at Tobruk, drove for Egypt. For the next year and a half, British and German forces drove back and forth along the coast of Cyrenaica, limited by the length of supply lines and what the respective governments deigned to send for supplies. They were also limited by the range of air cover: Halfway into Egypt the British could dominate from bases in Cairo and Alexandria, but halfway into Libya the Germans could dominate from Benghazi or Tripoli. Reaching those limits, usually timed with an arrival of reinforcements for the enemy, forced advances and withdrawals over the same ground in what came to be known as the "Benghazi Handicap."

Wavell was removed from command, although it was the lack of support from home that hurt him, not his generalship. British forces continued to be pushed back, although their new commander, Sir Claude Auchinlek, received better support from Britain. Still, Rommel was on the offensive through most of 1941. In November, Auchinlek counterattacked an overextended Rommel and drove back into Libya, but a large German supply convoy in January 1942 stiffened the Axis forces and Rommel was back on the offensive immediately. Again the British spent the summer months going backward, and again Rommel reached the limits of his supply lines by the fall. The Nazi invasion of Russia drew so much attention, and therefore supplies, that Rommel was unable to maintain himself, though he was ordered never to retreat.

Churchill's new commander in Egypt, Sir Bernard Montgomery, was in command when the climactic battle at El Alamein took place in September and October 1942. Rommel could not break through to Alexandria and was forced to withdraw in the face of a British counteroffensive.

This was the last leg of the Benghazi Handicap. Logistical superiority for the British, as well as the American invasion of North Africa in early November, put the Axis in the middle of a vise. By May 1943 the Allies controlled all of North Africa and used it as a base for further invasions to Sicily in July 1943 and Italy in September. The failed Italian invasion in September 1940 led to their ultimate removal from

Africa and the loss of their colonies. Never again could Italy mount offensive actions, and within six months of their defeat in Africa they surrendered unconditionally to the Allies. Even though the British did not lose Egypt militarily, they did abandon it as a protectorate after the war. Only French Algeria remained a European colony, but it was only a matter of time before that country, too, became independent. Egypt has undergone a number of political changes since, flirting with communism, pan-Arabism, and finally peaceful cooperation and attempts at national internal improvement. One of the longest-lasting legacies, however, is a byproduct of the nature of the war in the desert. Both Axis and Allies liberally used land mines, and as late as the 1970s an average of one person a day was still being hurt or killed by them.

*See also* Ethiopia, Italian Invasion of [157]; France, Nazi Invasion of [161]; Italy, Allied Invasion of [167]; Mussolini, Benito [175]; North Africa, U.S. Invasion of [177]; Sicily, Allied Invasion of [186]; Soviet Union, Nazi Invasion of the [191].

References: Barnett, Corelli, *The Desert Generals* (London: Viking Press, 1960); Heckman, Wolf, *Rommel's War in Africa* (Garden City, NY: Doubleday, 1981); Jewell, Derek, ed., *Alamein and the Desert War* (London: Times Newspapers, 1967).

## EISENHOWER, DWIGHT DAVID

156

Dwight Eisenhower was born in 1890 in Denison, Texas, but raised in Abilene, Kansas. He entered West Point at age 21 and graduated in 1915, going into the infantry as a second lieutenant. His World War I experience was completely in training and he saw no combat, but he rose to the wartime rank of lieutenant colonel commanding a tank battalion at the army's first tank training center at Camp Colt, Pennsylvania. After the war he met Colonel George S. Patton and, together with other tank advocates, developed armored warfare doctrine. They produced tactics calling for speed, mass deployment, and surprise; such ideas would be adopted by World War II.

Eisenhower reverted to a peacetime rank of major in 1920 and spent the next decade working his way through the necessary slots for advancement, graduating at the top of his class at the Command and General Staff School in 1926, then from the Army War College in 1928. The following year he was assigned to the office of the secretary of war, where he served as executive assistant for four years, participating in plans for the nation's industrial mobilization in time of war. In February 1933 he became personal assistant to Army Chief of Staff General Douglas MacArthur. For the remainder of the decade, he worked directly under MacArthur, writing speeches, lobbying Congress, and drafting annual reports. He followed MacArthur to the Philippines in 1935 when the general took the position of President Quezon's military adviser. Eisenhower was pessimistic concerning the abilities of the Filipino army, but MacArthur forced him to write a more optimistic assessment to go to Quezon. The stress of working for MacArthur and the Filipinos made him glad to leave the country in late 1939.

In the United States, Eisenhower was made chief of staff of the Third Division, then of the IX Corps. In late 1941 he received his first promotion in 16 years, to the temporary rank of colonel. He was next assigned to become chief of staff at Third Army headquarters at Fort Sam Houston in San Antonio, Texas. During this tour of duty he participated in the Louisiana maneuvers, the largest war games yet held by the U.S. Army. During these exercises he learned the problems of dealing with logistics, training, communications, equipment, and junior officers.

A week after the Japanese attack at Pearl Harbor, Eisenhower was assigned to Washington, D.C. He was directed by the army chief of staff, General George Marshall, to the War Plans Division as chief planner. They agreed on a "Europe First" strategy, whereby the major American effort would be directed toward the war against Adolf Hitler, while a defensive posture would be taken in the Pacific. In June 1942, Eisenhower, now a major general, arrived in London as commander of American forces in Europe. He and Marshall favored an immediate attack on France, but Prime Minister Winston Churchill and the British chiefs of staff convinced them that Allied forces were not yet strong enough or sufficiently trained to undertake such an operation. Instead, they would strike the Germans where they were weaker—in North Africa and the Mediterranean. In July, Eisenhower was promoted to lieutenant general and named commander of Allied forces for the U.S. invasion of North Africa. During the operation in North Africa he commanded U.S., British, and Free French air, sea, and land forces. His first experience with coalition warfare was successful.

Eisenhower received his fourth star in February 1943, and by May the Axis forces were driven from North Africa. He directed the operations to invade Sicily in July and Italy in September. In December he was named commander of Operation Overlord, the Allied invasion of France, the largest combined operation undertaken to that time. Eisenhower decided to launch the invasion during a break in bad weather on 6 June 1944. The diversions and disinformation the Allies had fed to the Germans were successful in keeping enemy forces away from the landing areas, and the beaches were secured in short order. The fighting through the hedgerow country of Normandy was slow, but on 1 August the Allied forces broke through and raced across France.

Eisenhower took direct command of the ground forces on 1 September. He now had to make a hard decision on the manner of assaulting German territory. Limited supplies forced him to choose between the options of a narrow front with more impact and a broad front for more widespread pressure. He decided on the broad front as a more conservative and less costly strategy; German offensives would be less apt to succeed, shorter supply lines could be used, and a stronger reserve could be built up. The decision was also politically correct, in that both Americans and British would share more equally in the final victory. However, the British favored a single thrust, using their forces under the command of Field Marshal Bernard Montgomery; they felt that the broad front would lengthen the war and its ensuing financial burden.

Eisenhower's decision stood. After a brief scare in December 1944 when Hitler launched an offensive through the Ardennes Forest, the wide front proceeded forward. American forces secured a bridgehead across the Rhine in March 1945; a week later, Allied forces all along the front had crossed. Again, Eisenhower resisted British pressure for a drive on Berlin because the territory that would be gained at the cost of British and American lives would have to be turned over to the Soviets according to agreements made by the political leaders at the Yalta Conference in February. Allied forces under his command cleared out pockets of resistance in the western part of the country and captured as many prisoners, cities, and factories as possible.

After the war, Eisenhower commanded the occupation forces in Germany, then became army chief of staff in November 1945, a position he kept until his retirement in 1948. As chief of staff, he oversaw the demobilization of the American armed forces. He spent a short time in retirement before returning to command NATO forces in Europe in 1950; he stayed in that post until mid-1952, when he retired to run for president. As president he favored peace, a balanced budget, and a strong deterrent force to combat the growing arms race with the Soviet Union. He proposed the "New Look" military: army and navy budget and manpower cuts, with priority being shifted to the air force, nuclear weapons, and delivery systems.

Though Eisenhower was never a battlefield commander, he was an efficient, outstanding general/statesman. He was an able strategist, a conciliator and compromiser between divergent national interests and goals, and a commander with the ability to draw the best from his subordinates.

—James L. Iseman

*See also* France, Allied Invasion of [159]; Hitler, Adolf [165]; MacArthur, Douglas [170]; North Africa, U.S. Invasion of [177].

References: Ambrose, Stephen, *Eisenhower: Soldier and Statesman* (New York: Simon & Schuster, 1990); Carver, Sir Michael, *The War Lords: Military Commanders of the Twentieth Century* (Boston: Little, Brown, 1976); Eisenhower, Dwight, *Crusade in Europe* (Garden City, NY: Doubleday, 1948).

## 157 ETHIOPIA, ITALIAN INVASION OF

Italy established a trading post at the Red Sea port of Assab, along the coast of Eritrea, in 1882. Three years later, the Italians occupied Massawa, Ethiopia's outlet on the Red Sea. In 1888, Italy claimed a protectorate over the area now known as Somalia. In the 1890s, Italy demanded the right to annex large parts of Eritrea, a region that Ethiopia had always claimed. When the Ethiopians resisted Italian demands, war followed in 1896. Lacking maps and good communications between the three attacking columns, Italian failure was inevitable. At Adowa, Italy lost over 4,000 men, and the remainder of their force was captured. The greatest disaster in European colonial history, it would play a major psychological role in Italy's future goals in the area.

When Benito Mussolini came to power in Italy in 1922, he dreamed of reestablishing the Roman Empire; Ethiopia looked like an easy conquest. Though Mussolini sponsored Ethiopia's membership in the League of Nations and concluded a friendship treaty with the country in 1928, he continued to stockpile arms and build up troop concentrations in Eritrea and Somalia. Inside Ethiopia, the domestic situation was unstable. The emperor, Haile Selassie, had succeeded to the throne after a series of factional battles and the mysterious death of the previous empress. In the mid-1930s, Mussolini suggested to the League of Nations that Ethiopia be expelled because of the lack of unity within the country. Italy seemed primed for intervention, and the other European powers did not care to stop the Italians. Britain and France rebuffed U.S. president Roosevelt's attempt at mediation, hoping to court Italy's support against the rising power of Adolf Hitler in Germany.

Before Italy could begin a war with Ethiopia, it was necessary to create an "incident." This took place at Walwal, an oasis of a few dozen acres in the middle of a scrub-covered desert. Contemporary maps were sketchy concerning the borders in this area, but all agreed that it was well within Ethiopian territory. When an Anglo-Ethiopian commission studying grazing rights found Italian troops at the oasis in December 1934, the Ethiopian government demanded Italian withdrawal and ordered up their own army. Shots were fired on 5 December; more than 200 Ethiopians died, while the Italians and Somalis lost 30. Mussolini's invasion came before the end of the month; tanks and aircraft were ordered into action to halt an Ethiopian "counterattack." Selassie appealed to the league, which debated into the following year.

The Italian expeditionary force numbered over 200,000 officers and men, armed with thousands of machine guns, 700 artillery pieces, 150 tanks, and an air force of 150 bombers and fighters. The Ethiopian army was basically a tribal assemblage with personal loyalty to a chief. The regular army numbered about 100,000 men, but only the Imperial Guard, a few thousand strong, was well trained. They were armed with a mixture of old and new rifles, a few hundred old machine guns, and an air force of 12 planes, all transports. Local levies were often armed with little more than spears, and female soldiers carrying swords were seen riding mules into combat.

Wanting to prove that Italy was the aggressor, Haile Selassie ordered his people not to resist. Some league sanctions were imposed on Italy, but none seriously enforced. The league failed to embargo oil, which Italy was obliged to ship via the Suez Canal to fuel its military. Members of the league were split over how to respond, so little happened, except that they managed to offend Italy by allowing Haile Selassie to address the league in Geneva, an action that (coupled with the mild embargo) provoked Italy's resignation.

Gaining no support from the international community, Ethiopia went on the offensive. They were occasionally successful, using their superior knowledge of the terrain to ambush Italian forces. Ultimately, however, Italy's modern weaponry, including poison gas, was too much to overcome. Ethiopian generals lost too many troops trying to fight the Italians directly. Though successful at ambush, whenever large numbers of Ethiopian troops gathered to fight they were badly hurt by Italian airpower. After losing a series of hard-fought battles, Haile Selassie was forced to admit defeat and flee from the capital at Addis Ababa in early May 1936. Organized resistance was broken, but local leaders continued to operate independently with guerrilla tactics. Ethiopians often controlled the countryside, allowing the Italians to own the cities.

Italian success was short-lived, not lasting much longer than the outbreak of World War II. When Mussolini declared war on Britain and France in June 1940, he had 91,000 troops in East Africa, along with 200,000 local troops. With these forces Italy went on the offensive against the British in the Sudan, Kenya, and British Somaliland. After a poor beginning under General William Slim, British forces under General Archibald Wavell prepared to remove Italy from the Horn of Africa. Three columns, including one of Ethiopian troops under British officers, invaded in November 1940. By January 1941, Haile Selassie was back in his own country, and by 5 May, the fifth anniversary of the fall of Addis Ababa to Italian forces, he was back in the capital. British forces were able to occupy the country fairly easily; the Italian forces surrendered rather quickly upon hearing reports of atrocities committed on Italian women by Ethiopian irregulars. Ultimately, the British took 230,000 Italian and Somali prisoners.

Italy occupied Ethiopia for five years and left behind a positive legacy. Despite the bloodshed inflicted in the invasion and consolidation, Italian authorities began a program of internal improvements the likes of which the natives had never seen. Roads, bridges, buildings, hospitals, and schools were built all over the country, though the Italians did not have enough time to institute a broad educational program. The country was unified and developed at a faster pace than ever before, and the people began to gain a respect for law and order. The Italians laid the physical foundations for Haile Selassie's modern Ethiopia, but the people did not embrace the negative aspects of the occupation, such as fascism or racism.

References: Barker, A. J., *The Civilizing Mission* (New York: Dial Press, 1968); Schwab, Peter, *Haile Selassie: Ethiopia's Lion of Judah* (Chicago: Nelson-Hall, 1979).

## 158     FINLAND, SOVIET INVASION OF

For almost as long as there have been Finns and Russians, there have been disputes over their borders. It was not surprising, then, that the Soviet Union took advantage of a passive Nazi Germany to annex territory at Finland's expense in the winter of 1939–1940. A secret clause in the German-Soviet Nonaggression Pact of August 1939 allowed the Soviet Union a free hand in the Baltic States and Finland, in return for their assistance in Poland and the cession of the western half of Poland to Germany. Within two months of Poland's surrender, the Soviets were preparing to attack Finland.

The Soviet government staged an incident on 26 November to justify their invasion. After three days of diplomatic arguing, the Soviets launched their attack on 30 November. Why they wanted to make war in the depths of winter remains a mystery; the only justification appears to be their confidence that they could crush their opponents in less than two weeks. The Soviets had every reason for that surety: The Soviet military was overwhelming in its size, while the Finnish army was without heavy weapons, large numbers of aircraft, ammunition, training, or discipline. The Finns' only advantages were the bitterly cold weather, to which they adapted more readily than the Soviet military, and the brilliance of their commander, 72-year-old Marshal Gustav Mannerheim. Mannerheim had thoroughly familiarized himself with Soviet training manuals, and knew their tendencies and tactics. He believed that their dependence on frontal, steamroller attacks could be negated by defenses in depth, coupled with the actions of small guerrilla units that knew the countryside better than the invaders.

The Soviets attacked Finland at five points, stretching from the Arctic seaport of Petsamo to the southern Karelian Isthmus, which held the Soviet-Finnish border just northwest of Leningrad. The Soviets launched their heaviest offensive across the isthmus, exactly where the Finns were best prepared behind the Mannerheim line of entrenchments, antitank ditches, and open fields of fire. The Finns beat back repeated Soviet attempts to cross the isthmus, slaughtering huge numbers of Soviet troops in the process. In the north, the Finns engaged in scorched-earth tactics, which denied the Soviets any shelter in the increasingly harsh weather, and they quickly developed masterful abilities at setting booby traps. The swarming guerrilla units operating on skis chopped up formation after formation of Soviet infantry, while mines and Molotov cocktails took care of Soviet armor. In the air, the Finnish pilots, terribly outclassed in their obsolete aircraft, used nothing more than courage to down large numbers of Soviet planes—at a terrible cost to themselves.

The easy conquest was an illusion. The huge Soviet army was being embarrassed by a tiny force, and Soviet premier Joseph Stalin was not happy. He removed the top commanders, either by retirement or execution, and appointed Marshal Semyon Timoshenko to take over the campaign. Timoshenko halted the offensive and regrouped his forces, quickly training and disciplining his men for their task. In January 1940 he harassed the Finns in the Mannerheim line with small attacks and large artillery barrages while he prepared his forces. On 1 February he sent Soviet aircraft to bomb reserve positions behind the Mannerheim line and ordered a huge artillery barrage that shot some 300,000 shells into Finnish positions. Under a smoke screen he sent in six divisions to rush the dazed defenders; he kept up the pressure with assault after assault for days. Soviet lives were still wasted at an appalling rate, but the Finns were quickly running out of ammunition. Timoshenko's continuing pressure proved too much, and on 14 February, Mannerheim ordered his men to withdraw to a second line of defenses a few miles to the rear.

The withdrawal did little more than delay the inevitable. By early March, Soviet forces were breaking through everywhere along the isthmus, while pockets of Finns fought to the last man. When the Swedes refused to allow a force of 100,000 British and French soldiers to cross their territory, any chance of continued Finnish resistance collapsed. On 6 March the Finnish government opened negotiations. The treaty of 12 March cost the Finns one-tenth of their territory—25,000 square miles of land, including all the Karelian Isthmus and their access to the Arctic Ocean. It also cost Finland almost 25,000 dead and over 43,000 wounded; Soviet casualty estimates range from 200,000 to 1 million.

The chance for revenge was not long in coming. When the Nazis invaded the Soviet Union in June 1941, the Finns saw an opportunity to recover their lost territory. Though the Finns never allied themselves with Germany, and only occasionally cooperated with them directly, they took advantage of the Soviet retreat to reoccupy their lost territory. This "Continuation War" lasted until 1945, when the defeat of Germany brought a stronger and better trained Soviet military to Finland's borders. Again the Finns were obliged to accept the loss of the Karelian Isthmus and all claims to Lake Ladoga on their north shore.

The Finnish resistance provided the world with a heroic story of an underdog fighting against overwhelming odds, but it also exposed the illusion of Soviet military might. If a tiny and unprepared country such as Finland could deal the Soviets a disastrous beating, then certainly, Adolf Hitler thought, Nazi Germany could crush the Soviets with little trouble. Hitler went to war against the Soviet Union with the same overconfidence the Soviets had displayed in November 1939, and the persistence of a determined population and the ravages of the Russian winter cost the Germans just as dearly.

*See also* Hitler, Adolf [165]; Poland, Nazi Conquest of [183]; Soviet Union, Nazi Invasion of the [191].

References: Erfurth, Waldemar, *Warfare in the Far North* (Washington, DC: Center for Military History, 1987); Lundin, Charles, *Finland in the Second World War* (Bloomington: Indiana University Press, 1957); Wuorinen, John, ed., *Finland and World War II, 1939–1944* (Westport, CT: Greenwood Press, 1983).

# FRANCE, ALLIED INVASION OF

**159**

By November 1943 the Allied forces of the United States, Great Britain, and the Soviet Union seized the initiative from Nazi Germany and began to take the offensive on all fronts. That month, the three nations' leaders—Franklin Roosevelt, Winston Churchill, and Joseph Stalin—met in Teheran, Iran, to discuss future strategy. This was the first time Stalin had met with the other two leaders, and he was eager to have input into the planning against Germany. Stalin felt that his country had borne the brunt of Nazi aggression because of American and British hesitation about launching major offensives, and he was determined to force the two countries to strike hard at Germany.

Roosevelt and Churchill were agreeable to a major offensive, but the three leaders had difficulty deciding where such an assault should take place. Churchill favored an attack into the Balkans. Britain had been forced to abandon an ally when the Nazis invaded Greece in 1941, and Churchill felt obligated to liberate the area. He advocated an offensive against the "soft underbelly" of Europe, where German forces and defenses were weak. This would put American and British forces directly on the German flank and provide the Soviets with the most direct assistance. Stalin would have none of it. He argued in favor an Anglo-American landing on the coast of France. By striking the German rear, this would force Hitler to fight a two-front war rather than concentrate his troops only in the east.

Both plans had facets in their favor, but certainly Stalin and Churchill were also looking ahead at a postwar world. Having been invaded by Germany in 1914 and again in 1941, Stalin surely wanted to acquire as large a buffer zone as possible against any future aggression. If British and American forces occupied the Balkans, this would deny the Soviets that buffer zone and put a new potential enemy—the United States—and Great Britain, a nation long at odds with Russia, on his doorstep. Churchill apparently saw Stalin's plan also, and he did not like it. Britain had no aggressive designs on the Balkans or the Soviet Union, but Churchill did not want to see Communist power extended past the Soviet Union's borders. He tried to get Roosevelt to see this as well.

The question was, which plan would Roosevelt support? Roosevelt also saw into the political future, but his focus was elsewhere. In November 1943, U.S. Marines were just beginning their island-hopping campaign in the Central Pacific and had met fierce resistance wherever they fought the Japanese. The president's advisers had estimated an extremely costly campaign to capture the Japanese homeland, and Roosevelt wanted help. He reasoned that if he cooperated with Stalin on this strategy, he could get Stalin to provide troops to fight Japan when the war in Europe was completed. This hope influenced his thinking more than Churchill's views, so Roosevelt supported Stalin's demand for an invasion of France.

The United States had been massing forces in Great Britain for months. Though many of them had gone on to fight in North Africa or Italy, many more were on British bases waiting for the big one. American and British air forces had begun strategic bombing of industrial sites on the Continent, and in the first months of 1944 began hitting targets in France as well. Dwight Eisenhower, designated overall Allied commander in Europe, oversaw the the largest armada ever assembled. Warships and landing craft gathered off England's shores in preparation for the invasion. First scheduled for early May, poor weather postponed the operation until the first week in June.

Allied invasion of France.

The Germans were not unaware that something was afoot. They had brought one of their most skillful generals, Erwin Rommel, to supervise the construction of defenses along the English Channel coast. Concrete bunkers and gun positions covered the beaches from Calais to Cherbourg, with most of the works concentrated near Calais, where the Channel is narrowest and therefore the easiest location for bringing in supplies and reinforcements. The Allies went to great lengths to convince the Germans that they were defending the correct place. A huge disinformation campaign attempted to confirm the German belief in the Pas-de-Calais as the invasion site, using false radio traffic, troop movements, and even inflatable tanks and trucks all over southeastern England to give the impression of an Allied buildup there. The landing site in Normandy, farther southwest, was successfully hidden until the landings actually took place.

Despite threatening weather, Eisenhower ordered the forces to invade on 6 June. American and British airborne forces landed in the dark, with mixed success, to seize bridges and roadway junctions to slow or halt German reinforcement. When the naval bombardment opened at dawn, the Germans were completely surprised. Two American, two British, and one Canadian army landed at five beaches. Some were easily secured, others not. The American forces landing at the beach farthest west (designated "Omaha") met the most resistance and suffered the greatest casualties: one man killed or wounded per square yard of beach. But by the end of the day, all the armies had men into the nearby countryside and had secured a beachhead. On Hitler's orders, German reinforcements were not allowed to move from the Calais area to counter this invasion because the Nazi leader was convinced that the landing was a diversion. By the time German forces were released to counterattack two weeks later, it was too late.

Still, getting into France was not easy. Though the beachhead was secure and supplies began to flow in through artificial harbors created by the Allies, German resistance in the farm country of Normandy was intense. Each small field was surrounded by an impenetrable hedgerow, very easy to defend and extremely difficult to capture. Bulldozers and tanks had to break through the hedges one at a time, and the invasion was almost two months old before the Allies were able to break through. On 1 August a massive carpet of bombs from a huge air assault paralyzed the Germans, and an Allied armored attack broke through. The race was on.

The blitzkrieg with which the Germans had terrorized Europe was now used against them. Fast-moving American armored columns drove across France and took hundreds of thousands of prisoners. Paris was liberated in late August, by which time a second invasion had occurred along the French Riviera and American forces were racing northward to link up with troops of the first invasion. By September they had outrun their supply lines and had to halt along the German frontier.

Eisenhower ordered the Allied armies to consolidate their positions and dig in for the winter; once fully supplied in the spring, they would drive into Germany. Only a defeat at the Dutch city of Arnhem in September 1944 and Hitler's Ardennes offensive from mid-December 1944 through mid-January—the famous Battle of the Bulge—gave the Allies any pause. American forces crossed the Rhine in early March, but stopped at the Elbe River rather than drive on to Berlin, which had been promised to the Soviets at another three-power conference in the Russian resort city of Yalta in February 1945.

As Winston Churchill had foreseen, after the war the Communists established dominion over eastern and southeastern Europe. He was unable to remind Roosevelt of this, because the president died in April 1945. Thus, the liberation of France had results far beyond that nation's borders. Within France, the people had to face a postwar political reality that was hard to accept. Regarded as a major power for centuries, they had been reduced to no more than a second-rate country. France's poor showing during the Nazi invasion in 1940

left them with too small a force to be a factor in the liberation of their own country, though Charles de Gaulle, leader of the French government-in-exile and Free French forces, exerted what influence he could. France was not as physically devastated as it had been after World War I, but in 1948 the French had to accept aid through the American Marshall Plan to rebuild their economy. De Gaulle, as president of France, tried to give the illusion of independent strength with the development of a French nuclear bomb and limited cooperation with the North Atlantic Treaty Organization. He also attempted to maintain a French empire, but defeat in Indochina and resistance in Algeria robbed them even of that.

*See also* Algeria, French Occupation of [128]; Indochina, French Occupation of [135]; Eisenhower, Dwight David [156]; France, Nazi Invasion of [161]; Greece, Nazi Invasion of [163]; Italy, Allied Invasion of [167]; North Africa, U.S. Invasion of [177]; Pacific Islands, U.S. Conquest of [179]; Russia, German Invasion of [185]; Soviet Union, Nazi Invasion of the [191].

References: Ambrose, Stephen, *D-Day, June 6, 1944* (New York: Simon & Schuster, 1994); Carrel, Paul, *Invasion: They're Coming*, trans. E. Osers (New York: Dutton, 1960); Keegan, John, *Six Armies in Normandy* (New York: Viking, 1982).

**160**

# FRANCE, GERMAN INVASION OF

After the Franco-Prussian War of 1870–1871, France burned to avenge itself after the poor performance of its armies, the humiliation of paying reparations to Germany, and the loss of the provinces of Alsace and Lorraine. France soon began reforming its military by imitating the German General Staff concept of command. The French government also set about looking for allies. France signed an agreement with Russia, creating enemies for Germany in both the east and west in the event of war, and in 1905 allied itself with Great Britain, whose navy could effectively isolate Germany not only from its colonies but from the rest of the world. This Triple Entente seemed an effective grouping of nations to defeat Germany. With Plan XVII, France prepared to position its forces along the German frontier and thrust immediately into its neighbor's territory when war began.

Germany was not idle as France worked on these preparations. If France could create allies around Germany, Germany could strengthen itself in the middle by allying first with the Austro-Hungarian Empire and then with Italy, creating the Triple Alliance. The Germans also hoped to gain stature vis-à-vis the rest of the major powers by engaging in empire building; Germany claimed colonies in Africa and the Pacific Ocean, but they were not prime locations for raw materials or trading purposes. Germany began looking to build an inland empire—what came to be called *Mitteleuropa*, or Central European Customs Union. By working on the alliance with Austria-Hungary and strengthening ties with the aggressive new Committee of Union and Progress in the Ottoman Empire, Germany could stretch its economic power from the North Sea to the Persian Gulf. With German money and engineering, the Balkans' labor and raw materials, and the Middle East's oil, Germany could control everything it needed to create a powerful economy and have ocean access at northwestern and southeastern extremes. All of it could be tied together by the Berlin-Baghdad Railway, along which supplies and goods could be shipped in peacetime, and men and matériel could be shipped in wartime. *Mitteleuropa* would make overseas colonies extraneous.

There was one major problem in this plan: the oil of the Middle East. Though Germany was bidding on drilling sites in the Ottoman Empire, the only oil currently flowing in significant amounts was in Persia. The Anglo-Persian Oil Company made that oil available mainly to Great Britain, but Russia regarded Persia as being within its sphere of influence. Any German move toward Persia could provoke war with Russia, and that meant war with France because of the Triple Entente. Thus, by 1912, Germany saw that war with France was inevitable if Persian oil was to come under German control.

The German General Staff had been working on plans for a war with France. The plan was authored by Alfred von Schlieffen, who had been formulating it since the 1890s. He envisioned a massive sweep past the left flank of the French forces poised on the frontier, a maneuver that would bypass most French resistance and put German armies in Paris even more quickly than in 1870. The Triple Entente made it necessary to place a number of German forces in the east to oppose Russia, but a holding action there would give sufficient time for the German armies to knock France out of the war. Germany could then deal with Russia at leisure, and Persian oil would soon follow Russia's defeat. Since Great Britain and Russia had no great love for each other, the Germans assumed that Britain would do nothing if France was quickly *hors de combat*. Though the French plan called for a quick thrust into Germany, the ground on which they planned to attack was rugged and wooded; a German holding force there could keep them pinned down while the "right hook" swung down on Paris.

The Schlieffen plan seemed unbeatable, but by 1914 there were problems. First, von Schlieffen had died in 1905 and left the plan to the General Staff under Helmuth von Moltke the Younger, son of the main strategist of the Franco-Prussian War. He saw the potential for problems, and began to weaken the main assault in order to strengthen the holding forces in the east and along the French frontier. There were also diplomatic problems. To sweep around the French left flank, German armies would have to pass through Belgium, a neutral country. Violating a country's neutrality was not an action to be taken lightly, but there was no other way to drive quickly into France. Everything depended on speed, because France had to be neutralized before the Russians could mobilize their military. By 1914 both Germany and France seemed to be waiting for an excuse to go to war, one for power and the other for revenge.

The assassination of Austrian archduke Franz Ferdinand on 28 June 1914 became the excuse. Germany supported severe Austrian demands on Serbia, which they believed knew of or participated in the assassination. If Serbia went to war, its main supporter would be Russia; Germany would honor treaty commitments to Austria-Hungary through the Triple Alliance. Thus, Germany would have the excuse to fight Russia. When the Serbians did not give in to Austrian demands by 28 July, Austria declared war and the dominoes started to fall. Russia began mobilizing its army immediately. On 1 August, Germany declared war on Russia; on 3 August, Germany declared war on France; on 4 August the Schlieffen plan went into action. The attack through Belgium precipitated British reaction, because Britain had a long-standing defense treaty with Belgium. Only Italy remained out of the fray, for it had a nonaggression pact with Great Britain.

(Italy changed sides in 1915; the Ottoman Empire joined with Germany and Austria in November 1914.)

At first, all seemed to be going according to German projections. French armies along the frontier attacked but made little headway, while German forces raced for Paris. The one thing the Germans could not overcome, however, was the lack of roads with which to keep its forces supplied. German troops made rapid headway against relatively ineffective British resistance, but by the time Paris was in sight the German offensive ran out of steam. The soldiers were exhausted, and supplies were slow in getting to the front. The French General Staff, realizing that Plan XVII was useless, attempted to reverse its armies from the frontier to defend the capital. General Joseph Joffre called on Parisians to rally, and France had its proudest moment. Ferried to the Marne River in Paris taxicabs, the hastily formed units threw together a defensive line just as the German onslaught was faltering. Once the German forces overcame their exhaustion and were resupplied, they staged another flanking move, but to no avail. The rapidly arriving British forces in the north blunted moves to the German right, while moves to their left met French armies returning to their capital.

The attempts by each side to outflank the other, or keep from being outflanked, ultimately spread the offense and defense into lines stretching from the English Channel to Switzerland. Unable to move, the two sides began to dig in, and the Western Front was created. Most of World War I was fought in the trench lines of northern France, where neither German nor French planners ever expected the war to be. What was to have been a quick war became the least mobile and deadliest war ever. Germany was forced to fight on two fronts, a circumstance greatly to be avoided. In

France, four years of mud, barbed wire, poison gas, and millions of casualties were the results. Not until the Russians withdrew from the war in 1918, and the American forces arrived at the same time, did the deadlock break. The war devastated not only the French countryside, but the psyches of a generation of French, British, Germans, and Americans. The French were able to wreak some vengeance on Germany via the Versailles Treaty of 1919, but the result was exactly the same as the harsh peace of 1871: a desire for revenge—this time on the part of the Germans—that would provoke yet another war. The peace gained in 1919 lasted but two decades, and the memories of the horrors of war in the trenches of France paralyzed the British and French populations and governments when Germany rose again to prominence under the leadership of Adolf Hitler.

*See also* France, Prussian Invasion of (Franco-Prussian War) [133]; Hitler, Adolf [165]; Russia, German Invasion of [185].

References: Fischer, Fritz, *War of Illusions* (London: Chatto & Windus, 1975); Koch, H. W., ed., *The Origins of the First World War* (London: Macmillan, 1972); Tuchman, Barbara, *The Guns of August* (New York: Macmillan, 1962).

## 161 FRANCE, NAZI INVASION OF

While still fighting in Norway, the Nazis directed their attention to Germany's traditional enemy, France, in the spring of 1940. Since the breakup of Charlemagne's Holy Roman Empire the rulers of the principalities of north-central Europe had been at odds with the rulers of France. This situation was at its worst in the 1870 Prussian

invasion of France when German forces embarrassed the French army and imposed a harsh peace with severe reparations. It repeated itself in the 1914 German invasion of France, in which France came within a hair's breadth of another humiliation. Germany provoked the wrath of the world at that time for violating Belgian neutrality at the start of their assault, but they had found it necessary to break international law in order to gain a strategic advantage over the French defensive plans. Ultimate French victory in World War I brought resolution to be fully prepared for any future German aggression, and this manifested itself in the construction of the Maginot Line, a string of fortresses guarding the Franco-German frontier. This defense, coupled with a large air force and an army equipped with almost as many tanks as their opponents could muster, made France feel secure despite the diplomatic victories and military successes scored by Hitler through the late 1930s.

There were shortcomings in the French strategy. First, though the Maginot Line was universally regarded as impregnable, the string of forts did not stretch all the way across the French border, and thus failed to protect France completely. These gaps occurred not only because of the prohibitive cost of construction, but because a fortress line all the way to the English Channel would necessitate building forts that pointed not at Germany but at neutral Belgium, hardly a favorable public relations move. The French tried to include the Belgians in the construction effort, but with no success. In addition, though the French army was large on paper, it was neither well motivated nor well led. Many units were dedicated to manning defensive works, unable to operate in the fast-moving warfare that eventually took place. Late-developing defensive plans worked out by the French high command were not

German troops in the Place de la Concorde, Paris, 1940.

communicated to lower-ranking officers, and therefore failed to be properly implemented. Even as German forces were massing for the assault in early May, much of the French army was on leave. Further, France's equipment was no better than, and in many cases inferior to, that of the Germans, especially in the air force.

Therefore, when Germany launched its invasion on the morning of 10 May 1940, France and its allies were only partially prepared. They were also surprised by the German decision to disregard the neutrality not only of Belgium but also of Holland. Hitler wanted to control the coastline completely, so the Dutch became victims as well. The first attacks came against Dutch airfields, where the Germans repeated the successes they had scored early in the Polish invasion, destroying most of the aircraft on the ground. They advanced against little organized resistance and

achieved a major victory by securing the huge fortress at Eben Emael along the Dutch-Belgian border by the first-ever use of glider troops. As the Dutch retreated before the onslaught, the German air force began pounding the port city of Rotterdam. When the Germans continued their advances and also threatened aerial destruction of Amsterdam, the Dutch had had enough. They laid down their arms after four days of battle.

By this time the Germans were making their way into Belgium and beginning to meet some French resistance. Allied defensive plans began to be implemented, and in some cases showed effectiveness, but the effort suffered because of a lack of coordination between French, Belgian, and British troops who had arrived to assist their allies during the "phony war" period (October 1939–April 1940). The Germans were able to take advantage of the confusion and exploit the capture of a few intact bridges across the Albert Canal and the Meuse River. As more French forces were sent to assist, they unknowingly fell into a German trap. The Nazi plan called for an attack through Holland into the flat coastal plain of Belgium, which would draw the bulk of the Allied forces. When these had been committed, the Germans would launch an armored thrust through the town of Sedan, site of the major French defeat in 1870. The French were unprepared for this, believing the wooded terrain too difficult for armor to negotiate. The Germans knew better, and aimed their thrust through the Ardennes forest, just north of the final Maginot Line defenses in an area held only by poor-quality reservists. By 12 May they had reached Sedan with only light resistance and, after a devastating aerial attack, the Germans captured the high ground west of the Meuse River late the following day. With the bulk of the French and all of the British and Belgian armies to the north, the pathway was open for the armored blitzkrieg to show its effectiveness.

The cumbersome French chain of command suffered from a shake-up at headquarters in the midst of the campaign and the accidental death of the general commanding the French First Army in Belgium. The Germans moved too quickly for the French to react or, even if they did, for the Allied forces to respond cooperatively. At one point, French forces were ordered to withdraw from Belgium, and the British and Belgian generals learned of it only by accident. The one overwhelming aspect of the German invasion was its speed, and the Allied forces were never able to adapt to it, steeped as they were in the lessons of defense learned in World War I. Once past the Ardennes, German tank units raced northwestward for the Channel. They reached St. Quentin, the halfway point, on 18 May; the same day, the Belgian city of

Antwerp fell. The French government had already been considering the consequences. On 16 May, the French met with Winston Churchill, who had taken control of the British government six days earlier, and admitted they had no strategic reserve and could no longer mount an active defense. The French begged Churchill for as many troops and aircraft as he could spare, a request he ultimately denied. He could see that France was falling, and a further commitment of British resources would make the defense of his own country that much more difficult. On 19 May the French government replaced their commander in chief, Maurice Gamelin, with General Weygand, a 73-year-old veteran of the command structure that had saved France in 1914. He promised nothing when he took the job, which was a wise decision because the next day, news arrived that German tanks had reached the Channel at Abbeville. The French First Army, along with the British Expeditionary Force and the remnants of the Belgian army, was now isolated.

The rapid armored movement had succeeded in splitting the French military, as expected, but it put the Germans in a precarious position because their infantry had not been able to keep up and consolidate the ground. British and French attempts to seize the opportunity failed because their counterattacks were too slow or too weak, and they scored only occasional, moderate successes. During the remainder of May, the Allied forces in Belgium slowly crumbled under the weight of the German advance. The Belgians and British staged a hard-fought withdrawal, but they could only withdraw toward either the German armored columns or the Channel. By 26 May the British had been forced to the coastal city of Dunkirk, where they began a miraculous withdrawal across the ocean under the noses of German troops. They were assisted in this operation by Hitler himself. Already overly worried about the condition of his tanks, he responded favorably to a suggestion from the chief of Germany's air force, Hermann Goering. The air force, or Luftwaffe, could bomb the British into submission, Goering claimed, and there would be no need to risk the armor. Hitler agreed, and ordered the assault on Dunkirk to halt.

The British had been throwing together Operation Dynamo over the previous few days and had to draft every available boat to assist. When the port cities of Boulogne and Calais fell to the Germans, the harbor facilities at Dunkirk were damaged, and only shallow-draft boats could get right up to the coast and take soldiers onboard. Every yacht, pleasure craft, and ferry boat along the southeast coast of England was pressed into service to aid in the evacuation. Under cover of occasional bad weather and the effective action of the Royal Air Force, the operation continued around the clock for nine days, by which time more than a third of a million men left France for England. The operation had to be called off with some 40,000 men left behind, but the bulk of the British army, as well as refugees from the French and Belgian armies, lived to fight another day.

After an unbroken string of successes, Hitler had finally committed an error—a grave one. Had he allowed the German army to finish off the troops in the ever-shrinking pocket around Dunkirk, which they certainly could have, Britain would have had to build a new army virtually from the ground up. As it was, they now had a large force of veterans around which to expand their numbers and continue the fight.

Hitler did not see that at the time; he was too busy celebrating the victory on the Continent. Belgium unconditionally surrendered on 28 May, and the French were doomed, though they fought on. German forces attacked southward along a broad front and overcame or bypassed most of the French opposition. To compound the French problems, Mussolini brought Italy into the war on 10 June, although Italy did not invade until 20 June. Threatened by imminent encirclement, on 11 June the commander of French forces in Paris declared it an open city; the Germans entered it three days later. On 16 June a new French government was formed at Bordeaux under the leadership of World War I hero Marshal Philippe Pétain, and the next day he ordered the French to stop fighting. An armistice was signed on 22 June, and 400,000 French soldiers surrendered.

The French expected the worst, but it did not occur. The Germans offered lenient terms, which the French were glad to accept, especially when they remembered the cost of defeat at German hands in 1870–1871. Many blamed Britain for having abandoned France at Dunkirk and used the British as a scapegoat for the defeat. German occupation forces did little pillaging or looting, and even left the southern half of France apparently unoccupied.

The "unoccupied" section was under the authority of a French government in Vichy led by Pétain, a role into which the Germans forced him. Actually a puppet government, the Vichy regime gave the impression of independence for the sake of France's overseas possessions. The Germans hoped that the French possessions would continue to take orders from home, orders that would actually come from Germany. The only resistance to this action came from a young French general named Charles de Gaulle. He had escaped France when the British left, and in London announced that he was forming a French government-in-exile. He would lead the French resistance that would ultimately free his country, he claimed, and he ordered French possessions around the world

German troops patrol the streets of Paris on 23 June 1940.

to ignore the Vichy government and resist their orders. Most French people, both inside and outside France, had no idea who de Gaulle was, whereas everyone knew who Pétain was: the hero of the great battle of Verdun in World War I. This set the stage for a number of problems that Allied forces would have to face in the future. Whenever French-owned territory was attacked, such as Algeria in November 1942, would the inhabitants listen to Pétain or de Gaulle? Would they resist or cooperate? It varied. Under the direction of the Vichy government, the French administration in Indochina gave up control of that province to the Japanese in 1940 when Germany and Italy brought Japan into the Axis fold. Those who responded to de Gaulle's leadership and resisted, in France and in the colonies, became the first French people to support the man who would dominate French politics and society for two decades after the war ended.

Other than the normal lack of amenities that exists in any occupied country, the French did not suffer extensively until the Allied invasion in the summer of 1944 obliged the Germans to seriously enforce their will on the population. Only French Jews felt the wrath of Nazi policies on a regular basis. Still, an underground movement, the Maquis, did creditable work in harassing the German forces in France and offered much assistance during the Normandy invasion.

Postwar France, like postwar Britain, found itself a second-rate power. Without an empire, with only the memory of a humiliating defeat and a long occupation, France had little but faded glory to fall back on. Only de Gaulle's obstinacy maintained French prestige in international relations, and the chauvinism he practiced can still be seen to an extent in the French attitude toward their neighbors on

the Continent and in their relations with the United States.

*See also* Carolingian Dynasty [39]; France, Prussian Invasion of (Franco-Prussian War) [133]; France, Allied Invasion of [159]; France, German Invasion of [160]; Norway and Denmark, Nazi Invasion of [178]; Poland, Nazi Conquest of [183].

References: Horne, Alistair, *To Lose a Battle: France, 1940* (Boston: Little, Brown, 1969); Jackson, Robert, *Dunkirk: The British Evacuation, 1940* (New York: St. Martin's Press, 1976); Sweets, John, *Choices in Vichy France* (New York: Oxford University Press, 1986).

## GERMANY, SOVIET INVASION OF

**162**

Besides being the largest armor battle ever fought, the Battle of Kursk in July 1943 symbolized the changing fortunes of war for both Nazi Germany and the Soviet Union. The battle marked the beginning of the end for Nazi Germany as it was the last time that the once mighty German Wehrmacht mounted a major offensive in the East. The Soviets, on the other hand, learned many bitter lessons over the two previous bloody years and now possessed a well-trained, well-equipped, and well-led army. The Red Army never relinquished the initiative in the East after Kursk and launched an almost continuous series of offensives that pulverized what remained of the Wehrmacht. In fact, the offensives forced the Germans into the vicious cycle of committing newly trained replacements and refurbished panzer (armored) units into battle with progressively less training. This cycle ended with mere boys defending Berlin in May 1945.

Following the Battle of Kursk, the Soviets almost immediately launched their Summer Offensive, which lasted from 12 July to 26 November 1943. Utilizing massed armor, the Soviets attacked along a front from Smolensk to the Black Sea. German Field Marshal Erich von Manstein conducted a well-executed mobile defense until Adolf Hitler on 2 August ordered him to retreat no farther. Hitler's intervention deprived the Germans of their last advantage over the Soviets: the ability to conduct effective maneuver warfare at the tactical level. The Soviets broke through Manstein's lines the next day and threatened to destroy his army. In order to avoid this disaster, Manstein ignored Hitler's orders and abandoned the city of Kharkov on 23 August. Despite this loss, Manstein was able to keep his army intact as he fell back to the Dnieper River.

By the end of the Summer Offensive of 1943, the Red Army had advanced along their entire front. In the northern sector of the offensive, they had pushed the German Army Group Center back to the Pripet Marshes, liberated Smolensk on 25 September, and recaptured Kiev on 6 November. In the south, the Red Army had forced a bridgehead across the Dnieper River and had cut off 210,000 soldiers of the German 17th Army in the Crimea. Hitler had refused to allow the peninsula's evacuation.

The Soviet Winter Offensive of 1943–1944 began almost where the Summer Offensive had left off. Only the unseasonably mild weather of December, which left the small lakes and waterways above the Pripet Marshes unfrozen, gave the German army any respite. The main thrust of the Soviet Winter Offensive ran the entire length of the front from the Pripet Marshes to the Dnieper River. From 29 January to the end of March 1944, the newly renamed Soviet First Ukrainian Front (under Marshall Georgi Zhukov) and the Second Ukrainian Front (under General Ivan Konev) continually battered Manstein. By mid-February the two Soviet fronts had encircled two German army corps near Cherkassy, inflicting over 100,000 casualties. By 1 March, Zhukov's First Front had crossed the 1939 frontier of Poland and was threatening Lvov.

The Germans also suffered defeats in the north around Leningrad and in the south in the Crimea during this time. In Leningrad, the forces broke through the German 18th Army and lifted the 900-day siege on 26 January. The three Soviet fronts continued to attack until they were stopped on 1 March at the line of Narva-Pskov-Polotsk by a combination of spring thaws and Field Marshal Walter Model's hard-pressed Army Group North. In the Crimea, the Soviet Fourth Ukrainian Front attacked across the widened Crimean Kerch peninsula on 8 April and soon trapped the German 17th Army in Sevastopol, which was evacuated from 4 to 8 May 1944.

In a little over four months, the Soviets had broken the siege of Leningrad, liberated the Ukraine and the Crimea, destroyed 16 German divisions of at least 50,000 soldiers, and reduced a further 60 divisions to skeletal strength. In addition, the Germans had weakened the only stable sector of their line, Army Group Center, by siphoning off troops to the collapsing flanks. As a result, the weakened Army Group was positioned in a huge salient without a large reserve. It was at this spot that the Soviets launched their next offensive.

The Summer Offensive of 1944 opened on 22 July, three years to the day after Hitler's invasion of the Soviet Union. The Soviet First, Second, and Third White Russian fronts attacked along a line 350 miles wide, stretching from Smolensk to Minsk to Warsaw. Since the German air force had been sent west to protect the homeland from Allied bombing, the Soviets gained complete air superiority. With this, they were able to mass their artillery and soon opened a 250-mile-wide gap in the German lines. Soviet formations quickly liberated the cities of Vitebsk (25 June), Bobruisk (27 June), and Minsk (3 July). By 10 July, Zhukov had enlarged the gap and was advancing toward Warsaw. His right flank attacked northward and began to trap German Army Group North against the Baltic Sea. The Germans were able to slow the First White Russian Front just short of Warsaw, but were unable to halt the First Ukrainian Front's drive in the south. It captured Lvov on 27 July and reached the upper Vistula River at Baranov on 7 August. The 450-mile Soviet advance only halted when the fronts outran their supply lines. The Germans lost over 450,000 men (including 300,000 in one 12-day period), 2,000 tanks, 10,000 artillery pieces, and 57,000 motor vehicles. The heart of the once-mighty Wehrmacht was torn out.

For the remainder of 1944 and into early 1945, Soviet forces continued to advance, especially in the north (where they trapped over half a million Germans in Courland) and in the south (where they pushed into the Balkans and removed Nazi satellite countries from German influence). This set the stage for the final act of the war, the attack on Berlin. Over a third of the USSR's 6,461,000 soldiers were committed for the advance on Berlin; the Germans had less than 2,000,000 soldiers left in the East, of which 500,000 were trapped in Courland.

The Soviet attack on Berlin began on 16 April, when Zhukov's and Konev's fronts crossed the Oder River. They faced stiff, desperate German resistance but by 19 April both were ready to assault Berlin itself. On 20 April the guns of the Sixth Breakthrough Artillery Division shelled the streets of Berlin and on the next day Zhukov's tanks entered the city's northern suburbs. Despite fierce German opposition and the efforts of the German Twelfth and Ninth Armies to try to rescue the city, the Soviets surrounded Berlin on 25 April and prepared for the coup de grace. The Soviets continued to advance house by house into Berlin with the Germans, by 27 April only holding a salient three by ten miles.

Hitler, fearing that he would be captured alive, committed suicide on 30 April. That evening, just after ten o'clock, two Red Army soldiers planed the Red Victory banner over the dome of the Reichstag, the German Parliament building; that signaled the end of the battle, although mopping-up operations continued through 2 May. Germany's unconditional surrender was announced on 8 May.

Nazi Germany's defeat left the country shattered physically, emotionally, and financially. The Allied leaders had met at the Russian resort city of Yalta in February 1945 to discuss postwar Germany. At that time President Franklin Roosevelt, Prime Minister Winston Churchill, and Premier Joseph Stalin drew lines on the map designating areas that the forces of each nation should occupy. Decisions at Yalta profoundly affected the postwar world, for the eastern portion of Germany and the nations of Eastern Europe were captured and occupied by Soviet troops. Decisions made at Potsdam, in July and August 1945, gave the occupied areas to the capturing nation until each country was prepared to embark on an independent course.

That meant, for eastern Germany and Eastern Europe, Soviet occupation and domination for 45 years. Believing that they had suffered the most of any nation during the war, the Soviets felt justified in looting the remaining assets of the occupied countries for the reconstruction of their homeland. They also launched a campaign to convince the people of those occupied nations that Soviet communism was the ideal system of government. That need to convince the population doomed the people of East Germany, Poland, Bulgaria, Hungary, Czechoslovakia, and the Baltic States to decades of privation and hopelessness, cut off from the outside world. The USSR refused to allow any of its occupied countries to accept money from the United States offered under the Marshall Plan of 1948. Thus, industrialization in those countries was extremely slow and the factories never matched the quality of those in the West.

The East Germans might well have suffered the most, for in their midst the city of Berlin was divided into four occupation zones, and three of them were managed and aided by France, Great Britain, and the United States. As those three sections rebuilt and progressed, they proved the value of a capitalist economy over a communist one and were a constant reminder to the inhabitants of the East of the oppression of Soviet rule. Soviet forces occasionally intervened when subject nations believed they had reached the point of independence: Czechoslovakia was invaded in 1948, Hungary in 1956, and Czechoslovakia again in 1968. Only the collapse of communism in the Soviet Union freed the people of Eastern Europe, and they faced the mixed blessings and problems of capitalism and democracy for the first time since World War II.

—Edward L. Maier III

See also Hitler, Adolf [165]; Soviet Union, Nazi Invasion of the [191].

References: Duffy, Christopher, *Red Storm on the Reich: The Soviet March on Germany, 1945* (New York: Atheneum, 1991); Glantz, David, and Jonathan House, *When Titans Clashed* (Lawrence: University of Kansas Press, 1995); Ziemke, Earl, *Stalingrad to Berlin: The German Defeat in the East* (Washington, DC: Center for Military History, 1968).

# GREECE, NAZI INVASION OF

**163**

After seeing his ally Adolf Hitler triumph easily in both eastern and western Europe, Italian dictator Benito Mussolini decided his country needed some simple glory as well. The German war machine had conquered all its foes from Poland to France, and German diplomacy was reducing Balkan resistance. German troops were "invited" into Rumania after German guarantees against further dismemberment of that nation, and Hitler was pressuring Yugoslavia, Hungary, and Bulgaria into cooperation or alliances. Italy could not let Germany dominate so close to home, so a quick victory was in order. What could be easier, Mussolini thought, than capturing the small nation of Greece? Italy had never had close relations with the country, and was in a good position to launch an invasion from Albania, which Italy had conquered in 1939. In the fall of 1940, Mussolini made demands on the Greek government that he knew they would reject; indeed, he did not even wait for a reply to his final ultimatum of 28 October before sending his troops across the Greco-Albanian border.

The Italian military greatly outnumbered and outgunned the Greek army, but poor discipline, morale, and leadership in the Italian army, coupled with an invasion into the Greek mountains at the beginning of the winter, served to subvert Mussolini's scheme. After early successes, the Italian army was drawn into mountain passes far from their supply depots and ambushed by

Greek units. Before the year was out, the Italians were not only defeated, but lost a quarter of Albania as well to a Greek counteroffensive. Hitler, as he was concurrently doing in North Africa, sent German forces into the Balkans to bail out his Italian ally.

The German invasion was not just a rescue attempt for a fellow Fascist. The Greeks had close ties with Great Britain, and British aircraft had begun to operate out of Greek airfields in support of their war against Italy. Hitler did not want British aircraft in range of his newly acquired oil fields in Rumania, nor did he want a future British offensive out of Greece that would threaten the upcoming Nazi invasion of the Soviet Union. To secure his southern flank, and to put himself in a position to drive into the Middle East if the opportunity presented itself, Hitler sent forces to Greece in the spring of 1941. He concentrated the German 12th Army in Bulgaria, and bullied the Yugoslavians into allowing safe transit of German forces through their country. The agreement with Yugoslavia was short-lived; a day after Prince Peter signed the treaty with Germany, his military overthrew him and placed his brother Paul on the throne. Never one to brook resistance, Hitler ordered his army to take Yugoslavia as well.

The German General Staff quickly reorganized their plans, reassigning units to drive for Belgrade from Bulgaria while sending in more troops from Austria. On 6 April two German invasions took place, both unstoppable. Within 11 days Yugoslavia surrendered, though a strong resistance movement immediately sprang to life. In Greece, the German invasion flanked the main Greek defensive positions and encircled them by driving down the Vardar River valley to Salonika. A second thrust swung eastward through southern Yugoslavia, then southward into northwestern Greece, bypassing the British forces that

had come to Greece's aid. Almost 60,000 British Empire troops had left Egypt for Greece in a futile effort to stop the Germans, who outnumbered them almost ten to one. Outflanked just as the Greek forces had been in the east, the British had to withdraw to avoid encirclement, then withdraw again to the south coast with the Germans hot on their heels. The Royal Navy had to evacuate the army in a second Dunkirk, but this time without air cover, while the German air force pounded them. Still, some 43,000 men got away to Egypt or Crete.

Hitler had taken the rugged country of Greece with the same blitzkrieg tactics that had served the Germans so well in Poland and France. The defenders had been sure that tanks could not operate effectively in the Greek terrain, but they learned differently. Without antitank weapons or an air force to speak of, the Greeks were unable to stand up to the onslaught. The hastily assembled British force was little better equipped or prepared. The rapid conquest embarrassed the British and gratified Hitler, but the Germans were not yet finished. With the support of German air force commander Hermann Goering, German general Kurt Student convinced Hitler that it was further necessary to capture the island of Crete. This would give the Germans a strong position in the eastern Mediterranean, and it could be used as a base for possible operations against the Middle East or the Suez Canal.

Student assured Hitler that an amphibious force would not be necessary, that he could do it with parachute troops. German airborne forces had proven their worth in the capture of key positions in Holland in May 1940, but to capture an entire island without follow-up infantry advances had never been done—until then. Crete was full of British troops, some in garrison and some newly arrived from the Greek disaster, but they were poorly supplied and equipped. German paratroopers landed on 20 May and fought to gain control of the island's major airfield. The Germans lost heavily, but well-timed reinforcements captured the field, and troop transports landed more men, who came out of the planes directly into battle. British morale broke, and the Royal Navy staged yet another evacuation, again harassed unmercifully by German aircraft. The defending force of Greek and British troops numbered more than 40,000, but only 18,000 troops got off the island, and the Royal Navy had 9 ships sunk and 13 damaged. The cost to Germany was 6,000 dead and wounded.

The stunning German victories in the Balkans had side effects, and one of the most immediate was in North Africa. Because the British had sent troops to Greece for the campaign against Italy in Cyrenaica, they were unable to deliver the death blow in North Africa that could have given them control of the African coast before any German troops could show up to stop them. Instead, Erwin Rommel and the Afrika Korps threw the British out of Libya and drove into Egypt. No one believed that the British could stop the Germans in Greece, and the Greeks even asked the British not to help them fight the Italians because they believed it would provoke a German response. Thousands of men died on a fool's errand, and thousands more had to fight and die in North Africa because the campaign was not quickly drawn to a close.

Another result of the German involvement in the Balkans is the subject of some debate: the effect it had on the German invasion of the Soviet Union. The German troops involved in Greece and, more importantly, in Yugoslavia had been dedicated to Army Group South in the invasion. Hitler had ordered his forces to be prepared by 15 May 1941 for the invasion, but the

assault did not begin until 22 June. The strong German armored forces used in the Balkans had to be refitted for the Russian campaign, and that certainly slowed down the timetable. However, late spring rains left Poland and western Russia deep in mud, through which the Germans could not drive their armies. The decision to postpone the invasion, however, came before the effects of the weather were completely known. Whether because of the Balkan campaign or the weather, Hitler sorely missed that extra month of campaigning in Russia.

Another, longer-term result must be discussed: the German occupation of Yugoslavia. Much of the postwar and late-twentieth-century conditions in this area date to the German occupation. Some ethnic groups welcomed the Germans as liberators and fought alongside them against neighboring factions. The underground movement led by Josip Tito hurt the Germans badly, and forced them to keep forces in the country throughout the war. That Tito was supplied and assisted by the Communists more than by the West was to prove a pivotal factor after the war. His leadership role led to political power after the war, and his Communist government ran the country until his death. Tito ruled with such an iron hand that the country's ethnic factions suppressed their hostilities, but after his death the country began to break up. In the mid-1990s, the country divided into numerous groups claiming land and killing other former Yugoslavs. Retribution for actions during the Nazi occupation, for or against the occupying power, was a major factor in the continued fighting.

The Greeks also staged a stout resistance to the Germans. After the war they had to wage another political struggle against Communist groups that, like Tito, tried to use their wartime actions to lead to political gains. In 1947, American president Harry Truman made economic and military aid available to Greece to stabilize their economy and thus combat Communist influence. It was successful, and led to the Truman Doctrine, that the United States would "support free peoples who are resisting attempted subjugation by armed minorities or outside pressures." That stand became the pillar of American foreign policy for four decades.

See also Albania, Italian Conquest of [147]; Egypt, Italian Invasion of [155]; France, Nazi Invasion of [161]; Hitler, Adolf [165]; Mussolini, Benito [175]; Soviet Union, Nazi Invasion of the [191].

References: Cervi, Mario, *The Hollow Legions: Mussolini's Blunder in Greece,* trans. Eric Mosbacher (Garden City, NY: Doubleday, 1971); Higham, Robin, *Diary of a Disaster: British Aid to Greece, 1940–41* (Lexington: University of Kentucky Press, 1986); Van Creveld, Martin, *Hitler's Strategy 1940–41: The Balkan Clue* (Cambridge: Cambridge University Press, 1973).

## GRENADA, U.S. INVASION OF

164

Grenada, a tiny island in the Caribbean at the southern tip of the Windward Islands, was long a British possession. It became independent in 1974, but from 1979 was ruled by a Marxist party under the leadership of Maurice Bishop. The United States is traditionally leery of any Communist-leaning government, especially in the Western Hemisphere, and Grenada's close ties to Castro's Cuba and anti-American votes in the United Nations worried Presidents Jimmy Carter and Ronald Reagan. Bad matters worsened in 1983, when Bishop

was overthrown and the coup installed an even more communistic government.

President Reagan became convinced that Grenada held the potential to become another Soviet satellite like Cuba. To forestall that possibility, he ordered American forces to invade the island, arguing the need to protect American medical students attending school there and to rid the island of Cuban soldiers. Early on the morning of 25 October 1983, the United States launched Operation Urgent Fury. For some unknown reason, 1,250 Marines and two Army Ranger battalions landed on opposite ends of the island, far from the main city and its objectives. Nevertheless, they were backed with an impressive array of Navy, Marine, and Army airpower, as well as armored vehicles.

The invasion was a case of overkill. A mere 43 Cuban soldiers were garrisoned on Grenada, in addition to almost 600 construction workers, and they had no air support or heavy weapons. Despite this almost nonexistent defense force, three days were needed to declare the island secured. The invasion showed a marked lack of interservice coordination and planning, a factor addressed by congressional action within a matter of months. The reforms instituted in response to this action were showcased in 1991 during the U.S. invasion of Panama.

In the wake of the American invasion, the people of Grenada were able to hold elections for a parliamentary-style government, which has operated without mishap since 1984.

See also Panama, U.S. Invasion of [180].

References: Adkin, Mark, *Urgent Fury: The Battle for Grenada* (Lexington, MA: D. C. Heath, 1989); Bolger, Daniel, *Americans at War, 1975–1986: An Era of Violent Peace* (Novato, CA: Presidio Press, 1988).

## 165       HITLER, ADOLF

The most important figure of the twentieth century was born in Branau-am-Inn, Austria, on 20 April 1889. His upbringing is the subject of some debate. Hitler claimed to be the impoverished son of a minor bureaucrat, but later research suggests that his father was fairly well-to-do and that he was actually raised in middle-class surroundings. As the first surviving son, he was spoiled by his mother, and any poverty in which he lived would have come after his father's death, because he freely spent his mother's inheritance. He harbored desires for an artistic career and moved to Vienna, where he was an irregular student. The surviving artwork shows a talent that was more technically than aesthetically good. Some historians argue that when Hitler was rejected for admission to an art school in Vienna, he blamed the Jewish directors of the school, beginning or reinforcing his anti-Semitic stance.

He lived in Vienna in poor housing on the income from selling paintings; the story that he hung wallpaper for a living is a myth. He left his home country for Germany in 1913 when called up for the Austrian draft. In Munich he lived much as he had in Vienna, though a deep, long-felt love for Germany raised his spirits. When World War I broke out in August 1914, he volunteered for a Bavarian unit and went to fight in France. Four years in the trenches brought a mixture of success and failure. He had the duty of messenger, running communications from the front to the rear headquarters when telephone lines were out, which was often. It was a dangerous job that carried a life expectancy of about two weeks, and he did it throughout the war. He was wounded in battle, decorated, and received quite positive reports from his superiors. Nevertheless, he rose only to the rank of corporal. Merely by surviving the deaths of so many around him should have made him an officer, one would think, but those same superiors who wrote good reports about him also noted that he lacked leadership ability. What could those officers have thought in later years?

After the armistice was signed in November 1918, Hitler remained in the army for a while. He spoke for the army to demobilized soldiers, encouraging them not to get involved in the political chaos that ran through Germany in the months after the war, but to wait for calmer times when Germany could reassert itself. Hitler showed some speaking talent in this position, and was later asked by the army to do some spying. The army kept watch on the growing number of political parties in postwar Germany, placing agents in each to watch for signs of danger should a political group prove threatening. Hitler was assigned to join the Socialist Workers Party, an extremely small group operating in Munich. He found himself interested in their political philosophy and, when he was released from the army in the wake of the Versailles Treaty, he decided to go into politics. He quickly took control of the party, renaming it the National Socialist German Workers Party. Under his direction, the Nazi party (so called because the opening word, *National,* is pronounced Naht-see-o-nal in German) slowly grew.

In late 1922 and throughout 1923, Germany suffered the worst inflation in history. Lack of hard currency, owing to the damage payments imposed by the Versailles Treaty, forced the German government to print money, and print they did. By November 1923 it took 40 billion marks to buy one dollar. Money was literally not worth the paper it was printed on. Millions of Germans had their savings wiped out and faced poverty or starvation. Desperate times call for desperate measures, thought

Hitler, so he decided to overthrow the government of the state of Bavaria and place himself in charge. In the Beer Hall Putsch of November 1923, Hitler stormed into a rival political party meeting, and at gunpoint coerced a promise from the city mayor and the state governor to give him power. When his forces marched on the capitol building the next day, they found soldiers waiting for them. Shots were fired and Hitler was wounded, then taken captive.

History could have changed at this point, but unluckily for the world, the trial judge favored Hitler's political views and allowed him to use his trial as a forum. He was found guilty of treason, but was sentenced to only nine months of minimum-security confinement. During this time he dictated *Mein Kampf* (My Struggle), the book in which he told the story of his upbringing and laid out his plans to return Germany to respect and its rightful position in the world.

This rambling, difficult work boils down to a few points. First, Germany did not lose World War I, but was forced into surrender when the government could no longer get loans to finance the war from Jewish bankers. So, getting rid of the Jews was a top priority. Second, all German-speaking people needed to be under one government. Third, Germany needed *lebensraum* (living space). The land they had captured in the east in World War I—most of European Russia—was rightfully German, and Germany should use this land to settle its hardworking people. Fourth, the people who lived in this area were *untermensch* (subhumans), who would be killed or used for slave labor for the superior German race. He spelled out his racial views and his plans for expansion for all to see. Why, then, was all that happened later a surprise to the world? Because *Mein Kampf* was so bad, nobody read it. It was not widely read in Germany until after Hitler came to power

in 1933, and not read outside Germany until much too late.

After his release from prison, Hitler decided that force was not the way to gain power. He spent the remainder of the 1920s building his party, gaining the support of business contributors who liked the idea of Germany being great again. The Nazi role in the government grew with each election, though Hitler himself held no office. After the election of 1932, Hitler was approached by the Social Democratic party to form a coalition government. He agreed, as long as he could hold the number two position, chancellor. Because the Social Democrat president would retain most of the power—and that would be World War I Field Marshal Paul von Hindenburg—Hitler could be kept under control, so the agreement was made. Hitler became chancellor at the end of January 1933.

Within a few months Hitler announced that Germany would no longer pay the reparations demanded by the Versailles Treaty. When Britain and France refused to go to war to force payment, Hitler knew that the Versailles Treaty was "a scrap of paper." After Hindenburg's death in August 1934, Hitler forced bills through a Nazi-dominated special session of Parliament that achieved two important things: The positions of president and chancellor were combined, and all political parties but the National Socialists were banned. Political resistance was brief because vocal opponents soon found themselves in prison. With dictatorial power, Hitler began wholesale violations of the Versailles Treaty. He expanded the army past the prescribed 100,000 men, he built an air force, he built warships. No one outside Germany resisted him, because public opinion would not allow more war so soon after the horrors of the last one.

He began to follow the plan laid out in *Mein Kampf*. Jews were soon restricted in their rights, then openly persecuted. He used the army to reoccupy the industrial area of the Rhineland in 1936. Later that year, he lent his air force to Francisco Franco, who used it to begin the Spanish Civil War. German pilots got on-the-job training fighting with Franco through 1939. Hitler supported, then allied himself with, Benito Mussolini, dictator of Italy. In March 1938 he threatened Austria with war if the government would not give itself up to him; they did, and Austria became a German state. In September 1938, he threatened war over the Sudetenland, the western province of Czechoslovakia, which held a large German population. France and Britain would not honor defense treaty commitments to the Czechs, and the land was conceded without a fight. Hitler occupied the remainder of the country in May 1939. The threat to use force over access to Danzig in Poland finally brought outside resistance. In Europe, World War II began 1 September 1939.

Hitler's political intuition had brought him the prewar gains, but that same intuition began to fail him in wartime. Bad decisions cost him strategic victories during the Battle of France and the Battle of Britain, while his support of Mussolini's failures diverted valuable men and matériel from more important ventures. His determination to destroy European Jewry brought the concentration and death camps, and transport dedicated to that use was siphoned from desperately needed military use later in the war. His decision to fight a two-front war and his declaration of war on the United States proved his ultimate undoing. Germany was overwhelmed by manpower and weaponry that negated the German army's advantages of training and experience. Hitler grew more paranoid and more self-assured as the war progressed. He was convinced that no one could accomplish what he could, and no one had his vision, so he trusted fewer and fewer people. He ended the war in an underground bunker as Soviet and German troops destroyed Berlin over his head. Until the last, he directed the movements of units long since destroyed, but which he would not believe had ceased to exist. He committed suicide on 29 April 1945 rather than be humiliated by his captors.

Hitler came to power by sheer force of will, and that will destroyed not only himself and his country, but altered the entire world. The long-expected death of the British Empire, the rise of two superpowers, the passing of French influence, and the Cold War with all its repression and confrontation since 1945 can be directly traced to World War II, which was Hitler's war. He is remembered for his cynical political actions, his naked aggression, and, of course, for the Holocaust. Like Tamurlane, Attila the Hun, and Genghis Khan, his name became synonymous with terror and destruction. The German people have yet to emerge from his shadow, and he still has the ability to frighten the modern world, for his views live on in a lunatic fringe that revere his name and his dreams.

*See also* Genghis Khan [47]; Tamurlane [76]; Austria, Nazi Occupation of [148]; Britain, Nazi Invasion of (Battle of Britain) [149]; Czechoslovakia, Nazi Occupation of [152]; Egypt, Italian Invasion of [155]; France, Nazi Invasion of [161]; Greece, Nazi Invasion of [163]; Mussolini, Benito [175]; Poland, Nazi Conquest of [183]; Soviet Union, Nazi Invasion of the [191].

References: Bullock, Alan, *Hitler: A Study in Tyranny* (New York: Harper, 1953); Payne, Robert, *The Life and Death of Adolph Hitler* (New York: Praeger, 1973); Shirer, William, *The Rise and Fall of the Third Reich* (New York: Simon & Schuster, 1960).

## ISRAEL, ARAB INVASION OF (YOM KIPPUR WAR)

**166**

After the 1967 Six-Day War, Israel occupied the entire Sinai Peninsula (previously Egyptian), the Golan Heights (previously Syrian), and the West Bank territory between Jerusalem and the Jordan River (previously Jordanian). The added territory gave the country some buffer zones to protect its population centers, but at the cost of administering large numbers of hostile Palestinian residents. On the defensive ever since its independence in 1948, Israel became even more of an armed camp. Combat against the Arabs in 1948, 1956, and 1967 convinced the Israelis of their superior military abilities.

Ever since the Six-Day War, the Arab states had been carrying on a terrorist campaign against Israel, waiting for the best time to recover their lost territories. Rearmed with Soviet weapons and better trained by Soviet advisers, Egypt led the Arab states in plotting revenge. After Gamal Abdel Nasser's death in 1970, the new Egyptian president, Anwar Sadat, directed the Arab coalition with as much determination, if not the bluster, of his predecessor. By October 1973, he thought they were ready.

Israeli intelligence warned the government of the impending Arab assault, and Defense Minister Moshe Dayan had to make the decision whether to strike first, as they had done in 1967, or absorb the first blow and take the moral high ground with the international community. Against the wishes of many of the generals, the government decided to wait. The Arabs timed their attack for the Sabbath day that began Yom Kippur, 6 October. Though the generals and the government knew of the coming attack, the population did not. The government thought that mobilization would be interpreted by the international community as provocative, so there was none. The decision to accept the first blow almost caused Israeli defeat.

Israel was attacked from two sides simultaneously: The Egyptians crossed the Suez Canal to regain the Suez Peninsula and the Syrians swept down on the Golan Heights. Syrian forces numbered almost 1,000 tanks in the assault, with another 500 in reserve, and the early attacks overran some Israeli positions. An airborne assault by helicopter forces quickly captured the main Israeli post on Mount Hermon, robbing them of the highest ground. Israel had no more than 200 tanks on-site to defend themselves, but they were well positioned and did the Syrians a great deal of damage. Israeli forces gave ground slowly and at great cost for four days, but by 10 October had regained the upper hand and began a counteroffensive.

In the meantime, Egyptian forces enjoyed great success. The Israelis had built a series of guardposts along the canal, but the Egyptians cleverly avoided them by using high-pressure water hoses to destroy the embankments between the outposts, then building pontoon bridges to cross over. The lightly held outposts were soon cut off by two Egyptian armies swarming between and behind them. The Egyptians prepared for the expected counterattack by building 130-foot-high antitank positions on the western bank to fire down and past the lower embankments on the eastern side. Israeli casualties in men and tanks were high because of this Egyptian tactic, plus the fact that almost the entire Israeli air force was dedicated to the Syrian front. Israeli generals held the three key passes (Mitla, Gidi, and Khatmia) into the peninsula while they concentrated forces for the counteroffensive. Successes against Syria allowed Israel to transfer some air support to the Sinai, and they began probing attacks on 10 October.

On the Syrian front, the Israelis also built up their forces behind the tenacious defense the garrison forces had been conducting since the outbreak of the war. With hundreds of Syrian tanks and armored vehicles charred and smoking along the frontier, the Israelis drove through them toward the Syrian capital of Damascus. A force of Iraqi tanks attempting to join the battle by striking the Israeli flank found themselves trapped in an ambush and destroyed in a night battle illuminated by a full moon. The Israelis drove to within 20 miles of Damascus when they received word of the Syrian acceptance of the UN-sponsored cease-fire. The cessation of hostilities on the northeastern front allowed the Israelis to focus on the Sinai.

With massive Egyptian forces across the canal, the defending Israeli units were extremely hard-pressed. On 14 October the Egyptians launched a massive assault to gain the passes. The two sides engaged in a tank battle on a scale not seen since Kursk in 1943, with some 2,000 tanks engaged. In their defensive positions the Israelis held off the assaults and shocked the Egyptians with their gunnery. By the end of the day, the Israelis had lost only 6 tanks while destroying 264. With their forces gathered and with increased air support, the Israelis decided to cross the canal themselves and get behind the Egyptian thrust, cutting it off from its supplies. While some forces fought desperate battles against the Egyptian beachheads on the eastern shore, one Israeli thrust drove to the canal at the north end of the Great Bitter Lake. During a night of hard fighting on 15–16 October at Chinese Farm on the eastern shore, the Israelis managed to build a bridge across the canal. No Egyptian forces were to be found on the western bank, and the Israelis ran amok.

Armored forces swiftly drove south along the Great Bitter Lake and secured the western shore of the canal beyond it, cutting off the Egyptian Third Army on the Sinai. Egypt soon called for a cease-fire as well.

The United States, the Soviet Union, and the United Nations had been proposing cease-fire plans for some days, but the Arabs rejected them early in the conflict and the Israelis rejected them later. Not until Israeli units were well in control of the situation did the Israeli government agree to stop fighting. The Soviets, who had been aiding the Arabs since the 1950s, saw their clients losing matériel at a fantastically high rate, and within a few days of the war's start the Soviet government began resupplying them. The United States saw the same thing happen on the Israeli side, and responded with tanks and aircraft. These actions strained the relationship between the two great powers at a time when they had begun to thaw, but neither side wanted to intervene directly and expand the war. Eventually, pressure from the United States and the USSR was the primary factor in bringing the fighting to a halt, though a UN peacekeeping force was formed (without their participation) to stand between the two armies during disengagement.

The Yom Kippur War taught lessons for many nations. The United States and the Soviet Union were able to see their respective weapons systems in action and judge their effectiveness against their major rival. The American equipment tended to dominate, but the Egyptians and Syrians badly hurt the Israeli air forces with Soviet surface-to-air missiles. The two superpowers also learned what modern war does to men and matériel: It eats them up in huge amounts, needing rapid repair and/or replacement.

The Israelis learned that the Arabs could fight much more effectively than they had

suspected. The air of invincibility the Israelis had built around themselves proved
false. Even though the Israelis won hand-
ily in the end, they were sorely pressed at
the beginning and surprised by the skill and
tenacity of Arab forces. They also realized
the need for territory; had they not held
the Sinai, the Golan Heights, and the West
Bank, the Arab forces would have overrun
Jerusalem and Tel Aviv. The closeness of
the conflict hardened Israeli resolve not to
return any captured lands.

The Arabs learned that fighting with
Israel was perhaps too expensive a propo-
sition. Soon after the war, Egypt began to
make tentative moves toward a reconcili-
ation. Through the efforts of U.S. Secretary of State Henry Kissinger, tensions
began to ease somewhat through the mid-
1970s, and Israel slowly began to consider
the return of Arab land in return for guarantees of safety. In 1977, Egypt recognized
Israel as an independent nation, the first
Arab country to do so. In return, the Egyptians got the Sinai Peninsula back, beginning a long process that by the early 1990s
brought about similar Arab actions. Israel,
a nation born in battle, seems by the middle
1990s to be more secure in its borders and
cooperative, if not overly friendly, with its
Arab neighbors. Some radical Arabs, however, continue the old campaign to bring
Israel's existence to an end.

See also Germany, Soviet Invasion of [162];
Sinai, Israeli Invasion of, 1967 (Six-Day
War) [188].

References: Badri, Hasan, The Ramadan
War, 1973 (Boulder, CO: Westview
Press, 1978); Dupuy, Trevor, Elusive
Victory: The Arab-Israeli Wars, 1947–
1974 (New York: Harper & Row,
1978); Herzog, Chaim, War of Atone-
ment, October 1973 (Boston: Little,
Brown, 1975).

In World War II, the British and Americans invaded Italy almost by accident. After clearing North Africa of Axis forces and
securing the island of Sicily at Italy's southern extremity to control Mediterranean
shipping, the veteran troops had little to
do other than wait several months for the
invasion of France. Because the fall of Sicily had occasioned Benito Mussolini's
downfall, the Italians were eager to withdraw from the war. Their new prime minister, Pietro Badoglio, had no desire to see
his homeland become a battleground, so
he covertly contacted the Allies through
agents in Portugal, even as he publicly assured his countrymen and the Germans
that Italy would fight on. Italy secretly
signed surrender papers on 2 September
1943, and several days passed before the
news was made public. Upon learning of
the withdrawal, German forces disarmed
the Italian troops with them and prepared
to fight for the country.

The German commander in Italy,
Field Marshal Albert Kesselring, was one
of few Germans who wanted to fight in
Italy. Even as he withdrew forces from the
southern tip of Italy in accordance with
orders from Berlin, he prepared defensive
positions to slow or stop the Allied advance. With the Appenine Range running down the peninsula's spine and often
reaching all the way to either coast, the
terrain presented Kesselring with a multi-
tude of opportunities to achieve his desire.
He persistently lobbied Hitler to allow
him to fight south of Rome, which all
other German military authorities counseled against. When Hitler finally gave
him that permission, Kesselring was ready
to act. He had to do so in a hurry.

British forces crossed the Straits of
Messina into Italy on 2 September, and

Allied invasion of Italy.

made rapid headway against the withdrawing Germans. On 9 September, British and American forces landed at the port city of Salerno, 200 miles down the coast from Rome. The landings went smoothly at first, but Kesselring's retreating forces joined with reserves rushed down from Rome and quickly counterattacked. For a few days it looked as if the Allies were going to suffer another Dunkirk, but they managed to solidify their beachhead by 14 September. Made cautious by the German resistance, the Allies moved slowly inland, giving the Germans time to man their mountain defenses, called the Gustav Line, which ended any chance that Italy would fall quickly.

Kesselring used not only the mountains but the swift-flowing rivers cutting through them as defensive strongholds. His men dug into the hillsides overlooking successive rivers, and were able to pound any attacker who tried to cross. As the American and Commonwealth troops tried to break through along both coasts, they had to face withering fire expertly directed from hidden observation posts in the mountains. The Sangro, Rapido, Garigliano, and Liri rivers stopped the Allied advances and made them sitting ducks for German artillery. Throughout the autumn and into the winter of 1943–1944, troops of multiple nationalities pounded against the German lines and were repulsed. American, Free French, French colonial, British, New Zealand, South African, Australian, and Polish soldiers each took turns dying in the Italian mountains.

The most difficult of the battles was along the Rapido River, which was overlooked by Monte Cassino, site of the original Benedictine monastery. Convinced that the Germans were occupying it for observation purposes, the Allies debated whether to attack it. The decision to bomb the historic shrine went all the way to Supreme Commander of Allied Forces Dwight Eisenhower, who reluctantly approved the attack at the urging of the New Zealand force commander whose troops were slated to attack the mountain. The air attack took place on 15 February 1944 and the monastery was leveled. Subsequently, the Allies learned that the Germans had not occupied it, but had been using observation posts camouflaged on the mountainside. After the bombing, however, reluctance to violate the sanctity of the monastery was moot, and the Germans turned the rubble into a much more difficult objective than the hilltop would have been otherwise.

As Eisenhower pondered the fate of Cassino, American forces staged another amphibious landing. The need for shipping for the upcoming Allied invasion of France robbed the Italian campaign of necessary transport and landing craft, so the landings at Anzio were a somewhat haphazard affair. General John Lucas commanded the 50,000-man force that went ashore on 22 January 1944 against an undefended beach. The Germans were unprepared for the landing, but Lucas gave them time to regroup. He spent a few days digging in and making sure his beachhead was secure; by the time that was done, Kesselring had shifted reserves to Anzio and launched his own attack. Though the Allies were once again on the verge of being pushed into the sea, they held on. They could not make a relatively quick move off the beaches as they had after the Salerno attacks because this time the Germans were not in the process of withdrawing, but had come to stay. The Anzio beachhead went nowhere for

four months, and any assistance it may have rendered to the troops in the south was minimal.

The Allies finally broke through the Gustav Line in the spring of 1944. The British Eighth Army attacked up the eastern coast, drawing the German reserves to that end of the line. A few days later, the American Fifth Army again challenged the Rapido River and Monte Cassino, while French Moroccan forces fought through the mountains in between. The Moroccans and the Poles scored the first breakthroughs, and the race was on. With the Germans finally dislodged and pulling back, General Lucian Truscott (now in command of the forces at Anzio) attacked eastward, hoping to block the fleeing Germans and hold them as the advancing Allies pushed north. It almost worked. As Truscott's men were about to reach the Liri River valley and cut off the German line of retreat, he was ordered to turn northward instead and take Rome before British troops could reach the city. Rome, declared an open city by the Germans, fell without a fight on 4 June; the German army slipped away to a new defensive line in the north.

The Allies captured all of central Italy in a matter of weeks, then ran into the Hitler and Gothic lines, where the Germans again stopped them cold. Another fall and winter passed with Allied forces struggling against mountain strongpoints, and they were doing it with fewer and fewer men because many troops were drained off for operations in France. Only because the German government collapsed in the spring of 1945 did the German resistance break in Italy, but it had forced the Allies into a much costlier campaign than had ever been anticipated. Much debate has ensued about just how vital the campaign was. True, it forced Italy from the war, but after Sicily the Italians were on the verge of giving up anyway. The fighting gave the Allies air bases from which to attack targets in southern France and the Balkans, which assisted in the invasion of France in the summer of 1944 and also hurt German oil refining in Rumania. Germany was obliged to shift men from the Balkans, France, and Germany to aid their effort in Italy, which could have had a significant effect because they were then unavailable to counter the Normandy invasion. It was a murderous campaign that resembled the fighting experienced in World War I in the slow progress of advances and the numbers of men lost for the amount of ground gained. Italy did not suffer as much as many other countries because most of the fighting was in limited areas in the mountains, but in some cases the destruction was significant. Rome saw no fighting at all, and the treasures of the city were saved. The same can be said for most of the major historic cities, but historic treasures such as Monte Cassino can never be replaced. Italy's losses were more economic than physical, and the democratic government that replaced the Fascists after the war has provided Europe with the most varied of political arenas.

See also Egypt, Italian Invasion of [155]; Eisenhower, Dwight David [156]; France, Allied Invasion of [159]; France, Nazi Invasion of [161]; Mussolini, Benito [175]; North Africa, U.S. Invasion of [177]; Sicily, Allied Invasion of [186].

References: Clark, Mark, *Calculated Risk* (New York: Harper, 1950); Majdalany, Fred, *The Battle of Cassino* (Boston: Houghton Mifflin, 1958); Morris, Eric, *Circles of Hell* (London: Hutchinson, 1993).

## 168 — KUWAIT, IRAQI INVASION OF

In 1990, Iraqi leader Saddam Hussein invaded his neighbor on the Persian Gulf, Kuwait. He claimed that in Ottoman times Kuwait had been part of territory controlled by Baghdad, so it should return to Baghdad's control as the nineteenth province of Iraq. Actually, this had not been the case; Kuwait was a separate sheikhdom under the Ottoman Empire, and Baghdad had merely served as the district capital for the Ottoman governor. It seems likely that Hussein's real reason for invasion was control of the Kuwaiti oil fields, as he was intent on being the major factor in the pricing of Middle Eastern oil. Kuwait appeared to be the first target of his expansion, and the United States in particular did not want to see other, more friendly oil producers come under Hussein's control. Hussein had made threatening gestures toward Kuwait for weeks, but the United States thought it was nothing more than saber-rattling.

Earlier, when Hussein made war against Iran, the United States had opened its military largess to him. In addition, when Iraq first made complaints about Kuwait's oil-pricing policies, the United States told Hussein that any Middle East "border dispute" was none of its business. Once the invasion took place, however, American president George Bush became the leader of an international coalition not only to resist further Iraqi expansion but to restore Kuwait's independence. In response to calls for aid from other Arab countries, notably Saudi Arabia, Bush sent American troops and cajoled the United Nations into aiding him in dealing with Hussein. European allies joined in with troops, but other nations dependent on Middle East oil, such as Japan and Germany, were barred by their post–World War II constitutions from sending troops outside their borders; they instead offered financial aid. Operation Desert Shield, organized under the command of American general Norman Schwarzkopf, put almost half a million men along the Saudi-Iraqi border by January 1991.

Much has been made of Bush's motives for Desert Shield and its successor, Operation Desert Storm. Certainly American and world dependence on a stable Middle East oil supply was a factor. As a member of the generation that had fought in World War II, Bush saw Saddam Hussein as a latter-day Adolf Hitler who needed to be stopped rather than appeased. Stories of Iraqi brutality in Kuwait further increased his resolve to resist totalitarian aggression. Also, because communism was collapsing in the Soviet Union and Eastern Europe, Bush saw an opportunity for what he called a "New World Order," where peace-loving nations would cooperate to maintain sovereign borders against flagrant expansionism. The international response to Bush's pleas was remarkable. Even such hostile nations as Cuba and Libya voted to condemn Iraqi aggression. Hussein tried to court Arab assistance by attacking Israel, but only the Palestinians gave him any support.

Throughout the second half of 1990, the coalition forces massed along the Iraqi and Kuwaiti borders. Rather than launch a preemptive strike, Hussein allowed the forces to grow; meanwhile, he began building a defensive line along the border, and dared the coalition to attack it. Schwarzkopf gave the impression that he would do just that, then planned a major turning movement through the desert along the Iraqi right flank. Economic attempts to pressure Hussein to leave proved futile, and by the end of December, President Bush gave Iraq a 15 January deadline to withdraw from Kuwait. Last-minute negotiations proved

fruitless, and Schwarzkopf received word to turn Desert Shield into Desert Storm.

Shortly after 3:00 A.M. local time on 17 January, a massive air assault struck the Iraqi capital and key locations across the country. Cruise missiles, Stealth fighters, and laser-guided "smart" bombs took out military installations with pinpoint precision. Iraqi command, communication, and control were paralyzed and then destroyed by 38 days of air attack. Hussein responded by launching "Scud" missiles against Israel, hoping to provoke an Israeli response that would attract Arab support to his side. Israel took relatively light damage, and did not respond militarily. That restraint effectively isolated Iraq, as did the Scud attacks on Saudi Arabia.

Hussein still refused to accede to international demands, so the land war finally began. It lasted a mere 100 hours until President Bush called it to a halt. The Iraqi army displayed what was possibly the poorest performance in all of military history. Anecdotes are told of soldiers surrendering to drone observation aircraft and news correspondents. Thousands died, and tens of thousands surrendered; coalition casualties numbered less than 800 dead and wounded. Kuwait was liberated in hours, and the massive defenses the Iraqis had spent months constructing were first outflanked and then easily pierced when the defenders gave up.

Many around the world believed that Bush stopped the war too soon, that the coalition should have completely destroyed the Iraqi military, driven to Baghdad, and removed Hussein from power. Because none of those things happened, the defeat of the Iraqi army proved to have accomplished little. Saddam Hussein retained power and the core of his military, and soon he was persecuting Arabs around Basra and Kurds in the north. Hussein had ordered oil spilled into the Persian Gulf to thwart an amphibious attack, and retreating Iraqi forces set fire to most of the Kuwaiti oil wells. The environmental damage was huge, but quick response by fire-fighting teams put the fires out sooner than expected. An international embargo remained for years as the United Nations awaited the extremely slow revelation of Iraq's atomic and chemical warfare capabilities. Through the middle 1990s, Hussein retained power, while the people of Iraq suffered extreme economic hardship because minimal imports were allowed and no Iraqi oil was exported.

In Kuwait the political administration of the emir suffered some discontent from Kuwaitis who had remained in the country during the occupation and conducted resistance action. They demanded some representation in the government, which came about by 1994. The large resident population of Palestinians, who had worked as laborers in Kuwait, was persecuted because the Palestine Liberation Organization had supported Iraq. Almost all were driven from the country in a matter of months.

*See also* Hitler, Adolf [165].

References: Blackwell, James, *Thunder in the Desert* (New York: Bantam Books, 1991); Friedman, Norman, *Desert Victory* (Annapolis, MD: Naval Institute Press, 1991); Woodward, Bob, *The Commanders* (New York: Simon & Schuster, 1991).

## LATIN AMERICA, U.S. INTERVENTIONS IN

**169**

Since the 1820s, the United States has viewed itself as something of a Western Hemispheric policeman. In response to the possible reconquest of Spanish colonies in Latin America, President James Monroe and Secretary of State John Quincy Adams formulated the Monroe Doctrine. This stated that the Western Hemisphere was closed to colonization, that any attempt to interfere in the internal affairs of a Western Hemisphere country would be viewed as an unfriendly act, and that the United States would not meddle in European affairs. No European power made good on the threat of reconquest (more because of British threats than American), so the United States came to view itself as the protector of the Americas.

What began as basically a defensive stance became, over time, more interventionist. President Theodore Roosevelt added the Roosevelt Corollary, stating that the United States would act preemptively to keep Europeans out of Latin America. In 1934, President Franklin Roosevelt created the Good Neighbor Policy, wherein the United States promised retaliation against any invasion and also reserved the right to intervene when local disturbances threatened American lives or interests. With and without that reservation, the United States has often sent forces into Latin American countries to protect its interests (strategic or economic) or to support friendly governments from internal resistance.

American naval forces were sent to Chile in 1891 to enforce payment of damages demanded by the U.S. government from the Chileans when American sailors were killed in a riot. To many Latin American nations it seemed like extortion, but no country was in a position to challenge the action. The United States made itself a mediator in a Venezuela–British Guiana border dispute in the middle 1890s; at first, Venezuela invited the United States to protect them from British claims to gold fields, but when the American mediators sided with British claims, the Venezuelans refused to abide by the decision.

## CUBA

The United States removed Spanish control from Cuba in 1898, and in 1901 a democratic government was established and the first president elected. After losing the following election, the president refused to cede power, so American troops went in and oversaw new elections. This oversight became an ongoing exercise until 1934, when President Franklin Roosevelt instituted the Good Neighbor Policy and withdrew from the Cuban political scene. The result was the establishment of a dictatorship in Cuba, put in place by Fulgencio Batista (with U.S. military and economic aid). Batista oversaw a regime as corrupt as any in Latin America, establishing close ties to organized crime (through casinos) and American businesses, which exploited most of the island's agriculture and raw materials. In the 1950s, Fidel Castro led a revolution, and in 1959 he succeeded in overthrowing Batista. Castro turned to the United States for economic assistance but was rebuffed by President Eisenhower. On the advice of some left-leaning lieutenants, Castro turned to the Soviets, who were more than happy to establish influence so close to the United States.

Castro, rejected by the Americans, now became their number one enemy. His expulsion of organized-crime figures and those who had profited under Batista created a group of disgruntled Cubans in exile in the United States. They appealed to Eisenhower for help, and he ordered the CIA to aid them in returning to Cuba, where they promised a popular uprising against Castro. President John Kennedy inherited the operation, but gave it inconsistent support. When the Cubans landed at the Bay of Pigs on Cuba's south coast in April 1961, the invasion was a fiasco. Though Kennedy ransomed the 1,100 prisoners, Cuban exiles were convinced he had not done enough to aid them in their attempt to reestablish control. An embargo on Cuba, long tied to the American economy, hurt them even more than the invasion.

The Soviet Union's 1962 attempt to install in Cuba offensive missiles capable of carrying nuclear warheads brought the island once again to Kennedy's attention. Plans were considered for bombing targets in Cuba or perhaps an invasion, but Kennedy instituted a "quarantine" around Cuba to stop Soviet ships. Soviet premier Nikita Khrushchev publicly announced his intention to break the quarantine, and nuclear war seemed imminent. It is not overly dramatic to say that the world held its breath until, at the last minute, Khruschev decided not to push his luck. The Soviets agreed to remove the missiles if the United States promised not to invade Cuba.

## THE DOMINICAN REPUBLIC

The United States has sent forces to the Dominican Republic more than once. In 1907 the two countries signed a treaty giving the U.S. the right to collect Dominican taxes and customs. President William Taft sent troops to the island to dislodge a corrupt leader and oversee new elections. A few years later they were back, protecting the island from a possible German attempt to establish a naval base there during World War I. More importantly, however, President Woodrow Wilson sent troops into the Dominican Republic to maintain internal security. While Cuba and the Philippines seemed to be progressing along democratic lines, Caribbean island nations remained politically unstable. Although Wilson said he wanted to "teach the South American republics to elect good men," he established a military occupation that oversaw no elections.

When Warren Harding became president, he began the withdrawal of American forces from the Domincan Republic in

1922. Supervised elections were held in 1924 and the Marines left, although the Americans retained control over customs revenues to relieve the republic's debt. A civil war soon broke out, however, and the Marines went back in 1927. They stayed until President Franklin Roosevelt announced his Good Neighbor Policy in 1934, in which the U.S. agreed with the Montevideo Conference resolution against intervention. The realization that we were militarily supreme in this hemisphere ended the traditional argument that control over Caribbean nations guarded access to the Panama Canal.

The Dominican Republic came under the dictatorship of Raphael Trujillo, who was succeeded after his assassination in the early 1960s by Juan Bosch. When Bosch was overthrown in 1963, President John Kennedy withdrew American diplomatic recognition and financial support, which he had made available through his Alliance for Progress, a Latin American Marshall Plan to stabilize the economies of Latin American countries. Another civil war in 1965 saw the arrival of 21,000 American Marines and airborne troops, sent by President Lyndon Johnson. This met with a negative response by the Organization of American States, which Johnson finally convinced to agree to an Inter-American Peace Force. The Americans, who provided the largest part of that force, favored a military junta with an openly anti-communist stance, although they were not democratically elected. Finally, through the efforts of the Organization of American States, fair elections were held in 1965 and 1966 and the troops were removed. American economic aid returned and the communist threat, real or imagined, receded.

## EL SALVADOR

The United States showed little interest in El Salvador prior to the 1970s, when re-

form movements rebelled against a coalition of the upper class and the military. When the military began using death squads to suppress the revolt, President Carter cut off U.S. aid. Moderate military officers attempted to institute some reforms by staging a coup in 1979, but they failed. In 1980, José Napoleon Duarte returned from exile to the presidency and tried to quiet both the extreme right and left. However, in time he had to lean more heavily on the military, and soon the repression returned. Carter again cut off aid to Duarte, then reinstated it because of a strong revolutionary offensive. The struggle turned into a long, low-intensity fight that killed thousands on both sides and ruined what had been one of Central America's strongest economies. President Reagan sent in forces to aid Duarte in putting down the rebellion, but succeeded only in pushing more people into the rebels' camp. After a nullified election in 1982, Duarte was finally reelected president in 1984. He seemed to have widespread support, but he could not institute the land reforms so desperately needed. The military resumed the death squads, and the right wing took power in the elections of 1989, continuing the death and destruction.

## GUATEMALA

The U.S. government had little interest in Guatemala, but by the 1940s the United Fruit Company of Boston owned 42 percent of the land. In 1944 a reform-minded revolt overthrew the government, and in 1951 Jacobo Arbenz Guzmán was elected to the presidency. He and his wife María set out to improve the educational and health conditions of the country's poor. Arbenz planned to confiscate a quarter-million acres of land from United Fruit, though he offered to pay for it. The administration of President Dwight Eisenhower, however, became convinced that this was a pro-Communist action. No proof of Communist collaboration existed, but in 1954 the Eisenhower administration acted (without the cooperation of the Organization of American States) by ordering the Central Intelligence Agency (CIA) to train a group of disaffected Guatemalans. Arbenz turned to the Soviet Union for arms, and that proved to Eisenhower that communism was in the neighborhood. The CIA-trained force invaded and overthrew Arbenz, executed his followers, and stopped the reform movements. The leader of the coup, Carlos Castillo Armas, made himself dictator and established a three-decade string of strongmen in power.

## HISPANIOLA

The island of Hispaniola, site of Spain's first colony in the New World, was later divided into two nations: Haiti in the west and the Dominican Republic in the east. Both nations have had their share of internal troubles, and no other nation has been occupied by the United States as much as these two.

Haiti became an independent nation in 1803 under the leadership of Toussaint L'Ouverture. It remained independent throughout the nineteenth century, but with a long string of increasingly corrupt leaders. Haiti was unable to repay foreign loans, and U.S. president Woodrow Wilson was forced to intervene to forestall possible European intervention. When negotiations failed and President Guillaume Sam was assassinated in July 1915, U.S. Marines landed and occupied Port-au-Prince. The United States impounded tax revenues, and demanded the right to appoint tax officials and policemen. The Haitians rather reluctantly agreed, and the United States kept troops in the country for 19 years. A constitution was adopted in 1918, but it provided for little more than an American-backed dictator. More dic-

tators followed, further impoverishing the country for their own benefit. In the early 1990s a president was elected, but the military forced his exile. In 1994, American troops were once again in Haiti to maintain order, break up a corrupt police force and military, and oversee new elections.

The Dominican Republic, established after a revolution against Haiti in 1844, was also the site of many dictators and much corruption. Almost constant revolution had indebted the nation to many European countries, and President Theodore Roosevelt intervened to forestall the arrival of European forces. Roosevelt entered into an agreement with Dominican president Morales whereby American officials would collect customs duties and take the responsibility of distributing them to the country's creditors. By 1911 the country was financially solvent and public works were being constructed. It was too good to last; in 1911 the president was assassinated, and the country returned to factional infighting. When the Dominican government rejected President Wilson's attempt to return to the original peaceful era, he sent in troops and ordered the establishment of a military government, run by an American navy captain. For six years the navy ran the government, with no hint of Dominican involvement.

President Coolidge removed American forces, and Franklin Roosevelt's Good Neighbor Policy, along with the formation of the Organization of American States (OAS), established freedom of action in Latin American countries. In 1965, however, President Lyndon Johnson sent American forces back into the Dominican Republic, claiming a possible Communist takeover in the wake of a 1963 revolution. With minimal OAS support, a compromise government was installed and the 21,000 U.S. forces withdrawn.

## NICARAGUA

Nicaragua has probably seen more American intervention than any other Latin American country. When the United States learned that Britain had acquired possible rights to a canal site in the 1840s, it acted to gain an equal share. Cornelius Vanderbilt convinced the Nicaraguan government in 1848 to cede transportation rights to the country's waters to the United States. One of Vanderbilt's employees killed a Nicaraguan, which sparked a local protest ending in an American bombardment of the port of Greytown. The arrival in 1855 of William Walker, an idealist American reformer, again brought American attention to the country. In an attempt to bring democracy to the country, Walker worked with some of the local political factions and Vanderbilt to conquer Nicaragua. Foolishly, he ceded mineral and land rights to American business interests, who in turn aided in his overthrow in 1857. In 1912 the United States supported the assumption of power by Adolfo Díaz, who offered his country as an American protectorate. When his countrymen rebelled at this decision, American troops landed to protect his regime. American banks and business interests owned much of Nicaragua, including 51 percent of the railroads; they advanced Díaz more loans in 1913 in return for the rest of the rail system. Secretary of State William Jennings Bryan negotiated the Bryan-Chomorro Treaty (ratified in 1916), which gave the United States the rights to build a canal through Nicaragua (rights that are still retained). By this time the country was almost exclusively under American control.

U.S. Marines stayed in Nicaragua through the middle 1920s, until President Calvin Coolidge ordered their return. Within a few weeks, fighting flared up, and the Marines were back. The major opponent to a negotiated settlement was Augusto Sandino, who led a guerrilla operation out of the mountains for years. American forces were harassed continually by the Sandinistas, costing hundreds of lives on both sides. American public opinion finally demanded the Marines' withdrawal in 1933, at which point Sandino laid down his arms and negotiated with the Nicaraguan government. Its American-trained national guard, under the direction of American-educated Anastasio Samoza, immediately took Sandino prisoner and executed him. The military now in his power, Samoza seized control of the government in 1936; with American assistance he stayed in power until the 1970s, when his corruption and greed proved too much for the people. A guerrilla movement fashioned after the Sandinistas of the 1920s and 1930s was reborn and carried on a brutal resistance to Samoza. In 1979 he was forced from power and into exile. While the American Congress debated an aid package to the bankrupt nation, the revolutionaries appealed to Cuba, and the promised elections were postponed. Under President Ronald Reagan, the United States openly and later covertly supported the "Contra" movement against the Sandinistas, but with little positive outcome. Finally, Oscar Arias Sánchez of Costa Rica offered a peace plan, which began to have good results. The American-backed Contras, unable to win in the field, finally won in the peace talks and elections of the late 1980s.

## PANAMA

American relations with Panama have usually been close but sometimes stormy throughout this century. Theodore Roosevelt was active in assisting the Panamanians in winning their independence from Colombia in 1903, using a timely naval and marine force to bar the reinforcement of Colombian troops. Within hours of their independence the United States recognized the new country, and within days had arranged to build a canal through the country at a price less than that demanded by Colombia. The negotiator for Panama was Phillipe Bunau-Varilla, a Frenchman who had a financial stake in the canal and who had secretly financed the revolution. He named himself ambassador to the United States and negotiated a treaty before any Panamanian representatives arrived in Washington. This treaty gave the United States sovereign rights in the canal zone, a strip of land ten miles wide from Atlantic to Pacific. In the administration of President Jimmy Carter, new treaties were negotiated to return the zone to Panama in 1999, but even now, disagreement over control remains. In President Ronald Reagan's administration, the United States sent troops into Panama to unseat dictator Manuel Noriega, who was accused of trafficking in illegal drugs.

After the establishment of formal relations with Latin American countries upon their declarations of independence in the early 1800s, American relations with the rest of the hemisphere steadily deteriorated. The Monroe Doctrine, formulated to meet a onetime potential threat, by accident became the dominant feature in hemispheric relations. The United States often tried to assist Latin American countries, but usually wound up aiding the more corrupt factions (with which U.S. companies cooperated) to the detriment of the majority of the population. U.S. companies have consistently dominated Latin American economies, and through this their governments, and an intent that often began as beneficial turned into local corruption and massive poverty. The American determination to resist communist expansion in the post–World War II era often made bad matters worse: The United States would aid any corrupt dictator who took an anti-

Communist stance. The vast majority of people in the affected countries suffered death, privation, and persecution, while a small number of powerful people benefited from the close relations with the power of the U.S. military and business.

*See also* Caribbean, European Occupation of [87]; Panama, U.S. Invasion of [180].

References: Collins, John, *America's Small Wars* (Washington, DC: Brassey's, 1991); LaFeber, Walter, *The American Age* (New York: Norton, 1989); Smith, Gaddis, *The Last Years of the Monroe Doctrine, 1945–1993* (New York: Hill & Wang, 1994).

## 170 MacArthur, Douglas

Douglas MacArthur was born into a military family in Little Rock, Arkansas, on 26 January 1880. His father, Arthur, had distinguished himself as a Union general in the Civil War. MacArthur attended the U.S. Military Academy at West Point, where he graduated first in his class (with the highest marks ever received by any student) in 1903. He was commissioned a second lieutenant of engineers, and spent the years prior to World War I in a number of teaching and staff positions, including one in Asia with his father and another with President Theodore Roosevelt. He was attached to the General Staff in 1913, and participated in the Vera Cruz expedition the following year.

When the United States entered World War I in April 1917, MacArthur was with the General Staff. He assisted in organizing the multistate National Guard "Rainbow" Division and was its chief of staff when it was assigned to France in October 1917. He served as a general during the Aisne-Marne campaign, commanding the

84th Brigade at Saint-Mihiel (September 1918) and the Meuse-Argonne offensive (October–November). MacArthur was one of the last commanders who believed in leading from the front, and he received ten medals for valor and two Purple Hearts. He stayed with the occupation forces until his return home in April 1919.

He became one of the youngest superintendents of the Military Academy in June 1919, and he initiated a number of reforms: codification of the Honor Code, revitalization of the curriculum, emphasis on the humanities and social sciences in addition to the "hard" sciences, and an attempt to end hazing. With these reforms, MacArthur tried to reflect the citizen-soldier nature of the cadets. His term ended in 1922, when he received orders for the Philippines. Three years later, he returned to the United States to command the Third and Fourth Corps areas in Baltimore and Atlanta, respectively. He faced the problems of a shrinking military budget, obsolescent equipment, decrepit facilities, and a low reenlistment rate. Three years later, in 1928, he was again in the Pacific as commander of the Department of the Philippines.

MacArthur held the position for two years; in November 1930 he was back home as army chief of staff. His experience in the Corps commands served him well in dealing with the even more stringent military budgets of the Great Depression. Though he focused on plans for industrial mobilization and manpower procurement, he became involved in political affairs as well. In 1932 he convinced President Herbert Hoover to send in troops to dislodge from Washington, D.C., the Bonus Army, a group of World War I veterans attempting to gain promised compensation from the government.

He was again in the Philippines in 1935, preparing that colony's military for independence. When he was ordered home in 1937, before the job was completed, he chose instead to retire and stay in Manila. He was appointed field marshal in the Philippine Commonwealth Army. When war against Japan seemed imminent in 1941, MacArthur was recalled to active duty and appointed commander of U.S. Army Forces in the Far East (USAFFE). As Philippine field marshal, MacArthur seemed to overestimate the abilities of his adopted army, while underestimating those of the Japanese. He learned the difference on 8 December 1941 when most of his air forces were destroyed on the ground by surprise Japanese attacks. He ordered a fighting withdrawal from Japanese forces landing on the island of Luzon, and spent the next months preparing defensive positions on the peninsula of Bataan and the island of Corregidor. He begged the U.S. government for reinforcements and supplies, but the decision in Washington was to write off the Philippines and defend Australia. MacArthur was ordered by President Franklin Roosevelt to evacuate the islands with his family and staff, which he did on 11 March 1942. U.S. and Filipino forces held out another month before their surrender to the Japanese.

In Australia, MacArthur was named supreme commander of the Southwest Pacific area. He secured the lines of communication by denying the Japanese a base at Port Moresby. With limited troops and support craft, he repulsed the southward Japanese advance across the island in the summer of 1942. He and Admiral Chester Nimitz, commander in chief, Pacific Fleet (CINCPAC), worked on strategy to carry the war to Japan's home islands. With army troops and naval support, MacArthur would stage leapfrogging amphibious landings along the western Pacific islands to bypass or cut off large Japanese fortifications or troop concentrations. The strategy proved successful as American forces worked their way northwest up the Solomon Island chain, New Guinea, and to the Philippines. Nimitz meanwhile used Marines and naval forces to "island hop" across the Central Pacific, bypassing major Japanese strong points. Both commanders used the growing American superiority in aircraft and warships to neutralize Japanese bases.

MacArthur argued for an early invasion of the Philippines to fulfill his promise to the population that he would return. He overcame the Washington leaders who preferred an assault on Formosa, and ultimately Roosevelt and the Joint Chiefs of Staff agreed. MacArthur and Nimitz carried out a joint operation in October 1944 against the island of Leyte. It was a daring plan, attacking the central section of the archipelago to split the defenders occupying the islands and prevent them from unifying. MacArthur was then able to separately defeat both Japanese forces. He spent the remainder of the war organizing the redeployment of his troops to areas outside his command and launching cleanup operations against the bypassed Philippine islands. On 2 September 1945 he presided over the Japanese surrender aboard the USS *Missouri*.

Now a five-star general, MacArthur was appointed military governor of occupied Japan. He transferred his headquarters to Tokyo on 8 September and began his oversight of the political and economic reconstruction of Japan. As supreme commander of Allied Powers, he directed the writing of a new Japanese constitution. His term as governor can be described as one of the most efficient, honest, and fair of all military occupations in history. Much of Japan's condition today can be attributed to the foundations MacArthur laid in the late 1940s.

On 25 June 1950, North Korean forces attacked across the 38th parallel into South Korea. The weak nature of the South Korean military and the inability to provide sufficient reinforcements left only the southeastern corner of the country around the port city of Pusan uncaptured. MacArthur was named supreme commander of United Nations forces on 8 July. His immediate goal was to prevent the fall of Pusan, so he brought in as many American troops as were available from occupation duty in Japan, and he ordered American airpower to support the forces trapped in what came to be called the Pusan Perimeter. While the area was being held by General Walton Walker's Eighth Army, MacArthur argued for newly arriving forces to be committed to a daring assault of Inchon, the harbor city serving the South Korean capital of Seoul on the peninsula's west coast. Again, MacArthur's influence and persuasiveness overcame Pentagon objections, and the landings on 15 September were an overwhelming success.

The United Nations expanded the scope of the conflict by permitting South Korean forces (closely supported by UN forces) to invade North Korea. The Communist Chinese government threatened intervention if their border was threatened, but MacArthur was certain they were bluffing; at Wake Island in mid-October, he assured President Harry Truman that the Chinese would not get involved. On 25–26 November 1950, the Chinese launched a massive assault that pushed UN forces south of the 38th parallel. Just as he had underestimated the Japanese in the late 1930s, he repeated his mistake in 1950. From the beginning, MacArthur and Truman could not agree on a strategy. Truman feared an escalating conflict that could become World War III, while MacArthur continued to believe in the goal of liberating North Korea. In addition to their personal differences, MacArthur began to publicly criticize Truman's foreign policy; he felt his hands were tied because the president would not let him increase air operations, blockade Chinese ports, deploy Nationalist Chinese forces from Formosa, or possibly use nuclear weapons. Truman began to depend on the advice of Field Commander General Matthew Ridgeway, and MacArthur's continuing critical tone and public statements released against orders proved too much for the president. MacArthur was relieved of his command on charges of insubordination on 11 April 1951. He returned to an adoring public and talk of the presidency in 1952, but his increasingly aggressive statements soon turned the public against him. He retired to West Point where (as he informed Congress of an old ballad common at the academy) he, like other old soldiers, faded away.

—James L. Iseman

*See also* New Guinea, Japanese Invasion of [176]; Pacific Islands, U.S. Conquest of [179]; Philippines, Japanese Invasion of the [181]; Philippines, U.S. Invasion of the [182]; South Korea, North Korean Invasion of (Korean War) [190].

References: Carver, Michael, ed., *The War Lords: Military Commanders of the Twentieth Century* (Boston: Little, Brown, 1976); Costello, John, *The Pacific War, 1941–1945* (New York: Quill, 1982); Manchester, William, *American Caesar* (Boston: Little, Brown, 1978).

## MANCHURIA, JAPANESE INVASION OF (1904) (RUSSO-JAPANESE WAR)

**171**

In the late nineteenth century, the major powers of the world divided the coast of China into spheres of economic influence. Great Britain, France, Germany, Holland,

Russia, and Japan had exclusive rights to trade within their spheres. In 1899 the United States convinced these countries to cooperate, rather than compete, by the adoption of the Open Door policy. Under this plan, the whole of China would be open for free trade, and the spheres of influence would gradually fade away.

The Russians held sway in Manchuria, and had laid claim to Vladivostok as the base for its Pacific fleet since the 1860s. After the Sino-Japanese War ended in 1895, Russia, France, and Germany put diplomatic pressure on Japan to withdraw from Korea, which the Japanese did under protest in what seemed to them a humiliating concession. Therefore, Russia and Japan were already unfriendly when in 1903, Russia failed to give up its rights in Manchuria, in which Japan was intensely interested. Russia promised to leave within six months, but instead reinforced its army, strengthened fortifications, and sent additional warships. This buildup not only gave the lie to their Open Door promises, but also gave the impression of threatening Korea, where Japan was keeping its pledges to open trade. Anticipating that Russia might prove recalcitrant, in 1902, Japan had entered into a defense agreement with Great Britain stating that either country would come to the aid of the other if one of the countries were fighting two enemies. The Japanese estimate seemed accurate, because the Russians refused to negotiate in good faith and continued their military buildup. By January 1904 the Japanese were convinced that further negotiation was futile, so military action seemed the only alternative.

On 8 February the Japanese navy struck the Russian fleet based at Port Arthur. Torpedo boats sneaked into the harbor, flashing Russian signal lights, then torpedoed two battleships and a cruiser. The next day the Japanese fleet stood outside the harbor and shelled the ships and facilities inside. The Russian ships that survived did little to challenge the Japanese. The Russian fleet commander realized his sailors were not well trained in fleet maneuvers, so he decided not to challenge the Japanese in open water. Leery of the coastal defenses around Port Arthur, the Japanese hesitated to draw close enough to the harbor to destroy the Russians. Both sides kept a close eye on each other for some months.

The Japanese army was in action as well, landing on 8 February at Inchon, Korea, then moving slowly up the peninsula over bad roads. Russian resistance was minimal, and the Japanese worked their way northward toward the Yalu River, the border between Korea and Manchuria. The Japanese staged a brilliant river crossing in April, which established them in Manchuria and forced the Russians to withdraw into the mountains. With bridges under their control, the Japanese were prepared to invade Manchuria from Korea as well as from the south. Japanese forces landed on the peninsula above Port Arthur on 5 May and rapidly sealed off the city from reinforcements. Japan hoped to capture Port Arthur easily, as they had done in the war against China ten years earlier, but the Russians mounted a much stouter defense. More and more men were committed to breaking through the well-prepared Russian defenses, and the siege lasted months longer than anticipated. Trench networks, massed artillery barrages, machine guns in defensive positions—all brought about massive loss of life on both sides in a preview of France in World War I.

In Port Arthur the Russians were in deep trouble. The fleet attempted to attack the Japanese in August but failed, leaving the navy demoralized. The Russians anchored their ships and moved the sailors to man the defenses on land. Through the fall of 1904, the Japanese continued their assaults on the city, inflicting and receiving huge casualties but edging ever closer. By December the highest point overlooking the city was in Japanese hands, and artillery placed there finished off the Russian fleet. The defenders, though killing more men than they themselves were losing, realized that there was no hope of relieving forces from the north. The Russian commander surrendered the city on New Year's Day 1905. The Japanese fleet could now go home for repairs, and the Japanese army marched north to aid their comrades near Mukden.

In late February the largest battle started. Just over 200,000 Japanese attacked almost 300,000 Russians in a double envelopment at Mukden. It was a long, slowly developing battle with poor leadership decisions and hesitant generalship on both sides. On 9 March the Russians withdrew the bulk of their forces before being surrounded, leaving behind 90,000 casualties. More aggressive action on the part of the Japanese would have captured the entire force, but the Russians re-formed 40 miles northward. It made little difference, as no more major land fighting took place.

The final major battle of the war took place at sea. In October the Russian government had dispatched the Baltic fleet to sail to Vladivostok and engage the Japanese fleet. It finally arrived in late May 1905 and ran into the Japanese in the narrows between Japan and Korea at Tsushima Strait. The Russian fleet was old and manned by inexperienced crews, and the battle was no contest. The more modern Japanese ships pounded the Russians in a day-long battle that cost the Russians 34 of their 40 ships, either sunk or captured. The Japanese capital ships all took heavy damage, but only three destroyers were sunk. After the devastation at Port Arthur and Tsushima, the Russian navy virtually ceased to exist.

The Japanese were winning every battle, but financially they were unable to continue fighting. The Russians lost every battle, but they continued to send men and supplies 5,000 miles down the Trans-Siberian Railway to keep the war going. The news of the losses, however, fomented discontent in Moscow, and the Russian government had to deal with revolutionary rumblings. Since the outbreak of the war, American president Theodore Roosevelt had offered to mediate, but both sides had refused. After Tsushima, the Japanese secretly informed him that if he would again offer his services, the Japanese would agree to talk. The Russians agreed to Roosevelt's new proposal on the condition that the Japanese publicly agree first, and that only representatives of the belligerents conduct negotiations. Roosevelt provided a venue for talks in Washington, D.C., in August 1905, but after no progress was made he moved them to the more comfortable site of Portsmouth, New Hampshire. Though not allowed into the conferences, Roosevelt worked behind the scenes to assist the negotiations, and he was able to bring them to a successful conclusion. The Portsmouth Treaty recognized Japan as the premier power in Manchuria, but the Japanese had to return captured Russian ships and not demand reparations payments from Russia. For his efforts Roosevelt received the 1905 Nobel Peace Prize.

The Japanese people were not happy with the treaty. They felt that they deserved more spoils of war, and blamed Roosevelt for the shortfall. Coupled with anti-Japanese legislation passed in California, relations between the two countries became strained. Roosevelt's personal influence in both California and Tokyo defused the situation, but he saw that Japan was a new power to be reckoned with. His dispatch of the American battleship fleet on an around-the-world cruise in 1907 was aimed primarily at flexing American muscles in the Pacific while concluding the Root-Takahira Agreement, which spelled out American and Japanese spheres of influence in the Pacific region. The two nations remained fairly friendly until the 1930s.

The war itself was an omen for any soldier who would see it. Observers in Manchuria, especially German General Staff members, saw the devastating effects of machine guns, and incorporated the knowledge into their military views. What almost everyone failed to see, however, was that the improved defensive capabilities called for new offensive doctrine. Many of the elements of destruction the Europeans inflicted on one another in World War I made their appearance in Manchuria.

In Russia, the czarist government's days were numbered. The poor handling of the war by both generals and governmental leaders, plus the cost in money and men, encouraged the radicals in Moscow and St. Petersburg to preach revolution. The 1905 uprising, which the government suppressed, laid the groundwork for the revolution of 1917, again brought on by military disasters.

In Japan, the people and government reluctantly accepted the peace, but they savored a taste of victory that encouraged future military ventures. Their success in 1904–1905 over the heavily favored Russians reinforced the long-standing traditions and training of the Japanese military and established a tradition for their navy. Their introduction to the modern industrialized world a mere 50 years earlier made the Japanese realize they needed raw materials that their country did not possess and, whether it was Manchuria or elsewhere, military action was a proven method of gaining them. Participation in World War I to obtain German possessions in the Pacific, as well as aggression in the 1930s in China, can both be traced to the successes of 1904–1905.

See also Korea, Japanese Invasion of (Sino-Japanese War) [136]; China, Japanese Invasion of [151].

References: Coonaughton, R. M., *The War of the Rising Sun and the Tumbling Bear* (London: Routledge, 1991); Walder, David, *The Short Victorious War* (London: Hutchinson, 1973); Warner, Denis, *The Tide at Sunrise* (New York: Charterhouse, 1974).

## MANCHURIA, JAPANESE INVASION OF (1931)

**172**

The Open Door policy had been the economic rule in China since 1899: All nations had equal access to China's markets. When the Russians would not cooperate in Manchuria, Japan went to war with them in 1904, and from 1905, Japan held a predominant economic position in Manchuria, within the Open Door framework. In 1914, Japanese forces captured the Shantung Peninsula, which the Germans had leased from the Chinese. With Japanese troops on Chinese soil, Japan attempted to press its advantage by making demands of the Chinese government that would give the Japanese virtually exclusive economic and political rights in China. Their Twenty-one Demands were withdrawn under American pressure, but the Japanese focus was now on China as its future. Poor in natural resources but rich in population, Japan saw its huge neighbor to the west as a source to be controlled and tapped.

This idea faded a bit in 1922. In Washington, D.C., Japan signed the Nine-Power Agreement, which recognized the Open Door policy and guaranteed Chinese territorial integrity. The Japanese government was dominated by moderates, but the moderates were increasingly in conflict with army leaders, who demanded expansion. The uneasy relations between government and army strained to the breaking point in 1930 when the prime minister was assassinated, and in 1931 when a group of officers narrowly failed in staging a coup d'état.

In China, the disorganized governmental situation brought on by revolution finally solidified in 1926 under the leadership of Chiang Kai-shek and his Nationalist Party, the Kuomintang. Chiang began moves designed to assert more Chinese control over Manchuria, which was, after all, Chinese territory. When the warlord in control of Manchuria was assassinated in 1928, his son took power and openly allied himself with Chiang. Growing Chinese influence in the area would certainly be detrimental to Japanese plans for growth.

To further complicate matters, Japan was also having trouble with the United States. The United States had initiated the Open Door policy, and had had friendly relations with China ever since. Should hostilities begin, this spelled a potential Japanese-American rivalry. Further, a long-standing Japanese agreement to unilaterally restrict emigration to the United States was overturned by the U.S. Congress in 1924, when an immigration policy was established specifically excluding all Asian immigration. The Japanese took that as an insult. Negotiations over the next few years eased tensions somewhat, but the growing strength of the military in Japan at the expense of moderates in the government kept the rift from healing.

In September 1931 the Japanese army decided to act independently of their government before more international concessions might be negotiated. On the night of 18 September, an explosion on the Japanese-owned and -operated South Manchurian Railway destroyed a mere 31 inches of track. The culprits have never been identified, but most authorities assume the Japanese did it, perhaps through the agency of Chinese radicals. Whoever was responsible, Japan blamed the Chinese; the Japanese immediately moved on the Manchurian capital at Mukden, seizing the city and its 10,000-man garrison. Japanese troops soon captured other strong points along the railroad right-of-way.

Chiang's government in Nanking appealed to the United States and the League of Nations for assistance, but found little. The powerless league called for Japanese withdrawal, but had no ability to force such a move. The U.S. secretary of state, Henry Stimson, hoped to deal with the moderates in the government and not provoke the Japanese military, but the government was losing or had already lost control over the army. The league sent an investigation commission to look into rival Japanese and Chinese claims, but the Japanese were already seizing all of Manchuria, which they accomplished by February 1932. In that month the state of Manchukuo declared its independence from China and was soon recognized by Japan as a sovereign state. It was, in fact, a puppet government full of Japanese.

The Lytton Commission presented its report to the league in October 1932, stating that the people of Manchuria did not want the new Manchukuo government and calling for Japanese troop withdrawal. The report did not call for complete Japanese withdrawal, however, but for a Sino-Japanese treaty to address the interests of the two nations and an outside peace-keeping force to maintain order. When the league accepted the report and voted that none of its members should recognize the independence of Manchukuo, Japan resigned from the international organization. Shortly afterward, Henry Stimson announced the Hoover-Stimson Doctrine, which declared that the United States would not recognize any political act that came about as the result of aggression.

Japan ignored both the league and the United States, and proceeded to launch attacks into China past the Great Wall. Japan also invaded Shanghai to force China to withdraw its boycott of Japanese goods. Both acts of aggression ended with Japanese withdrawal, but all of Manchukuo and the eastern provinces of Mongolia were under Japan's thumb. The Chinese lost large numbers of soldiers during the fighting, but proved too difficult for the Japanese to completely overpower. Chinese resistance so angered the Japanese that they engaged in widespread looting, rapine, and destruction. Condemnation of Japan for violations of the Nine-Power Treaty or the 1928 Kellogg-Briand Pact, which outlawed the use of force as national policy, fell on deaf ears.

Japan exploited the coal, iron, copper, lead, and other natural resources of Manchuria/Manchukuo and used the territory as a release valve for population pressures, but the new country did not prove as economically stimulating as Japan had hoped. To feed its growing nationalist and militarist desires, Japan needed all of China, and that attempt was not long in coming.

*See also* China, Japanese Invasion of [151]; Manchuria, Japanese Invasion of (1904) (Russo-Japanese War) [171].

References: Nish, Ian, *Japan's Struggle with Internationalism* (New York: K. Paul International, 1993); Tuchman, Barbara, *Stilwell and the American Experience in China* (New York: Macmillan, 1971); Yoshihashi, Takehiko, *Conspiracy at Mukden* (New Haven, CT: Yale University Press, 1963).

# MESOPOTAMIA, BRITISH INVASION OF

**173**

When the Ottoman Empire joined the Central Powers in November 1914, British interests in the Persian Gulf were threatened. For decades Great Britain had had close ties with the sheikhs of the area, maintained extensive economic interests, and controlled piracy in the gulf. The gulf sheikhs had little love for the Ottoman government and welcomed British forces who landed at Bahrain late in October. British oil interests in Persian Arabistan have been traditionally viewed as the main reason the British went into action in Mesopotamia, but economic investments and a fear that the Turks would raise a holy war that would spread to India were equal, if not greater, motivations for making war against the Turks.

British forces landed at the mouth of the Shatt-al-Arab on 6 November, and quickly made their way to the port city of Basra. Few Turkish troops were stationed in the region, and within a few weeks British and Indian troops consolidated the river and approached Kurna, where the Tigris and Euphrates meet to form the Shatt-al-Arab. By March 1915, Indian Expeditionary Force D occupied Shaiba (south of Basra), Kurna, and Ahwaz in Persian Arabistan, where the oil pipeline to Basra originated. These actions were really all that was necessary to maintain a secure British hold, but the government in India, abetted by an aggressive new commander in Mesopotamia, General Sir John Nixon, could not leave well enough alone. Using the British government's fear of a holy war, Viceroy Hardinge and General Sir Beauchamp Duff, the commander in chief in India, urged an expansion of the campaign so that the local Arabs would not rise up, thinking the British were afraid to advance. This rationale moved the secretary of state for India in London to authorize advances up both the Tigris and Euphrates. These actions took place in the heat of summer, and the British and Indian troops suffered immensely, but that mattered little to Nixon, the commander in Mesopotamia. When the Sixth Division captured 'Amara, 450 miles up the Tigris from Basra, the lure of Baghdad, another hundred miles up river, was too much for India and London to resist.

There was a problem, however. The Force D troops moved ever farther up the rivers, but received supplies less often because their transport craft had farther and farther to go, and they were given no additional river craft. With less matériel, both military and medical, to sustain themselves, their ability to hold the territory they had captured became increasingly tenuous. Both General Nixon in Mesopotamia and the government in India later claimed to be aware of the need for more transport, but no one informed London. In October 1915, the British cabinet decided that the capture of Baghdad would be immensely prestigious and would help to erase the disappointment of the recent failure at Gallipoli. The British government therefore approved an attack on Baghdad, not knowing that Nixon had grossly overestimated the ability of his own forces and underestimated that of the Turks.

In November the Sixth Division attacked Ctesiphon, just outside Baghdad, and was unable to break the Turkish defensive lines. The resultant retreat, with greater than expected casualties and too little transport, forced incredible suffering on the troops involved. Within a week they were surrounded by Turkish forces at Kut-al-'Amara. The Turks penned the Sixth Division inside the town, dug into extensive defensive positions astride the Tigris, and succeeded in stopping British attempts to break the siege. General Charles Townshend, Sixth Division commander in Kut-al-'Amara, maintained a solid defense through April 1916, but was ultimately forced to surrender because of a lack of food. At 149 days, Kut marked the longest siege in British history.

The British government took control of the campaign away from India and began to provide the necessary matériel to maintain a defensive position for the rest of the war. Reports on the suffering of the troops led to a Parliamentary Commission, which condemned the Indian leaders but punished no one. Conditions improved in Mesopotamia, but defense was the order of the day until the new commanding general, Sir Stanley Maude, convinced the General Staff to let him advance. Sure of his supplies and transport, Maude retook Kut in February 1917, then captured Baghdad in early March. After resting his troops through the summer, Maude secured the area around Baghdad in the fall, but a bout of cholera took his life in November. His replacement, General W. R. Marshall, completed Maude's consolidation and reached the Mosul oil fields as the war ended in November 1918.

The British had hoped throughout the war to incorporate Mesopotamia into their empire, either directly or as a sphere of influence. Secret negotiations in 1915 with the French and Russians had divided the Ottoman Empire among the three countries. The early publication of that agreement by the Soviets, when they left the war in November 1917, showed that British and French claims in the secret negotiations did not match promises made to the Arabs to secure their support against the Turks; thus, Britain was forced to deny any claims to the area. However, the British received Mesopotamia as a mandate in the Treaty of Versailles at the end of the war, so they maintained a presence in the country afterward, and in the 1930s presided over its

change into modern-day Iraq. Britain left the country to its own devices after World War II.

*See also* Turkey, British Invasion of [192].

References: Barker, A. J., *The Neglected War* (London: Cassel & Co., 1967); Davis, Paul, *Ends and Means: The British Mesopotamia Campaign and Commission* (Rutherford, NJ: Fairleigh Dickinson University Press, 1994).

## 174 MIDWAY, JAPANESE INVASION OF

Like the Spanish Armada in 1588 and the Battle of Britain in 1940, the battle for Midway resulted in the repulse of an attempted invasion, the failure of which was significant. By early June 1942, the Japanese seemed virtually invincible, having invaded and conquered targets throughout the South Pacific in the hectic seven months following the bombing of Pearl Harbor. Only a setback at the Coral Sea, northeast of Australia, in early May 1942 marred an otherwise perfect record. The thrust to Midway was designed to set up a Japanese base in the Central Pacific from which they could invade Hawaii, thus denying the United States its most strategic anchorage and its forward base of operations against Japan. If Hawaii fell, the U.S. Navy would have to operate out of San Diego on the West Coast, adding almost 2,000 miles to any Pacific action. Indeed, Hawaii's fall might be the blow necessary to convince the United States to make peace with Japan.

In order to mount an invasion of the Hawaiian Islands, however, Japan needed Midway. An invasion fleet escorted by a large naval force, including four of Japan's largest aircraft carriers, seemed sufficient for the job. The Americans had only one significant advantage: They had just succeeded in breaking the Japanese military code and knew exactly what their intentions were. Admiral Chester Nimitz concentrated his forces to meet the threat. He could muster three aircraft carriers and their support ships, hoping that surprise and the broken code would give him the edge.

On 3 June, American scouting aircraft based at Midway located the Japanese fleet and launched an attack of heavy bombers and torpedo bombers, neither of which inflicted any damage. The following day proved to be the day of decision, marked by a series of missed opportunities that could have tipped the balance to either side. The Japanese struck first by launching an air attack on the facilities at Midway. When the bombers returned to rearm for another attack, Japanese commander Chuichi Nagumo learned of the presence of the American aircraft carriers. Most of the bombers were ready for the next attack on the island when the crews were ordered to rearm with torpedoes in order to attack the American fleet. While the changeover was taking place, American carrier-based aircraft arrived. American torpedo bombers attacked from several directions, but failed to score any hits and lost a majority of its force to antiaircraft fire and swarming Japanese fighter planes. An apparent disaster for the Americans proved to be just the break they needed. By forcing the Japanese fighter cover to low altitudes to deal with the torpedo bombers that attacked at wave-top heights, the skies above the Japanese fleet were unprotected when American dive bombers arrived. They were able to strike the Japanese virtually unhindered, and succeeded where every other assault had failed. Within a matter of minutes, three of Japan's four aircraft carriers were hit and sinking. The fate of the Japanese operation was sealed; unable to launch the

aircraft necessary to destroy the American fleet or to recover all the fighter planes that had been airborne, their strike force was crippled. Bombers from the remaining carrier launched a strike against the American fleet and badly damaged the USS *Yorktown,* but it was too late. American follow-up attacks on 5 June finished off the last Japanese carrier and inflicted damage on other capital ships. Without the strength of its airpower, Japan could not hope to launch a successful landing on Midway, so the fleet was ordered home.

The Japanese scored the final success in this battle when one of their submarines finished off the *Yorktown,* but it was small consolation. The destruction of four of Japan's best aircraft carriers and, just as importantly, the death of so many of their most experienced pilots were losses they would not overcome. The battle for Midway became the turning point of World War II in the Pacific. Japan was now unable to mount major offensives, obliged instead to consolidate its gains. The United States, on the other hand, could go on the offense and keep Japan reeling. Two months after Midway, U.S. Marines would land on Guadalcanal and begin the strategy of island-hopping that ultimately brought them to a position from which they could invade Japan itself.

Had Japanese timing been a little better concerning their ability to locate the American fleet, vital time would not have been lost rearming their aircraft and exposing themselves to American attack. Had they been able to launch the first strike instead of receiving it, the battle almost certainly would have gone the other way, and the U.S. Navy would have been crippled to the point of impotence. Japan would have easily captured Midway because the garrison there could not have put up a significant defense, and Hawaii would have followed within a matter of months.

One can only conjecture what the United States would have done in this situation, but the outcome of the war and the shape of the postwar world would almost certainly have been radically altered.

*See also* England, Spanish Invasion of (Spanish Armada) [93]; Britain, Nazi Invasion of (Battle of Britain) [149]; New Guinea, Japanese Invasion of [176]; Pacific Islands, U.S. Conquest of [179].

References: Layton, Edwin, *"And I Was There": Pearl Harbor and Midway— Breaking the Secrets* (New York: Morrow, 1985); Lord, Walter, *Incredible Victory* (New York: Harper & Row, 1967); Prange, Gordon, *Miracle at Midway* (New York: McGraw-Hill, 1982).

## 175  MUSSOLINI, BENITO

The man who would lead Italy into World War II was certainly a product of his time. Born in 1883, Benito Mussolini was raised by a socialist father and schoolteacher mother in a time when Italy was virtually stagnant while the rest of Europe was progressing. While Britain, France, and Germany built or expanded empires and also enjoyed industrial growth, Italy remained a poor agricultural community with few resources. They also had little luck in trying to gain resources in futile expeditions against African nations like Ethiopia. Class struggles within Italy did nothing to promote progress and a frustrated nation looked for answers.

Mussolini followed in both his parents' footsteps, becoming an elementary schoolteacher and a socialist. He spoke and wrote forcefully about Italy's needs, but could not do much himself until World War I started. Although officially allied to Germany, Italy remained neutral at the war's outset. In-deed, Italy's main quarrel was with Germany's main ally, Austria-Hungary. Italy had long desired the cities of Trento and Trieste at the head of the Adriatic Sea and, as Austria was busy fighting a war with Serbia, it seemed an opportune time to grab some land. Mussolini loudly argued for Italian involvement in the war on the Allied side, and it alienated his socialist comrades. He was fired from his job editing the socialist newspaper *Avanti,* so he started his own paper and pushed for Italian expansion. When the Allies convinced Italy to join them in 1915, Mussolini joined the army and fought until 1917, when he was wounded.

Although the war brought Italy territorial concessions, it also brought a huge loss of life and continued political controversy. In March 1919, Mussolini started the Fascist party, blending conservative nationalist desires with socialistic government control of the economy. The Fascists promised all things to all people: a tradition of greatness, a change from disordered politics yet protection from the radical change of communism, opportunity for the poor, wealth for the nation, justice for the oppressed, and, above all, order. His party grew rapidly until, in October 1922, his supporters marched on Rome and demanded control of the government. While this march may not have been the reason for the change, King Victor Emmanuel asked Mussolini to organize a new government.

Calling himself "Il Duce" (the Leader), Mussolini used a growing military to maintain himself in power and crush opposition. He seemed to the outside world to be good for Italy. The economy improved and unemployment was low, but at a cost of freedom. The law and order he promised appeared, as did the decline in political corruption since there was only one political party. He was recognized in the United States by *Time* magazine as Man of the Year and will forever be remembered for the tribute, "He made the trains run on time." He also urged Italian women to have more children, for he needed soldiers to rebuild the Roman Empire.

Empire-building lay at the heart of his dream to bring about Italian greatness, and he focused on the Mediterranean area as his bailiwick. In 1935 he flaunted international condemnation by invading Ethiopia, a fellow member of the League of Nations. The only supporter for this expedition was Adolf Hitler in Germany, and the two concluded an alliance in November 1936, after which Mussolini stated that from that time forward, "the world would revolve around a Rome-Berlin axis" (hence, the Axis powers of World War II). The two countries cooperated in aiding Francisco Franco in the Spanish Civil War and Mussolini stood by while Hitler occupied Austria and Czechoslovakia. He did, however, feel that Italy was losing some of the limelight, so he invaded Albania to remind the world Italy was not to be ignored, and to try to influence Balkan politics.

It was Italy's role in World War II, and Mussolini's continuing attempts to gain territory for his empire, that brought about his downfall. Mussolini ordered the invasion of Greece and Egypt, but had to beg Hitler for assistance when his armies were defeated in both arenas. Mussolini, the senior dictator, became the alliance's junior partner once the war started. He watched his troops do little more than support German armies in North Africa and then in Sicily. When the Allied forces captured Sicily in August 1943, Mussolini's days were numbered. the British invasion of the toe of Italy in early September brought about Mussolini's forced abdication, then imprisonment. Hitler ordered Otto Skorzeny, his commando leader, to rescue his Italian partner from prison, then set him up in a pup-

pet government in the north of Italy until the war's end. In the spring of 1945 he fled for Switzerland, but did not reach the border before he was captured by Italian resistance fighters, who assassinated him and his mistress, then took the bodies to Milan for public display.

Mussolini was somewhat of an aberration in Italian politics, a ruthless strongman who dominated a nation that seems to revel in provincial differences and rivalries. No one before or since has exercised such power in Italy, but neither has anyone brought about such shame and despair. The Italian countryside and economy were badly damaged by World War II and Mussolini was the man who took Italy into that war. Unlike Hitler, he had no racial policies to condemn him, but like his German partner he left behind a legacy that some in Italy to this day would like to see restored.

*See also* Albania, Italian Conquest of [147]; Hitler, Adolf [165].

References: Collier, Richard, *Duce!* (New York: Viking, 1971); Dabrowski, Roman, *Mussolini: Twilight and Fall* (New York: Roy Publishers, 1956); Gallo, Max, *Mussolini's Italy,* trans. Charles Markmann (New York: Macmillan, 1973).

## NEW GUINEA, JAPANESE INVASION OF

**176**

Because the island of New Guinea lies due north of Australia, its location, rather than any inherent value, made it a target for Japanese aggression at the opening of World War II. The Japanese military spread across the western Pacific, and forces under the command of Major-General Horii landed on the north shore of the island early on

23 January 1942. As they had experienced elsewhere, the invaders had little serious opposition from the defenders—in this case, badly outnumbered Australian troops. The Australians withdrew inland, closely pursued by Japanese troops. At the same time, the Japanese secured the major port of Rabaul on the island of New Britain, the real prize in the area. New Guinea was to serve mainly as a guard for the bastion soon created at Rabaul. Japanese control of Rabaul made Allied possession of New Guinea vital as well, and brought the immediate attention of Douglas MacArthur, commander of Allied military forces in the Southwest Pacific.

The Japanese quickly secured the northern half of the island and established bases at Hollandia, Wewak, Madang, and Lae. Their next target was Port Moresby, on the southern shore of the peninsula forming the eastern part of the island. It was lightly defended and would have provided little difficulty for the invaders, but they never arrived. The Japanese force sailing around the eastern tip of the island met a combined American and Australian naval force in early May in the Coral Sea. The battle was unique at the time: It was the first naval battle in which ships never engaged one another. Instead, the battle was fought totally between carrierborne aircraft and enemy ships. For three days, opposing bombers and fighters fought it out over enemy shipping, and both sides lost roughly equal numbers of ships, including one aircraft carrier each. The battle was a tactical draw but a strategic victory for the Allies—it was the first time the Japanese failed to accomplish a mission. The Japanese fleet turned back and the tide of war began to turn.

Despite the naval reverse, the Japanese continued their victories on land, driving into the Owen Stanley mountain range that forms the spine of the island. They drove the Australians back across the range and to within a day's march of Port Moresby, but could go no farther. Reinforcements of Australian and American troops massed along the southeastern part of the island, and the jungle through which the forces fought took its toll on the ill-supplied Japanese army. American aircraft arrived and achieved air superiority, which meant that Allied troops could get supplies into the mountains without the need of "humping" it through the extremely rugged terrain. The Australians fought their way back up the mountains via the Kokoda Trail, entering the town of Kokoda along the ridge line on 2 November 1942. The large numbers of dead attested to the Japanese inability to survive the jungle on meager supplies, and the Allied offensive picked up some steam heading down the northern slope. By January 1943, the Australian and American troops owned the northern shore of Papua, thereby controlling the eastern half of the island.

Through 1943 the U.S. Navy and Air Force dominated the area. The battle of the Bismarck Sea in March 1943 was a victory of American airpower over Japanese attempts to bring in large numbers of reinforcements. As Rabaul was sealed off by American sea power, MacArthur made plans to work his way west along the New Guinea coast. With the use of large landing craft, MacArthur's forces made a series of landings along the coastline, capturing Japanese-held towns and airfields. They captured or bypassed all four Japanese strongholds, and established a bomber base on the island of Biak, just off New Guinea's northwest corner. This not only gave them complete aerial domination over New Guinea but provided a major base for MacArthur's ultimate goal, the U.S. invasion of the Philippines.

By the autumn of 1944, the focus of the war shifted to the Philippines and farther north, but New Guinea was not completely quiet. Japanese forces fought on even after the war was over; not until mid-September 1945 did they receive word of the atomic bomb drops and their government's surrender. The Japanese left behind a somewhat positive legacy in the construction of good roads and airfields, which remain in use even now. Though thousands of Japanese, Australian, and American soldiers were killed in fighting on the island, relatively few natives were directly involved. Over 50,000 were conscripted as laborers for the Allies, but very few engaged in fighting. However, they suffered from Japanese atrocities and sustained collateral damages from the fighting. The lack of men in native villages forced some hardships on those who remained, but the increased contact with the outside world had some positive side effects on an island that had been remote and isolated. Tribal enmity, already on the wane as more Europeans came to the islands in the first part of the century, diminished even more. The discovery of manufactured goods changed the lives of many in the mountains, for good or ill. In some remote areas, the first arrival of parachuteborne equipment seemed heaven-sent, and the rise of what came to be known as the "cargo cults" lasted for some years after the war (some natives became convinced that certain rituals would bring back the largess provided from the sky).

See also MacArthur, Douglas [170]; Philippines, U.S. Invasion of the [182].

References: Mayo, Linda, *Bloody Buna* (Garden City, NY: Doubleday, 1974); Robinson, Neville, *Villagers at War* (Canberra: Australian National University, 1981); Vader, John, *New Guinea: The Tide Is Stemmed* (New York: Ballantine, 1971).

**177**

# NORTH AFRICA, U.S. INVASION OF

Once the United States entered World War II in the wake of the 7 December 1941 Japanese bombing of Pearl Harbor, Hawaii, and the German declaration of war on 10 December, President Franklin Roosevelt was anxious to begin operations against the Axis powers. At the Atlantic Conference the previous August, he and British prime minister Winston Churchill agreed that if and when the United States became engaged in the war, Hitler's Germany would be the primary enemy, no matter who else became involved. Soviet foreign minister Molotov also urged rapid American action, hoping to get early relief from the Nazi invasion of his country. Roosevelt was anxious to commit troops before the end of 1942, but could not agree with the British on the target. Britain balked at the idea of an early invasion of France, afraid of the consequences if it failed. They preferred an assault on northwestern Africa to aid their campaign against German and Italian troops. Most American planners disagreed with the idea, but when an invasion of France was definitely rejected, they reluctantly accepted. The operation was code-named Torch.

Before the invasion could begin, two major questions had to be answered. The first: Where should the landings take place? British planners wanted landings that would quickly seize Tunis and Bizerta, the major German supply points in Tunisia; therefore, landings should take place as far east along the Algerian coast as possible. The Americans thought that idea too risky. Without a strong hold on the area around Gibraltar, Spanish air forces or Italian shipping might cut that supply route and leave the landing forces cut off. An invasion on the Atlantic coast around Casablanca would give the safest supply situation, the

Americans argued. The main problem with that idea was that Tunis was more than a thousand miles away.

The second question: What would the defending French troops do? Would they accept the orders of Marshal Pétain in Vichy or aid the Free French movement led by Charles de Gaulle in London? The Allied planners did not want to kill French troops if they were going to cooperate, but they did not want to send troops ashore into stiff resistance if they were not. The American diplomatic representative in Algeria sounded out some friendly French officers, who asked for a meeting with a ranking American. General Mark Clark, second in command of the landing operation, went ashore in late September to assist the French with their decision. They would not totally commit to aiding the landings, partly because Clark would give them little or no solid information on when and where they would take place. Thus, when the troops went ashore, they were still unsure of their reception.

The Anglo-American planning staff finally chose to land at multiple sites, ranging from Casablanca on the Atlantic coast to Oran and Algiers along the Mediterranean coast. The French commanders onshore had been told that General Giraud, a well-known officer close to Pétain but anti-German, would take command of French forces once the Americans landed. The units that landed on 8 November were either totally American or an Anglo-American mix, as the appearance of British units alone might not be acceptable to the French. The landings met sporadic resistance, but most of it was either token fighting to ensure the safety of officers' families in France, due to slow communications concerning the landings, or because of the occasional pro-Vichy officer who wanted to fight. The ranking French officer in North Africa, Admiral Darlan,

ordered all resistance to cease on 10 November. Darlan was given overall political command of the French forces and Giraud was to command the military, but Giraud took over complete control when Darlan was assassinated on Christmas Eve by an anti-Vichy gunman.

The landings were a complete success. Against scattered opposition the Americans lost less than 2,000 men killed and wounded and were in a strong position to begin advancing eastward to support the British, who were now driving German commander Erwin Rommel before them through Libya. The British forces involved in Operation Torch, the First Army, moved along the coast road while the Americans basically paralleled them to the south. Within three days after the original landings, the British captured Bougie (120 miles east of Algiers) and Bone (270 miles east of Algiers). On 17 November the British ran into serious German opposition at Tabarka, halfway from Bone to Tunis. Meanwhile, Rommel was in full retreat from Montgomery's advance, but that actually helped the Germans by placing them closer to their supply bases, while the British moved farther away from theirs. In January heavy rains fell, which halted the British advance and gave Rommel time to reorganize. Pressed from east and west, he was able to use his interior lines of communication to quickly transfer troops from one front to the other, holding the British at the defensive lines he had built at Mareth while striking a devastating blow to the Americans at Kasserine Pass in mid-February.

It was not enough. The Americans recovered and won a clear victory at El Guettar, and the British flanked the Mareth Line at the end of March. Rommel became ill and left in March for Germany; he did not return. General von Armin, left in command, could do little more than delay the inevitable, and the British capture of Tunis and Bizerta in early May sealed their fate. Many Germans and Italian were able to withdraw from those ports before they fell, but some 250,000 Germans and Italians were taken prisoner, making the total North African loss to the Axis almost 1 million men over two years.

With all of North Africa in Allied hands, the next step was to decide where to go next. When Prime Minister Churchill and President Roosevelt met in Casablanca in January 1943, they agreed on two things: The Allies would accept only unconditional surrender from the Axis powers, and the next offensive should be the invasion of Sicily. North Africa served only as a supply base for the rest of the war, and reverted to its prewar situation after 1945. France returned to Algeria and tried to reassert its authority after the fiasco with the Vichy government, but the seeds had long since been sown for an independence movement.

See also Algeria, French Occupation of [128]; Egypt, Italian Invasion of [155]; France, Nazi Invasion of [161]; Sicily, Allied Invasion of [186].

References: Brewer, William B., *Operation Torch* (New York: St. Martin's Press, 1985); Gelb, Norman, *Desperate Venture: The Story of Operation Torch* (London: Hodder & Staughton, 1992); Howe, George F., *Northwest Africa: Seizing the Initiative in the West* (Washington, DC: Office of the Chief of Military History, 1957).

## 178   NORWAY AND DENMARK, NAZI INVASION OF

In the wake of the Nazi conquest of Poland, very little happened. The fall and winter of 1939–1940 were known as the *sitzkrieg*, or phony war; war was declared, but little fighting took place. The only major military action was the Soviet invasion of Finland from November 1939 through March 1940. Germany and the Soviet Union had signed a nonaggression pact in August, so the Germans did nothing when the Soviets occupied the Baltic states of Lithuania, Latvia, and Estonia, and attacked Finland. However, the aggression provoked British interest in the Finns. Britain's attention to Scandinavia, along with the German need for iron ore from Sweden, made war over Norway inevitable, and war over Norway made the German occupation of Denmark inevitable.

Germany imported some 10 million tons of iron ore from Sweden, 90 percent of which was shipped through the Norwegian port of Narvik. At first, Germany felt that a neutral Norway was sufficient to maintain the flow of ore, but when Britain approached Norway about the possibility of traversing its territory in order to aid Finland, Germany saw the potential for trouble. There was also the problem of the German navy. In World War I they had been bottled up by a very effective British blockade of Germany. If, in 1940, the Germans could gain control of Norway, this would give them an extended coastline and make a British blockade much more difficult. The final motivation came from a visit to Berlin in December 1939 from Major Vidkun Quisling, former minister of defense in Norway. Fearful of a Communist victory in Finland and a possible Communist spread through Scandinavia, Quisling told Hitler that he headed up the Norwegian National Socialist Party and would do what he could to assist the Germans protecting his country from the Soviets. Though Quisling was somewhat mentally unbalanced and his claims imaginary, the idea piqued Hitler's interest. He ordered the German High Command to begin studying the possibility of invading Norway.

German troops in Denmark hold a parade to celebrate Hitler's birthday in 1940.

In February 1940 the British gave Hitler a potential reason for mounting the assault. A German ship, the *Altmark,* was in Norwegian waters carrying British POWs captured from British shipping destroyed in the South Atlantic by the German pocket battleship *Graf Spee.* A British cruiser and two destroyers stopped the *Altmark* in a fjord along the south Norwegian coast on 16 February and demanded to board and search it. When the *Altmark* grounded in an attempt to get away, the British boarded it and released 299 prisoners. This was not only a violation of Norwegian neutrality, but an illegal boarding under international law. It provided the provocation Hitler needed to decide finally on the invasion.

The Germans were not depending on Quisling's questionable aid. They planned to assault Norway in five places, from Oslo in the southeast to Narvik in the far north. A combination of landings along the coast and paratroop operations against airfields would seize the key cities. Norwegian defenses were few and not well directed. Even when informed of the imminent German invasion, the Norwegian government refused to mobilize, thinking it would be provocative. When they finally decided to mobilize on 8 April, the government directed it to be done secretly; the forces were informed by letter to report for duty. Since the invasion was scheduled for 9 April, this was of little use. Other than a few coastal defense vessels and a handful of fighter, bomber, and scout aircraft, Norway had little in the way of heavy weapons for their defense. A nation that had been at peace since the days of Napoleon was in no way prepared for a modern war.

The invasion took place just before dawn on 9 April 1940. The Germans met little or no resistance in four of their attacks; only the assault on Oslo experienced trouble. The German heavy cruiser *Blucher* was sunk by coast artillery, which convinced the troop ships to withdraw. Only when a handful of paratroopers landed against orders and captured the Oslo airport did the assault continue. It was successful by the first afternoon.

The Norwegian government fled before the German advance, and the newly appointed minister of defense attempted to mobilize Norwegian forces to resist from the interior of the country. They had little chance of holding out for long against a much larger and better equipped army. Still, they fought hard, and got some assistance from Britain and France. The British Royal Navy was successful in sinking and damaging a number of German ships and landing troops along the coast. The British chose to concentrate their efforts at the northern port city of Narvik, though they also attempted to capture the central coastal city of Trondheim. They were not prepared for the weather conditions (still snowy in much of the country) or the large numbers of German troops. Without tanks or much artillery, the British could do little more than the Norwegians. Nevertheless, the early fighting on land and the British successes at sea gave Hitler a scare; he considered withdrawing from the country within a week of the invasion. However, German forces gained control of the road network and linked up to provide a more concerted effort than the British could muster. By 1 May, British troops around Trondheim were withdrawn.

British forces near Narvik, supported by forces from the French Foreign Legion and French and Polish *chasseurs*, lasted a bit longer. Through May, the Allied forces in cooperation with the Norwegians managed to push German troops back. Foreign Legion amphibious landings surprised the Germans and gained some successes. British aircraft were beginning to arrive and operate from fields around Narvik. The city was captured by French and Norwegian troops on 28 May, but even as it fell, the Allies were making plans to evacuate. The Germans had launched their invasions of Holland and France on 10 May, and all military strength available had to meet this threat. The last British and French soldiers sailed away on 8 June, along with Norwegian king Haakon and the Norwegian government. A cease-fire went into effect the next day, and the Norwegian soldiers were allowed to go home.

Hitler set up a puppet government in Norway under the direction of Vidkun Quisling. This action made his name synonymous with the word *traitor* in Europe, much as Benedict Arnold is viewed in the United States, and he did not long survive the defeat of Germany in 1945. With Norway under his control, Hitler could count on the iron ore shipments that Sweden continued to provide; the Swedes saved themselves from invasion by maintaining the trade. Their neutrality worked to the advantage of the Allies as well. The crews of many American bombers damaged during raids over Germany flew their aircraft to Sweden to be interned for the duration of the war.

Denmark had little role in the Norwegian operation. Knowing they had absolutely no chance of putting up any sort of defense against Germany, the Danish king announced the surrender of his country almost as soon as German forces entered it on 9 April. Germany needed the country as an air base to assist the invasion of Norway, and occupied the country in a matter of hours. The ease of conquest belied the nature of the occupation, however. The Danes mounted one of the most effective underground resistance movements of any occupied country, and provided the Germans with a major headache in attempting to control it.

*See also* Napoleon Buonaparte [118]; Finland, Soviet Invasion of [158]; France,

Nazi Invasion of [161]; Poland, Nazi Conquest of [183].

References: Churchill, Winston, *The Gathering Storm* (Boston: Houghton Mifflin, 1948); Nissen, Henrik, *Scandinavia during the Second World War,* trans. Thomas Munch-Petersen (Minneapolis: University of Minnesota Press, 1983); Petrow, Richard, *Bitter Years: The Invasion and Occupation of Denmark and Norway* (New York: Morrow, 1974).

## PACIFIC ISLANDS, U.S. CONQUEST OF

**179**

Even before the United States entered World War II, American president Franklin Roosevelt met with British prime minister Winston Churchill in August 1941 at a secret conference off the coast of Canada. At this Atlantic Conference, the two decided that no matter who should join the Axis powers, the primary enemy was Germany and all planning should take place with that in mind. The policy of "Germany first" would be sorely tested when Japanese aircraft bombed Pearl Harbor in December 1941 and the United States became a full participant in the war.

As Japanese forces expanded through Southeast Asia and through the Central and South Pacific, American planners began to call for more and more supplies and manpower to be diverted to the war against Japan. The postponement of a proposed invasion of France from 1943 to 1944 allowed the redistribution of American forces to the Pacific. In Washington and in the Pacific theater, however, there was little agreement on how those forces should be deployed. American general Douglas MacArthur was based in Australia after the successful Japanese invasion of the Philippines. He had promised the people of the Philippines that he would return to liberate them, and his plans were designed toward that end. But U.S. Navy leaders did not want to turn their ships over to army command or risk them in the distant waters of the Southwest Pacific. Admiral Chester Nimitz, commanding the Pacific Fleet, with the support of Chief of Naval Operations Admiral Ernest King, preferred a plan that had been developed prior to the war. Plan Orange called for action across the Central Pacific toward the Philippines. Neither King nor MacArthur seemed to concede much to the "Germany first" plan and, in planning conferences held with the Americans, the British continued to press for fewer troops to the Pacific in favor of operations in Europe.

MacArthur had a prestigious career and many friends in Washington, but he could not directly influence decisions there as long as he stayed in Australia. Thus, he had to demand as much as he could and hope for the best. Because of the navy's resistance to the idea of committing too many valuable aircraft carriers to support army operations, someone had to make the decision, and it fell to the Joint Chiefs of Staff in Washington. With a modicum of navy support, MacArthur would direct the operations of American, Australian, and New Zealand forces in the Southwest Pacific with the primary aim of regaining control of New Guinea and the Japanese-held Solomon Islands to the east. The U.S. Navy, with its Marine Corps, would go through the Central Pacific.

Before the war and after their conquests in the first six months of the war, the Japanese had fortified islands virtually too numerous to mention. Recapturing every island would be an overwhelming task, so the navy planners decided that many could be bypassed and cut off, saving valuable time and manpower. By this strategy, some of Japan's most powerful bases would prove utterly useless to them. American forces would need only to capture key islands with good airfields or anchorages in order to control an area. With the expanding U.S. submarine fleet and air superiority established with carrier-based and then island-based planes, Japanese strongholds would be denied reinforcements or supplies. Regular bombing would destroy their air forces and runways, so the strongholds would be neutralized and unable to impede American progress or assist the Japanese war effort.

## THE SOLOMON ISLANDS

The first American offensive operation against Japan was against the island of Guadalcanal in the Solomons on 7 August 1942. The Japanese were unprepared for the landings, and U.S. Marines gained a

quick beachhead. The Japanese responded with a vengeance, and the Americans learned for the first time of the tenacity and aggressiveness of the Japanese soldier. Whatever lessons army forces may have learned when the Philippines fell went unheeded, so the Marines had to deal with an enemy of unexpected ferocity. The Japanese military were trained under a strict code of conduct, the ancient Bushido warrior's code, which taught that victory was everything and surrender was not an option. Unlike troops of virtually every nation in the world, Japanese forces would not admit defeat, and fought to the death in every engagement. Prisoners were few and far between.

The struggle for Guadalcanal was one of the longest in the Pacific war. The Japanese scored an early naval victory, which

U.S. conquest of the Pacific Islands.

forced the United States to withdraw its support of the Marines on the island. The Japanese regularly brought in reinforcements from bases farther up the Solomon chain, and used their navy to pound American positions. Ultimately the Americans won with a stubborn air defense and an even more stubborn force of Marines, and the island was declared secure in February 1943. Fighting in jungle conditions was a new experience for Americans, but it continued in the other battles in the Solomons. In July 1943, Marines assaulted New Georgia, northwestward up the chain, and on 1 November, the largest island, Bougainville. By Christmas most of the airfields were captured, and by mid-January 1943 the invading marine forces were relieved by army occupation forces to finish the job. Christmas landings also took place on New Britain, home of the largest Japanese base in the Southwest Pacific, Rabaul. Three months of fighting in the jungles brought American conquest of only a third of the island, but with airfields in hand they could pound Japanese defenses and isolate the garrison. MacArthur continued his offensive by securing New Guinea, which put him in a position to plan for his return to the Philippines.

## THE GILBERT AND MARSHALL ISLANDS

As the Marines moved up the Solomons, Admiral Nimitz got his Central Pacific campaign under way. The first target was Tarawa Atoll in the Gilbert Islands, northeast of the Solomons. The landing would be unlike anything the Americans had ever attempted, since this was a small collection of coral islets surrounded by reef. The Japanese had approximately 4,800 men defending Betio, 3 miles long and no more than 600 yards wide. Betio was the site of the airfield, so this was the target. The Japanese had spent a year building bunkers of

concrete, palm logs, and sand, so well constructed that only a direct hit by the largest naval shells could harm them. Every square foot of the beaches had been zeroed in by mortars and artillery.

The landing was preceded by a three-day naval bombardment, and the Marines were in trouble from the start. Most of the landing craft could not get past the reef, and the men had to wade 700 yards across a lagoon in water up to their necks under crisscrossing machine-gun fire. Those who managed to reach the beach found themselves under intense mortar fire and unable to advance because of a seawall. For most of the first day, 20 November 1943, they were pinned down, unable to advance or retreat. Once they broke through the seawall, the Marines had to reduce each bunker, one at a time, with explosive charges placed against the concrete and through the gunports. The interlocking Japanese fields of fire made each assault extremely difficult. Within 76 hours they secured the island, though the short time period belies the adversity. Only 146 prisoners were taken, most of them Korean laborers. Virtually the entire Japanese garrison had to be killed, at a cost to the Marines of 1,000 dead and 2,000 wounded. Nearby Makin Island, another atoll in the Gilbert group, was easier to capture, costing the lives of another 66 soldiers while defeating more than 400 Japanese defenders.

The Tarawa landing became a proving ground for future amphibious operations. From now on, longer preinvasion bombardments would take place. The Marines who fought here, already veterans of jungle warfare at Guadalcanal, learned how to fight on coral sand with no cover, lessons that were put to good use shortly. A mixed marine and army force landed at Majuro and Kwajalein atolls in the Marshall Islands, north of the Gilberts. The Japanese had not been able to reinforce this island group because of heavy losses in other areas, and the Americans made fairly short work of this island chain. Landings began on 30 January 1944, and the largest island, Kwajalein (site of the world's largest lagoon), was declared secured by 4 February. Eniwetok, the westernmost atoll in the Marshalls, was attacked on 18 February and the islands of the atoll were declared secured by 23 February. Control over the Gilberts and Marshalls gave the United States secure bases for the most difficult of operations to come: the Caroline Islands and the huge Japanese base at Truk. As it turned out, that invasion proved unnecessary. An American carrier raid against the harbor in February destroyed so many Japanese aircraft and ships that the bulk of the fleet stationed there was withdrawn farther west to the Palau Islands. Truk—indeed, the entire Caroline group—was bypassed.

## THE MARIANA ISLANDS

With the outer rim of Japanese defenses pierced or controlled, the inner ring came under attack in the summer of 1944. The Marianas contained fine harbors and airfields, and included Guam, an American possession since 1898 that was lost to the Japanese at the start of the war. Possession of islands here would put the U.S. Air Force within range of the Japanese home islands. Also, the connection between Japan and its bases in the Southwest Pacific would be severed. To avoid this, the Japanese prepared for a huge naval battle, which they were confident they could win if they could bring their capital ships into contact with the American fleet. The naval battle took place, but the tradition of Tsushima in the Russo-Japanese War, or even the surface victories off Guadalcanal, was not to be repeated. The aircraft carrier was the dominant player and, since Midway, the United States owned the advantage in these ships.

To avoid tipping his hand as to the location of the next strike, Nimitz used 15 aircraft carriers to strike everywhere at once. They supported MacArthur's landings on the north coast of New Guinea, struck Truk again, and then struck the Palaus. The carriers hit targets at Saipan and Guam in the Marianas and made a side trip to Iwo Jima, halfway to Japan, to interdict any reinforcements from the home islands. Saipan was a target of the first landings on 15 June 1944. When the landings began, the Japanese imperial navy knew just where the American fleet was, and they gathered their strength for the major clash they envisioned.

What ensued—later called the Battle of the Philippine Sea—became more popularly known as the "Marianas Turkey Shoot." Rather than leave the landing force unprotected, U.S. admiral Raymond Spruance stayed near Saipan and waited for the Japanese fleet to come to him. With advance warning provided by submarines, the Americans were prepared to protect their ships with swarms of fighter aircraft when Japanese bombers and fighters arrived on 19 June. Of the 430 planes onboard his five heavy and four light carriers, Japanese admiral Ozawa lost 328 on the first day and 75 on the second. Two Japanese carriers were sunk by American submarines; another was sunk and two damaged by American aircraft. These losses, plus the damaging of a battleship and cruiser, forced the Japanese to withdraw. The Japanese navy was now in tatters.

Meanwhile, the Marines and soldiers on Saipan were victorious as well. The island was declared secured on 7 July, and the island of Tinian, just south of it, was invaded 24 July and secured on 1 August. Landings on Guam, at the southern end of the island chain, took place on 21 July, and the island was totally in American hands by 10 August. Now the long-range B-29 bombers had a base from which to begin the strategic bombing of Japanese cities.

## IWO JIMA AND OKINAWA

MacArthur returned to the Philippines in October 1944 after the Marines had occupied Peleliu, the main island in the Palau group southwest of Guam and due east of the Philippines. These islands acted as a staging area for MacArthur. As American forces fought to regain the Philippines through the end of 1944 and the first months of 1945, Nimitz and the navy prepared plans for another offensive.

The air forces had been losing a significant number of damaged aircraft returning from raids on Japan, and the high command decided that possession of Iwo Jima, due south of Japan, would allow the crippled bombers to land and save large numbers of aircrew. Accordingly, the invasion began in February 1945. Iwo Jima was a volcanic island covered with sulfurous ash. The Japanese had had years in which to dig in, and their time had not been wasted. More than 20,000 men garrisoned the island, often entrenched in caves where naval gunfire could not reach. When the Marines landed to light resistance, they hoped for an easy time, but instead they saw a replay of Tarawa in the accurate, predetermined targeting of Japanese artillery. The rugged terrain and entrenched enemy conspired to make this the Marines' most deadly operation to date. It took five weeks to secure the island and months to flush out the last Japanese defenders. Ultimately, it took more than 6,000 dead and 18,000 American wounded to defeat the Japanese garrison, who fought as ardently as their comrades on every other island. More than 2,400 damaged B-29s landed here, saving many thousands more lives than were lost in the battle.

The invasion of Okinawa, scheduled for 1 April 1945, was a preview of the invasion of Japan itself. Okinawa had long been a Japanese province, and its inhabitants were officially Japanese citizens. Fighting here would give the Allied high command a taste of what it would be like to fight Japanese civilian resistance. Further, they expected a hard-fought struggle for the first territory of Japan proper.

They got what they were looking for. Many civilians either fought the Americans or committed suicide rather than become prisoners, believing the propaganda they had heard concerning American atrocities. Most of the fighting took place on the southern half of the island, a honeycomb of caves that had to be cleared one at a time. The Japanese garrison of 117,000 fought to the finish, the resistance lasting through July. The Japanese tactic of *kamikazes*, suicide aircraft attacks against American shipping, which had been introduced in the Philippines, proved to be a major headache for the U.S. Navy. They lost 34 ships sunk and more than 350 damaged, but it was not sufficient to turn them away.

The capture of Okinawa put the United States (plus the Allied forces of Britain and the Soviet Union once Germany was defeated in May) in a position to invade Japan. Plans were under way for a November invasion, but it never came about. President Harry Truman's decision to use newly developed nuclear weapons brought the war to an abrupt end. The island-hopping campaign demonstrated the ability of amphibious troops to land and overcome any prepared defenses, provided reinforcements and naval support were sufficient. Lessons learned here would be repeated again in just five years, when MacArthur again ordered Marines to go ashore at Inchon during the Korean War.

*See also* MacArthur, Douglas [170]; Manchuria, Japanese Invasion of (1904) (Russo-Japanese War) [171]; Midway, Japanese Invasion of [174]; New

Guinea, Japanese Invasion of [176]; Philippines, Japanese Invasion of the [181]; Philippines, U.S. Invasion of the [182]; South Korea, North Korean Invasion of (Korean War) [190].

References: Dunnigan, James, and Albert Nofi, *Victory at Sea* (New York: Morrow, 1995); Leckie, Robert, *Strong Men Armed* (New York: Random House, 1962); Morrison, Samuel E., *The Two-Ocean War* (New York: Little, Brown, 1963).

## 180 PANAMA, U.S. INVASION OF

The United States has had a long and intimate relationship with Panama, being the main factor in bringing about Panamanian independence from Colombia in 1903. That action, necessary in President Theodore Roosevelt's eyes, brought about a treaty that gave the United States generous terms for the construction of an isthmian canal: permanent lease on a strip of land ten miles wide stretching from the Atlantic to the Pacific for $10 million down and $250,000 a year. By 1914 the canal was completed, and U.S. forces were stationed on-site to protect it.

The American forces occupying Panamanian bases since that time brought the small nation security and income. Not enough income, apparently, because the population began agitating for cession of the canal to Panama. In 1978, American president Jimmy Carter negotiated a new treaty with Panama, promising to give them control of the canal in the year 2000. Until then, the United States would increase its yearly payments and maintain a military presence.

Ten years after the Carter treaty, political troubles in Panama changed American attitudes. The Panamanian president tried to remove the head of the Panamanian military, General Manuel Noriega, and for his efforts was overthrown in a coup. Noriega consolidated his power by authorizing the activity of personal, secret military enforcers. To pay for this increase in the military, he allied himself with international drug traffickers. Though he conceded to international demands for a supervised election in 1989, he refused to recognize its legitimacy when he was voted out of office.

A year earlier, U.S. courts had indicted Noriega for his involvement in international drug dealing. When he refused to seat the duly elected officials in May 1989, the United States froze Panamanian assets held in U.S. banks. President George Bush increased the American military presence in Panama and encouraged the Panamanian citizenry to oust Noriega, but too many people feared the consequences of trying. Tensions remained high throughout 1989 and reached a crisis point with the death of an American soldier in December, in addition to the arrest and abuse of a navy lieutenant and his wife. Noriega announced that he had been named "maximum leader for national liberation," waved a machete, and declared that a state of war existed with the United States, apparently believing that the Americans would not strike directly at his country. It was an assumption soon proven wrong.

A well-coordinated land-air assault, Operation Just Cause, struck Panama City, and Noriega's support soon evaporated. Though only 24 American servicemen were killed in action, the United States received severe criticism for the relatively high number of civilian casualties, many of whom were innocent bystanders and not Noriega's troops. Despite that, most Panamanians approved of the American action. Noriega ran for asylum to the Vatican Embassy while the officials elected several months previously were installed in office. After a few days, he surrendered to American authorities and was taken to Florida, where he stood trial on the charges brought against him in 1988. He was convicted in 1992.

Panama returned to peaceful conditions under elected officials who had sworn to uphold the country's constitution. This invasion followed much the same pattern the United States had often shown in Latin America, wherein American forces intervened to overthrow a ruler hostile to American interests. This time, it was a much more widely accepted intervention because it was short, effective, and fulfilled the needs not only of the United States (often the only motivation in the past) but also of the local population. The Organization of American States leveled some criticism at the United States for this unilateral action, but it was not condemned.

*See also* Latin America, U.S. Interventions in [169].

References: Donnelly, Thomas, Margaret Roth, and Caleb Baker, *Operation Just Cause: The Storming of Panama* (New York: Lexington Books, 1991); Flanagan, Edward, *The Battle for Panama: Inside Operation Just Cause* (McLean, VA: Brassey's, 1993); Woodward, Bob, *The Commanders* (New York: Simon & Schuster, 1991).

## PHILIPPINES, JAPANESE INVASION OF THE

**181**

When Japan received permission from the Nazi-controlled French Vichy government in July 1941 to occupy French Indochina, the United States began to worry even more seriously about Japanese intentions.

The Americans had been trying to negotiate with the Japanese to stop their aggression in China, but without success. With Japanese troops along the southern Chinese coast and then in Indochina, the Philippine Islands, controlled by the United States since 1898, appeared to be in the process of being surrounded. The Filipino army, recently under the training command of American general Douglas MacArthur, was incorporated into the U.S. Army, and MacArthur was given command of USAFFE: U.S. Army Forces in the Far East. The combined Filipino-American forces were primarily concentrated on the main Philippine island of Luzon at the north end of the archipelago, mostly along the western coast between Manila and Lingayen Gulf. USAFFE was made up of ten infantry divisions, five coastal and two field artillery units, and a scout force of cavalry and scout cars. All in all, they numbered (at least on paper) some 150,000 men.

When the news reached Manila early on the morning of 8 December 1941 of the attack on Pearl Harbor, the USAFFE in the Philippines was only partially prepared. Though American intelligence analysts considered the Philippines the most likely American target of Japanese aggression, the islands were not well fortified. Indeed, there being so many islands with such long and winding coasts, choosing a possible landing site to defend was difficult. Thus, when Japanese forces under General Masaharu Homma made ready to land, there was little resistance on the many beaches where his troops came ashore.

The Japanese assault was at once masterful and lucky. The planned surprise air attack against naval and air facilities around Manila was delayed by fog, which grounded the aircraft operating from Formosa. Thus, USAFFE commanders knew that war had started, and would not be caught unawares. They immediately launched aircraft to search for oncoming Japanese, then recalled those aircraft to refuel and arm for an attack on the Japanese base at Formosa. The timing could not have been worse for the USAFFE. Just as American aircraft were completely fueled and armed and preparing for takeoff, the fog-delayed Japanese air attack took place. The destruction of the American air forces, designed to be accomplished by surprise early in the morning, was just as completely achieved by a quirk of the weather. The Japanese bombers and fighters wrought havoc at the main air base at Clark Field, north of Manila, destroying B-17 bombers and P-40 fighters on the ground and setting most of the hangar and repair facilities on fire. Never during the invasion would the Japanese air superiority be seriously threatened.

Subsequent air attacks in the next two days finished off most of the remaining defending airplanes, while the last of the B-17s were ordered to withdraw to Darwin, Australia. The navy also feared for its capital ships, and ordered the cruisers and destroyers based at Cavite on Manila Bay to flee the area. On 10 December, the first Japanese troops landed on the northern and northwestern beaches of Luzon against virtually no resistance. They quickly captured two airfields, which made their air operations even simpler since they no longer had to fly down from Formosa. The Japanese advanced easily through northern Luzon against sporadic defenses, while the bulk of the USAFFE military remained around and north of Manila. With their attention focused on the north, MacArthur was unable to mount any serious opposition to more landings on 12 December at the southern end of Luzon, nor on 20 December to Japanese forces coming ashore at Davao on Mindanao, the southernmost Philippine island.

All the early Japanese landings were carried out by relatively small units, General Homma betting that MacArthur would not try to be everywhere at once. He gambled correctly, and was able to grab beaches and airfields with little troop expenditure, while conserving the bulk of his force for the major invasion that landed on 22 December at Lingayen Gulf. The landings were slowed by rough seas more than by gunfire; only one machine gun was on-site, and only two large artillery pieces shot at the oncoming landing craft. Where the Japanese ran into Filipino or American troops they were slowed, but they were able to establish and expand beachheads with little problem. Despite the fact that Homma's forces totaled just two divisions, their brilliant placement in multiple landings kept the USAFFE commanders guessing and unable to commit overwhelming forces anywhere. When yet another landing took place on 24 December at Lamon Bay south of Manila in the center of Luzon, MacArthur decided to pull his forces back to a central location and make the Japanese come to him. On Christmas Day he announced he was abandoning Manila, declaring it an open city. He began massing his forces across Manila Bay on the peninsula called Bataan.

MacArthur pleaded for reinforcements, but none were coming. The U.S. Navy was still reeling from the shock of Pearl Harbor, and few troops were ready to depart from the United States even if transport was ready and willing. Japan had total air and naval command of the Southwest Pacific, and nothing could get through from the United States. MacArthur's forces far outnumbered the Japanese, but they were outfought or outmaneuvered and had no air or naval support. The smaller Japanese forces could easily outflank American and Filipino units and force their withdrawal. Therefore, MacArthur took his men on to

Bataan, where outflanking was impossible. Unfortunately, so was retreat.

On 2 January 1942, the Japanese began to follow the retreating defenders onto the peninsula. Whatever success the Japanese had over the infantry was usually negated by outstanding American and Filipino artillery fire. Bataan is extremely rugged and easy to defend, and the Japanese assault soon bogged down. Some 80,000 troops and 26,000 civilians were on the peninsula, but with six-month provisions for only 40,000, and food and fuel were soon in short supply. USAFFE forces held the high ground, and their artillery dealt the Japanese severe damage, but the defenders soon learned the nature of the Japanese military code of conduct: Surrender was not an option; victory was more important than life. The Japanese kept coming.

It took four months for the Japanese to secure Bataan, a finger of land some 20 by 30 miles. Difficult as the constant combat was, the worst enemies were hunger and disease. Food and medicine were unavailable for the thousands of defenders. American forces surrendered on 9 April, but that did not end the resistance. About 13,000 troops had been stationed on Corregidor, a fortified island in Manila Bay, and about 2,000 soldiers, nurses, and civilians managed to escape there as Bataan fell.

Douglas MacArthur was no longer there to direct the defense. On 12 March, at the direction of American president Franklin Roosevelt, MacArthur was spirited away via torpedo boat and aircraft, accompanied by his wife and son and 17 staff members. General Jonathan Wainwright was left in command. Upon reaching Australia, MacArthur stated in a radio broadcast to the Filipinos, "I came through and I will return."

Through the early fighting on Luzon, the garrison on Corregidor was untouched. The Officer's Club operated, and soldiers kept themselves inspection-ready. On 29 December they came under Japanese fire. General Homma began an air campaign against Corregidor and the three other fortified islands in Manila Bay. Planes bombed the targets at irregular intervals, depending on the need for air support over Bataan. When that peninsula fell, Homma could focus his entire attention on the Americans' last retreat. He brought up every artillery piece that could reach the island and began pounding it. The American artillery returned fire and dealt some serious blows to the Japanese, but they could not replace their spent shells. Just like on Bataan, the defenders of the Manila Bay islands could expect no resupply of ammunition, food, or medicine. The artillery duel that lasted through the month of April gradually became more one-sided, and with total air superiority, Japanese bombers joined in the destruction. Even though Corregidor boasted extensive underground hospitals, barracks, storehouses, and magazines, the guns had to be on the surface and they numbered fewer every day.

By early May the defenders knew their days were numbered. Heavily fortified ammunition dumps finally gave in under the pounding and exploded. Intense artillery and air bombardment removed virtually every American cannon. On 5 May, Homma ordered his Fourth Division to land on Corregidor. Stiff currents blew the landing craft farther down the coast than intended and, as they drifted, the last few Americans guns blasted them. More than half the landing craft were sunk, but enough Japanese got ashore to begin the maneuvering and outflanking tactics that had served them earlier. Even though the final count of invaders was only 1,000 men against almost 15,000 defenders, the lack of coordination and communication, coupled with the weakened state of the sick and starving soldiers and Marines, spelled disaster.

With too few boats to bring in substantial reinforcements, Homma could only hope for the best. The men that got ashore proved sufficient because General Wainwright broadcast a message the second day, 6 May, signaling the surrender of his forces. The soldiers destroyed their weapons and remaining ammunition. Corregidor, the "Gibraltar of the East," believed invincible by everyone except General Homma, did not survive the onslaught of months of explosives.

The Japanese occupation of the Philippines proved horrific. The first disaster for the defeated Filipino and American forces was the removal of those forces who surrendered on Bataan. Without food or water, under intense heat, they were forced to walk miles to prisoner camps in what came to be known as the Bataan Death March. The Japanese, whose code would not condone surrender for their own men, could not conceive that anyone who surrendered was worthy of the least consideration. Hundreds died of exhaustion or execution along the way. American civilians taken prisoner were not as badly treated, and life assumed something like normality during the occupation. The men were separated from their wives and children, but in their respective camps they did the best they could with schools, musical and theater groups, and other imitations of peacetime pieced together from what little the Japanese allowed them to salvage or collect. Filipino civilians became laborers for the army of occupation, and suffered from overwork and abuse. Filipino and American soldiers who managed to avoid capture went into the hills and began guerrilla activities that lasted until the U.S. invasion of the Philippines in the autumn of 1944.

*See also* MacArthur, Douglas [170]; Philippines, U.S. Invasion of the [182].

References: Hartendorp, A. V. H., *The Japanese Occupation of the Philippines* (Manila: Bookmark, 1967); Toland, John, *But Not in Shame* (New York: Random House, 1961); Young, Donald, *The Battle of Bataan* (Jefferson, NC: McFarland, 1992).

## PHILIPPINES, U.S. INVASION OF THE

**182**

After the American surrender to Japanese forces in 1942, General Douglas MacArthur dedicated himself to fulfilling his pledge to the country that he would return. Since the fall of the Philippines, he had been based in Australia and was in command of U.S. Army forces in the Southwest Pacific, forces trying to regain control of New Guinea and fighting in the Solomon Islands northeast of Australia. By the late summer of 1944, MacArthur's naval counterpart, Admiral Chester Nimitz, had used the U.S. Navy and Marines to capture Japanese-held islands across the Central Pacific. With the Mariana Islands under attack in September 1944, and their bases about to be used for air attacks on Japan itself, American forces were in a position to attack the Philippines as well. Historians have debated the need for recapturing the Philippines, but by doing so, Japan would be cut off from whatever raw materials it had been able to access in the East Indies.

Before the invasion could take place, however, the Americans had to secure the Palau Islands to control sea access from the Marianas to the Philippines. A combined force of 20,000 soldiers and Marines had to dig Japanese soldiers out of caves honeycombing the mountain that dominated the island. For a loss of 7,900 dead and wounded, the Japanese defense force of more than 13,000 was killed; they gave up

Members of the Army's First Cavalry Division cross a water tank-trap set up as an obstacle by retreating Japanese forces to impede the advance of American troops in the Philippines in 1944.

only 400 prisoners. This was the highest percentage casualty rate of any American amphibious assault in history.

The American invasion of the Philippines was remarkable for its similarity to the Japanese invasion in 1941. This time, however, the roles were reversed, with the United States having command of the sea and air around the islands. MacArthur decided to assault the island of Leyte first to give the United States a central position in the archipelago from which to base its airpower. Accordingly, amphibious landings took place on 20 October. Though the Japanese could muster 350,000 men to defend the islands, they knew they could not repel the Americans without control of the sea. Therefore, the Japanese impe-

rial navy planned to stop the invasion by destroying the transports near the beach.

The Japanese sent a force of aircraft carriers southward from Japan to draw the American carriers and surface fleet away from the landing zones. They planned to strike the unprotected transports in two thrusts, from north and south, with ships sent from Singapore and the East Indies. However, American submarines sighted one of the Japanese fleets sailing from the Indies to the west of the Philippines. They sunk and damaged a number of cruisers, and alerted the invasion force to the coming attack. The bulk of the U.S. Navy under Admiral William Halsey had swallowed the northern bait and had sailed to strike the diversionary force, leaving the transports protected only by escort aircraft carriers and aging battleships (some resurrected from the bottom of Pearl Harbor). The battleships parked themselves at the end of Surigao Strait and waited until one of the Japanese fleets sailed into their guns and was destroyed. The second was able to get through the islands and into the area where the landings were taking place. They dealt some damage to the escort carriers, but turned back before attacking the defenseless transports; Halsey's ships to the north had destroyed much of the diversionary force with aircraft and then turned south to try to catch the retreating Japanese. Though Halsey was much criticized for chasing the diversionary force with the majority of his ships, they dealt extensive punishment to the empty Japanese aircraft carriers and returned south in time to seriously damage the retreating Japanese. The Battle of Leyte Gulf, actually three separate battles, destroyed the Japanese imperial navy as an effective fighting force: Three battleships, four aircraft carriers, ten cruisers, and nine destroyers were sunk for the American loss of three destroyers and two escort carriers.

From this point forward, the Americans controlled the sea and air. The only way the Japanese could challenge the U.S. Navy was through the introduction of *kamikazes,* suicide pilots flying bomb-laden airplanes into American shipping. Translated as "divine wind," kamikaze referred to the storms that twice destroyed Mongol invasion fleets attacking Japan in the 1300s. The Japanese hoped that this storm of dedicated flyers would perform the same task. More of a psychological weapon than an effective means of destruction, the tactic would be used by Japanese air forces for the remainder of the war in every succeeding American invasion. In this case, the kamikazes managed to sink a few ships, but not enough to deter the invaders, and it used up the last of Japanese aircraft in the islands.

Japanese general Tomoyuki Yamashita wanted to abandon Leyte after the naval defeat, but was overruled from Tokyo. He reinforced as best he could with the few transports he could get past American air cover, and the Japanese troops fought as hard there as everywhere else. With no air cover and inadequate transport, the Japanese were obliged to fight from a series of defensive lines, which took the Americans two months to overcome. Not until late December was Leyte declared secure; the mopping up of isolated pockets of resistance went on four months longer.

In mid-December, American forces landed on the small island of Mindoro, off the main island of Luzon, in order to establish closer airfields for the main battle. On 9 January they came ashore on Luzon from Lingayen Gulf, just as the Japanese had in 1941. The Americans drove across the central plains toward the capital at Manila, both to recapture the city and to free the large numbers of civilians who had been held in prisoner camps. The undernourished and abused condition of these civilians steeled American resolve to fight to the finish. Unlike 1942, when MacArthur had declared Manila an open city, Yamashita fought for it street by street. The Americans finally captured a city in ruins in March 1945. During this battle, Japanese soldiers committed a number of atrocities for which Yamashita was held responsible; after the war, he was executed as a war criminal. By the middle of March, Luzon was in American hands, but the rugged nature of the terrain allowed the Japanese to continue fighting from the hills and jungles, and the fighting in the Philippines did not end until the Japanese government surrendered in August 1945. The Americans lost 14,000 dead and another 48,000 wounded, while the Japanese lost all 350,000 to death or capture.

*See also* Dutch East Indies, Japanese Invasion of [153]; New Guinea, Japanese Invasion of [176]; Pacific Islands, U.S. Conquest of [179]; Philippines, Japanese Invasion of the [181]; Singapore and Malaya, Japanese Conquest of [189].

References: Breuer, William, *Retaking the Philippines* (New York: St. Martin's Press, 1986); Friend, Theodore, *The Blue-Eyed Enemy: Japan against the West in Java and Luzon, 1942–1945* (Princeton, NJ: Princeton University Press, 1988); Smith, Robert, *Triumph in the Philippines* (Washington, DC: Office of the Chief of Military History, 1963).

## POLAND, NAZI CONQUEST OF

**183**

Hitler's armies occupied the remainder of Czechoslovakia in the spring of 1939, in the wake of a promise that he had no more territorial ambitions in Europe after acquiring the Czech province of the Sudetenland. European leaders finally stiffened their resolve to resist further German expansion. Hitler, of course, assured them that he wanted nothing else after he gained the small Baltic port of Memel in late March from the Lithuanians, who had received the city as part of the Versailles Treaty. Control of Memel extended the coast of East Prussia farther north and gave Germany a port on the Baltic.

Both Britain and France alerted Poland in April 1939 that they would honor their defense treaty, unlike their actions concerning Czechoslovakia. This guarantee of Polish sovereignty created a huge amount of tension through the spring and summer of 1939, because to protect Poland the Western democracies had to have the support of the Soviet Union; what form that support would take was the overriding question. Britain wanted Soviet leader Joseph Stalin to announce a similar guarantee of Polish sovereignty, but Stalin wanted more: an alliance with the West, a ten-year mutual-defense agreement. The British government thought this would be too provocative to Germany, making war more likely, and the British still wanted to deal with Hitler through diplomacy. The Soviets saw Britain's hesitation as a rejection of their country as a serious power. Further, Britain and France sought to guarantee the sovereignty of Rumania as well, and Stalin saw this as a Western ploy to gain control over eastern Europe, which Stalin considered his sphere of influence. When he could not gain the agreement he desired from the Western powers, Stalin began to look to Germany for common ground.

In the 1920s Germany had fairly close ties to the new Soviet Union. The German military had trained at Russian bases and cooperated in producing poison gas. That relationship had come to an end when Hitler came to power in 1933 and signed a nonaggression pact with Poland. By the spring of 1939, however, it looked as if those ties might be renewed. If the Western powers could not guarantee Soviet dominance over eastern Europe, perhaps Hitler would. After all, Germany's military alliance with Italy, the "Pact of Steel" signed in late May, was clearly directed against Britain and France; certainly Hitler would not be interested in eastern Europe anytime soon. As Soviet relations with the Western powers deteriorated, relations with Germany reopened.

If Hitler had to fight Britain and France, the last thing he wanted was a two-front war. Therefore, Germany started the

Nazi parade in Warsaw, Poland.

process by having Foreign Minister Ribbentrop send out feelers to new Soviet foreign minister Molotov. The two conducted secret negotiations throughout the summer as Anglo-Soviet relations deteriorated.

In the meantime, Hitler prepared for aggression against Poland. In creating an independent Poland, the Versailles Treaty gave the country a seaport on the Baltic at Danzig. While termed a "free city," Danzig was totally German in its population. Further, Poland was granted land on either side of the city, the so-called Danzig Corridor, an action that created a detached German state, East Prussia. Using the same rationale he had used in overtaking Austria and the Sudetenland, Hitler began agitating for all German-speaking people to be under one government. In this case, that meant Danzig and the corridor. If Poland would merely cede the city and area to Germany, Hitler claimed that he had no more territorial demands in Europe. Such an action would make Poland landlocked.

This demand brought the British and French guarantees to Poland; they had no desire to look the fools again after the Sudetenland debacle. The only problems were: (1) Hitler did not believe the Western democracies now any more than he had earlier, and (2) Poland was so isolated that direct British and French intervention would be nearly impossible. Hence, Soviet aid was vital, but the Western powers would not give Stalin what he wanted. The Soviets continued to play both ends against the middle, waiting for the best offer from either side. They finally signed a nonaggression pact with Germany on 23 August, an agreement that shocked the world. Ever since Hitler had entered politics, he had been virulently anti-Communist, and Stalin had never expressed any love for Nazism. The Polish government was in a state of panic; they had assumed that Stalin would never allow Nazis on his doorstep,

and now Poland was stuck in the middle of these strange bedfellows. With this agreement in hand, Hitler ordered Nazis in Danzig to provoke an incident with Poland.

There was no formal declaration of war. Early on the morning of 1 September, German aircraft flew into Polish airspace and attacked airfields, road junctions, troop concentrations, and command centers. Fast-moving armored columns with close infantry support crossed the border just before dawn. The Poles were the first to be on the receiving end of the *blitzkrieg*, or lightning war. This strategy of using rapid thrusts to surround and cut off troop formations or defensive strong points, then letting them starve or be mopped up by infantry, had been theorized by British military thinkers between wars, but German theorists perfected it. The close air support, which assisted the attacking columns once the strategic targets were destroyed, was highly successful because most German air crews had had on-the-job training in close support operations while assisting Franco's forces in the Spanish civil war.

The Polish army, though 3 million strong, was unprepared for this style of warfare. Because the Polish forces were called to protect the capital city of Warsaw, the defenseless countryside gave Soviet troops an easy opening to come pouring in from the east on 17 September. Unknown until that moment was a secret clause in the nonaggression pact Hitler and Stalin had just signed that called for Poland to be divided between the two countries so that each could have a buffer zone from the other. Attacked from two sides and hopelessly outclassed, Polish authorities were obliged to surrender. Warsaw fell on 28 September, and all fighting ended by 1 October.

Britain reluctantly fulfilled its obligations to Poland, in a manner of speaking. The British government declared war on

Polish prisoners of war in 1939, camp name unknown.

3 September, with the French government following suit soon thereafter, but did nothing to help the Poles. The Poles did not see one British or French soldier, aircraft, or ship. All they got from the alliance was the knowledge that the world was going to war over them.

The German occupation was a harsh one because Hitler soon began implementing his "final solution" for European Jews. Occupied Poland was the site of most of the Nazi death camps, including the infamous Auschwitz and Treblinka camps. Poland was also the staging ground for later German aggression. When Hitler decided to invade the Soviet Union in the summer of 1941, Poland provided the base for German army groups heading for Leningrad, Moscow, Kiev, and the Caucasus. When the tide turned and Soviet troops entered Poland in 1944, the German occupation forces in Warsaw put down a massive uprising in the Jewish ghetto by destroying virtually every building and killing every person in that area. Classed as *untermensch* (subhumans), according to Hitler's racial theories, all Poles, Jewish or not, suffered simply because of their heritage. A nation crisscrossed by armies since the time of the Roman Empire endured yet another brutal experience at the hands of foreign soldiers.

*See also* Czechoslovakia, Nazi Occupation of [152]; Germany, Soviet Invasion of [162].

References: Guderian, Heinz, *Panzer Leader* (New York: Dutton, 1957); Liddell Hart, Basil, *History of the Second World War* (New York: Putnam, 1970); Shirer, William, *Rise and Fall of the Third Reich* (New York: Simon & Schuster, 1960).

## RHINELAND, NAZI OCCUPATION OF THE

## 184

One of the results of the Versailles Treaty, which brought about the end of World War I, was that the territory known as the Rhineland was to be occupied by Allied troops for a period of time and demilitarized indefinitely. No German troops, military installations, or fortifications were to be located in the demilitarized zone, which included all German territory west of the Rhine, along with the territory on the east side of the Rhine River to a depth of 50 kilometers. Though the Germans were forced to accept these terms in 1919, in 1925 they willingly agreed to a demilitarized Rhineland when they signed the Locarno Pact.

As early as May 1935, Adolf Hitler ordered the German High Command to create a plan for the reoccupation of the Rhineland. During this period, the French government received reports that the Germans were constructing barracks, ammunition depots, airfields, rail lines, and roads in the demilitarized zone, but failed to do anything about these warnings. By the beginning of 1936, Hitler believed the time was nearing for a German move into the Rhineland. Hitler watched closely how the League of Nations dealt with Mussolini's aggressions in Ethiopia. He rightly concluded that if the league could not get together on this problem, they would lack the resolve needed to confront Germany for its violations of the Versailles and Locarno treaties.

On Hitler's command, General Blomberg, the minister of war and commander in chief of the armed forces, issued on 2 March 1936 the preparatory orders for the reoccupation, code-named *Winterubung* (Winter Exercise). Three days later, on 5 March, the date for Z-Day (D-Day) was set for Saturday, 7 March. Historians believe that Hitler purposely planned many of his important actions to begin on Saturdays to take advantage of the long weekends enjoyed by many European diplomats.

The military leaders, including Army Chief of Staff General von Fritsch, did not believe the army was ready for such a move, and that the French and British would easily force the German troops out of the Rhineland. At this time the German army was inferior to the Allies in numbers, equipment, and training, and a German defeat would be a severe blow to Germany's rearmament program and growing political strength. On the day of and immediately after the invasion, the German generals urged Hitler to recall the troops west of the Rhine for fear of French reprisals. This was the first open conflict between Hitler and the army, and after the success of the German reoccupation, Hitler placed less value on his generals' opinions and more on his own intuition.

At dawn on 7 March, elements of the German army moved into the Rhineland, supported by two squadrons of fighter aircraft. These soldiers entered the zone undeployed for battle. Only three battalions of infantry crossed the Rhine River, and German panzers never entered the demilitarized zone. The total number of German troops was 36,000, which included 14,000 local police organized as infantry.

The consequences of the reoccupation were enormous. First, many historians believe that France and England could have easily prevented Germany from fortifying the Rhineland. If France alone or in conjunction with England had used force against the Germans, the German army would have been forced to retreat. In fact, the soldiers on the west side of the Rhine had orders to conduct a fighting withdrawal if they encountered French troops. However, the only response from the Allies was a formal protest to the League of Nations.

A number of important consequences occurred by allowing Germany to regain control of the Rhineland. The Allies failed to strike a crucial blow against the rising power of Nazi Germany and Hitler's influence at home by failing to act against Hitler's aggression. After the reoccupation of the Rhineland, a plebiscite was conducted in Germany that showed a 98.8 percent approval rate for Hitler and his actions. The German fortification of the Rhineland allowed Germany's western frontier to be protected with only a minimum number of soldiers, and provided cover for Germany's industries and mineral deposits located in the Ruhr, thus providing security for Germany's rearmament program. With Germany firmly entrenched in the Rhineland, France could no longer come to the aid of its allies in central and Eastern Europe. Now, with the remilitarization and reoccupation a *fait accompli,* Hitler would be able to begin expansion in the east to achieve *lebensraum* for the German people with little interference from the Western allies.

—James L. Iseman

*See also* Ethiopia, Italian Invasion of [157]; Hitler, Adolf [165].

References: Kagan, Donald, *On the Origins of War* (New York: Doubleday, 1995); Shirer, William, *The Collapse of the Third Republic* (New York: Simon & Schuster, 1969); Taylor, Telford, *Munich: The Price of Peace* (Garden City, NY: Doubleday, 1979).

# 185 RUSSIA, GERMAN INVASION OF

Germany went into World War I planning to quickly defeat France through its long-anticipated Schlieffen Plan, finishing off Russia at its leisure. This would give them, with assistance from the Ottoman Empire, access to oil in Persia, a country under Russia's economic dominance. Coupled with the raw materials of central and Eastern Europe and German financial and management abilities, Persian oil would be the final necessary addition for an empire under German dominance stretching from the North Sea to the Persian Gulf. When Archduke Franz Ferdinand, heir to the throne of Germany's ally Austria-Hungary, was assassinated in June 1914, a chain of events was set into motion that brought the world into war.

Germany urged Austria to blame the Serbian government for the act of terrorists and to demand concessions so intense that Serbia could not comply. When Austria declared war on Serbia on 28 July, Russia rallied to the aid of its fellow Slavic country. Germany declared war on Russia on 1 August, followed by another declaration on Russia's ally France on 3 August. The following morning, German troops violated Belgian neutrality on their way around the French army's flank, and by doing so brought Great Britain to Belgium's assistance.

Most of Germany's forces were dedicated to the offensive in France; the German Eighth Army remained in the east to maintain an active defense for a predicted-to-be-slow Russian mobilization. When Russian forces scored a small early success in Poland, two infantry corps and a cavalry division were transferred from France to East Prussia. A new commander was also brought in: Paul von Hindenburg, a veteran of the Franco-Prussian War. He was assisted by a very able chief of staff, Erich Ludendorff, and inherited the talents of Chief of Operations Max Hoffman. The Eighth Army faced the Russian First and Second armies in Poland and had just retreated from the more northerly enemy, the First. Hindenburg and Ludendorff took control just as the Eighth was repositioning itself to attack the Russian Second Army to the south. The result was a huge German victory at Tannenberg at the end of August. Within two weeks they had pivoted northward and destroyed the Russian First Army at the battle of Masurian Lakes. These victories did not result in momentum, for the exhausted German troops soon found more Russians in their path; they retreated to East Prussia.

In the meantime, the Austrians had not had good luck against Russia. They attacked northeast into Galicia, and at first made good headway against the Russians, but the overconfident Austrian commander, Count Conrad von Hötzendorff, attacked Russian forces who were not as broken and demoralized as he had believed. By the end of August, as the Germans were winning at Tannenberg, the Austrians were in full retreat and did not stop until they reached the Carpathian Mountains in mid-September. Against Russian casualties of 250,000, the Austrians lost 450,000, virtually half the army with which they started the war.

German forces attempted to capture Warsaw in October, but ran into fierce Russian resistance, which forced Hindenburg's men back to their starting point. Though he continually faced superior numbers, Hindenburg had the advantage of a superior intelligence staff who regularly intercepted Russian wireless transmissions. Using this knowledge of Russian plans and troop dispositions, Hindenburg shifted forces to attack Lodz, which the Germans captured after difficult fighting in December. Throughout the last months of 1914, Hindenburg begged for more men, but could get few from Erich von Falkenhayn, army chief of staff, who was dedicated to the Western Front. For the most part, the Eastern Front got reserve divisions, but enough new troops arrived to make up three armies (the Eighth, Ninth

and Tenth) by the end of the year, with Hindenburg in overall command.

In 1915 the Germans scored their greatest successes. In late January, Austrian forces attacked in terrible weather, and after early success, ground to a halt in the snow. In a second battle east of the Masurian Lakes in mid-February, the German Ninth and Tenth armies captured 55,000 Russians and drove off the remainder of the Russian Tenth Army, though they did not have the ability to press farther. The German successes could not convince the High Command to send more troops, but the Austrian difficulties brought a new army to the east. Falkenhayn sent the newly formed Eleventh Army to aid the Austrians, and together (with massed artillery preparations), they broke through the Russian defensive positions in Galicia in May. The Russians fought bravely but lacked the necessary ammunition; Russian transport was woefully inadequate. By 22 June, the Germans and Austrians were at the Bug River. Hindenburg favored a huge pincer operation with his forces, idle in the north, swinging around to meet the Austro-German force and capturing the Russian army. Falkenhayn and Kaiser Wilhelm settled instead for a smaller pincer that won battles but failed to surround the Russians. Even with the addition of a fourth army, the Twelfth, to Hindenburg's eastern force, they were unable to destroy their enemy. By the autumn of 1915, the Russians had extracted themselves from any encirclement and saved their army, though they were forced to take up new positions deep in their own territory. The Germans had captured vast tracts of land, but Falkenhayn refused to maintain the momentum and withdrew several divisions from the east to return to France. Hindenburg was told to go on the defensive.

The Russians conducted a scorched-earth withdrawal and forced the residents of the abandoned countryside to flee with them. This actually aided the Germans, who did not have to worry about feeding or keeping an eye on a hostile population. It hurt the Russians by burdening their overtaxed supply system, and the waves of refugees spread defeatism. Despite this negative development, the Russians had time to recover their strength when the Germans went on the defensive. New but short-term minister of war Aleksai Polivanov raised and trained 2 million conscripts and got Russian industry up to the task of producing weapons and ammunition. He reorganized the Russian army into three fronts, but the commanders of two of them were incompetent. Only Aleksei Brusilov, commanding the Southwest Front against the Austrians, was an inspired choice. He saw the potential for success in the south and exploited it.

The Austrians, Brusilov believed, were a broken reed. They had recently removed many of their Slavic troops to fight their new enemy, Italy, which meant that the hold on their section of the front would be weakened. A Russian offensive in the north in mid-March 1916 had come to naught, and the front commanders there never again mounted serious attacks against the well-entrenched Germans. Nevertheless, German attention was focused in the north, and that meant that Brusilov was able to prepare his offensive more easily. After a 24-hour bombardment, the Russians attacked five Austrian armies on 5 June; they were unstoppable. The Austrian armies on the flanks broke, and the Russians took 200,000 prisoners in the first week. Brusilov called a halt to regroup. Had the commanders of the two northern Russian fronts launched attacks at this time, the German force, which had been spread thin by the transfers to France, would have been unable to hold on. After the failure in March, however, they would

not move until too late. Hindenburg was able to shift men to the south to stiffen the Austrians just in time to stave off disaster. By October, Brusilov had reached the Carpathians and overlooked the Hungarian plains, but he could go no farther. The well-trained men with whom he had begun the offensive were now dead, and their replacements were too green.

Brusilov's offensive had far-reaching effects. The Habsburg monarchy in Austria-Hungary was faced with increasing ethnic tension that affected the army as well as the civilians. Emperor Franz Josef died in November 1916, and his successor, Charles, began secret negotiations to take Austria out of the war, but the Germans would not allow it. There were negative side effects in Russia as well. The loss of 1 million men in the offensive, on top of the quarter-million casualties per month the Russians had lost in the first year and a half of the war, was causing unrest on the home front. The addition of Rumania as an ally had no positive results; their army was useless and their country overrun in four months. Russia was ripe for revolution.

On the German side there were changes as well. The setback with Austria brought an end to Falkenhayn's tenure as chief of staff, and he was replaced in August 1916 by Hindenburg and Ludendorff. Max Hoffman became the commander of German forces in the east. After pleading so long for increased attention to the Russian front, the two new leaders shifted their attention to France. They finally learned just what had been occurring for two years in the west, and they had to deal with British and French offensives that kept men away from Russia. It looked as if the Eastern Front would become inactive while both sides tried to recover.

Russia broke first. Bad news from the front, coupled with food shortages, brought riots in March 1917. The troops ordered to quell the riots joined them instead, and Czar Nicholas was obliged to abdicate in favor of a democratic government under the leadership of Alexander Kerensky. He tried to keep the war effort going, but proved no more successful than the czarist government. The German foreign office tried to negotiate a separate peace with Kerensky, but the lack of German military activity gave hope to the new Russian leader. He kept the army going for another few months, long enough for the new commander in chief, Brusilov, to launch a new offensive in the south in the summer of 1917. It soon petered out, and Hoffman counterattacked in mid-July, making strong gains in Galicia. He ordered his forces in the north to attack the Russian flank at Riga, and captured that city easily in September.

The German successes caused friction between Kerensky and his new commander in chief, Lavr Kornilov. Kerensky believed that Kornilov was plotting against him, so Kerensky was forced to ally himself with the Bolshevik leaders he had kept in jail. They turned against him and overthrew him in six weeks. The Bolshevik leader, Vladimir Lenin, called for immediate peace talks, but balked at Ludendorff's demands for huge territorial concessions. A new offensive in February 1918 changed Lenin's mind, and the Treaty of Brest Litovsk removed Russia from the war. Hundreds of thousands of men were transferred to France for the spring offensive of 1918, but the timely arrival of American forces blunted Germany's last great hope in the west. If the occupation forces kept in the east had also been shifted, it may have had a decisive effect, but that can never be known.

Ultimately, the German invasion was successful only until November 1918, when Germany was forced to sign an armistice. The Versailles Treaty that was forced on the Germans in the summer of 1919 took away all their eastern conquests as well as their overseas possessions. The greatest effect of their offensive was not on Germany but on Russia, because the war hastened the downfall of the Romanov dynasty and brought the Communists to power. Their reoccupation of the Ukraine brought about such hostility that the local population would ever after chafe at Communist control and yearn for the day they could be free of it. It also left the Germans with a grudge—the land they had won was taken from them. Hitler's dreams to reconquer that land would bring on another world war.

*See also* France, Prussian Invasion of (Franco-Prussian War) [133]; France, German Invasion of [160].

References: Rutherford, Ward, *The Russian Army in World War I* (London: Gordon Cremones, 1975); Showalter, Dennis, *Tannenberg: Clash of Empires* (Hamden, CT: Archon Books, 1991).

## SICILY, ALLIED INVASION OF

**186**

Having successfully completed the occupation of North Africa, British and American leaders pondered the next target in their campaign against the Axis. American president Franklin Roosevelt and British prime minister Winston Churchill met in Casablanca, Morocco, in January 1943 to discuss this and other strategic matters. Two options presented themselves for a continued campaign in the Mediterranean area: (1) Corsica or Sardinia, to set up an invasion of southern France, or (2) Sicily, to set up an invasion of Italy. The two leaders decided to feint at Sardinia and plan the operation for Sicily. Occupation of the island would open up the sea-lanes of the Mediterranean to the Suez Canal and save time over the Cape of Good Hope route then in use. Hopefully, it would also force Germany to divert troops from the Russian front to counter the southern threat.

More than 400,000 German and Italian troops defended the island, which was known for its rugged terrain. The British Eighth Army under General Sir Bernard Montgomery was to land on the southeastern corner of the triangular island and drive up the coast to Messina, cutting off any Axis retreat into Italy. The American Seventh Army under General George Patton was to land in the central part of the south coast and clear the middle and western parts of the island of the enemy as well as drive north parallel to the British attack.

Early on the morning of 10 June 1943, American airborne troops landed for their first-ever combat operation. Their mission was to seize road junctions and delay any reinforcements that came up the few roads available on the island. The Germans had decided to hold back most of their troops from the beaches and respond to the Allied initiatives as though there were too much seacoast to defend. The initial landings went smoothly, but a German armored counterattack the next day put severe pressure on the American positions. It was ultimately driven back, and by the fourth day of the invasion, the Allies had a secure beachhead.

As Montgomery's forces encountered severe resistance along the coast road, they gradually had to move farther and farther inland, pushing American forces farther west. Patton took it upon himself to send his forces northwest to capture Palermo, then drive eastward along the north coast road, thus putting pressure on the retreating Axis troops from two directions. By the end of June, the Germans had decided to abandon the island, and began a fighting withdrawal toward the port of Messina. Despite constant pressure from the British

attacking overland and Patton staging amphibious flanking moves, the Germans managed to extricate themselves according to plan. When Allied forces entered Messina on 17 August, they found the city empty; the Germans had evacuated 100,000 men and 10,000 vehicles.

While not the crushing victory for which the Allies had hoped, the capture of Sicily had major results. It accomplished its primary mission of securing the sea-lanes through the Mediterranean. More importantly, it put such a strain on Italian morale that Mussolini was overthrown, and the new Italian government secretly approached the Allies to talk peace, ultimately agreeing to the demand for unconditional surrender called for by the Allies at the Casablanca Conference. This action was no surprise to Hitler; he had been sending German troops into the country for some months in anticipation of the Italian defection. Though the Italian army was no longer a factor in the war effort, the Germans did not abandon the countryside. The defense the Germans mounted after the landing of British troops in September 1943 continued until the end of the war. The Germans fought a slow and costly (for both sides) withdrawal up the entire peninsula, and were still fighting hard in the far north of the country when the surrender was signed in Germany in May 1945.

The invasion of Sicily caused a large amount of destruction, particularly around the cities of Palermo and Messina. The island's inhabitants were glad to see both the war and the Fascists go. The Allies were welcomed, if for no other reason than that they brought food and medicines. The lack of a fascist government structure left a power vacuum behind, which was filled by leaders of the local Mafia families. They backed a popular separatist movement until 1946, when Italy granted the island a large measure of local autonomy. The new relationship with Italy was further strengthened by the inclusion in the new Italian constitution of a clause instituting land reform; the largest landowners had to break up their holdings or be subject to government intervention. With land to work and universal suffrage, the Sicilians found their postwar condition much improved.

*See also* North Africa, U.S. Invasion of [177].

References: Birtle, A. J., *Sicily* (Washington, DC: U.S. Army Center of Military History, 1993); Garland, Albert, *Sicily and the Surrender of Italy* (Washington, DC: U.S. Army Center of Military History, 1965); Smith, Denis Mack, *A History of Sicily* (New York: Viking, 1968).

## SINAI, ISRAELI INVASION OF (1956) (SUEZ CRISIS)

187

In 1954 Egypt came under the control of Gamal Abdel Nasser, who dreamed great dreams for his nation: He wanted to modernize his country and make it the leader of the Arab world. To modernize Egypt, he proposed the construction of a dam on the Nile to bring hydroelectric power to his people and improve their living standards. To lead the Arab world, he proposed to make life difficult for Israel. In 1956 he set about accomplishing both these tasks.

The United States and Britain were interested in making money available to Egypt for the dam project, and worked with the World Bank to secure funds for Nasser. American president Dwight Eisenhower reconsidered the offer when he learned that Egypt had just contracted with Czechoslovakia, a communist state, to buy arms. Nasser had been sponsoring terrorist activity in Israel, and hoped with increased weaponry to have an army sufficient to defeat Israel. But if Nasser wanted to deal with Communists, Eisenhower reasoned, he could not have American money for his dam. The United States withdrew its support for the project without first notifying the other party involved, Great Britain, which was also obliged to back out. Nasser responded quickly and shockingly. Was there not a ready source of income in Egypt already, the Suez Canal? Why should the British and French stockholders be making money on this waterway when it was within Egyptian territory? Nasser announced that Egypt would nationalize the canal.

Britain and France did not care to lose income on a company they had owned since the 1870s, nor did they want to lose control of such a strategic waterway. If Egypt leaned toward the Soviet Union, their control of the canal could badly hurt European trade and troop movement. Moreover, France was upset with Nasser because of his support of revolutionaries in Algeria. Over and above all of this, however, was the humiliation of being outdone by a Third World leader. The British and French wanted their canal back, and just when they needed a handy ally, one appeared: Israel.

The Israelis had long wanted to do something to stop the Egyptian harassment of their country, and they feared what Nasser might do with the new supply of weapons he had just acquired. Egypt had been blockading the Straits of Tiran at the mouth of the Gulf of 'Aqaba, the branch of the Red Sea that reaches Israel's southern border. Since all three countries wanted to hurt Nasser, they made common cause. If Israel would invade the Sinai Peninsula and drive for the Suez Canal, the British and French would give them aid. Once the invading Israelis approached the canal, the Europeans would recommend a United Nations resolution to keep both Israeli and Egyptian troops ten miles from the canal. Then, Britain and France would volunteer to provide a peacekeeping force to guarantee that the canal stayed open. By coincidence, that would also put them in control again. If the United Nations or Egypt rejected the offer, the Europeans would invade and enforce their will. All of this planning was done in secret in Paris.

On 29 October 1956, Israeli troops went into action. They quickly drove down the west coast of the Gulf of 'Aqaba to seize the Egyptian post at Sharm al-Sheikh. They also landed parachute forces at Mitla Pass in preparation for an advance on the southern end of the Suez Canal, while an armored force was prepared to drive down the Mediterranean coast road to seize the northern end. When Egypt rejected Britain and France's offer of a peacekeeping force and a halt of belligerents ten miles either side of the canal (which the Israelis were not yet near), the second phase of the plan went into operation. British and French aircraft bombed Egyptian airfields, and ships were en route with an amphibious force, which landed at Port Said on 5 November. In the meantime, Israeli troops overran Egyptian defenses along the coast road, though Egyptian forces put up a much stiffer resistance deeper in the Sinai.

The United Nations condemned the invasions but could do little to stop them; both Britain and France were able to veto any Security Council resolutions. The real pressure came from the United States and the Soviet Union. President Eisenhower privately and publicly accused the British and French of colonialism, and suggested an embargo of Latin American oil to slow the invaders down. The Soviet threat was more to the point: They were willing to commit "volunteers" to aid Egypt, and possibly target Paris and London with nuclear missiles. That the Soviets would start World War III over Egypt was hard to believe, but neither the British nor the French were willing to call their bluff. They withdrew.

That left the Israeli army deep in Egyptian territory without the promised support, but they were loath to give up their gains. The United Nations committed a peacekeeping force to the Sinai Peninsula to protect Israel from further Egyptian incursions, and the Israelis achieved the security they wanted—at least until 1967, when the peacekeeping force was withdrawn. The British and the French got nothing but embarrassment and governments voted out of office. Nasser lost almost all his newly purchased weapons and saw his army badly handled by the Israelis, but he kept the canal and got Soviet money to build his dam. Because he seemed to have humbled the British and French, he was the big winner; he gained higher status in the Arab world, and was encouraged to keep planning actions against Israel. Relations between the United States and its allies were strained for some time, but Eisenhower's refusal to support them in what could possibly turn into nuclear holocaust was a wise move. The worst aspect for the Americans was their seeming cooperation with their archrival, especially since, concurrently with the Suez crisis, the Soviets were brutally suppressing a revolt in Hungary. To an extent, what this incident really proved was that Britain and France were not the powers they once were.

*See also* Algeria, French Occupation of [128]; Eisenhower, Dwight David [156].

References: Beaufré, André, *The Suez Expedition, 1956,* trans. Richard Barry (New York: Praeger, 1969); Bowie, Robert, *Suez, 1956* (London: Oxford University Press, 1974); Ovendale, Ritchie, *Origins of the Arab-Israeli Wars* (London: Longman, 1984).

## SINAI, ISRAELI INVASION OF (1967) (SIX-DAY WAR)

**188**

For ten years after the Suez crisis, the Middle East remained relatively peaceful. The United Nations emergency force kept the Egyptians and the Israelis at a distance, but they could not interfere in the diplomatic connections maintained by the Arab nations. Egypt's President Nasser still wanted to make his country the leader of the Arab world and, after ten years of Soviet military and economic assistance, he was establishing contacts with the other Arab nations to bring pressure on Israel. Nasser had helped bring the Palestinian Liberation Organization into existence, and they were carrying out guerrilla and terrorist raids into Israel that Egypt could no longer mount. The nations of Syria, Jordan, Lebanon, and Iraq supported the Palestinians to one extent or another, so Israel was under increasing pressure from all sides. When Nasser demanded and received the removal of the UN forces from the Sinai in May 1967, he occupied Sharm al-Sheikh and closed the Straits of Tiran (Israel's access through the Gulf of 'Aqaba to the Red Sea). Israel knew that a more serious attack was imminent.

Israeli prime minister Levi Eshkol gave in to pressure and appointed Moshe Dayan to the post of defense minister. Dayan had been one of the heroes of the 1956 conflict and was well known for his aggressive views of Israeli security. On 3 June, Dayan publicly announced Israel's intentions to carry on diplomatic efforts at peace, but he was secretly mobilizing the military and making plans. Increasing terrorist activity and threatening statements from its Arab neighbors gave Israel sufficient cause to strike first, Dayan believed. He did not think the United States would condemn him, nor did he think the Soviet Union would directly interfere. The official alliance of Jordan with Egypt on 1 June and the passage of an Iraqi division through Jordan were the last straw for Israel.

Just after 8:00 A.M. in Cairo on 5 June, Israeli aircraft came in low over the Mediterranean and attacked Egyptian airfields, destroying the vast majority of their combat aircraft on the ground. (The Egyptian pilots thought it terribly unfair to be attacked during breakfast.) Within a few hours, Israel had air superiority over the Sinai Peninsula, and its army was on the move. Three columns attacked Egyptian positions in and south of the Gaza Strip, meeting occasionally heavy resistance, but moving deep into the Sinai by the end of the first day. The Egyptian army fought hard at almost every defensive position, but were beaten or outflanked at every one. The Egyptian commander ordered his forces to withdraw to a line 50 miles east of the Suez Canal to defend the three passes covering the approach to the canal.

On Israel's western flank, operations were equally successful. The Iraqi and Jordanian forces were no match for Israeli armor, and soon the Arab forces withdrew to the east bank of the Jordan River, giving the Israelis control of the entire city of Jerusalem for the first time. Again, Israeli air forces were dominant in this area, winning air battles by destroying most Arab aircraft on the ground. The quick Israeli success, coupled with their air superiority, convinced the Syrians not to mount an invasion, but to remain in defensive positions on the Golan Heights, from which they could lob artillery fire into the area of Galilee.

By 8 June, the fourth day of the war, Israeli forces were within striking distance of the Suez Canal. Stubborn Arab resistance at the Mitla and Khatmia passes slowed them down, but outstanding Israeli tank gunnery and close air support made all the difference. That evening, the

Egyptian government issued a call for a cease-fire, so Israeli commanders ordered a mad dash for the canal to establish the best strategic and tactical position possible before the fighting ended. Israeli forces managed to reach the canal and control the entire western bank, including Port Tewfik, dominating the southern end.

Syria's acceptance of a proposed cease-fire, to go into effect early on 9 June, motivated the Israeli defense minister. Though Israel had not been invaded from the north, Dayan ordered his army to capture the Golan Heights before the cease-fire went into effect. Throughout 8 June, after the armistice was supposed to have begun, Israeli troops fought for the high ground. That night they dug in and waited for counterattacks that did not come. On the morning of 9 June, they heard explosions; the Syrians were destroying their fortifications and withdrawing. Dayan managed to get the cease-fire time extended long enough to secure vital road junctions to hold the Golan.

The Israeli victory was overwhelming. At a cost of some 800 killed, Israel extended its borders across the Sinai Peninsula (making control of the Gulf of 'Aqaba a certainty), secured land up to the west bank of the Jordan River (including the whole of Jerusalem), and gained the strong defensive position of the Golan Heights. Militarily, it was as impressive as any operation in history. Politically, it had its drawbacks. Though the war was halted, the fighting did not stop. No Arab nation made peace with Israel, and terrorist attacks intensified, both inside and outside the country. The United Nations, the United States, and the Soviet Union all tried their luck at assisting the peace process, and all failed. The Soviets replaced the lost Arab military equipment and argued that no negotiation could take place until Israel withdrew from their conquered territories. The United

States supported Israel, calling for guarantees of Israeli rights before withdrawal. Both Arabs and Israelis carried on a war of attrition that lasted until 1972.

Israel's new lands held almost 1.4 million Arabs, who chafed at the control of their new overlords. The Israeli government had a huge refugee problem, as well as the task of administering territory three times the size of its land area prior to the war. The long-standing hostility against the Jews, intensified by the army of occupation governing them, was a recipe for civil unrest and terrorism. No Arab nation would recognize Israel's right to exist, and after 1967 Israel was in too strong a position to negotiate without solid guarantees to its rights.

*See also* Israel, Arab Invasion of (Yom Kippur War) [166]; Sinai, Israeli Invasion of (1956) (Suez Crisis) [187].

References: Byford-Jones, W., *The Lightning War* (Indianapolis, IN: Bobbs-Merrill, 1968); Dupuy, Trevor, *Elusive Victory: The Arab-Israeli Wars, 1947–1974* (New York: Harper & Row, 1978); Gruber, Ruth, *Israel on the Seventh Day* (New York: Hill & Wang, 1968).

# SINGAPORE AND MALAYA, JAPANESE CONQUEST OF

**189**

Singapore was the pride of the British Empire in Southeast Asia, its fortifications bringing it the nickname "the Gibraltar of the East." The British had controlled the island since the early 1800s and had protectorate rights over the remainder of Malaya south of Thailand. Singapore served as the major British port for trade and defense, and the huge artillery protecting the island from invasion made the defenders feel impregnable.

The Japanese had other ideas. Certainly the big guns were daunting, but they had one serious drawback: They pointed to sea. If the Japanese could invade down the Malay Peninsula, the back door to Singapore should be easy to enter. The British had little concern over this possibility, for there were only two roads down the peninsula, and the remainder was impenetrable jungle and swamp. To Japanese planners on the island of Formosa prior to World War II, the jungle could be penetrated and the British beaten. Specialists in jungle warfare developed tactics to move men through the rough terrain, and by the end of 1941 the Japanese had trained in Formosan jungles and had become the finest jungle fighters anywhere.

As war approached in late 1941, the British commanders in Singapore begged London for an increase in men and aircraft. As only a few ships could be spared to the Indian Ocean, the British thought that air power was their best defense from invasion. However, because of the demands of British forces in Europe and Prime Minister Winston Churchill's focus on that theater, little could be spared for Singapore and Malaya. Some Indian army troops were sent to bulk up the defense forces, but they were not well trained or equipped. Australian troops were the primary defense forces in Malaya.

The British commanders in Singapore were sure that when war came to their area, the Japanese based in Indochina would be sending men their way. There were only three likely points of invasion along the eastern shore of the Malay Peninsula, and two of those sites were in Thailand. Plans were prepared for British forces to move first and seize the towns of Patani and Singora before the Japanese could land there, but London decided that any move prior to Japanese action would be provocative, so the preemptive strike never happened. The three Japanese divisions detailed for the invasion, under the leadership of General Tomoyuki Yamashita, landed in Thailand to no resistance, and only limited defenses at the Malay port of Kota Bharu.

Japanese landing craft went ashore just after midnight on 8 December through waters that were almost too rough in which to operate. They overcame the resistance of Indian army forces at Kota Bharu, and moved inland. At Patani and Singora, the Japanese quickly established themselves and moved south across the peninsula along the two roads that led to the western shore. The only serious British defense was mounted at Jitra by the 11th Indian Division, but they were amazed to find the enemy moving through the jungle and outflanking them. On 12 December the British withdrew, and from that day forward the Japanese were unstoppable. The Commonwealth forces were insufficiently prepared for the attack, and soon their spirit broke. The demoralized forces often withdrew even against inferior numbers, and they took casualties far out of proportion to those they inflicted.

The British withdrew rapidly down the peninsula, stopping to fight at each river crossing, then destroying the bridge and pulling back. Anticipating this tactic, the Japanese had brought more than the usual number of engineers and bridge-building units, and they quickly built bridges and continued the pursuit. The British were never able to stand at one spot long enough to dig in and stage a serious firefight. When the terrain became too difficult even for the specially trained Japanese, they staged amphibious landings to outflank the British and keep them on the run. By 31 January 1942 the Japanese occupied the entire peninsula, and the British, Indian, and Australian forces withdrew to the island of Singapore.

Yamashita had staged an impressive march, but he was still dissatisfied. His superiors disliked him for political reasons, and did not provide him with the support he deemed necessary. One of his three divisions was commanded by a general who was continually insubordinate. His entire command had never trained together, and his staff had been created only a few weeks prior to the invasion. Those factors made his success even more phenomenal, but he still had to take Singapore. He spent four days reconnoitering before launching his assault. He ordered one division to feint across the eastern end of the strait and draw the British reserves to that end of the island. He sent the other two divisions in landing craft against Singapore's western shore.

The heavy artillery on the island's southern shore did the best it could, but not all the guns could be traversed to meet the attack from the north, and even those that could had difficulty doing significant damage, because the range of 15 miles or more made observing and targeting almost impossible. The units assigned to beach defense tried to fight the landing craft in the dark, but the Japanese units came in along such a wide front that they were again able to penetrate and outflank the defenders. Orders came from Churchill to fight to the last man in the rubble of a destroyed city, but the fighting did not go on that long. A lack of water, caused by the aerial destruction of the pumping machinery, brought the defenders to a rapid crisis. Yamashita also faced a crisis: He was running out of ammunition. He decided to keep fighting as hard as possible, rather than scale back his attack and give the British an indication of his problem. His ruse worked; the British raised the white flag on 15 February and surrendered unconditionally.

The 73-day campaign cost the Commonwealth 9,000 dead and wounded and 130,000 prisoners. The Japanese lost a mere 3,000 killed and 7,000 wounded in the

entire campaign. The British commander, Lieutenant-General A. E. Percival, had asked for and received promises from Yamashita that the civilian population would remain unharmed, but the Japanese occupation was not pleasant. Food was scarce and the currency became worthless; the locals, especially those of Chinese descent, were treated harshly and forced into labor gangs for the Japanese. One source mentions that 70,000 Chinese were arrested, then executed—by being tied together and thrown into the sea. Anyone suspected of or caught in the act of espionage was tortured and beheaded. The British had left some men behind Japanese lines, somewhat by design, and they organized resistance groups that operated out of the jungle throughout the war. They did not do much damage, but they trained the locals for action when the Allied reinvasion took place. These units did not coordinate their activities too well, but they were in contact with British authorities in India, who kept them supplied with weapons and equipment through air drops. Along with these British-sponsored units was a Communist organization, the Malayan People's Anti-Japanese Army (MPAJA).

By June 1945, Australian forces were working their way through the East Indies toward Singapore and Malaya, and plans for the invasion of the peninsula were well advanced. The atomic bomb drops in early August made the invasion unnecessary. The Australians were not prepared to immediately come in and take over, so the MPAJA came in from the jungles and tried to establish control, using the time of disorganization to execute those whom they suspected of collaboration. The Japanese favoritism toward the Malays during the occupation, coupled with their persecution of the Chinese, led many guerrillas to believe that collaboration was widespread. The British military administration set up in September, and ran Singapore in the absence of a civil government for some months. The Colonial Office in London had plans to offer Malaya independence by 1946.

It took many months before production of goods and services could be reestablished. Even though the Japanese had invaded the peninsula to take advantage of its natural resources of tin and rubber, they had produced virtually none of either. The economic disorganization was matched by political disarray. Prior to the war, the peninsula was called the Unfederated Malay States, and for years the London government had planned on independence for this area based on states' rights. However, the constitution they imposed in 1946, the Malay Union, created a strong central government, which the factions in Malaya were unwilling to support. The union did not include Singapore because it remained vital to British strategic needs, and its dominant Chinese population would not fit well with the peninsular groups. Resistance to this government was widespread and even criticized in Parliament, so in 1948 a conference was held to fine-tune the document. The strong central government would be replaced by a confederation in which Malays held the dominant citizenship privileges. The state governments would exercise major power, while participating in a central legislature. The new Malay government came from the efforts of political moderates after left-wing groups were banned. By 1951, Malay and Chinese banded together in political parties.

First, however, the Communists had a try at taking over. Since they had operated out of the jungles throughout the war, they were accustomed to the terrain, and used it well. British antiterrorist units were brought in; by relocating the population away from the guerrillas and treating them well in relocation camps, the Communist

movement was crushed. A state of emergency lasted from 1948 through 1955. By 1957 the citizens of the peninsula had drafted a constitution, and independence was granted in August.

The British were hesitant to grant independence to Singapore because of their strategic interests. A city council was granted, which formed the first political parties on the island. The Communists, though not as violent as on the mainland, agitated through labor unions and Chinese schools. Not until 1958 did the island get self-rule and control over its economy and trade; Britain retains only defense rights. Singapore has developed into the fourth largest port in the world and one of the world's premier banking centers.

See also Singapore, British Occupation of [143].

References: Caffrey, Kate, *Out in the Midday Sun: Singapore 1941–1945* (New York: Stein & Day, 1973); Ienaga, Saburo, *The Pacific War, 1931–1945* (New York: Random House, 1978); Ryan, N. J., *A History of Malaysia and Singapore* (Oxford: Oxford University Press, 1976).

## SOUTH KOREA, NORTH KOREAN INVASION OF (KOREAN WAR)

**190**

Numerous foreign powers occupied Korea throughout its history, but the peninsula had always been the home of one nation. This changed for the first time at the end of World War II. At the Yalta Conference in February 1945, American president Franklin Roosevelt, British prime minister Winston Churchill, and Soviet premier Joseph Stalin agreed on zones of occupation for their forces at war's end. On the

Korean peninsula, a line was drawn at 38° north latitude to designate which forces would accept the surrender of Japanese troops: the Soviets above the line, and the Americans below it. Soviet forces entered Korea in early August 1945 and soon announced that the inhabitants requested their assistance in creating a Communist government. Koreans below that line, oddly enough, made no such request. The matter was sent to the new United Nations, which decided, in August 1947, that internationally supervised elections should be held throughout the country to determine the will of the people. The Soviet-occupied northern half of the country refused to cooperate, and announced the formation of the Democratic People's Republic of Korea. The inhabitants of the south formed a democratic government, the Republic of Korea.

Thus, a nation that had never been divided was split in half. The Soviets provided the North Koreans with military training and heavy weapons, while the Americans assisted the South Koreans in creating a lightly armed defense force. For almost three years there was unrest along the border. The critical point in relations between the two Koreas came in January 1950. U.S. secretary of state Dean Acheson announced the creation of a "defense perimeter," areas of the world the United States considered vital to its security and therefore would quickly defend. Areas outside that perimeter, which included South Korea, were told to appeal to the United Nations if threatened by outside forces. Coupled with a gradual withdrawal of American occupation forces, the North Koreans saw this as an admission that South Korea was not important to the United States. North Korean leader Kim Il Sung traveled to Moscow to ask Stalin for permission and assistance in attacking the south, and plans were made for an invasion.

On 25 June 1950, 175,000 heavily armed North Koreans invaded the south. Within a few days, the republic's capital at Seoul was captured, and South Korean forces, along with the few remaining American troops, were in retreat. South Korean president Syngman Rhee appealed to the United Nations for assistance. At American urging and in the absence of a Soviet delegate boycotting the organization, the United Nations voted to ask for world nations to volunteer forces to aid the Republic of Korea. Sixteen countries ultimately offered aid in one form or another, but the vast majority of troops came from the United States.

American president Harry Truman ordered American forces in Japan under the command of General Douglas MacArthur to assist South Korea immediately. MacArthur immediately had U.S. aircraft based in Japan giving direct support to retreating Allied forces and attacking North Korean troops and supply lines. U.S. forces in Japan were ferried to the south coast port of Pusan and began to set up a defensive line along the Naktong River while troops were being mobilized in the United States. From late July to mid-September, American and South Korean troops fought a tenacious defense against almost constant Communist North Korean attacks in what came to be known as the Pusan perimeter.

What was needed was an attack in the North Korean rear to isolate their forces and cut off their supply lines. MacArthur proposed landing U.S. Marines at the port of Inchon, just west of Seoul. Because most of the North Korean effort was concentrated along the Pusan perimeter, few troops would be in the rear to fend off such an assault. The problem with this idea was the target city itself. Inchon is the site of the largest tidal swell in the world—30 feet between high and low tides. Ships would have to unload very quickly during high tide to avoid being stranded in the mud and exposed to hostile fire at low tide. MacArthur overcame Washington's resistance to the idea and staged the landing on 15 September. It turned out to be a huge success. Within two weeks, U.S. forces had crossed the peninsula and cut off virtually the entire North Korean army. Coupled with an offensive out of the Pusan perimeter, the invading troops were almost completely captured between the two forces.

At this point, the UN mission had been accomplished. By the first week in October, South Korea was again free. President Truman decided to fulfill the UN mandate of 1947 to hold supervised elections all across the country. On his own, with the immediate approval of Syngman Rhee and the hesitant approval of the United Nations, Truman ordered MacArthur to lead UN forces into the north. On 7 October, South Korean troops backed by UN forces entered the north on a mission of reunion. This action led to a dangerous response. China was traditionally xenophobic, and did not like the idea of foreign troops approaching its borders. The Communist Chinese government, in power for only a year, warned the United Nations that if China felt threatened, its government could not stop "volunteers" from crossing the Yalu River into North Korea to assist their Communist brethren. MacArthur assured Truman that this was a bluff; the Chinese could not possibly commit enough troops to make any difference. With this assurance, Truman ordered the advance into the north to proceed.

By late November the operation seemed nearly complete. Because of a mountain range running north-south through the peninsula, the forces advanced in two columns that were not in direct contact with each other. UN forces on both sides of the mountains had almost reached the North Korean border with China at the Yalu River.

The presence of Chinese troops was minimal, and the advance halted so the troops could enjoy a Thanksgiving dinner in the field on 25 November; MacArthur guaranteed the men that they would be home by Christmas. The next day, 180,000 Chinese Communist forces swarmed down from the mountains, surrounding and decimating large numbers of UN troops. To make matters worse, extremely cold weather struck. Allied troops had to make a fighting withdrawal in subfreezing temperatures against Chinese troops that were everywhere at once. By early 1951, UN forces were in full retreat and crossed the 38th parallel heading south. Seoul was again captured by Communist forces. MacArthur denied any responsibility, and blamed Washington for not allowing him to use air power to interdict Chinese men and matériel at or beyond the Yalu River. Truman refused to sanction any attacks on Chinese soil, so MacArthur was not allowed to attack anything unless it was already in Korea. When he complained to the press about the restrictions put on his decisions, and did so contrary to orders from Washington, he was relieved of his command in April 1951 and replaced by General Matthew Ridgeway.

In the spring of 1951, Ridgeway was able to solidify the UN resistance some 50 miles south of Seoul. He counterattacked, and by June had recrossed the 38th parallel going north, but could go no farther. Trench warfare ensued, looking more like World War I than the fast-moving fighting of the previous year. When neither side could make headway against the other, they began considering peace talks. The first attempt at negotiations bogged down in July, and the fighting continued. By November the two sides were talking at the border village of Panmunjom as the killing went on. Negotiations stalled on the question of prisoner exchange. Most of the prisoners captured by UN forces, both North Korean and Chinese, expressed the desire to remain in the south rather than go back to their forces or their country. When the United Nations promised them that they would not be forcibly repatriated, the Communists cried foul. They demanded the return of all the prisoners, not believing the UN claim that so many did not want to be returned. No agreement could be made, so the fighting went on until June 1953.

That was the date of Joseph Stalin's death in Moscow. He had been the major supporter of the North Korean effort and, in the ensuing struggle for power in the Soviet Union, the Korean War fell low on the list of priorities. At this point, the Communists in Panmunjom agreed to take back only those prisoners who wanted to return, and an armistice was signed. Negotiations continued on a treaty to bring about peace and an official end to the conflict. Those negotiations were still going on 40 years later, with no end in sight.

The Republic of Korea maintained its democracy and reestablished close ties with the United States. By the 1990s, it had become an economically expanding nation with a growing export market in the mold of Japan: electronics and automobiles. The people enjoy a high standard of living and are active in Asian affairs. North Korea, on the other hand, has not enjoyed the same success. Tied to the Soviet Union throughout the Cold War era, its people lived under the iron hand of Kim Il Sung, who established a personality cult dominating every part of their society. The North Koreans continued to harass the border along the cease-fire line, and attempted to make life generally miserable for the south. Their hard-core Communist government remained one of the last such regimes in the wake of the collapse of the Soviet Union and the downfall of communism throughout most of the world. An isolated nation, cut off from most of the world's trade and political relations, the country has advanced very little since the end of the conflict.

References: Fehrenbach, T. R., *This Kind of War* (New York: Macmillan, 1963); Langley, Michael, *Inchon Landing* (New York: New York Times Books, 1979); Stokesbury, James, *A Short History of the Korean War* (New York: Morrow, 1988).

## SOVIET UNION, NAZI INVASION OF THE

**191**

Early in his political career, Adolf Hitler wrote *Mein Kampf,* spelling out his ideas on how to make Germany great again after the disaster of World War I. One of the necessities was to regain land that the Germans had captured from Russia in that war, but which had been taken away from them by the Treaty of Versailles. This land was rightfully theirs by conquest, Hitler argued, and Germany needed that land as *lebensraum,* or living space. Since they had conquered almost all of European Russia, and been ceded that territory by the Communists through the Treaty of Brest-Litovsk in early 1918, invading Russia would simply be a reoccupation of land legally belonging to Germany. Of course, this was the best land the Soviet Union owned: the great farm country of the Ukraine, the industrial and economic centers of Kiev and Minsk, and the Baltic ports.

Hitler successfully hid his intentions from the Soviets. Though he openly attacked communism in his speeches and backed Franco's forces in the Spanish civil war while the Soviets supported the government cause, he made no open threats against the Soviet Union. He was quick to exploit the hesitancy of the British and

French in the summer of 1939 when they would not treat the Soviet Union as an equal partner. Soviet premier Joseph Stalin had not expected this rebuff, and it resulted in the signing of the German-Soviet Nonaggression Pact, or Molotov-Ribbentrop Treaty, in August 1939, just days before Hitler invaded Poland. That agreement amazed the world because the Soviets seemed to be just as violently anti-Nazi as Hitler was anti-Communist. Even more shocking, the world soon learned that a secret clause of the nonaggression pact was an agreement to cooperate in Poland's dismemberment. The Soviet invasion of Poland in mid-September 1939, just as the entire Polish military was focused on the defense of Warsaw, was one of the most blatant stabs in the back in all of history. Stalin and Hitler, the strangest of bedfellows, each had half of Poland to act as a buffer zone against the other. Further, Hitler promised Stalin that Germany would not interfere with the Soviet Union's attacks on the Baltic States or Finland, which the Soviets undertook in November 1939. This diplomatic marriage of convenience was off to a great start.

With his rear covered, Hitler made war against the West in the spring and summer of 1940, invading Norway, Denmark, the Low Countries, and France, then spent the next few months in a fruitless attempt to bring Britain into the Nazi fold. Only after September 1940, when he postponed indefinitely the invasion of Britain, did Hitler turn back toward the East and his dream of lebensraum. From the fall of 1940 through the spring of 1941, he made preparations for the invasion, all the while dealing with unexpected sideshows such as aiding Italy in North Africa and Greece. These diversions, which included an airborne attack on Crete, served to delay the invasion of the Soviet Union. A one-month suspension of the start, until 22 June 1941, was quite possibly the reason Hitler's attempt on Mother Russia failed.

Stalin remained blissfully unaware of Hitler's intentions, even though there were attempts to warn him. Britain's code-breaking machine, ULTRA, gave the Western allies a look at Germany's plans. Britain was officially at war with the Soviet Union, but British prime minister Winston Churchill nevertheless tried to alert Stalin to Hitler's intentions—to no avail. Stalin was busy purging his own military and had no time to worry about anyone else's. Certainly, Stalin thought, Churchill was just trying to sow some discontent between allies.

Thus, Hitler's generals were able to amass three army groups for the invasion eastward. Army Group North was directed to drive through the Baltic States to secure the port city of Leningrad. Army Group Center's target was the Soviet capital city of Moscow. Army Group South was to drive for the Caucasus and its oil fields. All three got off to outstanding beginnings. The unprepared Soviet government watched in horror as entire Soviet armies were surrounded and captured in a matter of days. The German blitzkrieg, perfected in Poland and France, proved itself once again on the plains of Belorussia and the Ukraine. The initial attacks were so successful that Hitler spurned an opportunity that arose early in the invasion. He found that Belorussians and Ukrainians so despised the Communist regime that they would gladly assist the Germans in deposing it. These people viewed the Germans more as liberators than invaders. The German army thus had the opportunity not only to gain ground, but to gain size; as they drove deeper into enemy territory, they could actually build a larger army—an army full of motivated soldiers familiar with the Soviet military.

Instead, Hitler was married to the racial policies spelled out in Mein Kampf. The *lebensraum* was to be for Germans only, so the *untermensch,* or subhumans, who lived there were to be removed. Therefore, the would-be volunteers were either killed, rounded up for slave labor, or—if they were Jewish—shipped to extermination camps. Those who managed to escape those fates headed for the hills and forests to organize guerrilla partisan movements, and these partisans made a great difference to Hitler's ultimate fate in the East. At the height of the German advance, when they were engaged heavily at Leningrad, Moscow, and Stalingrad, they were obliged to maintain almost half their army in the rear to guard their supply lines. Instead of building his army as he went, Hitler was forced to cut in half the army he had in order to deal with the Ukrainians and Byelorussians he had rejected.

Perhaps Hitler's grasp on reality was beginning to fade, or perhaps it was the overwhelming success of his invasion that dictated his attitude toward the people he conquered, because his opening successes were phenomenal. German armies raced over vast tracts of land; the only defense the Soviets could mount because of their huge losses in manpower was a scorched-earth policy. By denying the Germans the ability to live off the land and by partisans harassing the ever-lengthening supply lines, the Soviets finally forced the German army to move not as it wished, but as its dwindling logistics dictated. Still, by September the port city of Leningrad was being surrounded and besieged, Moscow was virtually within German artillery range, and German armies were in the Crimea and poised to move into the oil-rich Caucasus. Another month of good weather, denied them because of the delay in starting the invasion, might have put the German army in warm cities when the winter came. By using rather than abusing the local volunteers, easier transport and supply lines could well have put them in those same cities. Instead, German soldiers had to face Mother Russia's oldest ally, Mother Nature.

Virtually every invader over the centuries has learned to his dismay that few winters can match those found in Russia. When Napoleon invaded Russia in 1812, he found himself in weather reaching −32°C, and 1941 proved to be 1812's rival. German forces had to survive in their summer uniforms because Hitler had been positive their goals would be reached before winter uniforms were necessary. Warm clothing was available in Germany, of course, but the increasing difficulty of moving matériel over guerrilla-infested supply lines kept most of that clothing out of German hands. Military activity basically ground to a halt until the following spring. Though the Germans suffered, so did the Russians. The 2 million people besieged in Leningrad (and another million in outlying areas) had to survive two successive winters with virtually no contact with the outside world. But survive they did, in one of history's most heroic defenses. Just over half a million people were in the city when it was liberated in January 1944.

The spring of 1942 brought the return of German successes in the south, but Hitler's maddening habit of withdrawing units from the south to reinforce the other army groups, especially around Moscow, limited Army Group South's effectiveness. Advance German units reportedly saw the Caucasus oil fields in the distance, but the Nazis never reached them. Instead, the major portion of the force went to capture Stalingrad, on the Volga River. Because the city was named for the leader of his enemy, Hitler demanded that there be no withdrawal until Stalingrad was captured. Stalin, equally prideful, demanded his forces fight just as hard and long.

The German Sixth Army went into Stalingrad in late summer 1942, and never returned. Some 350,000 German soldiers fought to capture the city, and only 5,000 ever saw Germany again. Combat was street by street, house by house, room by room, mostly in the dead of winter. Russian tank factories rolled tanks off the assembly line, put a crew inside, and sent them around the corner or down the street directly into combat. Desperate to save his city, Stalin decided to withdraw forces from the Far East, where he had been awaiting a possible Japanese offensive. Those troops, transported across the breadth of Russia, finally surrounded and destroyed the Sixth Army and blunted Germany's thrust toward Russian oil. Hitler ordered his forces in the city not to break out: "Where the German soldier has once set foot, there he remains." He promoted the army's commander, Frederick von Paulus, to field marshal, since no German field marshal had ever been taken prisoner. The orders doomed the Germans, because a tactical withdrawal might have linked up with forces fighting to relieve the Sixth Army and made a later capture of the city possible.

By the spring of 1943, German forces had driven almost as far as they ever would. They had made little headway against Leningrad or Moscow and, after Stalingrad, they were forced onto the defensive in the south. Hitler's dream of *lebensraum* died in the light of military realities: insufficient logistics, a hostile civilian population, inconsistent command from Berlin. The one overriding factor, however, was one that Hitler had preached against after the German experience of World War I: fighting a two-front war. Trying to supply men and matériel to both the Eastern Front and to North Africa, then Sicily and Italy, and finally to France after June 1944, proved impossible, just as it had in 1917–1918. Too many enemies at once, both from abroad and among the conquered territories, proved to be more than any country could handle.

The fighting in the Soviet Union created long-term results for the people defending the country and ultimately for the world. In the Soviet Union, this conflict was referred to not as World War II, but as the Great Patriotic War. People who hated Stalin and communism ultimately fought for them—not out of ideology, but out of love for their country. There is an almost mystical tie between the Russian people and their land, and Stalin played on that throughout the war and afterward. From the time he met with President Franklin Roosevelt and Prime Minister Churchill in Teheran in November 1943, Stalin accused the West of delaying a major European invasion so that the Nazis and Communists would kill each other. That accusation became the justification for almost all his actions through the end of the war and into the postwar period. Russia suffered, so Russia should benefit by capturing Berlin, taking control of Eastern Europe, and exploiting the German people and territory they had captured. Stalin's appeal to patriotism saved the country in 1942 and 1943, but it set up a confrontational attitude throughout the Cold War.

*See also* Russia, Napoleon's Invasion of [122]; Britain, Nazi Invasion of (Battle of Britain) [149]; Egypt, Italian Invasion of [155]; Finland, Soviet Invasion of [158]; France, Nazi Invasion of [161]; Greece, Nazi Invasion of [163]; Hitler, Adolf [165]; Norway and Denmark, Nazi Invasion of [178]; Poland, Nazi Conquest of [183]; Russia, German Invasion of [185].

References: Carrell, Paul, *Hitler Moves East, 1941–1943* (Boston: Little, Brown, 1965); Clark, Alan, *Barbarossa* (New York: Morrow, 1965); Guderian, Heinz, *Panzer Leader* (New York: Dutton, 1957).

## 192

# TURKEY, BRITISH INVASION OF

By the end of 1914, the war in France had settled into a deadlock. With both Allied and Central powers anchoring their flanks on the English Channel and the Swiss border, defenses in depth were the rule. Some in the British government believed that the war might have to be won elsewhere, or that at least the Allies should pose a sufficient threat to make Germany withdraw troops, weakening their position in France. The Russians were having little success against Germany, so that front seemed unlikely to bring any luck. First Lord of the Admiralty Winston Churchill suggested an attack against Germany's ally, Turkey. Turkey had its fingers in many pies: a new attack against the Caucasus to threaten Russia, an abortive move against the Suez Canal, and a defensive stand against a British force moving up from the Persian Gulf. Certainly, Churchill argued, a direct thrust against the Turkish capital at Constantinople should be enough to disrupt the Turkish military and panic their government into surrender. Secretary of State for War Lord Kitchener blocked any attempt to siphon off soldiers from the fighting in France, so Churchill stated that the victory could be won by the Royal Navy alone.

Churchill proposed to destroy the forts that guarded the Dardanelles, the passageway to Constantinople and the Black Sea, after which a naval force could cruise up to the Turkish capital and bombard the city at leisure. He was certain that naval gunfire could destroy the forts. When the Turks had joined the war the previous November, a British naval raid against the straits met virtually no resistance from the obsolescent Turkish defenses, so the Turkish government should surrender at gunpoint with little trouble. Once Turkey had been removed from the war, Churchill argued,

a direct supply line to and from Russia would be open, and the Balkan States that had allied themselves with Germany should cave in quickly to Allied pressure and threaten Germany's other ally, Austria-Hungary. The British cabinet reluctantly approved.

The force that gathered at the Greek island of Lemnos in February 1915 was made up of both British and French battleships. Though they were allies, the French had no intention of allowing Britain to control the straits alone. Under overall British command, the armada sailed to the mouth of the Dardanelles and began bombarding the forts. Little did the British know that the previous November's raid had alerted the Turks to the weakness of their defenses and, under the direction of German adviser Field Marshal Colmar von der Goltz, they had been working steadily ever since to improve their fortifications.

The Allies began bombarding the forts, and were surprised to find no return fire until they drew close to shore. The first few hours of shelling had had little effect, and the Allies withdrew to wait out some bad weather. When they returned on 25 February, the shelling continued with irregular results. Some forts were silenced by the naval guns, then blown apart by landing parties. Others survived erratic shelling with little problem. Turkish return fire was bothersome, but not dangerous. It was not artillery fire, however, that turned the tide, but mines. The Allies knew the Turks had sown the straits with mines, and had brought along minesweepers to take care of the problem. But the art of minesweeping was in its infancy, and a secret Turkish operation in a previously cleared area proved the Allies' undoing. On 18 March the ships sailed in to run the length of the straits and ran straight into the new minefield. Within a few hours, three ships were sunk and three badly damaged; the naval forces withdrew.

Had they pushed forward past this point, the mission may well have been successful, because the Turks were almost out of ammunition. The navy had failed, and called for the army.

Oddly enough, the government in London had been preparing forces for the campaign. Kitchener's early resistance turned to grudging acceptance, and 75,000 men, many from the Australia and New Zealand Army Corps (Anzacs), were assigned to land on the Gallipoli Peninsula. Sir Ian Hamilton was given command of the operation, though he was given little time to prepare; the government wanted results in a hurry. Hamilton found the base at Lemnos unfit for a major operation, and he redirected the troops' convoys to Alexandria, Egypt. The ships had to be unloaded and reloaded in an attempt to repair the haphazard loading done in England. Finally, the expedition got under way in mid-April 1915. Hamilton decided to land forces at five spots along the peninsula, plus a French diversionary force on the Asiatic side of the mouth of the straits. This multiple landing would provide the troops to swarm over the peninsula and capture the forts, giving the navy the opportunity to sail by unhindered. Rarely has the expression "So close and yet so far" had such meaning in military history as it did on 25 April 1915. The Turkish defenders, though outnumbering the attackers, were mostly held in reserve at the neck of the peninsula. At some beaches, stiff resistance forced slow progress, but at others there was little or no resistance. The Turks were unprepared for multiple landings, and aggressive action would have given the Allies an easy victory. Hamilton, onboard ship, had reports from all the beaches, but he preferred to have the local commanders respond to individual circumstances. Local commanders were operating on a preset timetable, and did not take advantage of opportunities because inland advances were scheduled for later. While the British, Anzacs, and French stayed on the beaches, whether through Turkish resistance or lack of leadership, the Turks were able to reinforce. By the time assaults were made, the Turks shot down the attackers in huge numbers. The quick, easy operation soon turned into a miniature version of the trench warfare of France.

Through the summer of 1915, the men on the beaches made little or no headway against Turkish defenses, which grew constantly stronger. Reinforcements sent in August repeated the failings of April: easy landings against little resistance, followed by enough hesitation to allow the Turks time to react. The 35,000 men committed in August ended up stuck on the beaches under punishing fire just like their comrades earlier. From beginning to end, the operation to force the straits suffered from a lack of planning and preparation. For example, the navy was sent in to capture Constantinople, though it is impossible for ships to take or hold targets on land. The amphibious operations were experimental to a great extent because the troops taking part had no previous training. Actually, the landings were successful; it was the push off the beaches that failed. The troops, both British and Anzac, were recent inductees in combat for the first time, and their lack of experience led to much confusion during and immediately after the landings. Both Allies and Turks made mistakes, but the Turks made fewer and won the battle. The men were successfully evacuated in December.

The invasion reinforced Turkish morale and strengthened their resolve to support Germany. Now veterans with a success under their belts, the Turkish troops transferred to Mesopotamia to take part in the successful siege of Kut-al-'Amara, in which the Sixth Indian Division was captured after the longest siege in British history. For the losing side, there are only a series of might-have-beens. As the battle took place, representatives of Britain, France, and Russia were dividing up the Ottoman Empire between them; Constantinople and the straits were to have gone to Russia, and the Russians would have attained their centuries-old dream of warm-water access for their navy. If the Western Allies could have used this passage to reinforce or re-supply the Russians, would the Eastern Front have held? Would the Russian Revolution have taken place? Would the Balkan States have abandoned the Central Powers in order to grab what they could from a struggling Austria-Hungary? The future of Eastern Europe may well have been much different had the British Royal Navy in March or the soldiers on the ground in April 1915 seized opportunities that would have given them a relatively easy victory.

*See also* Mesopotamia, British Invasion of [173]; Russia, German Invasion of [185].

References: Bush, Eric, *Gallipoli* (London: George Allen & Unwin, 1975); Fewster, Kevin, *A Turkish View of Gallipoli* (Richmond, Victoria, Australia: Hodja, 1985); Moorehead, Alan, *Gallipoli* (New York: Harper & Brothers, 1956).

# BIBLIOGRAPHY

Abbot, John S. C., *Life of Napoleon,* 4 vols. (New York: Harper & Brothers, 1855–1856).

Adams, James Truslow, *Building the British Empire* (New York: Scribner's Sons, 1938).

Addington, Larry, *Patterns of War through the Eighteenth Century* (Bloomington: Indiana University Press, 1990).

Adkin, Mark, *Urgent Fury: The Battle for Grenada* (Lexington, MA: D. C. Heath, 1989).

Alden, Richard, *The American Revolution* (New York: Harper & Row, 1954).

Allan, John, *The Cambridge Shorter History of India* (Delhi: S. Chand, 1964).

Allsen, Thomas, *Mongol Imperialism* (Berkeley: University of California Press, 1987).

Ambrose, Stephen, *D-Day, June 6, 1944* (New York: Simon & Schuster, 1994).

———, *Eisenhower: Soldier and Statesman* (New York: Simon & Schuster, 1990).

Arbman, Holger, *The Vikings* (New York: Praeger, 1961).

Armstrong, Karen, *Holy War* (New York: Macmillan, 1988).

Arnold, James, *Napoleon Conquers Austria: The 1809 Campaign for Vienna* (Westport, CT: Praeger, 1995).

Arrian, *The Campaigns of Alexander,* trans. Aubrey de Selincourt (New York: Penguin, 1958).

Audric, John, *Angkor and the Khmer Empire* (London: R. Hale, 1972).

Badri, Hasan, *The Ramadan War, 1973* (Boulder, CO: Westview Press, 1978).

Bagnall, Nigel, *The Punic Wars* (London: Hutchinson, 1990).

Baines, J., and J. Malek, *Atlas of Ancient Egypt* (New York: Facts on File, 1980).

Baker, G. P., *Hannibal* (New York: Barnes & Noble, 1967).

Balsdon, J. P. V. D., *Rome: The Story of an Empire* (New York: McGraw-Hill, 1970).

Barker, A. J., *The Civilizing Mission* (New York: Dial Press, 1968).

———, *The Neglected War* (London: Cassel & Co., 1967).

Barker, Elizabeth, *British Policy in Southeast Europe in the Second World War* (New York: Barnes & Noble, 1976).

Barker, John, *Justinian and the Later Roman Empire* (Madison: University of Wisconsin Press, 1966).

Bar-Kochva, Bezalel, *The Seleucid Army* (London: Cambridge University Press, 1976).

Barnes, Timothy, *The New Empire of Diocletian and Constantine* (Cambridge, MA: Harvard University Press, 1982).

Barnett, Corelli, *The Desert Generals* (London: Viking, 1960).

Barraclough, Geoffrey, *The Crucible of Europe* (Berkeley: University of California Press, 1976).

Bartha, Antal, *Hungarian Society in the Ninth and Tenth Centuries,* trans. K. Baazs (Budapest: Akademiai Kiado, 1975).

Basham, A. L., *The Wonder That Was India* (New York: Taplinger, 1954).

Beaufre, Andre, *The Suez Expedition 1956,* trans. Richard Barry (New York: Praeger, 1969).

Beny, Roloff, *Island Ceylon* (London: Thames & Hudson, 1970).

Berdan, Frances, *The Aztecs of Central Mexico* (New York: Holt, Rinehart & Winston, 1982).

Berton, Pierre, *The Invasion of Canada* (Boston: Little, Brown, 1980).

Best, Geoffrey, *War and Society in Revolutionary Europe, 1770–1870* (New York: St. Martin's Press, 1982).

Beven, Edwyn, *A History of Egypt under the Ptolemaic Dynasty* (London: Methuen & Co., 1927).

Bidwell, Shelford, *The Chindit War* (New York: Macmillan, 1980).

Bilgrami, Ashgar, *Afghanistan and British India, 1793–1907* (New Delhi: Sterling Press, 1972).

Birtle, A. J., *Sicily* (Washington: U. S. Army Center for Military History, 1993).

Blackwell, James, *Thunder in the Desert* (New York: Bantam Books, 1991).

Bolger, Daniel, *Americans at War, 1975–1986: An Era of Violent Peace* (Novato, CA: Presidio Press, 1988).

Bona, Istvan, *The Dawn of the Dark Ages: The Gepids and the Lombards* (Budapest: Corvina Press, 1976).

Borza, Eugene, *In the Shadow of Olympus: The Emergence of Macedon* (Princeton, NJ: Princeton University Press, 1990).

Bosworth, A. B., *Conquest and Empire* (New York: Cambridge University Press, 1988).

Boulger, Demetrius, *The History of China*, 2 vols. (Freeport, NY: Books for Libraries, 1898).

Bowie, Robert, *Suez, 1956* (London: Oxford University Press, 1974).

Bradford, Ernle, *Julius Caesar: The Pursuit of Power* (New York: Morrow, 1984).

Breuer, William, *Retaking the Philippines* (New York: St. Martin's Press, 1986).

Brewer, William B., *Operation Torch* (New York: St. Martin's Press, 1985).

Briggs, Lawrence, *The Ancient Khmer Empire* (Philadelphia: The Philosophical Society, 1951).

Brion, Marcel, *Attila: The Scourge of God* (New York: Robert McBride & Co., 1929).

Britt, Albert Sidney, *The Wars of Napoleon* (Wayne, NJ: Avery Publishing Group, 1985).

Brown, R. Allen, *The Normans* (New York: St. Martin's Press, 1984).

Browning, Robert, *The Byzantine Empire* (New York: Scribner, 1980).

———, *Justinian and Theodora* (London: Weidenfeld & Nicolson, 1971).

Bullock, Alan, *Hitler: A Study in Tyranny* (New York: Harper, 1953).

Bullough, Donald, *The Age of Charlemagne* (New York: Putnam, 1965).

Burn, A. R., *Persia and the Greeks: The Defence of the West* (London: Arnold, 1962).

Bury, J. B., *The Invasion of Europe by the Barbarians* (New York: Russell & Russell, 1963).

Bury, J. B., S. A. Cook, and F. E. Adcocks, eds., *The Cambridge Ancient History: The Assyrian Empire* (Cambridge: Cambridge University Press, 1923–1939).

Bush, Eric, *Gallipoli* (London: George Allen & Unwin, 1975).

Buxton, David, *The Abyssinians* (New York: Praeger, 1970).

Byford-Jones, W., *The Lightning War* (Indianapolis: Bobbs-Merrill, 1968).

Byng, Edward, *The World of the Arabs* (Plainview, NY: Books for Libraries, 1974).

Byron, Robert, *The Byzantine Achievement* (New York: Russell & Russell, 1964).

Caesar, Julius, *Commentaries,* trans. John Warrington, (New York: Heritage Press, 1955).

———, *The Gallic War,* trans. H. J. Edwards (Cambridge, MA: Harvard University Press, 1966).

Caffrey, Kate, *Out in the Midday Sun: Singapore, 1941–1945* (New York: Stein & Day, 1973).

Cain, P. J., *British Imperialism: Innovation and Expansion, 1688–1914* (London: Longmans, 1993).

Campbell, J. B., *The Roman Army, 31 B.C.–A.D. 337* (London: Routledge, 1994).

Cannon, Terry, *Vietnam: A Thousand Years of Struggle* (San Francisco: People's Press, 1969).

Capon, Edmund, *Tang China* (London: Macdonald Orbis, 1989).

Carmichael, Joel, *A History of Russia* (New York: Hippocrene Books, 1990).

Carr, William, *The Origin of the Wars of German Unification* (London: Longman, 1991).

Carrasco, David, *Moctezuma's Mexico* (Niwot: University of Colorado Press, 1992).

Carrell, Paul, *Hitler Moves East, 1941–1943* (Boston: Little, Brown & Co., 1965).

———, *Invasion: They're Coming,* trans. E. Osers (New York: E. P. Dutton, 1960).

Carrion, Arturo Morales, *Puerto Rico, a Political and Cultural History* (New York: Norton, 1983).

Carver, Sir Michael, *The War Lords: Military Commanders of the Twentieth Century* (Boston: Little, Brown & Co., 1976).

Cate, Curtis, *The War of Two Emperors* (New York: Random House, 1984).

Caven, Brian, *The Punic Wars* (London: Weidenfeld & Nicolson, 1980).

Cawkwell, George, *Philip of Macedon* (Boston: Faber & Faber, 1978).

Ceram, C. W., *The Secret of the Hittites,* trans. Richard Winston and Clara Winston (New York: Alfred A. Knopf, 1956).

Cervi, Mario, *The Hollow Legions: Mussolini's Blunder in Greece,* trans. Eric Mosbacher (Garden City, NY: Doubleday, 1971).

Chamberlain, Muriel, *Britain and India* (Hamden, CT: Archon Books, 1974).

Chambers, James, *The Devil's Horsemen* (New York: Atheneum, 1979).

Chandler, David, *The Campaigns of Napoleon* (New York: Macmillan, 1966).

Charles, E., *A History of Spain* (New York: Free Press, 1966).

Charles-Picard, Gilbert, and Collette Picard, *The Life and Death of Carthage,* trans. Dominique Collon (London: Sidgwick & Jackson, 1968).

Charol, Michael, *The Mongol Empire: Its Rise and Legacy* (London: George Allen & Unwin, 1961).

Chattopadhyay, Bhaskar, *Kushana State and Indian Society* (Calcutta: Punthi Pustak, 1975).

Chejne, Anwar, *Muslim Spain: Its History and Culture* (Minneapolis: University of Minnesota Press, 1974).

Chidsey, Donald B., *The War in the North: An Informal History of the American Revolution in and Near Canada* (New York: Crown Publishers, 1967).

Chirovsky, Nicolas, *A History of the Russian Empire* (New York: Philosophical Library, 1973).

Churchill, Winston, *The Gathering Storm* (Boston: Houghton Mifflin, 1948).

Clark, Alan, *Barbarossa* (New York: Morrow, 1965).

Clark, Mark, *Calculated Risk* (New York: Harper, 1950).

Claypole, William, *Caribbean Story,* 2 vols. (San Juan, PR: Longman Caribbean, 1989).

Codrington, Humphrey, *A Short History of Ceylon* (Freeport, NY: Books for Libraries, 1926).

Coedes, G., *The Making of Southeast Asia,* trans. H. M. Wright (Berkeley: University of California Press, 1966).

Cohen, Daniel, *Conquerors on Horseback* (Garden City, NY: Doubleday, 1970).

Coles, Harry L., *The War of 1812* (Chicago: University of Chicago Press, 1965).

Collier, Basil, *Japan at War: An Illustrated History of the War in the Far East* (London: Sidgwick & Jackson, 1975).

Collier, Richard, *Duce!* (New York: Viking, 1971).

Collins, John, *America's Small Wars* (Washington: Brassey's, 1991).

Collins, Robert, *Europeans in Africa* (New York: Knopf, 1971).

Connelly, Owen, *Blundering to Glory* (Wilmington: Scholarly Resources, 1987).

Connor, Seymour, *North America Divided* (New York: Oxford University Press, 1971).

Conroy, Hilary, *The Japanese Seizure of Korea, 1869–1910* (Philadelphia: University of Pennsylvania Press, 1960).

Coonaughton, R. M., *The War of the Rising Sun and the Tumbling Bear* (London: Routledge, 1991).

Costello, John, *The Pacific War, 1941–1945* (New York: Quill, 1982).

Cotterell, Arthur, *The First Emperor of China* (London: Macmillan, 1981).

Crankshaw, Edward, *Maria Theresa* (New York: Viking, 1969).

Cunliffe, Barry, *Rome and Her Empire* (London: Constable, 1994 [1978]).

Curtin, Jeremiah, *The Mongols: A History* (Westport, CT: Greenwood Press, 1972).

Dabrowski, Roman, *Mussolini: Twilight and Fall* (New York: Roy Publishers, 1956).

Davis, Paul K., *Ends and Means: The British Mesopotamia Campaign and Commission*

(Rutherford, NJ: Fairleigh Dickinson University Press, 1994).

Diaz del Castillo, Bernal, *The Discovery and Conquest of Mexico* (London: Routledge, 1928).

Diffie, Bailey, *A History of Colonial Brazil* (Malabar, FL: R. E. Krieger, 1987).

Donald, A. H., *Republican Rome* (New York: Frederick Praeger, 1966).

Donnelly, Thomas, Margaret Roth, and Caleb Baker, *Operation Just Cause: The Storming of Panama* (New York: Lexington Books, 1991).

Dorey, T. A., and D. R. Dudley, *Rome against Carthage* (London: Secker & Warburg, 1971).

Dorries, Hermann, *Constantine the Great* (New York: Harper & Row, 1972).

Dowart, Jeffrey, *The Pigtail War* (Amherst, MA: University of Massachusetts Press, 1975).

Drinkwater, J. F., *Roman Gaul* (London: Croom Helm, Ltd., 1983).

Dudley, David, *The Romans: 850 B.C.–A.D. 337* (New York: Knopf, 1970).

Duffy, Chris, *The Military Life of Frederick the Great* (New York: Atheneum, 1986).

Duffy, Christopher, *Red Storm on the Reich: The Soviet March on Germany, 1945* (New York: Atheneum, 1991).

Duffy, James, *Portuguese Africa* (Cambridge, MA: Harvard University Press, 1968).

Dunnigan, James, and Albert Nofi, *Victory at Sea* (New York: Morrow, 1995).

Dupuy, R. E., *An Outline History of the American Revolution* (New York: Harper & Row, 1975).

Dupuy, Trevor, *Elusive Victory: The Arab-Israeli Wars, 1947–74* (New York: Harper & Row, 1978).

Dyer, Gwen, *A History of the Vikings* (Oxford: Oxford University Press, 1968).

Earl, Donald C., *The Age of Augustus* (New York: Crown, 1968).

Eccles, W. J., *France in America* (East Lansing: Michigan State University Press, 1990).

Eddy, J. J., *Britain and the Australian Colonies* (Oxford: Clarendon, 1969).

Edwards, I. E. S., ed., *The Cambridge Ancient History* (Cambridge: Cambridge University Press, 1980).

Eisenhower, Dwight, *Crusade in Europe* (Garden City, NY: Doubleday, 1948).

Eisenhower, John, *So Far from God* (New York: Random House, 1989).

Erfurth, Waldemar, *Warfare in the Far North* (Washington: Center for Military History, 1987).

Errington, R., *The Dawn of Empire: Rome's Rise to World Power* (New York: Cornell University Press, 1972).

Fage, J. D., *A History of West Africa* (London: Cambridge University Press, 1969).

Falls, Cyril, *The First 3000 Years* (New York: Viking, 1960).

Farwell, Byron, *Queen Victoria's Little Wars* (New York: Harper & Row, 1972).

Fehrenbach, T. R., *This Kind of War* (New York: Macmillan, 1963).

Ferreira, Eduardo, *Portuguese Colonialism in Africa* (Paris: UNESCO, 1974).

Fewster, Kevin, *A Turkish View of Gallipoli* (Richmond, Victoria, Australia: Hodja, 1985).

Fieldhouse, D. K., *The Colonial Empires* (New York: Dell, 1966).

Finley, M. I., et. al., *A History of Sicily* (New York: Viking Penguin, 1987).

Finnegan, Richard, *Ireland: The Challenge of Conflict* (Boulder: Westview Press, 1983).

Fischer, Fritz, *War of Illusions* (London: Chatto & Windus, 1975).

Flanagan, Edward, *The Battle for Panama: Inside Operation Just Cause* (McLean, VA: Brassey's, 1993).

Florinsky, Michael, *Russia: A History and an Interpretation* (New York: Macmillan, 1947).

Foster, Edward, *Alexandria: A History and a Guide* (Gloucester: Doubleday & Co., 1968).

Franzius, Enno, *History of the Byzantine Empire* (New York: Funk & Wagnalls, 1968).

Freeman, Edward, *The History of the Norman Conquest of England* (Chicago: University of Chicago Press, 1974).

Friedel, Frank, *The Splendid Little War* (New York: Dell, 1962).

Friedman, Norman, *Desert Victory* (Annapolis, MD: Naval Institute Press, 1991).

Friend, Theodore, *The Blue-Eyed Enemy: Japan against the West in Java and Luzon, 1942–1945* (Princeton: Princeton University Press, 1988).

Frost, Alan, *Convicts and Empire* (Oxford: Oxford University Press, 1980).

Fry, Plantagenet, *Roman Britain, History and Sites* (Totawa, NJ: Barnes and Noble, 1984).

Fuller, J. F. C., *Military History of the Western World*, vol. 1 (New York: Minerva, 1954).

Furneaux, Rupert, *The Battle of Saratoga* (New York: Stein & Day, 1971).

———, *The Invasion of 1066* (Englewood Cliffs, NJ: Prentice-Hall, 1974).

Gabriel, Richard, *The Culture of War* (New York: Greenwood Press, 1990).

———, *From Sumer to Rome* (New York: Greenwood Press, 1991).

Gallo, Max, *Mussolini's Italy*, trans. Charles Markmann (New York: Macmillan, 1973).

Garland, Albert, *Sicily and the Surrender of Italy* (Washington: U. S. Army Center for Military History, 1965).

Gates, John M., *Schoolbooks and Krags: The United States Army in the Philippines* (New York: Greenwood Press, 1973).

Gaubert, Henri, *Moses and Joshua, Founders of the Nation* (New York: Hastings House, 1969).

Gelb, Norman, *Desperate Venture: The Story of Operation Torch* (London: Hodder & Staughton, 1992).

Gibbs, M. B., *Napoleon's Military Career* (Chicago: Werner Co., 1895).

Gimbutas, Marija, *The Slavs* (New York: Praeger, 1971).

Glantz, David, and Jonathan House, *When Titans Clashed* (Lawrence: University of Kansas Press, 1995).

Glick, Thomas, *Islamic and Christian Spain in the Early Middle Ages* (Princeton: Princeton University Press, 1979).

Gokhale, Balkrishna, *Ancient India: History and Culture* (Bombay and New York: Asia Publishing House, 1959).

Gordon, David, *The Passing of French Algeria* (London: Oxford University Press, 1966).

Grant, Michael, *The History of Ancient Israel* (New York: Scribner, 1984).

———, *The Rise of the Greeks* (New York: Scribner's Sons, 1987).

Green, Peter, *Alexander of Macedon* (Los Angeles: University of California Press, 1991).

Gregory of Tours, *History of the Franks*, trans. Ernest Brehaut (New York: Norton, 1969).

Griffiths, P. J., *The British Impact on India* (Hamden, CT: Archon Books, 1965).

Gruber, Ira, *The Howe Brothers and the American Revolution* (New York: Atheneum, 1972).

Gruber, Ruth, *Israel on the Seventh Day* (New York: Hill & Wang, 1968).

Gruen, E. S., ed., *Imperialism in the Roman Republic* (New York: Holt, Rinehart & Winston, 1970).

Guderian, Heinz, *Panzer Leader* (New York: E. P. Dutton, 1957).

Hahn, Emily, *Raffles of Singapore, a Biography* (Garden City, NY: Doubleday, 1946).

Haidar, Muhammad, *A History of the Moghuls of Central Asia* (New York: Praeger, 1970).

Haines, C. G., and R. J. S. Hoffman, *The Origins and Background of World War II* (New York: Oxford University Press, 1947).

Hallenbeck, Jan, *Pavia and Rome: The Lombard Monarchy and the Papacy in the Eighth Century* (Philadelphia: American Philosophical Society, 1982).

Hallett, Robin, *Africa to 1875* (Ann Arbor: University of Michigan Press, 1970).

Hamilton, Allen Lee, *Sentinel of the Southern Plains* (Fort Worth: TCU Press, 1990).

Hammer, Ellen, *The Struggle for Indochina* (Stanford: Stanford University Press, 1955).

Hammond, N. G. L., *Alexander the Great: King, Commander, and Statesman* (Park Ridge, NJ: Noyes Press, 1974).

Hamshere, Cyril, *The British in the Caribbean* (Cambridge, MA: Harvard University Press, 1972).

Harlow, Vincent, ed., *History of East Africa*, 2 vols. (Oxford: Clarendon Press, 1965).

Harrison, John, *Akhbar and the Mughal Empire* (St. Paul, MN: Greenhaven Press, 1980).

Hartendorp, A. V. H., *The Japanese Occupation of the Philippines* (Manila: Bookmark, 1967).

Hartog, Leo, *Genghis Khan, Conqueror of the World* (New York: St. Martin's Press, 1989).

Hassel, Arthur, *Louis XIV and the Zenith of French Monarchy* (Freeport, NY: Books for Libraries, 1972).

Hatada, Takahashi, *A History of Korea*, trans. Warren Smith and Benjamin Hazard (Santa Barbara: ABC-Clio, 1969).

Hatton, R. M., *Charles XII of Sweden* (London: Weidenfeld & Nicolson, 1968).

Hawkes, Jacquetta, *Pharaohs of Egypt* (New York: American Heritage, 1965).

Hayes, W., *The Scepter of Egypt* (Cambridge, MA: Harvard University Press, 1959).

Heather, Peter, *Goths and Romans* (Oxford: Clarendon, 1991).

Heckman, Wolf, *Rommel's War in Africa* (Garden City, NY: Doubleday, 1981).

Held, Joseph, *Hunyadi: Legend and Reality* (New York: Columbia University Press, 1985).

Henderson, Keith, *The Fall of the Aztec Empire* (Denver: Denver Museum of Natural History, 1993).

Henissary, Paul, *Wolves in the City: The Death of French Algeria* (New York: Simon & Schuster, 1970).

Henthorn, William, *Korea: The Mongol Invasions* (Leiden: E. J. Brill, 1963).

Hepple, Alexander, *South Africa: A Political and Economic History* (London: Pall Mall Press, 1966).

Herzog, Chaim, *War of Atonement, October 1973* (Boston: Little, Brown & Co., 1975).

Hi, Hsi-sheng, *Nationalist China at War* (Ann Arbor: University of Michigan Press, 1982).

Higham, Robin, *Diary of a Disaster: British Aid to Greece, 1940–41* (Lexington: University of Kentucky Press, 1986).

Hignett, Charles, *Xerxes' Invasion of Greece* (Oxford: Clarendon, 1963).

Hiskett, M., and Nehemia Levtzion, *Ancient Ghana and Mali* (London: Methuen, 1973).

Holder, P. A., *The Roman Army in Britain* (New York: St. Martin's Press, 1982).

Holland, Jack, *The Order of Rome* (London: Cassell, 1980).

Holt, P. M., *The Cambridge History of Islam*, 2 vols. (Cambridge: Cambridge University Press, 1970).

Hookham, Hilda, *A Short History of China* (New York: St. Martin's Press, 1970).

Horne, Alastair, *Napoleon, Master of Europe, 1805–1807* (New York: Morrow, 1979).

———, *To Lose a Battle: France, 1940* (Boston: Little, Brown & Co., 1969).

Hosch, Edgar, *The Balkans*, trans. Tania Alexander (New York: Crane, Russak & Co., 1972).

Hough, Richard, and Denis Richards, *The Battle of Britain* (New York: Norton, 1989).

Howard, Michael, *The Franco-Prussian War* (New York: Collier, 1961).

Howarth, David, *1066: The Year of the Conquest* (New York: Viking Penguin, 1977).

Howe, George, F., *Northwest Africa: Seizing the Initiative in the West* (Washington: Office of the Chief of Military History, 1957).

Hoyt, Edwin, *Guerrilla* (New York: Macmillan, 1981).

Hsu, Immanuel, *The Rise of Modern China* (New York: Oxford University Press, 1975).

Huart, Clement, *Ancient Persian and Iranian Civilization* (New York: Barnes and Noble, 1972).

Hucker, Charles, *The Ming Dynasty: Its Origins and Evolving Institutions* (Ann Arbor: University of Michigan Press, 1978).

Hyma, Albert, *A History of the Dutch in the Far East* (Ann Arbor, MI: George Wair Publishing Co., 1953).

Ienaga, Saburo, *The Pacific War, 1931–1945* (New York: Random House, 1978).

Innes, Hammond, *The Conquistadors* (New York: Knopf, 1969).

Isadore of Seville, *The History of the Goths, Vandals and Suevi*, trans. Guido Donini and Gordon Ford (Leiden: E. J. Brill, 1970).

Israel, Jonathan, *Dutch Primacy in World Trade, 1585–1740* (Oxford: Clarendon, 1989).

———, *The Dutch Republic: Its Rise, Greatness, and Fall, 1477–1806* (Oxford: Oxford University Press, 1995).

Jackson, Robert, *Dunkirk: The British Evacuation, 1940* (New York: St. Martin's Press, 1976).

James, Edward, *The Franks* (New York: Blackwell, 1988).

Jewell, Derek, ed., *Alamein and the Desert War* (London: Times Newspapers, 1967).

Jones, A. H. M., *Augustus* (New York: Norton, 1970).

Jones, A. H. M., and Elizabeth Monroe, *A History of Ethiopia* (Oxford: Clarendon, 1955).

Kagan, Donald, *On the Origins of War* (New York: Doubleday, 1995).

Kamen, Henry, *The War of Succession in Spain, 1700–15* (Bloomington: Indiana University Press, 1969).

Karnow, Stanley, *In Our Image: America's Empire in the Philippines* (New York: Random House, 1989).

Kee, Robert, *Ireland: A History* (New York: Little, Brown & Co., 1982).

Keegan, John, *The Mask of Command* (New York: Viking, 1987).

———, *Six Armies in Normandy* (New York: Viking, 1982).

Keen, Benjamin, and Mark Wasserman, *A Short History of Latin America* (Boston: Houghton Mifflin, 1984).

King, Anthony, *Roman Gaul and Germany* (Berkeley: University of California Press, 1990).

Kinross, Patrick, *The Ottoman Centuries* (New York: Morrow, 1977).

Koch, H. W., ed., *The Origins of the First World War* (London: Macmillan, 1972).

Koprulu, Mehmet Fuad, *Islam in Turkey after the Turkish Invasion* (Salt Lake City: University of Utah Press, 1993).

———, *The Seljuks of Anatolia*, trans. Gary Leiser (Salt Lake City: University of Utah Press, 1992).

Kumar, Baldev, *The Early Kusanas* (New Delhi: Sterling Publishers, 1973).

Kwanten, Luc, *Imperial Nomads* (Philadelphia: University of Pennsylvania Press, 1979).

Laessoe, Jorgen, *People of Ancient Assyria, Their Inscriptions and Correspondence* (London: Routledge & Kegan Paul, 1963).

LaFeber, Walter, *The American Age* (New York: Norton, 1989).

Lamb, Harold, *The Crusades*, 2 vols. (Garden City, NY: Doubleday, 1931).

———, *Cyrus the Great,* (New York: Doubleday and Co., 1960).

———, *Hannibal* (New York: Doubleday, 1958).

———, *March of the Barbarians* (New York: Literary Guild, 1940).

———, *Tamurlane, the Earth Shaker* (New York: R. M. McBride, 1928).

Lane Fox, Robin, *The Search for Alexander* (Boston: Little, Brown, & Co., 1980).

Lane-Pool, Stanley, *Medieval India under Muhammadan Rule* (Calcutta: Susil Gupta, 1951).

Langley, Michael, *Inchon Landing* (New York: New York Times Books, 1979).

Lasko, Peter, *The Kingdom of the Franks* (New York: McGraw-Hill, 1971).

Lawson, Philip, *The Imperial Challenge: Quebec and Britain in the Age of the American Revolution* (Montreal: McGill-Queens University Press, 1990).

Layn, H. R., *The Vikings in Britain* (Oxford: Blackwell, 1995).

Layton, Edward, *"And I Was There": Pearl Harbor and Midway—Breaking the Secrets* (New York: Morrow, 1985).

Leckie, Robert, *Strong Men Armed* (New York: Random House, 1962).

Leckie, William, *The Military Conquest of the Southern Plains* (Norman: University of Oklahoma Press, 1963).

Lee, Maurice, *Road to Revolution: Scotland under Charles I* (Urbana: University of Illinois Press, 1985).

Lehman, Johannes, *The Hittites: People of a Thousand Gods*, trans. J. M. Brownjohn (New York: Viking, 1977).

Levack, Brian, *The Formation of the British State* (Oxford: Clarendon, 1987).

Lewis, Michael, *The Spanish Armada* (New York: Thomas Y. Crowell, 1968).

Liddell Hart, Basil, *History of the Second World War* (New York: Putnam, 1970).

Lineberry, William, *East Africa* (New York: Wilson, 1968).

Liss, Peggy K., *Mexico under Spain, 1521–1556* (Chicago: University of Chicago Press, 1975).

Liu, F. F., *A Military History of Modern China* (Princeton: Princeton University Press, 1956).

Logorici, Anton, *The Albanians* (Boulder, CO: Westview Press, 1977).

Lone, Stewart, *Japan's First Modern War* (New York: St. Martin's Press, 1994).

Lord, Walter, *The Dawn's Early Light* (New York: Norton, 1972).

———, *Incredible Victory* (New York: Harper & Row, 1967)

Lossky, Andrew, *Louis XIV and the French Monarchy* (New Brunswick, NJ: Rutgers University Press, 1994).

Lowe, C. J., and F. Marzari, *Italian Foreign Policy, 1870–1940* (London: Routledge & Kegan Paul, 1975).

Lundin, Charles, *Finland in the Second World War* (Bloomington: Indiana University Press, 1957).

Macartney, C. A., *The Magyars in the Ninth Century* (Cambridge: Cambridge University Press, 1968),

Macaulay, Neill, *Dom Pedro* (Durham, NC: Duke University Press, 1986).

Macksey, Kenneth, *Invasion* (New York: Macmillan, 1980).

MacMullen, Ramsay, *Constantine* (New York: Dial Press, 1969).

MacQueen, J. G., *The Hittites and Their Contemporaries in Asia Minor* (London: Thames & Hudson, 1968).

MacQueen, James, *Babylon* (New York: Praeger, 1965).

Mahon, John K., *The War of 1812* (Gainesville: University Presses of Florida, 1972).

Majdalany, Fred, *The Battle of Cassino* (Boston: Houghton Mifflin, 1958).

Manchester, William, *American Caesar* (Boston: Little, Brown & Co., 1978).

Manz, Beatrice, *The Rise and Rule of Tamurlane* (Cambridge: Cambridge University Press, 1989).

Markham, Felix, *Napoleon* (New York: New American Library, 1963).

———, *Napoleon and the Awakening of Europe* (London: English Universities Press, 1954).

Marks, Richard, *Cortes: The Great Adventurer and the Fate of Aztec Mexico* (New York: Knopf, 1993).

Marlowe, John, *Cromer in Egypt* (London: Elek, 1970).

Marques, A. H. de Olivera, *History of Portugal* (New York: Columbia University Press, 1976).

Marsden, John, *The Fury of the Northmen* (London: Kyle Cathie, 1993).

Martin, Colin, *The Spanish Armada* (New York: Norton, 1988).

Mason, R. H. P., and J. G. Caiger, *History of Japan* (New York: Free Press, 1972).

Mason, Philip, *A Matter of Honour* (London: Jonathan Cape, 1974).

Massie, Robert, *Peter the Great, His Life and World* (New York: Knopf, 1980).

Matthew, Eva, *The Mediterranean World in Ancient Times* (New York: Ronald Press, 1951).

Mattingly, Garrett, *The Armada* (Boston: Houghton Mifflin, 1959).

Mayo, Linda, *Bloody Buna* (Garden City, NY: Doubleday, 1974).

McKenzie, W. M., *Outline of Scottish History* (London: Adam & Charles Black, 1907).

McLeod, A. L., *The Pattern of New Zealand Culture* (Ithaca, NY: Cornell University Press, 1968).

Means, Philip A., *Fall of the Inca Empire and the Spanish Rule in Peru, 1530–1780* (New York: Gordian Press, 1971).

Meyer, W. C., and W. L. Sherman, *The Course of Mexican History* (New York: Oxford University Press, 1979).

Miles, William, *Imperial Burdens* (Boulder, CO: L. Rienner Publishers, 1995).

Miller, James, *A History of Ancient Israel and Judah* (Philadelphia: Westminster Press, 1968).

Miller, Stuart, *"Benevolent Assimilation": The American Conquest of the Philippines* (New Haven, CT: Yale University Press, 1982).

Millis, Walter, *Martial Spirit* (New York: Literary Guild, 1931).

Minns, Ellis, *Scythians and Greeks* (Cambridge: Cambridge University Press, 1913).

Mintz, Max, *The Generals of Saratoga: John Burgoyne and Horatio Gates* (New Haven, CT: Yale University Press, 1990).

Mokhtar, G., *Ancient Civilizations of Africa* (Paris: UNESCO, 1990).

Mookerji, Radha, *Chandragupta Maurya and His Times* (Delhi: Motilal Banarsidass, 1966).

Moorehead, Alan, *Gallipoli* (New York: Harper & Bros., 1956).

Morgan, David, *The Mongols* (Oxford: Blackwell, 1986).

Morris, Donald, *The Washing of the Spears* (New York: Simon & Schuster, 1965).

Morris, Eric, *Circles of Hell* (London: Hutchinson, 1993).

Morris, William, *Hannibal: Soldier, Statesman, Patriot* (New York: Knickerbocker Press, 1978).

Morrison, Samuel E., *The Two-Ocean War* (New York: Little, Brown & Co., 1963).

Mukherjee, Bratindra, *The Rise and Fall of the Kushana Empire* (Calcutta: Firma KLM, 1988).

Muller, Herbert, *The Loom of History* (New York: Harper & Bros., 1958).

Newitt, Marilyn, *Portugal in Africa* (London: Longmans, 1981).

Nish, Ian, *Japan's Struggle with Internationalism* (New York: K. Paul International, 1993).

Nissen, Henrik, *Scandinavia during the Second World War*, trans. Thomas Munch-Petersen (Minneapolis: University of Minnesota Press, 1983).

North, Martin, *The Old Testament World* (Philadelphia: Fortress Press, 1962).

Nuttingham, Anthony, *Scramble for Africa: The Great Trek to the Boer War* (London: Constable, 1970).

O'Ballance, Edgar, *The Algerian Insurrection* (Hamden, CT: Archon Books, 1967).

Obolensky, Dimitri, *Byzantium and the Slavs* (London: Variorum Reprints, 1971).

Oliver, Roland, *A Short History of Africa* (New York: New York University Press, 1962).

Orel, Harold, ed., *Irish History and Culture* (Lawrence: University of Kansas Press, 1976).

Ovendale, Ritchie, *Origins of the Arab-Israeli Wars* (London: Longmans, 1984).

Owen, David E., *British Opium Policy in China and India* (Hamden, CT: Archon Books, 1968).

Painter, Sydney, and Brian Tierney, *Western Europe in the Middle Ages* (New York: Knopf, 1983).

Pakenham, Thomas, *The Scramble for Africa* (New York: Random House, 1991).

Palmer, Alan, *Napoleon in Russia* (New York: Simon & Schuster, 1967).

Palmer, John J. N., *England, France, and Christendom, 1377–99* (Chapel Hill: University of North Carolina Press, 1972).

Parker, Geoffrey, ed., *The Thirty Years War* (London: Routledge & Kegan Paul, 1984).

Paul the Deacon, *History of the Langobards*, trans. W. D. Foulke (Philadelphia: University of Pennsylvania Press, 1974).

Payne, Pierre, *The Holy Sword* (New York: Harper, 1959).

Payne, Robert, *The Life and Death of Adolph Hitler* (New York: Praeger, 1973).

Payne, Stanley, *A History of Spain and Portugal* (Madison: University of Wisconsin Press, 1973).

Pearson, Michael, *Those Damned Rebels: The American Revolution as Seen through British Eyes* (New York: Putnam, 1972).

Perlman, Samuel, *Philip and Athens* (New York: Barnes & Noble, 1973).

Petrow, Richard, *Bitter Years: The Invasion and Occupation of Denmark and Norway* (New York: Morrow, 1974).

Porter, Bernard, *The Lion's Share* (London: Longmans, 1975).

Prado, Caio, *The Colonial Background of Modern Brazil* (Berkeley: University of California Press, 1967).

Prange, Gordon, *Miracle at Midway* (New York: McGraw-Hill, 1982).

Prawdin, Michael, *Builders of the Moghul Empire* (London: Allen & Unwin, 1963).

Procopius, *The Secret History of Justinian*, trans. Richard Atwater (Ann Arbor: University of Michigan Press, 1961).

Randle, Robert, *Geneva 1954* (Princeton: Princeton University Press, 1969).

Rice, Eugene, *The Foundation of Early Modern Europe, 1460–1559* (New York: Norton, 1970).

Rice, Tamara, *The Seljuks in Asia Minor* (New York: Praeger, 1961).

Richter, Michael, *Medieval Ireland* (New York: St. Martin's Press, 1988).

Ritter, E. A., *Shaka Zulu* (London: Longmans, 1955).

Ritter, Gerhard, *Frederick the Great, a Historical Profile* (Berkeley: University of California Press, 1970).

Robb, Theodore, ed., *The Thirty Years War* (Lexington, MA: Heath, 1972).

Robert, Michael, *Sweden's Age of Greatness, 1632–1718* (New York: St. Martin's Press, 1973).

Robinson, Neville, *Villagers at War* (Canberra: Australian National University, 1981).

Robinson, R. E. and J. A. Gallagher, *Africa and the Victorians* (New York: Macmillan, 1961).

Roeder, Ralph, *Juarez and His Mexico*, 2 vols. (New York: Viking, 1947).

Romanus, Charles, *Time Runs out in CBI* (Washington: Office of the Chief of Military History, 1958).

Rossabi, Morris, *Khubilai Khan: His Life and Times* (Berkeley: University of California Press, 1987).

Rostovtzeff, M., *Iranians and Greeks in Southern Russia* (New York: Russell & Russell, 1969).

Rutherford, Ward, *The Russian Army in World War I* (London: Gordon Cremones, 1975).

Ryan, N. J., *A History of Malaysia and Singapore* (London: Oxford University Press, 1976).

Saggs, H. W. F., *The Might That Was Assyria* (London: Sidgwick & Jackson, 1984).

Salmon, Edward, *A History of the Roman World from 30 B.C. to A.D. 138* (London: Methuen, 1972).

Salway, Peter, *Roman Britain* (New York: Oxford University Press, 1981).

Saunders, J. J., *The History of the Mongol Conquests* (New York: Barnes & Noble, 1971).

Savory, Roger, *Iran under the Safavids* (New York: Cambridge University Press, 1980).

Schwab, Peter, *Haile Selassie: Ethiopia's Lion of Judah* (Chicago: Nelson-Hall, 1979).

Scullard, Howard H., *A History of the Roman World: from 753 to 146 B.C.* (London: Methuen & Co., 1969).

Searle, Eleanor, *Predatory Kinship and the Creation of Norman Power* (Berkeley: University of California Press, 1988).

Seignobos, Charles, *The World of Babylon* (New York: Leon Amiel, 1975).

Selby, John, *Shaka's Heirs* (London: George Allen & Unwin, 1971).

Sen, Siba Pada, *The French in India* (Calcutta: University of Calcutta Press, 1947).

Serjeant, R. B., *Studies in Arabian History and Civilisation* (London: Variorum Reprints, 1981).

Severin, Timothy, *The Golden Antilles* (New York: Knopf, 1970).

Sharma, G. N., *Mewar and the Mughal Emperors* (Agra: Shiva Lal Agarwala, 1962).

Shaw, A. G. L., *Convicts and the Colonies* (London: Faber & Faber, 1966).

Shaw, Stanford, *The History of the Ottoman Empire and Turkey* (Cambridge: Cambridge University Press, 1976).

Sherwin-White, Susan, *From Samarkand to Sardis* (London: Duckworth, 1993).

Shirer, William, *The Collapse of the Third Republic* (New York: Simon & Schuster, 1969).

———, *The Nightmare Years* (New York: Little, Brown & Co., 1984).

———, *The Rise and Fall of the Third Reich* (New York: Simon & Schuster, 1960).

Showalter, Dennis, *Tannenberg: Clash of Empires* (Hamden, CT: Archon Books, 1991).

Singletary, Otis, *The Mexican War* (Chicago: University of Chicago Press, 1960).

Slim, William, *Defeat into Victory* (New York: D. McKay, 1961).

Smith, Dennis Mack, *A History of Sicily* (New York: Viking, 1968).

Smith, Gaddis, *The Last Years of the Monroe Doctrine, 1945–1993* (New York: Hill & Wang, 1994).

Smith, Jonathan Riley, *The Crusades* (New Haven: Yale University Press, 1987).

Smith, Robert, *Triumph in the Philippines* (Washington: Office of the Chief of Military History, 1963).

Smith, Woodruff, *The German Colonial Empire* (Chapel Hill: University of North Carolina Press, 1978).

Sonino, Paul, *Louis XIV and the Origins of the Dutch War* (New York: Cambridge University Press, 1988).

Spence, Jonathan, ed., *From Ming to Ching* (New Haven: Yale University Press, 1979).

Spielman, John, *The City and the Crown: Vienna and the Imperial Court, 1600–1740* (West Lafayette, IN: Purdue University Press, 1993).

Stannard, David, *American Holocaust* (New York: Oxford University Press, 1992).

Steeds, David, *China, Japan, and Nineteenth Century Britain* (Dublin: Irish University Press, 1977).

Steele, Ian, *Warpaths: Invasions of North America* (New York: Oxford University Press, 1994).

Stephens, Morse, *The Story of Portugal* (New York: AMS Press, 1971).

Stokesbury, James, *A Short History of the Korean War* (New York: Morrow, 1988).

Sweets, John, *Choices in Vichy France* (New York: Oxford University Press, 1986).

Sydenham, M. J., *The First French Republic, 1792–1804* (Berkeley: University of California Press, 1973).

Sykes, Sir Percy, *Persia* (Oxford: Clarendon, 1922).

Tarle, Eugene, *Napoleon's Invasion of Russia in 1812* (New York: Farrar, Straus & Giroux, 1971).

Tarn, W. W., *Alexander the Great* (Cambridge: Cambridge University Press, 1948)

Taylor, F. L., *The Art of War in Italy, 1494–1529* (Cambridge: Cambridge University Press, 1921).

Taylor, Keith, *The Birth of Vietnam* (Berkeley: University of California Press, 1983).

Taylor, Telford, *Munich: The Price of Peace* (Garden City, NY: Doubleday, 1979).

Thompson, E. A., *The Goths in Spain* (Oxford: Clarendon, 1969).

———, *Romans and Barbarians* (Madison: University of Wisconsin Press, 1982).

Thompson, Virginia, *French Indo-China* (New York: Macmillan, 1937).

Thomson, Arthur, *The Story of New Zealand* (New York: Praeger, 1970).

Toland, John, *But Not in Shame* (New York: Random House, 1961).

Tompkins, Stuart, *Russia through the Ages* (New York: Prentice-Hall, 1940).

Tong, James, *Disorder under Heaven* (Stanford: Stanford University Press, 1991).

Townsend, Mary Evelyn, *Origins of Modern German Colonialism* (New York: Howard Fertig, 1974).

Trask, David, F., *The War with Spain in 1898* (New York: Macmillan, 1981).

Treasure, G. R. R., *Seventeenth Century France* (London: Rivington's, 1966).

Tresidder, Argus, *Ceylon: An Introduction to the Resplendent Land* (Princeton, NJ: Van Nostrand, 1960).

Trimingham, J. S., *Islam in West Africa* (London: Oxford University Press, 1962).

Tuchman, Barbara, *The Guns of August* (New York: Macmillan, 1962).

———, *Stilwell and the American Experience in China* (New York: Macmillan, 1970).

Twitchett, Denis, and John Fairbank, eds., *The Cambridge History of China,* vols. 9 and 10 (New York: Cambridge University Press, 1993).

Twitchett, Denis, and Michael Loewe, eds., *The Cambridge History of China,* vol. 1, *The Ch'in and Han Empires* (New York: Cambridge University Press, 1978).

Utley, Robert, *Frontier Regulars* (New York: Macmillan, 1973).

Vader, John, *New Guinea: The Tide Is Stemmed* (New York: Ballantine, 1971).

Vale, Malcolm, *English Gascony, 1399–1453* (London: Oxford University Press, 1970).

Vambery, Arminius, *Hungary in Ancient, Medieval and Modern Times* (Hallandale, FL: New World Books, 1972).

Van Creveld, Martin, *Hitler's Strategy 1940–41: The Balkan Clue* (Cambridge: Cambridge University Press, 1973).

Van Seeters, J., *The Hyksos* (New Haven: Yale University Press, 1966).

Vlekke, Bernard, *The Story of the Dutch East Indies* (Cambridge, MA: Harvard University Press, 1945).

von Moltke, Graf Helmuth, *The Franco-German War of 1870–71* (New York: Harper Brothers, 1901).

Walder, David, *The Short Victorious War* (London: Hutchinson, 1973).

Waley, D., *The Italian City-Republics* (New York: Longmans, 1988).

Warmington, B. H., *Carthage: A History* (London: Robert Hale, 1960).

Warner, Denis, *The Tide at Sunrise* (New York: Charterhouse, 1974).

Warren, Harris, *Paraguay and the Triple Alliance* (Austin, TX: Institute of Latin American Studies, 1978).

Wedgwood C. V., *The Thirty Years War* (Gloucester, MA: P. Smith, 1969).

Wei, Cheng, *Mirror to the Son of Heaven,* ed. and trans. Howard Wechsler (New Haven: Yale University Press, 1974).

Wheatcroft, Andrew, *The Ottomans* (London: Viking, 1993).

Wheeler, Radha, *Early India and Pakistan* (New York: Praeger, 1959).

Wheeler, Robert, *Early India and Pakistan to Ashoka* (New York: Praeger, 1959).

White, John, *Cortez and the Fall of the Aztec Empire* (New York: St. Martin's Press, 1971).

Williams, John, *The Rise and Fall of the Paraguayan Republic* (Austin, TX: Institute of Latin American Studies, 1979).

Wiseman, Anne, and Peter Wiseman, *Julius Caesar: The Battle for Gaul* (Boston: David R. Godine, 1980).

Wolpert, Stanley, *India* (Englewood Cliffs, NJ: Prentice Hall, 1965).

Wood, Derek, and Derek Dempster, *The Narrow Margin* (New York: Coronet, 1969).

Woodward, Bob, *The Commanders* (New York: Simon & Schuster, 1991).

Wourinen, John, ed., *Finland and World War II, 1939–1944* (Westport, CT: Greenwood Press, 1983).

Wright, Ronald, *Stolen Continents* (Boston: Houghton Mifflin, 1992).

Wrong, George McKinnon, *Canada and the American Revolution* (New York: Macmillan, 1935).

————, *The Rise and Fall of New France* (New York: Octagon Books, 1970 [1928]).

Yoshihashi, Takehiko, *Conspiracy at Mukden* (New Haven, CT: Yale University Press, 1963).

Young, Donald, *The Battle of Bataan* (Jefferson, NC: McFarland, 1992).

Ziemke, Earl, *Stalingrad to Berlin: The German Defeat in the East* (Washington: Center for Military History, 1968).

# ILLUSTRATION CREDITS

# INDEX

D0169349

# Virtual Leadership and the ISO9000 Imperative

# Virtual Leadership and the ISO9000 Imperative

## Tom Taormina

For book and bookstore information

http://www.prenhall.com

Prentice Hall PTR
Upper Saddle River, New Jersey 07458

**Library of Congress Cataloging–in–Publication Data**

Taormina, Tom.
   Virtual leadership and the ISO9000 imperative / Tom Taormina.
      p.    cm.
   Includes index.
   ISBN 0–13–237074–3
   1. ISO 9000 Series Standards.   I. Title.
  TS156.6.T36   1996
  658.562—dc20
                                        96–5251
                                          CIP

Acquisitions editor: Bernard Goodwin
Cover designer: Talar Agasyan
Cover design director: Jerry Votta
Manufacturing buyer: Alexis R. Heydt
Compositor/Production services: Pine Tree Composition, Inc.

© 1996 by Prentice Hall PTR
Prentice-Hall, Inc.
A Simon & Schuster Company
Upper Saddle River, New Jersey 07458

The publisher offers discounts on this book when ordered in bulk quantities.

For more information contact:
  Corporate Sales Department
  Prentice Hall PTR
  One Lake Street
  Upper Saddle River, New Jersey 07458

  Phone: 800–382–3419
  Fax: 201–236–7141
  email: corpsales@prenhall.com

Printed in the United States of America
10  9  8  7  6  5  4  3  2  1

ISBN 0-13-237074-3

Prentice Hall International (UK) Limited, *London*
Prentice Hall of Australia Pty. Limited, *Sydney*
Prentice Hall Canada, Inc., *Toronto*
Prentice Hall Hispanoamericana, S.A., *Mexico*
Prentice Hall of India Private Limited, *New Delhi*
Prentice Hall of Japan, Inc., *Tokyo*
Simon & Schuster Asia Pte. Ltd., *Singapore*
Editora Prentice Hall do Brasil, Ltda., *Rio de Janeiro*

*To Midge, my partner in life and my reality check*

> "We trained hard, but, it seemed that every time we were beginning to form up into teams, we would be reorganized. I was to learn later in life that we tend to meet any new situation by reorganizing, and a wonderful method it can be for creating the illusion of progress while producing confusion, inefficiency, and demoralization . . ."
>
> —Petronius, circa 100 A.D.

# Contents

# *Foreword*

Rarely does an executive get an opportunity to read a book that is written in a personal discussion style as if listening to a friend providing invaluable information. This is not the characteristic style of most consultants; but it is the unique style of Tom Taormina. He provides the most concise presentation of what ISO9000 really is and yet includes the essentials of what any leader needs to know as a basic foundation for running a business. This book should be read by board members; CEOs; vice-presidents; first-, second-, and third-level managers; and any employee involved in a company's commitment to quality and survival.

This book could have been entitled, "What Every Leader Wants to Know, But Didn't Know Who to Ask." One of the strengths of Tom's writing style is his honesty in depicting of the realities of ISO9000 and not supporting the myth of an European anti-American effort to avoid U.S. imports until Europeans ". . . get their act together as a unified financial forum." To incorporate the knowledge acquired from his vast experience, the book addresses exactly what ISO9000 is and isn't. Although he de-

scribes the technical verbiage of the ISO9000 guidelines, he does it with common sense. His applicable examples are easily understood by leaders and employees alike.

Contrary to early rumors about ISO9000, when implemented as a strategic quality tool, it has consistently increased employee commitment, clarified direction and understanding of the importance of the employees' consistency in fulfilling job requirements, and fostered a renewed sense by the American workforce that upper management is truly interested in improving quality. In this book, it becomes clear that "Quality" is no longer a buzzword from the 1980s.

Every executive in America will identify with Tom's introduction of Virtual Leadership through his metaphor of wild geese in flight. In short, virtual leadership is placing the ownership of processes lower in the organization in order for job holders to be held accountable for the quality of their implementation. In the past, companies have attempted to do this with standardized training skills, but the future now requires a paradigm shift which places responsibility and accountability on today's workforce through direct modeling of executive leadership. He addresses what leadership style changes are necessary to support the understanding of employees and the culture in which they operate. He does not demand that any organization restructures in a specific way, as often emphasized by organizational consultants, but companies must structure the way they do business according to their own unique organizational culture. As a reader you are left to decide for yourself if Virtual Leadership or the certification process for ISO9000 is what is best for your company.

The practical "how to's" provided by Tom's experience include how to implement a step-by-step procedure regarding leadership changes and the ISO9000 certification process and how to position your best people, not necessarily by highest ranking, to implement a plan for improving quality. The content of his information touches on the roles of the steering team, management representatives, the importance of the conducting structured management reviews, what happens during an ISO9000 assessment audit, and what preparation is required by the company in anticipation of an official assessment.

As a storyteller and conversationalist, his how-to style of communicating such a vast amount of information in a limited number of pages will be seldom exceeded by an author. Although he does not mandate that you follow his approach, his common sense explanation of sequencing the necessary steps and the importance of employee involvement is the best I have heard from any organizational consultant specialized in Total Quality Management, ISO9000 or the Baldrige Award assessments.

Seldom do business leaders find straightforward explanations, suggestions and descriptions of the vast array of applied quality improvement tools. This book is for leaders who need to understand why their managers are using specific tools to meet specific requirements. Tom is a very strong advocate for companies to avoid a preoccupation with Statistical Process Controls (SPC), Just-In-Time (JIT), or Quality Functional Deployment (QFD), which has lead to a loss of focus as to why we use any tools, especially those, so strongly emphasized in the mid 1980s. Rather than use tools just because they are available, Tom emphasizes that the tools should be implemented only to the degree that the tools support a company's goals and culture. Too many companies use tools for the sake of using tools.

The benefits of the ISO9000 certification process can be best summarized by companies that have experienced the process. These include the stimulation of creative thinking by employees, employees finding new and better ways to operate processes, reduction of waste and redundancy and the laying of a sound foundation for teamwork, which was not understood at the floor level, but too often as a managerial perk with free donuts and coffee.

The simple consistent message throughout the book can be summarized in three points:

◆ Write down what you do.
◆ Do what you write down.
◆ Verify that you are doing it.

In conclusion, the best reason for being informed of the ISO9000 certification process is the improvement that can be realized from

the process of becoming certified. It is refreshing to know that Tom's position is not advocating everyone be ISO9000 certified, but has interactive knowledge of ISO9000, the Baldrige criteria, and recommended readings on Total Quality Management which cannot help but provide a sound foundation for any organization wishing to remain competitive in today's marketplace.

Thomas E. Ollerman, Ph.D.
INNOVA, Inc.

*Tom Ollerman is President of Innova in Mesa, Arizona. He is an internationally recognized leader in innovative organizational change. He is currently serving as a coach to IBM and their development of its worldwide executive leadership program. He is also working with the United States Naval Air Command in their team-building efforts.*

# *Preface*

I was raised in a traditional Italian-American home, by traditional Italian-American parents. My life was, by tradition, predestined. My father decided for me that I was to get a degree in engineering, work for a big company with a fat government contract for forty years, and retire as a senior manager. I was programmed to marry young, have at least one male child, and continue the traditions and values of autocratic leadership, at home and in the work force. I didn't turn out exactly as my father had planned for me.

I had my first job when I was 13, sorting parts in an electronics surplus store. Since I was underage, the store owner suggested a business arrangement whereby he would pay me $5 a day and I could have any electronic components that I could successfully smuggle out of the store. I needed the parts for my hobbies, and my father assured me that this was an acceptable business agreement because we lived "in a dog-eat-dog world, and we had to look after number one." The underhanded and adversarial arrangement I had with my first boss always left me anxious. I never much cared for that feeling of anxiety and my first job lasted only a month.

The union work ethic of the 1950s and 1960s was modeled for me. I regularly heard the union battle cry "get every penny out of them that you can get for as few hours of work as possible." I watched my father's union strike every few years for more vacation, more benefits, shorter hours, more pay, and more commissions. The company usually capitulated, but warned that someday they would have to close the plant if the union didn't stop raising the ante.

I quietly fought my parental programming and modeling throughout my adolescent life. I had several jobs working in hostile, dictatorial environments and each made me resolve to break with the traditions that were ordained for me. It was my dream to be a part of the space program, and, on my nineteenth birthday, I left the family nest in New York and moved to Houston. The transition from an environment of fear, unionism, intimidation, and mistrust to "boom town," where million-dollar deals were made on a handshake, was my first culture shock. At an early age I learned that traditional wisdom may not be the path to the future.

I did attend engineering school, and I also worked my way through the ranks at Philco (Philco-Ford/Ford Aerospace) as we built and manned NASAs Mission Control Center in Houston. In 1969, I had a unique invitation to join an emerging discipline called "Quality Control Engineering." Our charter was to develop systems and processes that would prevent defects, rather than inspect and detect them. We were also chartered to train people who affected the product quality. I soon was a Certified Material Review Engineer and a Certified NASA Soldering School instructor. It wasn't long before I realized that training, facilitating, synthesizing, and improving quality were what I was meant to do in this life. I had a difficult time explaining all that to my father, as his company was furloughing all salesmen and he was to become unemployed at age 53.

I volunteered to head up "supplier quality." My job was to visit potential suppliers to determine their capability to meet the quality requirements levied by NASA (nowadays called capability audits). The NASA requirements were published and widely distributed. I was armed with a checklist and a clipboard, given a plane ticket, and sent on my way to audit potential suppliers who knew exactly what was on the checklist. At each facility, the sce-

nario was the same. Before lunch, the company had demonstrated the existence of all the controls that NASA required, and I was headed back to the airport with another compliant checklist and a new supplier added to the Approved Vendor's List.

It didn't take long before I was getting the same unsettled feeling that I remembered from my first job. I was doing what I was asked to do, but there was sometimes a gap between what I was told and what I observed as right and wrong. In some facilities, I was discouraged from talking with the workers. I would see assemblers working with no documentation in front of them. The person who was introduced as the QC Supervisor was nowhere to be seen on the shop floor. The work area was cluttered and dirty. The stockroom was behind a big cage, but people were walking in and out at will.

After about six months of seeing the same quality manual, the same procedures, and the same workmanship manual in every plant I visited, I had a revelation that *compliance to a checklist* and *capability to provide acceptable products and services* were often two separate conditions. I retired the checklist and started writing narrative reports of what I had observed in the suppliers' facilities. I evaluated their TOTAL capabilities, not just the toll-gate issues on the checklist. This procedural departure caused some real gas pains with our contract monitors and for several months, NASA sent auditors with me to find out what I was up to. The traditional government suppliers weren't thrilled about this new approach. When I visited a company, I would talk with the workers, not the salespeople. If the job holders used "we" instead of "us and them," there would usually be a high quality of workmanship in evidence. If they were proud to show off their facility and their products, there was usually a trail of superior craftsmanship visible. If there was one inspector for each five workers, there would also be a nonconformance area that had more material in it than was on the production floor. If the job holders wouldn't look you in the eye when explaining a process, the procedures were most times not being followed. Over the next ten years, I pioneered supplier auditing. My group developed an evaluation method that judged total capability. We solicited and approved partners instead of peddlers, and purchased for total cost of ownership, not just from the lowest bidder.

It isn't often that one can pinpoint critical moments in a life, but my observations and beliefs about the potential of the human spirit were galvanized on April 13, 1970. I was working swing shift (3 PM to 11:30 PM) at NASA, JSC, Houston, Building 30, Operations Wing, Second Floor. My office was directly across the hall from the Mission Operations Control Room (Mission Control for Apollo 13). During missions, the job of a quality control engineer was to monitor critical hardware systems and to be present to certify that any repairs done during a mission did not compromise flight success. If all went well, we had nothing to do during a mission except drink coffee and listen to the various communications circuits within the Control Center. At 9:08 PM CST that night, I was smoking my pipe, drinking coffee, and listening to the air-to-ground communications loop when Astronaut Jim Lovell spoke the fateful words heard around the world, "Houston, we have a problem." I enabled every communications loop available in our office and listened as the problems aboard Apollo 13 unfolded.

Within minutes, there were astronauts, scientists, and programmers streaming into Building 30. Within an hour there were classroom chairs lined up in the corridors outside the Control Room with mission specialists calculating trajectories and life support functions. About 10:15, Astronaut Frank Borman came into my office and asked who I was and what I was doing. I explained and he directed me to find a Polaroid camera and all the film I could gather. For the rest of the night, my job was to photograph the calculations they made on a chalkboard, then erase the board so they could make more calculations.

In one evening, I clearly understood the awesome potential of common vision, training, leadership, modeling, and teamwork. To this day, I can say without fear of contradiction that motivated, talented, and trained individuals can accomplish virtually anything they set their minds to do, as long as the vision is clear and empowerment is given and accepted.

I was indeed fortunate to have been a part of the Apollo Program at NASA and to have visited over 150 companies in ten years. I became a sensitive observer and a synthesizer and got to be part of one of the most dramatic demonstrations of teamwork in our Country's history (Apollo 13). From my experiences at NASA and in the field, I formed my own humanistic checklist for

determining supplier capability. I was able to document the attributes that were successful and those that led to disaster.

Over the next seven years, I distilled my observations and experiences and utilized them to start quality programs at two successive companies. In both cases, I ultimately had total operational responsibility for manufacturing and combined the quality and manufacturing functions. Again, this departure from tradition was looked at with jaundiced eyes. "Son, you've sent the fox to guard the henhouse," or so I was told. In both cases, I proved that the people were the keys to success, not traditional procedures and conventional management. I trained the job holders, I trusted them, and I gave them the responsibility for productivity and quality. I challenged them and rewarded them and we were successful together. The union environment that was modeled for me and the rigid rules of NASA proved to be unnecessary when I learned to trust, train, and empower people.

It is now over 25 years since I first became a Quality Control Engineer and a quality pioneer. I have visited over 300 companies and implemented a *humanistic* approach to success in several more companies. I have been a facilitator in implementing total quality cultures and I now consult, write, and coach on teamwork and quality. I have refined my experiences and observations into a cultural shift that I call Virtual Leadership. In essence, **Virtual Leadership removes the overhead of unnecessary management and replaces traditional hierarchical leadership with empowered job holders.** Over the last six years, I have also been active in ISO9000 implementation and have discovered that by using ISO9000 as a launching pad for strategic quality initiates, Virtual Leadership can be attained in almost any company environment, no matter how traditional.

I didn't turn out the way my father had planned, but neither did the world evolve as he predicted it would. His union work ethic came crashing down around us and we are faced with global economic challenges never dreamed of a decade ago. Just as I was a resolved team member who helped put man on the moon, I am equally resolved to help the team that will be successful in the global marketplace, through pioneering cultural changes and the through the limitless power of the human resource.

# 1

# Continuous
# Quality Improvement

> *The reasonable man adapts himself to the world; the unreasonable one persists in trying to adapt the world to himself. Therefore, all progress depends on the unreasonable man!*
>
> —George Bernard Shaw

The American democracy has its obvious flaws, but it is one of the most successful governments in the history of mankind. We have survived wars, scandals, financial disasters, national catastrophes, and the ravages of nature. The infrastructure is enmeshed in bureaucracy. Our leadership changes every four to eight years. The national credit card is way over its limit. Yet with all of its problems, the republic endures. We have to give much of the acclaim for its success to the founding fathers

and the genius of the Constitution. We have to give the recognition for its endurance to the American people. With all of its flaws, we've stood behind our democracy, without reservation, for over two centuries. We've raised ourselves from humble beginnings to the world leaders in industry and technology. We've successfully fought off some of the most tyrannical oppressors in history. Why, then, are we now struggling so painfully to deal with the challenges of the "New World Economy"?

History and self-examination reveal the simple answer. We have achieved our greatest successes overcoming crises. There is no more formidable success team than a wave of American Marines hitting a beach head. We are galvanized and excel in the face of war, disaster, and turmoil. Our greatest technological advances are the result of the needs of war and the race to the moon. As a people, the harder we are challenged the more resolve we display and the more inventive we become. When threat is removed, we fall into complacency and have a difficult time proactively pioneering the future. We model peace, yet we thrive on crisis. As a result, we have evolved a project-based culture that has endured and has been extremely effective, but is riddled with inefficiencies.

Our industrial might is the result of responding to challenges and, often, overwhelming odds. Our corporate culture is largely the product of customer driven requirements from World War I, the Depression, World War II, the Korean conflict, the cold war, the Vietnam conflict and the space race. Advances in technology for mankind are mostly spinoffs of military and space projects. We are conditioned to throwing vast quantities of money and bodies at a problem, reaching a victorious outcome, lighting a cigar, and patting our full tummies. In the ensuing months we assuage our consciences by publishing a list of ancillary benefits that mankind has reaped from the massive project that we just completed.

The continental United States has not seen the face of war since the 1860s. Most of those with whom we now compete in the international marketplace have had their industrial machines leveled by war within the last fifty years. They have had an opportunity to take a hard look at what went wrong and build a new industrial infrastructure that would compete with the runaway

American industrial giant. Their task was formidable, but not impossible. Not only did we give them a model and a target, we subsidized their recoveries! They've had every opportunity to succeed. They were already at the bottom and they really couldn't fail by trying new ideas. In the meantime, we were succeeding in spite of ourselves and growing more massive and more complacent with each passing year. We were waiting for the next "project" to come along while they were making long-range plans not to succumb to another war or national crisis.

In recent years, we have been losing our world industrial domination. We are fat and driven by the American Dream. Our competitors are lean and driven by survival and the model that we broadcast around the world by satellite TV. We've been smug in our successes and shared them with the world. For years, we were excellent teachers and lousy students. Our competitors took everything we gave them, learned from our successes, and fit them into their cultural evolution. When pioneers like Dr. W. Edwards Deming became a student of their successes, most of us were too egocentric to listen and harvest a payday from our investments.

To shoot ourselves in the other foot, we've been busy making money by manipulating money and real estate. Many of our great business minds produce no commodities of value. The Wall Street approach to financial success requires winners and losers. The stock moguls and the foreign real estate investors are the apparent winners. The rest of us are the losers. Our competitors are providing products and services of value, where everyone in the delivery process wins. We are selling off our national resources to the rest of the world for a quick buck. This time, I doubt we will be able to buy Manhattan back for $24 in trinkets.

We are now in the third decade of the "Silent Crisis."[1] How do we become lean and compete with the Pacific Rim and the European Community in the World Market? The solution is cultural, systemic and requires gradual change and unbending resolve to a

---

[1]The Silent Crisis is a metaphor for the challenges placed on American business by our international competitors. They are subtle and quiet, but extremely efficacious.

long range set of national goals. Like our government, our business infrastructure is flawed, but it has survived and it has the most potential of any in the world. The unwavering patience that we have demonstrated, for the last two centuries, in the evolution of our system of government has to make the transition to our business culture. If we had taken the "fast hit and quick fix" approach to government that we have evolved in business, we might be flying a different-colored flag these days. The nationalistic commonness of purpose that exists in overt crises must become the battle cry of the Silent Crisis.

## Only a Wet Baby Likes Change

Our great, self-motivated, inventive minds are still out there grinding out new ideas, but we are having only limited success bringing these ideas robustly to market, with intrinsic quality, on time and at a competitive price. The problem we face is not motivation or dedication, it is complacency from the perceived lack of a national threat or crisis. As a nation we've been afflicted by "corporate obesity," as a by-product of success. We do not lack in motivation or talent, we are lethargic, unwilling to change our cultural habits, and conditioned to throw money at our problems. We are programmed to complete a project and then move on to the next project, a little fatter, with more toys, but no wiser.

We wait until any given situation deteriorates to a critical state and then we look for the fast fix, albeit the magic diet pill, that will help us lose 60 pounds in six weeks. Every few years, someone offers us such a miracle. We jump at it, have some short term success, and ultimately wind up losing all the progress that we've made, and then some. The parallel between our personal health and our business health is amazing. You see, we are just beginning to understand how it all really works.

As a society, we've been raised to believe that fullness is wellness. When a baby cries, you put something in its mouth. When we are good, Mom makes our favorite meal. When we entertain friends, we demonstrate love with copious quantities of food. Most family and social activities revolve around food. In

business, we have power breakfasts, we "do lunch," and we encourage dinner meetings.

When we are hungry, we call it "pain." When we are full with food or drink, we feel no pain. We don't just eat to survive, we eat enough to feel satisfied, or beyond. For years, we didn't monitor what we put into our bodies, as long as it tasted good and made us feel good. We consumed, felt satisfied, and there were no overt side effects, other than occasional indigestion.

The more we ate and drank, the fatter we got. Not only did we have more glorious foods to choose from each year, we had new labor-saving devices to limit our physical activities. Excess calories turned to fat. As a nation we became obese. We built systems that encouraged that lifestyle (fast foods, prepared foods, family picnics, office parties, the neighborhood tavern), until crises arose. We suddenly were plagued with cardiovascular disease, diabetes, gout, liver disease, and Madison Avenue told us we didn't look healthy any more.

We responded, as we do to most need for change, with the search for the quick fix. We assaulted our bodies with intense exercise. No pain, no gain became the battle cry. That works until you become ill or the weather turns bad or you can't make the payments on the health club membership. The alternative is chemical stimulation and starvation dieting. Everywhere you look there are folks willing to take your money to help you stop doing what you enjoy so much, eating to feel well. You don't really believe in any of this, but you will endure it until you have overcome the crisis.

Our bodies are not so easily or quickly taken by the quick fix. They respond to gradual change. It took a long time to become obese and for your muscles to reach a supine state. When you assault your body with sudden exercise, things break and the doctors of sports medicine prosper. When you deprive your body of food, the brain senses starvation, burns lean muscle, and saves fat for the famine it senses. You feel tired, are prone to headaches, and get discouraged easily. If you persist with will power or chemical stimulation, the body reacts defensively. When you return to "normal" caloric intake, the internal thermostat resets

| The Business World Has Changed | | |
|---|---|---|
| **20 Years Ago** | **5 Years Ago** | **Today** |
| Local markets | Regional markets | International markets |
| Local competition | Regional competition | International competition |
| Entrepreneur run | Management run | Employee run |
| Think-tank design | Marketing-driven design | Customer-driven design |
| Customers were victims | Customers were gullible | Enlightened consumers |
| Customer at the end | Customer rebellion | Customer first |
| Over-design | Designed obsolescence | Robust design |
| Good reliability | Planned reliability | Exceptional reliability |
| Stable product lines | Changing product lines | Upward compatibility |
| Product loyalty | No loyalty | Shopping for value |
| Peddlers and customers | Suppliers and consumers | Partners |
| 10-year product life | 3-year product life | 18-month product life |
| 20-year employees | 5-year employees | Contract workers |
| Blue-collar | White-collar | Open-collar |
| No standards | Industry standards | International standards |
| Hire trained employees | OJT | Continuous training |
| The Quarterly report | Posturing for acquisition | The long run |
| Unions and pensions | Stock programs | Self-directed investment programs |
| Quality police | Preventative quality | Total quality |
| Knowledge is power | Management is power | Group intelligence |
| Cloak and dagger | Management by objective | Employee involvement |
| Worker bee employees | Motivated employees | Hands and minds |
| Big business | Losing business | Leading business |

in an attempt to regain the lost fat and prepare for future starvation by adding more reserve fat. The cultural system that we have devised is, inevitably, self-destructive.

The only answer to physical health is eating the correct foods in reasonable proportion and engaging in regular moderate exercise, forever. The change must be systemic, cultural, and continually improving. We must listen to our bodies and give them long-term health, not short periods of feeling full. Once we've purged our bodies of excess fat and achieved some muscle tone, the feeling is euphoric. We have difficulty explaining how good we feel

| Our Personal World Has Changed | | |
|---|---|---|
| **20 Years Ago** | **5 Years Ago** | **Today** |
| Japan emerging from junk status | Standard for quality | Competing with America |
| 10 miles per gallon | 20 miles per gallon | 25 miles per gallon |
| Carburetors | Fuel injection | Northstar |
| Calculators | Spreadsheets | Integrated software |
| DEC PDP-11 | 386-16 MHz | Pentium 120 MHz |
| Holerith cards | 1.2 Mb floppy disks | 135 Mb removable diskettes |
| Room-size disk drives | 80 Megabyte hard drive | 1 Gigabyte hard drive |
| Dot matrix printers | Laser printers | Color printers |
| TWX | Thermal FAX | Paper FAX |
| LP albums | Compact discs | DAT |
| Super 8 movies | Camcorders | Digital photography |
| AM/FM stereo | Theater sound | Prologic Surround and THX |
| Ping-pong | Super Mario | Virtual reality |
| U.S. mail | Federal Express | Electronic mail |
| Union mentality | Self-actualization | Individual entrepreneurs |
| Work is necessary | Work is a means to an end | Work is fun and challenging |
| Women stay home | Women professionals | Women leaders |
| Swiss watches | Electronic watches | Wrist data centers |
| Patience | Instant gratification | Entitlement |
| Movies painted fantasy | Movies mimic life | Life drives movies |
| Credit cards | Debit cards | Electronic funds |
| TV, VCR, cable | Pay-Per-View | Interactive entertainment |
| Loran | Inertial navigation | Global positioning |

and how we are ready to cope with any new challenges life throws at us. It is also nearly impossible to communicate the dedication and commitment that achieving our goals requires when the old way is comfortable and is acceptable to so many.

The parallel between the American body and the American corporation is uncanny. Substitute dollars for food and massive profits for wellness. Throw money at those who cry and at those whom we like. Substitute bureaucracy and empire building for our social culture. Equate hunger with negative cash flow and fullness with fat dividends. We supplied whatever commodities

were in demand, as long as the money flowed. There were no apparent ill effects from uncontrolled capitalism.

Our corporations grew fatter with technological innovations that saved labor. Our corporate culture encouraged large vertical organizations and fat budgets, until we were plagued with foreign competition, poor quality, slow reaction time, and outsiders holding a mirror to corporate America. We didn't like what we saw, so we looked to the miracle diet of cutting overhead. We exercised strenuously with quality circles and cellular manufacturing. Our corporate bodies reacted by breaking down and by turning on their defense mechanisms. Once the crisis temporarily ebbed, silos went up and bureaucracies fattened themselves, preparing for future starvation. Management quit dieting and exercising and was afraid to try any other miracle cures to our corporate ills.

The solution is not in a diet cookbook nor in short-term strenuous activity. Our long-term corporate health will only come from cultural and systemic change to a lean and healthy body. That body will consume just what it needs to be healthy, do all things in moderation and dedicate itself to continuous improvement, forever. It will plan for its long-term well-being, and sacrifice some quick hits. It will feel euphoric because all of its vital organs are being treated well and are being developed for a lifetime of productive activity. It will be a contributing member of society, not a lethargic couch potato. It will react to outside threat because it is trained and prepared, not because crisis is its usual corporate mode of operation. The imperatives of continuous improvement are, as Tom Peters suggests, get lean, get fast, or die.[2]

The motivation to change what we are currently doing is the realization that what has made us successful in the past may not be the path to a successful future. To compete in the global market place we must dismantle traditional vertical management and remove functions that add no value to the delivery system. We have to replace ego-driven design with satisfying, delighting, and exciting our customers. We have to replace crisis management with leadership by logical necessity. We have to embrace

---

[2]From Tom Peter's video, *Speed Is Life: Get Fast or Go Broke,* Video Publishing House, 1991.

change and make it our motivator not our enemy. We have to benchmark and learn from the best examples how we can improve processes and stimulate productivity. We have to deal with the human issues, not just the trials and tribulations of hardware and software.

I recently made a presentation to a group of Air Force officers. I was amazed and shocked to learn that the group I was working with was a model for continuous improvement. Their mission was to protect the American people (their customers) from foreign aggressors within a given budget. Their methods were Total Quality Management, training at all levels, improvement by using the Malcolm Baldrige assessment criteria. They were working to make the troops part of an empowered, self-motivated team. If our military can see the light of continuous improvement, there is hope that American industry can see the imperatives of change (burp!). The tables on pages 6–7 dramatize the incredible advances that make continuous quality improvement the battle cry of American business imperative for the next century.

# *Virtual Leadership*

O n a recent spring morning the usual pastoral quiet outside my office was shattered by the drone of disassociated screeching. Just above was a large group of snow geese. They were not flying in the graceful vee formation that we are accustomed to seeing. Neither were they chanting their usual rhythmical cadence.

After studying the chaotic flight, it was obvious that their work structure had broken down. They were flapping their wings and making noise, but they weren't going anywhere. They expended great effort to maintain altitude, yet they were flying in circles. They shrieked, as if they were calling for their leaders to guide them on a meaningful course. After a few minutes, they disbanded and returned to the nearby rice marshes where they had wintered. While I will probably never be absolutely certain, the dominant theory around the courthouse square is that a group of hunters with high-powered rifles was responsible for the ill-fated flight of snow geese. Since there were several days of poor hunting, the frustrated "sportsmen" attempted to shoot down a flight

of geese already flying in formation. Once again, apparently, human intervention upset the functionality of nature.

I managed to videotape some of the activity with the intent of adding it to my collection of what we can learn about ourselves from nature. You see, migrating geese are usually models of teamwork and I've found the example to be a useful metaphor in teaching leadership and team building.

As the theory goes, no individual goose can make the biannual migration on its own. By traveling in a vee formation, their flapping wings create a draft that helps each bird behind the leader gain lift and sustain flight. As the leader needs to renew its strength, another bird takes the lead. If a bird becomes ill or has to leave the formation, several others will follow it to the ground. When it is ready to travel again, a new migrating team forms and the journey is continued. Whether or not the aerodynamics of the theory is totally valid, the role that leadership and teamwork play in a successful migration is indisputable. If the metaphor were accurate as a success tool, what lesson is there to be learned from the failure that I had observed that spring morning?

## Flapping Our Wings

As I read the monthly trade journals, I usually find at least one article about how XYZ Company just saved over $2 million by implementing TQM, followed by another article that claims that TQM is dead. In another journal, there will be a similar story on the positive impact that ISO9000 is having on moving American companies into the international marketplace, immediately following an editorial warning that the ISO9000 locomotive is running out of steam. I read about quality circles being dead and quality circles coming back to life. Each time I read these apparent dichotomies, I am now reminded of the wing-flapping and screeching of the snow geese. We flap our wings and honk in cadence when we have a positive experience. Whenever we experience a setback in our journey, we flap our wings and make lots of noise.

There's nothing wrong with displaying our plumage when we are successful and sharing our accomplishments, as long as we do not become fanatics. When we fail, however, we screech and broadcast that we are innocent and the failure was due to some external fault. We are inclined to find blame and point fingers until the failure mode is obscured and only the symptoms remain. Instead of regrouping, returning to base, learning from our failures, and launching a new offensive, we make enough noise to convince everyone who will hear that we were given a faulty flight plan and we were led off course. Studying the geese makes me wonder what fails in the human model; the plan, the processes, or the players?

## The Search for the Secret of Flight

I have been a student of human nature for most of my adult life. I have also been a trained observer of American industry for over twenty-five years. I've been fortunate to have visited over 300 different companies and to have studied their successes and their failures. In all of my travels, I can identify perhaps three companies and ten individuals that are truly success models. They are on a never-ending migration. They fly straight and true, from one fruitful feeding ground to the next. They occasionally crash and burn, but they learn from the experience, regroup, and fly on with renewed commitment.

The vast majority of companies, however, expend their resources and energies on a futile search for quick fixes, cookbook programs, gurus to follow, and instant productivity. They search for "the secret of flight" during the moments when they are not preoccupied with solving daily problems.

They are experts at solving problems, yet they seldom admit that anything failed. These companies employ MBO, SPC, JIT, TQM, and every other acronym on the "program du jour" list. They fly on the hot air that discussing these programs produces, rather than using the lift of teamwork. Each company has a cadre of very talented people who are constantly flying in circles and screeching loudly. These caring people are the ones who read the

conflicting articles in the trade magazines as they search in vain for the secret of flight instead of looking for the clues of success. Their search usually stops short of discovering what failed.

## We are Superior to the Birds, but Can't Fly

Alas, we were not born to fly. We were given, instead, the attributes of reason, intellect, compassion, greed, avarice, lethargy, genius, jealousy, rage, rapture, and disappointment. We were not born with instincts to follow. Instead, we are armed with these human attributes, tempered by what has been modeled for us. Instead of conditioned behavior, we have the superior intellect that allows us to analyze symptoms and prescribe solutions based on logic, tempered with the dominant emotion of the day, and the agenda created by our modeling.

There are very few of the helpful "flight plan" authors who have looked beyond the system or methods that gave them flight. They are mostly dispensing advice and solutions based on symptomatic results. The readers are looking for the quick hit and the fast fix and haven't the time to dig out the underlying causes and effects of successes and failures. When the "program du jour" succeeds, it yields more than just positive results. It leaves a trail of evidence for the trained observer to model. When it appears to fail, those same observers have learned to decide first if the players failed in execution before condemning the processes or the plan. **Programs succeed and fail most often due to the interaction of scores of human emotions, not because of the quality of the processes or plan.**

## Success Isn't for the Birds

My definition of a success model may be a bit different from most, so it is worth stating here. It is:

♦ Providing total customer satisfaction
♦ Sustaining a creative environment where work is fun and challenging

Constantly setting the pace and taking risks

Challenging conventional wisdom

Having a positive effect on everyone

Propagating win-win scenarios

Continually improving every person and process

Rewarding all who contribute

Why is it that only about one out of 100 of the companies that I have studied is clearly successful (with the migrating geese, I suspect the ratio is nearly inverse)? Are these companies led by managerial geniuses? Do they have an unlimited source of capital? Actually, most of them deal in mundane commodities and they are led by unpretentious people who have no golden goose. **Their only secret is their ability to cast off the traditional managerial veneer and stimulate the full potential of everyone around them**. They lead and initiate the updraft needed to sustain their team. The leader is at the helm when he or she is needed there. At other times, he or she is back with the working troops, flying with the team momentum. When a team member falls behind, some of the team stays behind and helps the straggler until he or she is ready to pull his or her own weight. No individual can sustain flight alone, so there is no place for individual superstars who aren't team members. People work together and all reach their destination. They model success instead of reading about it. They are skilled at finding the clues that other successful people leave behind. They learn from their failures and regroup, instead of complaining to the world that the flight plan is bogus. **Most of all, successful leaders understand the complexities of the interaction of humans**, either innately or by training. They observe the migration of geese, the possibilities of ISO9000, the agenda of TQM, the teachings of Juran and Deming, and they select the tools that can help them achieve their goals **within their own unique human culture.**

If we had no human frailties, we could pattern work cultures directly from the snow geese and expect companies to work at peak efficiency. If companies had no fear of change, ISO9000 implementation would be a breeze and everyone would win the

Malcolm Baldrige National Quality Award. If we were all in a state of mind where there were no jealousies or egos, TQM would be the dominant mode of operation. We do, however, have those frailties and we choose to shoot the messenger when the latest success strategy is less successful than we expected.

## The Tenets of Virtual Leadership

There is a lesson to be learned from virtually every observation of nature. The migration of the snow geese has an elegant and profound one: **Geese don't have management! They have leaders.** Their work system is managed, but there is no single team member with the sole responsibility to provide lift and direction for the entire team. They don't need to be told when they are successful or when they are in trouble. They have shared, visual, effective measures of success. When they are on their flight plan, they are graceful and harmonious. When trouble arises, they may fly in circles for a while, but they quickly regroup and set out on a more fruitful course. They have the positive organization and discipline of being managed without the burden of management.

Managing *(directing, controlling, handling, administrating, and regulating)* has long been accepted as vital to the efficient operation of a company. Business people traditionally accomplish this function by *making* (others) *submissive.* They also *contrive and arrange,* which changes the gerund *managing* into its noun form. When it becomes a noun, it no longer materially adds value to the delivery system and it becomes an overhead expense. It exists merely to control anarchy. By definition, it requires a police force. It spends much of its time reacting to adversarial behavior and to sustaining itself.

Leadership does not imply the overhead that managing does. During a performance, an orchestra leader cannot do the work for a team member. He or she cannot regulate or contrive the activities of those being led. The maestro stands among very talented and well trained players and sets the pace and the tempo and keeps them on the strategic plan. If the verb lead changes to a noun, it loses its meaning and becomes a heavy load.

## *Man•age:*

*(verb) To direct, control, or handle. To administer or regulate. To make submissive.*

*To contrive or arrange.*

## Lead:

*(verb) To guide on a way. To direct on a course or in a direction. To direct the operations or activity or performance <~ an orchestra>.*

## Vir•tu•al:

*(adjective) Existing in effect or essence though not in actual fact or form.*

By adding the modifier *virtual* to *leadership* we can symbolically highlight the cultural change that must evolve to return *manage* to its functional status as a verb rather than the expensive noun called *management*. By practicing *Virtual Leadership,* enlightened managers and jobholders become dynamic partners in business success. By dismantling traditional adversarial roles, Virtual Leadership becomes a value-added activity instead of an overhead entity.

## Modeling Success

Virtual Leadership is the model for successful businesses of the new century. Those who practice Virtual Leadership will be those who take responsibility for their own actions. Each will be a contributor and a beneficiary. Each will be an individual with a vested interest in the success of everyone. The value delivery system will be comprised of process operators who have clear missions, adequate resources, and success models provided by visionary leaders. They will be trained by facilitators, supported by coaches, and they will have a single barometer for success: customer satisfaction. They will be the pioneers of the future rather than the victims of it. They will have a clear vision of the lessons of teamwork in nature, but they will allow for the frailties of humans. They will modify the flight plan when it fails and not blame the author for its shortcomings. They will fly in a formation that sustains lift and is in a constant state of change as it moves on a never-ending journey from harvest to harvest.

# CHAPTER 3

# The Imperative of ISO9000

## We Learn from History

World War II is over and most of Europe is in physical and economic ruin. Before being defeated, the Axis powers managed to destroy most of the Allied ability to manufacture durable goods. In the final battles, the Allies bombed away much of the manufacturing might of the Axis. In the Pacific, Japan is also a country in ruin. Meanwhile, the United States is celebrating victory by retooling its wartime manufacturing plants for cars, refrigerators, and consumer electronics. Even with the interruption of the Korean conflict, American industry is becoming fat and sassy, because it is the only game in town.

It doesn't take long for the Europeans to realize that, if they do not get back in the game, the Americans will position themselves to monopolize the industrialized world. They are also uncertain of what will rise from the ashes in post-war Japan. The Europeans have protected their vital defense interests by forming the North Atlantic Treaty Organization (NATO) in 1949 and the European Coal and Steel Community in 1951 (Figure 3.1). It is

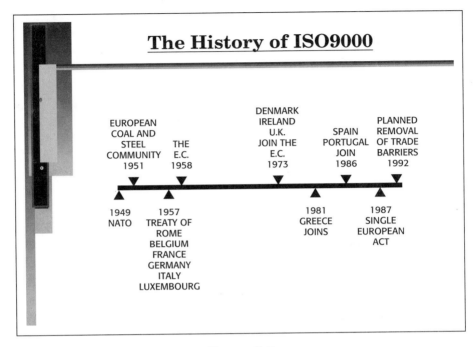

**Figure 3.1**

now 1957. Basic human needs are being met and it is time to look to the future. In a bold step toward becoming viable competitors, Belgium, France, Germany, Italy, and Luxembourg all signed the Treaty of Rome, leading to what we now know as the European Community. The EC will be the beginning of an effort to form a competitive bloc of consumers and manufacturers that will challenge the Americans and expedite the economic recovery in Europe.

As the EC devises its plans for economic recovery, it realizes that it need not be bound by the old ways learned through the industrial revolution. Since there is nothing to lose, it made sense to seek out the best methods and processes available. If the Americans want to help the economic recovery, why not learn from them and everyone else who has technology and methodology to share?

The EC did well with its early benchmarking and process re-engineering efforts. Even though the final currency barriers did

## The Growing Marketplace

- **The twelve countries of the E.C. (345 million consumers)**
- **Ongoing discussions with EFTA (Austria, Finland, Iceland, Liechtenstein, Norway, Sweden, Switzerland)**
- **Also looking at joining with the EEA (Poland, Hungary, Czech Republic, Slovak Republic)**
- **Potential to join with the former Soviet Republics in the future**

**Figure 3.2**

not come down as planned at the end of 1992, the EC has been, by all measures, successful in its unification efforts, with 345 million consumers and $6 trillion in buying power. In the late 1990s, they will likely align with the other bloc groups such as EFTA,[1] EEA,[2] and the former Soviet Republics to form a unified base of close to 800 million consumers (Figure 3.2).

While all of this revitalization was going on, the United States was taking a 25-year nap. We were of the omnipotent mindset that our wasteful business practices were bullet proof. We were so arrogant that we ignored the warnings of one of our visionary thinkers, Dr. Edwards Deming, for nearly thirty years! Since we wouldn't listen, he went to Japan and helped them build the industrial success model they enjoy today. Our successes in the space program further bolstered our industrial arrogance. To

[1]European Free Trade Association.
[2]European Economic Area.

outsiders, the successes of the Gemini and Apollo programs may appear as an archetype of quality and reliability, but it was actually the result of expensive double and triple redundancy and individual initiative by thousands of dedicated workers. We finally got the wake-up call, albeit late. For the last decade or so, the United States has been scrambling to cut costs, improve efficiency, and enhance quality before the Europeans and the Pacific Rim drive us out of the manufacturing business.

## The Contribution of the European Community to Quality

The effort to unify Europe was formidable on many fronts, but the most obvious obstacles were centered around the enormous diversity of peoples in such a small geographic area. Each of the major cultures had developed independently. There was no commonality of language, currency, regulations, laws, and little similarity in technology. As the EC developed its unification strategy, it became apparent that there was a need for a single standard for quality. Not only would such a standard have to translate a wide diversity of languages, it would also have to yield the same outcome, regardless of culture. This was definitely new ground to be plowed and sown.

The EC contracted with the International Organization for Standardization in Geneva to design such a standard. ISO,[3] as the International Organization for Standardization is now known, has 91 member countries and 173 active technical committees, and has published over 8,000 nonbinding international standards and technical reports. In 1979, ISO created Technical Committee 176 to undertake the writing of a unified quality standard. In 1987, ISO made the first release of the ISO9000 documents. The standard (Figure 3.3) consisted of guidelines for selection and use (ISO9000), guidelines for implementation (ISO9004), and the three quality system standards (ISO9001, 9002, and 9003).[4]

---

[3]ISO is the Greek word for "equal," not an acronym, and is pronounced "eye-soh."
[4]The standards are discussed in detail in Chapter 6.

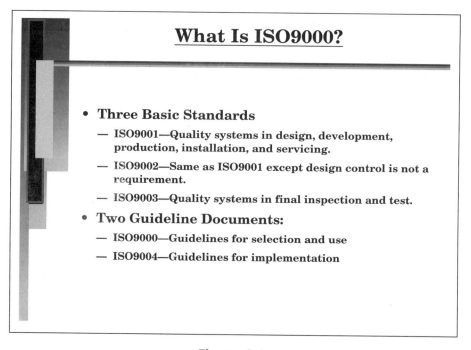

**Figure 3.3**

TC-176 devised a design for a basic quality management system that is nonprescriptive and nonjudgmental. In essence, it says:

◆ Write down what you do
◆ Do what you write down
◆ Verify that you are doing it

The genius of the content of ISO9000 is that it transcends language and cultural barriers. It does not require companies to change what makes them successful, just to document it and measure it. It is standardization of processes, not the dilution of culture. Whether one is manufacturing gaskets in Madrid, coating pipes in Athens, or distributing natural gas in Scotland, the process of ISO9000 certification is the same.

## The Quality Road Started In Europe

Becoming certified to ISO9000 involves subjecting a company to a quality management system audit by a third-party auditing firm. Once again, ISO and the EC have led the way in establishing certification criteria. Through the European Community, each country of the EC has an accreditation organization that is either part of the government or a prestigious national organization with close ties to the government (Figure 3.4).

Each of these accreditation bodies has the right to accredit registrars who can perform quality system audits and issue certificates of conformance to ISO9000. Within the EC, common recognition of third party audits isn't a problem. Outside the EC,

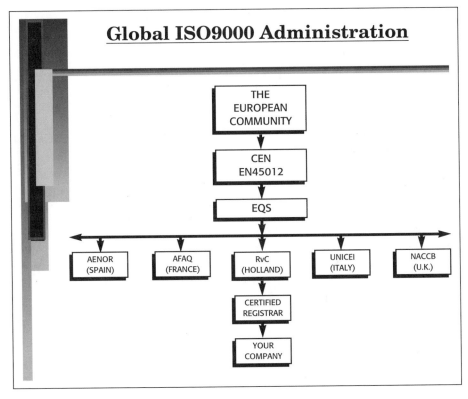

**Figure 3.4**

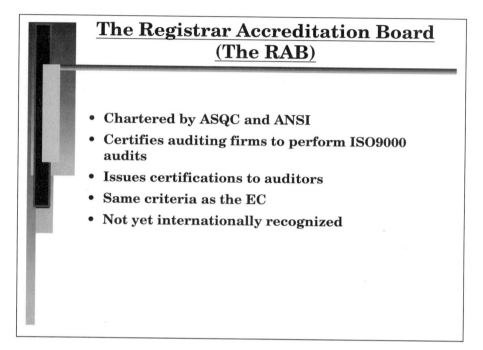

**Figure 3.5**

there are an ever growing number of *memoranda of understanding,* allowing organizations to recognize each other's auditing credentials. This entire process is in its infancy and companies should be careful when selecting a third-party auditor: Formal credentials back to the EC are seen as a highly desirable attribute when becoming certified, and many auditors do not have those credentials.

The RvC[5] in Holland and the NACCB[6] in the UK have pioneered the certification of third-party auditors outside their countries. In the United States, the Registrar Accreditation Board (RAB) (Figure 3.5) is vying to become the accreditation body; however, as of this writing, it still is not universally recognized.[7]

---

[5]The Dutch Council.

[6]The British Certification Agency has recently been privatized and is now the IRCA.

[7]Selecting a third-party registrar will be discussed in Chapter 9.

The Entire ISO9000 registration process is continually evolving. What is gospel today may be ancient history in a few months. As a rule, contracting with a third-party registrar is a long-term commitment. Surveillance audits are generally conducted every six months and complete recertification is usually required every three years. As the number of registrars grow and the needs of the customers drive the process, new schemes are surfacing regularly that vary the surveillance audit periods and recertification periods. A lesson learned early in Europe was to chose a registrar wisely, because starting over with a new registrar is a very expensive undertaking (you essentially start the certification process over).

## ISO9000 Spans the Globe

ISO9000 may have started as a single quality standard for the European Community; however, it has been accepted in over 81 countries around the world. As a platform, it translates and works in virtually every industrialized country. It is written about in trade journals from London to Singapore. Professional organizations are promoting its use to help standardization of quality systems within an industry, especially industries that do business in global markets.

## It's Not the Program du Jour

At the foundation of many of the strategic quality initiatives that have come and gone (like quality circles or zero defects) is academic modeling, a unique cultural experience or a practitioner's synthesis. That is, a number of models came from academia with little practical application, others were based on a single success model, and still others were synthesized from a success model without proofs in diverse industries and cultures. Unlike these initiatives, ISO9000 evolved from a "need to push the envelope" and fill a specific void. ISO9000 is the consensus of many learned quality practitioners, refined into a brief, concise standard. Although it treads on virgin territory, it has swallowed the globe in

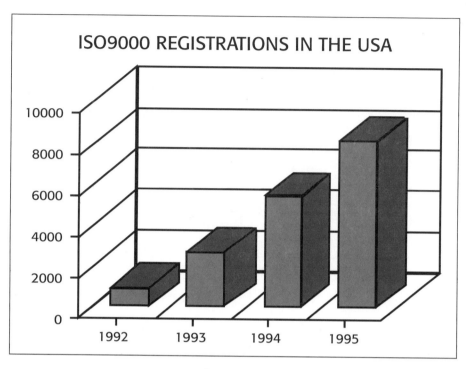

**Figure 3.6**

less than a decade. It is not the ultimate quality management system, but it has initiated the concept of a level playing field in the quality discipline. Its forward inertia and energy cannot be ignored by intelligent business leaders. The steady rise of ISO9000 registrations in the United States alone is dramatized in Figure 3.6. As we will see in the next chapter, what started as a European approach to standardization has taken over the globe because of its simplicity and its ability to adapt and be viable in any environment.

# ISO9000:
# Friend or Foe?

T he universal acceptance of ISO9000 can be traced directly to the simple elegance of its fundamental tenets:

◆ Document what you do
◆ Do what you documented
◆ Verify that you are doing it

More specifically, ISO9000 encourages each company to distill what makes it successful and document the success formulae in the form of process procedures. It compels companies to systematically follow those procedures until procedures no longer support their needs. As processes evolve and change, the process owners must continually change the procedures to reflect the new methods. To verify that the documented procedures are being followed, it suggests that companies build a nonadversarial system of internally auditing those processes and procedures, regularly and forever. While some critics of ISO9000 claim that the standard says nothing about continuous improvement, I have seen it proven re-

peatedly that the three steps of ISO9000 are *innately* a pattern for continuous improvement. **How can you not continually improve if you audit your processes regularly?** If you are constantly and objectively evaluating your value delivery system, you are, by design, honing and polishing that which makes you successful. In this chapter we will build on these basic tenets and explore the frequently asked questions about ISO9000. We will dispel the myths and rumors surrounding the standard and its implementation. We will show how it can help your company's strategic quality initiative and continuous improvement efforts and, ultimately, your business goals and profitability.

## ISO9000: What It Is and What It Isn't

The downfall of most quality initiatives is that they rely on a system of checks and balances, rules and remedies, prevention and detection, doers and checkers (Figure 4.1). There is always an action followed by a reaction. Traditional quality systems assume that the job holder is going to make mistakes and it erects ever-growing walls to contain defects. Within these walls are small doors, tended by learned individuals who can judge which avenue the defective material shall journey. These guardians of quality pass judgment on which products shall pass, which shall be reworked, which shall be repaired, and which shall be banished to the scrap heap.

Conventional quality wisdom assumes that workers are capable only of rote, repetitive actions and that more highly trained individuals downstream must ensure that all previous steps were accomplished successfully before products or services can move forward in the value delivery system. In a manufacturing environment, classic quality programs include: Receive - Inspect - Kit - Inspect - Subassemble - Inspect - Final Assemble - Inspect - Test - Inspect - Pack - Inspect - Ship. Traditional service organizations are structured: Operation - Check - Next Operation - Check - Next Operation - Check - Final Operation - Check - Supervisor Approval - Complete. Each time a process is added, the bureaucracy to support it has to be designed into the system. If a company is held compliant to a military, NASA or federal quality

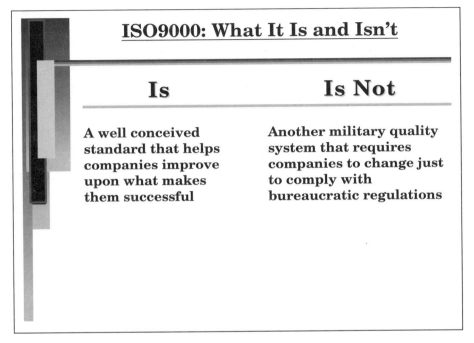

**Figure 4.1**

standard, there are specific prescriptive steps required for their quality system to be approved to the appropriate standard. Compliance often includes changing the way a company does business, adding detective and preventive steps to a process and adding specific police functions to ensure compliance. I have seldom seen a prescriptive quality system that did not add cost to the value delivery system. I have also witnessed few that added any significant value to product or service quality. Inevitably, I have never seen a rigid quality system that didn't systematically reduce productivity and worker morale.

If you have an existing quality management system, ISO9000 will not compel you to dismantle it. In fact, many companies have concurrent standards that exceed the basic requirements of ISO9001, 9002, or 9003. To achieve certification, these companies need only verify compliance with ISO9000 and provide evidence that their system is compliant and effective through examination of quality records and surveillance audits. If your quality management system is effective in producing consistent re-

sults, your journey to certification may be painless and inexpensive. In my experience, however, most companies fail to document their processes, have old and ineffective operational procedures, or do not follow what is documented. In these cases, ISO9000 implementation becomes a value-added, cathartic process of systematically replacing ineffective procedures, adding new productive ones, and streamlining operations. Here are several quotes from ISO9000 that summarize the nonprescriptive approach it offers to quality management:

> . . . the supplier's organization wants to install and maintain a quality system that will strengthen its own competitiveness and achieve the needed product quality in a cost-effective way . . .[1]

> The quality system of an organization is influenced by the objectives of the organization, by the product or service, and by the practices specific to the organization and, therefore, the quality system varies from one organization to another.[2]

Despite what rumors abound about the process of ISO9000 implementation, there aren't any prescriptive elements that you will have to implement that do not make sense for your business culture! You need only address those elements that are germane to your business. If you have disdain for bureaucratic procedures that stifle creativity and productivity, then ISO9000 is the quality system for you. If you would like to dismantle the walls of inspection and find more productive use for those talented guardians of quality, please read on (Figure 4.2).

In most companies, operational procedures are written by Quality Engineering, Manufacturing Engineering, Sustaining Engineering, Human Resources, or all of the above. The procedures are often written in a form that demonstrates the prosaic skills and furthers the writing career of the author. They are written in the most stylish form of the language of the discipline of the author. If they are written by quality engineering, they are full of quality buzzwords. If they are written by Human Resources, they

---

[1]From ISO9000, 1987, Page 2, Paragraph 5.
[2]From ISO9000, 1987, Page1, Paragraph 0.

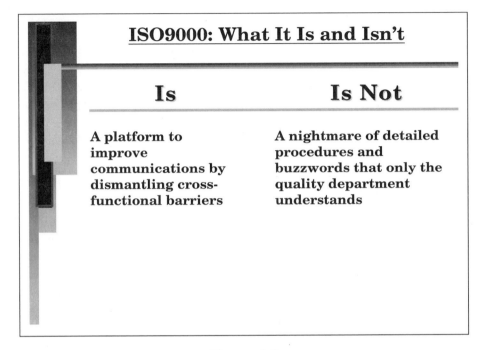

**Figure 4.2**

are full of kinder and gentler rules of conduct that can be changed in a heartbeat. They are seldom written in a form that concisely communicates policy or establishes brief, definitive procedures. They are usually full of pseudo-legalistic terminology designed to cover every nuance. In fact, the more convoluted contingencies a procedure writer can cover, the more his or her perceived worth may be. Most procedures I have read establish clear boundaries and erect organizational silos. Some really verbose procedures actually dig moats around departments and isolate them from the rest of the world.

Another truism that I have found is that procedures are seldom read by anyone other than the author. They are reviewed for form, nitpicked for detail, approved in a vacuum, and filed away until something blows up. When there is a crisis, procedures are usually read by a witch hunter searching for evidence to support a case against some poor job holder that will lead to a "burning at the stake."

If the documentation requirements of ISO9000 are followed, the results will be a concise quality manual that establishes basic policies, supported by second- and, as required, third-tier job descriptions and process procedures that reflect, in few words, how things are actually done. The best procedures are the most brief (It took eight years to write ISO9001, yet it is less than seven typed pages in length). As I help companies write procedures, I often share this quote with them:

> *I have made this letter rather long only because I have not taken the time to make it shorter.*
>
> —Blaise Pascal, 1656

ISO9000 requires that operational procedures deal with how all the functions within the value delivery system interact. This mechanism is usually one of the most beneficial in the implementation process. By objectively looking at the association of processes and the functions of various departments, I often uncover duplication of activities, expensive crutches constructed to patch a crisis and never removed, and often find holes in the system that no one is responsible for. It is not unusual to find costly redundancies that are continually overlooked because they are done by the same people, day in and day out, without ever questioning why they are being done.

My reality check for an effective ISO9000 documentation system is: "Can you take a skilled worker off the street and effectively and efficiently train him or her in a job and processes?" I encourage the job holders to write the procedures they use.[3] This approach greatly simplifies procedures and gives ownership to the people who do the work (even if the author is the only one who reads it, mission accomplished!).

---

[3]This process is explained in detail in Chapters 5 and 10.

The third step in the ISO9000 tenets, "Verify that you are doing it," is accomplished through a methodical system of regular internal audits of processes compared to procedures. The internal auditing scheme ensures that the procedures are understandable and accurate. At the end of the day, the language of ISO9000 becomes the language of your company, silos are dismantled, moats are filled in, and job holders actually talk to one another about improving processes.

In most classic quality systems, ownership of processes is vested in managers and delegated to job holders. Since accountability is usually delegated without adequate authority, the rules of ownership have to be strict and toll gates must be in place to ensure compliance with the canons of conduct. A typical scenario might be a design draftsperson who is given a project by an engineer. He or she usually has strict rules from the engineer on how the project is to be documented. Although the draftsperson is expected to read the engineer's mind and correct subtle oversights, that person is often discouraged from including an opinion on how a design might be optimized. That creative work is reserved for the engineer, although the designer may have years more practical experience. In most design cycles, the draftsperson has a formal checker (besides the engineer); however, the engineer is seldom the subject of a reality check until the design is in its prototype stage.

In the successful implementation of ISO9000, ownership of a job and of processes is vested in those who perform the job or process (Figure 4.3). In the last example, the engineer would have a clear set of expectations of what is expected of him or her before the detail work is turned over to the next process owner. Both the engineer and the designer would have distinct job descriptions and proven process procedures that are complementary. The designer would have clear boundaries and would be the internal customer of the engineer. Well-written procedures encourage them to collaborate to improve both jobs and make the final product of their efforts the best it can be. There is no need for a checker for the draftsperson nor an added-cost step for the engineer if the entire design process follows the tenets of ISO9000. Unnecessary overhead is reduced, adversarial relationships are dismantled, and costly rework is all but eliminated in an effective ISO9000 quality system.

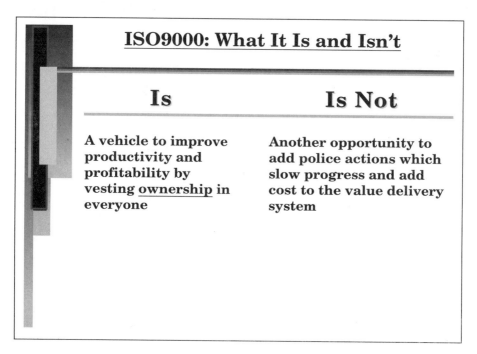

**Figure 4.3**

One of the absolute key elements of ISO9000 is *training* (Figure 4.4).

What an odd requirement to place in a quality management standard! Of course we are all trained. We went to school and have been training on the job all of our careers. The big guy must have lied to us when he said ISO9000 wasn't prescriptive, because now he's saying we have to do training! Anyway, we've been going to do training, but our development and production schedules have been so hectic that we haven't gotten around to it, but it's going to be in next quarter's budget, besides, I just sent my secretary to school to learn DOS. . . .

ISO9000 says that job holders must be trained and they must be continually learning the skills needed to do their jobs. The reasoning is that we so often neglect formal training and assume that process operators know what is expected of them. If job holders are going to be responsible for their own work, they must be trained in what is required. As technology advances, jobs

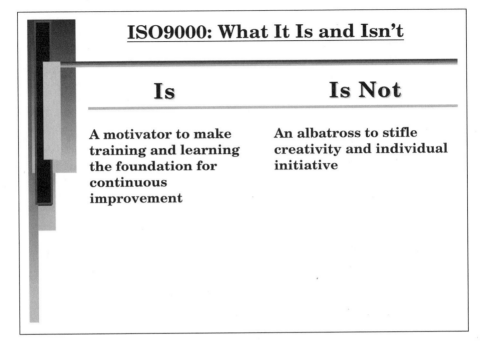

**Figure 4.4**

change and processes change. Training must continue or the quality management system will stagnate and lose its effectiveness. Perhaps one of the reasons you are reading this book is because your management and quality training are a bit rusty. My unofficial research has yielded the following hypothesis of technical training. Thirty years ago, training was good for ten to fifteen years. Twenty years ago it was good for eight to ten years. Fifteen years ago it was good for five to eight years. Ten years ago, it was good for three to five years. Five years ago it was good for two to three years and today it is good for one to two years. My assertion is that in each span of time specified, there would be quantum changes in technology that would make it imperative to have additional training to be able to function in a technically based industry. Look at the evolution of the personal computer. In its first ten years of existence, there were four quantum changes in platforms (the XT/AT, the 286/386, the 486, and the Pentium). Each change caused the previous technology to be virtually archaic. Software is evolving on an annual basis. A major manufacturer of

two-way radio equipment told me recently it was their design goal to evolve and add features to their products so that consumers will want to buy a new radio every eighteen months! The point is that our society is changing too rapidly to put training on the back burner.

Much of the criticism of ISO9000 comes from the engineering community that claims it stifles their creativity with cumbersome procedures. When closely analyzed, that translates to "I want to play with technology without a rule book" and "I don't want anyone to know how much of my R&D time is spent in reinventing the wheel." I have been involved in this arena most of my career and I have witnessed the geometric progression in technology causing engineers to resist discipline more than when they smoked briar pipes and kept hard-covered laboratory note books! It is unreasonable to not have a formal system of design that involves everyone in the value delivery system. It is wasteful not to keep detailed design development and design review notes so that the wheel is not continually reinvented. It is suicide not to have configuration engineering and sustaining engineering keeping up with the evolution of current products. Rather than stifling creativity, ISO9000 reduces wasted time and motion and keeps the design goals clear as technology changes halfway during product development.

The bottom line is that ISO9000 is an *evolutionary* step in the Industrial Revolution, not a *revolutionary* step to instant success (Figure 4.5). It is the platform to launch a new phase in business maturity through process control and internal auditing. It is a cultural shift away from adversarial management systems and toll gate inspections. It is not the program du jour to lose 60 pounds in six weeks. ISO9000 offers structure in which to work and continually improve. It is not a system of police actions that require many dollars of overhead to sustain. It is boundaries that keep you out of the ditches with policies and a mission statement that reflects the path you have chosen to follow. It is not the anarchy of everyone traveling a different path looking for the City of Oz. ISO9000 is discipline without bureaucracy. It provides a set of rules without requiring empires to enforce them. Properly done it instills a sense of urgency in its process owners, replacing the panic of missed schedules, rejected orders, and lost profits. It re-

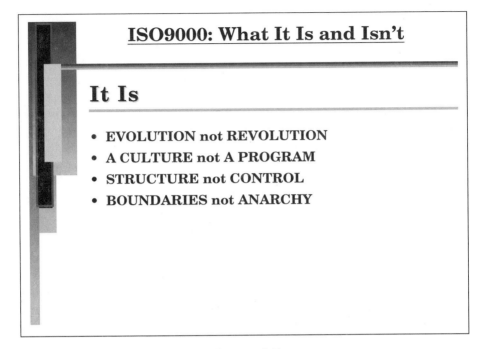

**Figure 4.5**

places damage control management with management by fact. That is, it drives out the tradition of moving from grass fire to grass fire with operating a business by dealing with the issues that are of most importance first (Pareto management?).[4] It is all about achieving sustaining quality, not just meeting arbitrary objectives and bogeys. It is commitment by all who participate in the quality management system, not compliance to rules owned by the quality department. It is shielding customers from receiving defective products and ineffective services, rather than continually using the customer as an unwilling beta test site. It encourages you to get rid of vendors and peddlers and replace them with partners in the future of your company. At the end of the day, ISO9000 is the platform to launch your future, not the end of your worries.

[4]In Pareto analysis, events are identified in rank order, usually from the most significant to the least.

## The Language of ISO9000

Have you ever been with a group of professionals and tried to reach a consensus on the definition of a technical term? How many times have you read the glossary in a technical document? Where did the definitions you hold near and dear come from? How do you define quality (Figure 4.6)? Some often given answers include:

◆ Fitness for use
◆ Compliance to specification
◆ Excellence (Rolls Royce versus Chevrolet)
◆ Goodness (Reliability)
◆ Customer satisfaction

Take those five common answers from the American English vocabulary and culture and translate them into the languages and

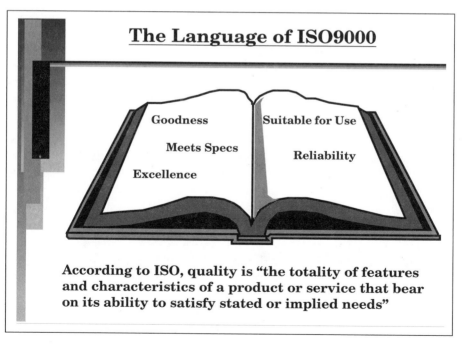

**Figure 4.6**

cultures of the 81+ countries that have adopted ISO9000 and consensus becomes just a dream.

Another insightful contribution of the European Community's effort to implement a universal quality standard is ISO8402, *Quality Vocabulary*. This standard complements ISO9000 by defining the terminology of ISO9000 in concise verbiage and then translating it into French and Russian in a single document. Just as ISO9000, it is not the last word, nor will everyone agree with the definitions, but it does make the playing field even more level. For instance, ISO8402 defines quality as: *The totality of features and characteristics of a product or service that bear on its ability to satisfy stated and implied needs.* Chances are you will have to read that about ten more times to fully appreciate the definition and then you will file it away with the rest of the glossaries in your technical library (after all we don't want to confuse our beliefs with new input!). The significance of the ISO8402 definition is that, when it is used in the context of ISO9000, *quality* can be universally translated from Brooklyn to Fort Worth and from Silicon Valley to the Ruhr Valley.

## Why Is It the Topic du Jour?

We've discussed what ISO9000 is, what it isn't, and some of its benefits. So far, we've created a lot of hype for a quality management system. Why has this European quality standard become the topic of discussion from board rooms to locker rooms around the industrialized world (Figure 4.7)? After all, it was originally supposed to be just a two-party certification system within the EC![5]

In my experience, the cream that rises to the top is that everyone is looking for qualified suppliers. In the past, every aspect of supplier selection was either a total crap-shoot or a costly process of qualification, selection, and newlywed growing pains. ISO9000 removes one of the variables from the equation. If a company is certified, it has, at least on a given day, demonstrated

---

[5]The original intent of ISO9000 was for companies within the EC to certify their supplier's quality management system. Some European companies even paid to have their suppliers certified. The third-party auditor scheme was a mutation of the original intent.

# Why Is ISO9000 the Topic du Jour?

- Everyone is looking for qualified suppliers
- ISO9000 has moved beyond Europe and become the defacto quality standard around most of the world
- ISO9000 makes selecting new suppliers much more objective and much less costly
- Required or not, it is turning up in bid packages, RFQs
- Some companies are requiring their suppliers to become certified
- Some European companies are even subsidizing the cost of certification for their suppliers

**Figure 4.7**

a viable baseline quality management system that meets a known set of tenets. Wouldn't it be comforting if when you went to buy a car, you knew that each of the manufacturers had a compliant quality system? You could reduce one of your selection criteria and concentrate on price, comfort, ride, and value without wondering if they even test their product or audit their assemblers. Caution! There is no guarantee that you aren't going to buy a lemon, but your chances are far less than by the random system we now have. Chances are good that an ISO9000 certified company is going to have more focus on customer satisfaction than one chosen for you by your cousin's father-in-law. There are a number of lists of ISO9000 certified companies[6] that are published and those lists are becoming the "yellow pages" for companies looking for new suppliers.

---

[6]"The ISO9000 Registered Company Directory" is published by CEEM Information Services, 1501 Braddock Rd., Fairfax VA 22032, 800-745-5565. Available by subscription.

As I have implied, ISO9000 has become the de facto quality standard around the United States and around the world. I regularly interview salespeople and ask how often it shows up as a requirement in bid packages and requests for quotation. A few years ago, it was just a question on a few bids. Now, it is mandatory for some companies and most larger companies ask if you are certified and if not, when you plan to be. I have witnessed a number of ISO9000 implementations that were sponsored by the sales staff and marketing groups because they were either not qualifying to respond to certain bids or they saw the handwriting on the wall that their customers were gradually cutting back their potential supplier pool to ISO9000 certified companies. If you have not seen questions about ISO9000 show up on bid requests, you may be in an industry that is domestic and has a limited customer base. Some cottage industries will never see ISO9000 requirements; however, our globe is shrinking every day and we are all looking for the most competitive advantage we can muster to keep our position and to get our share of the marketplace.

It must be stated at this point that ISO9000 is not an iron-clad requirement in most environments (Figure 4.8). Any company that makes it a requirement is doing so to promote its own quality goals. Anyone who threatens you with "ISO9000 or else" is feeding some self-serving interest. The one area where it is a requirement is when selling certain "Regulated Products" to the European Community. These products include toys, medical devices, personal protective equipment, and construction products (Yes, the Lego Company is ISO9001 certified!). Before products are placed on specific lists in these groups and are qualified to be sold to the EC, they must have the "CE Mark" on them, much as many devices in the United States must have the Underwriter's Labs (UL) mark and similar Canadian products must have the CSA mark. ISO9000 certification in these companies is just a prerequisite to exhaustive product testing by agencies that work for the EC. When testing is complete and the product proven, the CE mark may be placed on the product (Unlike the marks of ISO9000 registration, which are specifically prohibited from being displayed on products). To make the universe of companies required to be ISO9000 certified even smaller, there have been very few directives released for certified products. This is a painfully slow

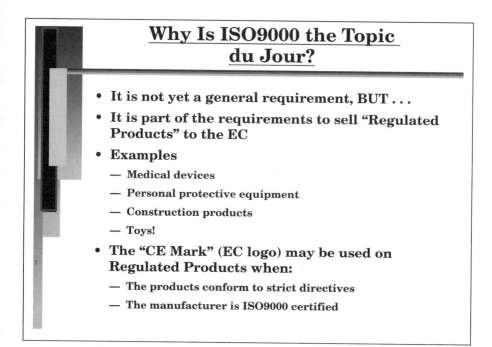

**Why Is ISO9000 the Topic du Jour?**

- It is not yet a general requirement, BUT . . .
- It is part of the requirements to sell "Regulated Products" to the EC
- Examples
  - Medical devices
  - Personal protective equipment
  - Construction products
  - Toys!
- The "CE Mark" (EC logo) may be used on Regulated Products when:
  - The products conform to strict directives
  - The manufacturer is ISO9000 certified

**Figure 4.8**

process that is taking far longer than anyone in the ISO9000 community imagined. This lack of mandatory requirement is one of the reasons that ISO9000 implementation is a hot topic in some areas and lukewarm in others. As you will discover, **the best reason to become ISO9000 certified is the improvement realized from the process of becoming certified.**

The process of ISO9000 implementation (Figure 4.9), done well, is an incredibly cathartic undertaking. It roots out activities that are not producing results. As existing procedures are revised or developed, wasteful methods are identified. As internal audits are performed, holes in the system are recognized and fixed. As the process repeats itself, continuous improvement is inevitable.

ISO9000 involves virtually everyone in the organization in the quality management system. As process operators are trained and quality awareness is heightened, product quality improves. As groups work together to document and refine processes, they always find areas of productivity improvement and ways to elimi-

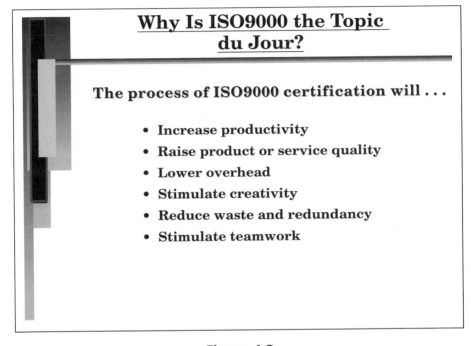

# Why Is ISO9000 the Topic du Jour?

## The process of ISO9000 certification will . . .

- Increase productivity
- Raise product or service quality
- Lower overhead
- Stimulate creativity
- Reduce waste and redundancy
- Stimulate teamwork

**Figure 4.9**

nate duplication of effort. As job holders become responsible for their own actions, layers of bureaucracy are dismantled, toll gate inspection is virtually eliminated and overhead is reduced.

By having the job holders revise or write their own procedures, creativity is stimulated. Ad hoc committees brought together to document processes often find new and better ways to operate those processes because synergism is a powerful tool of ingenuity. These cross-functional groups also reduce waste and redundancy because they identify crutches that have been built into processes by those who didn't take the time and the energy to look at the interaction of all operations within a system. Bringing job holders together to make ISO9000 work often lays the foundation of teamwork in companies that have had a difficult time getting ownership in the team-building process.

As a result of the process of ISO9000 implementation, many companies cite improved documentation, positive cultural impact, higher perceived quality and faster development time. Many use

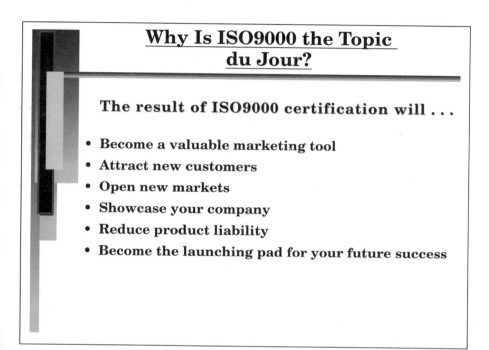

**Figure 4.10**

ISO9000 implementation as the rationalization for continuous improvement and the launching pad for strategic quality initiatives that will sustain and not become another program du jour.

When you successfully complete initial certification, you will receive a nice certificate to hang in the lobby. If you are like many companies, you will commission a banner or post a billboard outside your facility proclaiming your certification to ISO9001 or ISO9002. While the process is the most valuable part of ISO9000 and the certification party may be the most fun, the **result** of ISO9000 certification (Figure 4.10) certainly is a big reason to make the journey. You can use the various marks[7] on your stationery, on your sales brochures, and in your advertising to attract new customers. You can use it in your marketing efforts (as

---

[7]The Registrar you use will provide artwork from the various agencies that they are authorized to issue to you (such as the Dutch Council, the NACCB and/or the RAB).

long as you do not affix a mark to a product). You can use it to open new markets outside your traditional sphere of influence by approaching companies as an ISO9000 certified addition to their supplier base. You can use it to showcase your company by opening up your processes for benchmarking by other companies. Some ISO9000 companies even provide consulting and auditing services to their suppliers.

There have been a number of cases reported in trade journals where ISO9000 has been used as part of the legal defense of companies involved in product liability suits. The premise is that a company that has an ISO9000 certified quality system has a definable minimum quality standard. I don't see an entire new field of legal services starting based on ISO9000; however, it is an interesting aside to throw into the list of reasons for becoming ISO9000 certified.

A more lofty reason for becoming certified is the "we can do anything" culture fostered by the lengthy road to ISO9000 certification. Companies that matriculate from the initial certification begin to look to state and national quality award criteria to see where their next challenge will come from. If ISO9000 certification can be the impetus to achieve higher and higher levels of excellence, it was worth the price of admission.

In this chapter, we've given a host of reasons to become ISO9000 certified. We would be remise if we didn't pause at this point and give some very valid reasons why you should not pursue ISO9000 certification (Figure 4.11).

If you are a local or regional "mom and pop" business or cottage industry, there is little reason to actually seek certification. The model for an ISO9000 quality management system is certainly valid; however, the formal certification process is a fairly expensive outlay for a small business.

Another reason not to seek certification is that you are content with the status quo, you are happy with your quality management system, and you are comfortable with your market share. Not every company wants to grow and some are content with staying with the tools that made them successful. Still others are what I call *limited perpetuity companies*. That is, their owners are planning to sell or they are ripe for a buyout. In those

## Reasons Not to Seek Certification

- Because it is the <u>topic du jour</u>
- You are a <u>regional</u> or <u>local</u> business
- You are content with the status quo
- Someone told you "<u>you have to</u>"
- For a quick fix

**Figure 4.11**

cases, spending money on anything new and changing cultures are not indicated.

The absolute *best* reasons not to seek certification include:

◆ Someone told you had to
◆ You are looking for a quick fix to some endemic or systemic problem

If a customer or your senior management has waved its magic wand and ordered your facility certified **and you have no vested ownership** in the decision, it is the wrong thing to do. Unless everyone is convinced (or at least supportive and receptive) that ISO9000 certification will help them in their journey of productivity and quality improvement, it will be a horrendous waste of money and manpower and will result in frustration and failure. Everyone in the quality management system must own their processes to be effective and to pass a certification audit. If you think implementation of ISO9000 is a magic pill to cure your

productivity or quality woes, it isn't. It will exacerbate existing cultural problems, unless you plan to deal with those problems first and make the needed changes. Early in my career, I was fortunate to meet a very wise salesperson who taught me the following lesson. When bar coding first came in vogue, I wanted to bar code everything in my inventory and every piece moving around the production floor. I saw it as the magic panacea to solve my inventory inaccuracies and my work-in-process tracking problems. I usually shun salespeople, but I solicited this one to show me bar coding equipment so I could do a budgetary estimate and shake out the money to buy the equipment. Before he opened his catalogs, he asked if I would give him a tour of the manufacturing area. When we returned to my office, he started to pack his briefcase. In amazement, I asked what was up. He told me that, as much as he would like to sell me the equipment, I needed about six months of getting my existing system cleaned up and operating correctly before I ever thought about adding another variable to the system. He said that, unless the manual systems were working, bar coding would create an even bigger mess than I had already.

I never forgot that lesson and I give the same advice to potential clients when they want to use ISO9000 as a tool to cover up a mess that should be fixed at its root cause. ISO9000 is not a quick fix for anything. The process, by design, takes from six months to over two years. It requires a gradual cultural change for most companies, not an overnight re-engineering job.

Finally, there are no magic pills in the ISO9000 medicine cabinet. It is just common sense and hard work. If your personality is one of instant success or slash and burn, please close this book now and leave it in the library of your local business school.

## Why Us and Why Now?

The reasons to do it NOW include:

◆ The world is shrinking. Most industries now have global competitors where just a few years ago the major threat was regional or local.

## Why Us and Why Now?

- Global competitors
- Opportunity to sell in an international marketplace
- Stimulus for long delayed documentation
- Rationale for training
- Demand for excellence
- New "yellow pages"
- Need for growth and continuous improvement
- End of adversarial relationships

**Figure 4.12**

♦ The marketplace is expanding. For the same reason that we have global competitors, reasonable transportation and the information superhighway give us access to an international marketplace.

♦ There is a growing demand for excellence. We are not accepting the premise that high value products and services are throw-away items. As consumers, we place a high value on quality and reliability.

The fiscal reasons for becoming ISO9000 certified are clear (Figure 14.13). The need to keep and grow market share is also clear. To begin the journey, ISO9000 provides the stimulus to start the long-awaited quality improvement initiatives or to restart existing efforts that stall every time there is a hiccup in the market. It helps launch the process of continuous growth and improvement. It dismantles adversarial relationships and makes work more interesting and fun.

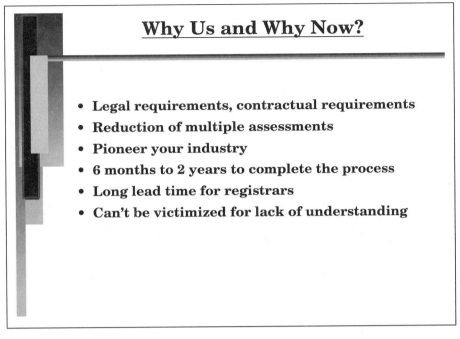

## Why Us and Why Now?

- Legal requirements, contractual requirements
- Reduction of multiple assessments
- Pioneer your industry
- 6 months to 2 years to complete the process
- Long lead time for registrars
- Can't be victimized for lack of understanding

**Figure 4.13**

As we mentioned earlier, there are very few instances where ISO9000 is a contractual or legal requirement, *yet.* Since the process of becoming certified is lengthy, proactively implementing ISO9000 is far less costly and painful than waiting until it is mandatory. A number of the more well-known certified registrars also have a backlog because the demand for their services is high. Some quote three- to six-month lead times in scheduling certification audits. In industries such as chemical refining, ISO9000 is being implemented *now* because it eliminates costly assessments that are historically performed by every major customer. Some process plants had full-time staffs to host audits and assessments. Since ISO9000 has become widely accepted in this industry, companies are saving large sums of money by not having to perform quality audits and not having to host them.

Another good reason to begin the process of ISO9000 certification now is **what you don't know can hurt you**. There is a great deal of misinformation being spread by those who are casually familiar with ISO9000 and set themselves up as experts.

There are also those who would exploit any opportunity for a profit. On a recent morning I received a call from a client who had just begun the ISO9000 journey. A salesperson had told that person that if he did not buy a particular product that he was peddling, his company would never be able to be ISO9000 certified. The allegation was, of course, absurd. I wonder how many times he had used that threat on others and made a sale.

The final reason that I offer to begin your ISO9000 implementation now is my favorite. Most of the companies I work with want to be the leaders in their industry or field. They want to be able to boast that they were the first on the block to achieve certification. It is exhilarating to work with folks who want to excel at what they do and it's fun to watch the ISO9000 process enhance their productivity, quality, market share, and profitability.

Oh, yes, one more thing. One of my favorite Texas euphemisms: "When you ain't the lead dog, the view don't change much" (Figure 4.14).

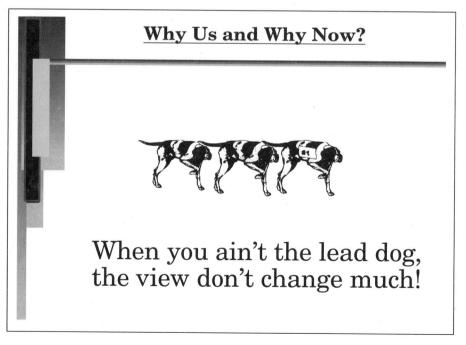

**Figure 4.14**

## Is It an Investment or an Expense?

One of the most frequently asked questions is "How much will it cost?" The ISO9000 champion is usually on his or her feet with "we will save more than it will cost," but that seldom gets by the folks who control the purse strings. As true as the assertion is, the question is relevant and companies must start the process with their eyes open and budgets established.

By far, the greatest cost is the internal cost of documenting procedures, training, and performing internal audits. Many implementors are hesitant to point these costs out or try to measure them at the onset. I firmly believe that if you don't know where you are, you can't know where you are going. Spend some up-front time documenting the cost of quality, the cost of rework, productivity, and whatever metrics make sense for your environment (Figure 4.15). Establish a benchmark set of numbers at the time you start the ISO9000 process and track them on a regular

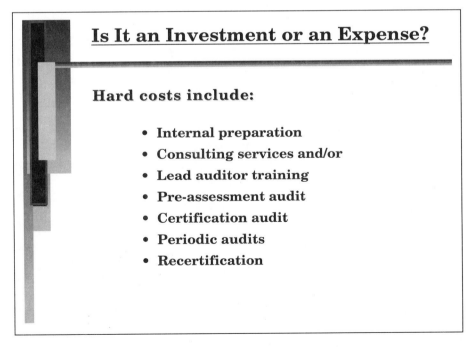

**Is It an Investment or an Expense?**

**Hard costs include:**

- Internal preparation
- Consulting services and/or
- Lead auditor training
- Pre-assessment audit
- Certification audit
- Periodic audits
- Recertification

**Figure 4.15**

basis. Without a score, a football game is pointless and without statistics, you can't make corrections during the game.

Develop a budget based on how many ad hoc hours of work you anticipate and with what labor mix. Be sure that those who control the budget agree with the budget and with the benchmark.

---

## Success Snapshot

The Benefits of Strategic Quality Initiatives
Robert Holiday, Corporate Director of Quality
Megahertz Corporation

Our company, in the last eighteen months, implemented a Total Quality Management system with ISO9001 as a foundation. We passed ISO9001 certitification audit with eight minor findings and recognition of three of our processes as "Best in Practice." The effect of this initiative, just over the last year, while we were in the process of implementing the quality system and while the company was growing 100%:

- ◆ Surface mount defects—DOWN 50%
- ◆ Hardware defects—DOWN 12 times
- ◆ Test defects—DOWN 71%
- ◆ Packaging defects—DOWN 87%
- ◆ Out of Box defects—DOWN 72%
- ◆ Scrap dollars—DOWN 90%.

These are not "soft costs." They are hard dollar savings that go straight to the bottom line. This is just a start, but it shows what a good quality system can do if quality is taken seriously by company management. Our three-year goal is to achieve a score of 700 points against the Malcolm Baldrige National Quality Award criteria.

If you have a viable quality group within your company, you may be able to launch your ISO9000 efforts by sending representatives to seminars, workshops, and lead auditor training. Include these costs in your startup budget. Also include time for them to observe successes in other companies and to continually learn about ISO9000, because the world of ISO9000 is changing daily.

If time is of the essence and you want to implement ISO9000 with a minimum of startup problems, then you will need a consultant[8] who has a number of successful ISO9000 implementations behind him or her or, as a steering committee member put it to me recently, "This ain't your first rodeo, is it?" A good consultant will help you get launched on your own as quickly as possible, and keep you from making costly startup mistakes. He or she will show you how to reduce cost and how consultants will pay for themselves many times over (spoken like a true consultant) in demonstrating the most painless ways to develop your processes and procedures. If you hire a consultant to do the entire implementation process for you, it will be an extremely expensive effort. The expense will not just be in the consulting fees. The big cost will be in the fact that you will not, in all probability, achieve your goals because the consultant will own the processes, not the job holders, and you will not pass an assessment audit. I use and recommend the "yellow pad" approach. That is, I have the job holders write their own procedures on a yellow tablet. The consultant can put their words into procedural format, but the people who do the work are the only ones who really know the processes. I also recommend that internal auditors come from the ranks of the workers. When people own what they do, they will do it gladly and costs will be minimized.

[8]We will discuss selecting a consultant in Chapter 10.

# ISO9000:
# The Launching Pad
# for Strategic
# Quality Improvement

I have visited with, literally, scores of companies that have started and stopped strategic quality initiatives repeatedly. Most of them have reacted to the latest fad, such as Quality Circles or TQM, and have been disappointed with the results. In every case, the failures were due to a lack of commitment and follow through. Most of the companies that had experienced successes in their strategic quality initiatives were motivated by some financial or customer-driven disaster that drove them to seek an alternative to *crisis management.*

If we face our human need for some form of significant motivation to begin self-improvement, ISO9000 can be the catalyst that companies need to kick their stalled quality initiatives off the launching pad and into high gear. Of the companies I have worked with, a few have embarked on the ISO9000 continuum for the benefits it offers as a minimal quality system. Most, however, feel the pressure from their clients in the form of questionnaires and requests for quotation that ask subtle questions like "Are you presently certified to ISO9001 or ISO9002? If not, by what date do you plan to be certified?" Some have even stronger motivation

such as "We are reducing our supplier base over the next year and we will be requiring ISO9000 certification of all of our remaining suppliers." It doesn't take a rocket scientist to realize that ISO9000 is here to stay and that it could become a crisis very quickly if your customers start dropping you from their supplier and bidder lists. I wonder how often the following conversation has happened in the last few years:

> The CEO calls the Quality Manager and says; "Hey, the marketing folks are getting a lot of RFQs asking if we are ISO9000 certified. Are we?" After the Quality Manager comes to attention and realizes his moment in the sun is about to come to fruition, he says; "No, J. W. Remember, we talked about this in the last budget planning meeting and you told me to study it some more and get back to you next year." The next part of the scenario usually goes; "Well, work me up some numbers and let's get this thing off the ground. Can you get it done by the end of the quarter?"

Those who understand the benefits of company-wide strategic quality initiatives live for the moment when we gather the doubters into the revival tent and have their undivided attention. If it takes an external threat to finally get them into the tent, then let's seize the moment. Once they have their receivers on and tuned in, it doesn't take long for the win-win scenario of ISO9000 implementation to convert the doubters into soldiers of quality.

## ISO9000: The Launching Pad for Continuous Improvement

It has become a cliché that all ISO9000 demands is that we write down what we do, do what we write down, and verify that we are doing it. At the end of the day, it really is that simple and we will discuss that in more detail when we get into the nuts and bolts of ISO9000 implementation in later chapters. Most small and medium-sized companies that I have dealt with have very little written down about what they do every day. If they do, it is a quality manual written by a "quality professional" for the quality

department. The only time anyone outside the quality department has seen the thing is when the president was asked to sign the first page. Many medium and larger companies have volumes of convoluted, cryptic, and arcane quality and operational procedures designed to keep the quality and process engineers employed until age 65. These epistles are usually locked away until a potential customer sends a survey team to audit their "quality procedures." I have found only a very few companies that actually have meaningful quality and operational procedures that reflect their day-to-day business and are used to train new employees. "We just don't have time for all that bureaucratic paperwork." "It stifles our creativity." "We need to be flexible to respond to our customers' needs." These are a few samples from my list of industrial-strength lies about why companies do not have documented quality management systems. Why is this so?

General George Patton said: "I only want to pay for this real estate once!" When I was in manufacturing management, I needed clear guidelines of how our processes worked so I didn't have to reinvent the wheel every week. I also didn't want to have to scrap my processes when the guy who knew the formula for our secret sauce quit and moved to South America. To me, simple, concise, accurate, and timely operational procedures are vital to any organization. Alas, my view is still a minority opinion.

## Building the Infrastructure

Given the resistance to documenting operational procedures, the first step in ISO9000 implementation can be the most painful. Who is going to write down what we do? The quality manager (or whomever the ISO9000 champion may be) is having cold sweats at this point as he or she sees another twenty hours of work each week on top of the sixty hours she now has. Conventional wisdom will usually lead to one of the following:

1. Go to ISO9000 lead auditor training school (one week, $4K) and do it all myself.
2. Read the ISO9000 "how to" books or go to a seminar and then do it all myself.

3. Get the usual committee of overworked managers together to do it.
4. Hire a full time ISO9000 coordinator and/or staff of auditors.
5. Have a consultant come in and do it all.

None of these alternatives is usually appealing, especially the ones requiring a big outlay of capital and ones having folks out of the plant for days and weeks at a time. If the ISO9000 champion is the only expert, he or she then has to do the work and train everyone. If an ad hoc management committee is assembled, the implementation process will be only as high a priority as the lowest priority grass fire. Again, if the managers become the experts, they will have to train everyone else. Hiring overhead people is totally counterproductive to the benefits of ISO9000 implementation. Even if you have a large organization with strict union rules, you do not need any more police officers on your staff. Having a consultant come in to do the whole thing will be great exercise for the consultant, but, when they are through, the consultant will be the only one who understands the procedures or processes.

The ISO9000 champion should certainly be schooled in the tenets and methods of ISO9000. In my experience, the next step is to seek out the help of a consultant who has lived the implementation process many times. Not only should that person have lived the process, he or she should be a facilitator in using the process as the foundation for strategic quality improvement. That consultant should have glowing recommendations from companies he or she has helped become ISO9000 certified. The referrals should speak not just to their certificate, but to the fact that the consultant coached them to new heights in productivity, quality, and teamwork. The agreement with the consultant should be to take you step-by-step through the implementation process as a trainer and coach and not have to actually move in with you and write procedures or make policy. The consultant should be itinerant, but high profile, until you have a highly committed team of ISO9000 champions.

The next step in building that team is to empanel an ISO9000 steering committee. This should NOT be the same group of managers who always get volunteered for every ad hoc assign-

ment. They need to be five or six individuals from diverse sections of your organization. They should be worker-level folks who have a thorough knowledge of their area and of the company. They do not have to be the most vocal and they do not have to have any meeting or writing skills (the consultant should teach meeting skills early on). They should be chosen because they produce results and they are passionate about their jobs and about the company. The "passion" doesn't necessarily have to be positive, either. A good steering committee needs a rebel with a burr under his or her saddle to keep the momentum going.

The quality coordinator will be part of the committee and the consultant should lead it through the first couple of months. Meetings should be no more than once a week and held to one hour in length. The committee will be schooled in ISO9000 and each member will be assigned responsibility for one or more of the nineteen or twenty key elements of ISO90002 or ISO90001 (depending on which has been selected). The consultant and ISO9000 coordinator may help to write the policy portion of the quality manual; however, each member will have at least one area that he or she must own. This ownership does not mean these people have to write the procedures, it means they will be the ones who seek out the experts in your organization and solicit them to write their own procedures, which brings us to the next piece of our success story.

## Vesting Ownership with the Job Holders

In my various assignments as manufacturing manager and quality manager, I never had a staff of process and quality engineers to write procedures. I did have the incredible talent base of the people who actually performed the processes. Who knew the processes better? Who owned them? Who used them? Who were the experts? Process operators don't have to be writers to scribble down on a yellow pad how their processes work. They would write out, in their own words, what they did. I would do the wordsmithing, type, and spellcheck the procedures. I gave them back a draft copy to verify that I wrote what they said. I then asked them to get with their co-workers and figure out if the procedures made any sense. After several revisions and a host of good ideas

to improve the processes, we had a real "live" quality manual or operations manual that the job holders owned and maintained. I did little but operate a word processor, facilitate, and coach.

In order to successfully pass an ISO9000 third-party audit, the workers in the trenches have to be able to demonstrate that what they do is documented and that they follow the documented procedures. How much more easy can it be to follow the ISO9000 cliché than to have the quality and operational procedures written (or rewritten) by those who use them every day? Here are the challenges I offer the troops to make documenting processes painless and profitable:

1. If you do not have clear direction in what is expected of you, you can't be fairly reviewed and rewarded.
2. If you have a better idea for doing your job, it can't be evaluated until we know what you are doing now.
3. You can't be promoted if you are the only one who knows how to do your job.
4. I am asking you to do it because you are the expert, not me.
5. If you don't have time to do it, how are we going to know how overloaded you are until you document what you are doing?
6. If you believe that there is an inequitable division of work, encourage everyone to document what they do so that it can be more fairly divided.
7. If you feel we are stifling your creativity, think of how much more creative time you will have when you don't have to process changes resulting from poor communication or incomplete and inaccurate documentation.
8. We would rather pay you to do this than help the consultant pay off his mortgage.

Read the list again, several times, because the first time through, the points might come across as trite, parochial clichés. They aren't. The challenges are real. They are right on the target for process owner buy-in. If you can't discuss these points with your workers, you have a more serious issue of trust and loyalty to work out. If they are involved from the very beginning, you do not have to train them on procedures that someone else wrote. You

*"Operations procedures? I'm not sure about that. Bubba showed me how to do this before he retired in '79 . . ."*

don't have to ask them to buy into your program. You don't have to be petrified of what they might tell a third-party auditor.

## Internal Auditing: The Catalyst for Teamwork

The third ingredient in using ISO9000 as a launching pad for strategic quality improvement is the internal audit. That which separates ISO9000 from more traditional quality systems is that it suggests verifying compliance can best be determined by continually auditing processes from within. Actually, it is more prescriptive than suggestive in this area, noting that audits shall be conducted regularly, their results recorded, and that follow-up audits must verify the effectiveness of any corrective action taken from previous audits.

Most companies use toll gate inspections and systems of checks and balances to verify that processes are operating properly. By nature, these are adversarial and punitive. They rely on one team member to find defects caused by other team members. Even in progressive work environments, where proactive steps are taken to vest ownership in processes with the job holders, variations on toll gate inspection wind up somewhere in the work flow. There is a strong paradigm that says you can't send the coyote to guard the chicken house, so someone has to put the final seal of approval on your products or services. Classic management systems also rely on management to enforce procedures such as document control and contract review. This provides job security for managers, but adds little to the value delivery system. It also does not lend itself to regular review of overhead processes, fostering empire building, redundancy, archaic procedures, and territorialism.

The process of regular internal audits takes an entirely different tact to verification. It says that, on a regular basis, each process in the value delivery system will be reviewed for effectiveness. This includes not only operational procedures within the product or service flow, but areas such as the operation of the quality management system itself, document and data control, and quality records. The process of internal auditing is nonconfrontational. It involves a team of auditors who use the existing process procedures as a checklist to verify that processes are being conducted per those procedures and that the results are verifiable. Internal audits are scheduled in advance, so they are never a surprise. Auditors are trained to stick to the agenda and not to use the opportunity to conduct a witch hunt. Both auditors and auditees are trained in using the experience as a catharsis to flush out latent problems in the system, not as a game of "gotcha." Audits are documented and any nonconformities are transcribed to a corrective action request that is formally processed. Corrective action takes the form of fixing the immediate problem, locating the root cause of the problem, and then following up to ensure that the corrective action was effective.

On the surface, this activity doesn't appear to vary dramatically from classic toll gate inspection. Some companies I have worked with have made it an adversarial overhead activity by ap-

pointing full-time internal auditors from within the quality department. What the Virtual Leadership approach does to make this a team-building function is to select internal auditors from the ranks of the job holders. Team members are volunteered on their ability to be objective and nonconfrontational, not on their technical skills. They are recruited from as diverse a mixture of the work population as is possible. The only selection processes is verifying that individuals do not perform audits within their own areas of responsibility. They are trained in auditing skills, specifically in how to ask questions that will determine the effectiveness of the processes being audited. They are trained to not let their personal experiences prejudice their objectivity. They are coached in not jumping to conclusions or assuming they know what is really happening before they have completed their checklist. They are trained to recognize the importance of this activity to the person being audited. They also fully understand that tomorrow they will be audited by a co-worker whose job is to help them be the best they can be at their particular job function. The Virtual Leadership approach to Internal Auditing has been proven to be effective in a wide variety of companies. Some observed benefits include:

1. The need for toll gate inspectors is diminished or eliminated.
2. Those who do the work become more responsible for the quality of their own work.
3. Job holders develop a deep appreciation for their internal customers,[1] what their co-workers do and how the whole system works interdependently.
4. Managers who do nothing but control people and processes can be phased out to work on more value-added activities.
5. Static processes become dynamic with new eyes looking at them regularly.
6. Team building and TQM initiatives receive a big boost in acceptance and buy-in.

---

[1]The concept of the *internal customers* is discussed in length in Chapter 10. It is the belief that each job holder has a customer who is the recipient of the product or service they produce.

# Success Snapshot

Magnetic Instruments, Inc., Brenham, TX
180 person precision job-shop machine shop

MIC was run as a patriarchy for twenty years. It was managed by fear and intimidation. It grew to command a respectable market share; however, quality and delivery problems were rampant. There was a major log jam around each month end at final inspection. The true scrap rate unknown and was hidden by the workers. The customers and employees were both unhappy.

A strategic plan was developed to replace patriarchy with a management team using ISO9002 as a platform. Managers developed their strategic quality plan on weekend retreats. They formed a management council that meets weekly and a cross-functional steering committee to implement ISO9000. They had the job holders write their own process procedures. They trained everyone in the quality management system and in needed job skills. They selected internal auditors from the ranks of the job holders. They developed a skills-based reward system. Responsibility for workmanship and production was pushed downward to job holders. The floor supervisors were turned into trainers and leaders.

The results were impressive. MIC achieved certification to ISO9002 in one year. They passed their initial audit with only three minor findings. On-time deliveries went up from 40 percent to over 90 percent in less than eighteen months. The scrap rate dropped dramatically. Workers are empowered and responsible for their own work and the log jam no longer exists at final inspection. The number of inspectors was reduced from six to two and the number of lead men was reduced from nine to four. Existing petrochemical service customers are seeking long-term partnerships. Their ISO9000 certification has also helped them land contracts in aerospace and biomedical markets. Their steering committee is now a process improvement team, and, after the second year of their strategic quality initiative, they have grown another 20 percent and are setting record sales and profit levels.

Internal audit systems work best when the entire quality management system is dissected into its functions and each key element placed on an annual calendar-based matrix. Noncritical functions can be audited annually. More critical processes should be scheduled for audit as frequently as good business sense dictates. The audit dates should be published annually for the next year. They should be no more detailed than within a month timeframe. To ensure the schedule isn't the whipping boy for all other schedules, it should be required that audits be performed within a two-week window of their scheduled date. Audit teams should be selected at random. I have had great success having the teams name themselves and rotate one member in and out each quarter. Depending on the size and complexity of the company, audit teams should not have more than four audits to perform each year. Formal audit training should be offered as an elective course as part of jobholders' ongoing training.

One final reminder about internal auditing: The nay-sayers of ISO9000 have preached that it does not specify that continuous improvement be part of the quality management system. I submit to them that, if you did nothing else in the area of continuous improvement, by auditing the entire quality management system at least annually, you cannot help but improve by building on the results of previous audits! When you examine each process regularly, there is very little chance that processes will remain static and not progress at least at the same rate your business and its culture progress.

If we go back to the ISO9000 cliché:

♦ Write down what you do
♦ Do what you write down
♦ Verify the results

Clearly the Virtual Leadership approach of vesting ownership in the job holders is a critical element in ISO9000 implementation and in strategic quality initiatives. The case study on page 64 illustrates the point.

CHAPTER

6

# The Structure of ISO9000

To this point, we've discussed the tenets of ISO9000 in generalities. We will now look at the International Standard itself and talk about how it is written and what it says. It should be noted that we continually refer to ISO9000, however, companies are certified to ISO9001, ISO9002, or ISO9003. Table 6.1 shows the relationship between the standards. More to the point, in the United States, companies receiving the RAB Mark[1] are often certified to Q9001, Q9002, or Q9003.[2] If you do not have official copies of these documents (1994 version), it is suggested that you obtain them. In this book, we will not repeat the verbiage in the standards. We will communicate, in plain American English, what the standards literally mean to you and to your company.

[1]Registrar Accreditation Board.

[2]Q9001, Q9002, and Q9003 are the United States version of the ISO standards. They are word-for-word the same, except for the differences between British spelling and American spelling of certain words. Q9000 is written by the American National Standards Institute and is available through ANSI or through the American Society of Quality Control (ASQC).

| Paragraph | Title | ISO9001 | ISO9002 | ISO9003 |
|---|---|---|---|---|
| 4.1 | Management Responsibility | ✓ | ✓ | ✓ |
| 4.2 | Quality System | ✓ | ✓ | ✓ |
| 4.3 | Contract Review | ✓ | ✓ | ✓ |
| 4.4 | Design | ✓ | | |
| 4.5 | Document and Data Control | ✓ | ✓ | ✓ |
| 4.6 | Purchasing | ✓ | ✓ | |
| 4.7 | Control of Customer Supplied Product | ✓ | ✓ | ✓ |
| 4.8 | Product Identification and Traceability | ✓ | ✓ | ✓ |
| 4.9 | Process Control | ✓ | ✓ | |
| 4.10 | Inspection and Testing | ✓ | ✓ | ✓ |
| 4.11 | Control of Inspection Measuring and Test Equipment | ✓ | ✓ | ✓ |
| 4.12 | Inspection and Test Status | ✓ | ✓ | ✓ |
| 4.13 | Control of Non-Conforming Product | ✓ | ✓ | ✓ |
| 4.14 | Corrective and Preventative Action | ✓ | ✓ | ✓ |
| 4.15 | Handling, Storage, Packaging, Preservation, and Delivery | ✓ | ✓ | ✓ |
| 4.16 | Control of Quality Records | ✓ | ✓ | ✓ |
| 4.17 | Internal Quality Audits | ✓ | ✓ | ✓ |
| 4.18 | Training | ✓ | ✓ | ✓ |
| 4.19 | Servicing | ✓ | ✓ | |
| 4.20 | Statistical Techniques | ✓ | ✓ | ✓ |

In the structure of the standards, ISO9000 is the guideline for selecting which standard is appropriate for your facility. ISO9004 is also included in the standard as a guideline for implementation of ISO9001, ISO9002, and ISO9003. ISO9001 contains twenty paragraphs in Section 4.0 (Quality System Requirements). These have come to be known as the "key elements" of ISO9001. ISO9002 and ISO9003 are a subset of ISO9001 and the relationship of the paragraphs and the standards is shown in Table 6.1.

The official titles of each standard are:

**Q9001** Quality Systems—Model for Quality Assurance in Design, Development, Production, Installation, and Servicing

**Q9002** Quality Systems—Model for Quality Assurance in Production, Installation, and Servicing

**Q9003** Quality Systems—Model for Quality Assurance in Final Inspection and Test

Although there appears to be a hierarchial structure to the standards, they are really designed for different purposes. ISO9001 is for companies that provide a total product or service, from design to delivery and servicing. ISO9002 is for companies that do not have design as a primary part of their business. Such companies might include custom assembly houses, branches of larger organizations, service companies, and job shops. ISO9003 is designed primarily for warehouses and distribution centers. Although it is popular in Europe, ISO9003 is seldom used in the United States. A company can move from ISO9003 to ISO9002 to ISO9001 as the scope of their business changes; however, there is no need to achieve ISO9001 certification unless design is critical to your product or service (ISO9001 is not *better than* ISO9002).

We will discuss the twenty key elements of ISO9001 because they are all inclusive. The same interpretations are accurate for ISO9002, except Paragraph 4.4 is not required. The same general interpretations of the key elements apply to most of ISO9003; however, some are abbreviated (such as 4.10, which deals only with final inspection in ISO9003). Again, I will **interpret** the twenty key elements, rather than quote them. These interpretations are based on extensive experience in how they are usually implemented and how certified registrars decode them. While there is some philosophical and practical variation in interpretation, I will attempt to cover most common applications. Keep in mind that the registrar who performs your third-party audit may have a slightly different spin on the ball; however, the information in this chapter has stood the scrutiny of a number of the major registrars. The entire business of ISO9000 certification is also still in its infancy and specific nuances of the interpretation of the key elements are being discovered regularly. At the end of

this section, however, you will be armed with a working knowledge of what it will take to design or customize your quality management system to meet the key elements of ISO9000 (Figure 6.1).

Paragraph 4.1 says that senior management should have in place a viable quality management system. The very first requirement of a quality management system is for the company to have a quality policy. This is usually one or two sentences that states the charter and value system that is the essence of the company. It is usually followed by several other bullets to form a complete mission statement. The quality policy becomes the focal point that all employees can use to define their primary objectives. On the surface it sounds like we are starting our look at ISO9000 with an arbitrary and banal requirement. Nothing can be further from the truth.

One of my clients is Microwave Data Systems. When they launched into the world of continuous improvement, we spent

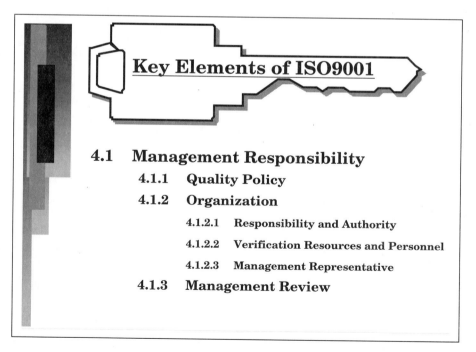

**Key Elements of ISO9001**

**4.1    Management Responsibility**

    **4.1.1    Quality Policy**

    **4.1.2    Organization**

        **4.1.2.1    Responsibility and Authority**

        **4.1.2.2    Verification Resources and Personnel**

        **4.1.2.3    Management Representative**

    **4.1.3    Management Review**

**Figure 6.1**

considerable effort in developing a quality policy/mission statement. In fact, the senior managers cloistered themselves for several days developing a policy that reads: "Microwave Data Systems is dedicated to producing the best microwave data radios in the world." I know what you are saying to yourselves; "The big guy is losing it if he thinks that parochial cliché is hot stuff . . ." It is, by design, a rote statement, but it says a great deal. First, the employees can remember enough of it to keep the spirit of it with them at all times. Second, it defines the focus of the company's universe. They build microwave data radios. If they receive a bid for a VHF data radio or a bid for a computer modem, they bounce it against the quality policy/mission statement to see if it is in the scope of their business. If it isn't, they either no-bid the request, or they know that they will have to add resources beyond those dedicated to designing and building microwave data radios. As their business grows and technology changes, they use the quality policy as a sounding board for strategic planning. It also says that they want to be the best. Every time an employee expends energy, they have the guidance of the quality policy/mission statement and give it the reality check; "Is it the best it can be?"

At Magnetic Instruments, their quality policy is "We will meet the customer's stated and implied requirements." Each time an employee mills a block or turns a shaft, he or she is required to ask him- or herself, "I know am I meeting the customer's stated requirements, but am I meeting their implied requirements?"

There is nothing more powerful than a well conceived quality policy and mission statement. If it is relevant to the organization's goals and the customer's requirements, it can set the pattern for excellence and success. If it is glossed over, the rest of ISO9000 implementation will be very difficult to keep in focus. We will deal with this at length in Chapter 7.

The second element of 4.1 states that the responsibility, authority, and interrelation of all those who manage, perform, and verify work shall be documented. This tenet requires a company to look closely at how each job function and each process in the value delivery system interrelates. Often, positions and processes evolve from crises rather than as the result of logical necessity. As you document your quality management system and begin to fit the various job functions and processes together, you may find

gaping holes in some areas and redundancy in others. This is a cathartic process that is one of the great values of the journey of implementation of ISO9000. Once you have clearly identified the players in the value delivery system, you must ensure that each has the authority and resources to carry out his or her assigned tasks and that no key processes can be completed without all required steps being followed.

The third section of 4.1 states that trained personnel shall be assigned to manage, perform, and verify work. This seems self-evident; however, training is one of the most often neglected areas in business today and ISO9000 keeps it a high priority.

Paragraph 4.1 goes on to state that management shall delegate a person to be responsible for the quality management system. If you do not have a quality manager (and it doesn't make sense to have a dedicated job function), the quality representative can be someone who has other responsibilities, but is also the guardian of the system. He or she will be responsible for ensuring that the quality management system is viable and continues to meet the requirements of ISO9000, and that the quality policy is carried out. The quality representative will also be the focal point for activities such as the management review. Speaking of which, 4.1 prescribes that on a regular basis (usually, at least once per year) the management team get together and review the quality management system. This meeting must be formal and documented. Most often, the quality representative will set an agenda that includes a review of internal audit activity, nonconformance reports, corrective actions, and customer issues. Management will determine, by this review, if the quality management system continues to be viable, continues to meet the quality policy and ISO9000, and provides a cost-effective basis for continuous improvement (I threw in the continuous improvement part; however, the agenda should point in that direction on its own). This should also be a time to review the direction the ship is headed and make any course corrections deemed necessary. At the very least, management should follow up on audits and corrective actions that they consider serious or have the potential to not be efficacious. This one meeting, done well, can be a vital role in strategic planning. At the very least, the management staff will be the first group audited by your registrar, and this meeting

arms them with the tools they will need to be audited. Chapter 7 details how to run an effective management review.

Paragraph 4.2 (Figure 6.2) deals with the entity I have been referring to as a *quality management system (QMS)*. It says that a company must have a documented system that ensures that products and services meet specified requirements. Unlike traditional systems, an ISO9000 compliant quality management system covers every activity in the value delivery system, not just inspection and test. In most companies, the only areas that fall outside the value delivery system are personnel and accounting. Everyone else is a part of the quality management system and the must know his or her role and responsibilities. It goes on to say that you must prepare a quality manual to document your QMS. This manual must ensure compliance with ISO9000 and the stated quality policy. The complexity of a company and its products/services will dictate how detailed this quality manual will be, but there must be such a document. The most successful

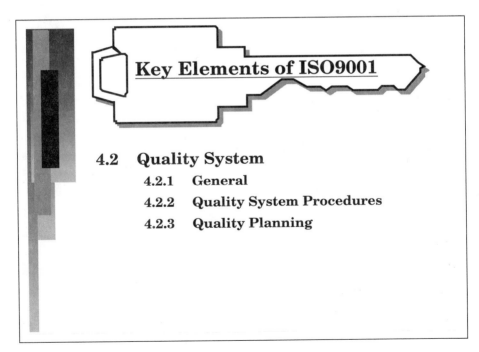

**Figure 6.2**

approach is to have a Level 1 Quality Manual that does no more than set policy. This document is submitted to your registrar as evidence of compliance with and understanding of ISO9000. It may be supported by Level 2, 3, and 4 documents, as needed, to fully document your processes. Again, these documents need be no more complex than is needed to run your company. If you build pacemakers or fighter jets, your process procedures are likely to be complex. If you deliver fertilizer, your procedures should be very short and concise. The examples of quality manuals enclosed in Appendixes A and B are examples of "auditor friendly" manuals written around the key elements of ISO9000. If you have an existing manual that works, you need only build a compliance matrix to show your internal and external auditors how it complies with ISO9000.

The final section of 4.2 deals with quality planning. It requires that you plan and document how you will meet your own requirements for quality. For many companies who build repetitive commodities or provide consistent services, the level-two procedures often are all that is required to satisfy the need for quality planning. These procedures document, in sufficient detail for skilled operators to follow, how processes are carried out. If your company is more dynamic, you may need third-level plans that are project specific or, are unique for certain customers or products.

Paragraph 4.3 (Figure 6.3) deals with how you and your customers agree upon what you will do for them. It simply says that you will document the procedures you use for communicating with your customers. If you use a formal system of purchase orders and/or contracts, you must document how those are solicited, received, and agreed to. If you use verbal or computerized order-taking system, that's not a problem as long as you document what steps are taken to ensure that what the customer requires is what you intend to deliver and that you have the capability to deliver it. It goes on to say that you should resolve any differences before the contract is agreed upon.

One of my clients buys and sells petroleum products. Often times, the exact quantity delivered isn't known until a tanker is unloaded. There are times when required dates are at the mercy of the weather and the delivery date is changed on the day it is

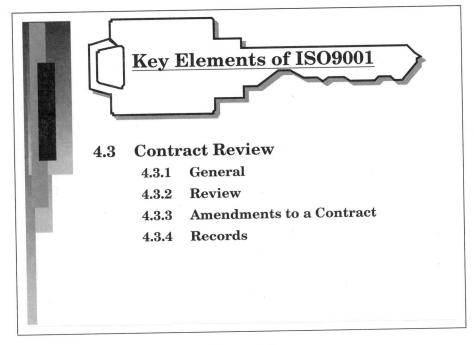

**Key Elements of ISO9001**

**4.3    Contract Review**

    **4.3.1    General**

    **4.3.2    Review**

    **4.3.3    Amendments to a Contract**

    **4.3.4    Records**

**Figure 6.3**

actually delivered. All of these contractual variations are documented in their procedures and are acceptable, because it is innate to their business. However you do business, you must document your procedures for coming to agreement with your clients. You must also document how you will deal with any changes that occur during a contract and how those changes will be communicated to the affected organizations within your company. If you deliver your products or services within hours of order receipt, this may not be an issue. If you have year-long contracts, changes may be constant and costly. Whatever is right for your culture, it must be documented, followed, and leave an audit trail.

Ah, the dreaded Paragraph 4.4, Design control (Figure 6.4). No other paragraph is so misunderstood and feared. No other tenet is singularly responsible for ISO9000 implementation efforts winding up on the scrap heap. If there is any part of ISO9000 that is perceived as prescriptive, this is it! I can't tell you how many times I have heard "You're going to stifle my creativity," or "You're going to double or triple development time

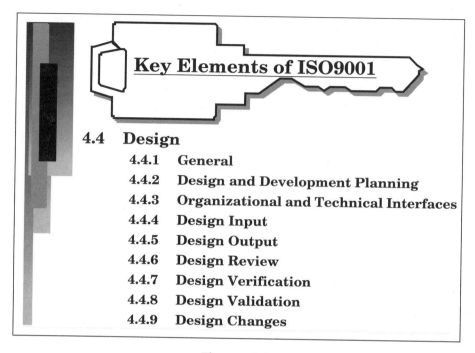

**Key Elements of ISO9001**

**4.4   Design**

    **4.4.1   General**

    **4.4.2   Design and Development Planning**

    **4.4.3   Organizational and Technical Interfaces**

    **4.4.4   Design Input**

    **4.4.5   Design Output**

    **4.4.6   Design Review**

    **4.4.7   Design Verification**

    **4.4.8   Design Validation**

    **4.4.9   Design Changes**

**Figure 6.4**

with all those procedures," or "This is a bureaucratic nightmare!" Traditionally, those who perform research, design, and development for a living have worked in think tanks, locked behind doors, and veiled in secrecy. Companies' creative geniuses are often labeled eccentric and temperamental. Outsiders are warned to go to extremes to put up with antisocial or unpredictable behavior. Suicidal tendencies would be evident in those who challenged a company guru in his or her area of expertise. Having spent some time in those smoke filled rooms, I can report that most of the mystique is a cover-up for R&D people not wanting anyone to know how many times they have chased their tails in circles, reinventing the same problem. Creativity is often synonymous with lack of discipline. Eccentricity is often a manifestation of a fear of being challenged.

Since R&D money most often comes from profit dollars, it would appear that management would want to maximize the effectiveness of this effort. ISO9000 offers a workable outline that establishes discipline in the design function to enhance its effec-

tiveness and minimize waste and redundancy. It does this through a systematic framework of design, verification, and validation. It suggests involving everyone who has a stake in the design and development process. It stresses design for manufacturability and establishment of formal steps of design process maturity. It suggests measurable milestones and documentation of all successful and unsuccessful experiments. It states that design changes must be controlled and point of effectiveness determined. This sounds like good business sense to me, not an attempt to impede your next great technological breakthrough.

Paragraph 4.5 (Figure 6.5) says that whatever documents or data (i.e., computer data) you prescribe as part of your quality management system should be controlled to the extent that makes sense for your culture. If you have controlled drawings and specifications, they must be cataloged, filed, and revision controlled. The same is true for computer software, industry specifications, even sales brochures that contain specifications and per-

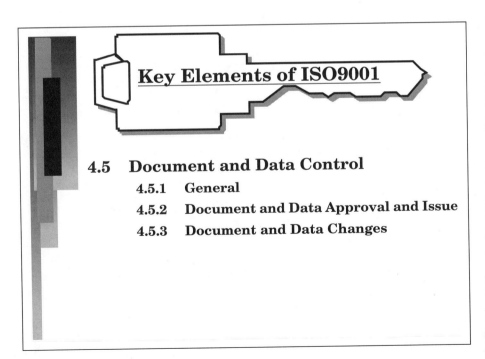

**Figure 6.5**

formance claims, if the possibility of using an incorrect revision or outdated document can affect quality. Forms that cross departmental lines should be controlled if their revision level is relevant. The quality manual and related procedures must be controlled as to storage, issue, and revision. Those who are responsible for generating and approving procedures and documents must be in the approval cycle for release and revision of controlled documents and specifications. When controlled documents and data are changed or revised, all functions that use the documents or data must be notified of the change and point of effectiveness must be specified. Sounds formidable, doesn't it?

Again, if the nature of your business requires you to use controlled documents and data, the system should make sense for your culture. I have clients that just leave the door to the print room open and let everyone make their own copies. They claim that this is a very cost-effective way to run a business because they aren't burdened with a lot of unnecessary bureaucracy. That theory holds water right up to the point where someone builds something to an old revision drawing because that's the drawing they had in the desk drawer. The rubber meets the road when a customer phones in a verbal change that makes the revision "D" product the mirror image of the revision "C" product and the telephone message gets lost on the back of a lunch sack. If you presently have no system for controlling drawings and specifications, Document and Data Control can be another tool you need to replace anarchy with discipline.

We are now a quarter of the way through the ISO9001 key elements and it's time for a reality check. So far, do any of the key elements sound like they are arbitrary, prescriptive, and demanding? Do any of them sound like paperwork for the sake of bureaucracy? Do any of them require hiring a rocket scientist? Don't they make good business sense? If you answered negatively to any of these questions, I suggest you go back and identify the areas you disagree with. There's no sense planning to implement the tenets of ISO9000 if they make no common sense to you or if they will require you to change what makes you successful. Before you scrap ISO9000 or fire everyone on your staff, however, please give me a call and we'll discuss it!

Paragraph 4.6 (Figure 6.6) deals with how you acquire the commodities you use in the value delivery system. If you use nothing more than office supplies to run your business, you can move by this section quickly. If you purchase components, assemblies, and supplies to support a production operation, then you need to deal with how you acquire those commodities in a uniform manner consistent with the nature of your business. Once again, ISO9000 asks that you document the system that you use to select suppliers, approve and disapprove suppliers, maintain control of suppliers and document how you generate and approve purchasing paperwork. This area often raises controversy because it adds structure to an area that many companies have left to the creative devices of anyone who could fill out a purchase order or place a phone call to a distributor. On careful analysis, an unstructured purchasing policy is often wasteful, expensive, and yielding a warehouse full of stuff that you have no idea what it was purchased for. ISO9000 suggests that you analyze the com-

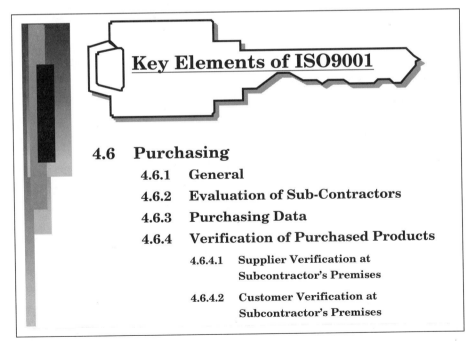

**Key Elements of ISO9001**

**4.6    Purchasing**

  **4.6.1    General**

  **4.6.2    Evaluation of Sub-Contractors**

  **4.6.3    Purchasing Data**

  **4.6.4    Verification of Purchased Products**

   **4.6.4.1    Supplier Verification at
               Subcontractor's Premises**

   **4.6.4.2    Customer Verification at
               Subcontractor's Premises**

**Figure 6.6**

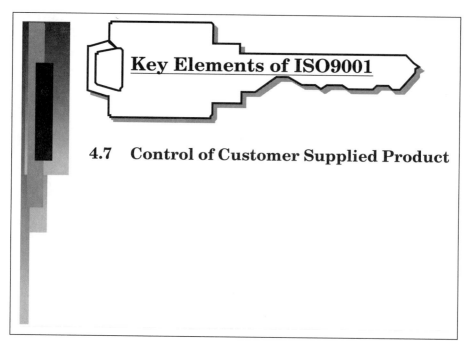

**Figure 6.7**

modities that you purchase and document a system that ensures that you get what you order, every time. It discusses in some detail the selection of suppliers and their ongoing performance. It does not prescribe formal surveys or reams of statistical data. It does require you to chose an objective system for supplier approval and then follow that system. The last part of 4.6 is called "Verification of Purchased Product." The title is misleading because it exists only to ensure that you and your customers reserve the right to perform on-site inspection at your suppliers, whenever that need is indicated.[3]

Paragraph 4.7 (Figure 6.7) exists to ensure that any supplies, equipment, fixtures, or parts furnished to you by your cus-

---

[3]In the 1987 version of ISO9000, this paragraph was often misinterpreted to mean that companies were required to verify all parts received against the purchase order requirements. This type of inspection is usually covered under paragraph 4.10.

tomer are handled with the same control that you would handle your own materials and equipment. This section has always reminded me of the old GFE (Government Furnished Equipment) paragraphs of military and aerospace contracts. Government equipment was always segregated and stored in bonded facilities. Those requirements always struck me as paranoia that a company would take government equipment and sell it as contraband or mishandle and abuse it. While there was certainly abuse of GFE, this paragraph of ISO9000 speaks to a kinder and gentler business environment. It is less prescriptive than the old mil specs and affects relatively few companies.

Paragraph 4.8 (Figure 6.8) is another common sense element of ISO9000. It states, simply, that you should be able to identify your products at all times. Literally, it means that you should have effective controls over the identification of piece parts and assemblies, from the receiving dock to the shipping dock, to the

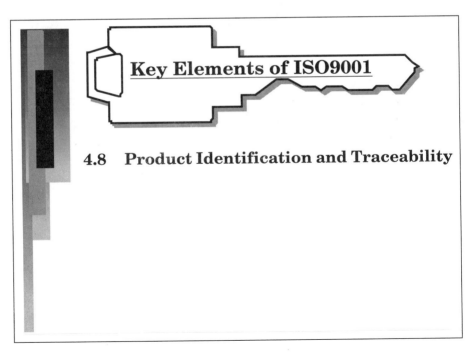

**Figure 6.8**

degree it makes sense for your business. This can manifest itself from high-cost, highly sensitive parts that have part numbers and serial numbers on each piece, to a bin full of wood screws with a size and length written on the box. Again, document what you do. Paragraph 4.8 also goes on to suggest that you have traceability of parts and assemblies to the degree that make sense. If you make heart pacemakers, you will need detailed traceability for each and every part so that you know who manufactured the part and have evidence that it was successfully tested. When I was training manager at a company that built expensive electronics assemblies used in oil and gas drilling, we started a system of naming the equipment with people's names and tracking them all over the world. "Sam" and "Janice" each had a book with their complete history, traceability, and repair record and the books were kept up until the equipment was scrapped or lost in a well. I have also seen many applications where the products were extremely inexpensive and noncritical and traceability was not an issue.

Paragraph 4.9 (Figure 6.9) will be the most voluminous part of most quality management systems. It deals with how you control your processes, and processes are virtually everything you do in the value delivery system. Soldering is a process. Handling an insurance claim is a process. Operating an engine lathe is a process. Developing a photograph is a process. Any activity that has steps that result in value being added is a process. Process procedures should be only as complex as they absolutely must be. My basic guideline is "Can you take a skilled person from outside the area and, in a reasonable amount of time, train that person to perform the process successfully?" If the response is positive, you have a good process procedure. If the procedure is too simplistic, you will have to use "cheat sheets"[4] to get the job done. If the procedure is too cumbersome, you will not be able to train someone in "a reasonable amount of time."

Paragraph 4.9 goes on to suggest distinctive treatment for "special processes." A special process is one whose outcome cannot be fully evaluated without destructive testing. An example might

---

[4]See my definition of "cheat sheets" in the sidebar on page 83.

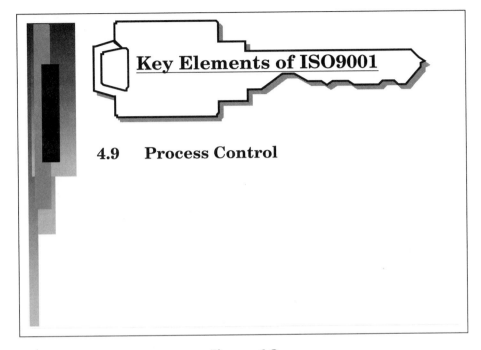

**Figure 6.9**

be molding a rubber tire. By visually examining the finished tire, it is impossible to determine if the rubber was mixed in proper proportion, if the temperature settings were correct, or if the pressure in the mold was within prescribed limits. In the case of special processes, ISO9000 discusses controlling the critical aspects of the process before and during the process. This might include logging the temperature readings or running a chemical analysis of the rubber before molding the tire. It also indicates that special process operators must be trained to follow the process steps as prescribed to obtain the desired outcome. Section 4.9 often becomes the training manual as well as operational procedures.

Paragraph 4.10 (Figure 6.10) speaks in some detail about the steps that companies should incorporate into their product or service verification scheme. Many words used in this element are fa-

# NEWS
## DIGEST

by Dirk Dusharme

## Avoid ISO 9000 Cheat Sheets

Cheat sheets, those invaluable informal notes, hints or tips that help you do your job, are the bane of controlled documentation, say ISO 9000 auditors and consultants.

"Cheat sheets are just another attempt to circumvent the intent of ISO 9000," says consultant Tom Taormina. "They're usually lazy work-arounds for inadequate procedures."

The problem starts when procedures are written by engineers, technical writers or a person other than the employee who performs the task, explains Taormina. These procedures, although under document control, may not include important set-up information or hints useful to performing a particular task. Consequently, operators often write notes to themselves on how a procedure should *really* be done.

For instance, a lathe operator might make notes on setting up a lathe for a particular part. The problem, says Taormina, is that these notes are often written on uncontrolled copies of controlled drawings, which stops ISO 9000 auditors dead in their tracks.

One solution is to let the process operators themselves write down how they perform a process, explains Taormina. It is then the engineer or technical writer's job to verify the operator's written procedure and incorporate it into an official document. Because the operator has written the procedure, he or she is more likely to take ownership of the job and always follow the procedure, a controlled document.

*Source: Quality Digest,* p. 8, April 1995.

miliar to those who have been involved in classic quality control systems. If conventional wisdom prevails, this section can lead to or reinforce archaic adversarial steps of toll gate inspection. ISO9000 does not mandate that a separate police force of overhead-intensive individuals be responsible for verification. Classic systems of checks and balances often bog down ISO9000 implementation, just as they bog down most manufacturing and service processes. I have had great success incorporating the verification steps within the processes themselves. That suggests that the process owner be responsible for his or her own verification. If a system of "internal customers" is established that requires each process owner to verify conformance before handing a product or service on to the next step in the value delivery system, the need for detective quality methods is virtually eliminated. Again, your culture and your product or service will determine how verification is performed and how accountability is established. Just keep

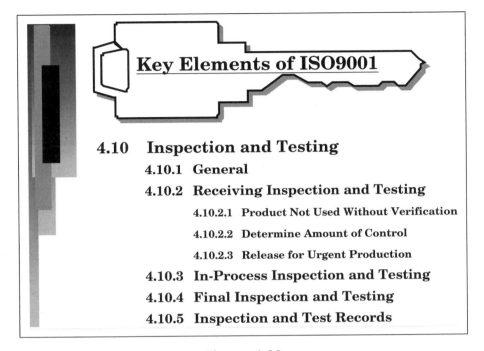

**Key Elements of ISO9001**

**4.10   Inspection and Testing**

**4.10.1  General**

**4.10.2  Receiving Inspection and Testing**

      **4.10.2.1  Product Not Used Without Verification**

      **4.10.2.2  Determine Amount of Control**

      **4.10.2.3  Release for Urgent Production**

**4.10.3  In-Process Inspection and Testing**

**4.10.4  Final Inspection and Testing**

**4.10.5  Inspection and Test Records**

**Figure 6.10**

an open mind when reading 4.10 because ISO9000 does not force you to perform any activities that do not support your value delivery system.

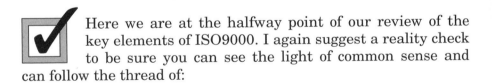 Here we are at the halfway point of our review of the key elements of ISO9000. I again suggest a reality check to be sure you can see the light of common sense and can follow the thread of:

◆ Write down what you do
◆ Do what you write down
◆ Verify the results

Everything we have discussed thus far supports those fundamental tenets. If it appears to be cumbersome or prescriptive, please reread those areas of concern, or forge ahead to the chapters com-

ing up where we will discuss practical implementation ideas and offer success strategies that you can implement in your unique environment.

Paragraph 4.11 (Figure 6.11) deals with another area of ISO9000 that affects different companies in varying degrees. If you publish measurable specifications for your product, you must have some method to ensure that the equipment you use to validate the published claims is capable of accurately reporting quantitative results. This usually manifests itself with various pieces of test equipment periodically having to be calibrated to standards traceable to the National Institute of Standards and Technology (NIST). It can also mean that if you sell your commodities by the foot or yard, your measuring equipment must be of known accuracy. The same is true if you sell it by the gram or pound. More subtle areas that fall within this key element are computers that are used for automatic testing and diagnostics and measuring gages that are part of the manufacturing processes. Comput-

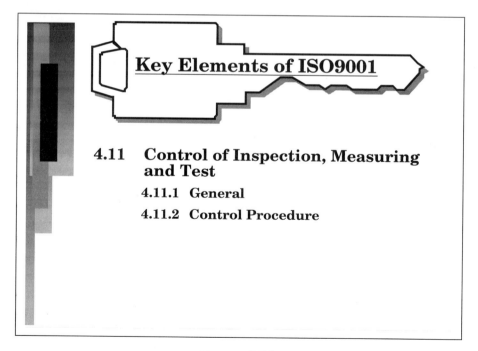

**Figure 6.11**

ers that are used for word processing and measuring cups that are used to put water in the coffee machine do not fall under these guidelines. I have witnessed companies that go to great lengths to measure their precision test equipment and then base the outcome of a test on an old power supply that has never been calibrated. ISO9000 causes you to take another look at how inspection, measuring, and test equipment are controlled at your facility. It suggests that you weigh the criticality of the measurements and tests being taken and then implement appropriate procedures to ensure that you consistently achieve your desired results.

Paragraph 4.12 (Figure 6.12) is another tenet of ISO9000 that appears, at first blush, either to be self-evident or not applicable to your operation. This section suggests that if you are going to inspect and test your products, that you should be able to tell, at any given moment, which inspections and tests have been performed and whether they were satisfactory or not. A classic exam-

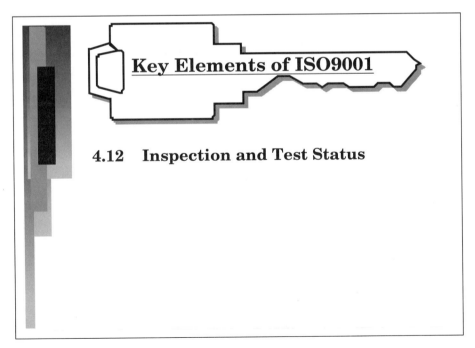

**Key Elements of ISO9001**

4.12   Inspection and Test Status

**Figure 6.12**

ple might be affixing inspection stamps to products that have passed functional test. Many companies use routing sheets to show the sequential steps of fabrication and assembly and each step must be signed off before the next one may commence. In a company processing insurance claims, there may be a check-off sheet stapled to the paperwork that indicates a process has been completed and the claim is ready to move to the next step. In more sophisticated operations, commodities and/or paperwork may be bar coded and scanned into a computer to indicate their inspection and test status. As with Identification and Traceability (4.8) this is a fundamental step in a functional quality management system that is often overlooked or handled poorly for the sake of expediency. ISO9000 makes it an auditable part of the system.

Paragraph 4.13 (Figure 6.13) deals with segregating nonconforming product from the work flow to protect the customer from receiving a defective commodity or service. The standard gives

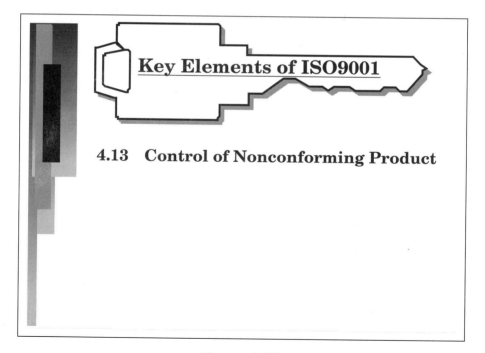

**Key Elements of ISO9001**

**4.13   Control of Nonconforming Product**

**Figure 6.13**

guidelines for removing a nonconformity as soon as it is discovered, expeditiously arriving at a remedy, and assuring that (if it can be salvaged) it is returned to the work flow in an acceptable condition. Once again, ISO9000 does not prescribe how this process is to be done, it is only concerned with auditable results. Under some of the classic military systems, companies were required to have bonded and segregated areas for nonconforming material. They were required to empanel formal material review board meetings to disposition the defective products. ISO9000 assumes that you have responsible employees who are anxious to ship only acceptable products. It does not require added-cost punitive measures because of human error or random perversity.

Every business uses some form of corrective and preventive action. Paragraph 4.14 (Figure 6.14) is one of the key elements of ISO9000 that, done well, adds a great deal of value to the implementation process because it gives structure and meaning to corrective and preventative action. Too often, corrective action takes

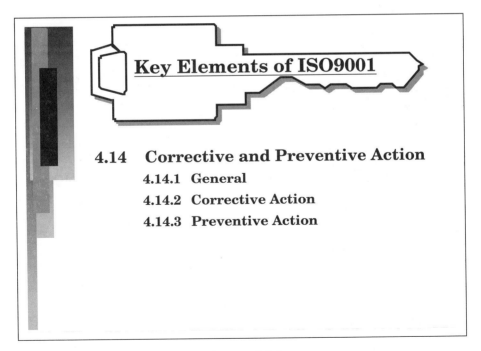

**Figure 6.14**

the form of "If you do that again you are fired" and preventive action becomes "I told you not to do that again—you're fired!" ISO9000 suggests that you define the need for corrective action based on the criticality of the nonconformity or deviation from procedure. Routine production variations are usually covered under 4.13, Control of Nonconforming product. Corrective action is initiated when the same nonconformity repeats itself or when it is the result of a process procedure breaking down. The degree of corrective action is directly proportional to the impact the problem has on your company or on your customer. The key to making the process successful is to document corrective action. By documenting each occurrence of corrective action, you can build a database that shows subtle trends of problems you never knew existed. This written data also provides evidence for building a case to change procedures or to take other proactive remedial action. ISO9000 also dwells on preventive action. We all believe that we take preventive action, however, unless corrective action is followed up, religiously and repeatedly, problems will continue to recur and cost you money. A good preventive action program will ensure that the same battlefield is not visited repeatedly. The data from corrective and preventive action is also one of the key indicators that should be digested at every management review meeting.

A thumbnail synopsis of Paragraph 4.15 (Figure 6.15) might be, if you are going to go through the trouble to build and test a product, don't damage it or lose it before it gets to the customer. The subparagraphs are self-explanatory and any good inventory control system will satisfy this key element. Once again, the standard disclaimer applies; these topics should be treated only to the degree that they make sense in your company. One company I work with loads tank trucks from railroad cars. They do not store, package, or preserve anything, so these paragraphs are not applicable to their operation.

Paragraph 4.16 (Figure 6.16) causes more findings in audits than any other key element. The reason is that it is overlooked or taken for granted. Hands in the audience: How many of you have boxes of records stacked in a corner of the warehouse that haven't been looked at in years? How many have mountains of records on top of an office ceiling that are about to cause a cave-in? How many of you could find a project file from three years ago in less

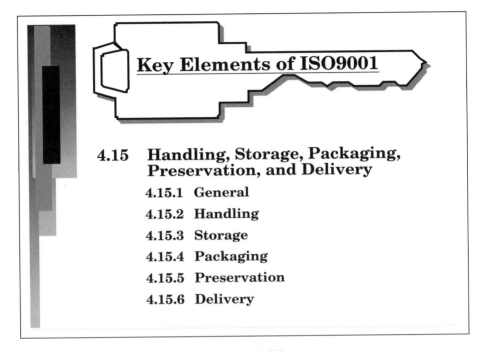

**Key Elements of ISO9001**

**4.15   Handling, Storage, Packaging, Preservation, and Delivery**

4.15.1   General

4.15.2   Handling

4.15.3   Storage

4.15.4   Packaging

4.15.5   Preservation

4.15.6   Delivery

**Figure 6.15**

than an hour? Earlier, we defined the Quality Management System as virtually every function in a company with the possible exclusion of personnel and accounting (I say "possible" because many personnel offices keep training records, which **are** quality records). The records generated in the routine operation of the value delivery system are all considered quality records. Records that are no longer active should be kept legible and retrievable, in case you should need to access them. As product liability becomes more of an issue, accurate quality records are about the only viable defense a company has. If you have a systematic process of retention and disposition, you should dispose of old records in a timely manner (evidence of properly disposed quality records also brings a smile to a defense attorney). If you do upgrades or retrofits of equipment or systems you produced in past years, accurate quality records can save time, money, and endless aggravation. Records that aren't legible and retrievable are useless. Along with Document and Data Control, Quality Records is included in almost every third-party audit.

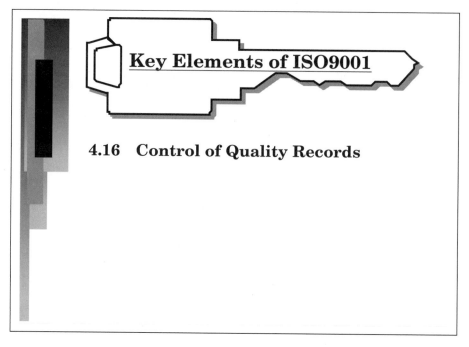

**Figure 6.16**

Paragraph 4.17 (Figure 6.17) is the third bullet of the three fundamental tenets of ISO9000:

◆ Document what you do
◆ Do what you document
◆ Verify that you are doing it

Internal audits are the secret weapon of ISO9000. They keep the players doing what they have documented or cause them to change procedures to reflect what they are actually doing. The word "audit" can strike fear in the hearts of most taxpayers. Unlike IRS audits, in the context of ISO9000, audits do not have a punitive purpose. Not only are you assumed to be innocent, but audits should never be personal. Internal audits are a review of process and procedures, not a witch hunt for individuals. They should never be a surprise and you can't be thrown in jail for failing an audit! Internal audits are scheduled and systematic. They

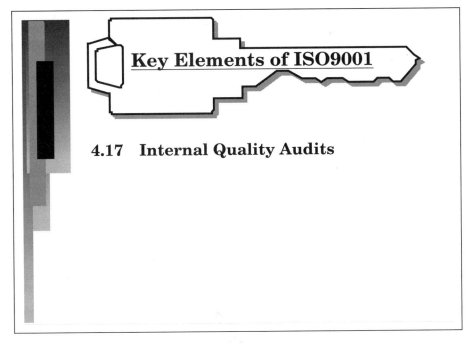

**Figure 6.17**

are conducted by trained auditors who are sensitive to conducting nonconfrontational examinations. They are documented. Findings are recorded and become the subject of corrective and preventive action. Common practice is to establish an annual audit schedule where each element in your quality management system is audited at least once a year. When you have critical processes, they should be audited as often as good business sense dictates. In Chapter 10, we will discuss how internal auditing can become an extremely powerful team building tool. It is such an important topic that we have included an entire internal auditor training course in Appendix C.

Many first time readers of ISO9000 are surprised to see Training as a topic in a quality standard (Figure 6.18). After all, companies hire trained people who were educated in school and trained in their former jobs, don't they? In Chapter 3, we dealt with the compelling reasons to begin strategic quality initiatives. Nowhere are we more negligent than in the area of training.

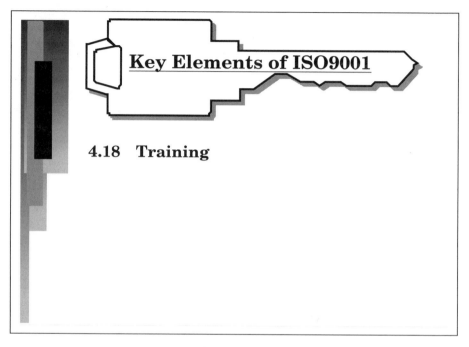

**Figure 6.18**

ISO9000 says that all personnel who affect quality should be trained. That does not imply that you must send a twenty-year machinist to school to become a machinist. It does compel you to verify that those who presently hold jobs actually meet the minimum training and experience requirements set forth in your procedures. It also implies that you must have a system in place to train (and/or verify training of) all new employees. Since ISO9000 is alien to most companies, a minimal training program for everyone usually starts with an introduction to the quality management system. Other helpful training might include "how to be audited," because registrars will talk to the working folks as they conduct their certification audits. The real benefit to establishing a training program is to help workers keep up with the quantum leaps in technology. There are computer-based systems that can be tremendous productivity improvement tools, when training is accomplished. These same systems can be a nightmare when operators are left to their own devices to figure out how to operate

them. Managers and leaders need to be aware of the host of new quality improvement tools available to them. ISO9000 can become the excuse you needed to get that badly needed training program (that has been postponed for the last few years) under way at last.

Paragraph 4.19 (Figure 6.19) is another that appears arcane and is seldom applicable. It deals with service contracts. If your company actually provides "service for hire," then you may have to deal with 4.19. I say "may" because most companies that offer service of some type usually document that service as a process procedure under 4.9. This paragraph is often misunderstood to mean warranty services. It does not apply to after-the-sale warranty-type service.

The final key element of ISO9001 is 4.20 (Figure 6.20). It simply says that if you have a need for statistical techniques, you should have documented procedures to support them. Again, ISO9000 does not require you to use control charts and sampling

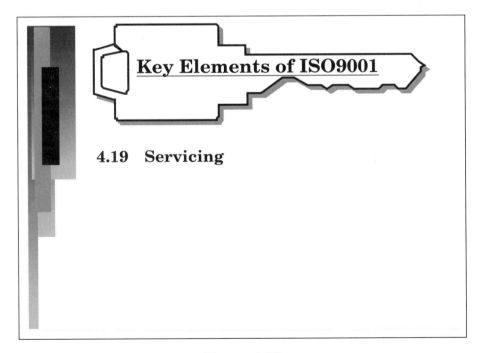

**Key Elements of ISO9001**

**4.19   Servicing**

**Figure 6.19**

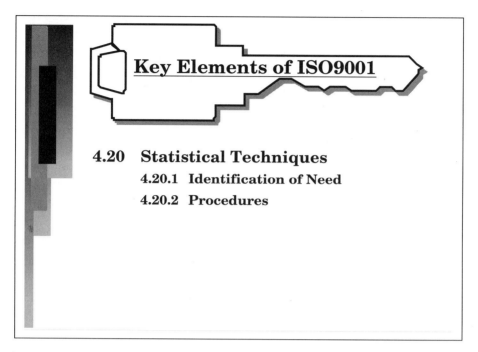

**Key Elements of ISO9001**

**4.20    Statistical Techniques**
   **4.20.1  Identification of Need**
   **4.20.2  Procedures**

**Figure 6.20**

procedures if they do not make sense for your operation. At the same time, I observe many companies making this paragraph "not applicable" when they really do need a family of measures to operate their business. Too many companies have the "bottom line" as their only statistic and, it is not only ancient history by the time it is available, it does not accurately reflect how you got there. As with each key element of ISO9000, you get to chose how your system runs. If you are in obvious need of data to support your processes, you might be challenged on this element by your third party auditor.

## The Rest of the Story

A review of the key elements of ISO9000 would not be complete without a look at how it all fits in the continuum of time and evolution. ISO9000 is not a static standard. Technical Committee 176 (TC-176) of the International Organization for Standardiza-

tion is a sitting committee with representatives all over the world. It is constantly working on interpretations of ISO9000 and planning for future revisions. The next formal revision is due in 1999 or 2000. TC-176 is also involved in regularly releasing supplemental standards that help with ISO9000 implementation. Some of the ISO standards that have been published include:

| | |
|---|---|
| **ISO9000-3** | Application to Software |
| **ISO9004-2** | Guidelines for Service Companies |
| **ISO9004-3** | Guidelines for Processed Materials |
| **ISO9004-4** | Guidelines for Quality Improvements |
| **ISO10003** | Application of ISO9000 to software |
| **ISO10011** | Standards for Auditing |
| **ISO10012** | Control of Measuring and Test Equipment |

Other ISO standards that are in various stages of development and review include:

| | |
|---|---|
| **ISO9004-5** | Quality Assurance Plans |
| **ISO9004-6** | Project Management |
| **ISO9004-7** | Configuration Management |
| **ISO9004-8** | Quality Principles |
| **ISO10013** | Quality Manuals |
| **ISO10014** | Economic Effects of the Management of Quality |
| **ISO10015** | Continuing Education and Training |
| **ISO10016** | Inspection and Test Records |

It must be noted that all of these standards, released and pending, are only to assist in planning the implementation of quality management systems and in interpreting the key elements of ISO9000. Audits must be conducted **to the exact wording of** the key elements of ISO9000 and those will not change until the next revision. As each of these ancillary documents is released, however, the nature of the beast is for registrars to modify and update some of their interpretations of ISO9000. As an example, before ISO10003 was released, registrars had to make their own interpretation of how certain key elements affected software. Now

## The Future of ISO9000

*Vision 2000*
 **TC-176's long range strategic planning group**

 • Striving for universal acceptance
 • Looking at current capability
 • Looking at forward capability
 • Looking at forward flexibility

that there is a guideline, some of those assumptions have been changed. When these guidelines are released, registrars will often take another look at a particular part of a quality management system using the new guidelines. The best practice is for companies certified to ISO9000 to keep abreast of what is happening in the world of ISO9000 either through newsletters, magazines, or via the Internet.[5]

That's the short range "rest of the story" for ISO9000. There is another group within TC-176 that is called Vision 2000. Their charter is to figure out how ISO9000 should evolve. They are looking at current capability and considering issues such as universal acceptance, forward capability, and forward flexibility. The are also looking at how much emphasis should be placed on adding continuous improvement initiatives to ISO9000. There is a lot of controversy surrounding keeping ISO9000 a minimum system versus upgrading it to be more exacting and of higher standards. Vision 2000 is wrestling with those issues, as well.

[5]Sources will be discussed in Chapter 10.

Moving from the world of the European Community and the International Organization for Standardization, ISO9000 has spawned a lot of change that forms "the rest of the story" in the United States. To begin, the Big Three auto manufacturers (GM, Ford, Chrysler) have released QS90000. They are compelling their major suppliers to have their quality management systems in compliance with this offshoot of ISO9000. The are also releasing TE9000, which they will require of their third-tier subcontractors. NASA has done away with their NHB5300 set of standards and replaced them with NASA-HDBK-9000. The Department of Defense is doing away with MIL-I-45208 and MIL-Q-9858A and has replaced them with MIL-HDBK-9000. The Food and Drug Administration is considering replacing their GMP Standard with their version of ISO9000. Who will be next? The Nuclear Regulatory Commission? The American Society of Mechanical Engineers? The American Pipe Institute? Stay tuned, ISO9000 is still in its infancy.

# CHAPTER

**7**

# *The Quality Management System (QMS)*

In Chapter 5, we brought together the tenets of Virtual Leadership and the tenets of ISO9000. In Chapter 6, we had our first look at the structure of ISO9000. In this chapter, we will begin to build a quality management system around ISO9000 and Virtual Leadership.

Most of the 280+ companies I have audited are either not satisfied with the effectiveness of their existing quality management system or they do not have one. Based on that sample, we will make the assumption that you are going to rework your QMS around ISO9000 or you intend to build a new system around ISO9000. If you already have a viable quality management system in place, this chapter will help you to utilize some of the Virtual Leadership tools to help enhance your present system. It will also help you begin to build a compliance matrix between your system and ISO9000.[1]

---

[1]In order to facilitate internal auditing and to minimize the audit time required by your Registrar, developing an ISO9000 compliance matrix is a valuable tool for companies with existing quality management systems and those who choose to structure their system in a format other than ISO9000.

## Definition of a Quality Management System

Since the definition of a QMS is new to most readers, it bears repeating here. **A quality management system is a documented system of policies and procedures that guide all those who can affect product or service quality in the execution of the value delivery system.** It is a structured approach to maintaining uniformity in products and services. It establishes a baseline system for predictability, repeatability, and improvement. An ISO9000 QMS can be no more complex than documenting what you do and verifying that you do what you documented. In a culture of Virtual Leadership, a QMS places the responsibility for the success of the company on each job holder. It assures a baseline from which to grow and continually improve. It is a foundation from which a culture of total quality can expand. It provides for growth and flexibility without having to scrap and rebuild the infrastructure each time technology or customer requirements change. A Virtual Leadership Quality Management System places the customers and the job holders at the top of the food chain. It dismantles adversarial systems of checks and balances and replaces them with a network of interdependent internal customers and suppliers. It is an archetype to dismantle ineffective departmentalized work and replace it with a seamless and efficient value delivery system. That all sounds like pretty lofty pie-in-the-sky from some post-graduate textbook. It really isn't. We will take these definitions and put them into practice, so let's begin at the beginning.

## The Charter

Many of you who are reading this are investigating for the first time the possibilities of implementing ISO9000 and/or a strategic quality initiative in your organization. Some of you are working in a system that is not functioning very well and you are looking to make some breakthroughs in quality and productivity. Some readers are CEOs and senior managers who are looking for help

in moving to the next step in their company's evolution. If you are reading this for the first time, then please contemplate this section carefully. If you are ready to begin implementation or re-design, then roll up your sleeves because you can't go much further without a clear charter.

Key element 4.1 of ISO9000 is entitled *Management Responsibility* and it deals with the executive's roles in the quality management system. The need for senior management to be crystal clear about their commitment to the strategic quality initiative is defined in paragraph 4.1. Freely translated, it says that they must provide a charter that will give the quality management system the authority to administer the value delivery system. It compels them to define the interrelationship of the players involved. It states that they shall provide adequate resources to allow it to work effectively. It compels them to appoint a management representative to be responsible for the QMS. Finally, it holds them accountable for the quality management system through a system of regular management reviews. ISO9000 requires that senior management be actively involved and committed. ISO9000 notwithstanding, good business sense dictates that all strategic effort be enabled from the top.

- What authority is going to empower your strategic initiative?
- Who will authorize your QMS as defined in ISO9001 or ISO9002, paragraph 4.1?
- Who is controlling the budget?
- Who will determine how much time is invested in this effort?
- Who will resolve issues of priority?
- Who is the enabler and the facilitator?
- Who can give you the road map you need?
- Who will be your champion?

That series of questions is not designed to find out who the boss is, you already know who sits in that chair. The questions are designed to help you acquire the tools you will need to succeed, not just obtain tacit approval from mahogany row. Let's look at the outcome that you will need to proceed.

### *The Quality Management System Charter*

1. Establishment of a perpetual Quality Management System that has the clear and unambiguous authority to direct the operation of the value delivery system.

2. Assignment of a quality representative who has the stated responsibility of establishing the QMS, maintaining it to ISO9000, and reporting its viability to management on a regular basis.

3. Management's definition of responsibility and authority for all those who work within the QMS and within the value delivery system.

4. Management's commitment to establish, enforce, and live by the quality policy and mission statement.

5. Management's commitment to provide the resources necessary to effectively operate the QMS.

6. Management's commitment to be the champions of the QMS.

7. Management's anticipated outcomes.[2]

How easily you obtain an effective charter will depend a great deal on where the impetus is coming from to build or rebuild your quality management system. One of the following scenarios is probably true in your organization:

> **It came from on high, Version A . . .** The CEO, President, COO, and so on, discovered the benefits of ISO9000, quality improvement, and the like, and he or she has directed that the company begin a strategic initiative. He or she is convinced that the future of the company will best be served by taking a leap of faith and this person is willing to champion the effort and lead the initiative.

> **It came from on high, Version B . . .** Same scenario as Version A, except the CEO has delegated the implementation to the working managers. He or she wants to be kept abreast of the progress, but will not be directly involved.

> **It came from middle management . . .** Some dedicated and motivated stakeholder(s) in the management or profes-

---

[2]Such as improved quality, reliability, new markets, and customer satisfaction.

sional ranks see a compelling need for the company to change course. They have studied a variety of success stories and have a proposal ready to submit to the head shed.

**It's a grassroots effort . . .** Some of the working troops, who are really dedicated to the success of the company, have taken it upon themselves to study ways to help productivity and quality. They have a plan, or want to recommend a consultant, or wish they could get senior management to go to a seminar. They've found a champion who is willing to take their recommendations up the ladder.

Which most closely resembles the culture in your company? If it is the first scenario, you are in great shape. Senior management has seen the light and is dedicated to moving forward. They may already have drafted the charter before initiating the effort. The second scenario is similar, only different. Senior management knows something needs to be done and may even have a direction in mind. They are viewing this initiative as something that they can delegate, as they would an R&D project or development of a new market. They have been in the revival tent, heard the message, but believe that they can change the way they do business without having to change what has made them successful. For example, if the company is a thirty-year patriarchy, you are likely to get permission to develop teamwork, as long as the CEO can still run the place with an iron hand. You may get a charter that reads very much like the sample, but item 6, *The Champion*, is usually missing.

In larger companies, leadership of a successful strategic quality initiative can be delegated to the level of management that has P&L responsibility for the operation. There are even some companies who have charismatic middle managers that can successfully take a surrogate role as the *QMS Champion*. In most companies, however, unless the senior management is a viable part of the QMS, it will not be very successful and it might cause the company not to pass an ISO9000 certification audit. As part of internal and third party audits, the auditors will talk first with senior management. The Registrar will be looking for a commitment to the quality charter, **and** he or she will be looking for signs of leadership in the QMS, as defined in ISO9000, paragraph

4.1. If there is not evidence of compliance and of commitment, they can (and do) identify a lack of leadership as a major finding and a hold point.[3] As a practical matter, management commitment and a clear charter are vital to the success of a strategic quality initiative. If you are trying to build culture of Virtual Leadership, all six elements of the charter must be present and viable if you are to succeed.

The third and fourth scenarios are very common. Their chances of success are strictly dependent on whether senior management will fall into the first or second scenario. About once every six months I will get a phone call that goes something like this. "The guys have taken up a collection to pay your fees and travel expense if you will come and talk to our boss about (Total Quality, ISO9000, SPC, Self Directed Work Teams). Can you help us help him or her see the light?" I always graciously decline the offer. You can't drag an unwilling subject into the revival tent. If senior management is not going to strongly empower a strategic quality initiative, it probably will not work. If they are willing to give you the latitude to begin pilot projects, then seize the opportunity. Do not be lured into believing that you can convert a manager to your new religion by demonstrating a few successes, however. We each look at our worlds with our programmed paradigms firmly in place and we seldom are willing to look beyond what has worked for us in the past when the new method is unproven. In Chapter 10 we will deal with some of the success tools that might help you obtain a clear charter. In the meantime, if you do not have the first scenario in your company, find a copy of Joel Barker's video *Discovering the Future: The Business of Paradigms* and play it every lunch hour in the executive dining room.

## The Quality Policy and Mission Statement

After you have a clear charter, the first step in implementing a QMS is to develop a Quality Policy and Mission Statement. We discussed the importance of the quality policy in Chapter 6 under

---

[3]A hold point is where the auditor has found a major problem that compromises the integrity of the quality management system and usually causes the certification to be withheld pending evidence of corrective and preventive action.

key element 4.1. Its importance cannot be overstated, so let's look at it more closely. Here is the quality policy and mission statement from the sample quality manual in Appendix B.

### 4.1.1   *Quality Policy*
*XYZ Company is committed to meeting the customers' stated and implied requirements.*
### *4.1.1.1 Mission Statement*
1. *XYZ Company provides turnkey services in electromechanical assembly, including a full complement of technical support, inspection, and testing services.*
2. *XYZ Company is committed to meeting our customers' stated and implied requirements. Our success is measured in customer satisfaction, not in profits.*
3. *Our employees are empowered to place product quality as their first priority and they are dedicated to shielding the internal and external customer from receiving defective materials.*
4. *Our success is based on our ability to look at any new challenge as an opportunity to excel. Our history is to find innovative solutions to impossible problems.*
5. *Our future is dependent on the partnerships we enjoy with our customers, our suppliers, and our job holders (employees). Only by working together in an environment of trust and respect can we succeed.*
6. *XYZ Company embraces ISO9000 as a platform for total quality and continuous improvement. It is the cornerstone of our company-wide quality management system.*
7. *We are committed to the belief that continued learning is essential to the mind and ongoing training is essential to the hands.*
8. *Our people are the Company. We provide a positive work environment, the tools and training to perform their jobs, and the support and encouragement for each person to achieve his or her full potential. We reward on achievement, not on activity. We learn from mistakes, not punish for them.*
9. *XYZ Company is dedicated to being a contributing member of our industry, our community and our nation.*

A great deal of thought and consensus thinking went into writing those ten paragraphs. The charter to the management of that company was to develop a set of principles that would guide the company through its daily business, through its key decision points and in its strategic planning. Let's look at what they wrote:

### 4.1.1 Quality Policy

*XYZ Company is committed to meeting the customers' stated and implied requirements.*

In all of its actions, this company has dedicated itself to not only meeting the needs stated by its customers (in the form of contracts, purchase orders, and specifications), but they will look beyond what the customer asked for and meet their implied requirements. For each job holder, from the salesperson making the quotation to the truck driver loading for delivery, they are constantly reminded to look for ways to give the customer not just what he or she expects, but also give the extra value that will delight the customer and keep him or her coming back for more.

1. *XYZ Company provides turnkey services in electromechanical assembly, including a full complement of technical support, inspection, and testing services.*

This mission statement clearly defines what the company does. It also forms the "Scope" for their ISO9000 certification.[4] It is a sounding board each time a request for quotation is received, to ensure the company is quoting services that it has the capabilities to provide.

2. *XYZ Company is committed to meeting our customers' stated and implied requirements. Our success is measured in customer satisfaction, not in profits.*

This paragraph reinforces their quality policy and it also states that they realize that profits are the result of happy customers, not the result of measuring the bottom line every month.

---

[4]Your registrar will ask you to write a "scope" describing the processes and services covered by your certification to ISO9001, 9002, or 9003.

3. *Our employees are empowered to place product quality as their first priority and they are dedicated to shielding the internal and external customer from receiving defective materials.*

As each employee carries out his or her daily duties, he or she can refer back to this statement for the empowerment needed to take all reasonable steps to ensure that the internal and external customers are shielded from nonconformities. There can be no excuse for compromising quality when individuals and teams have a charter this clear.

4. *Our success is based on our ability to look at any new challenge as an opportunity to excel. Our history is to find innovative solutions to impossible problems.*

This company made its reputation on being able to solve impossible customer problems with innovative ideas and techniques. They historically take on jobs that others "no-bid" and turn them into acceptable products and services. This paragraph perpetuates that spirit and ensures that everyone continues to look for challenges that makes the company invaluable to its customers.

5. *Our future is dependent on the partnerships we enjoy with our customers, our suppliers, and our job holders (employees). Only by working together in an environment of trust and respect can we succeed.*

They acknowledge the need for everyone to work together as team members and as partners. This reminder prevents walls from being built and it nurtures an environment of mutual respect and trust.

6. *XYZ Company embraces ISO9000 as a platform for total quality and continuous improvement. It is the cornerstone of our company-wide quality management system.*

This paragraph affirms the company's dedication to utilize ISO9000 as its platform for continuous improvement.

**7. We are committed to the belief that continued learning is essential to the mind and ongoing training is essential to the hands.**

This company discovered the power of training and learning as they were implementing their QMS and adopted a philosophy of continually training everyone, forever.

**8. Our people are the Company. We provide a positive work environment, the tools and training to perform their jobs, and the support and encouragement for each person to achieve his or her full potential. We reward on achievement, not on activity. We learn from mistakes, not punish for them.**

This company embraced the tenets of Virtual Leadership and included this paragraph to encourage all job holders to achieve their full potential. They also used the opportunity to remind the employees that they will be rewarded and not punished for taking risks.

**9. XYZ Company is dedicated to being a contributing member of our industry, our community, and our nation.**

So often, companies can become so preoccupied with the task of making money for their shareholders that they lose sight of the need to share their successes with the community that fuels them. This company chose to make a statement that compels them to give back some of the good fortune they have worked for over the years.

If you think these statements are banal window dressing, you'd best not begin the process of quality improvement. A quality policy and mission statement are the conscience of your business. They establish guidelines and boundaries. They empower job holders to be the best they can be. They eliminate the need to waste time making political decisions instead of making productive decisions. More and more companies that I visit issue their quality policy and mission statement to employees on laminated cards for them to keep handy. Even if they are used only to clean

up spilled sugar or scrape snow from a windshield, they are reminders of the value system that the job holders have become
trained to enforce and defend. A word of caution, however. These
truisms about quality policies and mission statements are only
valid if everyone in the company believes them and lives by them.
The first time management makes an arbitrary decision that is
clearly outside the scope and mission, trust will be broken and
the long journey of rebuilding will have to begin anew.

You can use the above model, but I encourage you to brainstorm your own company culture and take the time to develop a
quality policy and mission statement that are meaningful to your
organization and to your culture. To pass an ISO9000 audit, you
will have to have a written quality policy and you will have to
demonstrate that it is understood and followed by everyone. Your
senior managers will also have to validate them in management
reviews and they will be asked about them in your certification
audit. Why not make it the opportunity to develop a flight plan
that will take you into the next century with a dynamic and responsive infrastructure manned by motivated and empowered
employees?

## The Organization

The next step is to take a hard look at your organization and ask
some probing questions. Get a copy of your organization chart (or
make one up). Eradicate the names and just look at the job titles.
Study the flow, without regard to the personalities that fill the
boxes. Does it make sense? Does it work smoothly today? Does it
flow or is it convoluted with mazes and tiers of bureaucracy? Will
it support the quality policy and mission statement? Will it support the key elements of ISO9000 (as outlined in Chapter 6)? Was
it created by logical necessity or are there chairs established because someone needed a place to sit? Is the subject of how the organization is structured even open to question? Is there a job description for each job?

After taking your first hard look at the existing organization,
you need to look at the job descriptions for each functional block.
In building an ISO9000 QMS, job descriptions are a vital part of

the documentation structure. They delineate the credentials of each job holder and specify the skill set that is required to perform the processes associated with each job. With well-written job descriptions, process procedures can be extremely brief and to the point because they assume that the operator of the process is trained with the necessary skills to do the job. Take a look at Figure 7.1. Do your job descriptions read something like the example? If they do not exist, your job is to go to each job holder and have them write his or her own job description based on the example in Figure 7.1.

Now it's time for the rubber to meet the road. Take your notes from the reality check you did in the first part of the paragraph (Does it make sense, does it flow, etc.) and your draft job descriptions and let's do a gap analysis. The first step is to use

**Job Name**
1. **Principal function performed (outcome related)**
2. **Daily assigned duties (key processes for which you are responsible)**
3. **Weekly/Monthly/Quarterly duties**
4. **Other assigned duties**
5. **Skills and background required**

**EXAMPLE**

**Senior Chef**
1. **Prepare dinner meal as ordered by customers.**
2. **Supervise kitchen, purchase vegetables daily, keep inventory up to date, ensure kitchen is clean and sanitary.**
3. **Help plan menus. Help with decoration of the restaurant. Interview candidates for kitchen help.**
4. **Conduct internship program for new chefs.**
5. **Formal training of at least 3 years in a culinary school. At least 3 years experience as a chef or saucier.**

**Figure 7.1** Sample Job Description

the ISO9000 check list in Appendix E and compare your notes and job descriptions to paragraph 4.1.2, *Organization*. Does your organization meet the requirements as written? Identify the areas of clear conformance, clear nonconformance, and areas that are ambiguous. Don't worry too much about the *Management Representative* at this point—we will deal with that person in detail in a few minutes. For those positions that do not meet the requirements of paragraph 4.1.2 and those that are ambiguous, you will have to develop a strategic plan to make your organizational structure compliant.

*Whoa, big guy! I thought you said we weren't going to have to change the way we do business to become ISO9000 certified?* I come from the village of the truthtellers. The only way your organization will not meet the requirements of ISO9000 is if it has some elements that are ineffective, dysfunctional, or missing. These elements are vital to the effective operation of a business and may have been crutched in your organization, or they may not have been addressed and are causing you ongoing problems. The only way your organization might not be compliant is if it does not clearly define the interrelationship of the organizations and functions that affect the value delivery system, or if it doesn't provide adequate resources to support your products or services. If your organization is not firing on all cylinders, you need a plan to fix it before contemplating ISO9000 certification.

If you are implementing a cultural shift to Virtual Leadership, you have some more homework to do. You will need to look at each job description closely. How many of them are full of functions such as: "Prepare weekly production report"; "Supervise inspection personnel"; "Attend daily production planning meeting"; "Prepare monthly activity charts"; "Review daily production figures"; or "Reduce and interpret budget reports"? How many job descriptions add any value to the delivery system? **How many of them are VERBS (producing action) and how many are NOUNS (existing as an entity)?** You will need to prepare a summary of the job functions that are nouns and those that are verbs. Integrate this summary with the results of the reality check about the logic of your existing organizational structure. Revisit Chapter 4 for the basic tenets of Virtual Leadership and form a strategic plan that will be the archetype for your Virtual

Organization. Experiment with organizational structures that replace layers of overhead with job functions that add value to the delivery system. Go back to the job holders and find out exactly why each function is performed and eliminate those that are redundant, nonproductive, punitive, and prescriptive. Replace those functions with a culture that places ownership for the job with the job holders. Redefine each job description until it reads like the example in Figure 7.1 and contains nothing but verbs that contribute to the value delivery system. Use the tools in Chapters 9 and 10 to help you develop a lean and productive organization structure that will support ISO9000 and will be the model for your future success. Train your present managers to be Virtual Leaders, facilitators, coaches, and trainers instead of a group of meeting attenders and report readers.

## The Management Representative

ISO9000 says that a company will have an individual who is responsible for the quality management system. In larger companies that have the need for a *quality department*, the quality manager usually fills the job of management representative. In other companies, the management representative can wear nearly any hat, as long as that person has been appointed by senior management and empowered to carry out the quality policy. There is no need to have a full-time individual appointed as management representative unless that makes sense for your company. One of my clients appointed a senior commodities dealer as quality representative. Another appointed the warehouse manager and yet another designated an inside salesperson to the post. In all these cases, their clear mandate was that they would oversee the QMS and be responsible to senior management for its integrity (and perform their other job duties). Depending on the depth of resources in your organization, the early stages of implementation of a viable quality management system can place a lot of demands on the management representative. Most times, the implementors are chosen because they get things done, which means they are already burdened with a heavy workload. The management representative often spends a great deal of time pro-

viding the motivation for the implementors to complete their tasks on time, because they are burdened with their normal assignments. He or she may also have to keep the momentum going on mahogany row. Managers like to delegate and not be burdened with too many details. A viable quality management system has to change that paradigm and the management representative is usually the agent of change. The management representative is often the liaison with a consultant or has to become schooled in ISO9000 and/or quality management techniques. These tasks are also time consuming and burdensome until the benefits of improvement begin to outweigh the overhead of changing the ineffective systems of the past.

## The Steering Committee

Implementing a quality management system can be approached in many ways. Some rely on consultants to build their infrastructure. Some approach it as an engineering project, complete with milestones, design reviews, and PERT charts. Still others have the *quality department* design all the elements and (inevitably), force feed them to the other departments. In my experience, the most efficacious and cost-effective approach is to empanel a cross-functional steering committee. This committee will have the clear charter to implement the QMS and (usually) to guide the company through the process of ISO9000 certification. Its members are often charged with the responsibility of making sure that key elements are implemented and effective. They generally have sections of the quality manual and operations procedures assigned to them for review and revision, or to have them solicit authors where no procedures exist. The steering committee members will often become trained as the first internal audit team to review corrective and preventive action. The management representative usually heads up the steering committee, although a good consultant might sit at the head until the momentum gets going and the mission is clear.

The makeup of the steering committee is critical. I am always insistent that "the usual managers" not be part of the committee (you know, those who always get stuck with the ad hoc as-

signments). I suggest finding unlikely candidates from the working troops. I select members who are outspoken and who aren't, as long as they are dedicated. They must have a positive attitude and be open to change. They should represent the key functional areas of the company (engineering, production, documentation, purchasing, inventory, etc.). They should be an unlikely combination, with diverse personalities. I usually ask for candidates who exhibit a restless nature with the status quo and those who often suggest different ways of doing business. Of course, if you have job holders who have experience with building a QMS or with ISO9000, you might want them on the team. Avoid candidates with totally dominating personalities and those who will not contribute. Discourage management from being regular participants because they often intimidate creative thinking from the newcomers to meetings and committees.

Have the committee meet once a week for one hour. Be sure there is an agenda so that the participants will know what to be prepared for. Be sure that there are written minutes and action items and that the action items are the first order of business at the next meeting.

The committee's charter must be clear. It will likely include writing or rewriting the quality manual, coordinating writing of the operational procedures and job descriptions, reviewing and reality-testing written procedures, learning how to audit, performing internal audits, defining training needs, and being the champions of quality. The committee will have the authority to empanel ad hoc committees to help them with specific assignments and problem areas. They will often help select the ISO9000 registrar. When their charter to become ISO9000 certified is complete, they often form the nucleus of a continuous improvement team or of the group that keeps up with the audit and certification scheduling.[5] Selection of a viable steering committee is vital to success of the QMS and of the ISO9000 certification process. They can accomplish a great deal because the tasks are spread out around the company and not burdening any one overhead center. The members take the new information and culture back

[5]ISO9000 registered companies are usually audited every six months and recertified every three years.

to their areas and propagate optimism and sign up their co-workers for the quality movement. The process helps potential leaders bloom and flourish in an environment where they are empowered and challenged.

## The Management Review

Another powerful tool spawned by ISO9000 is the management review meeting. ISO9000 says that senior management will regularly review the effectiveness of the quality management system and this has most often manifested itself in the management review meeting. This key element of the QMS provides the impetus for management to set time aside from the daily business of doing business to look at what has actually been accomplished since the last review (aside from the financial reports). It also helps to ensure that the ship is still sailing in the right direction. The meeting is held at least annually. In my experience, as the senior managers discover how powerful a tool this is, they will schedule the meetings semiannually and even quarterly.

In most cases, the management representative prepares an agenda and the meeting is attended by all senior managers who have responsibility for the quality management system.[6] The agenda should include items such as:

◆ A synopsis of available performance data
◆ A review of trends in nonconformities and customer complaints
◆ A detailed review of internal audit findings, corrective actions taken, and preventive actions initiated
◆ A review of corrective actions ordered by the last management review
◆ A review of the quality policy and mission statement
◆ An analysis of the effectiveness of the quality management system

---

[6]Divisions of larger companies need only include those managers with P&L responsibility for the division or facility being reviewed.

◆ Plans for continuous improvement activities
◆ Unveiling new business opportunities and objectives
◆ Assignment of action items and corrective action

The meetings are most effective when held off site and under a gag order (no incoming or outgoing phone calls during the meeting, no beeping pagers or cell phones). A ground rule I always suggest is that everyone check their badge of rank at the door and approach the review as a team that is going to optimize the effectiveness of the business (without fear of reprisal). Smaller companies may require only 4 hours for a management review meeting. Others may go a day or two, depending on the amount on the agenda and the scope of responsibility of the management group.

When performing an assessment audit, the ISO9000 auditors will usually interview the senior managers first. They will be looking for objective evidence that senior management has empowered the quality management system and that they review its effectiveness. Before initial assessment, I often schedule at least two management reviews. The first becomes an awareness ses-

## Success Snapshot

### Agenda for a Successful Management Review
Larry DePaoli, Management Representative
Morton International

Assemble statistical results from internal audits, corrective and preventive action, nonconforming product, employee suggestions, customer complaints and suggestions, etc. Review your quality policy. Use the measures you have available in order to determine how well you have complied to the quality policy. Review the annual quality plan. Use the measures you have available in order to determine how well you followed the plan. Highlight any extraordinary data from the above reviews. Record the results of the review. Use your corrective action procedures to deal with any nonconformances found in the review.

sion where the managers learn of the depth of their involvement in running the QMS. The second gets down to the business of actually determining effectiveness and initiating any corrective action needed.

As with many of the tenets of developing a quality management system, if you already practice strategic planning and systems review, a management review will be an integral part of your culture. If you are beginning your strategic quality initiative with ISO9000, the management review will be awkward at first. There will be resistance to spending the time when "the managers already know how the company is performing," until they find out that the monthly or quarterly report is only one small indicator of business performance.

We have now defined the basic components of a quality management system. In Chapter 8, we will look at some of the tools available to Virtual Leaders and quality professionals and in Chapter 9, we will bring it all together in a strategic implementation plan.

# CHAPTER

# 8

# *Quality Improvement Tools*

In this chapter, we will take a brief look at some of the tools available to implementors of ISO9000 and of strategic quality initiatives. We will not attempt to define *how* to use each of these instruments because there are many fine texts in print that can give you a nuts-and-bolts approach to implementing specific tools.[1] We will give you a universe of what is available, the application, and the strengths and weakness of each.

It should also be noted that a number of these tools can wind up being a strategic quality initiative in and of themselves and lose their meaning and purpose. In my experience, companies have become preoccupied with Statistical Process Controls (SPC), Just-In-Time (JIT), or Quality Function Deployment (QFD) and lost the focus of **why** they were using the tools. I have seen quality departments attempt to implement SPC in every conceivable area of a company and then spend all of their energies reducing

---

[1]Prentice Hall, One Lake St, Upper Saddle River, NJ 07458, 800-382-3419
Quality Press, P.O. Box 3005, Milwaukee, WI 53201, 800-248-1946
Productivity Press, P.O. Box 13390, Portland, OR 97213, 800-394-6868

and interpreting data, instead of running a quality management system. Please remember that each of these is a tool that has its place and should only be implemented to the degree that supports your goals and culture.

## Problem-Solving or Idea-Gathering Techniques

### Brainstorming

One of the most effective ways to solve problems, begin strategic initiatives, or stimulate new ideas is a brainstorming session, usually comprised of six to ten individuals in a meeting room, with a specific agenda and time period. The participants all have a vested interest in the topic being brainstormed and one is appointed scribe and moderator. When the outcome is clearly defined, each participant, in order, gives a spontaneous suggestion. The scribe records the inputs on a flip chart or white board. There is no discussion, criticism, or editing of the input. Answers must be candid, rapid fire, and continue around the room until there are no more inputs. Once there are no more inputs, the group ranks the ideas in any hierarchial order that yields the five to ten best answers. These become the foundation for moving forward with the initiative or for creating an action item list. Brainstorming encourages everyone to contribute without fear of ridicule. It stimulates creative thinking because the members fuel ideas for others in the group. It is a good start in *consensus thinking*, which is the key to viable business systems. Its drawbacks are only in the rules not being followed and the sessions becoming a nonproductive free-for-all. There is also a danger, if the members personalities are so much alike that "group think" takes over, that no original ideas are stimulated.

### Consensus Thinking

One of the legacies inherited from labor unions is the idea of reaching agreement by *compromise*. In a collective bargaining agreement, everyone gives and takes a little until there is an effective stalemate and everyone goes away equally dissatisfied.

The compromise contains bits and pieces of activities that are successful on their own, but totally unproven when married together. I analogize compromise to not being able to decide what to have for dinner and eating a little chop suey, pizza, coleslaw, and tacos all at the same meal. By themselves, each is okay, but together, they are unpalatable. Consensus thinking is often the outcome of brainstorming. As each approach to an issue is discussed, the pros and cons are weighed. The field of possible avenues of action is narrowed down to the few best ideas. To reach consensus, the group picks the one idea that is most agreeable to the group. Those who oppose it must agree to throw their full support behind the consensus idea chosen until it has had a fair chance to succeed or fail. With everyone pulling in the same direction around a plan that is known to be viable, chances of success are much greater than in a compromise. A down side to consensus thinking is when there are one or two strong personalities driving the decision. Instead of consensus, you stand the chance of winding up with dictatorship.

## Nominal Group Technique

NGT has a lot in common with brainstorming and consensus thinking, except that it is more private and scientific. Ideas are generated by a group in the form of anonymous written submissions. When all the ideas are received, they are posted on a flip chart or white board and each of their relative merits is discussed. After the discussion period, each idea is secretly ranked. The ballots are collected and the scores tabulated. The ideas are placed in rank order and the highest scoring is usually the solution recommended or adopted. This technique works well where there are a few dominant personalities who want to have only their ideas aired. It can stimulate some interesting ideas. Its limitation falls in using strictly a numerical score to determine outcome.

## Benchmarking

This relatively new tool is a radical departure from conventional wisdom when it comes to problem solving and process improvement. Benchmarking is defined as measuring your processes and

practices against the processes and practices of companies recognized to be the industry leaders or "best in class." If you wanted to upgrade your accounting system, instead of reading books and attending accounting seminars, you would seek out companies that were recognized for their outstanding accounting practices. You would then find one that was willing to host you and show you how their system evolved and how it works. You would then take the information and model your system around the best of the best.

It is interesting that benchmarking has become so popular in American business. It requires companies opening their doors (and often their records) to other companies, with no apparent direct benefit to the host company. The reason for its success is that companies that host benchmarking efforts are also seeking out companies to benchmark with as part of their own continuous improvement efforts. As benchmarking partnerships and networks grow,[2] there is a mutual benefit derived and the win-win scenario is encouraged. The downside to benchmarking is that it can be a very costly process with an uncertain outcome (you may not find what you are looking for!). Benchmarking is only as good as the measures you have established. If you have selected the wrong data to measure, your efforts will be in vain. Benchmarking is also a continuous process. It is not a cost-effective approach to putting out grass fires.

## Quality Function Deployment (QFD)

QFD is another relatively new tool to help resolve difficult problems. It is sometimes called a *house of quality* because it is graphically represented with an X-Y matrix resembling a house. The Y axis usually contains the various components of a process (the *what*). The X axis contains how those components are used (the *how*). The intersection of each X and Y coordinate is called a relationship matrix. The roof of the house is called a correlation matrix. The bottom usually has a place for scoring and ranking the results. Without getting into a great deal of detail, an example

---

[2]The American Productivity and Quality Center in Houston sponsors the leading benchmarking network called the International Benchmarking Clearing House. Membership is open to companies only.

that was used in the QFD course I attended may shed some light on how it is used.

An automaker was working on the design of the outside mirrors on an automobile. Outside mirrors are necessary from a safety standpoint, but they are often unsightly and they are an appendage that disrupts the sleek lines of a car. The matrix was constructed with all of the various attributes of an outside mirror down the Y axis and all of the ways to accomplish the task across the X axis. The QFD matrix was built around what was possible, what the customers would accept, and what was cost effective. Everyone from the customer to the design engineers had input into the matrix. At the end, they had a very scientific model for what they could and could not do with outside mirrors on their cars.

The downside to QFD is that it is extremely complex to operate. Each practitioner must be schooled in how the matrix works and how to operate it. It can also be very expensive. One of my clients flew customers from all over the world to help them build the QFD matrix. The process was to decide on what new products to build. It involved thousands of man hours of work on top of the travel expenses for their clients, and the company management did not accept the result of the study!

## Design of Experiments (DOE)

DOE (sometimes called Taguchi techniques) is a specific technique used to develop and/or improve products and services. It is a very structured scientific approach to maximizing design and improvement processes. Although it is rich in statistics and scientific proofs, it is built to provide managers empirical data from which they can make sound business decisions about new products or upgrading existing services. While the actual technique is too complex to outline here, those who deal in highly technical issues will want to explore DOE more deeply before deciding if it is a viable quality tool for their arsenal.[3]

---

[3]There is a valuable primer on DOE entitled "Staying on Target with Design of Experiments" on page 63, *Quality Digest,* December, 1994.

## Information Presentation and Analysis

Many of the tools presented in this section are considered statistical process controls (SPC). That is, they are used as statistical indicators of the effectiveness of processes.

### Flow Chart

Flow-charting is an extremely effective method for visually displaying how a particular process works. It uses symbols to define key events and decision points and uses interconnecting lines to show process flow. It is a logical picture of the events in a process and how they are performed. The process of drawing a flow chart is often very helpful in working through the logic of a situation in order to be able to visually display it. Well constructed flow charts can replace pages of written procedures. They can be used in group sessions to work through issues and to improve processes. The down side to flow charts is that they are not universally understood and you must know the capabilities of your audience before making flow charts a common tool. Nontechnical organizations may find flow charts too difficult to use.

### Cause-and-Effect (Fishbone) Diagrams

Cause-and-effect diagrams are laid out to look like a fish skeleton. Along the backbone are spines that contain all definable causes of a particular problem. The problems are listed from left to right and the head winds up being the *effect,* or the key issue, on the far right of the diagram. In group problem solving, each cause can be dissected and all contributing factors listed. The net result is usually a fairly complicated collection of information. Again, these diagrams are very useful in a group because they are very visual. Many will find difficulty using all the information provided. Also, the data will often have to be transcribed into a list of action items before it can be distributed and utilized.

### Run Charts

Run charts are any type of visual presentation of measurements versus time presented in an X-Y graphic format. Run charts can use lines, data points, or bars to indicate relative measures. They

are often used to display variations, trends, or lack thereof. They are used to plot actual data or averages. In each case, the axes are selected to best depict the data being presented and the dramatic result to be presented. For instance, a cycle count run chart would display inventory accuracy percentage up the Y axis and weeks or months along the X axis. If your desire was to show a stable process, your Y axis might be scaled 0 to 100 percent with your cycle count running between 90 and 95 percent accuracy. If you wanted to show the variations in monthly accuracy, you might want to make the Y axis scale 90 to 100 percent. Run charts are very common because they are contained in many spreadsheet, database, and word processing software packages. By constructing a simple spreadsheet of information, powerful software packages can design exotic run charts in a few key strokes. They can be seamlessly imported into documents and used in report presentations. The down side to run charts is that they can be designed to display the same data favorably and unfavorably, depending on the author's desired result. They can be misleading when trends and averages are used to plot processes that are out of control or have wide swings in performance.

## Control Charts

Control charts are a variation of run charts. They contain upper and lower control limits that are statistically determined to show the boundaries of acceptability of a particular process. They have a very narrow use; that is, to monitor consistency of processes and to show when and how often processes move out of control. They might be used, for instance, by a lathe operator turning down shafts. He or she would plot critical dimensions on a control chart for each piece as they are machined. As the tooling started to wear, the operator would see a trend develop toward one of the control limits. As the control limit was approached, the tooling could be replaced. If the data became erratic, there might be a material problem to investigate or a worn part on the machine to replace. Control charts can be very "math intensive" and should be carefully studied before use. The operators and those reviewing the data must be thoroughly trained in data collection, chart use, and interpretation.

## Pareto Chart

A Pareto chart is another specialized run chart. It is intentionally biased to show data in a "highest to lowest" or "worst to best" format to help prioritize which issues should receive the most attention or highest priority. A Pareto chart is usually a bar chart that has had the data sorted from left to right in order of diminishing importance. It graphically highlights the most significant data and gives a visual comparison of relative degree of importance to the other data on the chart. The down side to a Pareto chart is it does not emphasize the number of lesser problems shown on the chart. You may have one giant problem that can be resolved quickly and a hundred smaller problems that will take months to fix. The Pareto chart will only highlight the giant problem.

## Histograms

Another bar chart representation of X-Y data is the histogram. Unlike the Pareto chart, a histogram shows the distribution of a universe of data. A histogram displays the occurrences of events and the variability in a process. A large amount of raw data is first categorized into boundaries. The number of occurrences within each boundary is then plotted. As an example, you may want to plot the physical height of each member of your graduating class. You might categorize the data as: under 5′, 5′1″ to 5′3″, 5′4″ to 5′6″, 5′7″ to 5′9″, 5′10″ to 6′, and over 6′. You would then fit everyone in the class into one of the categories. The Y axis would be the number of people and the X axis would be your categories. The bar chart would, in all probability, show large numbers in the 5′4″ to 5′6″ and 5′7″ to 5′9″ and smaller numbers in the other categories. Like Pareto charts, histograms are very visual. They play well in public presentations or in reports. The downside to histograms is that they are a very relative comparison. They should not be used on face value to make precise determinations, unless the data used is categorized very precisely and in small steps.

## Scatter Diagram

Still another X-Y presentation tool is the scatter diagram. It plots two independent variables along the axes with single dots and allows the user to look for areas of correlation between the two vari-

ables. An example might be an analysis of the number of thunderstorms in your town and the average outside temperature. You might plot the number of storms on the Y axis and the average temperature on the X axis for a year and look for the trends. Once again, your data analysis will be very visual and not very precise. The appearance of the data may vary greatly with the number of data points and the scales selected. The amount of empirical data that you can extract from a scatter diagram is very limited.

## Stratification

This tool may be used in many X-Y chart presentations. It is a technique to present the data more precisely than can be shown on a simple X-Y chart. It takes complex data and depicts the elements that make it up by adding additional layers of data to a chart. For instance, if you were plotting the number of traffic accidents per year in your state, you might show the number per month on the Y axis and the months on the X axis. This might show the rise in accidents around the holidays, or a positive or negative trend, but little else. Instead of just showing the total number, you might include the major categories, such as DUI, weather, or mechanical failure below the main graph to show the components of the data plotted. The downside to stratification is that it can get very busy and you can quickly lose the readability of your chart.

## Pie Chart

A frequently used visual tool is the pie chart. It cuts segments out of a circle in relative proportion to the size of the circle. For example, a pie chart might be used to show the various agencies that receive monies from the federal budget. The Social Security System would stand out as a large piece of the pie, while other recipients might be much smaller wedges. The pie chart is another very visual tool, usually chosen to make dramatic comparisons in management level reports. It has little scientific or statistical use.

## Force Field Analysis

A lesser known and lesser used tool is the force field analysis. It is comprised of two lists. One is the forces driving a situation and the other is the forces restraining a situation. It is not unlike a list of positive and negative attributes you might make in decision making. If you did a force field analysis of "getting to work on time" you might have lists like the following:

| *Driving* | *Restraining* |
|---|---|
| Keeping your job | Like to sleep late |
| Pressure from co-workers | Stay up working on home computer |
| Customers' needs | Spouse gets home at midnight |

As you complete the lists, the information compels you to closely analyze the pros and cons. It helps you to set priorities and assign relative values to the forces. It should help you decide which forces are dominant and what actions you believe to be appropriate, based on the data. Force field analysis works well in group decision-making activities. As with brainstorming, caution is advised in allowing dominant personalities from skewing the data one way or another.

## Processes and Systems

### Cell Manufacturing

Traditional manufacturing systems are designed around making small pieces into bigger pieces on a moving assembly line. Although few assembly lines physically move, the concept is to build progressively larger subassemblies until the product comes together in a finished unit. Conventional wisdom is that subassemblies can be most cost effectively produced in lots or batches. These lots are then staged, awaiting their turn to be included in the next assembly step. This technique makes for very specialized job owners, inventory waiting to be processed, and complex controls of inventory and work-in-process (WIP).

The cell concept was the program du jour in the late 1980s. It is based on containing complete processes within one cell, rather than in a serial production line. If you are building a particular model of computer, a cell would assemble the components, build the system, install the software, and check out the unit all within one area. The workers would all be continually cross training to handle each job in the cell. Inventory and WIP turn much quicker in a cell and workers are less plagued by boredom and burnout (common in production lines).

One company I work with makes explosive charges used in the oil well drilling industry. They produce thousands of these assemblies each week. Each step in the assembly process is very repetitive and very boring. When dealing with explosives, boredom and burnout among employees can become more than just a productivity problem! The company broke the steps of manufacturing the charges into five operations. They moved all of the machinery from common areas into work cells. The employees in each cell spend one day per week on each operation, rotating on a schedule. The last step is to set off a sample of each lot of charges. No matter how repetitive the operation, each employee looks forward to his or her turn to work on the firing range and the quality levels from the cells has become outstanding. Their productivity is also extremely high because they have a cadre of cross trained operators that can cover for sick and vacationing team members. They also maintain a friendly competition with the teams in other cells.

As all good ideas seldom work in every situation, cell manufacturing has fallen from the limelight; cellular manufacturing is not for every company. It only works where there is an environment that can benefit from this approach. An intensive benchmarking effort should be undertaken before considering cell manufacturing for your company.

## Just-in-Time (JIT)

Another tool that is peculiar to manufacturing environments is JIT. As in the conventional wisdom examples already discussed, traditional manufacturing is based on having quantities of raw material and subassemblies on hand in a warehouse ready to

meet production needs. The material and subassemblies are purchased or assembled in quantity to, in theory, acquire them at the lowest cost. The problem is that the companies that have adequate inventories also have a lot of their working capital tied up in that material. They are also not very flexible to changes in products. Often times, traditional companies wind up "writing down" obsolete and excess inventories on a regular basis.

JIT is a system that calls for parts and subassemblies to be ready just in time for them to be assembled into the next assembly step. This technique requires very careful planning and partnering with suppliers. The suppliers have to be involved in the planning activities and sales so that they can respond quickly to the needs of the manufacturer. The manufacturer rewards JIT suppliers with loyalty and long-running contracts. The entire process revolves around a rapid response manufacturing system that is unique to each JIT company. A graphic example is one of the largest computer manufacturers in the United States. Each day's production is planned for every model and quantity on the point of sale information from the previous day. Key suppliers keep inventory in the company's stockroom and they are paid as the material is used. Every day, the company builds the exact quantity needed for the next day. From this example, it should be clear that JIT is not for everyone!

## Reengineering

One of the boldest quality improvement tools to come along has been reengineering. In the seminal work on this subject,[4] Hammer and Champy offer an alternative to the gradual continuous improvement philosophy that is the cornerstone of most strategic quality initiatives. Their proposed option is radical work process redesign. Taken to its extreme, a business would systematically design a new, more effective work structure around the reengineering principles and then, essentially, close the old business down on a Friday and open the new business on Monday morning. In my experience, this type of catharsis should be widely executed, but, alas, most senior executives will not take the chal-

[4]James Champy and Michael Hammer. 1993. *Reengineering the Corporation, A Manifesto for Business Revolution.* New York: Harper Collins Publishers.

lenge. A developing subset to reengineering the company is business process reengineering (BPR). It is a similar concept; however, it focuses on redesigning key processes and performing an "out with the old—in with the new" cathartic episode on a macro level. Many forward-thinking managers are very pleased with the results of discarding old processes that have atrophied and replacing them entirely with systematic and structured processes that can grow and change with the future. As with any radical change, effective assessment of the climate for change, careful planning, and training are the keys to success. If any of these three are not done completely and effectively, BPR and company-wide reengineering efforts could become catastrophic disasters.

## Family of Measures

A football game would be meaningless if no one kept score. If teams kept only the score, and didn't track first downs, yards rushing, yards passing, penalties exacted, penetrations, and individual performance, they could not make game plan corrections during the game. A large majority of the businesses I have audited have little more in place than tracking the "final score." That is, most companies focus on the monthly financial reports to indicate how well or poorly they are doing. Financial reports are ancient history. There is nothing can be done to make mid-course corrections after the month is over. You can't change your game plan on Monday morning after the game is lost. In fact, Monday morning quarterbacking in business is very dangerous, because financial results are often skewed by accounting wizards. Accountants may take advantage of tax laws, or spread losses around or manipulate overhead expenses to make numbers come out more palatable for the stockholders and give the managers a distorted view of the real picture. In virtually every management job I've ever held, the piles of green-bar paper that showed up in my office around the tenth of each month usually went in a binder or in the circular file. In manufacturing, quality, and training I always kept my own book of how my group was performing and I reviewed the information every week. I developed processes whereby data was entered routinely and as a business necessity, rather than as a batch overhead exercise. I shared the data with those who kept it so they saw the importance of a family of mea-

sures. When I became even more enlightened, I asked them to keep their own measures and report their results regularly. With real-time measures that they owned, the job holders fixed a lot of potential problems long before the problems made it to the run charts.

Each time I help a company begin a strategic quality initiative, Total Quality Management implementation, or ISO9000 registration effort, I ask what measures they have in place to know where they are today and what progress we will make as we move forward. Most have very few. I press hard to implement basic process performance measures, people productivity measures, defect tracking measures and corrective action effectiveness measures, but there is seldom priority given to launching a family of measures. The managers and executives get "warm fuzzies" from the progress we make, because they often compliment me on how much better things are now than they were before. That's great for my ego, but I would rather they had hard numbers kept by the job owners that demonstrate there were monies moved from overhead or waste to the bottom line. I would rather the workers knew how much better they were at their jobs after a year of ongoing training in the quality management system and in their job skills. I would rather that management see trends and make corrections before they spend dollars on waste and rework.

A family of measures is unique to each business. They may include statistical process controls (SPC), productivity measures, customer satisfaction indices, quality levels attained, cost of quality, schedule performance, and a host of other indicators designed to give a barometer of how well a particular process is working against some predetermined norms. The "family" concept is important. Just one or two measures may not give a clear picture of quality or productivity levels. For instance, you may consistently receive high marks from your customers' receiving inspection departments because there are seldom rejects, but you may be on the verge of losing a customer because your product is being replaced with newer technology. If you are just talking to inspection and not to those who specify your products, you may be getting only half the story and find yourself struggling to keep a "satisfied" customer. There are no real down sides to keeping a family of measures, unless you don't deal well with reality.

## Malcolm Baldrige National Quality Award

This is a curious topic to appear in a list of quality improvement tools, or is it? The MBNQA was launched in the late 1980s to recognize those companies in the United States that had achieved exemplary levels of quality and performance. The award criteria are very exacting and are refined every year. The volunteer examiners are very hard to convince that the applicants are really living the quality levels they report. In the first few years, the number of companies applying grew steadily, until one of the winners, the Wallace Company, declared bankruptcy after winning the award. Since that unfortunate incident, the actual number of applications has not been rising dramatically, but the number of companies requesting application packages has soared! You see, enlightened leaders have discovered that the MBNQA evaluation criteria make an excellent model for strategic quality improvement in all areas of a company! The MBNQA uses numerical indices to evaluate the effectiveness of key areas within a company. By regularly performing self-assessments, companies can determine where their weak points are and watch their numerical scores climb as they make process improvements. In fact, there is a growing subculture that advertises that "we are an MBNQA 500 company," or "we hope to be MBNQA 600 by next year," indicating the numerical evaluation to MBNQA criteria. Again, there is no real down side to this technique, unless you fall in the Wallace Company trap and forget to sell your products while you are improving quality!

As you thumb through the book catalogs mentioned previously, you will find titles that deal with quality improvement tools such as Kanban, Quick Changeover, Activity Based Cost Accounting, Total Productivity Maintenance, and other fine instruments and techniques. Room does not permit us to cover them here. Be curious. If one of them sounds interesting, pay a visit to the bookstore or post an inquiry on the Internet about the book, video, or compact disc. Be sure that you take each of them at face value until you have checked them out thoroughly.

We've also avoided listing tools that may be losing their popularity or are being retired because there are better ways. These

# Success Snapshot

Seven Step Approach to Implementing Statistical Process
    Control (SPC)
Dan O'Leary, Product Quality Manager
NMR Division, Picker International
Cleveland, OH

Implementing SPC is not easy, but it is well worth the effort. I use
a seven-step approach:

1. Define the process. Flow chart how the process works.
2. Determine the characteristics to be measured. The flow
   chart should identify two to five attributes to be measured.
3. Review the specifications. Make sure they are real.
4. Conduct a gage repeatability and reproducability study. Ensure that no more than 10 percent of the process variability
   is traceable to measurement variation.
5. Work on process capability.
6. Work on process performance. Estimate anticipated results
   and track them.
7. Work on process control maintenance. Expect this process
   to take one to two years!

Form a special project team made up of those who will use the
process, those who will benefit from the process, and an engineering representative (to help with the drawing changes that will
occur). Have the team follow the seven steps.

Select attributes to be measured near the end of the process
to measure overall health of the process. These attributes should
be "global" rather than "local." That is, they should tell you about
the process, not just about some part of it. Expect to change one
or more of the attributes selected before you finish the process.

Decide what kind of SPC charts to use. Xbar and R charts are
indicated for high volume environments while lower volumes
might warrant X and MR charts.

Do not computerize SPC data collection. If charts are not
maintained in real time by the operators, you are not controlling the
process. If you do not intend to empower the operator to collect
the data, plot the data, and react to the patterns shown, don't waste
the time to start the program. Don't make SPC into wallpaper.

Do reward accomplishments as the processes improve.

include Quality Circles and Zero Defects. If these tools work in your environment, do not scrap them just because they are no longer in vogue. Please do, however, look into some of the tools listed on these pages and examine if you can benefit by utilizing some of the new techniques that have been proven successful in the last few years.

A final note. We have also avoided including as quality improvement tools the teachings of the various quality gurus. There are many "Deming Companies" and "Crosby Companies" out there that have followed the teachings of Dr. W. Edwards Deming, Philip B. Crosby, or J. M. Juran. Companies that achieve success through dedicated practice of the tenets taught by these and other enlightened masters of quality are to be applauded. In fact, I encourage all practitioners to become familiar with Tom Peters', Deming's, Juran's, and Crosby's works. They contain many valuable tools and truisms. My advice to all companies, however, is to keep a broad focus because many breakthroughs in technology and techniques come from outsiders and not from those who are totally vested in one set of principles.

# The Strategic
# Implementation Plan

When we begin a new journey with a plan to achieve certain milestones, it is most desirable to have a road map of where we are and where we want to go. If we are out for a Sunday drive, a road map may detract from the spontaneity of the trip. In running a business, however, navigating by feel will almost certainly steer you into a ditch or cause you to arrive at a destination that was not planned.

We've looked separately at the culture, systems, and tools that make up a Virtual Leadership Strategic Quality Initiative. We will now try to bring all of the pieces together and see how they might fit into a road map that I call the Strategic Implementation Plan.

Before we begin, you may have noticed a ninth part in the puzzle (Figure 9.1). We haven't directly addressed this piece before. I call it *shared vision* and, in my experience, it is one of the most commonly neglected success attributes in the companies that I have worked with and those that I have audited. When companies begin, the principals usually have a very clear vision of why they started the new enterprise. There is often a com-

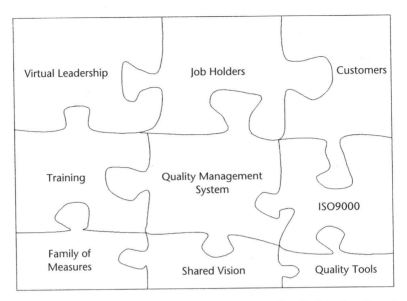

**Figure 9.1** The Pieces of the Strategic Quality Initiative Puzzle

pelling technical breakthrough or a market niche screaming to be filled, or a dissatisfaction with old ways of operating a business that launches a new company. Whatever the catalyst, those who are in on the ground floor are usually of one mind. They generate a synergistic energy that moves the business forward at warp speed. If the business survives infant mortality and continues to grow, the original vision is often skewed by customer needs, market changes, technological shifts, or by logical extension of the original ideas and/or products. An example of skewed vision can be illustrated with a computer company I work with. The company started with a vision of building computer systems and selling them to retail customers. Retail customers appreciated their personal attention and rapid response. Some of those retail customers had business needs that the computer company could fill. The small company could offer an attractive price and quick response, so they started building business systems. The businesses customers had custom needs that larger companies wouldn't respond to, so they began building custom systems. Then, the commercial customers wanted to network these systems, so the com-

pany is now in the networking business. They are doing so well in networking and custom systems that the retail sales are nearly nonexistent.

The vision of the founders was clear but they unconsciously agreed to skew the vision as they grew, by agreeing to enter the new markets and take on new challenges. They now have six employees and the vision of what they do is not so clear to those who weren't in on the inception and were not witness to the evolution of the business. The recent hires observe that the company is in the networked systems business and they tend to dismiss the needs of some of the older retail customers (who were the ones who introduced the company to the commercial opportunities). The principals awoke one morning to find some of their old retail customers have moved on to other shops, because they aren't getting the personal service that they once received. Overhead has grown and prices aren't as attractive as they once were. The principals are confused and the new employees are confused; the reason is that they do not have a shared vision of what is going on in their business.

If the example can be this dramatic with eight people, think of how poorly most companies with layers of management and scores of employees deal with shared vision. In my experience, those who have the vision are so far removed from those who implement the products and services that neither has a clue as to what either really does. To complicate the issue, those at the top seldom realize that they have an unconscious vision that drives them to make key business decisions and that this vision is not communicated openly nor is it shared. In classic autocratic businesses, the concept of a shared vision is contrary to absolute control, so it has historically not been an issue. As businesses decide to evolve from autocratic rule, the concept of shared vision is alien. That is why there are in-depth discussions of quality policy, mission statement, and management reviews in Chapters 6 and 7. When ISO9000 implementation is initiated, managers often find out they haven't a clue how the company runs, day to day, and the employees find out that their senior managers do not have a feel for the working person's job or needs. Lack of shared vision is epidemic in American business because the principals take it for granted that everyone shares their visions while the

job holders develop their own vision, based on their perception of what is modeled for them in the plant by their co-workers. To make it even more complex, the senior managers often do not have a clear picture of what their vision is and the perceived vision created in the work place seldom resembles any stated or implied grand plan.

As we move through building a strategic implementation plan, remember that a key part of the puzzle is involving everyone in the value delivery system in development of the plan. As the plan is hatched, defined, and refined, you will not lose the vision if everyone has the same road map. If you can lay out a logical, effective vision that everyone can follow, you will not wind up in any ditches or at any unscheduled destinations. As you are planning your shared route, do, however, allow for an occasional Sunday drive. They sometimes lead to opportunities that are not on any map.

## The Plan Outline

The strategic implementation plan is going to be very much an outline. We've defined the tenets of the strategic plan in the first eight chapters; we will discuss how to make each piece successful in Chapter 10; and we will bring the plan to life in Chapter 12. We have selected the bullets that need to be included in the plan outline and incorporated them into the following topical categories. Since we've selected the theme of using ISO9000 as the foundation for our strategic quality initiative, we will construct the strategic plan around it.

I. **The Infrastructure**
   A. **Define the quality policy and mission statement** (Chapter 7)
   B. **Build a functional organization chart** (Chapter 7)
      1. **Define the responsible leadership positions**
      2. **Define the organizational structure and interrelationship**

C. **Steering Committee** (Chapter 7)
1. **Define who will coordinate and implement the strategic plan**
D. **Appoint a management representative to be the quality coordinator** (Chapter 7)
E. **Define the scope of the plan.** Determine if the plan is to encompass the entire company and all of its business entities, or will it be specific to a plant, operation, product line, or service center.
F. **Define the boundaries.** Decide if the plan will be limited only to those functions and processes that directly effect the value delivery system, or will it be a strategic plan that encompasses all functions (Administration, human resources, and accounting are often not included in an ISO9000 quality management system).
G. **Define the budget issues.** If your company requires a specific budget for each department or project, determine how will the costs associated with developing the plan be budgeted and expensed and how you will you track cost versus budget.
H. **Set up a perpetual renewal plan.** Establish a charter that makes the strategic plan a perpetually evolving activity, regardless of who is occupying which chairs. Make the required budget part of your long range projections.
I. **Establish a management review system** (Chapter 7)
J. **Develop a tactical plan.** Determine how you will deal with short-term problems and issues while you are developing and implementing this plan.
II. **The quality management system** (Chapter 7)
A. **Document the quality management system**
B. **Document the strategic implementation plan**
C. **Set up a perpetual review and maintenance plan** (as in I.H)
III. **Human interface**
A. **Implement virtual leadership** (Chapter 4)
B. **Define the role of the job holders.** Determine if the job holders will be evolving into self-directed work teams, how they will be empowered to be responsible for their

own actions, how they will be rewarded, and what risks and remedies they will face.

C. **Define how everyone will be trained.** Develop a master training plan. Planning should include quality management system training, job related training, technical skills training (computers, software, etc.), and personal growth training and education.

IV. **Customer interface**

A. **Develop a plan for customer interface**

1. **Develop business partnerships.** Posture yourself to become a strategic partner with your customers, not just another vendor or peddler. Culturally evolve your customers as the focus of your business. Ask them what they need and show them what is possible.

2. **Control document and contract flow.** Ensure that there is no chance for miscommunication between you and your customers. Control their documentation and reach agreement on all contractual requirements.

B. **Develop a feedback loop for corrective and preventive action.** Develop a working level communication system with your customers to ensure that any problems are resolved quickly and equitably and that the same problems do not recur.

V. **Business operations**

A. **Design control**

1. **Document and control the design and development process.** Use the model in ISO9000 paragraph 4.0.

B. **Documentation control**

1. **Document the paperwork and/or data flow.** If it affects the quality management system, be sure that the flow of information is auditable.

2. **Develop a system of positive control.** Ensure that only the correct revision of documents are available for use in the value delivery system.

3. **Develop a change control system.** Ensure that any changes are positively communicated to those affected by the changes. Determine "point of effectiveness" for every change and document what is to be done with existing product and/or services.

    **4. Develop a method to control quality records.** The integrity of historical records must be maintained for them to be of any use in configuration management or liability control.

**C. Supplier interface**

    **1. Develop a plan for supplier interface**

        **a. Business partnership.** Replace peddlers and vendors with companies that will share your vision of success and support you through the ups and downs of your business.

        **b. Control document and contract flow.** Ensure that your partners control your documentation and specifications and that you reach agreement on all contractual terms.

    **2. Develop a feedback loop for corrective and preventive action.** Develop a working level communication system with your suppliers to ensure that any problems are resolved quickly and equitably and that the same problems do not recur.

**D. Inventory control**

    **1. Product identification and traceability.** As makes sense for your industry, be sure that all products and materials are identified and are traceable.

    **2. Control of customer-supplied product.** If your customers provide material, equipment, or supplies, be sure they are controlled and accounted for.

    **3. Handling, storage, packaging, preservation, and delivery.** Ensure that your methods of handling, inventory, packaging, preparation, and delivery maintain the integrity of your product.

**E. Process control**

    **1. Develop a plan for controlling all processes within the value delivery system.** Each activity that adds value to your product or service is a process. Each process should be documented to the degree necessary to measure its effectiveness and to the extent required to train new operators.

**F. Quality conformance**

    **1. Develop a plan for inspection and testing.** Each product and service must be verified compliant before

delivery to a customer. Systems for ensuring this compliance should be in place and effective.

2. **Develop a plan for controlling inspection measuring and test equipment.** Any equipment used to verify published specifications or used to demonstrate conformance should be controlled and calibrated to a source of known accuracy.

3. **Develop a plan to identify inspection and test status.** Identification of the stage of inspection and test of any product should be clear and evident to the degree that is indicated by the criticality of the commodities.

4. **Develop a plan for controlling nonconforming product.** Develop a system to segregate nonconformities from the work flow and a system to disposition them in a timely fashion.

G. **Corrective and preventive action**

1. **Develop a corrective action plan.** Ensure that deviations from policies and procedures are documented and resolved in a timely manner. Follow up to ensure effectiveness of the corrective action.

2. **Develop a preventive action plan.** Ensure that deviations and nonconformities do not recur.

H. **Internal audits**

1. **Develop an internal auditing system.** Develop an effective program of routinely verifying the effectiveness of the quality management system.

VI. **Develop a family of measures.** Implement a series of barometers that effectively measure the performance of all key processes in the value delivery system (Chapter 8).

# CHAPTER 10

# The Secrets of Success—ISO9000

In this chapter, I will try to share some of my experiences for successfully implementing ISO9000. I will also share with you some experiences that I have found to be sure-fire roads to disaster. Again, this is not meant to be a cookbook. These experiences span nearly thirty years and are from 300+ companies that I have visited, and a host of other companies that I have read about and heard about in seminars and workshops. Select the material from this chapter anecdotally when looking for proven ways to help your company. Take the object lessons rather than trying to duplicate the exact scenarios I describe. If the information fits your culture, give it a try instead of embarking on a totally unproven trail. If a technique is not germane to your environment, even though it sounds nifty, pass it by. I will highlight the most important secrets and I will highlight the deepest tank traps.

**Success Snapshot**

- Question everything that you do. There is no force more counterproductive than conventional wisdom.
- Hold a mirror up to every process. If you don't like what you see, it's time to change it.
- Test every procedure in your company for common sense. If you find some that make none, get rid of them!
- Consider how changes in your area will effect those with whom you interface.
- Involve everyone. Make everyone a virtual leader.

## The Infrastructure

### The Quality Policy and Mission Statement

We discussed the importance and structure of the quality policy and mission statement at length in Chapter 7. The secret to making them successful is finding the words that will have meaning to your culture. If they are not well thought out, they will be treated as meaningless rhetoric by the job holders. If they are too complex and lengthy, they will not be understood and they will not be lived. In an engineering firm, the quality policy *We want our customers back, not our products* would likely be treated as banal and meaningless. In a retail establishment with a young workforce, the same statement might be an effective reality check. Treat your quality policy as a "rally cry" might be used in the military or as a "fight song" might be used in a football game. It cannot build product or make a sale, but it can make the difference between a winning score and a losing one.

### Define the Leadership Positions

Also as discussed in Chapter 7, you must decide what functional leadership roles are required to run your company successfully. This entire subject may be academic if your infrastructure is cast

in stone. If it isn't, this success tool can greatly enhance your productivity and set the path by which your company will be guided into the future. I have found a good technique for this is to brainstorm it with your management team. Draw your organization chart on a white board without any names. Fill each box with the functions that position performs on a daily, weekly, monthly, quarterly basis. When you have run out of functions, extract from each box the tasks that say "attend _____ status meeting," "develop _____ report," "direct the operation of_____," "maintain control of_____," "evaluate_____," "analyze_____," measure_____," or "prepare status of_____." Make these a separate list entitled "Management Duties" and erase them from each box. What's left in the boxes? Are any of them empty?

Look again in each box. Determine which functions do not directly contribute to the value delivery system and start another list called "Overhead Functions." Some of these might include: "perform employee evaluations"; "prepare annual departmental budget"; "chair the cost reduction committee." Erase each of these from the boxes. Now how many boxes still have content? If a third or more of the boxes are empty, you have a bureaucracy on your hands. You have job functions that add no value to the delivery system and are being funded from the life-blood-draining overhead budget.

Go away, have lunch, play a round of golf, take the afternoon off or do something to purge your mind of what you just did. While you are gone, have someone transcribe your chart and your lists to paper and have them erase the white board. The next day go back to the white board and brainstorm a functional diagram of how your company works. Do a continuum of the work flow and include the support functions such as accounting and human resources. Your challenge, now, is to isolate each area that you believe must have a functional leader for the process to perform within acceptable norms. Perhaps you need a function that coordinates the output of several operations into one final product, or you need a leader to coordinate the activities of a team of sales professionals. When you make a decision to create one of these positions, ask the question, "If the workers were trained and were responsible for the quality of their own work, would I need this position?" If the answer is no, you don't need the position. If the position survives

that test, ask yourselves, "What would this person contribute to the value delivery system?" If the answer to that question is no more than "managing people" then it is not a valid leadership role.

When you are through, you should have a lean structure of functional leadership roles that add value to the delivery system. Now you can compare the new organization to the transcribed information from the day before. From the list of "management duties" and "overhead functions," how many of those exist because people can't be trusted to do their jobs right? How many are measures of performance that the people who do the work could better perform themselves? How many of them are really nonproductive bureaucratic busy work?

This is usually a very disturbing exercise. It raises a mirror that many do not care to gaze in. It sets up a challenge for you to redesign your management infrastructure to just include functions that serve a valuable purpose in the delivery system and kick the chair out from under those that do no more than support a wide tush.

## Define the Organization Interrelationship

Once you have designed the new leadership roles, you can see how the organizational structure fits the new roles. Are there toll gates and barriers that serve no purpose? For instance, if every worker is made responsible for the quality of his or her own work, do you need a cadre of quality inspectors? Are there convoluted production line processes that can be converted to single cell activities? For example, if you process insurance claims in a batch operation, would it not be more productive to have each person trained in all the review and approval steps? Are there log jams that cripple your productivity? An example might be a single point of order entry that delays orders being queued for production when the order entry person is backlogged. **The common thread to these success secrets is taking a cathartic look at every function, step, and person in the value delivery system and designing that function to be as lean and self-sufficient as possible. This is accomplished through a clear vision, a common mission, dedicated leadership, and everyone being responsible for his or her own actions.**

## The Steering Committee

We discussed the steering committee at some length. The importance of the steering committee cannot be stressed too strongly. It can make or break an ISO9000 implementation. The keys to success include:

◆ Recruit members from diverse backgrounds and disciplines throughout the company. Do not use the same management committee that is tagged for every ad hoc assignment that comes along.

◆ Recruit members from all levels, especially those who are most vocal and most likely to stimulate creative ideas.

◆ Do not try to select a purely harmonious group. A little bit of controversy helps the thought processes and avoids "group think" where everyone agrees to everything.

◆ Invite members of management only when you need their help with a specific issue or you want to report on progress. If the group is empowered and has a clear charter, you will not need permission or forgiveness on a regular basis.

◆ Change the makeup of the committee when it is warranted. The process of ISO9000 may take six months to two years. In all likelihood, you will not end up with the same group that you started with. Some members will not be comfortable with the committee and some will change job assignments. Some will grow restless and some will try to take control. Accept changing membership in stride.

◆ Keep the membership from five to nine people. Any more can't get anything done. Any less may put too much work on one individual. Remember, we are trying to minimize the impact to the work flow. I constantly remind committee members that their primary tasks come first, but their committee duties must come as part of their work day, not as an afterthought.

◆ Meet once per week for one hour. Do not routinely let the meeting go beyond the time limit. During particularly intense efforts, such as internal audit training, the meetings may be scheduled for longer periods. Everyone should have and is expected to do homework outside the meeting.

◆ Have a chairperson who sets the agenda and causes the group to stick to it. The chairperson may also be the guardian of the implementation schedule and may regularly remind the committee of the progress they are making within the agreed upon schedule.

◆ Have a person who is the scribe and is charged with recording and publishing the meeting minutes and action items in a timely fashion.

◆ Divide the twenty key elements of ISO9001 (or the nineteen key elements of ISO9002) among the committee members. Each should be responsible for those that are logically part of his or her job. The rest should be divided and assigned to those who are interested in the topic and/or who have special talents (i.e., training might be assigned to someone who has teaching experience). The assignment of these elements is not for the individuals to necessarily write procedures, but for them to be responsible for volunteering the help needed to get the procedures finished and audited.

◆ Use ad hoc committees to tackle particularly difficult areas. Often documentation requires a great deal of research and dissection to determine if your control systems are effective and compliant.

◆ Expose committee members to as much training in every aspect of the quality management system as they can absorb. They will be the champions and spokespeople for the QMS and for ISO9000 within their areas of influence. They may also grow to become permanent members of a quality improvement team.

◆ The leadership of the committee may not necessarily be just one person. A good consultant may direct the meetings for the first few months, until everyone is comfortable with the assignment and with their roles. The quality representative may logically chair the committee; however, I have seen successful groups that rotated the leadership just to keep the group dynamic and interested.

Much of the planning work may be done behind closed doors, especially in the early stages, but **the job holders must be involved in the development process as much as practical.**

**Have regular company meetings where the steering committee shares its progress and milestones with everyone. Regularly reward the committee with appropriate expressions of appreciation, such as a luncheon or a field trip. Celebrate significant milestones with everyone.**

Some sure-fire ways to have the steering committee fail are to:

◆ Not have a clear charter, an operating budget, and a time budget.
◆ Have meetings continually postponed and rescheduled.
◆ Have meetings that drag on for hours at a time.
◆ Put the initiative on hold every time the workload picks up.
◆ Have management dictate the activities of the committee or to have to seek management approval for every decision the group makes.
◆ Continually change the scope of the committee (like adding problem investigations for business related grass fires).

## Success Snapshot

Some tools for the Steering Committee:

◆ Reach consensus not compromise.
◆ Don't create victims and winners.
◆ Never lose sight of the fact that you are in business to make money.
◆ Work within the system while improving it.
◆ Measure your progress.
◆ You are the architects of the future. Don't let your paradigms blind you to what is possible.
◆ Success is a journey, not a destination.
◆ Walk the walk and talk the talk.

## Management Representative

Conventional wisdom is to appoint the quality manager as the management representative responsible for the operation of the quality management system. In larger companies that have an existing quality infrastructure, that decision is generally consistent with success because the quality department usually champions continuous improvement. As we mentioned in Chapter 7, there are many other good choices for a management representative from virtually any area of the company. The success attributes are for the person to be passionate about what he or she does, have leadership skills (or potential), and be analytical (rather than judgmental). Some sure-fire disaster candidates for the management representative include those who are highly opinionated, those who lose their composure at every bump in the road, those who see the efforts as a futile exercise, those who are absorbed with the process and never arrive at milestones, those who build the Queen Mary when a rowboat will suffice, and those who like the status quo.

## Develop a Tactical Plan

Beginning a strategic quality initiative can be very frustrating. I compare it to the experience of charging your credit cards to the limit and then having to find money to live on while you pay down your credit cards. Your system is probably overloaded and everyone has twice the work that can be performed in a day, yet you are now going to add to that workload by rebuilding the infrastructure of the organization. Not only is it additional work, but it is very challenging work that really can't be done between midnight and six in the morning (the only time you have left in the day). Strategic quality initiatives have to be implemented *along with* the daily work, not instead of the daily work (or not at all). Great initiatives are often paralyzed by continually rescheduling training sessions and committee meetings. The success secret is to have all people prioritize their tasks and work them in priority order (with the QMS having a high priority level). Making it happen takes a leap of faith because the process owners have to help dismantle the bureaucracy and implement the

strategic plans before they will be relieved of the wasteful and re-dundant tasks that occupy so much of their time. A sure-fire road to failure is to ignore the tactical issues and keep piling on new assignments. Another is to redesign a process and not have a plan for transition and phase-out of the old ways. Strategic plans without tactical solutions are incomplete and are a prelude to disaster.

## Document the Quality Management System

As we discussed in Chapter 6, the quality management system must be documented to ensure consistency and to meet a funda-mental tenet of ISO9000. The secret to success is to not document any more than is absolutely necessary to maintain process control and train new operators. The documentation system can be a sin-gle manual or a multi-tier system that resides on a computer, but the concept of *keeping it simple* should be followed regardless of the complexity of your operation.

First, write a quality manual that documents your quality policies. To make it auditor friendly, I suggest structuring it around the twenty key elements of ISO9000. This document will have to be submitted to your Registrar for a documentation audit before he or she audits your quality management system. Once the policies have been set, enlist the job holders in writing all supporting documentation. I call it the "yellow pad approach" and I touched on it briefly in Chapters 2 and 5. Explain to the job holders that you need them to document exactly how they per-form their job functions. Tell them to write it down on a yellow pad, without regard to form or style. Some will write paragraphs, others will write two-word sentences. From their input, translate the key ideas into a procedure format and make it grammatically correct. Hand it back to the job holders and ask, "Is this what you said?" Once you have ironed out the miscommunication and have agreement that what the procedure says is what they think they do, you can move on to the second step. Meet with small groups that work in the area affected by each procedure. Have them dis-cuss the content out loud and ask if it makes sense. At this point, there will usually be considerable disagreement on how a particu-lar job is done and how most people thought it should be done.

You may discover that you cannot "document what you do" because it doesn't make a lot of sense or it doesn't work very well. Form an ad hoc group from the workers involved to study the process and make recommendations for how it might be done well. An example comes from a company that I work with as they were trying to write a document control procedure. They have hundreds of customer catalogs and price sheets. If they would have documented what they thought they were doing, they would have had to inventory and mark every single price sheet and catalog. Such an exercise would have taken weeks of clerical labor and would not have been maintainable. An ad hoc committee was empaneled to come up with a clever way to be compliant and to reach the goal of only having the latest catalogs and price sheets in the work area. Their solution included declaring all existing price sheets and catalogs as "reference only" and starting from scratch with a new system of cataloging and controlling the documents.

After those who are directly involved are happy with the procedures, have them meet with the departments with whom they interface. Determine if the procedures are complimentary to the functions that the other departments depend upon. Be sure there is no redundancy and there are no holes in the system. This exercise builds teamwork and helps job holders understand the issues and problems that face others in the company, making them more effective at their own jobs.

Besides a low-cost method of documenting your quality management system, the yellow pad approach instills ownership in the people who perform the processes. When the procedure manuals are completed, they will require very little direct training to be "doing what you document."

A sure-fire way to fail at documenting your procedures is to let the quality department or engineering department write all the procedures and force-feed them to the workers. Another is to let a consultant write all of your procedures because no one in the company will own them, but you will help the consultant pay off his mortgage! The newest failure path is to clone procedures verbatim from the host of new documentation software that is now on the streets. The software makes a good template, but the content should be yours.

## The Role of the Job Holders

ISO9000 and Virtual Leadership are most effective when the job holders are working as self-directed work teams. The journey to self-directed work teams is long and difficult and it is not appropriate for every environment. While work teams should be considered as the best model, the most important success factor is determining exactly what role the job holders will play in the company culture. The key attributes to consider are:

◆ Be sure the risks and rewards are clear. Workers will not be self-motivated or team driven if there is not a clear benefit to being productive versus being nonproductive.

◆ Reward for accomplishments, not for activity. Dismantle compensation systems that are based on tenure or cost of living and replace them with systems that reward for accomplishments and for learning new skills.

◆ Develop a culture where it is "cool" to be good instead of it being "cool" to be bad. That is, develop incentives for employees to do things the right way and for them to place peer pressure on those who are not carrying their weight or those who are generating nonconformances. **There is no more awesome force in the workplace than peer pressure.**

◆ There must be open communication (see Figure 10.1) and mutual trust between the job holders and the leadership.

In an ISO9000 environment, the training activity can be used as a vehicle for restructuring the compensation system. Internal auditors should be selected from the job holders, encouraging everyone to perform well by peer pressure. The quality policy can become the rally cry for the troops. Process procedures should be written by the job holders so that they will own the processes. Inspection functions should be performed by the job holders, causing the dismantling of the toll gate inspection process.

Providing adequate training can become a monumental effort. For so many years, we have presumed that workers were hired for their training and they could learn every other skill they need "on the job." With the dramatic advances in technology, the evolution of work systems, and the proliferation of productivity

# Communications From A Male Perspective

Think about how many times you've told your children to "mow the grass" and the results you obtained were not exactly what you expected. If you do not have children, think about the same scenario with your parent telling you to "mow the grass." How may times were there missed spots, clippings not bagged, the mower left in the driveway, or the edging not done?

Who trained you and your children to "mow the grass?" Hasn't it mostly always been by *assumed observation* and some intuitive sense of what a properly manicured lawn looked like?

When you say "mow the grass, " aren't you really saying:

◆ Put on heavy boots and safety glasses.

◆ Inspect the mower. Verify the air filter is clean and the blade is tight.

◆ Be sure the level adjustment is set properly and all wheels are at the same height.

◆ Check the engine oil. Add as necessary.

◆ Fill the gas tank. Go get gas if there is none in the gas can.

◆ Start the mower and mow in a logical sequence.

◆ Be sure to cut all areas that you can reach with the mower.

◆ Inspect the edger. Add gasoline/oil mixture. Check to be sure there is enough cutting line in the edger and that it is properly wound.

◆ Run the edger around all perimeter areas. Be careful not to damage flowers, trees, or decorative trim.

◆ Rake up excessive grass clippings. Place clippings in compost bin.

◆ Inspect your work and verify the job was done correctly. Report any damage that occurred during mowing and edging.

◆ Clean the edger and mower and return them and all tools to their storage spaces. Report any observed problems with the mower or edger.

◆ Keep track of when the oil needs changing in the mower or there is sign of blade wear.

◆ Report any observed problems in the flower beds or with the trees and shrubbery or with insect infestations.

Do we communicate our needs, or do we assume that people understand what is expected of them?

**Figure 10.1** Training Everyone

# Success Snapshot

Successful ISO9000 Implementation in Two Small Companies
Bill Borusiewich, Consultant
ISO-Dyne
Scarborough, Ontario

Two of my clients are small companies that wanted to be ISO9002 certified. Company #1 has about thirty employees and has been in business for over sixty years. Company #2 has seven employees and has been in business twelve years. Both have found real benefits from the ISO9000 implementation process, although their experiences are significantly different.

Company #1 has its business processes well thought out and highly computerized. Their original motivation to seek ISO9002 certification was pressure from their customers. As they went through the implementation process, however, they found that the process improvements made the effort worthwhile. This company answered its customers' concerns and improved its own effectiveness.

Company #2 really struggled with the implementation process. While two of the seven people documented processes, their daily jobs were not being attended to. Very few processes had been documented previously and there was considerable disagreement among the employees as to exactly what the procedures were. Different operators performed the same process differently. Their computerization was not as mature or effective as the systems in Company #1. An example of the lack of control was that an accounting person was spending two hours per day searching for shipping addresses because that person had no faith in the computerized database. As ISO9000 drove the company to write operational procedures, the benefit they derived from the process was much greater than Company #1, while the implementation costs were proportionally higher.

In both cases, the actual paperwork required to implement the quality management system was not as great as expected (one of the major fears of small companies). Training was not conducted until the documentation was finished to minimize the amount of training required. When training was accomplished, the workers had a greater understanding of the ISO9000 standards, an appreciation of what it took to become certified, and training in the methods of the auditors.

improvement tools, constant training is no longer optional. Some success tools for training include:

◆ If you use computers, have everyone trained by a qualified instructor in the software packages that you use. So many of us have spent countless wasted hours hacking and learning computer skills by trial and error.

◆ Select job holders who have a talent for training and send them to schools on the equipment you use. Oftentimes, manufacturers provide very reasonable training courses on their own equipment. When the job holders return, have them conduct training for all others who operate the equipment.

◆ Make available training in quality tools, leadership tools, team building skills, production skills. Many local colleges offer reasonably priced training. Some colleges even build courseware for the needs of their local industries.

◆ Use lunch hours to provide voluntary training in team building and leadership. There are a host of effective and entertaining videos that can be run in the cafeteria during the noon hour. Equipment manufacturers often provide free videos of how to use their equipment that can also be run at lunchtime.

◆ Encourage professionals to be active in their professional societies and to seek training that the societies offer. Make time available to them to attend seminars and symposia in their fields of expertise. Oftentimes professionals will volunteer their time if the company will pay expenses.

If training is not used as part of the compensation reward system, then celebrate successful training with handsome certificates or "battle ribbons." Visible reminders always help motivation and pride. A sure-fire way to fail at training is to make it sporadic and used only to cure an immediate problem. Another failure mode is to make it a reward only for the favored few. Training must be ongoing, forever and for everyone.

## The External Customer

Virtually every business has customers. Customers are the recipients of the products and services businesses provide. Virtually every business succeeds by keeping existing customers happy and

by enticing new ones to use their products and services. Over the last two decades there has been a revolution by consumers. They are no longer satisfied with marginal commodities or services. They do not want to move from supplier to supplier looking for the best deal and the best value. They are tired of throwaway commodities that were not meant to be. Success in dealing with the external customer has taken on a new meaning for those who have become enlightened to the needs of the contemporary consumer. Some success tips include:

Be sure your products and services provide the value your customers expect at a competitive price.

If you want to keep existing customers, be sure your products and services provide some extra value that your customers can use. A guideline is that it is four times more expensive to gain a new customer than it is to keep an existing one happy.

Listen actively to what your customers tell you they want. Make every effort to provide what they say they need.

Anticipate customer needs through open dialogue with them. Don't design in a vacuum.

Potential new customers are often dissatisfied with their existing source. Be sure you offer them what they are not getting from their previous supplier.

Ensure that customer documentation is controlled, kept proprietary and secure. Ensure that you always have the latest documents and specifications that you need to provide the customer what they ordered.

◆ Be sure you have the capability to provide the products and services being ordered.

Ensure that all contracts and purchase orders are clear and complete. Resolve any differences in contracts before they become binding. Communicate in writing and keep accurate customer records.

◆ Whenever possible, keep an open channel of communication between the job holders in your company and those at your customers'. You will get regular feedback on problems before they become critical and you will be able to anticipate their needs in time to develop a solution before they need it.

Go out of your way to ensure that issues do not become problems.

## Success Snapshot

The following example of customer service happened at a Lexus Automobile dealership in Louisiana.

A lady customer had owned her new Lexus about a week when she returned to the dealership in distress. She wore only one brand of designer shoes and the heel of the right shoe would get wedged below the accelerator peddle, causing her to have difficulty with the accelerator and, ultimately, break the heel on the shoe. The service manager at the dealership recorded the problem and offered to make restitution for the shoes.

The woman assumed this would be the last she would hear from the Lexus dealer. A week later, however, a design engineer from the Lexus factory in Japan showed up at her doorstep. He asked to see the shoes and he made measurements and drew sketches of them. The engineer left without saying a word.

A month later, the woman was contacted by the Lexus dealer and asked to bring her car in. The engineer had redesigned the accelerator peddle to ensure that shoe heels would not get wedged any longer. They replaced the accelerator peddle in her car and that retrofit peddle is now standard in Lexus production.

## Design Control

Companies that perform design functions have a most formidable task of continually ensuring that they realize the best return from their research and development budget. Design is such an incredibly complex subject and it is so company specific that it would be ill advised to try to cover its intricacies in this text. A very viable model for design assurance is contained in Section 4.0 of ISO9001. There are also a series of guidelines on design in ISO9004 that are complementary to Section 4.0 of ISO9001. A sure-fire way not to survive in the high-tech, fast-response, rapid-deployment global marketplace is to **not have** your design function controlled and documented.

## Document and Data Control

**The most profound secret of document and data control is not to avoid it!** I am as guilty as anyone. In my office, I have hundreds of documents, books, and manuals and I have no idea how out of date some of them are! Invariably, if I need one for something other than general reference, I order a new one to be sure it is the latest revision. Even in a two-person company, I cannot excuse my lack of document control. Without a configuration control system, I pay the overhead of buying new documents when I need them. In most companies that I have audited, the result of lack of document and data control is much more costly because not everyone is disciplined to verify that they are using the latest or the correct revision. Here are some secrets to success in document and data control:

♦ Keep logs or databases of **all** documents that are used in the quality management system that have an issue date or a revision level. You will probably want to keep separate logs of customer drawings, industry specifications, internal forms and tags, software and operating manuals and procedures. Make an entry each time you receive a new document or each time a revision changes.

♦ Subscribe to services that automatically send you the latest revision of controlled documents and software. Regularly verify the revision levels of industry standards to be sure that there are not superseding documents released.

♦ If your system is uncontrolled and you have a large number of documents, don't mount a six-month effort to catalog each and every item. File them all in a dedicated "archive" area or "reference library." As you need each document, verify its revision, log it, and move it from the archives to the active document library.

♦ Lock your document control area, not because you can't trust people, but because the road to hell is paved with good intentions. The most dedicated employees are those who are most likely to wander off with an original drawing and wind up leaving it under a pile of papers on their desk. Have a librarian who issues controlled documents and logs them in and out.

Success Snapshot

The amount of time required to implement ISO9000 depends on:

◆ The imperatives to become certified
◆ The resources you have available to work on implementation
◆ The resources you are willing to commit to work on implementation
◆ The complexity of your processes and procedures
◆ The amount of outside expertise you use
◆ The realities of your business culture allowing you to implement ISO9000 in parallel with daily work

An almost certain way to have a major finding in an ISO9000 audit is to gloss over the issue of document and data control. This is one of the most often failed elements in an ISO9000 audit because companies resist methodically controlling their documents and data. There is not an immediate and visible reward to this discipline and the subject seldom comes up, until someone builds the wrong revision assembly from a print they had stored in their tool box!

## Supplier Partnerships

There are a number of secrets to successfully acquiring the commodities and services that your company needs to perform its stated mission. Most of them revolve around the same tenets we've discussed in dealing with your customers and dealing with your job holders. That is, dismantle adversarial relationships, develop open and honest communications, and arrive at mutually beneficial scenarios (the "win-win" relationship). As with your document control system, treat your supplier relationships systematically and with reasonable control. A worn-out phrase I have heard used over and over is "we must give our buyers the latitude to find hard-to-get commodities without a bunch of bureaucratic paperwork." **Supplier partnering techniques**

**prove that if you develop mutually beneficial relationships with suppliers who share your values, you will not need to be constantly on a hunt for hard-to-get commodities.**

- ◆ Visit each of your critical suppliers. If they are not ISO9000 certified, find out if they have a baseline quality management system in place. If they don't, they will sooner or later disappoint you with defective product, late delivery, or reliability problems.
- ◆ Pare down your supplier list to those who have exhibited evidence of sharing your value system.
- ◆ Develop strategic alliances with them by sharing your needs, goals, schedule, budget constraints, and quality requirements. Allow them to intelligently gear their capacity to your needs. Make long-term relationships based on both of you keeping your commitments.
- ◆ Regularly evaluate supplier performance and share it with the suppliers. Whenever practical, have the working people in your organization who use the commodities interface with the people at your supplier's plant that make the commodities.
- ◆ Resolve nonconformities in a nonpunitive fashion. Work with the supplier until you have discovered the root cause of the nonconformity and are assured that corrective and preventive actions are in place.

Failing at supplier relationships can be accomplished by treating your suppliers as adversarial vendors or peddlers, squeezing every penny out of them, and not paying them on time. You can contribute to failure by being fickle, using suppliers as pawns against one another, making unreasonable demands for delivery and quality, and changing your mind after beating them to death over price and delivery.

## Inventory Control

There are a number of success secrets that are unique to companies that deal with products, inventory, and manufacturing. The recurring theme is that success is directly tied to successfully con-

trolling your products, inventory, and manufacturing operations so that process variability is eliminated to the greatest extent practical. When inventory integrity is consistent and accurate, productivity increases and frustration decreases.

**Identification and Traceability.** Beyond the examples given in Chapter 6, the only secret to identification and traceability of material is to not implement a system that is more complex than your products warrant. Just because "identification and traceability" is a separate element in ISO9000, that does not imply that you must have some systematic method of serializing or date coding parts. Most manufacturing and distribution operations do, at least, include some kind of batch identification that helps them control inventory turns and may be useful if a run of product is found to be defective.

**Customer Supplied Product.** Another area that is a target for overkill is customer-supplied product. Unless your customers regularly furnish raw materials, subassemblies, tools, molds, fixtures, or consumables, this key element of ISO9000 requires only an honorable mention in your quality documentation. Don't invent a control system if the situation never comes up. You might mention in your level 1 documentation that, should the need arise, you will write a quality plan to cover the handling of customer-supplied product. If you do regularly deal with CSP, then separate quality plans is definitely a good idea. If you try to incorporate CSP procedures into your level 2 documentation, you will have to revise a number of procedures every time your customer has a change in their procedures.

**Handling, Storage, Packaging, Preservation, and Delivery.** It is a good idea to treat each of these topics as a separate procedure. Write procedures only for those that you actually do (or should do!). Document them to the extent necessary to keep your inventory under control. The handling procedure should do no more than ensure that you do not damage your inventory or products. Storage is the actual inventory function and may include activities such as shelf life control and cycle counting. Packaging is necessary if you package commodities. Warehouses and distribution centers will seldom have a need for this paragraph. Preserva-

tion is also a fairly limited use procedure. If you deal in volatile commodities or those subject to storage for long periods of time, then this area will need to be proceduralized. If you build computer systems that are delivered directly to the end user, then there will be little need to write a preservation procedure. Delivery will likely be the subject of operational procedures in most companies. Sooner or later, you give something to your customer in return for some compensation. Whether you physically deliver your products yourself, transmit them via computer, send them common carrier or mail them, you probably deliver something. Again, this procedure should cover exactly what you do. There is no need for a motor freight delivery procedure if you never use

## Success Snapshot

ISO9000 in a Large Company

Jacqueline Randler-Buxo
General Electric Industrial & Power Systems
San Juan, Puerto Rico

GE's main plant in Schenectady, New York was certified to ISO9001 in 1992. The company describes ISO9000 as a series of quality system standards that generically define how to establish, document and maintain a quality system. Their reason for seeking certification revolved around becoming certified before it was required by their customers; however, they also believe that it demonstrates to customers that they have a cohesive quality management system and a commitment to continuous improvement. Most importantly, they believe that an effective quality management system is required to improve productivity and reduce "cycles."

During the implementation phase of ISO9000 in San Juan, the Information Systems group provided the excellent support necessary to produce documentation and to help with interdepartmental communications, and to deal with their sales and operations subsidiaries around the world.

motor freight. The procedure should also give the inventory personnel sufficient latitude to choose delivery methods based on some predetermined (and proceduralized) criteria so that you do not wind up writing a separate procedure for U.S. Mail, UPS, Federal Express, and others.

## Process Control

Chapter 6 describes the basics of process control. The secret to success revolves around defining what a process is and how detailed the procedure should be. A good guideline is "Is this procedure adequate to train a skilled new operator?"

Process control consists of three parts. The first is an accurate job description of the process operator that covers all of the background and skills that person should possess. The second part is training and certification of the operator in the process to be performed. This includes classroom training or study as necessary followed by a demonstration of proficiency to someone who is authorized to evaluate the result of the training. The third element is the process procedure that lists the steps necessary to perform the process. Assuming the operator is skilled and will be judged proficient, you can make most process procedures fairly simple. You must also assume that you have adequate *product* documentation. That is, the shop order package or work order should contain the necessary released documentation to build a specific product. With all of the prerequisites in place, the process procedure for electronic assembly may be as simple as:

1. Review the contents of the Shop Order Package. Ensure that the released drawing, Bill of Material, and Router Sequence Sheet are present and that they all match the revisions on the Shop Order.
2. Lay out the job, identify and count the parts. If there is a discrepancy, process per procedure 246802.
3. Select the manufacturing fixture called for in the router package.
4. Read all the drawing notes.
5. Assemble per drawing and router instructions.

6. Inspect and test the product per procedures 123456 and 567890.
7. Sign and date the Shop Order and move all material and prints to the next Work Center identified on the router.

Again, simplicity is the key to successful process procedures. You will seldom need to write one that gets down to "insert tab 'a' in slot 'b'." If that level of detail is necessary, you need detailed work instructions to compliment the procedures.

Since ISO9000 discusses special processes, it is good to identify those process procedures whose outcome cannot be easily verified. These will often be more complex than most process procedures because there will be a number of steps that will require observation of process variables and, perhaps, recording data from process indicators.

A sure-fire way to fail at process control is to have your processes out of control, have no evidence of training of process operators, and have no job descriptions. **If you run your manufacturing operation by the seat of your pants, you will likely be in the hot seat when you audit the system to ISO9000.**

## Quality Conformance

Somewhere in your processes, whether they be product or service related, most companies have a need to verify that what they plan to do actually happens. Historically, this has manifested itself in toll gate inspections and independent testing. Often these processes are prescriptive and adversarial. An initial scan of ISO9000 paragraphs 4.10, 4.11, 4.12, and 4.13 may lead the reader to the conclusion that this standard perpetuates these methods of conformance verification. On closer examination, ISO9000 allows companies to select the verification methods that make sense for their culture. If you have prescriptive and punitive methods, ISO9000 implementation is a good excuse to phase them out in favor of less costly and more effective methods. If you have informal methods, ISO9000 can help you develop meaningful procedures that add value to the delivery system rather than digging into the profit to pay overhead inspection functions.

**Receiving Inspection.**    Success secrets for receiving acceptable products revolve around your relationship with your suppliers (see Supplier Partnering earlier in this chapter). If you can prevent problems from reaching your facility, the need for a toll gate receiving inspection group may be minimal or nonexistent. Some companies arrive at agreements where their suppliers perform all needed inspections and tests and supply data to the customer verifying those inspections and tests. This practice is called "dock to stock." Another new practice called "out-of-box audit" is becoming popular. It is a form of sampling, but it is often done by independent auditors (third parties) and replaces receiving inspection. If your supplier relationships are solid, you can, at a minimum, develop a history of acceptable performance that minimizes receiving inspection to sample audits. Whatever makes sense for your business, ISO9000 suggests that you verify compliance of the commodities you purchase before they enter the value delivery system. A sure-fire path to disaster is to perform cosmetic inspection and catch functional problems in assembly and test. Not will this not pass an ISO9000 audit, it is not good business practice.

**In-Process Inspection.**    Another classic relic of the industrial revolution is the inspection stations at key points in every factory, complemented by "roving" inspectors. Successful in-process inspection is a matter of the job holders being responsible for their own quality. If they are trained properly, each job holder should be able to certify that his or her products were inspected and tested and they should be able to forward the products to the next work center without need for independent verification.

**Final Inspection and Testing.**    The secret to final inspection and testing is not to do it. The final blessing as a product prepares to meet its customer should be no more than verifying that all previous steps have been accomplished. An effective production system should preclude nonconforming product from moving to the final inspection or testing area. The final audit should be a cursory step to ensure that human error did not inadvertently allow a defective product to make it this far. If you presently use final inspection and test as a road block, consider the fact that you have added maximum value to the product at this point and are now eating into profit dollars to send a complete product back for rework or repair.

**Inspection and Test Records.** The secret to dismantling toll gate inspection is to have the job holders keep complete and accurate records of all inspections and tests. These records should become permanent and be a viable configuration management tool. Quality records should be filed in such a manner that the data is retrievable and usable to repair products, update them, or perform traceability investigations. In these days of liability and lawsuits, accurate testing and inspection records are also invaluable defense tools.

**Inspection, Measurement, and Test Equipment.** Chapter 6 provides the ground rules for control of IMTE. The secret for success in this area is NOT to look for ways to circumvent calibrating test and measuring equipment. There is an unfounded belief in many companies that money spent on calibrating equipment is wasted because the equipment is seldom found to be out of calibration. That's like saying that your children should not have regular medical exams because they are seldom sick. The reason the equipment is seldom out of calibration is because you monitor it regularly! If you allow it to drift out of calibration before it is checked, you stand a good chance of shipping product that is out of tolerance. Not every piece of equipment has to be calibrated to the National Institute of Standards and Technology (NIST) for it to be considered calibrated. If there are industry standards or secondary standards that you establish that are suitable for your environment, then specify those standards for calibrating your equipment. When I worked at the Johnson Space Center, we built a new master clock for the Manned Spaceflight Network. It was so accurate that NIST could not provide a secondary standard that was more accurate to calibrate the clock, so we established our own standard. A sure-fire way to fail this requirement is to turn the calibration program over to a service and not specify what services you want performed. ISO9000 requires that you establish the standards that you want your IMTE calibrated to.

**Inspection and Test Status.** Success in this requirement is no more complex than ensuring that the acceptability of any product in the value delivery system is evident at all times. Most companies have systems in place to give evidence of acceptability before the product is moved to the next step in the process. Just as we discussed in Inspection and Test, this is vital to the traceability

required to eliminate costly toll gate inspections. A secret is that, in many noncritical environments, product that has no marking can be considered acceptable, as long as you can demonstrate that all nonconforming products are identified and segregated from those that are acceptable.

**Control of Nonconforming Product.**   There are several success secrets in this area. The first is to dismantle the punitive system of massive withholding areas that are locked and bonded. If you have an effective quality management system in place, job holders are motivated not to use products that are nonconforming, so a simple system of clearly marking defective parts is often acceptable and auditable. Another secret is to disband the classic material review board that sits in judgement over defective material. Turn the responsibility for determining the disposition of nonconforming product to the job holders that were responsible for the defect. Invite them to diagnose what went wrong and recommend remedies. If third parties (like the customer) have to be involved in repair or scrap decisions, have the workers contact them and explain the options. Job holders who have to explain their errors to a customer are less likely to repeat them. Have the job holders track their own nonconformances with some of the quality tools described in Chapter 8. Involve them in performing root-cause analyses to determine why repetitive defects occur.

## Corrective and Preventive Action

Along with internal auditing, corrective and preventive action are the keys to a successful quality management system. The secret to making this work is proactively correcting processes to keep nonconformities from recurring and methodical actions to ensure that the corrective action was effective. The distinctions and practical use can best be demonstrated with an example I use in *Root-Cause-Analysis* training. The example shows clearly how corrective and preventive actions can save a lot of money and a lot of grief if they are systematically and religiously utilized.

Corrective and preventive action must be more than stomping out grass fires. There is a wealth of savings to be realized when companies dig down and fix root causes and avoid repeat-

# Root-Cause-Analysis Investigation

You arrive home from work on a July afternoon and it is 95° in the house. You check your thermostat and verify that the air conditioning was left in the "on/automatic" position. You go to the breaker box and find that the main breakers for the compressor are tripped. You reset the breakers. You inspect the condensing unit and observe that the fan is running and there is warm air being exhausted from the unit. You go in the house and there is refrigerated air coming from the vents. By 9 PM the house has cooled down and the thermostat is cycling normally.

The next day, you arrive home and find the house is 95° again. You call the service technician. He hooks up his gages to the compressor and tells you that the unit is "overcharged" and that it is probably tripping out on high pressure. He removes some freon from the system and leaves. For the next few days, the air conditioner is running when you come home from work.

> What was the symptom?
>
> What was the symptomatic cure?
>
> What was the apparent cause?
>
> What was the fix?
>
> What was the corrective action?
>
> What was the preventive action?
>
> What was the root cause?

*Answers to Root Cause Analysis*

| | |
|---|---|
| Symptom | It was hot in the house even though the air conditioning was turned on. |
| Symptomatic Cure | Reset the circuit breakers and restart the air conditioner. |
| Apparent Cause | The unit was overcharged and tripping out on high pressure. |
| The Fix | Remove freon from the compressor. |
| Corrective Action | None. |
| Preventive Action | None. |
| Root Cause | Not investigated. |

If the technician had been better trained, he would have looked for the root cause and found that the evaporator coils were dirty and the unit was tripping out because the coils were freezing up. Preventive action would have been to inspect and clean the coils every six months and to install pressure limit switches on the compressor.

edly fixing symptoms. Certain death in an ISO9000 audit is to not have a documented trail of corrective and preventive action that is well executed and methodically followed through.

## Internal Auditing

As we just mentioned, internal auditing is another of the keys to a successful quality management system. Chapters 5 and 6 discuss the structure of internal auditing. The secret of effective internal auditing is to select the auditors from the work force, not from the quality department. In larger companies, there is a tendency to promote quality engineers to full-time auditing positions. All this accomplishes is moving adversarial relationships higher in the company structure (instead of line people interfacing with quality inspectors, the line people now must deal with quality engineers). Pick candidates who have an analytical personality. Select those who will not get rattled or frustrated when looking into "other people's business." Do not choose those who have an ax to grind or a hidden agenda. Auditing skills can be taught to willing candidates. I am so emphatic about the importance of internal auditing, I've enclosed a training course that you can use in your company (Appendix D).

## A Family of Measures

In Chapter 8 we discussed the importance of developing and keeping viable a variety of measures of the successes and failures of your quality management system. One of the secrets to success is ensuring that the measurements are real, accurate, and timely. Biased and late data is worse than none at all because no one trusts the information. Another is to share the measures with everyone so that the shared vision of where you are going is kept alive. Drive down collection of data to those performing the work. If they own the numbers, they will use them to improve their own processes and you will get more meaningful measures and a better product or service. Challenge every area to develop meaningful measures so that you can see progress on a regular basis and take immediate corrective action when a process has drifted out of control.

## Selecting a Consultant

When venturing into any new undertaking, one of the most cost-effective approaches to successful implementation is to seek the help of a professional consultant. A highly skilled consultant can facilitate implementation of strategic quality initiatives in far less time and with far less wasted effort than you can on your own. If you resist using consultants because they are costly or because you aren't comfortable selecting the "right" one, these tips should help you find a facilitator to help you achieve your goals.

First, have a clear set of expectations of what you hope to accomplish. For instance, the requirement may be to achieve ISO9000 registration in eighteen months and launch a total quality initiative at the same time. Estimate how long and how much it would cost to do it yourself. Be realistic with labor costs. Use hourly rates that include fringe, burden, and profit. Also be realistic about having the people to dedicate to the project. Also consider that hiring a consultant usually is motivation to keep the effort alive and on track. Will you have the same motivation if you do it in house? If doing it yourself requires external training, will you be able to schedule the time to go to the training with your present and projected work loads? Does your company have a history of starting projects and abandoning them when work loads get heavy? If so, a consultant can be very expensive because many of us base our fee structure on being able to keep a predictable schedule.

Once you have established a scope of work and a projected budget, you can begin looking for a consultant. I advise you not to pick one from the classified ads. Anyone can buy ad space. Call other companies that have successfully done what you want to do and ask for recommendations. If they give glowing praises that the consultant accomplished exactly what he or she was contracted to do, then you have a candidate. If the praises also include that the consultant gave more value than expected, you have a viable candidate.

Contact the consultant and have a phone interview. First impressions and chemistry are accurate barometers. If you don't get along on the telephone, you probably are not a match. If the initial contact is positive, the consultant should offer to meet with

you and discuss your needs with no charge for the first meeting. If he or she has to travel a long distance, it is etiquette for the company to pay travel expenses, but each of you should be risking your time for the first meeting. Go into the meeting with a list of questions. Ask about the consultant's approach. Determine if he or she is committed to getting you up and running on your own as quickly as possible or is he or she looking for a lucrative place to camp for a few years. Ask for a list of successes they have had in similar environments. If they can give you several people to call for referrals, you have a basis to continue. If they do not, you are on risky ground. Answers such as "This is very similar to some work I did five years ago," or "This is a logical extension of what I have done in the past," give clues that you had better dig deeper. Consultants have to start somewhere and you may choose to take that risk, but do so with your eyes open and your purse strings tightly controlled. Insist that the consultant generate a timetable with measurable milestones to be furnished with his or her proposal. Do get a written proposal with the scope of work and schedule clearly stated.

## Success Snapshot

ISO9000 implementation costs depend on:

- ◆ The amount of internal expertise available
- ◆ The effectiveness of the existing quality management system
- ◆ The existing level of documentation control
- ◆ The existing level of design control
- ◆ The innate cultural resistance to change
- ◆ The degree of desire to turn the effort into an investment
- ◆ The outside resources and expertise needed
- ◆ The complexity of your processes and procedures
- ◆ The cost of the certification and recertification process

Consultants should come across as confident and positive, but not cocky and prescriptive. If they have a packaged solution to each of your problems, you will not get the value that a consultant should bring to the table. Get a list of references and call them and interview them. They should all give glowing praises of how much better off they are since the consultant helped them.

Consulting fees can vary widely by services provided, market price, geography, expertise, and involvement. Someone who just facilitates ISO9000 implementation can run $250 to $750 per day. A facilitator that will help you build your quality management system may get $500 to $1,500 a day, and someone who can help in all phases of your strategic quality initiative may demand $1,000 to $3,000 per day. The worth of the consultant is directly tied to how many times over he or she will pay for themselves, not the daily fee.

## Selecting a Registrar

Selecting a registrar is every bit as critical as selecting a consultant. Once you have become certified, it would be a very expensive process to fire the registrar and start all over again (your certification is not transferable). As with the consultant, ask others who are certified what their experiences are with their registrar. Again, look for glowing reviews. Get three bids and ask for lists of clients to call for references. Call the references and spend some time with them on the phone. They are usually glad to talk about their successes and you may get some good tips from them on how to pass an audit.

Don't make your value judgment by name alone. The registrar must be a fit with your type of business. Many registrars have limited areas of expertise. Some try to deal in too many areas and you may wind up with auditors who have little familiarity with your business. Most registrars charge by the audit-day, so you want an audit team that doesn't spend one day just learning the language of your business. Be wary of travel charges. Most registrars have travel costs associated with their services. If you are fortunate to have several qualified registrars in your geographical area, it might make cost and access more attractive (all other factors being equal). Aligning yourself with a "new" regis-

trar (they are springing up every day) may look attractive in price, but will they be around in ten years? Again, everyone has to start somewhere and I am not opposed to giving new registrars a chance, but go into the arrangements with your eyes open. Even the new ones need to give you some assurances that they are competent and stable.

Each registrar should be certified to issue marks from one or more certifying bodies (such as the Registrar Accreditation Board [RAB] in the United States, NACCB in Britain, or RvC in Holland). If your particular industry places high value on one or more of these marks, then choose your registrar accordingly. Some of the newer companies are certified only by the RAB, which is still not universally recognized in the international arena. If you plan to deal with any companies in the European Union, you should have NACCB or RvC marks on your certificate.

The registrar business is highly competitive and highly responsive. Registrars are continually finding ways to make their services more attractive without compromising their standards. A few years ago, an ISO90000 registration was for a single site. Now, most registrars will issue certificates for multiple sites that have the same quality management system. One company I work with wants all of its branches around the world under the same certificate. That is a new concept today, but it may be common in a few months. Not too long ago, certification was for three years with periodic audits every six months. Some registrars now offer four-year certificates and surveillance audits on eight-month centers. What is industry gospel as this is being written may be history by the time you read it. Either rely on your consultant to help you separate current fact from fiction or perform your own research before believing that there is a level playing field among registrars.

## Internal Customers

Another valuable success tool is adapting the concept that every job holder has an internal customer that he or she must satisfy just as diligently as the external customer. The concept is based on the premise that each of us is responsible for our own actions and that when we hand off our product or service to the next per-

son in the value delivery system, that product or service should be correct and acceptable. What makes the internal customer culture work is that each of us is the customer of the person ahead of us in the value delivery system. If we want the product or service that we receive to process to be correct before we get it, we have to have good suppliers. To make it all work, we simply identify who our customers and suppliers are and treat them with the same respect we would treat our external customers. We also have to be good customers, letting our suppliers know when we have a problem with their work. If the system of internal auditing for ISO9000 is effectively implemented, the internal customer system is the ideal culture to make internal audits shine as the vehicle of continuous improvement.

# The Secrets of Success— Virtual Leadership

The secret to successfully implementing Virtual Leadership is a thorough understanding of the attributes of a Virtual Leader. We have defined Virtual Leadership as administering processes and people without the overhead of management. To evolve Virtual Leaders from managers, we have to have a clear picture of the attributes that a Virtual Leader must possess to be effective. If managers can perform a candid and honest self-analysis against these attributes, they can begin the process of personal growth and greater business success. If you are serious about beginning the journey, use of the following can help create a list of the personal attributes that you possess and formulate your individual strategy for change.

Virtual Leaders are:

1. Standards of truth
2. Patterns to model
3. Builders of teams
4. Producers of results

## Standards of Truth

The attribute of personal honesty transcends all others. If you can be trusted, you can open most any door and you can earn the respect and cooperation of most anyone. If you cannot be trusted, you can be an autocratic manager who spends a great deal of time keeping track of what was told to whom and watching your flanks. You see, honesty requires no maintenance. Historically, managers have been taught that little white lies go with the job. When you are in management, there are certain proprietary subjects that you are sworn to protect and you are bound to find creative ways to present answers to your employees without telling them the truth. How would you answer the question "Boss, are we going to have layoffs this year?" If you know that layoffs are an option to declining productivity and/or sales, the book of traditional management prohibits you from being honest and saying "We withhold the right to reduce staff as a last resort." Instead, you generally hear "It is not our policy to reduce head count," or "We've never laid off anyone in your department," or "Don't worry about it, you're one of the key people." In the honest scenario, the employees can watch production levels and begin to plan for a work slowdown by retraining or looking to other industries. The employees who had sunshine pumped up their skirts are constantly in a state of anxiety, knowing that they can't plan anything because you've placed quicksand around them. They will be less productive and overly sensitive to any changes. Their attitude will be "No matter what they say, I feel it coming, so I'm not going to kill myself." If they believe you when you honestly told them that layoffs are a last resort, self-motivated employees will work hard to cut costs and minimize waste so that they may help avoid a reduction in force. Who knows, they might even suggest new uses or new markets for your products and services!

## Self-Honesty

How honest are you with yourself? That's a strange question, on the surface, but it needs answering. Do you constantly tell yourself that you can quit smoking any time or that you will start exercising regularly next week? Do you rationalize the little fibs that you tell your employees? How much of what you tell people

to do are you modeling? Do you like yourself? Do you like your job and your boss? Do you avoid these kinds of questions at all cost?

To be honest with the world, you have to start with being honest with yourself. That process starts with a lot of introspection and a look into a mirror that may not reflect what you want to see. Start with a clean note pad and openly answer some simple questions. Answer the questions knowing that no one else will ever hear or see your answers. Use one sheet for positive answers and another for negative answers. Do you like yourself? Would you want you for a friend; boss; employee; mate? What are your positive attributes and what are your negative ones? What about you causes positive and negative behavior in the people around you? Do you accomplish the objectives you say or promise that you will? Are you goal driven or crisis driven? Are you argumentative and confrontational or are you a listener and a facilitator? Are you passive/submissive or do you stand by your values? What are the roadblocks to your really being successful?

You can tell a lot about how honest you are with yourself by analyzing the two lists you've just created. How many of the answers are the whole truth and how many are the public image you would like to project? How many of them are excuses? How many of them point blame at someone else? Do you like what you see? Remember, you can set fire to these lists when you are through.

How do you answer the question, Are you honest with yourself? Do you have behavioral traits that you need to change to be comfortable with your self-honesty? Are you likely to do the work to make the changes? How difficult will they be to change? Remember, the entire journey of virtual leadership is based on changing human behavior. If you can't start with yourself, there is no sense trying to change others.

Can you change by yourself or do you need help and support? Many times, becoming at peace with yourself is a matter of identifying the behavioral traits you do not like and making them into a list of affirmations. Affirmations that you regularly refer to and verbalize (to yourself) are very powerful self-improvement tools. They must be positive and they must portray a goal achieved, not one in progress. For example:

I always keep my employees abreast of the latest information.
I exercise at least three times a week and I feel great.
I spend at least one hour a week on self-improvement.
My employees can always come to me for an honest answer.
I am always on time for meetings.

I keep my list of affirmations in the back of my daytimer and refer to them at least once a week (another affirmation!). I read them aloud, when there is no one else around. With no other behavioral changes, I can keep most of my negative behaviors under control just through affirmations. That is, if I can't honestly verbalize an affirmation, I take steps to make sure that it is not a lie the next time I say it. Also, I constantly keep an internal dialogue going that questions my actions. As the late southern humorist Brother Dave Garner used to say, "You don't have to watch what you do, you just have to watch what you think!"

Another part of self-honesty is looking at what you are doing and deciding if you need to be here or somewhere else. Are you obsessive compulsive and really have little regard for people? If these traits are programmed in, then perhaps you are not destined to be a leader, coach or facilitator. Perhaps you are better suited to research or writing or some other solitary endeavor. Is your value system really based on a military system of rank and privilege? If it is, then you need to find an environment that appreciates those values because they are counter to the tenets of Virtual Leadership. Are you really happy at your job? Can you ever be happy in the type of culture that Virtual Leadership seeks to evolve? Perhaps you can't just quit your job because you aren't happy, but you can identify your strengths and your motivators and learn where you can help and where you must avoid being a negative influence on those around you.

## Honesty with Others

Once we have reached a tentative peace with ourselves, we've got to look at how we deal with others and how they perceive us. Do you regularly treat your employees as mushrooms (keep them in the dark and feed them manure)? Do you tell your boss what he wants to hear or do you always tell the unvarnished truth? Do

you give reports at meetings that are liberally sprinkled with half-truths (Stated: The Reproduction Department met its cost reduction goal last month. Not Stated: They did it by not fixing a broken copy machine)? Do you assign blame with every statement that you make ("It's late because I didn't get my input on time.")? If you participate in any or all of these activities, do you really believe that they are the best practice?

The last question is often the most difficult to answer. We set up dysfunctional systems of human behavior that allow and condone these management styles. The person who tells half truths believes that his tactics are effective because he gets results and no real feedback to the contrary. Those around him filter out the baloney and move on with their work, never telling him that his answers need to be strained through a sieve. In time, this co-dependent behavior becomes routine. Co-dependents can work together, live together, eat together, bowl together, and never be honest with each other. Moving up the ranks of management is often dependent on how well we have honed our wordsmithing skills so that we have our troops snowed and our bosses proud of us. How many of us know managers that are admired for being able to set out traps and snare others in little white lies? What prevents us (as managers) from being honest with each other and with our employees?

As there are in most industries, the early days of NASA saw huge inequities in pay between departments and even between employees in the same department. As I moved up the ranks from assembler to planner to engineer, I was always reminded never to discuss my pay with anyone and never to ask what anyone else made. My father had a white-collar union job where everyone made exactly the same base salary, and I was used to hearing salaries discussed all of my adolescent life. This dichotomy was always a source of irritation to me, and very few people would even discuss it. I had to wait until I joined the ranks of "management" to look for answers. I would draw up a question-and-answer session that revolved around the issue "Why can't I post a copy of my paycheck stub on the bulletin board?" I wish I had honed my Virtual Leadership skills back then because I only asked the question of myself and a few close confidants. I should have asked it of everyone. The consensus was that everyone had a

morbid curiosity about what everyone else made; however, they weren't willing to divulge their salaries in order to gain the information about everyone else. The reasons usually revolved around embarrassment about their salary being too low or too high. Some believed it would create a ranking system among those in the same job description. In one company, I inherited a purchasing agent that had bullied her way into making much more than her skills or training demanded. Most people I interviewed would have divulged their pay to learn what she made so they could dislike her even more than they did. Every time I answered the question for myself, it came down to embarrassment that I made three to four times what most of the workers made. It wasn't that I didn't deserve the compensation for 80-hour weeks and total P & L responsibility, it was that I added very little to the product delivery system. I attended a lot of meetings and analyzed a lot of reports. I also did a significant amount of training and mentoring, but that still didn't justify the inequities in salaries. At the end of the day, I always felt that salaries fell into the "little white lie" area of management and were always a stumbling block to me being totally honest with my employees.

I also had a standing rule that any direct question that was asked of me would receive one of three answers: 1) I would give you the answer. 2) If I didn't know the answer, I would find out and get back with you. 3) If I knew the answer and it was privileged information, I would tell you that I couldn't tell you. I felt that was being honest, but, in retrospect, that was a cop-out, just like the salary issue.

## How Honest Is Honest?

If you feel as though the honesty subject is being beaten to death, this is just a reminder of how critical it is to the success of Virtual Leadership. At the same time, we cannot set honesty on a pedestal above the realities of being fully human. We all have a history, a past, and a few skeletons in the closet. Psychologists tell us that white lies and half truths are part of the human reality. We bring about reaction in other people by the words we choose and the actions we model and very few of us are saints. In some cases, public figures are held to several sets of standards of honesty, depending on if we are for them or against them. The so-

cietal norms for honesty can be skewed for politicians, clergy, and criminals, if we allow it to happen. I do not believe that there are degrees to honesty; however, I think there are group norms and a baseline for what our society considers to be honest. In some companies it is expected that employees take pens and pencils home. In others, the same act is considered stealing. Some law enforcement groups allow an unspoken tolerance above the posted speed limit. If you regularly drive 7 miles per hour over the speed limit and never receive a citation, are you breaking the law? Each of us has to form a definition of what honesty means to our individual conscience and abide by that conscience. If your conscience fails you, your contemporaries will usually provide the feedback needed to ensure that your definition of honesty is the consensus definition.

Once we have a benchmark, each of us has to evaluate if we have what it takes to be honest with ourselves and with our job holders. We have to be willing to create an environment where we can comfortably post our paycheck stubs on the bulletin board. We have to retire the book of traditional management that contains the secrets that we aren't supposed to divulge. Impossible you say? Not so. At Johnsonville Foods in Wisconsin, everyone starts at the same salary. The only way to advance is to learn a new skill. The pay for each skill learned is posted and common knowledge. The company books are open to the job holders because they set production quotas and set their own budgets, so they know what everyone makes. They are wildly successful and there is a waiting list to work there. Their CEO, Ralph Stayer, is a Virtual Leader who gave trust to get trust and modeled honesty to establish an environment of honesty. The success of Johnsonville Foods is just one example that Virtual Leadership is not only possible, it works splendidly over the long haul!

## Patterns to Model

One of the certainties of human behavior is that we learn best by conduct that is modeled for us. We can read books, discuss philosophy, make lists of affirmations, set goals, and make resolutions to change how we act, but we are most influenced to behave as those around us behave. One of the most dramatic examples of

## Success Snapshot

*Trust and Cooperation*

Lee Royal, Organizational Development Specialist
Dallas Outsourcing Center
SHL, Inc. (Formerly FMC Corporation)
Dallas, TX

I worked very hard in my organization on a simple theory I call "do what you say and say what you do." It manifested itself in an unusual way:

1. The employees developed their own standards of conduct. They are behavioral guidelines centered around keeping commitments and treating each other with respect. The employees presented these guidelines to management, who accepted them.

2. Using company funds, the employees purchased a large plaque engraved with the standards. They then called an organization-wide meeting at which everyone (including the managers) ceremonially signed the plaque.

3. There is a copy of the plaque attached to everyone's company ID badge.

4. Through a peer review system and immediate feedback, everyone is held accountable to the standards.

In the first eighteen months this was in place, trust and cooperation has increased dramatically. There is more open access to information, people are keeping their commitments to one another, and many of the managers have experienced an increase in credibility.

modeling that I have seen is contained in Joel Barker's video *Discovering the Future: The Business of Paradigms*. While Joel is making a case for the power of paradigms, he depicts the life of the Tarahumara Indians in Northern Mexico. They regularly run 70 miles as part of a religious ceremony. For most of us, running 70 miles is totally unreal, yet, for generations, the parents have

modeled for the children how to run 70 miles at a time, and the children have learned from that modeling. You could write books and publish videos about how one runs 70 miles, but unless you lived in the environment where it was modeled for you, I submit that you will never be able to run more than the 20+ miles as historically modeled for us by the great runners of our culture in the United States.

It has been my observation that we learn either directly or the opposite of what is modeled for us. Many of my contemporaries grew up in dysfunctional homes with one or more alcoholic parents. Many of them are nondrinkers and a few are alcoholics. The nondrinkers learned that their modeling led to negative consequences and behave exactly opposite of how their parents acted. The alcoholics found it more to their personalities to follow in their parents footsteps.

Current conventional wisdom says that excessive compulsive behavior skips a generation and the grandchildren of alcoholics are more likely to be excessive compulsive than the children. My limited and nonscientific studies conclude that the obsessive compulsive behavior is learned from the model; however, it is often focused in another area (like overeating or workaholic behavior) in the children. Most children of excessive compulsive parents that I know exhibit some form of excessive compulsive behavior. Those that are usually socially acceptable (like eating and working) are often dismissed as positive attributes. Let's look at what this all has to do with leadership.

## Our Parent Tapes

For the vast majority of us, being leaders has to be learned because we grew up in homes that were benevolent dictatorships. One of the parents was usually dominant. There were arbitrary rules of the house established from what was learned from their parents. "Eat your spinach," "No TV before 7 PM," "Polish your shoes every Sunday night," "Take out the trash every Tuesday and Thursday," and "Speak only when spoken to" are a few arbitrary rules that many of us grew up with. They were not *suggestions* or goals, they were rules handed down by a benevolent dictator who loved you and punished you when you broke one of

them. The most arbitrary of all was (is) "Do it just because I told you to." That one statement led more to our autocratic upbringing than any other I can think of. The first time I heard myself saying it to one of my sons, I almost dropped to my knees and screamed from the frustration of having verbalized those words. In most homes, there was a boss who knew more than the workers who dispensed work assignments, judged the results, and took corrective action when the results were less than expected. Corrective action may have been a night without dinner or a spanking, but it was a motivational tool of consequence. That is, break a rule and you will be blamed, shamed, and punished to keep you from making the same mistake again.

When I lecture on this subject, I show a picture that I cut from an issue of the American Automobile Association's magazine. It shows a family sitting around the dining room table reviewing various brochures and specification sheets for new automobiles. The accompanying story is how to go about selecting the right vehicle for your family by reviewing safety, performance, and cost factors. Get real! Around my house, about every two years, Dad pulled in the driveway with a new family car, much to the surprise of everyone (including my mother!). There was no review of specifications or consensus thinking at my house! This never manifested itself more vividly than when he came home with a 1963 Peugeot station wagon with a 4-speed shifter on the steering column. The thing looked like a hearse! His rationale was that it came with steel-belted tires, got good gas mileage, and I wouldn't be able to speed in it. I would be relegated to borrowing this car from hell through my junior and senior year in high school. How could any self-respecting teenager drive a hearse with a shifter that pointed up in the air when it was in 4th gear? Did Dad ever know what he did to my adolescent love life with that one arbitrary, benevolent decision? Are you modeling for your children and employees what was modeled for you at home?

## Stand at Ease, Smoke 'Em If Ya Got 'Em

Another profound influence on our modeling, over the last few generations, is the U.S. military. If you or your model was a member of the military, your minds were formed around rank, command, obedience, and unquestioned following of direct orders.

You were stripped of individuality, convinced you were expendable, and modeled by a seasoned drill instructor. You saluted officers, marched to and from everywhere, learned skills by rote instruction, memorized creeds, and did exactly what you were told to do, no more, no less. You checked your brain at the bus station and often were discharged addicted to cigarettes, alcohol, and the power of giving orders (there is a lot of evidence that the military used nicotine (smoke breaks), alcohol, and permissive sexual behavior (Saturday night leave) as rewards for positive behavior). There is no doubt that some of the discipline taught in the military is positive and there is no doubt that "the military method" has been successful in making the United Stages *the* military super power. These days, however, there are major efforts to launch total quality in the military in an effort to break down the punitive modeling of the past. Strategic quality initiatives in the military are meeting substantial resistance, however, because the risk/reward/rank system is inflexible and historical modeling is hard to change.

## Pray for Us

The third behavioral model for many of us was our secular upbringing. I will not dwell on this topic; however, there is no organized religion that I am aware of that does not have a deity (or deities) and worshipers. The deity knows all, its disciples are unquestionably in control and the faithful follow the teachings without question. There is no teamwork or leadership modeled in most houses of worship, only reinforcement to respect those in charge so that you can, eventually, be in charge.

## What Did We Learn in School?

Ah, the great bastions of learning! The institutions charged by our society to teach our young how to function in the adult world! Surely our schooling would be progressive, learn from the past, and adopt the behavioral modeling that would make us more and more successful, wouldn't it? How many times in your academic carrier were you involved in designing a syllabus? How often did instructors call for a consensus on how the class would be structured? How conducive to team behavior was the system of grades and rank?

I received the full benefit of how schools model behavior with my first seven years in a parochial school taught by Catholic nuns. By the time I started eighth grade, I was fully programmed to follow arbitrary instructions (that were for my good and I would understand them later in life), take direct orders without question, don't draw outside the lines, sit up straight, walk quietly to the next class, and, if it is in a textbook, it is gospel. By the time my intellect began developing in high school, I started questioning the fact that the students were not part of the process, only the beneficiary (victim) of it. I was, once again, told that I would understand these "grownup things" later in life. Well, I'm now fifty and still do not understand why arbitrary rule and control is necessary to achieve positive results!

My models in college were equally dictatorial. I never even got a good look at my freshman and sophomore history professors, because I sat (alphabetically) in the back of an auditorium of 200+ students. I was never once asked for my input into how our two semester slide-rule interpretation class could be made more effective! I doubt that there were any ad hoc process improvement committees in the Cullen College of Engineering. I know there was no attempt to lower the barriers of rank between students, instructors, professors, and department heads. I currently have an association with a university that teaches advanced management principles, yet the inner workings of the staff has changed little since the industrial revolution. As with the military, change is difficult when rank and tenure are such an intrinsic part of the system. The tenure system virtually ensures resistance to dismantling barriers to communication and to replacing autocratic rule with high commitment interactive models. I do not intend to imply that schools at all levels aren't making great strides in internal improvement, they just have a long way to go to be practicing what they are preaching and modeling the behavior we need to learn to be leaders.

## All Things Considered . . .

When you look at how most of us were raised in this country over the last few generations, we really have no modelling for the kinds of leadership that we must exhibit to bring our companies successfully into the next century. Since our earliest experiences with our parents, through our secular training, primary school,

secondary school, college, and military lives, we have learned by modeling that there should be a vertical management system in place, those who know the most should be in charge, those who are learning should be submissive and do what they are told, and that we will be punished if we do not follow the rules. We also learned that, when we fail, we assign blame elsewhere and we are shamed for making a mistake. We were taught that we earn respect through rank and we gain privilege as we grow in the vertical hierarchy. Even though our mistakes grow in scope as we move up the chain of command, we have more tools at our disposal to push blame downhill. We lecture those below us on ac-

## Virtual Leadership Might Have Helped

Juan held up the First Bank of El Paso and headed across the border into Mexico. The Texas Rangers had been foiled by Juan crossing the border before, but this time they obtained permission to pursue him into the Mexican frontier. After weeks of searching, word came that Juan was holed up in the village of San Miguel. Sure enough, the Texas Rangers walked into the cantina in San Miguel and Juan was busy drinking and gambling.

"Tell me where the money from the bank robbery is hidden, Juan," demanded the senior Texas Ranger. There was no response. The bartender volunteered the fact that Juan spoke no English. "Get over here and interpret what I say," directed the senior Texas Ranger to the bartender. Once again, the Texas Ranger demanded that Juan tell him where the money was hidden. "I will never tell," spoke Juan. The Ranger demanded a translation from the bartender, who replied "He says he will never tell."

"Tell him that I will hang him in the town square at sunrise if he does not tell me where the money is hidden," barked the Texas Ranger, as he prepared a hangman's noose. The bartender translated the threat. Juan hesitated for a moment and replied, "Tell him the money is in the dry well at the edge of town." "What did he say?" demanded the Ranger of the bartender. "Juan is prepared to die rather than tell where the money is hidden" said the bartender.

ceptable behavior and then we sexually harass our secretaries (after all, we learned from the military that the favors of a woman are a perk for those who defend our shores).

## How Do We Develop Models of Virtual Leadership?

Since, for most of us, our programming is so well imprinted on our personalities, we have to seek out those models who have broken with their paradigms and have launched successful cultural transitions to success. We have to consciously question each of our behaviors to methodically modify how we deal with other people. We have to eat the elephant in small, bite-sized pieces. We cannot read this or any other book and expect to model Virtual Leadership. We have to seek out and benchmark from the models whose positive behavior we would like to emulate. Here are some examples of models of Virtual Leadership.

Once again, Johnsonville Foods comes to mind. Their primary product has always been sausage. For years, they were moderately successful in their local market. Although business was "okay," Ralph Stayer was not happy with the high turnover and low morale and he sensed that they could do better. Conventional wisdom would have been to attend a few seminars and install some productivity improvement tools. Instead, Ralph asked the workers why they had a poor attitude and why the high turnover. He was given a direct answer. Each day, he would sample the product for quality and judge if it was acceptable for shipment. The workers said that they were just as capable as he to judge the quality of the production and to pass it for shipment to the customers. He gladly turned the taste testing over to them and watched quality and morale improve. He went back to the workers and said, "Okay, what's next?" Their reply was that they couldn't stand the food in the vending machines! He empowered them to solicit bids and pick a caterer that would meet their needs. He found that listening and empowering are such powerful tools, that today, Johnsonville Foods virtually runs itself. The workers set their own quality and production goals. They hire and fire their own team members. They are compensated for results and for learning new skills. They are so successful that Ralph and his former head of Personnel, Linda Honold (they do not need a personnel department any more), spend much of their

time travelling the country sharing their experiences with other companies.

Eric Silverthorn is General Manager of IDB Systems, a major international player in the earth-station satellite communications business. Eric joined the company when it had less than ten employees. He was a field technician installing earth stations in some of the most remote corners of the world. The company grew and prospered because it was able to rapidly deploy systems for the various news agencies when news stories broke and there were no telephone or video circuits available. During the Gulf War, IDB provided most of the reliable phone and video circuits for CNN. Still in his thirties, Eric did not fall into the programming of "management." He knows what it is like to be watching Monday Night Football and two hours later being on an airplane to set up for a breaking news story in Somalia. He knows what kind of dedication everyone in the company must have to leave their families for six weeks and live in a van in Siberia, maintaining a dial-up phone line to Staten Island for an oil company. He is always in the production shop and in intimate contact with the customers. He trains, leads, and facilitates instead of giving orders and signing purchase orders. He turned total responsibility for ISO9000 implementation over to his administrative assistant because she asked for more challenges. He has small children and an intense sense of family and, last Christmas, sent all of his field people a plane ticket to come home and spend a few days with their loved ones. Recently, he and his family were invited to a contract-signing ceremony at the Great Wall in the Peoples Republic of China. Eric won the contract and was ceremoniously awarded it because he was the only bidder that did not tell the Chinese government that their people were untrainable and incapable of working on the installation of the earth station.

The common thread of these models is that they looked beyond their parent tapes and programming when they became managers. They treat others as they would like to be treated. They lead by example. They stay in touch with everyone in the company. They answer questions with questions. They empower everyone and don't revert to programmed behavior when the road gets bumpy. They reward for accomplishment and treat failure as

an opportunity for learning. They have consciously broken with the wasteful modeling of the past and are setting benchmarks of modeling for the companies of the new century.

## Builders of Teams

Another of the four key attributes of Virtual Leaders is that they are builders of teams. That may appear to be self-evident, but it goes deeper than being Vince Lombardi. When analogizing with famous team builders, we can be frustrated because they were born with a leadership gift and we weren't. It is also true that they gain public recognition as leaders by the results they get and not necessarily HOW they got to the national championships. True team builders aren't necessarily born that way and public results may not indicate how the team members feel about their leader's success. In other words, the means to the end may have been different than outward appearances.

Put simply, team builders create environments that encourage team members to achieve their greatest potential. The dynamics of that definition will vary with the people and with the environment. In this chapter we have already discussed honesty and modeling, so we will look at the other attributes a Virtual Leader exhibits as a team builder.

## All for One and One for All

Team builders must be absolutely convinced that they cannot succeed unless all of the team succeeds. They must be deprogrammed from their parent tapes that taught looking out for number one first. They must live and breathe the philosophy that sharing the work, the responsibility, and the rewards is the only way to succeed. A good analogy of a team leader is the maestro in a symphony orchestra. He receives the music that the musicians are to perform and works with each section leader to prepare the plan. He works with each team member as each one practices to perform. He helps nurture each one's individual strengths and works with those who need special assistance. He has the strength to remove those who cannot work as team members and

who will detract from the overall team performance. During the performance, he does little more than set the mood and the pace. He cannot play individual instruments during a performance. He cannot stop performers and correct them in the middle of a concerto. He is judged only on the overall team performance and he knows that without them he has no purpose.

Hold that analogy up to people whom you believe to be team leaders. If they are pseudoleaders, they will be trying to lead and to play a flute at the same time. Instead of standing on the podium with a baton, they are walking around the orchestra pit with a club. Rather than having the orchestra rise to take a bow after a performance, they will stand up, wave their baton and let everyone know that it isn't their fault that the oboe missed a bar.

Team leaders will always say *us* and *we* instead of *I* or *they*. The team will succeed as a unit or fail as a unit. Team leaders will allow no individual to be open to ridicule or blame, nor will they place one individual in a spotlight for the accomplishments of the team. I have observed pseudo-team leaders who have their private agendas that are being met by having people under them "act" as a team. This tactic seldom lasts because selfishness become transparent quickly and team members will revert back to protectionism if they sense that they are pawns in a game.

## Follow My Lead

Team builders must, by nature, exhibit the attributes that they wish their team to exhibit. As we discussed in Modeling, a team builder must set an example. Here are some archetypes of leading by example.

Builders have visions that are shared with everyone around them. These visions are of a clear goal or goals that are a year or two away from becoming reality. These visions drive their activities and set the agenda for all who are on the teams. Leaders by example work to that vision every day and publicly live by it for all to follow. Team members provide feedback that modifies and renews the goals. For example, if your vision is to capture the North American potato chip market within the next year, all of your actions must be focused on achieving that goal. You must visibly lead your team in only those activities that enhance and

# Success Snapshot

*Natural Teamwork*

Dave Dumas, Quality Engineer
Micron Technology
Bosie, Idaho

Too many teamwork approaches are aloof from the culture of a company. I strongly believe this is also true with TQM and is a reason why both initiatives flounder and lead to immense frustration.

At Micron Technology, teams have played a huge role in growth, profitability, innovation, and job satisfaction. We have had teamwork since our founding, yet, if you ask the Micron people, they usually say they do not have teams. In fact, our teams are so natural that the people move seamlessly in and out of teams as part of their normal job functions.

We don't have steering committees, team sponsors, self-directed teams, self-managed teams, or any other formal charters. The key to our teamwork is being totally focused on the business reason for our organization's existence. Our reason for existence is we want to be the lowest cost and highest quality manufacturer of semiconductor memory products in the world. When a yield or delivery issue arises, a team of people with complementary skills forms spontaneously to address the issue. When there is an opportunity for improvement in a process, the same spontaneous team dynamic happens. Our method might be called a variation of Nike's "just do it" that works for us.

When teams are tied to the business reason for existence, they are very organized and smooth without being bureaucratic. They are immensely flexible, very responsive, and exhibit an amazing speed in making decisions, which is critical in our competitive market. This culture exists at all levels in our company, even within the Board of Directors.

Since team performance is tied directly to the business reason for being a company, we reward the teams by distributing the profits back to the teams (In 1994, 10% of our $400M net income was distributed back to our 5,500 team members). The monetary reward is just part of the success story of our teams. The members learn new skills, have opportunities for advancement, and are recognized. These personal rewards cause them to go to amazing extremes to support the team.

Our teamwork has helped us reach our stated goal, as evidenced by the fact that our competitors are emulating many of our strategies. Your company can also realize success through teamwork by avoiding useless bureaucracy, giving people reasons to be team members, focusing on results instead of activity, and avoiding creating obstacles of teamwork that get in the way of the work that needs to be done.

further the goal. If you are busy building a cookie factory while you are telling your troops to capture the potato chip market, your are dictating, not leading, and your team will be less successful because you aren't modeling what you preach.

Leaders by example follow through with commitments. If you expect your team to be thorough and complete projects on time and within budget, you must set the example. These leaders are on time for meetings, prompt with responses for support or resources, attentive to the details of what they promised and when, and mindful of the needs of the team members. Leaders by example are highly visible. They are not up to their elbows in work that belongs to the team members, but they are constantly moving through the work areas interacting with the team members about what they are doing. Visibility means daily exposure to the actual work, not a speech at the monthly awards presentations. Visible leaders actively listen to what is being said and they share the benefits of their experiences, without being directive or patronizing.

Leaders by example broadcast energy and enthusiasm. An enthusiastic leader says "Good Morning, it's going to be a productive day," not "Isn't the rain ever going to stop?" They answer "How are you?" with "I'm terrific, how are you?" Even if they are under pressure or feeling lousy, the verbal affirmation of "I feel great" is powerful medicine for what ails you.

Leaders by example approach each opportunity with a sense of urgency. They start and complete tasks in a timely manner. They do not allow problems to drag on for days. They do not accept answers unless they include "I'll have it done by XXX day at XXXX time." They create an environment of kinetic energy that keeps momentum at a steady pace, heart rate slightly elevated, and exhilaration just around the next bend.

## Producers of Results

In sales, you are not a salesperson unless you can close a deal. In Virtual Leadership, you aren't really a leader unless you can produce measurable results. That statement may sound arcane, but it is true. I have observed literally hundreds of managers and

many of them produce little more than reports, meeting minutes, and performance reviews. Their time is occupied with summarizing the results of the accomplishments of others. They take pride in controlling and directing their troops. They seldom, however, personally contribute anything to the bottom line.

Virtual Leaders produce results through the synergistic relationship they have with their teams. As in the model of the snow geese, they all produce measurable results on a daily basis. As with an orchestra leader, the workers and the leaders perform together to produce a harmonious output. Virtual Leaders are always contributing to the value delivery system, not leeching from the overhead budget. Their efforts are focused on producing a product or service, not reporting about it. They are coaching, facilitating, and enabling their teams, not directing or controlling. Successful Virtual Leaders can be recognized for their accomplishments, not for activity or tenure.

# 12

## *Implementing Your Strategic Quality Initiative*

In Chapter 9 we outlined the elements that I suggest be included in a strategic plan. Since every company has a unique product, service, and culture, it would be presumptuous of me to suggest that you follow the outline as written. Conversely, it would be unwise for you to follow the outline, verbatim, as a pattern. The outline makes a good place to launch your initiative. It may even prove helpful in isolating key areas that you know need rework or redesign. It is critical, however, that you are intensely introspective about your company and your culture before drafting an initiative. You may not be able to separate fact from fiction without the help of a consultant. You may not be allowed to tamper with certain positions and processes. You may be able to devote a lot of time and resources to this effort or you may be forced to work on this after hours with minimum support. Each of these factors will determine how the initiative is put together. You may wind up with a prioritized shopping list or a total reengineering effort. The choice is yours. You can't force change.

There should be a great deal of creativeness that goes into building your strategic implementation plan. It is critical, how-

ever, that you implement it in the correct sequence. While there are no cookbooks to success, there are logical and chronological steps that must be followed to ensure that your strategic quality initiative will not become another exercise in futility.

**1. Management Awareness.** All managers must be aware of the options facing them in the future of your business. These options include every logical possibility from leaving the status quo to total process reengineering to selling the company. Whoever the champion(s) of this effort is, this person must use every tool (seminars, videotapes, consultants, plant visits, retreats, books, presentations) to make the decision makers aware of the options facing them as they prepare for a leadership role in the new century. Please do not make the fatal mistake of choosing a single path (such as Deming, Juran, Malcolm Baldrige) and presenting it as the only option. Intelligent leaders need to make informed decisions based on consensus thinking from the best of the best.

**2. Assessment of Readiness to Change.** Before embarking on any new path, there must be an honest and cathartic assessment of the climate for change within your organization. Are there certain rules and traditions that are absolutely sacred? Are there certain individuals and job slots that will be in place through the end of time? Is change okay, as long as it doesn't affect key individuals? Where do the decision makers spend most of their time? In the trenches with the troops? Putting out grass fires? In planning and strategy sessions? With a business broker? Talking with customers? Monitoring their investments? On the golf course? You must find the answer to the questions: To what degree will you be allowed to succeed in your strategic quality initiative? Who will be the champions, the nay sayers, the passive followers, and the silent saboteurs? Is there too much turmoil, right now, to even begin to change the culture? Will this effort be allowed to grow and evolve or will it be discarded when the next program du jour comes along?

A force field analysis (described in Chapter 8) might be the appropriate tool to help you in your assessment. List all of the forces that are driving change on the left and all those opposing change on the right. Assign the forces relative values (i.e., "The

CEO is a strict authoritarian" gets more opposing points than "Lack of a training program."). At the end of the brainstorming session, add up the points and see if you are positive, negative, or in the middle. A large negative score will not bode well for starting any dynamic, human-based changes. If your company is willing to address the opposing forces, then overcoming them becomes part of the strategic plan and adds to the time required. If there is no willingness to change, your strategic initiative is doomed before you get out of the gate.

**3. Develop a Strategic Plan.**   Using Chapter 9 as a guide, select the approach and tools that will best suit your culture then develop an implementation plan. Even if the plan is no more than a list of expected outcomes, it must exist in some form to provide a road map for your journey. If it is too restrictive or constrictive, it will be counterproductive. If only a few at the top know what it is, it will never work. The strategic plan is the shared vision that must be communicated openly, effectively, and repeatedly.

**4. Develop a Corporate Charter.**   Generate a quality policy and mission statement that will lead everyone in your organization into the future.

**5. Develop a Family of Measures.**   A football game isn't much fun without a scoreboard. As the game is being played, you need statistics to know how to make corrections to your offense and defense, before the outcome is certain. Keeping records from beginning lets you know where you were and where you are headed.

**6. Train Management in the Culture of Virtual Leadership and ISO9000.**   The only way to obtain buy-in is to educate your leaders in the whats and whys of your strategic quality initiative. They must be the walking and talking models of ISO9000. If you are working toward self-directed work teams, they must be working diligently on converting the top-down management structure into a model of Virtual Leadership.

**7. Train in Virtual Leadership at All Levels.**   The only way change works is if everyone sees the benefits to him- or herself and to the Company. Every employee must become responsible for his or her own actions. The only way to pass an ISO9000

audit is for everyone to be living the procedures as you wrote them.

**8. Implement the Strategic Plan.**   Keep the plan visible and visit the plan regularly. Have meaningful milestones and celebrate their achievement.

**9. Measure Results.**   Maintain a family of measures that gives a complete picture of how the company is running. The measures should be in real-time and accurate. The job holders should be the ones who generate most of the measures.

**10. Benchmark against the "Best in Class."**   Seize every opportunity to learn new and better methods. Implement those that make sense for your culture.

**11. Make Mid-Course Corrections Based on Measured Results.**   A strategic plan should be designed to be changed. Changes in technology, customer needs, job holder culture, and financial considerations are all valid reasons to make objective corrections to the master plan.

**12. Follow a Continuous Process of Planning, Training, Implementation, Measurement, and Evaluation, FOREVER!**

## Success Snapshot

The success of Virtual Leadership and ISO9000 in your company depends on:

◆ Realistic expectations based on realistic goals
◆ The empowerment to act
◆ The resources to make a difference
◆ The maturity to continually adjust your strategic plan
◆ Plus one giant leap of faith

## Making It Last

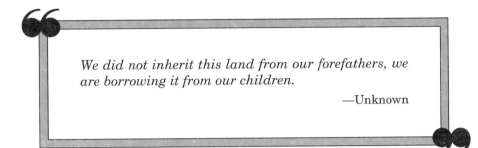

> *We did not inherit this land from our forefathers, we are borrowing it from our children.*
>
> —Unknown

Nothing lasts forever. The last few decades of sweeping cultural changes and massive technological breakthroughs have proven that to be true. The bottom line to Virtual Leadership is that it must constantly posture us to be proactively pioneering our future instead of the future driving us. We are on a journey without an end, but our nature is to want to arrive at one point, smell the flowers, and then start down another road. We have to learn to be smelling the flowers as they pass by. Our commitment to the future must be passion, not fashion. We have to make continuous improvement habitual. We have to train and educate on a perpetual calendar. We have to modify the old requisite of "learning something new every day" and add to that "evaluate its impact and take appropriate action." We have to plan to leave a legacy of self-perpetuating growth, not one of "the last one out, turn off the lights."

Finally, If you take nothing else from this book, remember this quote:

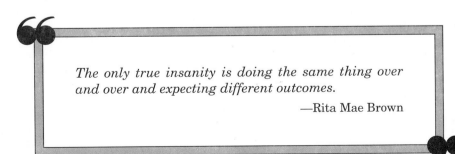

> *The only true insanity is doing the same thing over and over and expecting different outcomes.*
>
> —Rita Mae Brown

# APPENDIX
# A

## Sample Quality Manual, ISO9001

| | | |
|---|---|---|
| ABC<br>Services<br>Company, Inc. | **Quality Policy Manual** | Revision: 0.0<br>Issue Date: 00/00/00 |

## ISO9001
## Quality Policy
## Manual

This Manual establishes the policies of the Quality Management System at ABC Services Company Headquarters and Branch Offices. It is how business is conducted within the scope of the Quality Management System as defined in Section 1.0 of this standard.

### Controlled Distribution

Control #_____ Revision #_____

Issued to: _____

Date _____

| ABC Services Company, Inc. | **Quality Policy Manual** | Revision: 0.0 Issue Date: 00/00/00 |
|---|---|---|
| Section 0.0 | **Table of Contents** | Page 1 of 2 |

| ABC | **Quality Policy Manual** | |
|---|---|---|
| Services | | Revision: 0.0 |
| Company, Inc. | | Issue Date: 00/00/00 |
| Section 0.0 | **Table of Contents** | Page 2 of 2 |

These contents reflect the revision status of this manual. Any revision to any section of the manual will require a revised Table of Contents and a new cover page.

*Changes are indicated by italicized text.*

| ABC | **Quality Policy Manual** | |
|---|---|---|
| Services | | Revision: 0.0 |
| Company, Inc. | | Issue Date: 00/00/00 |
| Section 0.1 | **Statement of Policy** | Page 1 of 1 |

### Quality Policy

*"To become the touchstone of excellence in the consulting industry through customer communication and teamwork."*

Mission Statement

1. Coming together is a beginning, keeping together is progress, working together is success.
2. To provide the most professional and cost effective solutions available, with complete confidentiality.
3. To remain wholly committed to the aspiration of Total Quality Management.


Bill Brown, President
ABC Services Company, Inc.

| ABC | **Quality Policy Manual** | |
|---|---|---|
| Services | | Revision: 0.0 |
| Company, Inc. | | Issue Date: 00/00/00 |
| Section 1.0 | **Scope** | Page 1 of 1 |

The Quality Management System described in this Quality Policy Manual has been designed to integrate ABC Services' quality processes and the requirements of ISO9001 Quality System Standard. This system is the core quality management system utilized by ABC design and delivery of professional services.

| ABC | **Quality Policy Manual** | |
|---|---|---|
| Services | | Revision: 0.0 |
| Company, Inc. | | Issue Date: 00/00/00 |
| Section 1.1 | **Definitions** | Page 1 of 3 |

| | |
|---|---|
| ACCEPTANCE CRITERIA | Defined limits placed on characteristics, materials or products. |
| AUDIT | A systematic and independent examination to determine whether quality activities and related results comply with planned arrangements and whether these arrangements are implemented effectively and are suitable to achieve objectives. |
| CALIBRATION | Comparison and adjustment to a standard of known value/accuracy. |
| CONFORMANCE | Compliance with specified requirements. |
| CONTROL | To exercise authority over and regulate. |
| CONTROL FEATURE | A documented activity to ensure conformance with specific requirements of applicable specifications. |
| CORRECTIVE ACTION | Measures taken to rectify conditions adverse to quality and to eliminate recurrence. |
| DEFECT | The nonfulfillment of intended usage requirements. |
| DOCUMENTATION | Recorded information. |
| FAILURE | Any condition which prevents a product or service from performing its specified function. |
| FINDING | Objective evidence that a control feature of the approved Quality Management System was not implemented or was not being followed to the extent that compromise of the Quality Management System was possible. |

| ABC | **Quality Policy Manual** | |
|---|---|---|
| Services | | Revision: 0.0 |
| Company, Inc. | | Issue Date: 00/00/00 |
| Section 1.1 | **Definitions** | Page 2 of 3 |

INSPECTION — Activities such as measuring, analyzing, examining, testing, gauging one or more characteristics of a product and comparing these with specified requirements to determine conformity.

NONCONFORMITY — The nonfulfillment of specified requirements.

OBJECTIVE EVIDENCE — Facts that are observed and documented.

OBSERVATION — Evidence that a surveyable/auditable element exists that is not contrary to documented requirements, but may warrant further qualification or improvement.

OPERATING PROCEDURE — A document that specifies or describes what activities are to be performed. It may include methods to be used, equipment to be used, and sequence of operations.

PRODUCT — Any completed item or unit that can be used for its intended purpose without further processing.

QUALITY — Conformance to specified requirements.

QUALITY ASSURANCE — All those planned and systematic actions necessary to provide adequate confidence that a product or service will satisfy given requirements for quality.

QUALITY CONTROL — The operational techniques and activities that are used to fulfill requirements for quality.

QUALITY MANAGEMENT SYSTEM — Organizational structure, responsibilities, procedures, processes, and resources for implementing Total Quality Management.

| ABC | **Quality Policy Manual** | |
|---|---|---|
| Services | | Revision: 0.0 |
| Company, Inc. | | Issue Date: 00/00/00 |
| Section 1.1 | **Definitions** | Page 3 of 3 |

QUALITY MANAGEMENT SYSTEM REVIEW
: A formal evaluation by top management of the status and adequacy of the Quality Management System in relation to quality policy and new objectives resulting from changing circumstances.

SPECIFICATION
: The document that prescribes the requirements with which the product has to conform.

OPERATING PROCEDURE
: A document that specifies or describes what activities are to be performed. It may include methods to be used, equipment to be used, and sequence of operations.

SUPPLIER
: Any individual or organization who furnishes materials, products, or services. (ISO-9002 definition for subcontractor)

TRACEABILITY
: The ability to trace the history, application, or location of an item or activity, or similar items or activities, by means of recorded identification.

VERIFY
: To determine conformance to specified requirements.

| ABC | **Quality Policy Manual** | |
|---|---|---|
| Services | | Revision: 0.0 |
| Company, Inc. | | Issue Date: 00/00/00 |
| Section 1.2 | **Organization** | Page 1 of 2 |

1.2.1 Management personnel identified in the Organization Chart (1.2.3) are responsible for implementation and maintenance of the Quality Management System within their areas of responsibility. Each manager is responsible to develop and execute planning to provide processes, resources, equipment, skills and methods necessary to meet or exceed customer or regulatory requirements.

1.2.2 Any manager assigned responsibility for a function may delegate performance of that function to others. The individual originally assigned shall retain responsibility and accountability for the proper execution of the delegated activity. The manager shall assure that the delegate is properly trained and/or qualified per Section 18.0 of this manual.

1.2.3 Functional Organization Chart

1.2.4 Functional Departmental Responsibilities

1.2.4.1 President

Quality Policy

Organizational Structure

Responsibility and Authority

Resources

Chair Management Review

Quality Management System

Quality Policy Manual Approval

Quality Planning

Supplier Control

Customer Satisfaction

Branch Operations

| ABC | **Quality Policy Manual** | |
|---|---|---|
| Services | | Revision: 0.0 |
| Company, Inc. | | Issue Date: 00/00/00 |
| Section 1.2 | **Organization** | Page 2 of 2 |

1.2.4.2  Quality Coordinator

> Management Representative
>
> Quality Management System Procedures
>
> Document and Data Control
>
> Corrective and Preventative Action
>
> Control of Quality Records
>
> Internal Quality Audits
>
> Training
>
> Statistical Techniques

1.2.4.3  Operations Manager

1.2.4.4  National Marketing Manager

1.2.4.5  Administrations Manager

1.2.4.6  Financial Executive

1.2.4.7  Technical Manager

1.2.4.8  Project Manager

1.2.4.9  Marketing Manager

1.2.4.10  Branch Manager

Reference Procedures

1.2.XXXX   Job Descriptions

| ABC | **Quality Policy Manual** | |
|---|---|---|
| Services | | Revision: 0.0 |
| Company, Inc. | | Issue Date: 00/00/00 |

Section 1.3    **Control of Quality Policy Manual**    Page 1 of 1

1.3.1 Manuals may be controlled or uncontrolled. ABC personnel will use only controlled copies.

1.3.2 The Quality Coordinator is responsible for issuance and control of all controlled copies of the Quality Policy Manual, including revisions.

1.3.3 A log is maintained of all controlled copies of the Quality Policy Manual. The Quality Policy Manual Issue Log includes manual number, assignee, revision letter, date issued, and acknowledgment. Issuance of revisions to the manual shall be handled and documented in the same manner as the original issuance of the manual. Revision status of each section within this manual will be indicated in the Table of Contents.

1.3.4 Each controlled Quality Policy Manual issuance and revision requires an acknowledgment on the Quality Manual Acknowledgment form.

1.3.5 Latest changes to manuals will be indicated with *italicized text*, except when totally rewritten.

1.3.6 The Quality Coordinator will record a summary of all changes by paragraph/section. The Manual Revision Summary will be filed with a copy of the revision being replaced and will be available for review at all times.

Reference Procedures:

1.3.0100 Control of Quality Policy Manual, Operations Procedures and Work Instructions

| ABC | **Quality Policy Manual** | |
| --- | --- | --- |
| Services | | Revision: 0.0 |
| Company, Inc. | | Issue Date: 00/00/00 |
| Section 1.4 | **Resources** | Page 1 of 1 |

1.4.1 Each process within the Quality Management System has been identified and described in Operations Procedures or, as necessary, Work Instructions.

1.4.2 Personnel for management, performance of work, and verification activities, and equipment resource needs are identified and planned during management reviews (Reference Operations Procedure 1.01, Management Review). Ongoing evaluation for adequacy of resources is accomplished through monitoring and auditing.

1.4.3 All management, performance of work and verification activities for production and acceptance are performed by trained and/or qualified personnel.

| ABC | **Quality Policy Manual** | |
|---|---|---|
| Services | | Revision: 0.0 |
| Company, Inc. | | Issue Date: 00/00/00 |
| Section 1.5 | **Management Representative** | Page 1 of 1 |

1.5.1 The Quality Coordinator is assigned as the Management Representative and has the authority and responsibility for the day-to-day administration of the Quality Management System. This position is authorized to ensure that the Quality Management System is established, implemented, and maintained to the requirements of ISO9001 and to ensure that the Quality Policy is carried out. The Quality Coordinator is also responsible for reporting on the performance of the Quality Management System to management for review and as a basis for continuous improvement.

| ABC | **Quality Policy Manual** | |
|---|---|---|
| Services | | Revision: 0.0 |
| Company, Inc. | | Issue Date: 00/00/00 |
| Section 1.6 | **Management Review** | Page 1 of 1 |

1.6.1  The President is responsible to perform a Quality Management System review at least annually. This review is conducted to verify continued suitability and effectiveness of this Quality Management System in meeting the International Standard ISO9001, specific customer requirements and the Company's Quality Policy, Mission, and Values. Operations Procedure 1.6.01, "Management Review," describes the agenda and criteria for and conducting each review. Records of this Quality Management System review, any resulting corrective actions and verification of their implementation are documented.

Reference Operations Procedures:

1.6.0100  Conducting Management Reviews

| ABC | **Quality Policy Manual** | |
|---|---|---|
| Services | | Revision: 0.0 |
| Company, Inc. | | Issue Date: 00/00/00 |
| Section 2.0 | **Quality System** | Page 1 of 2 |

2.1 The Quality Management System described in this Quality Policy Manual is a three-tiered system of documentation utilizing the following:

Quality Policy Manual

Operations Procedures

Work Instructions

2.2 Quality Policy Manual

2.2.1 The Quality Policy Manual provides the policy and system structure necessary for the definition and application of requirements which ensure compliance to ISO9001.

2.2.2 Operations Procedures necessary for achieving compliance to the Quality Policy Manual are referenced within this manual.

2.3 Operations Procedures

2.3.1 The President is responsible to ensure that departmental activities and functions are described in Operations Procedures and Work Instructions.

2.3.2 Branches are responsible for employee training, implementation, and compliance with the Quality Policy Manual, Operations Procedures, and Work Instructions.

2.3.3 Methods used for documenting, maintaining, and distribution of Operations Procedures and Work Instructions are described in Section 5.0.

2.4 Quality Planning

2.4.1 Quality planning necessary to accomplish specified requirements is provided through integration and use of Operations Procedures and Work Instructions.

| ABC | **Quality Policy Manual** | |
|---|---|---|
| Services | | Revision: 0.0 |
| Company, Inc. | | Issue Date: 00/00/00 |
| Section 2.0 | **Quality System** | Page 2 of 2 |

2.4.2  All activities related to forecasting, acquisition of controls, processes, inspection/testing equipment, resources, skills, inspection, and testing technologies and suitable verifications are all part of the Quality Management System. Responsibility for providing these resources is described in Section 1.4 of this Quality Policy Manual.

| ABC | **Quality Policy Manual** | |
|---|---|---|
| Services | | Revision: 0.0 |
| Company, Inc. | | Issue Date: 00/00/00 |
| Section 3.0 | **Contract Review** | Page 1 of 1 |

3.1   All contracts received at ABC will be subject to review and acceptance. The Administrative Manager will coordinate review and acceptance of all contracts.

3.1.1 Contracts received at ABC will include (but not be limited to):

◆ Employee Service Contracts

◆ Client Contracts with ABC as sole contractor

◆ Client Contracts with ABC using subcontractors

◆ Client Contracts with ABC as a subcontractor

◆ Services Testing Service Contracts

3.1.2 Each contract will be reviewed to determine:

◆ If the work is within the scope of expertise of ABC Services Company

◆ If the content of the contract is acceptable in all aspects

◆ If the terms and conditions of the contract are acceptable to ABC

3.1.3 ABC will notify, in writing, the other parties in a contract when any of the provisions of 3.1.2 are unacceptable. Negotiations will be conducted until the contract is either acceptable or it is rejected.

3.2   Amendments to contracts will be handled as specified in 3.1, however, accepted changes will be communicated to those in ABC who are affected by the changes.

3.3   Records of all contract activities will be maintained as Quality Records (See Section 16.0)

Reference Operations Procedures:

3.0100  Contract Review

| ABC | **Quality Policy Manual** | |
|---|---|---|
| Services | | Revision: 0.0 |
| Company, Inc. | | Issue Date: 00/00/00 |
| Section 4.0 | **Design Control** | Page 1 of 1 |

4.1 Controlling the design of the services provided by ABC is essential to the success of the company. To that end, each step in the design process will be proceduralized, followed closely, and the results of each step will be documented.

4.2 A separate design plan will be developed prior to the inception of a new design project. The Quality Representative will work with Engineering to ensure each plan is complete.

4.3 Each plan will include specific expectations and assignments for each group in the Company. Engineering will not embark on "design-in-a-vacuum."

4.4 There shall be a Design Specification sheet released prior to any activity beginning. The responsible engineer will ensure that all contractual and regulatory issue are addressed in the Design Specification.

4.5 After critical design review, the Engineering Manager and the Quality Representative will make a final audit to ensure that the final design meets all requirements of the Design Specification.

4.6 There will be no less than three formal design review meetings conducted during any engineering project. They will include preliminary, prototype release, and critical design reviews.

4.7 In addition to the testing and verification steps specified in each Design Specification, appropriate alternative methods will be prescribed for testing critical parameters to ensure the validity of the testing methods.

4.8 A final validation will be conducted prior to critical design review. The responsible engineer will certify that all design steps have been followed and that all customer and regulatory requirements have been satisfied.

4.9 Design changes will be documented and controlled to ensure effectiveness and to provide an audit trail during the design process. Design documentation shall be considered Quality Records.

| ABC | **Quality Policy Manual** | |
|---|---|---|
| Services | | Revision: 0.0 |
| Company, Inc. | | Issue Date: 00/00/00 |

| Section 5.0 | **Document and Data Control** | Page 1 of 2 |
|---|---|---|

5.1 All Documents and data used within the Quality Management System will be approved prior to use and their issuance and use will be controlled.

5.1.1 Documents and data will include, but not be limited to:

◆ Databases used to conduct company business

◆ Reports used to conduct company business

◆ Interdepartment forms

◆ The Quality Policy Manual, Operations Procedures, and Work Instructions

5.1.2 The Operations Managers will be responsible for administering this procedure.

5.2 A database will be maintained that will list all controlled documents and data. This database will include (but not be limited to):

◆ Unique name or control number

◆ Current revision level

◆ Authorizing job function

◆ Date of issue

5.2.1 All documents and data will be approved by the issuing job function before use. This will be accomplished by signature or by positive control of computer documents and data.

5.2.3 Only the most recent revision of documents and data will be available for use. Obsolete versions will be purged from use, unless those previous versions are approved for use until the supply is exhausted.

5.2.4 Data and documents that are obsolete or for reference only will be appropriately and clearly marked as to their status or will be assumed "for reference only" if they have no ABC markings to indicate that they are controlled by this procedure. Uncontrolled documents and data include (but are not limited to):

| ABC | **Quality Policy Manual** | |
|---|---|---|
| Services | | Revision: 0.0 |
| Company, Inc. | | Issue Date: 00/00/00 |
| Section 5.0 | **Document and Data Control** | Page 2 of 2 |

◆ Informational literature

◆ Off-the-shelf business services

◆ Trade publications

5.3    Changes to documents and data controlled by this procedure will be controlled in the same fashion as a new document or data.

5.3.1  Any changes must be approved by the authority that originally approved the document or data for use.

5.3.2  Changes will be positively communicated to all those who are affected by the change.

5.3.3  Where practical, a change history file shall be maintained to give visibility to the history of change for a document or data.

Reference Operations Procedures:

5.0100  Document and Data Control

| ABC | **Quality Policy Manual** | |
|---|---|---|
| Services | | Revision: 0.0 |
| Company, Inc. | | Issue Date: 00/00/00 |
| Section 6.0 | **Purchasing** | Page 1 of 1 |

6.1 All materials, supplies, and contracted items purchased as part of the value delivery system will be controlled by this procedure. It is the responsibility of the President to ensure that purchases and contracts conform to all applicable requirements.

6.2 All materials, supplies, and contracted items that fall under this procedure will be purchased from sources that have been approved by ABC Services Company. Operations Procedure 6.01.01 will detail how suppliers and subcontractors will be evaluated and controlled.

6.2.1 A list of approved sources will be maintained by the Purchasing Manager. This list will be periodically reviewed, maintained, and objectively evaluated.

6.3 All materials, supplies, and contracted items that fall under this procedure will be acquired on a purchase order or contract document that clearly describes the expected outcome or deliverables. The purchase order or contract will be reviewed for adequacy prior to issue and approved before it is released.

6.4 ABC shall reserve the right to inspect and or test the materials, supplies, or contracted items at their source. ABC shall also reserve the right to have our customers inspect and or test the materials, supplies, or contracted items at their source. Such inspections and or tests shall not relieve the supplier of responsibility for conformance to purchase order or contract requirements.

Reference Operations Procedures

6.0100 Purchasing

| ABC | **Quality Policy Manual** | |
|---|---|---|
| Services | | Revision: 0.0 |
| Company, Inc. | | Issue Date: 00/00/00 |
| Section 7.0 | **Customer Supplied Material** | Page 1 of 1 |

ABC Services Company does not currently deal with any material or services supplied by our customers.

| ABC | **Quality Policy Manual** | |
|---|---|---|
| Services | | Revision: 0.0 |
| Company, Inc. | | Issue Date: 00/00/00 |
| | **Product Identification** | |
| Section 8.0 | **and Traceability** | Page 1 of 1 |

8.1 In the performance of certain proprietary services for its clients, ABC will take appropriate steps to ensure that all steps of the processes used are identified with appropriate nomenclature and that revision control will be used to ensure traceability.

Reference Operations Procedures

8.0100  Identification and Traceability

| ABC | **Quality Policy Manual** | |
|---|---|---|
| Services | | Revision: 0.0 |
| Company, Inc. | | Issue Date: 00/00/00 |
| Section 9.0 | **Process Control** | Page 1 of 1 |

9.1 All processes used within the Quality Management System will be documented by Operations Procedures or by Work Instructions. Processes include any specific steps that add value or can directly affect service quality. Where results of processes cannot be inspected or fully verified, sufficient controls shall exist to ensure that the process is inherently effective and that quality cannot be compromised.

Reference Operations Procedures

| | |
|---|---|
| 9.0100 | Engineer Recruiting, General |
| 9.0101 | Engineer Recruiting, Existing Customers |
| 9.0102 | Engineer Recruiting, Database |
| 9.0103 | Engineer Recruiting, Background Checking |
| 9.0104 | Engineer Recruiting, Standard Skills Testing |
| 9.0200 | Sales, General |
| 9.0201 | Sales, Existing Customers |
| 9.0202 | Sales, New Customers |
| 9.0300 | Engineer Services, General |
| 9.0301 | Engineer Services, Engineer Handbook |
| 9.0302 | Engineer Services, Performance Reviews |
| 9.0303 | Engineer Services, Location and Relocation |
| 9.0304 | Engineer Services, Sustaining Relationships |
| 9.0305 | Engineer Services, Exit Interviews |
| 9.0306 | Engineer Services, Hardware Requirements |
| 9.0400 | Branch Operations |
| 9.0500 | The ABC Supplier Partnership |
| 9.0600 | Engineering Performance Monitor |
| 9.0700 | Testing Services |

| ABC | **Quality Policy Manual** | |
|---|---|---|
| Services | | Revision: 0.0 |
| Company, Inc. | | Issue Date: 00/00/00 |
| Section 10.0 | **Inspection and Testing** | Page 1 of 1 |

10.1 Inspection and verification activities within Engineering will be covered in the detailed process procedures for each activity. There shall be included in each process procedure the checks and balances necessary to ensure that client requirements are met and that the requirements of the ABC Quality Management System are met. Records of inspections and verifications will be retained as Quality Records (See 16.0—Control of Quality Records).

10.2 Inspection and verification activities within services validation will be covered in the detailed process procedures and in the specifications agreed to with each customer for each testing activity. There shall be included in each process procedure and specification the checks and balances necessary to ensure that client requirements are met and that the requirements of the ABC Quality Management System are met. Records of inspections and verifications will be retained as Quality Records (See 16.0—Control of Quality Records).

| ABC | **Quality Policy Manual** | |
| --- | --- | --- |
| Services | | Revision: 0.0 |
| Company, Inc. | | Issue Date: 00/00/00 |
| Section 11.0 | **Control of Inspection, Testing & Measuring Equipment** | Page 1 of 1 |

11.1 As a general rule, there is no quantitative testing associated with the services performed by ABC Services Company and, therefore, no need for inspection, testing, and measuring equipment. Should such requirements occur, the method for ensuring the accuracy of such equipment will be determined within the specific contract or quality plan for that specific activity.

| ABC | **Quality Policy Manual** | |
|---|---|---|
| Services | | Revision: 0.0 |
| Company, Inc. | | Issue Date: 00/00/00 |
| Section 12.0 | **Inspection and Test Status** | Page 1 of 1 |

12.1 Inspection and test status will be covered in the detailed process procedures for each activity. There shall be included in each process procedure the information necessary to ensure that the status of any process, relative to inspections and tests, can be easily and accurately identified.

12.2 Inspection and verification activities within Special Services will be covered in the detailed process procedures and in the specifications agreed to with each customer for each testing activity. There shall be included in each process procedure the information necessary to ensure that the status of any process, relative to inspections and tests, can be easily and accurately identified.

| ABC | **Quality Policy Manual** | |
|---|---|---|
| Services | | Revision: 0.0 |
| Company, Inc. | | Issue Date: 00/00/00 |

| | **Control** | |
|---|---|---|
| Section 13.0 | **of Nonconforming Product** | Page 1 of 1 |

13.1 Control of nonconformances in the services provided by ABC Services will be covered in the detailed process procedures for each activity. There shall be included in each process procedure the procedures necessary to ensure that any deviations from customer requirements or the requirements of the ABC Quality Management System are documented and resolved in a timely fashion.

| ABC | **Quality Policy Manual** | |
|---|---|---|
| Services | | Revision: 0.0 |
| Company, Inc. | | Issue Date: 00/00/00 |

Section 14.0   **Corrective and Preventive Action**     Page 1 of 1

14.1 Deviations and variations discovered during formal audits, from casual surveillance and from repetitive nonconformances shall be subject to corrective and preventive action. Corrective action shall address the symptoms, uncover the root causes, correct the processes, train the operators, and ensure that all reasonable steps have been taken to preclude recurrence. Preventive action shall also provide for follow up audits of the effectiveness of the corrective action taken.

14.2 Corrective actions will be taken as appropriate to the severity of the deviation or variation found.

14.3 Formal requests for corrective action and all subsequent findings and remedies shall be documented on a Corrective Action Request Form (CAR).

14.4 The Quality Coordinator is responsible for follow-up to ensure that action was concluded and was effective in eliminating the cause of the nonconformance. Close-out of the CAR will be documented. CARs will be recorded on the Corrective Action Status Log.

14.5 Changes to Procedures resulting from CARs will be processed as described in Section 5.0 (Document and Data Control).

14.7 Customer complaints are documented and processed on a CAR form.

14.8 It shall be the responsibility of every ABC employee to identify areas of preventive action as they are discovered. These include any observed activities that may lead to a customer problem or a breakdown in the Quality Management System.

Reference Operations Procedures

14.0100  Corrective and Preventive Action

| ABC | **Quality Policy Manual** | |
|---|---|---|
| Services | | Revision: 0.0 |
| Company, Inc. | | Issue Date: 00/00/00 |
| | **Handling, Storage, Packaging,** | |
| Section 15.0 | **Preservation, and Delivery** | Page 1 of 1 |

15.1 As a general rule, ABC Services Company does not deal with any commodities that require handling, storage, packaging, preservation, nor delivery. Should any such requirements arise, they will be handled by a separate process procedure and/or customer contract.

| ABC | **Quality Policy Manual** | |
|---|---|---|
| Services | | Revision: 0.0 |
| Company, Inc. | | Issue Date: 00/00/00 |
| Section 16.0 | **Control of Quality Records** | Page 1 of 1 |

16.1 The Quality Coordinator is responsible for the control and maintenance of all quality records generated.

16.2 Records shall be legible, identifiable, and retrievable.

16.3 Records shall be protected from age deterioration, damage, or loss.

16.4 All records shall be maintained in file boxes, cabinets, electronic storage, or other secure means.

16.5 Provision shall be made for disposal methods for all quality records.

16.6 As a minimum, the following quality records will be kept:

 a. Training records

 b. Certification/qualification records

 c. Calibration records

 d. Document control

 e. Purchase orders

 f. Nonconformance records

 g. Audit records

 h. Corrective action request

 i. Management review

 j. Contract review

16.7 As requested by a specific customer, records will be maintained as described in the customer's Contract.

Reference Operations Procedures

16.0100  Control of Quality Records

| ABC | **Quality Policy Manual** | |
|---|---|---|
| Services | | Revision: 0.0 |
| Company, Inc. | | Issue Date: 00/00/00 |
| Section 17.0 | **Internal Quality Audits** | Page 1 of 1 |

17.1 The Quality Coordinator is responsible for developing a schedule of internal audits. Audit schedules will be documented and posted. Each area of the Quality Management System will be audited at least annually.

17.2 The Quality Coordinator or President may conduct or request unscheduled audits when cause exists, either internally or externally.

17.3 Audits are conducted by qualified personnel who do not have direct responsibility for or control of the area to be audited. The audit system and auditor qualifications are defined in Operating Procedure 17.0101, "Quality Audit System."

17.4 All audits are conducted utilizing a planned checklist.

17.5 Audit results will be documented and used for Management Reviews.

17.6 Copies of all audit reports, including corrective actions are forwarded to each level of management involved with the audit or corrective action.

Reference Operations Procedures

17.0100 Internal Quality Audits

| ABC | **Quality Policy Manual** | |
|---|---|---|
| Services | | Revision: 0.0 |
| Company, Inc. | | Issue Date: 00/00/00 |
| Section 18.0 | **Training** | Page 1 of 2 |

18.1   Qualification of Personnel

18.1.1 The Quality Representative is responsible to ensure personnel are qualified to ABC requirements and/or certified to applicable industry or regulatory requirements.

18.1.2 Qualifications shall be documented on the Qualification Record and include:

a. Description of qualifications required.

b. Documented approval that the individual in the position meets all of the qualification requirements.

18.2   Training

18.2.1 Each branch is responsible for definition, planning and conducting specialized or general job training for personnel within its organization.

18.2.2 The Quality Coordinator is responsible for coordination of all training and for implementing the Quality Management System training for all personnel assigned duties and responsibilities described in this manual. ABC Policy, Mission, and Values are included in the training program.

18.2.3 Records of training are required and will include:

a. Subject matter

b. Date of training

c. Duration of training

d. Instructor's name

e. Attendees

| ABC | **Quality Policy Manual** | |
|---|---|---|
| Services | | Revision: 0.0 |
| Company, Inc. | | Issue Date: 00/00/00 |
| Section 18.0 | **Training** | Page 2 of 2 |

18.3    Methods utilized for identification of training needs and documentation of personnel qualifications and training are described in Operating Procedures 18.0100, "Qualification" and 18.0200, "Training."

Reference Operations Procedures

18.0100   Qualification

18.0200   Training

| ABC Services Company, Inc. | **Quality Policy Manual** | Revision: 0.0 Issue Date: 00/00/00 |
|---|---|---|
| Section 19.0 | **Servicing** | Page 1 of 1 |

19.1 Key to the services provided by ABC Services Consulting is ongoing service contracts. These service contracts will be documented under Section 3.0 (Contract Review) and under Section 9.0 (Process Control).

| ABC | **Quality Policy Manual** | |
|---|---|---|
| Services | | Revision: 0.0 |
| Company, Inc. | | Issue Date: 00/00/00 |
| Section 20.0 | **Statistical Techniques** | Page 1 of 1 |

20.1 ABC does not currently utilize any statistical applications. In the event of future use, the selection and application of statistical techniques will be described in Operating Procedures.

# APPENDIX

# B

# Sample Quality Manual, ISO9002

|  | #: 1.0 | Rev: A |
|---|---|---|

| XYZ Company | Approved: _____ |
|---|---|
| **QUALITY MANUAL** | Date: _____1 March 1995_____ |
| **The XYZ Company Quality Manual** | Page 1 of 1 |

### 1.1 Purpose

The purpose of the Quality Manual is to set policy for the Quality Management System at XYZ Company. Detailed procedures implementing the Quality Manual are contained in the XYZ Company Operations Procedures Manual. All products and services provided by XYZ Company will be manufactured and performed in accordance with the Quality Management System described in the Quality Manual.

### 1.2 Authority

The Quality Manual is authorized by the President of XYZ Company and administered by the Quality Manager.

Reference Documents

2.0200  Quality Manual Approval/Issue/Change

| #: 2.0 | Rev: A |
|---|---|

XYZ Company                          Approved: _____

**QUALITY MANUAL**                   Date: _____1 March 1995_____

**Quality Standards and Specifications**            Page 1 of 1

### 2.1 Quality Manual Structure

XYZ Company's Quality Manual is written for maximum clarity, minimum verbiage, and ease of interpretation. It is structured around the key elements of ISO9002/Q9002 and is numbered to the 1994 revision to ISO9000 to facilitate compliance auditing (4.1, 4.2, etc.).

### 2.2 Conformance to Standards

XYZ Company's Quality Manual is designed as a model for compliance to:

| | |
|---|---|
| ISO 9002/ANSI Q9002 | Quality System—Model for Quality Assurance in Production and Installation |
| MIL-I-45208A | Military Specification, Inspection System Requirements |
| MIL-STD-45662 | Military Standard, Calibration System Requirements |

Quality Management System implementation will be consistent with those Standards.

### 2.3 References

| | |
|---|---|
| ISO9000/ANSI Q9000 | Quality Management and Quality Assurance Standards—Guidelines for Selection and Use |
| ISO9004/ANSI Q9004 | Quality Management and Quality Elements—Guidelines |
| ISO8402/ANSI A3 | Quality System Terminology |

| #: 3.0 | Rev: A |
|--------|--------|

XYZ Company                          Approved: _____

**QUALITY MANUAL**                   Date: _____1 March 1995_____

**Quality Vocabulary**                                Page 1 of 2

### 3.1  General Quality System Terms

The following terms will be used throughout the Quality Manual and Operations Procedures.

3.1.1  Conformance: An affirmative indication or judgment that a product or service has met the requirements of the relevant specifications, contract, or regulation; also the state of meeting the requirements.

3.1.2  Quality: The totality of features and characteristics of a product or service that bear on its ability to satisfy stated or implied needs; fitness for use or purpose; conformance to the requirements.

3.1.3  Quality Assurance: All those planned or systematic actions necessary to provide adequate confidence that a product or service will satisfy given requirements for quality.

3.1.4  Quality Audit: A systematic and independent examination and evaluation to determine whether quality activities and results comply with planned arrangements and whether these arrangements are implemented effectively and are suitable to achieve objectives.

3.1.5  Quality Control: The operational techniques and the activities used to fulfill requirements of quality.

3.1.6  Quality Management: That aspect of the overall management function that determines and implements the quality policy.

3.1.7  Quality Policy: The overall intentions and direction of an organization as regards quality as formally expressed by top management.

3.1.8  Quality Management System: The organizational structure, responsibilities, procedures, processes, and resources for implementing quality management.

3.1.9 Quality System Review: A formal evaluation by management of the status and adequacy of the quality system in
relation to quality policy and/or objectives resulting from
changing circumstances.

| #: 4.1 | Rev: A |
|--------|--------|

XYZ Company                Approved: _____

**QUALITY MANUAL**        Date: _____1 March 1995_____

**Management Responsibility**                    Page 1 of 4

4.1.1  Quality Policy

XYZ Company is committed to meeting the customers' stated and implied requirements.

4.1.1.1  Mission Statement

1. XYZ Company provides turn-key services in electromechanical assembly, including a full compliment of technical support, inspection, and testing services.

2. XYZ Company is committed to meeting our customers' stated and implied requirements. Our success is measured in customer satisfaction, not in profits.

3. Our employees are empowered to place product quality as their first priority and they are dedicated to shielding the internal and external customer from receiving defective materials.

4. Our success is based on our ability to look at any new challenge as an opportunity to excel. Our history is to find innovative solutions to impossible problems.

5. Our future is dependent on the partnerships we enjoy with our customers, our suppliers, and our job holders (employees). Only by working together in an environment of trust and respect can we succeed.

6. XYZ Company embraces ISO9000 as a platform for total quality and continuous improvement. It is the cornerstone of our Company-wide quality management system.

7. We are committed to the belief that continued learning is essential to the mind and ongoing training is essential to the hands.

8. Our people are the Company. We provide a positive work environment, the tools and training to perform their jobs, and the support and encouragement for each person to achieve

his or her full potential. We reward on achievement, not on activity. We learn from mistakes, not punish for them.

9. XYZ Company is dedicated to being a contributing member of our industry, our community and our nation.

### 4.1.2 Organization

The organization at XYZ Company is shown in Figure 4.1.2-1. Although distinct departments are defined in the organization, XYZ Company maintains flexibility in duties and responsibilities, without compromising the function of each department. The objectives of the organization's structure are to provide efficient operation or function of each department, reduce operating costs, limit the number of levels of management, and minimize departmental barriers.

### 4.1.2.1 Responsibility and Authority

All XYZ Company's employees are responsible for the quality of the products and services provided. Each employee has an individual responsibility to assure that his or her contribution to the product or service complies with customer requirements. Where necessary, XYZ Company may choose to delegate the responsibility for internal or external quality assurance. The company or persons so delegated will be independent of the activities reported on. The Quality Manager has the direct responsibility and authority to assure that the company complies with the company's quality system requirements and to verify products and services meet customer quality requirements.

### 4.1.2.2 Resources and Personnel

XYZ Company shall provide qualified and trained personnel for management, production and in-house verification, inspection, test, and monitoring of the production and installation of the process and/or products and audits of the quality system, processes, and/or products. Verification shall be conducted by personnel independent of those having direct responsibility for the

| #: 4.1 | Rev: A |

work being performed. All personnel and equipment used to verify conformity shall possess a level of skill or accuracy commensurate with the product, service, and/or specification.

### 4.1.2.3 Management Representative

The Quality Manager shall act as the management representative having defined authority and responsibility for ensuring the requirements of the quality standards, quality specifications, and quality manual are implemented and maintained.

### 4.1.3 Management Review

The quality system outlined in this manual shall be reviewed at appropriate intervals (1 year maximum), by the management of XYZ Company, to ensure its continuing suitability and effectiveness. Records of management reviews of the quality system will be maintained in accordance with quality record procedures.

Reference Documents

1.0100 Functional Work Flow Chart

1.0200 Employee Records

1.0300 Job Descriptions

1.0400 Management Review

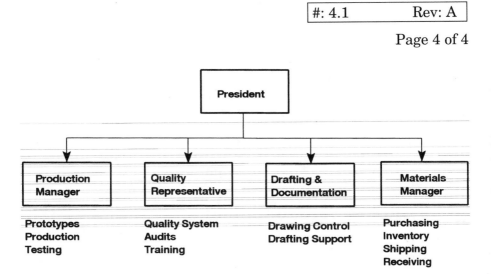

**Figure 4.1.2–1**

| #: 4.2 | Rev: A |
|--------|--------|

| XYZ Company | Approved: _____ |
|-------------|------------------------------|
| **QUALITY MANUAL** | Date: _____1 March 1995_____ |
| **Quality System** | Page 1 of 1 |

### 4.2.1  Scope

XYZ Company has established and maintains a documented quality system as a means of ensuring that products conform to specified requirements. The system includes:

a) Documented quality system procedures and instructions in accordance with the standards and specifications listed in Section 2.1 (Quality Standards and Specifications) of this manual.

b) The means to effectively implement the documented quality system procedures and instructions included in this manual.

### 4.2.2  Responsibility

All XYZ Company employees are responsible for assuring that the quality system, as defined by the Quality Manual, is maintained and revised as necessary. In addition, it is the responsibility of the customer to provide the appropriate information, materials, and support necessary to maintain the quality system. Quality Planning will ordinarily be accomplished through the Operations Procedure Manual.

Reference Documents

2.0100  Quality System Implementation

2.0200  Quality Manual Approval/Issue/Change

2.0300  Operations Procedures Manual Approval/Issue/Change

2.0400  Quality Results Measurement

| #: 4.3 | Rev: A |
|---|---|

XYZ Company

Approved: _____

**QUALITY MANUAL**

Date: _____1 March 1995_____

**Contract Review**

Page 1 of 1

### 4.3.1 Scope

All contracts and purchase orders received by XYZ Company shall be reviewed to ensure that:

a) the requirements are adequately defined and documented,

b) any requirements differing from those in the tender/quotation are resolved and

c) the capability to meet the contractual requirements exists within the company or by outside services.

### 4.3.2 Responsibility

Production is responsible for ensuring that all contracts, and their modifications and variations, are controlled and processed per these procedures. This includes maintaining and documenting all contractual events with the customers, verifying that all terms and conditions agreed to are understood and all contractual information is disseminated to those who are responsible for implementation and verification. Amendments to contracts will be handled in the same manner as new contracts, except that all affected areas will be notified when there is a change in scope. Contract documentation will be handled as quality records (See 4.16).

Reference Documents

3.0100  Order Entry

3.0200  Contract Files and Logs

3.0300  Deviations, Variations, and Changes

3.0400  Customer Contact Procedure

|  | #: 4.4          Rev: A |
|---|---|
| XYZ Company | Approved: _____ |
| **QUALITY MANUAL** | Date: _____1 March 1995_____ |
| **Design Control** | Page 1 of 1 |

XYZ Company does not presently engage in design of proprietary products or services.

| #: 4.5 | Rev: A |

XYZ Company                    Approved: _____

**QUALITY MANUAL**              Date: _____1 March 1995_____

**Document and Data Control**                    Page 1 of 2

### 4.5.1 Scope

The Document and Data Control procedure establishes the review, approval and control of all documents and procedures used in the XYZ Company Quality Management System.

### 4.5.2 Responsibility

It is the responsibility of Production Control to maintain the requirements of document control.

### 4.5.3 Document Approval

All required production documents shall be reviewed and approved for adequacy by authorized personnel prior to issue. Customer and/or industry association documents are assumed to have been authorized approval prior to issue. Customer documents are reviewed by XYZ Company in accordance with Section 4.3 (Contract Review). Documents that do not have clear approval shall be reviewed by Production Control, or the responsible support function/group, prior to release.

### 4.5.4 Document Storage

Original documents are to be stored in a location controlled or authorized by Production Control. Only authorized personnel shall have access to documents. Customer documents are to be stored by customer and document number. Industry association or military specifications/standards are to be stored by organization name and document number. Customer sketches, modifications, and/or prerelease documents are to be stored until the final revision is received/incorporated.

### 4.5.5 Document Release

Pertinent production documents are to be released/issued to manufacturing with the Production Work Order. All locations where operations essential to the effective functioning of the quality sys-

tem are performed shall have access to the necessary production documents. At the completion of the work order, production documents are to be returned to Production Control. Controlled Manuals and Procedures shall also be released/issued by Production Control.

## 4.5.6   Document Changes/Modifications

Changes or modifications to documents shall be reviewed and approved by the same functions/organizations that performed the original review and approval, unless specifically designated otherwise. The designated organizations shall have access to pertinent background information upon which to have their review and approval. Where practical, the nature of the change shall be identified in the document or the appropriate attachments. In addition, a master list or equivalent document control procedure shall identify the current revision of documents in order to preclude the use of nonapplicable documents. Documents shall be reissued after a practical number of changes have been made.

Changes or modifications affecting work-in-process are to be reviewed to determine impact. New or updated documents will be issued to manufacturing as applicable and previously released documents removed.

## 4.5.7   Obsolete Documents

Obsolete documents are to be marked "OBSOLETE" and stored in a location separate from current documents. Obsolete documents previously released to the shop floor shall be collected and archived. Since customers occasionally order old revision parts, the archived drawing file will be kept within the Document Control area.

Reference Documents

5.0100  Document Control

5.0200  Forms Control

5.0300  Document Changes/Modifications

| #: 4.6 | Rev: A |
|--------|--------|

XYZ Company                    Approved: _____

**QUALITY MANUAL**          Date: _____1 March 1995_____

**Purchasing**                                    Page 1 of 2

### 4.6.1 Scope

This procedure establishes a system to ensure materials, products, or services purchased for deliverable products and services conform to the specified requirements of XYZ Company and the company's customers.

### 4.6.2 Responsibility

Purchasing has the responsibility to administer the procurement requirements in this procedure and those of the customer. Assistance is obtained from the support functions/organizations and the customer, as necessary.

### 4.6.3 Assessment of Suppliers

XYZ Company selects suppliers on the basis of their ability to meet the required specifications or requirements, including quality. Purchasing shall maintain a record of acceptable suppliers. Where applicable, customer approved or specified vendors are used.

The selection of suppliers, and the type and extent of control exercised by XYZ Company, shall be dependent upon the type of product or service and, where appropriate, on records of the supplier's previous demonstrated capability and performance. Purchasing, with the assistance of the Quality Manager, shall ensure that the supplier's quality system controls are effective. Supplier surveys shall be performed as necessary.

### 4.6.4 Purchasing Data

Purchasing documents shall contain data clearly describing the product or service ordered, including where applicable:

    a) the type, class, style, grade, or other precise identification,

    b) the title or other positive identification, and applicable issue of specifications, drawings, process requirements,

| #: 4.6 | Rev: A |
|---|---|

inspection instructions, and other relevant technical data, including requirements for approval or qualification of product, procedures, process equipment, and personnel, and

c) the title, number, and revision of the quality system standard to be applied to the product or service.

Purchasing shall review purchase requests and review/approve purchasing documents for adequacy of specified requirements prior to release. Technical and quality support shall be provided as necessary.

## 4.6.5 Verification of Products and Services

Where specified in the contract or purchase order, XYZ Company or the company's representative shall have the right to verify at source or upon receipt that purchased products or services conform to the specified requirements. Verification by XYZ Company or the company's representative shall not absolve the supplier of the responsibility to provide acceptable products or services, nor shall it preclude subsequent rejection. When XYZ Company's customer or the customer's representative elects to carry out verification at the supplier's facility, such verification shall not be used as evidence of effective control of quality by the supplier.

Reference Documents

6.0100  Purchasing Procedure

6.0200  Assessment and Control of Suppliers

6.0300  Verification of Purchased Products

| #: 4.7 | Rev: A |
|---|---|

XYZ Company            Approved: _____

**QUALITY MANUAL**      Date: ____1 March 1995____

**Customer Furnished Materials**              Page 1 of 1

### 4.7.1 Scope

This procedure establishes a system to ensure the integrity of materials, products, or services supplied to XYZ Company by the Company's customers.

### 4.7.2 Responsibility

Purchasing has the responsibility to administer the requirements in this procedure and those of the customer. Assistance is obtained from the support functions/organizations and the customer, as necessary.

### 4.7.3 Customer Furnished Material

Prior to delivery, arrangements shall be made between XYZ Company and the customer for the shipment of customer furnished materials. This includes raw materials, parts, components, tooling, and gaging. XYZ Company shall verify, identify, store, and maintain property that is provided by the customer. Verification by XYZ Company does not absolve the customer of the responsibility to provide acceptable product. Customer furnished material shall be handled, stored, packaged, and delivered in accordance with Section 15.0 (Handling, Storage, Packaging, and Delivery). Any such product that is lost, damaged, or otherwise unsuitable for use shall be recorded and reported to the customer in a timely manner.

Reference Documents

7.0100 Customer Furnished Materials

| #: 4.8 | Rev: A |
|---|---|

| XYZ Company | Approved: _____ |
|---|---|
| **QUALITY MANUAL** | Date: _____1 March 1995_____ |
| **Identification and Traceability** | Page 1 of 1 |

### 4.8.1 Scope

All materials used in the manufacturing process shall be clearly identified from the time they are received at XYZ Company until they are received by the customer. All materials will be traceable to their origin and deliverable products will also be traceable to their manufacturing processes.

### 4.8.2 Responsibility

Production Control will be responsible for insuring that materials and products are identified at all times from receipt through manufacturing staging. During the manufacturing process, Manufacturing will share that responsibility with the Quality and Production Control Departments. They will each be responsible for insuring the traceability of materials and processes.

Reference Documents

8.0100  Material Identification and Traceability

| #: 4.9 | Rev: A |
|--------|--------|

XYZ Company                    Approved: _____

**QUALITY MANUAL**            Date: _____1 March 1995_____

**Process Control**                              Page 1 of 2

### 4.9.1 Scope

This procedure establishes the requirement to identify and plan the production and, where applicable, assembly processes that directly affect quality and to ensure that the processes are carried out under controlled conditions. Controlled conditions shall include the following:

a) documented work instructions defining the manner of production and assembly, where the absence of such instructions would adversely affect quality, use of suitable production and assembly equipment, suitable working environment, compliance with referenced standards/ codes and quality plans,

b) monitoring and control of suitable process and product characteristics during production and assembly,

c) the approval of processes and equipment, as appropriate, and

d) criteria for workmanship that shall be stipulated, to the greatest practical extent, in written standards or by means of representative samples.

### 4.9.2 Responsibility

Process control is the responsibility of Production Control, Manufacturing, Purchasing, and Inspection, as applicable. Responsibilities are assigned according to function and/or requirements.

### 4.9.3 Special Processes

These are processes, the results of which cannot be fully verified by subsequent inspection and testing of the product and where, for example, processing deficiencies may become apparent only after the product is in use. Accordingly, continuous monitoring and/or compliance with documented procedures is required to en-

sure the specified requirements are met. Special processes shall be qualified and shall also comply with the other requirements of this procedure. Records shall be maintained for qualified processes, equipment, and personnel, as appropriate.

Reference Documents

9.0100  Process Control

9.01XX  Process Procedures

| #: 4.10 | Rev: A |
|---|---|

XYZ Company                    Approved: _____

**QUALITY MANUAL**          Date: _____1 March 1995_____

**Inspection and Testing**                    Page 1 of 3

### 4.10.1 Scope

The inspection and testing of products and services provided by XYZ Company is controlled by this procedure. Products and services shall be properly inspected and tested, to ensure compliance to process and customer requirements, through all phases of production.

### 4.10.2 Responsibility

It is the responsibility of the Quality Manager to verify that products and services provided by the company meet the stated and implied requirements. Although the Quality Manager has the primary responsibility for assuring the quality of products and services, all XYZ Company employees shall be responsible for the quality of their own work.

### 4.10.3 Receiving Inspection and Testing

Incoming materials and products received by XYZ Company shall be verified prior to use in production, except as noted below. Receiving shall review incoming products and determine if the product and data supplied conforms, or provides verification of performance, to the requirements specified on the purchase order (see Section 4.6, Purchasing). Verification shall be to a level commensurate with the product and/or application of the product. Consideration shall also be given to the control exercised at source and the documented evidence of quality conformance provided. Any products determined to require additional inspection or verification, or requiring special inspection instructions, shall be forwarded to the Quality Manager or applicable support function/organization. Products which have been verified shall be identified and issued to manufacturing.

Where incoming product is released for urgent production purposes, it shall be positively identified and recorded, by Purchas-

ing, in order to permit immediate recall and replacement in the event of nonconformance to specified requirements.

### 4.10.4  In-Process Inspection and Testing

The purpose of in-process inspection and testing is to:

a) inspect, test, and identify product as specified by the quality plan or documented procedures,

b) establish product conformance to specified requirements by use of process monitoring and control methods,

c) hold product until the required inspection and tests have been completed or necessary reports have been received and verified, except when product is released under urgent conditions, and

d) identify nonconforming product.

During production, in-process inspection and testing shall be performed to ensure products are manufactured to specifications. In-process inspection and testing shall be performed by the operators and inspectors, as defined. Mandatory in-process inspections and testing shall be specified on the Work Order. All other inspections or tests will be performed as directed by procedures or work instructions.

### 4.10.5  Final Inspection and Testing

All products produced by XYZ Company shall be subject to final inspection, testing, and/or verification. During final inspection, all specified inspections and tests, including those specified either on receipt of product or in-process, must be completed and the data meet the specified requirements. Any products pulled from incoming or in-process inspection, due to urgent circumstances, must be inspected at final inspection.

The Quality Manager shall carry out all final inspections and testing in accordance with the quality plan, or documented proce-

dures, to complete evidence of conformance of the finished product to meet specified requirements.

No product shall be shipped until all the activities specified in the quality plan or documented procedures have been satisfactorily completed, the associated data and documentation is available, and shipment has been authorized.

### 4.10.6 Inspection and Test Records

XYZ Company shall maintain records that give evidence that the product passed inspection and/or test with defined acceptance criteria. Inspection Data Sheets, certifications, statistical data, and/or other applicable records shall be prepared and filed for each lot and/or work order of product produced. Upon request, inspection and test records will be supplied with the product.

### Reference Documents

10.100  Receiving Inspection and Testing

10.200  In-Process Inspection and Testing

10.300  Final Inspection and Testing

10.400  Inspection and Test Records

| #: 4.11 | Rev: A |
|---------|--------|

XYZ Company                          Approved: _____

**QUALITY MANUAL**                 Date: _____1 March 1995_____

**Inspection, Measuring, and Test Equipment**        Page 1 of 4

### 4.11.1  Scope

The purpose of this procedure is to establish and maintain control, calibration, and maintenance of inspection, measuring, and test equipment, whether owned by XYZ Company, on loan, or provided by the customer, to demonstrate the conformance of product to the specified requirements. Equipment shall be used, calibrated, and cared for in a manner that insures that the measurement uncertainty is known and is consistent with the required measurement capability.

### 4.11.2  Responsibility

The Quality Manager shall be responsible for the control, calibration, and maintenance of inspection, measuring, and test equipment.

### 4.11.3  Equipment Use

Equipment used to inspect, measure, and/or test product shall be appropriate for the characteristic, feature, or function inspected.

### 4.11.4  Calibration

Inspection, measuring, and test equipment owned by XYZ Company or its employees, on loan, and provided by the customer shall be identified and calibrated, prior to use and at prescribed intervals, against certified equipment having a known valid relationship to a nationally or internationally recognized standard(s). Where no such standard exists, the basis for calibration shall be documented.

### 4.11.4.1  Calibration Status

Inspection, measuring, and test equipment shall be identified with a label indicating, as a minimum, identification number, calibration date, calibration due date, and by whom calibration was performed. Equipment identification numbers shall correspond to

| #: 4.11 | Rev: A |
|---------|--------|

the appropriate calibration records. When it is impractical to apply a calibration label directly on an item (i.e., gage block), the calibration label may be affixed to the container or some other suitable measures may be used to reflect calibration status. Upon receipt of loan or customer inspection, measuring, and test equipment, the Quality Manager shall verify the proper calibration status is affixed to the instrument or container.

### 4.11.4.2 Calibration Records

XYZ Company shall maintain calibration records for inspection, measuring, and test equipment. The records shall document that established schedules and procedures are followed to maintain the accuracy of all equipment and measurement standards. The records shall include an individual record of calibration or other means of control for each item of inspection, measuring, and test equipment and measurement standards, providing a description or identification of the item, calibration source, calibration procedure used, calibration results, and calibration action taken.

### 4.11.4.3 Calibration Intervals

XYZ Company has established and maintains calibration intervals to assure acceptable accuracy and reliability throughout the established interval. Calibration intervals vary from prior-to-use to annually, depending on the type of equipment and usage. Intervals shall be shortened, or may be lengthened, when the results of previous calibrations indicate that such action is appropriate to maintain acceptable reliability. Records of calibration intervals are maintained and available from the Quality Manager.

### 4.11.4.4 Calibration Recall

Prior to the end of the calibration interval, the Quality Manager shall recall the equipment requiring calibration and recalibrate as necessary. Any equipment found out of calibration shall be sent to the Quality Manager. Equipment that is not currently in use to inspect product and/or is out of calibration shall be prop-

erly identified (i.e., Do not use). This includes equipment that is out of calibration and in storage. Provisions may be made for temporary extension of the calibration due date for a limited period of time under certain specific conditions, such as the completion of a test or job in progress.

### 4.11.4.5 Calibration Procedures

Calibration procedures are utilized for the calibration of all inspection, measuring, and test equipment. Each procedure is commensurate with the equipment type. The procedures are in accordance with manufacturer's specifications, Government, and/or published standard industry practices. Copies of the above procedure sources are available from the Quality Manager. Each calibration procedure shall specify, as a minimum, the measurement standard, equipment used, the required parameters, range, and accuracy of the standard at the acceptance tolerance of each instrument characteristic being calibrated. Where practical, safeguards shall be implemented that prevent equipment adjustment which would invalidate calibration settings.

### 4.11.4.6 Measurement Standards

Measurement standards used by XYZ Company for calibration shall be traceable to certified equipment having a known valid relationship to a recognized standard. Where no such standard exists, the basis used for calibration shall be documented. All deviations shall be documented.

### 4.11.4.7 Environmental Conditions

Inspection, measurement, and test equipment shall be calibrated and utilized in an environment controlled to the extent necessary to assure continued measurements of the required accuracy. Consideration shall be given to temperature, humidity, vibration, cleanliness, and other controllable factors. When applicable, compensation corrections shall be applied to calibration results obtained in an environment that departs from acceptable conditions.

## 4.11.5  Out-of-Calibration or Tolerance

When inspection, measuring, and test equipment is found to be out-of-calibration or tolerance, previous inspections and tests shall be assessed and documented to consider validity and impact.

## 4.11.6  Handling, Preservation, and Storage

Inspection, measurement, and test equipment and standards shall be handled, preserved, and stored such that the accuracy and fitness for use is maintained.

## 4.11.7  Test Hardware and Software

Test hardware, including jigs, fixtures, templates and patterns, and test software used for inspection shall be checked to prove that they are capable of verifying the acceptability of product prior to release for use during production and installation and shall be rechecked at prescribed intervals. Inspection of test hardware and software shall be in accordance with Section 4.11.4 (Calibration) of this procedure. Measurement design data shall be made available for verification that test hardware and software is functionally adequate.

Reference Documents

11.0100  Control of Inspection/Measuring/Test Equipment

11.0200  Calibration Procedures

11.0300  Calibration Records

| #: 4.12 | Rev: A |
|---|---|

XYZ Company                           Approved: _____

**QUALITY MANUAL**                    Date: \_\_\_\_\_1 March 1995\_\_\_\_

**Inspection and Test Status**                              Page 1 of 1

### 4.12.1  Scope

This procedure describes the methods used by XYZ Company to indicate the inspection and test status of products through production.

### 4.12.2  Responsibility

It is the responsibility of the person performing the manufacturing or inspection operation to provide the appropriate inspection and test status of products as they are produced. Included are both production and inspection personnel.

### 4.12.3  Identification

The inspection and test status of product shall be identified by using marking, authorized stamps, tags, labels, work order, inspection records, test software, physical location, and/or other suitable means, that indicate conformance or nonconformance of product with regard to inspection and tests performed. Unless otherwise specified, only nonconforming product will be physically marked. Markings should include a description of the nonconformance. Products with no physical markings shall be considered in conformance with specifications. The identification of inspection and test status shall be maintained, as necessary, throughout production and installation of the product to ensure that only product that has passed the required inspection and tests is shipped, used, or installed. Records shall identify the inspection authority responsible for the release of conforming product.

Reference Documents

12.0100  Inspection and Test Status

XYZ Company                           Approved: _____

**QUALITY MANUAL**                    Date: ____1 March 1995____

**Control of Nonconforming Product**                    Page 1 of 3

## 4.13.1 Scope

Control of nonconforming product shall be regulated by this procedure. This control is necessary to prevent the inadvertent shipping, use or installation of nonconforming product. Control shall provide for identification, documentation, evaluation, segregation when practical, disposition of nonconforming product, and for notification of the functions concerned. Field nonconformances are also handled by this procedure.

## 4.13.2 Responsibility

The proper control of nonconforming product is the responsibility of all employees of XYZ Company. The primary responsibility is with manufacturing and quality personnel; however, all support functions/organizations shall provide assistance as necessary.

## 4.13.3 Identification of Nonconforming Product

All nonconforming product shall be properly identified in accordance with Section 4.12 (Inspection and Test Status) to indicate the product does not meet the required specification(s).

## 4.13.4 Nonconformity Review and Disposition

Once a nonconforming product is discovered, a review and disposition of the nonconformity shall be conducted, as soon as possible, to prevent unnecessary processing or delivery impact. The review shall be conducted by Quality, Manufacturing, Production Control, Sales, and/or the customer, depending on the nature or severity of the nonconformance.

The nonconformance review and disposition shall include the following options:

| #: 4.13 | Rev: A |
|---------|--------|

a) Rework—The product may be reprocessed from a non-conforming to a conforming condition without violating customer specifications or requirements.

b) Use-as-is—The product will conform to the required form, fit, or function, however, does not meet all product specifications or requirements.

c) Repair—Provide additional processing and/or features that were not originally specified that will allow the product to comply with the required form, fit, or function.

d) Alternate use—Classify the product for an alternate use, revision, or grade that would result in the product complying with the requirements of the new classification.

e) Reject or scrap—The product cannot be brought to a condition that will provide the desired form, fit, or function.

Upon completion of the nonconformance review, the results shall be marked on the affected product or container. Steps should be taken to resolve all nonconforming product as soon as practical. Reworked and repaired product shall be reinspected to the original or revised requirements.

## 4.13.4.1 Nonconformance Notice

Where required by the customer, the proposed use or repair of product which does not conform to specified requirements shall be reported for concession to the customer or customer's representative. A nonconformance notice shall be completed and sent to the responsible authority of the customer. Upon review, the customer shall complete the disposition and return the notice to XYZ Company with the required action documented. For product that receives authorization to use-as-is or repair, a copy of the authorization shall be attached to the inspection data sheet. For urgent requests, a verbal authorization may be accepted, however, it

| #: 4.13 | Rev: A |
|---------|--------|

must be followed by written documentation. All other forms of customer authorization for nonconforming product shall be handled in accordance with this procedure.

Reference Documents

13.0100  Nonconforming Materials Procedure

| #: 4.14 | Rev: A |
|---|---|

XYZ Company Approved: _____

**QUALITY MANUAL** Date: _____1 March 1995_____

**Corrective and Preventive Action** Page 1 of 2

## 4.14.1 Scope

Corrective action (formal or informal) shall be taken when a non-conformance is discovered or a process is found to be out of control. Need for corrective action may be the result of inspections, audits, tests, or observations.

## 4.14.2 Responsibility

Initiating the corrective action process is the responsibility of all employees of XYZ Company. The primary responsibility for insuring resolution is with the Quality Manager; all support functions/organizations shall provide assistance as necessary.

## 4.14.3 Corrective Action

As a result of a nonconformance or audit, a corrective action evaluation shall be performed. The purpose of the corrective action shall be to:

a) investigate the cause of nonconformance and the corrective action needed to prevent recurrence,

b) analyze all processes, work operations, concessions, quality records, service reports, and customer complaints to detect and eliminate potential causes of nonconforming product,

c) initiate preventive actions to deal with problems to a level corresponding to the risks encountered,

d) apply controls to ensure that corrective actions are taken and are effective, and/or

e) implement and record changes in procedures resulting from corrective actions.

f) Preclude the nonconformity from recurring.

| #: 4.14 | Rev: A |
|---------|--------|

Page 2 of 2

Corrective action evaluations shall be conducted by quality and/or manufacturing personnel, depending on the cause, nature, or severity of the nonconformance. Feedback shall be provided to the source of the nonconformance and all functions/organizations that are affected. The initiating function/organization shall monitor the corrective action and recommend or implement changes as necessary. All functions/organizations shall support the corrective action process.

Reference Documents

14.0100  Corrective Action

| #: 4.15 | Rev: A |
|---------|--------|

XYZ Company     Approved: _____

**QUALITY MANUAL**   Date: _____1 March 1995_____

**Handling, Storage, Packaging,**
**Preservation, and Delivery**     Page 1 of 1

### 4.15.1 Scope

All materials and products will be handled, stored, packaged, preserved, and delivered in a manner that insures their inherent integrity, controls their issuance and movement, and maintains quality through delivery to the customer.

### 4.15.2 Responsibility

Ensuring the integrity of materials and products is the responsibility of all employees of XYZ Company. The primary responsibility for handling, storage, packaging, and delivery is vested with Production Control.

### 4.15.3 Handling

All materials and products will be handled in a manner that prevents damage and/or deterioration.

### 4.15.4 Storage and Preservation

All materials and products will be stored in areas that ensure their integrity and also afford adequate controls for issuance and receipt. XYZ Company shall utilize sound inventory control methods, including the verification of limited life materials and the first-in-first-out issuance of materials and products.

### 4.15.5 Packaging and Delivery

All products shall be packaged in a manner that ensures the integrity of the product through delivery to the customer.

Reference Documents

15.0100  Material Handling

15.0200  Material Storage and Preservation

15.0300  Material Packaging and Delivery

| #: 4.16 | Rev: A |
|---------|--------|

| XYZ Company | Approved: _____ |
| **QUALITY MANUAL** | Date: _____1 March 1995_____ |
| **Quality Records** | Page 1 of 1 |

### 4.16.1 Scope

All product and service related records produced within the Quality Management System will be considered Quality Records. This includes all internally generated and controlled forms, tags, computer records, and customer supplied documentation.

### 4.16.2 Responsibility

The Quality Manager will be responsible for the collection and the integrity of Quality Records.

### 4.16.3 Record Keeping

Orderly and retrievable records shall be kept as evidence that the Quality Management system is effective. Records shall be kept that provide traceability of products and processes, so that internal and external audits may efficiently follow work flow and production steps. Sufficient records shall also be kept for analysis of trends and as the basis for planning continuous improvement.

### 4.16.4 Record Disposal

Records shall be archived at intervals appropriate to the need to access them. Each family of records shall have designated intervals at which they may be properly disposed.

Reference Documents

16.0100  Quality Records Maintaining/Storage/Disposition

| #: 4.17 | Rev: A |
|---|---|

XYZ Company                    Approved: _____

**QUALITY MANUAL**            Date: _____1 March 1995_____

**Internal Quality Audits**                         Page 1 of 1

### 4.17.1 Scope

The infrastructure of the Quality Management System at XYZ Company is keyed to the Internal Audit System. Audits will be conducted by cross-functional team members who have been trained in auditing as a tool of total quality. Audits will be scheduled to cover each element of the Quality Management System at least annually. Critical areas will be audited more frequently. Audits may also be unscheduled, as needed to maintain system and process integrity.

### 4.17.2 Responsibility

The Quality Manager will be administer the internal auditing system. Audits may be conducted by any designated employee; however, the Quality Manager will have responsibility to see that the audit findings are acted upon in a timely manner and that all follow-up was performed effectively.

### 4.17.3 Scheduled Internal Audits

An internal audit schedule will be posted each calendar year by the Quality Manager. They will see that the schedule is followed and that audits are conducted in a professional and effective manner.

### 4.17.4 Unscheduled Audits

When there is reason to suspect a process is reaching its control limits or is out of control, when a customer requests corrective action, or when Management deems necessary, unscheduled audits may be conducted. Deficiencies detected will normally be referred for corrective action.

Reference Documents

14.0100  Corrective Action

17.0100  Audit Procedure

| #: 4.18 | Rev: A |
|---------|--------|

XYZ Company                Approved: _____

**QUALITY MANUAL**        Date: _____1 March 1995_____

**Training**                         Page 1 of 1

### 4.18.1 Scope

At XYZ Company, training is an investment in the future. Each employee who can effect product or service quality will receive the job-related training specified in his or her job description. Also, they will receive ongoing training in areas that will help them develop their skills and ensure that they support the Quality Policy.

### 4.18.2 Responsibility

Each functional supervisor will be responsible for ensuring that prescribed training is available to his or her team. Each individual will be responsible for seeking out the training that is necessary as a condition of continued employment.

### 4.18.3 Training

A master training plan will be published, maintained, and updated as necessary. The plan will be periodically reviewed for effectiveness, adequacy, and updated as necessary to support Company operations. Employees will receive training as a usual part of their jobs. Records of training will be maintained and retraining conducted as indicated by criticality of the process.

Reference Documents

18.0100  Master Training Plan

18.0200  Measuring Training Effectiveness

18.0300  Training Records

| #: 4.19 | Rev: A |
|---|---|

XYZ Company

**QUALITY MANUAL**

**Service**

Approved: _____

Date: _____1 March 1995_____

Page 1 of 1

XYZ Company does not presently engage in after the sale service.

| #: 4.20 | Rev: A |

XYZ Company                     Approved: _____

**QUALITY MANUAL**              Date: _____1 March 1995_____

**Statistical Techniques**                         Page 1 of 1

### 4.20.1  Scope

When statistical techniques are employed to determine product quality or process effectiveness, the methods used will be selected for their adequacy and ability to produce accurate analyses. If used for informational purposes, only, statistical techniques may be informal.

### 4.20.2  Responsibility

The Quality Manager will select and enact any statistical techniques used at XYZ Company.

### 4.20.3  Statistical Techniques

When statistical techniques are to be employed to measure process effectiveness or to determine product quality, the Quality Manager will choose techniques from those proven to be effective in the environment that they will be applied. The Quality Manager will ensure that the results of these techniques will be acted upon.

Reference Documents

20.0100  Sampling Plan

# APPENDIX

## C

# *Internal Auditor Training Course*

**Internal Auditor Training**

**Conducted by**
**Productivity Resources**

# Introduction

Our industrial revolution spawned a great many companies that were run by dominant, powerful leaders. They derived their power by knowing "everything" about their products and about their companies and by ruling by fear and intimidation. These autocratic leaders were taught by Fredrick Taylor that workers were capable of performing only mindless, repetitive tasks. This "production line" thinking was effective when workers were illiterate and when there were plenty of policemen to maintain order and to enforce the autocratic rules. The Taylor management style has been challenged only in the last few decades, and proven to be a dinosaur in just the last ten years. It no longer functions effectively because American workers are literate, educated, and want to be part of the success of the companies they work for. Job holders also want to be trusted, instead of working in a police state. Although business leaders have learned that they are not capable of knowing "everything" about their products and processes, the transition is a slow, painful process.

Your Company has taken a bold step forward, away from the traditions of manufacturing systems that have been in place since 1776. The process of ISO9000 certification is causing new and more effective methods of operating the Company to be implemented. They include controlling documentation and processes instead of controlling people. They also include placing responsibility for quality with the people who are performing the work.

Rather than pay policemen to tell us what is right and wrong, Internal Auditing will become the key tool in enabling the manufacturing process to run with minimum overhead and with maximum customer satisfaction. It involves workers helping each other to ensure that written procedures are effective, processes are operating as they should and that individuals are trained to perform their jobs.

## Contents

# 1. Definition of Internal Auditing

*Internal Auditing is the Objective Evaluation of a company's Quality Management System.*

Internal Auditing is:

- Performing systematic reviews of processes and procedures to evaluate system performance.
- Employees helping each other maintain the desired quality levels.
- Replacing wasteful adversarial roles with constructive team building.
- Creating a documented foundation for continuous improvement.

## 2. Why Internal Auditing?

- Routine and systematic verification that written procedures are being followed and are effective.
- Eliminates the need for high profile and high overhead tollgate controls.
- Empowers employees to help each other optimize their systems and performance.
- Tears down adversarial roles.
- Promotes "win-win" thinking.
- Processes are reviewed on a regular schedule lessening the chance for error to drift into products and services.
- Minimizes nonconformances and customer problems.
- Management gains objective evidence of system performance and of opportunities for improvement.
- Documentation and resolution of nonconformances prevents similar problems from recurring (Preventive action).

# 3. How Internal Auditing is Used

◆ Internal Audits are scheduled to review each area of the Quality Management System at least once a year. Critical areas are audited more frequently.

◆ Internal Audits are conducted when a process is suspected to be out of control.

◆ Internal Audits are used as a basis for changing and improving procedures and processes.

◆ Internal Audits are used as a database for Management to perform strategic planning and to take preventive action.

# 4. How Are Audits Conducted?

Audits are usually conducted by teams of two or more people who work outside the area that they are auditing. Scheduling of audits and types of audits will be discussed later, but they are never a surprise to the people being audited. They always have a specific agenda. They are focused on a specific procedure or process, never on an individual. The general format of an audit would be:

Select the procedure or process to be audited.

Determine who will be on the Audit Team.

Notify the person responsible for the area to be audited of the subject and schedule a mutually agreeable time.

Read the operating procedure or process procedure carefully and make up an audit checklist.

Conduct the audit, with a guide from the area being audited.

When you are finished, discuss your preliminary findings with the person responsible.

Complete an Audit Report and Corrective Action Reports, as necessary.

Follow the prescribed procedures for distribution, response, follow-up, and closure.

## 5. The Role of the Auditor

Auditing done well is very beneficial to everyone involved. Auditing done badly creates hard feelings and builds adversarial relationships. The most important elements of auditing are how the auditor perceives his or her role and how that perception is communicated to those being audited.

◆ The auditor must be convinced that the service he or she is performing is of value and that it is a win-win situation for all involved.

◆ The auditor must enter the situation with an open mind about what they may or may not find during the audit.

◆ The auditor must be patient and follow the audit logically to completion before arriving at any conclusions.

The most beneficial situation at any company is that every employee have an opportunity to be a member of an audit team and that every employee be involved in being audited. By being on both ends of an audit, there is closure and balance. There are some people who would rather not be auditors, however. There are also some whose personality and training do not lend themselves to auditing, so not everyone will have an opportunity to be an auditor. The attributes of an effective auditor are:

◆ Having enough technical background to understand the processes and procedures being audited. Being familiar with the Quality System and being comfortable with it.

◆ Being able to read a procedure and then observe the effectiveness of what was written.

◆ Being a sensitive and articulate interviewer and being able to write down an accurate account of what was said and observed.

◆ Being an effective listener. That is, being able to extract the significant information from what is being discussed.

◆ Being able to deductively reason through a situation or problem and arrive at a logical conclusion.

## 5. The Role of the Auditor (continued)

*There must be a little bit of Sherlock Holmes in an internal auditor's personality. That is, an internal auditor must be able to follow the trail of clues and logically deduce the realities of a situation. This trait is especially helpful when what appears on the surface isn't exactly what is happening.*

What you see and what is really happening can be interpreted differently by different people, depending on their point of view.

### WHAT DO YOU SEE IN THIS PICTURE?

## 5. The Role of the Auditor (continued)

There are also a number of ways for an auditor to turn an audit into an instant disaster. They include:

Being confrontational, argumentative, opinionated, and overbearing.

Dispensing advice or turning the situation into an opportunity to tell personal "war stories."

Accusing or attacking individuals. Offering ultimatums or promising revenge. Looking for victims and scapegoats. Using the audit for personal agenda items.

Being insincere, looking down, talking under your breath, seeming like you can't wait for this to be over.

Not listening, interrupting, drawing conclusions, comparing situations or individuals.

Not sticking to the audit agenda. Wandering off into witch hunts.

Being patronizing and too understanding. Not doing the job because of potential hurt feelings or potential confrontations.

Interpreting standards, negotiating deals, predicting outcomes.

Being an effective auditor is best summed up by a quote from Rudyard Kipling:

*I keep six honest serving men. They have taught me all I know.*
*Their names are What, Why, When, How, Where and Who.*

Being able to ask the right questions is the hallmark of a good auditor:

◆ What is supposed to be happening and what is happening?
◆ Why is it happening?
◆ When is it happening?
◆ How is it being done?
◆ Where is it happening?
◆ Who is doing it?

## 5. The Role of the Auditor (continued)

The answers to those questions will be the key to an effective audit. The questions must be followed by "Show Me" to verify that the answers really depict what was described in the interview. They may also be asked with "What would happen if . . . ?" when appropriate to clarify a procedure or process.

Finally:

An auditor has two ears and one mouth. They should be used approximately in that proportion.

## 6. How to Be Audited

Being the subject of an audit can be a rewarding experience or it can be pure hell, depending on how you perceive the audit and how well prepared you are. Internal Audits should always be approached as an opportunity to have a co-worker help you polish you skills and identify areas needing improvement.

Audits should never be a surprise and the topic should be published in advance, so take the time to review the procedures that will be audited.

Be sure that all equipment that should be calibrated is current and that there are no obsolete or unauthorized documents in the work area.

Be sure all records are up to date and current revisions are present.

Make sure that objective evidence exists of compliance with applicable procedures.

Be sure that all work in your area is being processed per the applicable procedures and that the documentation with the work is up to date and accurate.

Answer questions briefly, courteously and truthfully. If you don't know an answer, tell the auditor that you will find out.

Do not volunteer information that wasn't requested and do not tell war stories or unload personal issues on the auditor.

Do help the auditor understand the process completely.

Never argue with the auditor. Don't try to hustle or snow the auditor. Don't try to hide problems discovered during the audit.

Remember, treat the auditor the way you would like to be treated.

## 7. Types of Internal Audits

◆ Routine internal audits should be part of a complete annual audit schedule. Each Operations Procedure and each Quality Procedure should be audited at least once a year. Critical processes should be audited as often as necessary to be sure that the process stays in control.

◆ When a problem is discovered in a process or in a procedure that raises a question of adequacy of the process or adequacy of the training, an audit should be initiated to document the problem and to ensure that the problem is resolved.

◆ Management should schedule spot audits to ensure that routine audits are effective. Management may also schedule special audits based on customer input or on trends observed in data.

## Content Note

In the first seven sections, we have discussed internal auditing in a very generic fashion. For the remainder of this session, we will deal specifically with performing internal audits in an ISO9000 environment.

A Quality Management System designed around ISO9000 or designed to be compliant with ISO9000 will have certain unique attributes. To prepare the participants for their role as ISO9000 Internal Auditors, we will deal with many of the issues that are peculiar to an ISO9000-based Quality Management System in the examples and case studies that follow.

## 8. The Audit Checklist

Prior to conducting an audit, make a checklist of the items to be covered in the audit. Often, there are existing checklists used by the operators that can be adapted to help simplify the audit checklist. Other times, it may be necessary to take the procedure or process being audited and turn the written procedure around from statements to questions. For example, the procedure might say *Record the work order number on the Inspection Data Sheet.* The audit checklist might say *Is the work order number recorded on the Inspection Data Sheet?*

◆ Make a checklist of the various equipment that you want to look at while performing the audit.

◆ List the people whom you intend to interview during the audit.

◆ Note any problems found on previous audits of the same area, procedure, or process.

◆ Note paragraph numbers of applicable procedures on the checklist so that you do not continually have to refer to the procedure.

◆ Leave enough room on the checklist for notes about what was observed and what was discussed during the audit. Also leave room to record model numbers and serial numbers of equipment involved in the audit.

## Exercise 1

The first step in conducting internal audits is to construct an audit checklist. We will use key elements of ISO9002 to build several checklists. The first page includes an example of how to construct an audit checklist.

## ISO9002 Internal Audit Checklist

### Paragraph 4.3

1. *Are there documented procedures for contract review and for the coordination of contract review activities (4.3.1)?*

2. *Before contracts are finalized, are they reviewed (4.3.2)?*

   ◆ *Are requirements adequately defined?*

   ◆ *Are differences resolved?*

   ◆ *Do they verify capability to meet the contract requirements?*

3. *Are contract amendments transferred to the functions concerned (4.3.3)?*

4. *Are there records of contract reviews? (4.3.4)*

# ISO9002 Internal Audit Checklist

## Paragraph 4.5

## ISO9002 Internal Audit Checklist

## Paragraph 4.6

## ISO9002 Internal Audit Checklist

## Paragraph 4.8

## ISO9002 Internal Audit Checklist

## Paragraph \_\_\_\_\_

## ISO9002 Internal Audit Checklist

### Paragraph _____

# ISO9002 Internal Audit Checklist

## Paragraph _____

## ISO9002 Internal Audit Checklist

### Paragraph _____

# 9. Conducting Internal Audits

ISO9000 QUALITY MANAGEMENT SYSTEM AUDITS

The goal of a Quality Management System Audit (QMSA) is the completion of an objective evaluation of the company's quality management system. This audit includes, but is not limited to, the:

- —Organization
- —Procedures
- —Training
- —Equipment
- —Materials
- —Work areas
- —Operations
- —Processes
- —Final product
- —Documentation
- —Reports
- —Record keeping

QMS audits are usually conducted at several levels. First, the Quality Policy Manual is audited to ensure compliance with the ISO9000 Standard. Second, the second- and third-tier operational procedures are audited to ensure compliance with the policies set forth in the Quality Policy Manual. Finally, the items in the above list are audited to their respective procedures.

# 9. Conducting Internal Audits (continued)

ISO9000 QUALITY MANAGEMENT SYSTEM
AUDIT GUIDELINES

1. First, carefully review the documented procedures that describe the system being audited.

   —Quality Manual (Level I documentation)

   —Operations Procedures (Level II)

   —Step-by-step Work Instructions (Level III )

   —Forms and Records (Level IV documentation).

   —Do these documents meet the requirements of ISO9000?

2. Check for actual compliance with those documents.

   —Are the process operators doing what the procedures require?

   —Are all forms authorized and controlled?

   —Do the required records exist?

3. Always base your questions upon written statements. Track the issue back to the source.

   —Is the issue the lack of a necessary procedure, or is it actually inadequate training?

4. Avoid personal opinions. Stick to the actual requirements of the standard or documents that have been generated to support that standard.

5. Ask questions such as:

   —How do you know how to perform that operation?

   —Can you show me the records?

   —Where is this form authorized for use?

   —What is your system for . . . ?

   —Who can make that decision?

# 10. The Audit Report

Documenting the results of the audit is just as important as the audit itself. You must be able to communicate your observations and conclusions clearly, accurately, and in a manner that is constructive, rather than punitive or offensive.

Audit reports should contain the following:

**Observation:** Situations worth noting that are either commendations of processes that are working particularly well or processes that may warrant additional research. Observations are not indicative of any deviations or noncompliances.

**Minor Finding:** A deviation or noncompliance that indicates a system deficiency that does not put product or service quality at risk. These may also be a single lapse of a procedure. Minor Findings are also described as points of ongoing improvement.

**Major Finding:** A nonconformity that places product or service quality at risk. An absence of a required procedure. A total breakdown of a process or procedure. Major findings are also described as hold-points. Multiple minor findings in the same area may also be considered a hold point. A significant number of minor findings in an audit outing may also be considered a major finding.

## Audit Notes

During an audit, you may observe deviations or noncompliances that are outside the scope of your audit. These deviations or noncompliances should be noted and passed on for follow-up to the responsible job holders and to those responsible for scheduling audits.

The only other data that should be contained in an audit report is annotation of specific documents, products, and personnel that were part of the audit.

There is one simple rule that will make your audit report writing clear and concise every time:

◆ Describe what the situation *should be*.
◆ Describe what *it is*.

## 10. The Audit Report (continued)

If you cannot cite a process or procedure that states how a situation *should be*, then you cannot have a finding.

Example 1: A tool is found without a calibration sticker.

Right:

> Calipers found in Work Center 21 with no calibration sticker.
>
> All tools used for verification must be calibrated (11.0100, 7.2).

Wrong:

> Found Joe using one of his own calipers that he keeps in his tool box that nobody knows about. He ought to know better.

Example 2: An obsolete print is found in a job file.

Right:

> While auditing Work Order 654321 there were two prints in the master file, drawing #22-44567-33, one revision C, and one Revision D. Only the latest print should be in the master file (3.0200, 7.3).

Wrong:

> Order entry forgot to pull an old revision when the new one came in.

In each Right case, the finding was stated clearly and the procedure number and paragraph were cited. In the Wrong examples, the same problem became argumentative and judgmental. Never *try and convict* in an audit report.

In the words of Jack Webb (Sgt. Joe Friday from the *Dragnet* TV show):

> *"We want the facts, ma'am; just the facts!"*

## 10. The Audit Report (continued)

When the audit report is complete, discuss your findings with the person responsible for the area that has been audited. Be sure that you both agree on what was observed and what was documented. Be sure to verbally express any positive observations and compliment the process owners.

From the Audit Report, select the major and minor findings and write a Corrective Action Request (CAR) for each observed non-conformance or deviation.

## 11. The Corrective Action Report

A Corrective Action Request (CAR) is the vehicle for documenting deviations and nonconformities found during an audit. It not only states the findings of the auditors, it contains the necessary preliminary assessment data to enable a root-cause-analysis to be conducted. The amount of information provided on the CAR should be as thorough as the severity of the nonconformance. If it is a major issue, the auditor should defer the detail investigation to the responsible Manager. If the investigation crosses functional lines, the people responsible for the other areas should be included in the investigation. The objective of formally documenting findings on a CAR is to ensure problems do not recur. To that end, the CAR files should be checked to verify that this problem has or has not been documented in the past.

In the case of the previous examples, the following scenarios might be documented on the CARs.

Example 1:

Right:

> I interviewed Joe and he explained that he was under the impression that he could use any calipers while the job was running, but he always used calibrated ones when he was finished with the part. I explained that the procedure didn't make that distinction. It sates that any tools in the work area used for dimensional measurement must have a current calibration sticker on them. I also suggested that it made sense, because if his calipers were not accurate, he could get to the end of a job and find out the part was out of tolerance. I recommend that the lead men review the procedure with all of the shop workers in case this interpretation is shared by others.

Wrong:

> Joe tried to tell me that he didn't understand the procedure, but I was sure that he is one of those who is always trying to work around the system. The rumors are that he is a little slow to learn and that he hides his poor performance by crying that he hasn't been trained right. I recommend that he be put on probation until he straightens out and follows the rules.

# 11. The Corrective Action Report
(continued)

Example 2

Right:

> I discussed the print revision situation with Susie. She said that the new revision came in while the job was being run, so she left the old copy in the file in case the inspectors needed to see the old print. I showed her where the procedure states to archive the old print and that they could always go to the obsolete drawing file if they wanted to see the old revision. In discussing the contract filing system further with Susie, it is apparent that the system doesn't support production as well as it should. She says that she has to keep notes on a pad about revisions for the Martin Company, because they change revisions two and three times during a job. I recommend that the Order Change and Revision Procedure be reviewed to make sure that it supports what is actually happening with our customers.

Wrong:

> Susie had some lame excuse about making sure that both prints were available for the inspectors. Actually, she is just lazy and likes to keep her own records. Have you ever looked at the note pad she keeps? I think her filing system stinks. It was much better when we could go in and pull our own prints.

## 12.   Closing The Loop

Once a Corrective Action Report has been initiated, the responsible process owners must investigate the findings and respond to the CAR. The owners of the process should perform a detailed investigation and reply to the CAR with what was found, what steps will be taken to correct the problem, and what steps will be initiated to prevent recurrence. The rest of the Corrective Action Process is:

◆ The responsible manager returns the CAR to the Quality Representative for closure. The recommended corrective action is reviewed for completeness.

◆ A follow-up audit is scheduled to verify that the corrective action was effective.

◆ The CAR is not closed until all of the stake holders agree that the corrective action was completed and it will preclude the problem from recurring.

◆ As a part of Management Reviews, the Audit Reports and CARs are reviewed and sample independent reviews are performed by Management to ensure that the system is working as it should.

# 13. Auditing Exercises

The following exercises are designed to apply the internal auditing skills learned thus far. The examples will use the ISO9000 standards as the procedure manual being used for the audit. Refer to the audit checklists previously written and to ISO9002 as the governing requirements.

Form into teams of three to five people. Appoint someone to read the exercises and someone to write an audit report. After reading each situation aloud, discuss the situation and decide if there is:

◆ No finding
◆ A Minor Finding
◆ A Major Finding
◆ An Observation
◆ An Audit Note

Have the scribe record the results on an audit report. Have each team present their audit reports to the group and to the course leader. You may want to refer to Section 4 of this course on how audits are conducted.

Exercise 2 assumes that you are part of an internal audit team auditing a particular area within your company. In actual internal audits, it is usually a more efficient use of time to audit a particular area and cover all procedures that apply to that area. For this exercise, we have no process procedures, so we will be auditing to the key elements of ISO9002.

Exercise 3 is similar to Exercise 1, but takes place in a different environment.

Exercise 4 assumes that you are part of an ISO9000 audit team sent to perform an ISO9000 assessment audit of another company. It is similar to the experience you will share when an independent audit firm is retained to perform an ISO9000 assessment audit at your company. In this case, you will appoint a lead auditor to present your audit report to the president of the company being audited.

## Exercise 2

Your company builds electronic control systems to customer specifications. You are an audit team performing an internal audit of
the Documentation Control Area in your company. This area contains master copies of customer drawings, industry specifications,
internal procedures, and company engineering drawings.

1. As you approach the Documentation Control Room, you notice the door is open and a number of production workers are
   searching through a file drawer of obsolete drawings.
2. Roberta, the Document Control Specialist, greets you, and
   informs you that she will be your guide as you audit Documentation Control. She apologizes for the area being disorganized in appearance. She explains that she has been on vacation and the filing is a couple of weeks behind.
3. You ask to see examples of how customer drawings are controlled. Roberta takes you to the file cabinets containing
   drawings from the Smith Steel Works. You select five drawings to audit. You ask for the Master Document List and you
   check the revision levels of the drawings in the file against
   the master list. All but one are the correct revision. One
   drawing should be revision AB, per the master list, and the
   print in the drawer is revision AA. Roberta says that she
   thinks that the new drawing is in the stack to be filed.
4. You ask Roberta to see the procedure governing the filing of
   customer drawings. She says that she loaned her copy of the
   Operations Procedures Manual to another department, but
   she has a copy of the procedure laminated and tacked to the
   wall outside the door for all to read.
5. You ask Roberta how the Master Document List is controlled. She pulls up a spreadsheet on her computer showing
   you how she logs all new drawings as they are received. You
   ask if her computer is secured by a password or some other
   form of controlling access to the Master Document list. She
   responds that the door to the room is always locked when she
   isn't around.
6. You next ask to see how Engineering Changes are controlled
   and distributed. Roberta shows you the master file of Engi-

neering Change Notices. You ask to pull five examples. Only one of the five examples has a signature sheet indicating that she had distributed the change and received acknowledgements from those affected by the change. She explains that she has been short handed and has had to rely on the Engineering secretary to run copies for the production workers and that the secretary didn't always return the acknowledgments.

7. You notice a shelf of catalogs from various electronic distributors. You ask Roberta if these are controlled. She says that they are used only for reference and that they never leave the room. She says that the engineers use the computerized parts catalog when they need to publish parts specifications.

You thank Roberta and return to the conference room to write your audit report.

## Exercise 2

### Audit Report

1. Audit Note: Documentation Room door was open and production workers inside. Include a check for uncontrolled obsolete drawings in the Production Area in the next audit. Observation: Should the room be secure at all times?

2.

## Exercise 3

Your company provides engineering support services to the road construction industry. You are an audit team performing an internal audit of the Contract Area. This group reviews all incoming orders and prepares job orders for the engineers to work from.

1. Don is in charge of Contracts and he greets the audit team. You ask to start the audit by reviewing his job description and his copy of the Operations Procedure manual. His manual contains a controlled issue number. His job description is contained in the manual, but it has a number of changes that he has made to it penciled on the document in the manual. He explains that he intends to formally change the Job Description as soon as the workload slows down.

2. You ask to see three contracts from different construction firms. Each contract is in a master file folder with a checklist for the key areas that must be reviewed and signed off prior to contract acceptance. Don explains that this is checklist is a new form that his assistant invented to help them ensure that the procedures were being followed.

3. The first contract you audit has records of phone conversations with the client dealing with discrepancies in the State Construction Statutes cited in the contract. You ask how the discrepancies were resolved. Don explains the resolution in great detail and shows the Statutes listed on the Engineering Work Order, but he can find no documentation indicating the final agreement with the client.

4. The second file contained a formal Request for Bid form. The bid was submitted and all documents were in order; however, the bid acknowledgement form was still attached to the original document and had never been submitted.

5. The third job calls for a Certified Professional Engineer to sign off on each step of the contract. You see various names and initials on the sign-off sheets and you ask how we verify that these individuals are certified. Don says that he always assumed that Personnel keeps a copy of their Certificates on file.

6. You asked to see several examples of how revisions to Engineering Work Orders are controlled. Don said that the Engineering Manager required each engineer to keep his or her own log of revisions because it was too much to expect Don to keep up with all the changes. Don said that the engineers were pretty good about sending him copies of the changes.

# Exercise 3

# Audit Report

## Exercise 4

You are part of an audit team sent to Weston Industries to certify them as a new supplier. Weston is still in the process of obtaining certification to ISO9002. Had they achieved certification already, you would not have needed to perform a physical audit. Weston's Quality Director, Matt Denton, will be your guide.

1. Matt first takes the team to Purchasing where he shows you how they use Super Widget software for material control. The team asks Matt about an "Approved Vendor List" and Matt pulls up a screen of vendors. The approved subcontractors are coded "Q" and the disapproved subcontractors are coded "X". In looking over the AVL screen, you notice no distributor names. Matt explains that Engineering approves the manufacturers, not the distributors, of the components. You ask the Purchasing Manager, Diane Williams, about Weston-owned tooling at their subcontractors' locations, and Diane explains that the subcontractors maintain that tooling themselves. Weston periodically does a sample inspection on the material coming off of the tooling to see how it looks.

2. Matt then takes the team to the stockroom, which appears to be well organized, with its contents easily accessible and identified accurately. Matt comments that Maria Hernandez, who is responsible for this area, is out today on jury duty. He hopes that she will be back by the end of the week because there is not yet anyone cross-trained for her position. As you leave the area, you notice several boxes containing aluminum castings, stacked five-high and leaning toward the open stockroom door.

3. When Matt takes the team through the Marketing office, someone notices a xerox copy of a released specification. Matt explains that since this is the marketing area, it is not controlled within the document control system. He says that the Product Managers can tell from the specifications approximately when the document was released and if it is current.

4. The Planning office is located next to the Marketing Office, and Matt leads the team there next. They meet Weston's

planning staff while observing the department's activities. One of the planners, Tony Cerniglia, is working on Weston's build plan. In response to a question from one of the auditors, Tony explains that the build plan is now developed based upon information received from the vice president of Manufacturing, rather than from the Marketing department information as it used to be. Matt suggests that the team move on to Order Administration.

5. As you visit Order Administration where the new orders first arrive, supervisor Jane Andrews shows you a Sales Order just received. You notice a handwritten note from Jane to Planning that indicates that the customer ordered yellow inserts, but to ship blue ones, as that is the only color in which the insert is manufactured. When asked to describe how product pricing is established, Jane responds, "Well, Marketing seems to just pick a number out of the air."

6. Matt next takes the team to Receiving Inspection where the team is introduced to Inspector Bill James. You ask Bill how he knows that the material he is currently inspecting came from an approved subcontractor. Bill goes to his terminal and pulls up the same screen that you saw in Purchasing and explains about the "Q" and "X" coding next to the vendor names. You thank Bill and proceed to the production floor.

7. On the Production floor one of the members sees a yellow "Hold" tag on a system. When she inquires as to its purpose, Matt summons Quality Manager Steve Upton. Steve explains that this is just an informal way of identifying material that has failed one of the final tests and therefore should not be shipped. You ask to speak to the individual who completed the tag, and Steve says that it was one of the two Test Technicians, but he isn't sure which one.

8. Matt seems to be very intent on making sure that things are "done right the first time." You ask what system, if any, is in place to double-check the effectiveness of corrective actions. Matt explains that this is handled informally on a manager-by-manager basis. "This pushes the responsibility back where it belongs," he says.

9. Matt takes the team by the Human Resources department where you meet the director, Tim Dodd. Tim hands you a

sample file for inspection. You look through it and see several Performance Evaluations and Training Certificates. Tim explains that through close manager-to-employee interaction, they have been able to avoid having specific job descriptions. In talking with Tim, you also learn that there are no job grades or salary levels defined.

10. After the tour, you thank Matt for showing the team around and you suggest that the audit team meet with Weston's management at 4:00 to go over the results of the audit. Matt indicates that he will be ready.

## Exercise 4

## Audit Report

(After completing the audit report, The Lead Auditor should pre-pare to brief Mr. Weston (played by the Seminar Leader) on the audit findings, at a closing meeting).

# APPENDIX

# D

## THE 1994 REVISION TO Q9002 (ISO9002) COMPLIANCE CHECKLIST

4 QUALITY-SYSTEM REQUIREMENTS

4.1 MANAGEMENT RESPONSIBILITY

☐ **4.1.1 Quality policy**

*The supplier's management with executive responsibility shall define and document its policy for quality*, including objectives for quality and its commitment to quality. The quality policy shall be relevant to the supplier's organizational goals and the expectations and needs of its customers.

☐ **The supplier shall ensure that this policy is understood, implemented, and maintained at all levels of the organization.**

4.1.2 Organization

☐ **4.1.2.1 Responsibility and authority**

*The responsibility, authority, and the interrelation of personnel who manage, perform, and verify work affect-*

*ing quality shall be defined and documented,* particularly for personnel who need the organizational freedom and authority to:

a) initiate action to prevent the occurrence of any nonconformities relating to product, process, and quality system;

b) identify and record any problems relating to the product, process, and quality system;

c) initiate, recommend, or provide solutions through designated channels;

d) verify the implementation of solutions;

e) control further processing, delivery, or installation of nonconforming product until the deficiency or unsatisfactory condition has been corrected.

☐ **4.1.2.2 Resources**

**The supplier shall identify resource requirements and provide adequate resources,** including the assignment of trained personnel (see 4.18), for management, performance of work, and verification activities including internal quality audits.

*NOTE: ELEMENTS REQUIRING DOCUMENTATION ARE ITALICIZED*

☐ **4.1.2.3 Management representative**

**The supplier's management with executive responsibility shall appoint a member of the supplier's own management who, irrespective of other responsibilities, shall have defined authority for**

a) **ensuring that a quality system is established, implemented, and maintained in accordance with this American National Standard, and**

b) **reporting on the performance of the quality system to the supplier's management for review and as a basis for improvement of the quality system.**

NOTE 5 The responsibility of a management representative may also include liaison with external parties on matters relating to the supplier's quality system.

☐ **4.1.3 Management review**

**The supplier's management with executive responsibility shall review the quality system at defined intervals** sufficient to ensure its continuing suitability and effectiveness in satisfying the requirements of this American National Standard and the supplier's stated quality policy and objectives (see 4.1.1).

☐ *Records of such reviews shall be maintained* (see 4.16).

4.2 QUALITY SYSTEM

☐ **4.2.1 General**

**The supplier shall establish, document, and maintain a quality system as a means of ensuring that product conforms to specified requirements.**

☐ *The supplier shall prepare a quality manual covering the requirements of this American National Standard.* The quality manual shall include or make reference to the quality-system procedures and outline the structure of the documentation used in the quality system.

NOTE 6 Guidance on quality manuals is given in ISO10013.

☐ **4.2.2 Quality-system procedures**

**The supplier shall**

   a) *prepare documented procedures consistent with the requirements of this American National Standard and the supplier's stated quality policy,* **and**

   b) **effectively implement the quality system and its documented procedures.**

For the purposes of this American National Standard, the range and detail of the procedures that form part of the quality

system depend on the complexity of the work, the methods used, and the skills and training needed by personnel involved in carrying out the activity.

NOTE 7 Documented procedures may make reference to work instructions that define how an activity is performed.

☐ **4.2.3 Quality planning**

*The supplier shall define and document how the requirements for quality will be met.* Quality planning shall be consistent with all other requirements of a supplier's quality system and shall be documented in a format to suit the supplier's method of operation. The supplier shall give consideration to the following activities, as appropriate, in meeting the specified requirements for products, projects or contracts:

a) the preparation of quality plans;

b) the identification and acquisition of any controls, processes, equipment (including inspection and test equipment), fixtures, resources, and skills that may be needed to achieve the required quality;

c) ensuring the compatibility of the production process, installation, servicing, inspection, and test procedures and the applicable documentation;

d) the updating, as necessary, of quality control, inspection, and testing techniques, including the development of new instrumentation;

e) the identification of any measurement requirement involving capability that exceeds the known state of the art, in sufficient time for the needed capability to be developed;

f) the identification of suitable verification at appropriate stages in the realization of product;

g) the clarification of standards of acceptability for all features and requirements, including those which contain a subjective element;

h) the identification and preparation of quality records (see 4.16).

NOTE 8 The quality plans referred to (see 4.2.3a) may be in the form of a reference to the appropriate documented procedures that form an integral part of the supplier's quality system.

4.3  CONTRACT REVIEW

☐ **4.3.1  General**

*The supplier shall establish and maintain documented procedures for contract review and for the coordination of these activities.*

☐ **4.3.2  Review**

**Before submission of a tender, or the acceptance of a contract or order (statement of requirement), the tender, contract, or order shall be reviewed** by the supplier to ensure that:

   a) the requirements are adequately defined and documented; where no written statement of requirement is available for an order received by verbal means, the supplier shall ensure that the order requirements are agreed before their acceptance;

   b) any differences between the contract or accepted order requirements and those in the tender are resolved;

   c) the supplier has the capability to meet the contract or accepted order requirements.

☐ **4.3.3  Amendment to a contract**

**The supplier shall identify how an amendment to a contract is made and correctly transferred to the functions concerned** within the supplier's organization.

☐ **4.3.4  Records**

*Records of contract reviews shall be maintained (see 4.16).*

NOTE 9 Channels for communication and interfaces with the customer's organization in these contract matters should be established.

## 4.5  DOCUMENT AND DATA CONTROL

☐ **4.5.1  General**

*The supplier shall establish and maintain documented procedures to control all documents and data that relate to the requirements of this American National Standard* including, to the extent applicable, documents of external origin such as standards and customer drawings.

NOTE 10 Documents and data can be in the form of any type of media, such as hard copy or electronic media.

☐ **4.5.2  Document and data approval and issue**

**The documents and data shall be reviewed and approved for adequacy by authorized personnel prior to issue.**

☐ *A master list or equivalent document-control procedure identifying the current revision status of documents shall be established* **and be readily available** to preclude the use of invalid and/or obsolete documents.

This control shall ensure that:

a) the pertinent issues of appropriate documents are available at all locations where operations essential to the effective functioning of the quality system are performed;

b) invalid and/or obsolete documents are promptly removed from all points of issue or use, or otherwise assured against unintended use;

c) any obsolete documents retained for legal and/or knowledge-preservation purposes are suitable identified.

☐ **4.5.3  Document and data changes**

**Changes to documents and data shall be reviewed and approved by the same functions/organizations that performed the original review and approval,** unless specifically designated otherwise. The designated functions/organizations shall have access to pertinent background information upon which to base their review and approval.

Where practicable, the nature of the change shall be identified in the document or the appropriate attachments.

### 4.6  PURCHASING

☐ **4.6.1  General**

*The supplier shall establish and maintain documented procedures to ensure that purchased product (see 3.1) conforms to specified requirements.*

### 4.6.2  Evaluation of subcontractors

**The supplier shall:**

☐   a) **evaluate and select subcontractors on the basis of their ability to meet subcontract requirements** including the quality system and any specific quality-assurance requirements;

☐   b) **define the type and extent of control exercised by the supplier over subcontractors.** This shall be dependent upon the type of product, the impact of subcontracted product on the quality of final product, and, where applicable, on the quality audit reports and/or quality records of the previously demonstrated capability and performance of subcontractors;

☐   c) *establish and maintain quality records of acceptable subcontractors* (see 4.16).

☐ **4.6.3  Purchasing data**

**Purchasing documents shall contain data clearly describing the product ordered,** including where applicable:

   a) the type, class, grade, or other precise identification;
   b) the title or other positive identification, and applicable issues of specifications, drawings, process requirements, inspection instructions, and other relevant technical data, including requirements for approval or qualification of product, procedures, process equipment, and personnel;
   c) the title, number, and issue of the quality-system standard to be applied.

☐ *The supplier shall review and approve purchasing documents for adequacy of the specified requirements prior to release.*

4.6.4  Verification of purchased product

☐ **4.6.4.1  Supplier verification at subcontractor's premises**

**Where the supplier proposes to verify purchased product at the subcontractor's premises, the supplier shall specify verification arrangements and the method of product release in the purchasing documents.**

☐ **4.6.4.2  Customer verification of subcontracted product**

**Where specified in the contract, the supplier's customer or the customer's representative shall be afforded the right to verify at the subcontractor's premises** and the supplier's premises that subcontracted product conforms to specified requirements. Such verification shall not be used by the supplier as evidence of effective control of quality by the subcontractor. Verification by the customer shall not absolve the supplier of the responsibility to provide acceptable product, nor shall it preclude subsequent rejection by the customer.

☐ **4.7  CONTROL OF CUSTOMER-SUPPLIED PRODUCT**

*The supplier shall establish and maintain documented procedures for the control of verification, storage, and maintenance of customer-supplied product* provided for incorporation into the supplies or for related activities. Any such product that is lost, damaged, or is otherwise unsuitable for use shall be recorded and reported to the customer (see 4.16). Verification by the supplier does not absolve the customer of the responsibility to provide acceptable product.

4.8  PRODUCT IDENTIFICATION AND TRACEABILITY

☐ *Where appropriate, the supplier shall establish and maintain documented procedures for identifying the product by suitable means from receipt and during all stages of production, delivery, and installation.*

☐ *Where and to the extent that traceability is a specified requirement, the supplier shall establish and maintain documented procedures for unique identification of individual product or batches. This identification shall be recorded* (see 4.16).

☐ **4.9  PROCESS CONTROL**

**The supplier shall identify and plan the production, installation, and servicing processes that directly affect quality and shall ensure that these processes are carried out under controlled conditions.** Controlled conditions shall include the following:

   a) documented procedures defining the manner of production, installation, and servicing, where the absence of such procedures could adversely affect quality;

   b) use of suitable production, installation, and servicing equipment, and a suitable working environment;

   c) compliance with reference standards/codes, quality plans, and/or documented procedures;

   d) monitoring and control of suitable process parameters and product characteristics;

   e) the approval of processes and equipment, as appropriate;

   f) criteria for workmanship, which shall be stipulated in the clearest practical manner (e.g., written standards, representatives samples, or illustrations);

   g) suitable maintenance of equipment to ensure continuing process capability.

☐ **Where the results of processes cannot be fully verified by subsequent inspection and testing of the product and where, for example, processing deficiencies may become apparent only after the product is in use, the processes shall be carried out by qualified operators and/or shall require continuous monitoring and control of process parameters to ensure that the specified requirements are met.**

The requirements for any qualification of process operations, including associated equipment and personnel (see 4.18), shall be specified.

NOTE 11 Such processes requiring prequalification of their process capability are frequently referred to as special processes.

Records shall be maintained for qualified processes, equipment, and personnel, as appropriate (see 4.16).

## 4.10 INSPECTION AND TESTING

☐ **4.10.1 General**

*The supplier shall establish and maintain documented procedures for inspection and testing activities in order to verify that the specified requirements for product are met.* The required inspection and testing, and the records to be established, shall be detailed in the quality plan or documented procedures.

### 4.10.2 Receiving inspection and testing

☐ **4.10.2.1 The supplier shall ensure that incoming product is not used or processed (except in the circumstances described in 4.10.2.3) until it has been inspected or otherwise verified as conforming to specified requirements.** Verification of the specified requirements shall be in accordance with the quality plan and/or documented procedures.

4.10.2.2 In determining the amount and nature of receiving inspection, consideration shall be given to the amount of control exercised at the subcontractor's premises and the recorded evidence of conformance provided.

4.10.2.3 Where incoming product is released for urgent production purposes prior to verification, it shall be positively identified and recorded (see 4.16) in order to permit immediate recall and replacement in the event of nonconformity to specified requirements.

□ **4.10.3  In-process inspection and testing**

*The supplier shall:*

   a) *inspect and test the product as required by the quality plan and/or documented procedures;*
   b) *hold product until the required inspection and tests have been completed or necessary reports have been received and verified, except when product is released under positive-recall procedures* (see **4.10.2.3**). Release under positive-recall procedures shall not preclude the activities outlined in 4.10.3a.

□ **4.10.4  Final inspection and testing**

**The supplier shall carry out all final inspection and testing** in accordance with the quality plan and/or documented procedures to complete the evidence of conformance of the finished product to the specified requirements.

□ **The quality plan and/or documented procedures for final inspection and testing shall require that all specified inspection and tests, including those specified either on receipt of product or in-process, have been carried out, and that the results meet specified requirements.**

□ **No product shall be dispatched until all the activities specified in the quality plan and/or documented procedures have been satisfactorily completed and the associated data and documentation are available and authorized.**

□ **4.10.5  Inspection and test records**

**The supplier shall establish and maintain records which provide evidence that the product has been inspected and/or tested.** These records shall show clearly whether the product has passed or failed the inspections and/or tests according to defined acceptance criteria. Where the product fails to pass any inspection and/or test, the procedures for control of nonconforming product shall apply (see 4.13).

Records shall identify the inspection authority responsible for the release of product (see 4.16).

## 4.11  CONTROL OF INSPECTION, MEASURING, AND TEST EQUIPMENT

☐ **4.11.1  General**

*The supplier shall establish and maintain documented procedures to control, calibrate, and maintain inspection, measuring, and test equipment* (including test software) used by the supplier to demonstrate the conformance of product to the specified requirements. Inspection, measuring, and test equipment shall be used in a manner which ensures that the measurement uncertainty is known and is consistent with the required measurement capability.

Where test software or comparative references such as test hardware are used as suitable forms of inspection, they shall be checked to prove that they are capable of verifying the acceptability of product, prior to release for use during production, installation, or servicing, and shall be rechecked at prescribed intervals. The supplier shall establish the extent and frequency of such checks and shall maintain records as evidence of control (see 4.16).

Where the availability of technical data pertaining to the measurement equipment is a specified requirement, such data shall be made available, when required by the customer or customer's representative, for verification that the measuring equipment is functionally adequate.

NOTE 12 For the purposes of this American National Standard, the term "measuring equipment" includes measurement devices.

4.11.2  Control procedure

The supplier shall:

☐ **a) determine the measurements to be made and the accuracy required, and select the appropriate inspection, measuring, and test equipment** that is capable of the necessary accuracy and precision;

☐  b) **identify all inspection, measuring, and test equipment that can affect product quality, and calibrate and adjust them at prescribed intervals,** or prior to use, against certified equipment having a known valid relationship to internationally or nationally recognized standards. Where no such standards exist, the basis used for calibration shall be documented;

☐  c) **define the process employed for the calibration of inspection, measuring, and test equipment,** including details of equipment type, unique identification, location, frequency of checks, check method, acceptance criteria, and the action to be taken when results are unsatisfactory;

☐  d) **identify inspection, measuring, and test equipment with a suitable indicator** or approved identification record to show the calibration status;

☐  e) **maintain calibration records** for inspection, measuring, and test equipment (see 4.16);

☐  f) **assess and document the validity of previous inspection and test results when inspection, measuring, or test equipment is found to be out of calibration;**

☐  g) **ensure that the environmental conditions are suitable for the calibration,** inspections, measurements, and tests being carried out;

☐  h) **ensure that the handling, preservation, and storage of inspection, measuring, and test equipment is such that the accuracy and fitness for use are maintained;**

☐  i) **safeguard inspection, measuring, and test facilities, including both test hardware and test software, from adjustments which would invalidate the calibration setting.**

NOTE 13 The metrological confirmation system for measuring equipment given in ISO10012 may be used for guidance.

☐ **4.12 INSPECTION AND TEST STATUS**

**The inspection and test status of product shall be identified by suitable means,** which indicate the conformance or nonconformance of product with regard to inspection and tests performed. The identification of inspection and test status shall be maintained, as defined in the quality plan and/or documented procedures, throughout production, installation, and servicing of the product to ensure that only product that has passed the required inspections and tests [or released under an authorized concession (see 4.13.2)] is dispatched, used, or installed.

4.13 CONTROL OF NONCONFORMING PRODUCT

☐ **4.13.1 General**

*The supplier shall establish and maintain documented procedures to ensure that product that does not conform to specified requirements is prevented from unintended use or installation*. This control shall provide for identification, documentation, evaluation, segregation (when practical), disposition of nonconforming product, and for notification to the functions concerned.

☐ **4.13.2 Review and disposition of nonconforming product**

**The responsibility for review and authority for the disposition of nonconforming product shall be defined.**

Nonconforming product shall be reviewed in accordance with documented procedures. It may be

   a) reworked to meet the specified requirements,
   b) accepted with or without repair by concession,
   c) regraded for alternative applications, or
   d) rejected or scrapped.

Where required by the contract, the proposed use or repair of product (see 4.13.2b) that does not conform to specified requirements shall be reported for concession to the customer or

customer's representative. The description of the nonconformity that has been accepted, and of repairs, shall be recorded to denote the actual condition (see 4.16).

☐ **Repaired and/or reworked product shall be reinspected in accordance with the quality plan and/or documented procedures.**

### 4.14 CORRECTIVE AND PREVENTIVE ACTION

☐ **4.14.1 General**

*The supplier shall establish and maintain documented procedures for implementing corrective and preventive action.*

Any corrective or preventive action taken to eliminate the causes of actual or potential nonconformities shall be to a degree appropriate to the magnitude of problems and commensurate with the risks encountered.

☐ **The supplier shall implement and record any changes to the documented procedures resulting from corrective and preventive action.**

4.14.2 Corrective action

The procedures for corrective action shall include:

☐    **a) the effective handling of customer complaints and reports of product nonconformities;**

☐    **b) investigation of the cause of nonconformities relating to product, process, and quality system, and recording the results of the investigation (see 4.16);**

☐    **c) determination of the corrective action needed to eliminate the cause of nonconformities;**

☐    **d) application of controls to ensure that corrective action is taken and that it is effective.**

4.14.3 Preventive action

The procedures for preventive action shall include:

☐    **a) the use of appropriate sources of information such as processes and work operations which affect**

product quality, concessions, audit results, quality records, service reports, and customer complaints to detect, analyze, and eliminate potential causes of nonconformities;

☐ b) **determination of the steps needed to deal with any problems requiring preventive action;**

☐ c) **initiation of preventive action and application of controls to ensure that it is effective;**

☐ d) **confirmation that relevant information on actions taken is submitted for** management review (see 4.1.3).

## 4.15 HANDLING, STORAGE, PACKAGING, PRESERVATION, AND DELIVERY

☐ **4.15.1 General**

*The supplier shall establish and maintain documented procedures for handling, storage, packaging, preservation, and delivery of product.*

☐ **4.15.2 Handling**

**The supplier shall provide methods of handling product that prevent damage or deterioration.**

☐ **4.15.3 Storage**

**The supplier shall use designated storage areas or stock rooms to prevent damage or deterioration of product, pending use or delivery. Appropriate methods of authorizing receipt to and dispatch from such areas shall be stipulated.**

☐ **In order to detect deterioration, the condition of product in stock shall be assessed at appropriate intervals.**

☐ **4.15.4 Packaging**

**The supplier shall control packing, packaging, and marking processes (including materials used) to the extent necessary to ensure conformance** to specified requirements.

☐ **4.15.5 Preservation**

**The supplier shall apply appropriate methods for preservation and segregation of product** when the product is under the supplier's control.

☐ **4.15.6 Delivery**

**The supplier shall arrange for the protection of the quality of product after final inspection and test**. Where contractually specified, this protection shall be extended to include delivery to destination.

☐ **4.16 CONTROL OF QUALITY RECORDS**

*The supplier shall establish and maintain documented procedures for identification, collection, indexing, access, filing, storage, maintenance, and disposition of quality records.*

Quality records shall be maintained to demonstrate conformance to specified requirements and the effective operation of the quality system. Pertinent quality records from the subcontractor shall be an element of these data.

☐ **All quality records shall be legible and shall be stored and retained in such a way that they are readily retrievable** in facilities that provide a suitable environment to prevent damage or deterioration and to prevent loss.

☐ **Retention times of quality records shall be established and recorded**. Where agreed contractually, quality records shall be made available for evaluation by the customer or the customer's representative for an agreed period.

NOTE 14 Records may be in the form of any type of media, such as hard copy or electronic media.

☐ **4.17 INTERNAL QUALITY AUDITS**

*The supplier shall establish and maintain documented procedures for planning and implementing internal quality audits* to verify whether quality activities and related results comply with planned arrangements and to determine the effectiveness of the quality system.

☐ **Internal quality audits shall be scheduled on the basis of the status and importance** of the activity to be audited and shall be carried out by personnel independent of those having direct responsibility for the activity being audited.

☐ **The results of the audits shall be recorded** (see 4.16) and brought to the attention of the personnel having responsibility in the area audited. The management personnel responsible for the area shall take timely corrective action on deficiencies found during the audit.

☐ **Follow-up audit activities shall verify and record the implementation and effectiveness of the corrective action taken** (see 4.16).

NOTES

15 The results of internal quality audits form an integral part of the input to management review activities (see 4.1.3).

16 Guidance on quality-system audits is given in ANSI/ASQC Q10011-1-1994, ANSI/ASQC Q10011-2-1994, and ANSI/ASQC Q10011-3-1994.

☐ **4.18 TRAINING**

*The supplier shall establish and maintain documented procedures for identifying training needs and provide for the training of all personnel performing activities affecting quality.* Personnel performing specific assigned tasks shall be qualified on the basis of appropriate education, training, and/or experience, as required.

☐ Appropriate records of training shall be maintained (see 4.16).

☐ 4.19 SERVICING

Where servicing is a specified requirement, the supplier shall establish and maintain documented procedures for performing, verifying, and reporting that the servicing meets the specified requirements.

## 4.20  STATISTICAL TECHNIQUES

☐ **4.20.1  Identification of need**

**The supplier shall identify the need for statistical techniques required for establishing, controlling, and verifying process capability and product characteristics.**

☐ 4.20.2  Procedures

The supplier shall establish and maintain documented procedures to implement and control the application of the statistical techniques identified in 4.20.1.

# LOGICAL INDEX

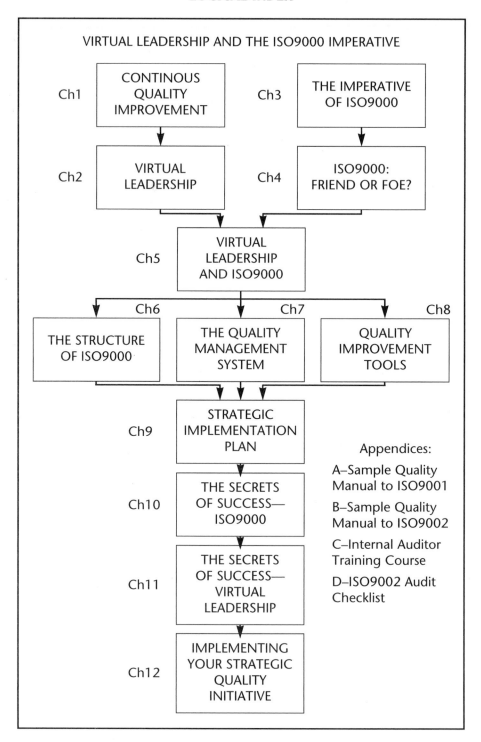

VIRTUAL LEADERSHIP AND THE ISO9000 IMPERATIVE

Ch1 — CONTINOUS QUALITY IMPROVEMENT

Ch3 — THE IMPERATIVE OF ISO9000

Ch2 — VIRTUAL LEADERSHIP

Ch4 — ISO9000: FRIEND OR FOE?

Ch5 — VIRTUAL LEADERSHIP AND ISO9000

Ch6 — THE STRUCTURE OF ISO9000

Ch7 — THE QUALITY MANAGEMENT SYSTEM

Ch8 — QUALITY IMPROVEMENT TOOLS

Ch9 — STRATEGIC IMPLEMENTATION PLAN

Ch10 — THE SECRETS OF SUCCESS— ISO9000

Ch11 — THE SECRETS OF SUCCESS— VIRTUAL LEADERSHIP

Ch12 — IMPLEMENTING YOUR STRATEGIC QUALITY INITIATIVE

Appendices:

A–Sample Quality Manual to ISO9001

B–Sample Quality Manual to ISO9002

C–Internal Auditor Training Course

D–ISO9002 Audit Checklist

# Index by ISO9000 Paragraph

*Numbers in parentheses represent ISO9000 paragraphs.*

# *Index*

*Numbers in parentheses represent ISO9000 paragraphs.*

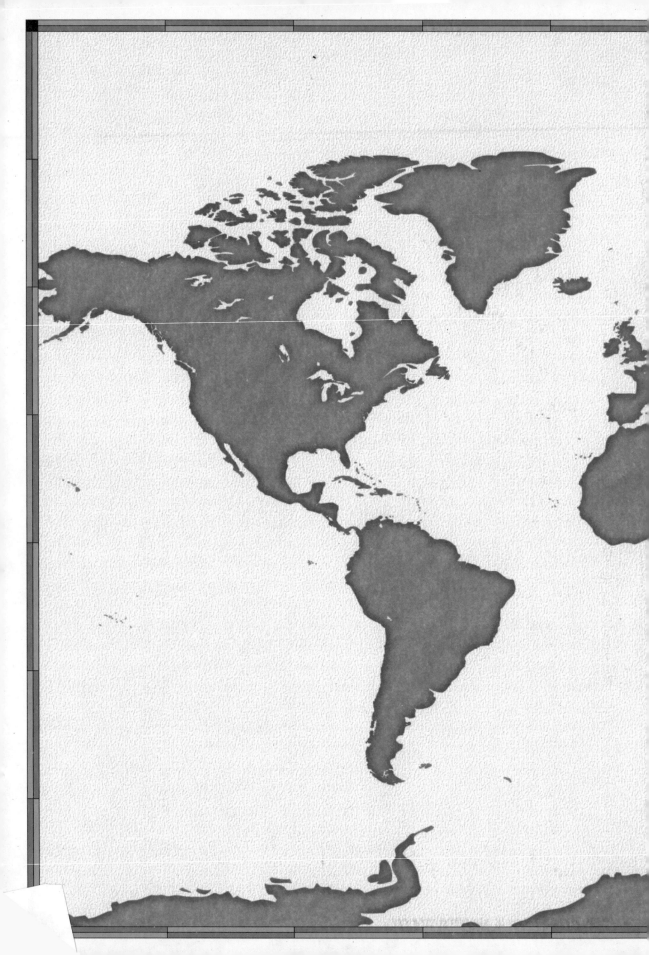